AQA(B) PSYCHOLOGY FOR A2

DONALD PENNINGTON
JULIE McLOUGHLIN

HODDER EDUCATION
AN HACHETTE UK COMPANY

Orders: please contact Bookpoint Ltd, 130 Milton Park, Abingdon, Oxon OX14 4SB. Telephone: (44) 01235 827720. Fax: (44) 01235 400454. Lines are open from 9.00–5.00, Monday to Saturday, with a 24-hour message answering service. You can also order through our website www.hoddereducation.co.uk

If you have any comments to make about this, or any of our other titles, please send them to educationenquiries@hodder.co.uk

British Library Cataloguing in Publication Data
A catalogue record for this title is available from the British Library

ISBN: 978 0 340 973516

First Edition Published 2009

Impression number 10 9 8 7 6 5
Year 2012

Hachette UK's policy is to use papers that are natural, renewable and recyclable products and made from wood grown in sustainable forests. The logging and manufacturing processes are expected to conform to the environmental regulations of the country of origin.

Cover photo © Nikreates/Alamy
Illustrations by Barking Dog
Typeset by Fakenham Prepress Solutions, Fakenham, Norfolk NR21 8NN
Printed in Dubai for Hodder Education, an Hachette UK Company, 338 Euston Road, London NW1 3BH

Contents

Acknowledgements

The authors would like to thank family, friends and colleagues for their support. Thanks also to Emma Woolf, Ruben Hale, Kate Short and Stephanie Matthews at Hodder Education for their guidance and advice. Finally, a special mention is due to the many A level students who have unwittingly helped in the preparation of this book.

Donald Pennington and Julie McLoughlin

How to use this book

This book has been designed for students and teachers following the GCE A2 level Psychology Specification B offered by the Assessment and Qualifications Alliance (AQA). There are seventeen chapters covering the topic areas in Unit 3 Child Development and Applied Options and Unit 4 Approaches, Debates and Methods in Psychology. Each chapter covers the specification content, and includes descriptions of concepts, theories and studies, along with summary evaluation points.

'How Psychology Works'

At the end of each topic chapter there are activities to aid understanding of 'How Psychology Works'. These are classroom activities to enable students to 'think like a psychologist' and apply their knowledge of practical methods in psychology. The skills acquired through these activities will be tested in the examinations where students are required to answer questions on research methods and data analysis. It is recommended that students keep a detailed record of practical activities in a separate section of their classroom folder and use these as part of their examination preparation.

Further reading

There are suggestions for further reading at the end of each chapter. The introductory texts should be accessible for all students. the specialist texts are more demanding and perhaps more useful for teachers, although they will also be useful and interesting for the more ambitious student.

Picture Credits

The author and publishers would like to thank the following for permission to reproduce material in this book:

Figure 1.2 PHOTO RESEARCHERS/SCIENCE PHOTO LIBRARY; Figure 1.8 Cynthia Johnson/Liaison/Getty Images; Figure 1.9 © Monkey Business – Fotolia.com; Figure 2.12 © Blend Images / Alamy; Figure 2.14 © wildman – Fotolia.com; Figure 3.4 Brian Smith / Rex Features; Figure 3.10 © Angela Hampton Picture Library / Alamy; Figure 4.12 AP/PA Photos; Figure 4.14 AJ PHOTO/SCIENCE PHOTO LIBRARY; Figure 4.3 EMPICS Entertainment/PA Photos; Figure 4.4 Everett Collection / Rex Features; Figure 4.5 JSSImages/BEI / Rex Features; Figure 4.7 Greg Williams / Rex Features; Figure 5.1 © Mary Evans Picture Library; Figure 5.2 Universal / Everett / Rex Features; Figure 5.16 © Photos 12 / Alamy; Figure 6.5 AARON HAUPT/SCIENCE PHOTO LIBRARY; Figure 6.12 WILL & DENI MCINTYRE/SCIENCE PHOTO LIBRARY; Figure 7.1 © LifeStyle / Alamy; Figure 7.3 Denis Closon / Rex Features; Figure 7.10 ISOPRESS SENEPART / Rex Features; Figure 7.12 Sven Doering / VISUM / Still Pictures; Figure 7.13 Patrick Frilet / Rex Features; Figure 7.14 Rex Features; Figure 8.1 PA Archive/PA Photos; Figure 8.4 © tom carter / Alamy; Figure 8.8a © 2000 PA / Topham / TopFoto; Figure 8.12 Larry McKee / Rex Features; Figure 8.14 Giles Moberly / PYMCA / Rex Features; Figure 8.16 ODD ANDERSEN/ AFP/Getty Images; Figure 8.17 Sipa Press / Rex Features; Figure 9.1 © Sam Tanner / Photofusion; Figure 9.2 Sipa Press / Rex Features; Figure 9.10 DEPT. OF CLINICAL CYTOGENETICS, ADDENBROOKES HOSPITAL/SCIENCE PHOTO LIBRARY; Figure 9.11 Jeremy Sutton Hibbert / Rex Features; Figure 10.2 TEK IMAGE / SCIENCE PHOTO LIBRARY; Figure 10.7 PHOTO RESEARCHERS/SCIENCE PHOTO LIBRARY; Figure 11.1 from *The Mentality of Apes*, Wolfgang Koehler © 1925 Kegan Paul, Trench, Trubner & Co. Reproduced by permission of Taylor & Francis Books, UK; Figure 11.3 © 2002 PA / Topham / TopFoto; Figure 12.7 The Granger Collection, NYC / TopFoto; Figure 14.1 © Steve Eason/Photofusion; Figure 14.9 DAVID GRAVES / Rex Features; Figure 14.10 © Greg Epperson – Fotolia.com; Figure 14.11 © Jack Hollingsworth/Photodisc/Getty Images; Figure 15.1 Alisdair Macdonald / Rex Features; Figure 15.3 © David Trainer/Photofusion; Figure 15.6 © John Powell / TopFoto; Figure 16.1 © 2009 photolibrary.com; Figure 16.3 © Galina Barskaya / Alamy; Figure 16.7 LOUISA GOULIAMAKI/AFP/Getty Images; Figure 16.14 © Stock Montage, Inc. / Alamy; Figure 16.19 Claudia Rehm / WestEnd61 / Rex Features; Figure 17.14 © Deco / Alamy; Figure 17.19 Sipa Press / Rex Features;

Every effort has been made to obtain necessary permission with reference to copyright material. The publishers apologise if inadvertently any sources remain unacknowledged and will be glad to make the necessary arrangements at the earliest opportunity.

Social development

Chapter 1

The topic of social development includes some key issues in developmental psychology, including research into early attachment and effects of loss of an attachment figure. Some psychological theory and evidence has suggested that children who do not receive continuous and loving care can grow up to be emotionally and cognitively damaged. This idea has led to a tendency to blame many of our adult problems on inadequate 'mothering'. In this chapter we shall consider psychological evidence and research into attachment and then look beyond early relationships between infant and caregiver to the development of later relationships with friends in childhood and adolescence.

1.1 Early relationships

The work of Schaffer

Attachment has been defined as 'a long-enduring, emotionally meaningful tie to a particular individual' (Schaffer, 1996). This affectional bond or tie is usually characterised by a desire for closeness or proximity to a particular individual and by separation distress when the tie is broken or disrupted. The attachment object, usually the mother, offers comfort and acts as a source of security. Schaffer and Emerson (1964) studied 60 Glasgow infants, carrying out observations and interviews with parents at regular intervals during the first 18 months after birth. They found that a particular pattern of attachment behaviour occurred and identified stages in the development of attachment.

1.1.1 The role of caregiver–infant interactions

Positive **caregiver–infant interactions** can function to develop and maintain attachment. In subtle and often unconscious ways, adults interacting with babies seem to be especially tuned in to the baby's needs, modifying their speech and actions accordingly. Even though a baby cannot speak, communication between

Stage/age	Type of attachment
Asocial (0–6 weeks)	Babies respond in a similar way to people and objects, although they prefer to look at human-like stimuli.
Diffuse (6 weeks to 6 months)	Babies show no particular preference for a specific individual and will be comforted by anyone.
Single strong attachment (7 to 12 months)	Babies show a strong preference for a single individual and will show a fear of strangers.
Multiple attachments (from 12 months)	Babies will show attachment towards several figures. By 18 months some infants have as many as five attachment figures.

Figure 1.1 *Stages of attachment identified by Schaffer and Emerson (1964) (see pages 19–20).*

caregiver–infant pairs is rich and complex. The following are examples of caregiver–infant interactions.

i) Immediate physical contact

Research in the 1970s suggested that mother and baby should have immediate contact after birth because skin-to-skin stimulation was important for the formation of a bond. Klaus and Kennell (1976) argued that mothers who cuddled their baby in a critical period after birth enjoyed better relationships with the child than those mothers who did not have that opportunity. In the short term at least it does seem that mothers who have immediate contact show more tender interactions with the child and spend more time looking at them than mothers who do not. However, longer-term effects of early contact are less reliably demonstrated, although in some cases early contact does appear to be related to general adequacy of parenting (Bee, 1989).

ii) Imitation

The capacity of even very young infants to imitate adults' facial expressions has provided some of the most convincing evidence that children are innately social beings and take an active part in relationship formation in the first months of life (see study below).

iii) Interactional synchrony

Condon and Sander (1974) noted how babies would co-ordinate their actions in time with adult speech, taking turns to contribute to the 'conversation'. Frame-by-frame analysis of film recordings of babies' movements was matched to sound recordings of adult conversation. It was found that the babies would move in time with the rhythm of the conversation, engaging in a subtle form of turn-taking. In real interactions between baby and caregiver this results in reciprocal behaviour, with both parties able to elicit responses from the other, even though only the adult can speak. Such synchronised interaction is sometimes likened to a 'dance' between mother and baby.

The importance of interactional synchrony in attachment has been demonstrated by Isabella *et al.* (1989), who found that securely attached mother–infant pairs were those who had shown more instances of interactional synchrony in home observations during the first year.

Aim

Melzoff and Moore (1977) investigated imitation of facial expressions in 2- and 3-week-old infants.

Method

Infants were presented with a set of three facial expressions (tongue pull, lip protrusion and open mouth) and one hand movement involving sequential finger movement. A dummy was positioned in the infant's mouth to prevent any movement before and during the modelling of the behaviour by the adult. After presentation of the behaviour by the model, the dummy was removed from the infant's mouth and the immediate response/behaviour was recorded on a close-up video. Independent judges were then asked to rate the infant's response for likeness to any of the four target behaviours. Raters were not aware of which expression or movement the infant had been exposed to.

Results

There was a significant association between the model's behaviour and the infant's behaviour, with infants able to imitate specific facial expressions or hand movements.

Conclusion

Very young infants will spontaneously imitate facial and hand movements of adult models. The same effect was later demonstrated in infants of less than 3 days old.

In order to demonstrate how the infant takes an active role in these interactions Murray and Trevarthen (1985) deliberately interfered with the interactional turn-taking. They asked mothers to adopt a 'frozen face' expression with their babies and found that the infants became extremely upset, turning away from the mother's face and crying. Furthermore, infants made deliberate attempts to draw the mother back into the interaction.

iv) Modified language or 'motherese'

Snow and Ferguson (1977) identified distinctive language patterns demonstrated by adults conversing with young children. Initially this was referred to as motherese, although it is sometimes referred to as 'parentese' or 'caregiverese'. Motherese differs from normal linguistic style in a number of ways, all of which help communication between adult–baby pairs and draw the child into the communication, perhaps helping to establish and cement a relationship.

Motherese is usually slow, high-pitched and repetitive, varied in intonation and comprises short, simple sentences. One of the most distinctive characteristics of motherese is the sing-songy nature of the communication, almost as if the speaker were singing rather than speaking. Papousek *et al.* (1991) found that Chinese, German and American mothers tended to use a rising tone to signal to the baby that it was his or her 'turn' in the interaction. 'Motherese' can therefore be seen as contributing towards the effectiveness of interactional synchrony.

1.1.2 Animal research

Human infants are not alone in their need for early social interaction. Animal research showed that baby rhesus monkeys that have been separated from their mothers prefer the warmth and physical comfort of an artificial cloth mother even though an artificial wire

Figure 1.2 *Harlow showed how infant monkeys would prefer to be close to the cloth mother even though the wire mother provided food.*

Evaluation of the role of caregiver–infant interaction in the development of attachment

- Myers (1984) suggested that immediate physical contact is neither necessary nor sufficient for the development of attachment.
- Critics of the imitation studies have suggested that young babies are not intentionally social and will respond in a similar way to inanimate objects such as an approaching pen (Jacobsen, 1979). However, Abravanel and DeYong (1991) found that 5- and 12-week-old babies would imitate tongue pulling and mouth opening in human models, but not when the expressions were simulated using objects.
- Interactional synchrony is not related to security of attachment in all cultures. LeVine *et al.* (1994) showed how mothers in Kenya rarely cuddle and interact closely with their babies, even though they are attentive to their needs and have secure attachments.
- Although 'motherese' undoubtedly serves to enhance communication between caregiver and infant, there is no evidence that it directly affects the formation or quality of attachment. Indeed, adults have been found to use 'motherese' with all babies and young children, and not just those with whom they have an attachment.

STUDY

Aim

Harlow (1959) studied the behaviour of infant monkeys separated from their mothers at birth to test the effects of the separation.

Method

Infant rhesus monkeys were taken from their mothers and kept in a cage with two substitute mothers: a 'cloth mother' covered with a soft blanket and a 'wire mother' incorporating a feeding bottle. The monkeys were kept in these conditions for a period of time, and then released into a cage with a group of normally reared monkeys.

Results

The infant monkeys preferred to spend time close to the cloth mother, even though they got their food from the wire mother. When returned to the company of other monkeys, Harlow's monkeys showed signs of inappropriate social behaviour and delinquency. They were aggressive towards other monkeys, unable to form normal relationships and attacked any monkey that tried to mate with them. If they did have offspring, the deprived monkeys were extremely poor, neglecting mothers.

Conclusion

Two conclusions can be drawn from Harlow's work. First, the study showed that physical comfort is more important for attachment than food. Second, it seems that lack of attachment results in delinquent and antisocial behaviour.

Evaluation of animal research

- According to Darwin's theory of evolution, all species are genetically related in some way and it therefore makes sense to generalise findings from one species to another because there is behavioural continuity. The field of comparative psychology involves studying other species and then making extrapolations or comparisons from those findings to human behaviour. In the case of Harlow's research, there is an especially close relatedness between humans and rhesus monkeys, but it could still be argued that human behaviour is much more complex than that of other species.
- Harlow's research has been criticised on ethical grounds for the distress caused to the infant monkeys. In defence of Harlow, deliberate separation is the only way to determine cause and effect, and it is not possible to carry out such research with human infants. In evaluating whether or not research is ethical, it is also important to consider the importance of the findings. In this particular case, Harlow's contribution to our understanding of attachment has been significant.
- The Harlow study was used to support Bowlby's hypothesis (page 15) that babies need a secure attachment by a certain age if they are to develop normally and be able to relate to others satisfactorily.

mother was the source of the food (Harlow, 1959). These baby monkeys were also found to be unable to form attachments when they were older, suggesting that infant–caregiver interaction is important for the development of attachment.

1.1.3 Function of attachment

Several theories have been proposed about the function of attachment.

i) Initially it was thought that human infants attach to the person who provides nurture in the form of food. This secondary drive theory of attachment or **'cupboard love' theory**, as it is sometimes known, can be criticised on several grounds, not least because babies do not necessarily attach to the person who feeds them. Note how the infant monkeys studied by Harlow preferred to spend time with the cloth mother even though they obtained their food from the wire mother.

ii) Evolutionary theorists suggest that attachment behaviour has a critical **survival value** for an infant, but not necessarily in the way that cupboard love theory would have predicted. Animals that are immediately mobile at birth, known as precocial species, need to remain close to the mother and have the protection of their group in order to avoid predators. Early views about attachment were often based on observations of other species – for example, Lorenz (1935) studied the innate following behaviour demonstrated by greylag geese. He reared young goslings away from other members of their species and found that they would follow and attach themselves to the first large moving object they saw. In normal circumstances this would usually be the mother, and so, this behaviour, known as **imprinting**, functions to keep the young gosling safe from harm. Thus, according to evolutionary theory, the innate following behaviour would confer survival value on members of the species that behave in this way. Psychoanalytic theorists have drawn on animal research to explain attachment in terms of an **innate, instinctual drive** to maintain proximity to the caregiver, who would most usually be the mother. Drawing on animal research and his own psychoanalytic background, Bowlby (1969) proposed that attachment was rooted in the need to maintain proximity or closeness, the chief benefit of which would be survival.

iii) Survival value of a different sort was proposed by Bower (1979) in his **communication theory** of attachment. According to Bower, infants are selective in their choice of attachment figure, choosing as their preferred figure whoever is best able to communicate with them. This need not be the person who spends most time caring for the child, but instead would be the person who the child can use most effectively as a means to accessing the things he or she needs. For example, the child would prefer an attachment figure who can recognise from a cry exactly what is required over someone who might often be present, but who is unable to interpret the child's attempts at communication. This theory about attachment can be linked to Ainsworth's views about sensitive responsiveness (pages 6–8).

iv) Aside from offering survival value to the infant, attachment may serve a function in the longer term. In 1969, Bowlby proposed that attachment provides the child with an **internal working model** of relationships. This model acts as an internal representation or mental view of the relationship with the primary caregiver – for example, a child who has a secure and loving attachment would have an internal representation of the

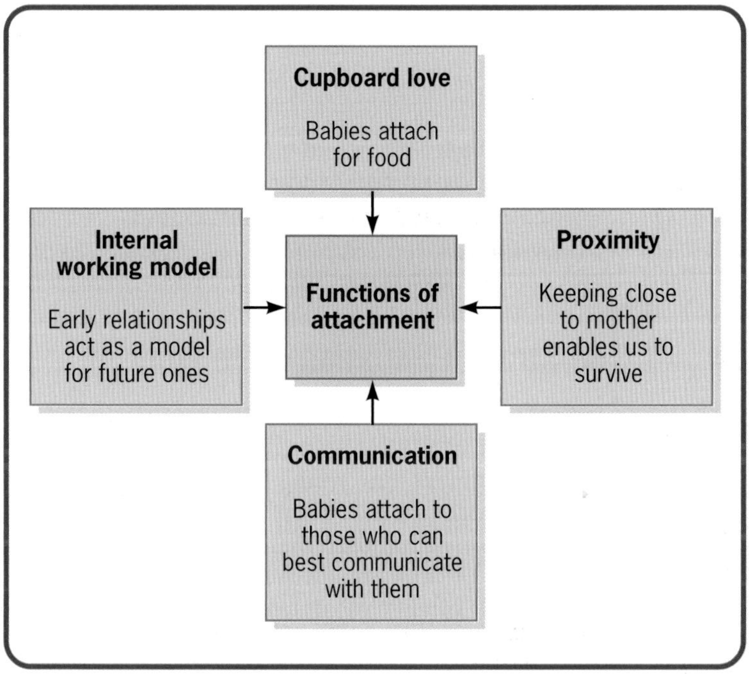

Cupboard love
Babies attach for food

Internal working model
Early relationships act as a model for future ones

Functions of attachment

Proximity
Keeping close to mother enables us to survive

Communication
Babies attach to those who can best communicate with them

Figure 1.3 *Attachment may serve several functions.*

caregiver as responsive and sensitive. This mental model enables the child to have expectations of the caregiver and makes future interactions easier and more predictable. As the child comes into contact with more and more people, the internal working model can be used as a framework on which to build other similar relationships. If this notion is correct, then quite simply, the child's earliest relationship sets the scene for all relationships that are to follow, for example, with teenage and adult friends, and in intimate relationships.

Evaluation of the internal working model function

- Whilst the idea that early relationships act as a foundation for later relationships is an appealing one, critics have argued that the internal working model is too general to be useful (Dunn, 1993).
- The notion of continuity in relationships also leads to a fairly pessimistic, determinist view suggesting that if your first relationships are unhappy and insecure then future relationships will be the same.
- The internal working model is attractive in that it combines several perspectives in psychology – for example, the cognitive perspective (understanding of attachment) and the behaviourist perspective (behaviours that are rewarding are likely to be repeated) (Barnes, 1995).

1.1.4 Measuring attachment – secure and insecure attachment

We all know what it feels like to be attached to someone because you know how you feel when you are separated from them. Adults can describe these feelings, but because most attachment research is carried out using infants and young children, psychologists have tended to use the observational method to study attachment. The sorts of attachment behaviours psychologists have observed can be seen in the adjacent box.

Observable attachment behaviours

Watching – the child will keep an eye on the attachment figure as they move about the room.

Crying – when the attachment figure moves out of sight.

Following – children who are mobile will try to keep contact with the attachment figure by following and clinging to them.

Using as a safe base – a child will play in close proximity to the attachment figure, perhaps venturing away to get a toy but returning frequently and playing close by. This behaviour is especially obvious when the child is startled by, or suspicious of, something. For example, a child playing in the centre of the room might run back to the mother and hold on to her if a stranger enters or a sudden noise occurs.

Greeting – the child will show obvious pleasure at the return of an attachment figure, smiling and holding up his or her arms as a signal to be picked up.

Stranger fear – the child will show a fear of strangers, demonstrated by turning away and resisting attempts to be picked up and comforted.

The Strange Situation – the work of Ainsworth

Ainsworth *et al.* (1978) devised a procedure for measuring attachment in young infants. The Strange Situation procedure has been replicated many times and has become a standard method for measuring type and quality of attachment. According to Ainsworth, the type and quality of attachment between mother and child is largely dependent on the mother's behaviour towards the child. She suggested that mothers of securely attached infants tended to be more sensitive to

Figure 1.4 *The Strange Situation involves a sequence of eight 3-minute episodes in which the child's reactions to mother and stranger are observed.*

STUDY

Aim

Ainsworth *et al.* (1978) studied the reactions of young children to brief separations from their mother in order to determine the nature of attachment behaviours and types of attachments. Ainsworth's procedure is known as the **Strange Situation.**

Method

In a controlled observation infants were exposed to a sequence of 3-minute episodes. The total observation period lasted for approximately 25 minutes. First the infant and mother were introduced to the observation room by the researcher, then the researcher left the room. After a while a stranger entered and had a brief conversation with the mother. The mother then left quietly, leaving the infant and stranger together for a maximum of 3 minutes. If the child became very distressed at this point the mother would return earlier than planned. This sequence of events was then repeated with a further 'stranger' episode. The child's behaviours were recorded throughout.

Results

Using a combination of behavioural measures, mainly proximity seeking and maintenance of proximity, Ainsworth classified infants as securely attached, anxious-avoidant or anxious-resistant. In middle-class US samples approximately 65% of infants were found to fall into the secure category, with around 15–20% in the other two categories. These three types are described in figure 1.5.

Conclusion

Ainsworth's research led her to two conclusions: a) there are different types of attachments and these types are differentiated in observed attachment behaviours, and b) the type of attachment between a mother and child is dependent upon the mother's sensitivity and responsiveness to the child.

the child's needs, more responsive, more co-operative and more accessible than mothers of either of the anxious types. Main *et al.* (1985) explored the relationship between the mother's behaviour and type of attachment and found that mothers who themselves had satisfactory attachment experiences would be more likely to have children who were securely attached.

Main and Solomon (1990) later proposed a fourth type of attachment, 'disorganised', which is characteristic of high-risk families where children have perhaps been abused or neglected. A child showing disorganised attachment will appear confused and apprehensive, with no consistent response to the events of the Strange Situation.

Attachment type	Behaviour typical of infant
Anxious-avoidant	Ignores mother, seems indifferent. Easily comforted by stranger. Treats mother and stranger the same.
Secure	Happy in mother's presence. Distressed when mother leaves. Calms on mother's return. Wary of stranger.
Anxious-resistant	Fussy, difficult, cries a lot. Distressed when mother leaves, not comforted on her return. Shows anger. Resists stranger.

Figure 1.5 *Attachment types identified in the Strange Situation.*

Evaluation – Ainsworth's work

- Ainsworth's procedure has been replicated many times to see whether (a) the classifications show good reliability over time with the same mother–child pairs and (b) the category percentages are similar across cultures. (See van Ijzendoorn below.) Although Ainsworth's own study (Ainsworth *et al.*, 1978) failed to show good test-retest reliability of classification, other studies have found fairly stable classification over time, certainly for those babies in the securely attached and disorganised categories (Hesse and Main, 2000). Looking further ahead, studies have shown there to be a relationship between the type of attachment observed in infancy and relationships in later life (Waters *et al.*, 2000).
- Bremner (1994) questions the assumption that proximity seeking and maintenance of proximity are key measures of security of attachment. Securely attached infants are often observed to be happy exploring their environment, and do not feel the need to maintain continual proximity to mother (Cassidy, 1986). Indeed it could be argued that proximity seeking is a sign of insecurity rather than a sign of a secure attachment.
- Belsky (1984) noted that Ainsworth focused on the mother's sensitivity and neglected wider influences on attachment. Additional factors that might affect security of attachment include the temperament of the child, the parent's background and health and the social context, including social support and the family's socio-economic status. According to some researchers, it is the baby's temperament rather than the mother's behaviour that determines the type of attachment.
- Fraley and Spieker (2003) argue that the fixed category system is oversimplified, suggesting that it is more sensible to consider attachment as a two-dimensional construct. The first dimension is proximity seeking versus avoidance; this represents the degree to which the child prefers to maintain closeness to the mother. The second dimension is anger/resistance versus emotional confidence; this represents the child's emotional response to the attachment figure. Figure 1.6 shows the relationship between the two dimensions and types of attachment.

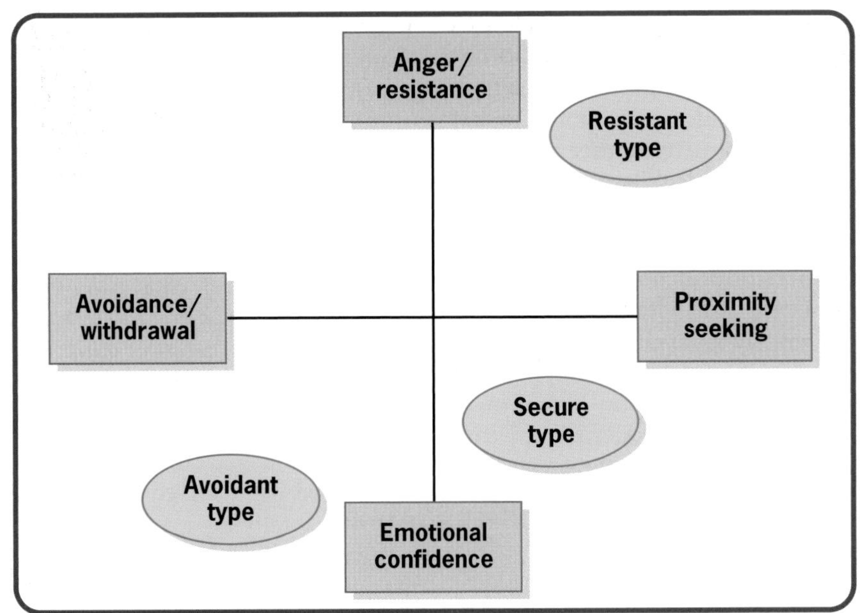

Figure 1.6 *The relationship between Fraley and Spieker's two attachment dimensions and Ainsworth's types of attachment (after Fraley and Spieker, 2003).*

The Strange Situation – the work of van Ijzendoorn

Cross-cultural replications of the Strange Situation indicate that the category percentages defined by Ainsworth using an American sample are not universal. van Ijzendoorn and Kroonenberg (1988) analysed Strange Situation data from 32 different studies in 8 different countries. This type of study, where data are collated from several different studies, is known as a meta-analysis. van Ijzendoorn and Kroonenberg found that German infants had the highest percentage of anxious-avoidant attachments, and Israeli and Japanese infants showed the highest percentage of anxious-resistant attachments. Takahashi (1990) suggested that this could be due to the excessive stress Japanese infants might experience during the Strange Situation separation, as infant–mother separation is not the norm in the Japanese culture. Overall the most common type of attachment found in all cultures was the secure type.

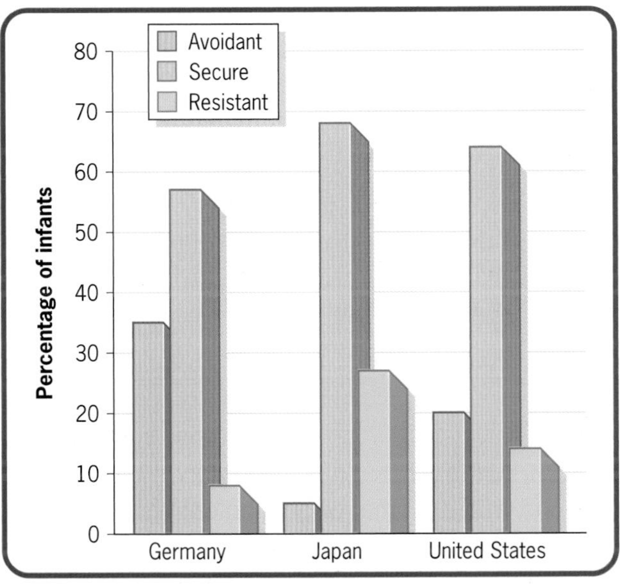

Figure 1.7 *The percentages of secure, avoidant and resistant attachments in German, Japanese and US cultures (van Ijzendoorn and Kroonenberg, 1988).*

In addition to noting cross-cultural differences, the researchers also found differences in patterns of attachment within individual cultures; in one Japanese study there were no anxious-avoidant babies and in the other 20% of the infants showed anxious-avoidant attachment. In all, van Ijzendoorn and Kroonenberg's research suggests that, although the Strange Situation is a highly useful tool for measuring attachment, differing child-rearing norms between and even within cultures will lead to varying percentages of types of attachment found in any individual study.

de Wolff and van Ijzendoorn (1997) have also considered Ainsworth's view that the type of attachment depends on the sensitivity shown by the mother. Sensitivity refers to the mother's ability to read signals from the baby and understand and respond to her baby's immediate needs. A sensitive mother is responsive, accepting and co-operative, whilst an insensitive mother tends to put her own needs before those of the baby. Again using the meta-analysis technique, de Wolff and van Ijzendoorn found that the quality of mother–infant interaction and sensitivity of the mother was only moderately associated with security of attachment. According to van Ijzendoorn *et al.* (1995), 'the impact of sensitivity on attachment appears to be only modest and not in accordance with its central position in attachment theory'.

Alternative ways of measuring attachment

The Adult Attachment Interview (Main *et al.*, 1985)

Main *et al.* (1985) devised a procedure for classifying adults according to their recollections of their own attachment experiences. The Adult Attachment Interview (AAI) lasts approximately 1 hour and consists of 15 open questions about the person's attachment experiences. Interview content is then analysed and coded according to four categories:

- insecure-dismissing: individuals whose attachment relationships are dismissed as of little concern
- autonomous-secure: individuals whose attachment experiences are recalled openly and objectively
- insecure-preoccupied: individuals who still actively struggle to please their parents
- unresolved: individuals who have experienced an attachment trauma or loss of an attachment figure and have not yet come to terms with it.

The AAI can be extremely stressful, particularly for those adults who had negative attachment experiences as children. Autonomous-secure adults, who discussed their own childhood experiences openly, were more likely to have children identified as securely attached in a Strange Situation. Dismissing and preoccupied adults, however, tended to have children identified as insecure in the Strange Situation. According to Main *et al.* (1985), a mother's own childhood experiences affect how she interacts with her child and the type of relationship established between the mother–child pair.

The Attachment Q-sort

Waters *et al.* (1995) devised a method for measuring attachment using a set of 90 behavioural descriptors on cards. The parent, teacher or child expert has to sort the cards into nine piles, according to how well each descriptor represents the child's behaviour. Items include:

If adult reassures, child will approach.
Child keeps track of adult's location.
Child actively goes after adult if upset.

To complete the test the sorter has to decide where to place the card on a scale of 1–9, where 1 is 'least like' the child and 9 is 'most like' the child. When all the cards have been sorted into the nine piles, there is a system for tallying a total attachment score; this score is then used to indicate the attachment type. Subsets of the cards are suitable for use with different people depending on their relationship with the child – for example, there is a subset suitable for teachers. Pederson *et al.* (1998) reported that classifications of type of attachment made using the Attachment Q-sort correspond well with classifications made using the Strange Situation procedure.

1.1.5 Privation and deprivation – the short-term and long-term consequences

Deprivation might be defined as losing something which a person once had, whereas privation might be defined as never having had something in the first place. Linking this idea to the concept of attachment, we can understand deprivation as having had a secure relationship or bond with a mother or attachment figure and then losing that relationship, and privation as never having had any secure and loving relationship with any attachment figure.

Definitions

Deprivation: losing a secure relationship or bond with a mother or attachment figure
Privation: never having had any secure and loving relationship with any attachment figure

Deprivation

In the short term, deprivation results in distress of the type observed when a child has to be separated from the carer for a short while, perhaps because of hospitalisation or an extended holiday. A commonly observed sequence of behaviours can be seen in this sort of separation. Initially the child will protest by crying and struggling to keep contact with the carer. This protest will then give way to despair where the child appears to be calmer, but perhaps cries quietly and appears very unhappy. Eventually, as the separation goes on, the child enters a period of detachment, showing little emotion towards others and being apparently unconcerned. If the attachment figure returns, the child often rejects contact and appears almost to resent the attachment figure, who is treated just like a stranger by the child.

An excellent illustration of the **protest-despair-detachment** sequence is presented by Robertson and Robertson (1968), who filmed separations of young children going into care for a short time. The Robertson studies illustrated the short-term effects of separation and had a significant impact on the way health and childcare professionals viewed children's needs in separation situations.

Not surprisingly, young children between 7 months and 3 years are most vulnerable to suffering from the distress of separation. However, Schaffer (1996) identified other characteristics that predispose children to suffer more in separation situations. Problems are more likely where the child:

- is male (in early childhood, although females suffer more in adolescence)
- has a 'difficult' temperament
- has a history of family conflict
- has parents who are psychologically unavailable
- suffers repeated separations.

Long-term effects of deprivation are difficult to determine because other variables may influence the child's behaviour. However, studies of children who have experienced separations suggest that one long-term consequence may be a fear that separation will occur again. This separation anxiety may be seen in a variety of behaviours, such as increased clinging, aggression

STUDY

Aim

Belsky (1988) investigated the effects of day care on attachment relationships.

Method

Using a meta-analysis, Belsky collated the results of a number of previously published studies. Data gathered included the time per week young children spent in non-maternal care and information about their type of attachment.

Results

Out of 464 children, 26% of those in day care for less than 20 hours per week showed insecure attachments, whereas 41% of those in day care more than 20 hours per week were categorised as insecure.

Conclusion

Belsky concluded there was some evidence that 20 hours or more per week in non-maternal care has a negative effect on attachment security. This effect was especially marked for children under 1 year. Barnes (1995) notes that these differences in attachment type may be due to other factors, such as the type of substitute care and the reasons for mothers needing to work longer hours.

towards the carer and physical stress-related reactions. In adulthood, separation anxiety may result in a general fear of abandonment or insecurity in relationships, making it difficult to trust other people.

One of the most common separation situations occurs when parents divorce. Studies of children of divorced parents show some negative life outcomes, such as lower academic attainment and a higher incidence of delinquency. However, such data are correlational and do not show that separation following divorce causes negative effects. Schaffer (1996) summarised the effects of divorce-related separations and concluded that several factors can help to reduce the effects of separation:

- regular contact with absent parent
- reduced parental conflict
- behaviour of the parent who has custody and his or her ability to provide stability
- lifestyle maintenance – many separated parents find themselves worse off financially, which affects continuity for the child
- avoidance of further disruption, such as moving school
- positive relationships with step-parent where there is remarriage.

It is also important to realise that not all children are equally affected by such separations, with many finding ways of coping with their loss. Jenkins *et al.* (1989), for example, found that a common coping mechanism for 9–10-year-old children separated from a parent after divorce was to increase contact with siblings and friends.

Privation

If children can be adversely affected by deprivation, then it is likely that there would be negative consequences where infants and young children have no chance to form an attachment relationship at all. Since it is not possible, for ethical reasons, to carry out controlled studies of privation with children, much evidence showing cause and effect has tended to come from animal research. One of the most influential studies of animal privation was the Harlow experiment with rhesus monkeys (page 4). Harlow's monkeys

STUDY

Aim

Koluchova (1991) followed the long-term development of twin boys who had suffered severe privation in early childhood. Between the ages of 18 months and 7 years the boys had been locked in a cellar and physically abused. The twins were discovered by the authorities and moved into care at the age of 7 years. At the age of 9 they were fostered with two sisters.

Method

In a longitudinal study the twins were assessed at intervals over 22 years for intellectual and social ability.

Results

At the age of 7 years the twins had no speech, were suffering from malnutrition and were totally lacking in social ability. By the age of 10 years they were attending a mainstream school and were assessed as having average intelligence and showing normal attachments to their adoptive family. In a follow-up study in 1991 they were reported to have totally recovered and showed no psychological problems. As adults both twins have completed vocational training, are married and have their own families.

Conclusion

The effects of years of severe privation can be overcome with appropriate treatment and care.

showed inappropriate and delinquent social behaviour when they were placed into the company of other monkeys: they were aggressive towards other monkeys, unable to form normal relationships and attacked any monkey that tried to mate with them. If they did have offspring, the deprived monkeys were extremely poor, neglecting mothers. Harlow's work illustrates the extreme consequences of privation, at least in monkeys.

Aside from the experimental work of Harlow, most evidence for effects of privation has come from case studies of children who have been raised in conditions of neglect. Some cases, for example the case of Genie (Curtiss, 1977), suggest that severe privation has permanent effects. Genie had been severely neglected and maltreated by her parents. At the age of 13 years she was unable to speak, physically underdeveloped and showed inappropriate emotional responses. Despite fostering and intellectual stimulation, Genie apparently never recovered from her years of privation, although there was a suggestion that other factors may have contributed to her problems. Certainly in other cases (see Koluchova study, page 12), children who have experienced severe privation seem able to overcome the effects of their early suffering.

1.1.6 Romanian orphan studies – privation and effects of institutionalisation

In the 1990s the world became aware of the severe conditions in Romanian orphanages, where large numbers of children were being held in inhumane conditions. The children were malnourished, had no toys and experienced minimal social interaction. Following an international outcry, many of the children were removed to enriched environments and adopted in the UK and other countries. The progress of the UK adoptees has been followed closely by the English and Romanian Adoptees study team at the Institute of Psychiatry led by Michael Rutter.

Figure 1.8 *The plight of Romanian orphans enabled psychologists to study the effects of severe privation.*

The age-related benefits of adoption – the work of Rutter *et al.*

Since 1998 children from Romanian orphanages have been studied many times to see whether the effects of their early privation are long-lasting. Although Rutter's original study (see page 14) suggested that severe institutional deprivation can be overcome, more recent research has not been as positive, especially for those children who are adopted after the age of 6 months.

Kreppner *et al.* (1999) reported that 104 Romanian children adopted into British families before the age of 2 years showed lower frequency of pretend play, role play and ability to appreciate other people's mental states than a UK control group. These differences did not appear to be related to general cognitive or verbal ability, so the negative outcomes were assumed to be due to their early privation.

Rutter *et al.* (2007) studied 144 children who had been raised in Romanian institutions and been adopted into UK families. The children were studied at 4, 6 and 11 years and compared with 52 UK adoptees not raised in institutions. Following general assessment, some of children were also tested for autistic-like symptoms at the age of 12 years – 9.2% of the Romanian institution-reared adoptees were found to show quasi-autistic symptoms compared with 0% of the UK adoptees. Quasi-autistic symptoms include communication difficulties and stereotyped behaviours. Approximately half of the children with quasi-autism also showed other symptoms such as disinhibited attachment and poor relationships with their peers. Disinhibited attachment occurs where children show little discrimination in their attachments, rapidly forming attachments with comparative strangers.

The Rutter team has also studied the long-term effects on cognitive functioning in Romanian orphans. Beckett *et al.* (2006) compared 131 adoptees from Romanian institutions with 50 UK-adopted children. The children were tested for cognitive functioning at the age of 11 years. Many of the Romanian children who were over the age of 6 months on arrival in the UK

STUDY

Aim

Rutter *et al.* (1998) investigated the progress of 111 Romanian orphans brought to Britain for adoption in the 1990s. These children had been raised in very poor institutions, with little chance to develop close attachments.

Method

The Romanian children were assessed for height, head circumference and general cognitive level (assessed using the McCarthy and Denver Scales) on arrival in Britain, and had periodic assessments until the age of 4 years. A control group of 52 British-adopted children was also tested to see whether it was separation from mother or the severe circumstances in Romania that was responsible for any negative effects.

Results

Approximately half the Romanian group showed intellectual deficits at the start and most of them were very underweight. The British children showed no such negative effects. Four years later the two groups of adopted children showed no significant differences in either intellectual or physical development; however, children who arrived in Britain before the age of 6 months tended to show more marked improvement.

Conclusion

Rutter *et al.* concluded that (a) the negative outcomes shown by the Romanian children could be overcome through adequate substitute care, and (b) separation from mother alone is not sufficient to cause negative outcomes, as the British children had been separated but were not developmentally delayed.

Evaluation

- The situation of the Romanian orphans provides a fairly unique opportunity for psychologists to study the effects of severe and sustained privation in a large sample of human participants. Prior to this, privation research had been limited to animal experiments or case studies with single individuals in extreme circumstances.
- Although not all of these children show developmental catch-up leading to equivalence with UK-raised controls, they nonetheless show a significant improvement in comparison to their non-adopted Romanian peers.
- Despite having been raised in extremely deprived conditions, the extent of human contact the Romanian children had experienced and the individual circumstances into which they were adopted varied considerably. This may have mediated the effects of privation for some individuals.
- More recent evidence raises questions about Rutter's original finding that the effects of early privation could be overcome. The general outlook seems to be less positive when adoption occurs after the age of 6 months.

continued to show marked adverse effects at the age of 11 years, although some catch-up was noted between ages 6 and 11 for those children at the very bottom of the ability range. The researchers concluded that there are continuing psychological deficits associated with institutional deprivation for children adopted over the age of 6 months.

1.1.7 Bowlby's theory of attachment

Bowlby was a psychoanalyst and psychiatrist who thought that many mental health and behavioural problems could be directly attributed to early childhood experiences. In 1951, the World Health Organization (WHO) published a document in which Bowlby stated that mother love in infancy is just as important for a child's mental health as are vitamins and minerals for physical health. In his 1953 book, *Child Care and the Growth of Love*, Bowlby stated the following:

> What is believed to be essential for mental health is that an infant and young child should experience a warm, intimate and continuous relationship with his mother (or permanent mother-substitute – one person who steadily 'mothers' him) in which both find satisfaction and enjoyment.

Remember how the psychodynamic approach emphasises the role of innate, instinctual drives in the motivation of our behaviour. This theoretical background led Bowlby to suggest that a child had an instinctual need to be close to the mother, which he called 'proximity seeking'.

The key points of Bowlby's (1951) theory are shown in the box below.

The implications of Bowlby's theory

- When the maternal deprivation hypothesis was originally proposed some mothers questioned their own childcare arrangements. Mothers who were in work felt guilty for leaving their children in alternative care and stay-at-home mothers probably thought that they should continue to do so for the good of the child. As such, Bowlby's work affected the way in which a generation of children was raised.
- In other areas too there were consequences for social and welfare policy and practice: some childcare workers reading Bowlby's work concluded that it was better for a child to be brought up by a 'bad' mother than to be sent to an institution or children's home.
- Bowlby's work also had positive consequences. Hospitals changed their practices so that mothers were encouraged to stay with their child in hospital and the importance of continuity of care was recognised for children in institutions.

Bowlby's theory of attachment and maternal deprivation hypothesis

- A child has an innate need to attach to **one main attachment figure.** This idea of the need for a single and exclusive bond became known as **monotropy** theory. Although Bowlby did not exclude the possibility of other attachments for a child, he did believe that there should be a primary bond which was much more important than any other.
- A child should receive the **continuous care** of this single most important attachment figure for approximately **the first two years** of life.
- If the attachment is broken or disrupted during the **critical two-year period** the child will suffer **irreversible long-term consequences.**
- **Maternal deprivation** would lead to **delinquency, affectionless psychopathy and intellectual retardation.** Affectionless psychopathy is an inability to empathise with other people, or, as Klein (1987) described it, 'permanent lack of feeling for others'.

Figure 1.9 *Bowlby's maternal deprivation hypothesis predicted damaging consequences for children who did not have the continuous care of a single attachment figure.*

Support for the maternal deprivation hypothesis came from a variety of sources. Drawing initially on the evidence from animal studies, such as that of Harlow and Lorenz, Bowlby then looked at research into the effects of institutional care. One such study was the work of Goldfarb (1943), who carried out a longitudinal study on 15 pairs of children up to the ages of 10–14. Children in one group were fostered soon after birth, whilst the other group spent 3 years in an institution and were then fostered. Goldfarb found that the institution group performed significantly less well on a range of emotional and cognitive measures, concluding that their deficits could be attributed to their lack of an attachment figure during their institutionalised years. However, lack of an attachment figure may not be the sole reason for the deficits observed in these children. In those days, institutional settings tended to be very unstimulating environments, with few toys and books. It is also possible that the 15 children who were chosen for fostering were chosen because they were brighter and more sociable compared with the institution group.

STUDY

Aim

Bowlby (1946) set out to investigate causes of delinquency.

Method

Bowlby interviewed 44 juvenile thieves at a clinic, asking them about themselves, their behaviour and their childhood experiences. Bowlby also interviewed members of their families about the boys' behaviour and aspects of family history, including whether the boys had been separated from their families in early childhood. A control group of non-delinquent young people was used as a baseline for comparison.

Results

The clinic group included 14 individuals identified as affectionless psychopaths, and of these, 12 had been separated from their mothers for a long period during their first 2 years. Only five of the delinquents who were not suffering affectionless behaviour had been similarly separated from their mothers, and only two of the control group had been separated for any prolonged period (see figure 1.10).

Conclusion

Bowlby concluded that delinquency is linked to childhood maternal deprivation, since the delinquents were more likely than the average population to have had a deprivation experience in childhood. Critics have argued that the retrospective interviews he conducted might have yielded unreliable data. Quite simply, the interviewees might not have been able to recall accurately events from many years ago.

	Control group	Juvenile thieves
Evidence of maternal deprivation	2	17
No evidence of maternal deprivation	42	27

Figure 1.10 *Table showing the association between cases of antisocial behaviour and maternal deprivation (Bowlby, 1946).*

Bowlby's research was conducted during the course of his work as a child psychoanalyst at an institution for juvenile offenders.

Evaluation of Bowlby's theory

Whilst not denying the importance of attachment, many people have criticised aspects of Bowlby's maternal deprivation hypothesis. The issues discussed here are:

- the concept of monotropy
- deprivation as the cause of delinquency
- the concept of a critical period and irreversibility
- the effectiveness of substitute care
- the role of the father.

i) Monotropy – the work of Schaffer

Bowlby's notion of a monotropic attachment has been criticised by Schaffer and Emerson (1964), who showed that children develop more than one strong attachment, and that attachment need not be to the mother but will be to those who are most responsive to the child's needs.

Schaffer and Emerson's research into multiple attachments is consistent with cross-cultural studies of childrearing. Schaffer (1996) also states that there is no evidence from societies where infant care is shared between members of the community that shared care is diluted care. Tronick *et al.* (1987) described the infant care arrangements of the Efe people from Zaire, where children are collectively cared for by members of the group, and where the average number of carers for a group of infants is 14.2. Such collective responsibility seems to have no damaging psychological effects on the children and brings many benefits, including the provision of various sources of security and wider social experience for the child.

ii) Deprivation as the cause of delinquency – the work of Rutter

Rutter (1981) argued that there is no simple cause-and-effect relationship between delinquency and maternal deprivation. He believed that other important variables need to be taken into account, such as the reason for the separation from the mother and the way the separation is handled. Not all cases of maternal separation result in delinquent behaviour. Rutter suggested that Bowlby had confused deprivation and

Evaluation – continued

privation (see 1.1.5). Deprivation happens when a child has had an emotionally satisfactory relationship which is then broken, whereas privation is never having had an emotionally satisfactory bond in the first place. Note the consistency between Rutter's suggestion that privation is the main cause of delinquency and Harlow's work with infant monkeys.

In 1970, Rutter *et al.* carried out a large-scale study of children on the Isle of Wight, using a rating scale to measure disturbed behaviour. Parents and teachers were asked to assess a child's character and behaviour by indicating agreement or disagreement with a series of statements such as, 'Often destroys or damages own or others' property' and 'Not much liked by other children'. Rutter *et al.* concluded that approximately 6% of 10- and 11-year-olds showed substantial emotional and behavioural problems. Subsequent investigation showed that these children had suffered from an accumulation of stresses, including, but not exclusively, separation from mother. The types of stresses identified by Rutter included marital discord, overcrowding, psychiatric illness in one or both parents and death of a close relative. Rutter concluded that maternal deprivation on its own was not a sufficient explanation for delinquency and that the reason for the separation of mother and child was a more important determinant of problem behaviour. Separations that were well handled and included satisfactory alternative emotional support for the child were much less likely to lead to delinquency than separations involving family discord and argument.

iii) Critical period for attachment and irreversibility

Bowlby asserted that 'good mothering is almost useless if delayed until after 2½ years of age'. However, Hodges and Tizard (1989) showed how children adopted as late as 7 years of age could establish strong affectional relationships with adopted parents. At the age of 16 years, the adopted children were found to have family relationships that were as good as those of children who had been raised continuously in their own families. Clarke and Clarke (1976) reviewed a large number of studies and suggested that children have a resilience which enables them to cope with and overcome even the most difficult circumstances. Despite these positive findings, some studies do seem to support Bowlby's notion that lack of attachment in early life can lead to negative psychological consequences. For example, Romanian orphan research indicates that enduring cognitive and behavioural effects of severe early deprivation are worse if the adoption takes place after 6 months of age (Rutter *et al.*, 1998).

Results of animal research might lead us to question Bowlby's ideas about the irreversible damage caused by maternal deprivation. In a follow-up study of Harlow's work with rhesus monkeys (page 4), Suomi and Harlow (1972) found that it was possible to socialise 6-month-old isolated monkeys by introducing female monkeys 3 months younger than themselves (monkey therapists). Using these monkey therapists, delinquent and stereotyped behaviours were found to be much reduced.

iv) The effectiveness of substitute care

Freud and Dann (1951) studied six war orphans who had been living in a concentration camp for 2 years before they were brought to Britain at the age of 3 years. Initially the children were hostile, had poorly developed language skills and were underweight. However, the children were relatively emotionally sound and had extremely close bonds with each other. Freud and Dann proposed that the children had survived emotionally because they had established bonds with peers who acted as an effective substitute for a primary attachment figure. Skuse (1984) reviewed several cases of deprivation and concluded that, with sympathetic care, such children have an 'excellent prognosis'. Most recently, work with Romanian adoptees (Rutter *et al.*, 2007; Beckett *et al.*, 2006) has indicated that whilst significant catch-up is possible for those children who have the benefit of early substitute care, later adopted children may not be able to fully recover.

Evaluation – continued

v) The role of the father

In the 1940s/1950s, when Bowlby was studying attachment, fathers had very little to do with childcare and childrearing. According to Bowlby, the child would have one attachment figure and most usually this would be the mother. However, with changes in social attitudes and employment patterns, fathers nowadays take an increasingly active role in the care of their children.

Studies have shown that some fathers are just as responsive to their infants as mothers are (Parke and Sawin, 1980). Since responsiveness is an important factor in the development of attachment, this might suggest that paternal attachments can be just as secure as attachments to mother. van Ijzendoorn and de Wolff (1997) have found that there is a positive correlation between the level of sensitivity shown by the father and the security of father–infant attachment, although the correlation is not as strong as it is for mothers.

In their research into multiple attachments, Schaffer and Emerson (1964) found that around half the infants in their Scottish study showed a stronger attachment to someone other than the mother, usually the father. Lamb (1997) found that babies will approach both mother and father equally to be held except when they are in distress, when the mother is usually the preferred attachment figure.

Lamb (1987) noted differences in maternal and paternal interactions with infants: time that fathers spend with their children is taken up with fun, playtime activity; mothers spend their time with the child carrying out care-focused duties such as cleaning and dressing. Despite these differences in type of interaction, evidence from fathering research indicates that fathers have a valuable role to play in attachment.

STUDY

Aim

Schaffer and Emerson (1964) investigated the number of attachment relationships infants have.

Method

In a longitudinal study of Scottish infants throughout their first 18 months, 60 infants were observed and mothers were interviewed about the child's responses to separation. Two aspects of attachment behaviour were considered: separation anxiety and stranger distress.

Results

By 18 months most children had formed more than one attachment figure and some children had as many as five. Although the mother was the most commonly selected attachment figure, 75% of infants also selected the father at 18 months.

Conclusion

Babies do not normally demonstrate monotropy and it is usual for a child to have several attachment figures. This finding is supported by other research. For example, Lamb (1977) noted how infants establish several attachments simultaneously.

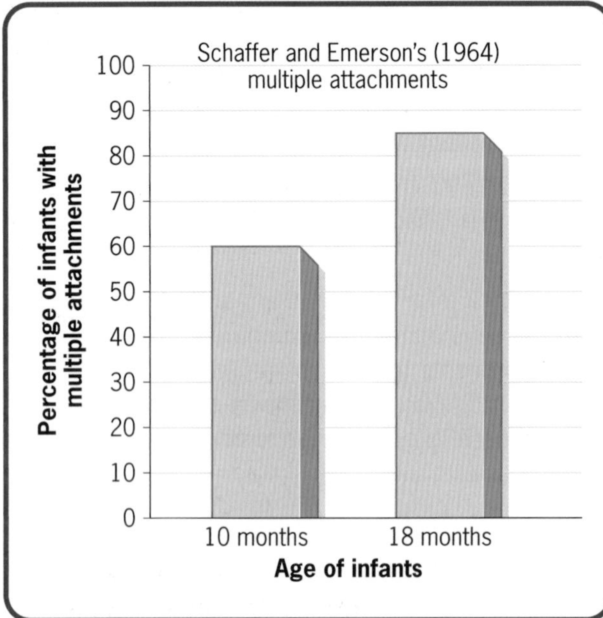

Figure 1.11 *The percentages of infants with multiple attachments at 10 months and 18 months (Schaffer and Emerson, 1964).*

1.2 Later relationships

Friendship in childhood and adolescence

Smith *et al.* (2003) describe friendship as 'a close relationship between two particular people, as indicated by their association together or their psychological attachment and trust.' According to Erwin (1998), children's friendships serve a number of important functions:

- friends allow for the development of interactional and cognitive skills
- friends provide an opportunity for intimacy
- friends enable us to exchange and test knowledge about people and the world
- friends can be an important emotional buffer in times of stress, for example, when parents are arguing and the child is unhappy at home.

Many studies have shown that friends tend to share personality traits, interests and backgrounds, perhaps because a relationship with someone similar to ourselves is rewarding and supportive. As the friendship progresses, friends start to become even more similar in attitude and behaviour.

STUDY

Aim

Damon (1977) investigated age-related differences in the understanding of friendship.

Method

Children were interviewed and asked a series of questions like 'Tell me about your best friend' or 'Tell me a story about two children who are friends'. The content of the replies was analysed and categorised into three levels of understanding.

Results

Children under 7 years expressed few feelings of like or dislike. For them, friends are just people they spend time with and friendships are quickly formed and quickly dissolved – for example, if a child takes away a toy from another. Between 8 and 11 years children described friendships based on shared mutual interests, with trust and responsiveness to others' needs, with kindness seen as an important criterion. From 12 years upwards friendships were described as deep, enduring relationships, with mutual understanding and sharing of intimacies.

Conclusion

Understanding of friendship becomes more complex with age as children become less egocentric and more concerned with mutuality. There is a gradual shift from focus on shared activities to focus on intimacy and reciprocal understanding.

1.2.1 Age-related change in friendship

Observation studies often show that 2-year-old children have a sustained preference for a particular playmate, and by the age of 4, approximately 50% of children have a preferred friend with whom they spend at least 30% of their time at nursery school (Hinde *et al.*, 1985). The number of friendships increases up until adolescence, when depth of relationship rather than number of friends becomes important. Levitt *et al.* (1993) found that even 7-year-olds reported 'feeling close' to friends as well as members of their family, and Buhrmester (1996) found that, whereas 7- to 10-year-olds are most likely to self-disclose to parents, 15-year-olds are most likely to self-disclose to friends.

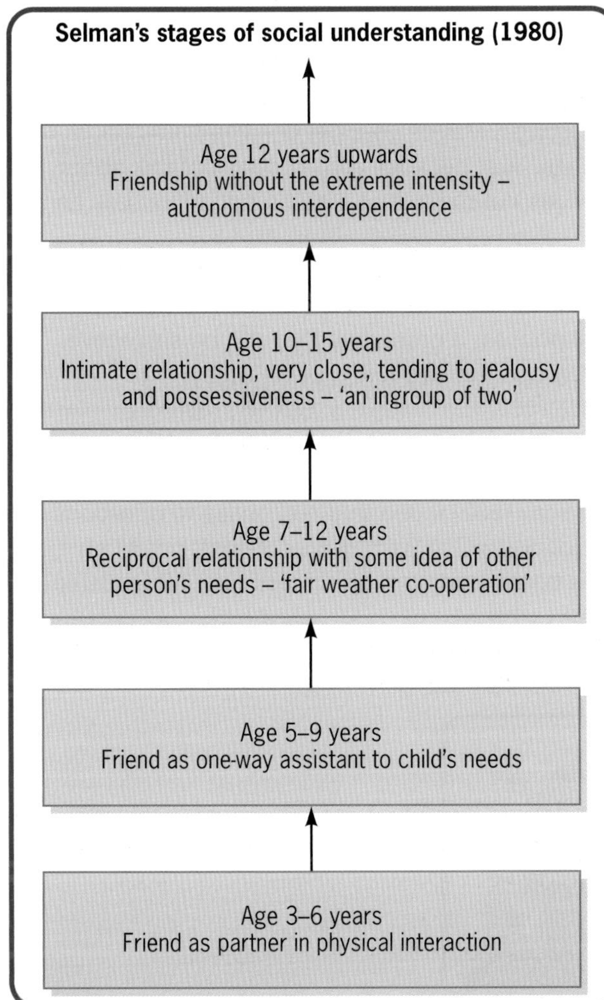

Figure 1.12 *Understanding of friendship becomes increasingly complex with age (Selman, 1980).*

Hartup and Stevens (1999) report a decrease in the number of friends after the early teens, with adolescents reporting they have between four and six friends and most young adults stating that they have one or two friends.

Just as children seem to value friends more as they get older and prefer the company of peers to the company of adults and family, so their understanding of friendship seems to change with age. This age-related change in understanding friendship might be explained

STUDY

Aim

Bigelow and La Gaipa (1975) studied how children's understanding of 'a friend' changed with age by analysing children's essays.

Method

Children from Scotland and Canada between the ages of 6 and 14 years were asked to write essays about 'a best friend'. There were 480 children in each sample. Researchers then analysed the content of each essay, rating the content on 21 dimensions, including reciprocity and sharing.

Results

The dimensions referred to in the stories changed as children got older. For younger children the emphasis was more on common activities, living nearby, general play and giving to a friend. For older children the focus was more on similarity, acceptance, loyalty and intimacy. No differences were observed between the samples from the two countries.

Conclusion

The understanding of the concept 'friend' becomes more sophisticated with age, with an increasing emphasis on psychological qualities rather than physical interaction. Children's views about friendship become less egocentric, with less focus on the child's own perspective, and more empathetic, with the child showing greater concern for the other person.

through lessening egocentrism and an increase in the ability to take the perspective of another person.

Damon (1977) studied how the understanding of friendship changed with age, identifying three levels of friendship understanding.

Cognitive representations of friendship were also investigated by Selman (1980) who presented children with a social dilemma. A typical dilemma might involve a story about a girl who lied to her friend because she did not want to go out with her. The story was then followed by interview questions about the characters in the story and about friendship in general. Selman categorised the responses and proposed five stages in social understanding of friendship (see figure 1.12).

1.2.2 Sex differences in children's friendship

Before 2 years, interaction between children tends to be in twosomes or pairs, with little evidence of same-sex preference. However, even before the concepts of 'boy' and 'girl' are properly developed, children start to prefer the company of their own sex, and by 3 or 4 years play mostly in same-sex groups (Erwin, 1998). This sex separation might occur because boys and girls prefer different sorts of activities – for example, boys engage in much more rough-and-tumble play. By 5 years of age boys show greater same-sex preference than girls and by 11 or 12 years groups have become very important and sex segregation is almost complete.

Evaluation

- The increasingly complex and abstract understanding of friendship shown in older children may be partly due to the increase in ability to express such ideas in language. Maybe younger children understand friendship in a complex way, but cannot express their ideas. Just because a child does not talk about characteristics like trust and empathy in their answer, it does not mean that they do not appreciate and recognise such qualities in a friend.
- Many studies involve the use of the clinical interview and lack formal structure and control. Usually the interview is followed by analysis and categorisation of responses, a procedure that can be subjective. This is especially likely where responses take a completely open-ended form like an essay.
- Hypothetical dilemma responses have been used in many contexts, including investigations of moral and pro-social reasoning, and it has often been suggested that hypothetical reasoning tends to be more advanced than real-life understanding. Interestingly, Serafica (1982) found that responses to questions about hypothetical friends and real friends yielded descriptions which were quite different; not all studies are testing the same thing – some ask about 'a friend', 'a best friend' and others ask about 'friendship', which is a complex and abstract notion for a young child.

Figure 1.13 *Boys are more likely to focus on the importance of the group, whereas girls are more concerned with forming close, intimate relationships.*

STUDY

Aim

To investigate social networks in 10-year-old boys and girls.

Method

Benenson (1990) asked 10-year-old children to rate their peers using friendship and play rating scales. The children were also asked to describe their peers using open-ended interviews.

Results

Boys were found to have more extensive social networks of interconnected friendships, whereas girls' friendships were based on small, more intimate groups or 'cliques', as shown in Figure 1.14. Benenson also noted that, in interviews, boys tended to focus on attributes that contributed to the status of the group, whereas girls tended to focus on attributes that were important for two-person or small-group relationships. No differences were found in the number of best friends reported by boys and girls.

Conclusion

Boys and girls have different types of social networks and have different ideas about the attributes that are important for friendship.

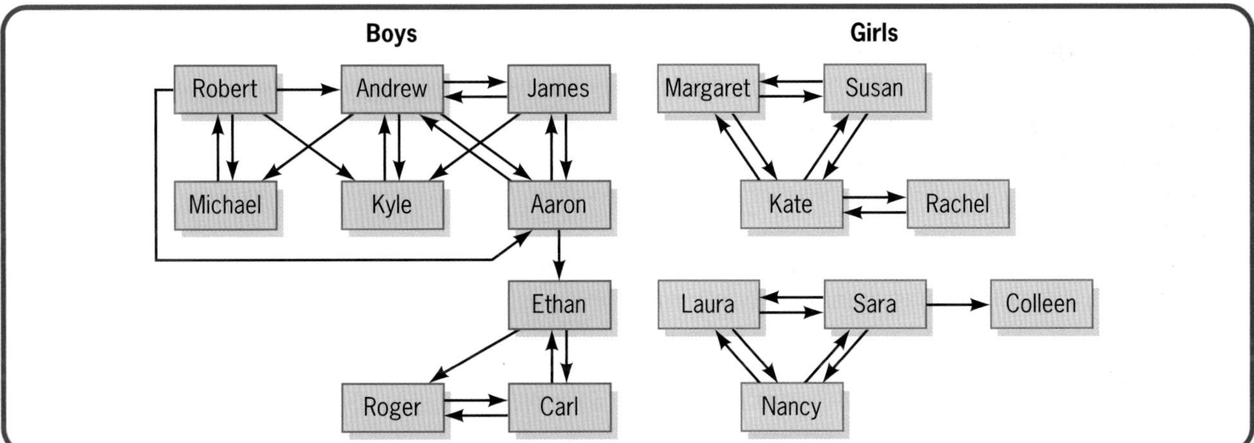

Figure 1.14 *Sex differences in social organisation in 10-year-old boys and girls. The direction of the arrows indicates who each child is friends with. Boys have been found to have more extensive friendships than girls (after Benenson, 1990).*

STUDY

Aim

Lever (1976) investigated sex differences in friendship attitudes and friendship behaviours.

Method

10-year-old boys and girls in American city and suburban schools were interviewed about their attitudes towards friends and their interactions with friends.

Results

Several sex differences emerged:

- girls were most comfortable with a single best friend, being less likely than boys to admit a third person into a friendship
- girls openly showed affection – for example, by handholding and writing notes – whereas such behaviour was rarely seen in boys
- girls were more sensitive to the fragility of the intimate relationship, worrying more about falling out with a friend
- girls shared personal intimacies, whereas boys shared group secrets and information about group strategy or rules
- girls were more likely to be jealous of a third party than boys.

Conclusion

Girls are more emotionally involved with friends and prefer more intimate two-person relationships, whereas boys' friendships are more open.

Waldrop and Halverson (1975) have described boys' and girls' peer relationships as extensive (boys) and intensive (girls). For boys, most time is spent in the larger group with the focus on shared activities or tasks. Boys view the friendship group as a collective entity and value its solidarity. Girls' relationships are described as intensive because they view the group as a network of intimate two-person friendships, with the focus on closeness and sharing of emotion rather than joint activities.

Sex differences in friendship during adolescence tend to be similar to those observed in younger children. Although there is no apparent difference in the number of friends that boys and girls have, boys are much less concerned with forming close, intimate relationships. Whereas girls see individual friends as confidantes and a source of emotional support, boys are more likely to focus on the importance of the group and allegiance to the group. Considering reasons for differences in social behaviour between adolescent males and females, Douvan and Adelson (1966) suggested that boys need the group to support the quest for autonomy and defy authority, whilst girls are not as defiant and do not need to focus on the group as a source of strength.

Early work by Lever (1976) showed that girls worry more about their friendships than boys. Researchers have recently investigated this aspect of sex differences in friendships and have confirmed that girls are much more sensitive to threats to a relationship and much more concerned about the breakdown of close relationships than boys (Benenson and Christakos, 2003).

STUDY

Aim

Benenson and Christakos (2003) investigated sex differences in young people's friendships.

Method

60 girls and 60 boys, aged between 10 and 15 years, were interviewed about their closest same-sex friendships.

Results

Several differences were noted: girls' friendships lasted for a shorter time than boys'; girls were more upset at the thought of the friendship ending than boys; girls were more likely than boys to recognise that they had already done something that could have prejudiced their friendship; girls reported having had more 'best friends' in the past than boys.

Conclusion

Girls appear to be very aware of the fragility and vulnerability of relationships with their same-sex best friend. Boys appear to be much less sensitive and much less concerned about the fragility of their best friend relationships.

Evaluation

- The male preference for larger friendship groups can be explained from the biological and evolutionary perspective in psychology; for males the large group offers a means of fulfilling the need to compete within the dominance hierarchy. Viewing social behaviour from this perspective might also explain why females prefer quieter activities using friends as a source of individual support, thus fulfilling the need to nurture and care.
- Traditional behaviourists would argue that sex differences in friendships occur because of operant conditioning. Males and females are reinforced for what is seen as sex-appropriate behaviour, so girls are encouraged to play quietly in twos and boys to play competitively in groups.
- Social learning theorists would suggest that boys and girls are simply copying the behaviour of adult models.

1.2.3 Popularity and rejection

Coie and Dodge (1983) carried out a sociometric study of primary-school-aged children in which each child was asked to identify who in the class they 'liked most' and who they 'liked least'. From the responses the researchers identified five types of children: popular children, average children, controversial children, neglected children and rejected children.

Neglected children are often well adjusted and quite socially skilled, apparently choosing to play alone rather than being forced into solitude because they are actively disliked by peers. Classmates often describe neglected children as shy. Controversial children do show some of the behaviours typical of rejected-aggressive children, but they compensate for these with positive and pro-social behaviours. As a result, the controversial child often has many friends, despite being

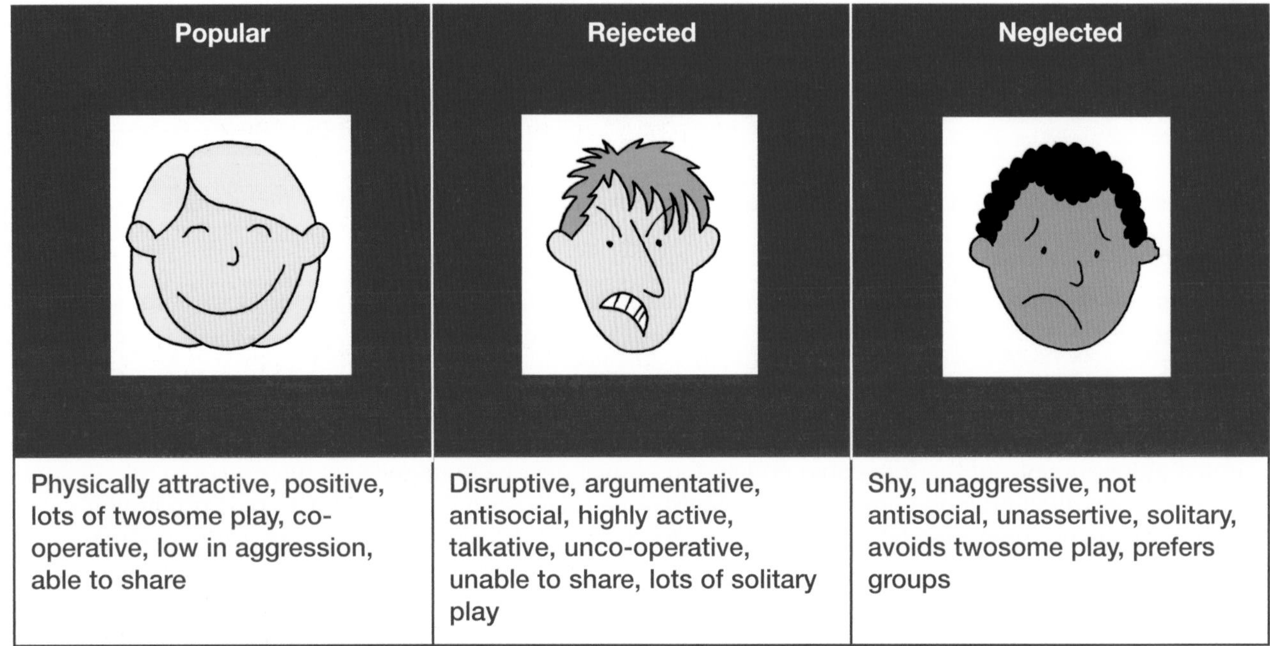

Figure 1.15 *Behaviours typical of popular, rejected and neglected children (Schaffer, 1996).*

disliked by some children. It is the rejected child that is a source of concern and rejected children have been the greatest focus of study for child psychologists.

Rejected children often have few friends or make friends with other unpopular children. Berk (2003) identifies two types of rejected child. **Rejected-aggressive** children often demonstrate serious behavioural problems because they are hostile, hyperactive and impulsive. They are very poor at social understanding, very often misreading the behaviour of others – for example, misinterpreting the behaviour of peers as hostile (Crick and Ladd, 1993). **Rejected-withdrawn** children are inhibited, passive and socially withdrawn. They show high levels of social anxiety and are concerned about being attacked by others. Such a submissive style often leads to them to being the target of bullying.

Causes of popularity and rejection

i) Attractiveness

Children prefer to be friends with those who are attractive, and even young children have been found to prefer to look at attractive rather than unattractive peers. Higher-status individuals and those who are perceived to be more competent – for example, those good at sport – tend to be more popular. Vaughn and Langlois (1983) found a significant correlation between ratings of physical attractiveness and popularity using a sociometric analysis with 59 preschool children. Whilst the results for the group as a whole were significant, there was a much more significant correlation between the two variables for the girls than for the boys.

ii) Similarity

Children will choose friends who live near or who are seen regularly. As we find similarity reinforcing, children will choose playmates from similar background, of the same sex, with similar interests and so on. Rubin (1980) refers to strong pressures to exclude the 'deviant' or different child. Kandel (1978) carried out a longitudinal study of adolescent friendships from the start to the end of a school year, which suggests similarity is important in friendship. Three types of friendships were identified:

- maintained friendships – existed at the start and the end of the year
- dissolved friendships – existed at the start, but not at the end of the year
- newly formed friendships – started up at some time during the year.

Kandel noted that maintained and newly formed friendship pairs were more similar in attitude, behaviour and interests than dissolved friendship pairs. He concluded that either similarity may be the key to friendship or successful friendships may be those

Type	Relationship characteristics
Secure	No trouble getting close to others Happy depending on others Comfortable if others are dependent Not worried about being abandoned Not afraid someone will get too close
Anxious-avoidant	Somewhat uncomfortable being close to others Difficulty trusting others Difficulty depending on others Nervous when anyone gets too close Feels partners want to be too intimate
Anxious-ambivalent resistant	Concerned partner will leave Disappointed other people will not get close enough Desire for intense closeness frightens others away Afraid others are not really committed

Figure 1.16 *Adult relationship characteristics displayed by secure and anxious types (Hazan and Shaver, 1987).*

STUDY

Aim

Dodge *et al.* (1983) investigated playground behaviour to see whether there were behavioural differences between popular and unpopular children.

Method

In a naturalistic observation, 5-year-olds were observed in the playground. Researchers focused on pairs of children at play and watched to see how a third child would approach and try to join in with the game. Behaviours such as the time spent watching, the types of verbal comments made and the style of approach were recorded.

Results

It was found that popular and unpopular children differed significantly in their approaches to the other children. Popular children watched and waited, made group-oriented statements and were gradually accepted. Neglected children watched but shied away from attempting interaction. Rejected children were highly active and aggressive, disrupting play of the others, being generally unco-operative and making critical comments.

Conclusion

The unpopularity of rejected and neglected children relates to deficits in social skills.

where partners come to adopt each other's interests and characteristics.

iii) Childhood attachment – the Internal Working Model

According to attachment theory and the internal working model, the relationship between child and mother figure sets the pattern for future relationships. Perhaps, then, the rejected child is one who has not had the satisfactory care of a single loving adult, and who therefore has no model on which to base future relationships.

Hazan and Shaver (1987) proposed that the three types of attachment shown in Ainsworth's Strange Situation (pages 6–8) are carried through to later relationships with other people, so that an infant defined as 'secure' type according to Ainsworth's category system, would grow up to be a person who has similarly positive experiences in later relationships. Although Hazan and Shaver relate the three types to later romantic relationships, it follows that the 'anxious-resistant' and 'anxious-avoidant' types would probably be more likely to have difficulty in childhood and adolescent relationships too. For example, the anxious-avoidant type would be afraid of getting too close to other people and tend to resist any attempts at intimacy from others, therefore finding it very difficult to sustain friendships.

iv) Personality characteristics

Rejected children do seem to show aggressive and disruptive behaviours, but it is very difficult to say whether these are a cause or a consequence of their rejection. To disentangle cause and effect, Dodge (1983) arranged for children aged 6–8 years who did not know each other to play together in organised play sessions over a number of weeks. The children were tested for personality characteristics before the play sessions began and were observed during the sessions. The observers recorded data about each child's popularity and interaction in the group. A clear relationship was found between the children's personality traits at the start of the study and their popularity within the group. However, it was also noted that once a child had been labelled as 'unpopular' by the group, the child's behaviour became even more negative. It therefore seems that personality traits may lead to unpopularity, which, once established, becomes self-fulfilling.

Evaluation

- There is no clear-cut cause-and-effect relationship between social inadequacy and rejection. Perhaps initial peer group rejection leads to an expectation of social failure. Because a child expects to be rejected he/she may then avoid social opportunities to practise peer social skills. As a result the child becomes more and more deficient at social interaction.
- Ladd and Golter (1988) followed 3- to 4-year-old children for a year to see whether they could detect a cause-and-effect relationship between social incompetence and unpopularity. They found that early argumentative behaviour predicted later unpopular status.

v) Social skills

Whilst attachment theory may explain why some children have difficulty relating to peers, there are other possible explanations. A number of studies have shown that one reason for rejection by peers may be that a child has poor social skills and therefore experiences difficulty interacting with others.

If poor social skills are at the root of the problem for an isolated child, then training in social skills ought to lead to an increase in popularity. Oden and Asher (1977) set up a programme of social skills training for 8 to 9-year-old isolates. The unpopular children were given coaching in the following skills:

- how to join in
- turn-taking
- sharing
- communication
- giving attention to others
- helping.

At the end of the programme they were no longer isolated from their peers, were more outgoing and more positive towards other people and had improved social status.

Consequences of popularity and rejection

Berk (2003) describes acceptance by peers as extremely important for a child's psychological adjustment. Whereas childhood popularity seems to be associated with positive life outcomes, evidence from several sources suggests negative long-term outcomes for unpopular children. Cowen *et al.* (1973) carried out a longitudinal study with 800 children to investigate the long-term effects of peer relationships on psychological well-being. It was found that children rated negatively by peers at 8 years old were more likely to suffer from a variety of psychiatric problems throughout childhood and adolescence and into their adult lives. Duck (1991) similarly found that rejected children were more likely to grow up to suffer from a range of behavioural and mental disorders, including alcoholism, depression, schizophrenia, delinquency and psychotic behaviour.

Kuperschmidt and Coie (1990) identified a link between sociometric status and a number of negative life outcomes, including truancy and being in trouble with the police. In a 7-year longitudinal study they found that children identified as rejected at the age of 11 were much more likely to drop out of or be suspended from school and three times more likely than averagely popular children to have been in trouble with the police by late adolescence. Interestingly, neglected children did not show any increased evidence of negative outcomes.

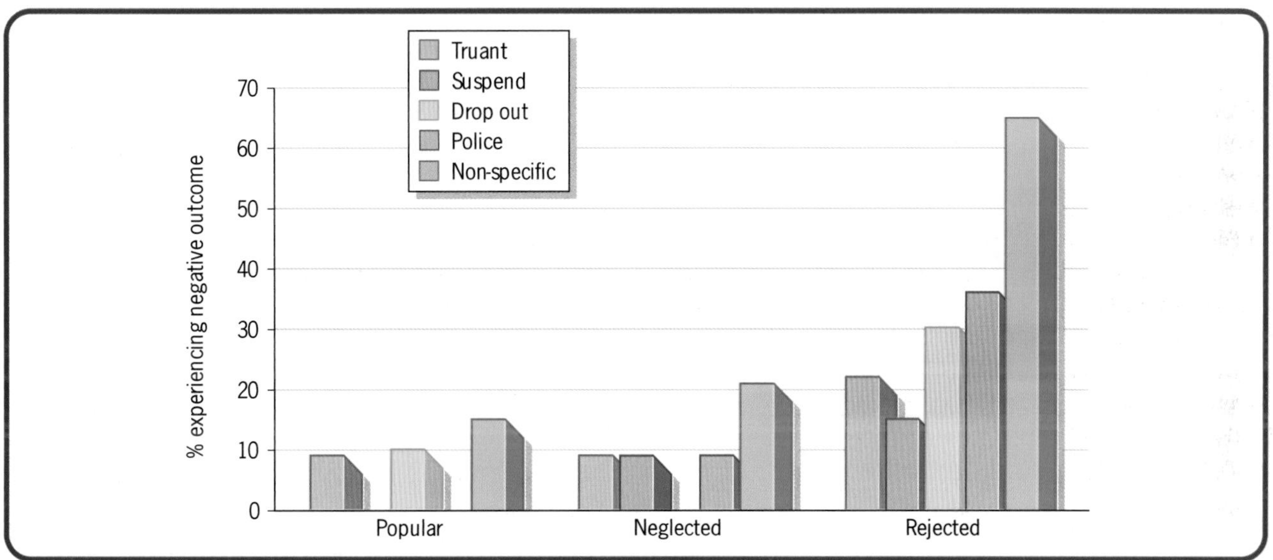

Figure 1.17 *Graph to show the relationship between popularity status and negative outcome (Kuperschmidt and Coie, 1990).*

Evaluation

- Although these studies suggest that rejection has serious consequences, determining a cause-and-effect relationship is impossible. It might be that these individuals were rejected as children because they already showed disordered behaviours and that the behaviour was a cause and not a consequence of their rejection.
- Schaffer (1996) discusses the role of aggressiveness in negative outcomes and suggests that an aggressive temperament may be a more reliable indicator of negative life outcomes than peer rejection.
- Only some of the rejected children in the Kuperschmidt and Coie study were identified as being aggressive and these were the children more likely to show social maladjustment.
- In most studies of rejected children, the rejected children are also friendless, but it is possible to be rejected by many and yet still have one or two friends. A study by Bagwell *et al.* (1998) suggests that the effects of rejection alone are different from the combined effects of friendlessness and rejection.

STUDY

Aim

Bagwell *et al.* (1998) investigated the effects of peer rejection and friendship in a longitudinal study.

Method

A large group of 334 US children aged 10 years were asked to name their three best friends and the three people in class they liked the least. From the large group, the researchers selected children who fell into two distinct subgroups: 58 'friended' children who each had a stable best friend and 55 'chumless' children who had no two-way friendship. These children were then given a peer rejection score based on the ratings from the whole group. At the age of 23 years the young adults from the two subgroups were assessed on several variables.

Results

Those who were rejected as children had poorer life status (job, etc). Those who had childhood friends had better family relationships and self-esteem. Those rejected and friendless as children showed symptoms of mental disorder. The quality of adult friendships was not related to either rejection or friendlessness as a child.

Conclusion

The long-term effects of rejection are not the same as the effects of rejection coupled with childhood friendlessness.

How Psychology Works

A questionnaire to investigate differences in friendship between males and females

First read the Benenson and Christakos (2003) study on page 25 in which sex differences in young people's friendships were investigated. The researchers noted several differences when they asked participants about relationships with their closest friends – for example, they found that girls' friendships lasted for a shorter time than boys'.

- Design a questionnaire to assess teenagers' understanding and experience of their relationship with their same-sex close friend. Aim to have at least ten questions. You will have to decide whether it is best to use open or closed questions. You might even decide to use some form of rating scale. You can look at the same issues as Benenson and Christakos and try some others of your own. Questions might focus on issues such as duration, sharing of activities, sharing of intimacies, source of support in time of crisis, response to arguments, frequency of contact and so on.
- Type out your questions with answer spaces if they are open questions, and response options if they are closed questions. At the top of the sheet you need to type some standardised instructions.
- Prepare a debrief suitable for use after respondents have filled in the questionnaire.
- Pilot your questionnaire with a couple of female friends and a couple of male friends.

- Check whether your findings are consistent with those of Benenson and Christakos, who found that a) girls were more concerned with the fragility and vulnerability of their relationship with the same-sex best friend, and b) boys seemed much less sensitive and much less concerned about the fragility of their best friend relationships.
- Consider the **validity** of the questions on your questionnaire. Do the questions measure what they are supposed to measure? They probably have 'face validity' because 'on the face of it' you thought that they did measure what you wanted to measure. Now ask an impartial colleague or your teacher to consider the validity of each item.
- Write three paragraphs to summarise your activity as follows:

Paragraph 1: Summarise your findings and compare them to those of Benenson and Christakos.

Paragraph 2: Write a brief discussion of the ethical issues that arose when carrying out this study, how you considered them and how you might address the issues differently if you were to carry out a full study on this topic in the future.

Paragraph 3: Write a brief discussion considering the validity of the items on your questionnaire. Discuss any items that you now think are unsatisfactory and explain how you might change the content of the questionnaire to make it more appropriate.

Further Reading

Introductory texts

Bee, H. (1999) *The Developing Child*, 9th edn., New York: Longman.
Berk, L.E. (2003) *Child Development*, 6th edn., Boston: Allyn & Bacon.
Harris, M. and Butterworth, G. (2002) *Developmental Psychology: A Student's Handbook*, Hove: Psychology Press.
Jarvis, M. and Chandler, E. (2001) *Angles on Child Psychology*, Cheltenham: Nelson Thornes.
Slater, A. and Bremner, G. (2003) *Introduction to Developmental Psychology*, Oxford: Blackwell.
Smith, P.K., Cowie, H. and Blades, M. (1998) *Understanding Children's Development*, 3rd edn., Oxford: Blackwell.

Specialist sources

Berryman, J.C., Smythe, P.K., Taylor Davies, A. and Lamont, A. (2002) *Developmental Psychology and You*, 2nd edn., Oxford: Wiley Blackwell.
Bremner, J.G. (1994) *Infancy*, 2nd edn., Oxford: Blackwell.
Dunn, J. (2004) *Children's Friendships*, Oxford: Blackwell.
Erwin, P. (1998) *Friendships in Childhood and Adolescence*, London: Routledge.
Rutter, M. (1981) *Maternal Deprivation Reassessed*, 2nd edn., Harmondsworth: Penguin.
Schaffer, H.R. (1996) *Social Development*, Oxford: Blackwell.

Cognitive development

Chapter 2

Cognitive development is the area of psychology concerned with how children's thinking develops. Developmental researchers carry out studies to investigate children's thinking processes, particularly changes in thinking processes with age. As we shall see, children's thinking is very different to that of adults and there are qualitative differences in children's thinking at different ages.

2.1 Piaget's theory of cognitive development

The first person to study cognitive development in a systematic way was Jean Piaget. Piaget (1896–1980) was born in Neuchâtel, Switzerland. He had a background in epistemology, the philosophy of knowledge, and went on to study biology at university. His theory of cognitive development was based on detailed observations of his children and the children of friends. He was particularly interested in the thinking errors that children make and thought that these could inform us about children's thinking processes. His clinical interview technique was essentially an open-ended conversation in which he studied children's responses to problems he gave them.

2.1.1 Schemas, adaptation, assimilation, accommodation

Schemas

A **schema** can be defined as an evolving unit of knowledge which we use to understand and respond to situations. Piaget believed that schemas were the key to cognitive development and he described how they were developed or acquired. An example of a complex adult schema might be an 'electricity schema'. This would contain all the information a person has about electricity – for example, it is a form of energy, it travels along wires or cables, it is used to light bulbs, it is dangerous, it can cause fires. Individual schemas are linked to other schemas to form an interconnecting system of knowledge. In the case of an electricity schema, the knowledge about electricity would be linked to other schemas about heating and power sources and so on.

According to Piaget, young babies have simple schemas for innate or inborn reflexes – for example, babies have a sucking reflex, which Piaget assumed involved a 'sucking schema'. Other reflexes, such as the grasping reflex, were also assumed to involve basic schemas. These simple schemas can be applied to a range of different situations, so that infants will use the sucking schema with blankets, fingers, toes and other objects.

Very quickly a baby will develop other schemas, such as a 'throwing schema', applying this to a variety of objects which can be thrown from the cot or the buggy. Repeating an action seems to be important in the development of new schemas. In this sense a schema

Figure 2.1 *Young babies have simple schemas.*

can be understood almost as a learned habit. To take the example of a throwing schema, a baby will at first let an object fall from the cot and observe what happens. Other objects will then be thrown out of the cot and the child will repeat the action over and over. This particular action is especially likely to be repeated because it usually results in the fun of someone else having to pick the object up.

Adaptation – assimilation and accommodation

Piaget referred to the process by which a child's schemas are developed to fit with their experience of the world as **adaptation**. As each child's knowledge is adapted to take account of his or her own unique experience and environment, each child will develop a different understanding of the world. According to Piaget, adaptation takes place through the processes of **assimilation** and **accommodation**.

Assimilation means adding to an existing schema, either by applying a schema to a new situation or by adding new information to an existing schema. For example, Sam has learned to play with toys that have wheels using a pull-along dog that he has in his toy cupboard at home. He has developed a 'pull-along' schema. When he goes to nursery he will use the same schema with a pull-along duck. In this way, the duck has been assimilated into Sam's 'pull-along' schema, and his knowledge of the world has been adapted and consolidated in the light of experience.

In other situations new information cannot so easily be absorbed into an existing schema. When confronted with a wind-up tractor, Sam may try to use his 'pull-along' schema, but this will not work. According to Piaget, when a child assimilates an object or situation using a schema that does not quite fit that situation, the child experiences **disequilibrium**. Disequilibrium might be defined as a state of cognitive imbalance that occurs when our understanding of the world is inconsistent with incoming information. In this case, disequilibrium is caused by the fact that the tractor will not move forward in the way that Sam expects it to. Balance or **equilibrium** can be restored by a process which Piaget called accommodation.

Other examples of assimilation

Using a grown-up spoon in the same way as a baby spoon.

Holding a pen in the same way as a pencil.

Using the same action to put on a pair of shorts as to put on a pair of trousers.

Stroking the neighbour's labrador in the same way as stroking the family spaniel.

Accommodation means changing a schema or developing a new schema in order to deal effectively with a new situation. In this case, Sam will need to develop a new 'wind-up' schema in order to get the tractor to move along. Having developed a new schema to cope with the new experience, Sam is once again in a state of equilibrium. Note that his cognitive ability has also been extended because he now has two schemas for dealing with toys with wheels, a 'pull-along' schema and a 'wind-up' schema, instead of just one. In the additional examples below we can see how each instance would lead to the development of a new schema.

Other examples of accommodation

A spoon grip needs to be modified to hold a fork.

A pencil grip needs to be modified to hold a paintbrush.

A sucking schema needs to be modified the first time a baby is presented with solid food.

A digging schema used with a toy spade will need to be modified if the child is given a toy hammer.

According to Piaget, a child's understanding of the world is actively constructed through experience and discovery. For this reason his views are sometimes referred to as **constructivist**. Piaget believed that it is important for a child to actively explore and experience objects and situations in order to learn about them; only through active discovery could a child's understanding develop properly. Piaget's notion of **discovery learning** has had enormous influence in

nursery and primary education, leading to methods that allow for self-discovery through play rather than learning by instruction.

Due to his emphasis on discovery learning it is sometimes suggested that Piaget neglected the role of other people in cognitive development. In fact he recognised that parents and teachers played an important part through their provision of stimulating experiences and materials to aid the development of cognition.

2.1.2 Piaget's stages of intellectual development and his research

Piaget proposed that cognitive or intellectual development takes place in four stages. He thought that the sequence of stages was **invariant**, meaning that each child passes through these stages in the same order. He also proposed that the stages were **universal**, meaning that the same sequence of development applies to children from all cultures. Although there are indicative ages for each stage, progression through the stages depends on the maturity of the individual's nervous system; as the biological structures involved in thought become more complex and sophisticated, so does the capacity to think and understand. At each stage the child's understanding of the world is qualitatively different; the child thinks differently, making different mistakes and using different strategies to solve problems.

Piaget's stages of cognitive development

The sensorimotor stage (0–2 years)

The pre-operational stage (2–7 years)

The concrete operational stage (7–11 years)

The formal operational stage (12 years +)

STAGE 1 The sensorimotor stage: 0–2 years

At the start of this stage, 'knowledge' consists mainly of simple motor reflexes such as grasping and sucking. There is no intentional behaviour and the child's cognition is limited to sensations and motor movements. The child simply responds to stimuli and has no **object concept** or person concept, meaning there is no awareness of objects or people that are outside the child's immediate present. A child in the early stages of the sensorimotor stage does not distinguish between self and others, apparently not recognising that objects and other people exist independently of him or herself.

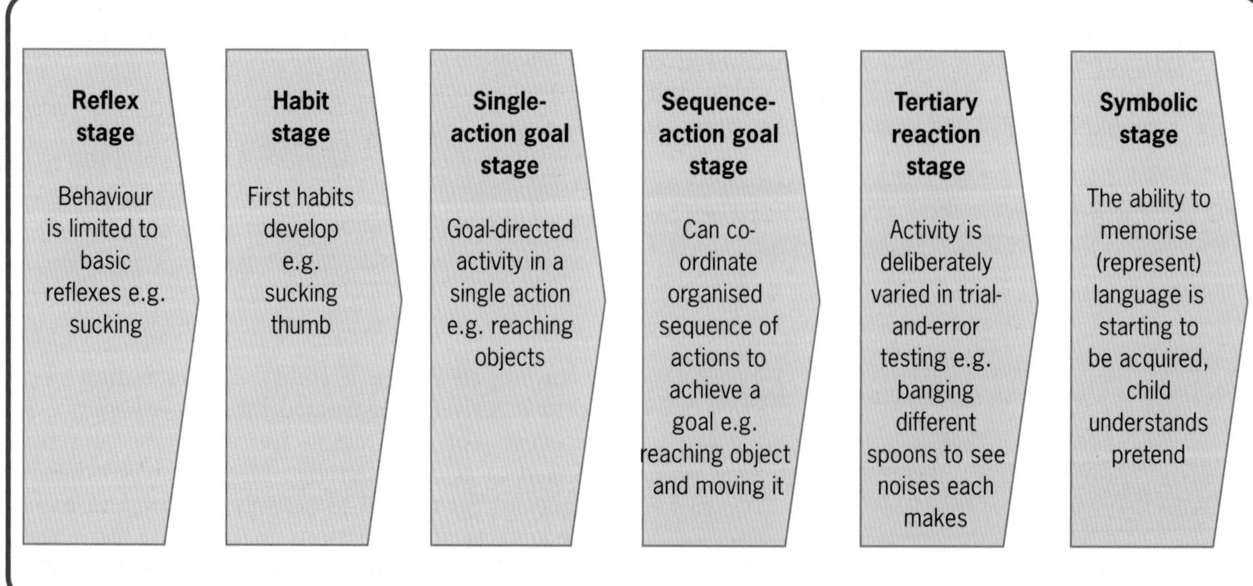

Figure 2.2 *Sub-stages of the sensorimotor stage.*

From around 8 months of age the child begins to act intentionally – for example, banging a spoon on the table to listen to the noise it makes. Trial-and-error behaviour is demonstrated – for example, the child might bang different objects on the table to see whether they make a noise too. Towards the end of the sensorimotor stage the child has acquired **general symbolic function**, which is the ability to understand that one thing can stand for another; this is linked to the development of language and the capacity for pretend play. The sensorimotor stage can be sub-divided into six sub-stages, as shown in Figure 2.2.

Object permanence

A key feature of the sensorimotor stage occurs at around the age of 8 months, when the child acquires an ability known as **object permanence**. Object permanence is the understanding that objects exist independently and continue to exist even if they cannot be seen. In order to have object permanence, a child needs to ability to hold a simple mental representation of the object. Essentially this means that the child needs to be able to remember. Piaget demonstrated object permanence in a simple study.

STUDY

Aim

Piaget (1963) investigated the age at which children acquired object permanence or object concept.

Method

Infants of different ages were tested individually. Piaget waited until the child was playing with an object. He then removed the toy from the child's grasp and hid it beneath a blanket whilst the child looked on. Piaget then observed whether or not the child searched for the hidden toy. If the child searched for the toy this would suggest that the child could understand that the object continued to exist even when it was no longer in sight, indicating object permanence.

Results

Under 8 months of the age the infant would not search for the hidden toy, apparently forgetting that the toy existed once it was out of sight. Infants of approximately 8 months would search for the hidden toy, showing that they had object permanence. Even when the infants had developed object permanence they were still fooled if Piaget moved the toy from under the blanket and hid it in a different place. Even though the infant had seen the toy moved from one hiding place to another he or she would continue to search for it in its original hiding place – under the blanket (the **A not B error**). At around the age of 12 months the infant would search for the toy in its most recent hiding place, showing a more advanced type of object permanence.

Conclusion

Simple object permanence develops at around 8 months, and by 12 months of age object permanence is complete.

Evaluation

- Perhaps infants under the age of 8 months did not search for the toy for other reasons: they lacked the necessary motor skills; they were not interested; the deliberate covering of the toy led them to infer that it was forbidden. Piaget's tests are sometimes described as lacking 'human sense'. For these and other reasons, critics have suggested that Piaget underestimated the age at which children develop object permanence.

Evaluation – continued

- Studies using alternative methods have shown that children as young as 3 months may have object permanence. Bower and Wishart (1972) made an object disappear by turning out the lights and then observed the child using an infrared camera. They found that the infants continued to reach for the object in the dark, suggesting they had object permanence. See 2.2.3 (page 54) for further work on early infant abilities that present a challenge to Piaget's views on object permanence.

Figure 2.3 *Piaget suggested that children under 8 months do not have object permanence.*

STAGE 2 The pre-operational stage: 2–7 years

Pre-operational children can use symbols, such as words and images, and can recognise that one thing can stand for something else – for example, a child can pretend that a big cardboard box is a car. However, there are many mental tasks that pre-operational children cannot perform. Indeed the stage is so named because children at this stage cannot perform mental operations, in other words they cannot logically manipulate information. As a result, there are many errors of thinking in the pre-operational stage. This stage can be divided into two sub-stages: the pre-conceptual period (2–4 years) and the intuitive period (4–7 years). By the time they reach the intuitive period children are beginning to carry out the mental operations involved in systematic classifying and ordering, although they do not really understand the principles involved and cannot explain them. According to Piaget, thinking errors that are typical of the pre-operational child are animism, centration and egocentrism.

Animism

Animism is the belief that inanimate objects have feelings and intentions. According to Piaget, animistic thinking indicates egocentrism because it suggests that the child is unable to distinguish between the psychological and the physical world. An example of animism might be a child who has hurt his leg on a chair saying 'Naughty chair!' as if the chair had intentionally caused harm. However, it is questionable whether or not the child really believes inanimate objects have human traits or is simply making the best use of their limited powers of expression. Although Piaget proposed that animistic thinking was a fairly dominant feature of thinking in the pre-operational stage, Shields and Duveen (1982) showed that even 3-year-olds could determine which of a farmer, cow, tractor and tree could eat, sleep, move about on its own, talk and be angry.

Centration

Centration means the ability to cope with only one aspect of a situation at a time. For example, if you ask a child to sort out the big, green bricks from a box of different coloured bricks of various sizes, a pre-operational child will tend to sort out all the green bricks or all the big bricks, focusing on just one characteristic (colour or size) at a time. Here the child is centred (or focused) on either 'bigness' or 'greenness', but cannot consider both simultaneously. Piaget thought that the ability to take account of more than one factor at a time is achieved at around the age of 7 years.

Egocentrism

Egocentrism is the inability to take another person's perspective. Piaget believed that the child at this stage thinks that other people's experience of the world is exactly the same as their own. This is nicely illustrated if you play a game of hide-and-seek with a pre-operational child, who will think that you cannot see them if they cannot see you. Smith *et al.* (2003) describe a typical conversation between an adult and a child which illustrates how the young child has difficulty in de-centring or seeing the world from another point of view.

Interviewer: 'Have you any brothers or sisters?
Boy: 'Yes, a brother.'

STUDY

Aim

Piaget and Inhelder (1956) investigated egocentrism in children aged 4–12 years.

Method

The researchers constructed a three-dimensional papier-mâché display of three mountains. One mountain had snow on the top, one had a house and the other had a cross. The child walked around the model and looked at it from each side, then sat down facing the model. A doll was then placed in various positions around the model. Ten images of the model from different angles were shown to the child, who had to pick out the view that the doll could 'see' from wherever it was positioned. Children who correctly picked out the doll's view of the mountain were said to be not egocentric. Children who picked out their own view rather than the doll's view were said to show egocentrism.

Results

Children aged 4–5 years chose the view from their own perspective. Six-year-olds quite often chose a view other than their own, but it was not always the correct view for the doll. By the age of 7–8 years children would consistently choose the view that the doll could see.

Conclusion

Pre-operational children are egocentric and the ability to de-centre arises at around the age of 7 years.

Figure 2.4 *Piaget's three mountains experiment. Piaget found that children under the age of 7 years could not choose the doll's view from a selection of pictures. He concluded that pre-operational children are egocentric.*

Interviewer: 'What is his name?'
Boy: 'Joe.'
Interviewer: 'Has Joe got a brother?'
Boy: 'No.'

Here the child can see the world from his own point of view and knows that he has a brother, but he cannot understand his brother's perspective because he cannot see that that his brother has a brother: him!

Piaget carried out a famous experiment to illustrate egocentrism in children at the pre-operational stage.

Evaluation of the three mountains experiment

- Donaldson (1978) argued that Piaget seriously underestimated the cognitive ability of young children. She proposed that his findings were a result of the way in which he carried out his investigations.
- Critics suggest that the three mountains task is not a valid measure of perspective-taking. One problem lies in the nature of the task; looking at a 3-D display of mountains is an unfamiliar situation for most children. Perhaps young children can de-centre in more realistic situations which have some personal relevance. Another problem might be that choosing a view from a picture is not as easy as choosing a real 3-D view. A further problem might be lack of motivation: perhaps children are not really interested in the mountains test. To take account of these problems, Borke (1975) used characters from a children's TV show, *Sesame Street*, in a test of perspective-taking using a variety of 3-D layouts. Instead of using pictures taken from different angles, children could rotate the layout on a turntable to show the character's viewpoint. Borke found that 3- and 4-year-old children could correctly identify the view of the *Sesame Street* character using a more realistic and familiar situation.
- Other research into egocentrism – for example, the Hughes' study below – has also shown that children can de-centre much sooner than Piaget would have predicted.

STUDY

Aim

Hughes (cited in Donaldson 1978) investigated egocentrism in pre-operational children using a more familiar situation similar to a game of hide-and-seek.

Method

Hughes presented 30 children aged 3½–5 years with a model of two intersecting walls in a cross layout. A boy doll and a policeman doll were placed in various locations around the model and the child was asked whether the policeman could see the boy doll. In practice sessions the child was given feedback about whether or not they had given the right answer. The child was then asked to hide the boy doll so that the policeman could not see him. A second policeman doll was then placed on the model and the child's task was to hide the boy doll where neither of the policemen could see him. This task was carried out with the policemen in different locations.

Results

Ninety per cent of children aged 3½–5 years could hide the boy doll successfully.

Conclusion

Children can de-centre much sooner than Piaget suggested if the task is clearly understood and familiar. In Hughes' experiment the child could understand the situation and the motives of the characters in what seemed like a game of hide-and-seek.

Figure 2.5 *Can the policeman see the doll? Hughes found that children as young as 3½ years could answer correctly, indicating that they were not egocentric.*

Conservation

In the latter part of the pre-operational stage (the intuitive period, 4–7 years) egocentrism begins to decline; however, the child still cannot perform mental operations. At this age thinking is mostly based on the appearance of objects, rather than on logical reasoning. This is particularly evident in the child's inability to conserve. **Conservation** is the ability to understand that properties of objects and materials remain the same despite changes in outward appearance. According to Piaget, young children cannot conserve because their thinking is dominated by how things look on the outside.

Conservation experiments

The most well-known of Piaget's tests of conservation is the conservation of volume experiment, but conservation also applies to other concepts such as mass and number.

Conservation of mass can be demonstrated using two equal balls of clay and asking the child whether one ball has more clay than the other or whether there is the same amount in each ball. When the child has answered the first question 'They are the same', one of

STUDY

Aim

Piaget and Szeminska (1941) investigated the age at which children could conserve volume.

Method

They showed children two identical beakers with the same level of water in each. The child was asked whether the amount of water in the beakers was the same or whether one beaker contained more than the other. Most children said that the two beakers held the same amount. The water from one of the beakers was then poured into a third, tall, thin beaker. The question was asked again – this is the post-transformation question.

Results

After the transformation, most of the children under 7 years old said that the tall, thin beaker contained more water. Older children, however, said that the two beakers had the same amount. Children were then asked to explain their answer.

Conclusion

There is an important change in cognitive ability at around 7 years, when the child develops the ability to conserve and moves from the pre-operational stage to the concrete operational stage.

Conservation experiments

Volume

Figure 2.6 a) *Children in the pre-operational stage usually say that the tall, thin beaker has more water.*

Mass

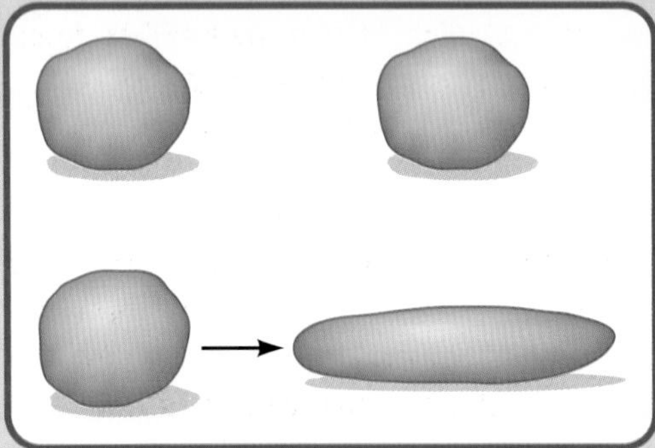

b) *Children in the pre-operational stage usually say that the long, thin sausage has more clay.*

Number

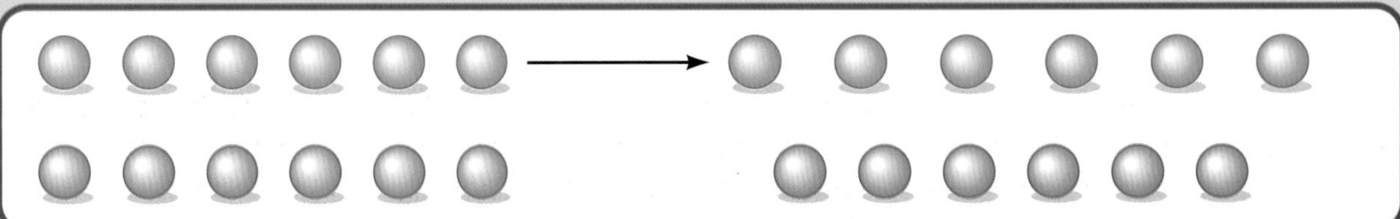

c) *Children in the pre-operational stage usually say that there are more beads in the spaced-out row.*

the balls is rolled out into a long sausage, and the question is asked again. In the post-transformation question children tend to say that the sausage shape has more clay.

Conservation of number can be tested using two sets of six beads arranged in two parallel lines of the same length. Again the child is asked whether one row has more beads or whether they have the same. After the child has answered 'The same', one of the rows is spaced out so that it is longer. When the post-transformation question is asked the child will tend to say that the spaced-out row has more beads. Conservation of number is usually acquired at around the age of 5 or 6.

STAGE 3 The concrete operational stage: 7–11 years

According to Piaget, a significant change in thinking occurs at around the age of 7 years when the child develops the ability to perform mental operations. An **operation** is a powerful internal schema that enables logical thought processes such as serial ordering, adding, subtracting, multiplying and dividing. The

Evaluation of Piaget's conservation experiment

- The language used in Piaget's volume experiment may have made it more difficult for the younger children to conserve. When children use the word 'more' they are probably using it in the sense of 'higher' or 'fuller' rather than in the adult sense of greater volume.
- Other researchers have shown that children can conserve at an earlier age if the task is presented differently.
- Rose and Blank (1974) thought that asking the same question twice was confusing. It might have led children to assume that their first answer had been wrong, and so they gave a different response the second time because they thought that was what the researcher wanted. Rose and Blank conducted the conservation of number test omitting the first question. They showed the child the two rows of beads in silence then spread one of the rows out. They then asked the question 'same or different?' Using only the post-transformation question they found that 6-year-olds made fewer mistakes than in the original two-question version of the study.
- McGarrigle and Donaldson (1974) suggested that seeing the adult deliberately transform the material in a conservation test might lead the children to believe that a different answer was required. A child would understand that there must have been a purpose for the adult's deliberate action and would therefore guess that the action must have changed something. In McGarrigle and Donaldson's version of the number experiment, 'Naughty Teddy' made a surprise appearance and messed up one of the rows of beads, spreading them out to be longer. The researcher pretended to be cross with Teddy and suggested to the child that Teddy should be put back in his box. In this way the child did not see the spreading out of the beads as intentional but rather as a consequence of Naughty Teddy's nuisance interference. Using this procedure, 60% of 6-year-olds could successfully conserve, compared with 16% in the original version.
- Clearly language and perceived intention influence success in conservation studies. For this reason the original conservation studies have been criticised for not making human sense. Perhaps Piaget underestimated children's ability to conserve and their capacity to make sense of the experiment as an interaction between two people. It is likely that young children are rather more capable of reading situations than Piaget thought.

Figure 2.7 *McGarrigle and Donaldson (1974) used 'Naughty Teddy' to show that children younger than 7 years could conserve if the task made more sense.*

operation that affects the child's ability to conserve is that of **reversibility**, that is, the ability to perform reversible mental operations. Whereas a pre-operational child cannot mentally reverse the transformation in a typical conservation study, a child in the concrete operational stage can mentally reverse the action of pouring the water into the long, thin beaker and can therefore understand that the amount of water is no different to what it was at the start. Similarly, the mental operation of compensation enables the concrete operational child to understand that one feature of the beaker, such as tallness, can be compensated for by another feature, such as width.

However, although the ability to perform operations leads to significant advances in the child's thinking, logical thought processes are limited to thinking about concrete objects and problems. For example, a child can think about fractions in relation to real objects such as a cake cut into quarters, but cannot perform abstract mathematical operations.

Class inclusion experiment

Between the ages of 7 and 10 years children become very aware of categories and classification of objects. This awareness is evident in play activities that involve collecting and sorting, such as collecting sets of cards, dolls or action figures. At this age children start to recognise the relationship between a general category and subcategories within that general category. With this understanding comes the ability to perform what are known as class inclusion tasks.

Examples of logical thought in the concrete operational child

Conservation – understanding that the properties of objects and materials can remain the same despite changes in outward appearance.

Compensation – understanding that one feature can compensate for another.

Serial ordering (seriation) – organising concrete objects into order. For example, ordering seven sticks of different lengths from shortest to longest.

Transitivity (mental seriation) – making inferences on the basis of information given. As an example, knowing that stick A is longer than stick B, and stick B is longer than stick C, the child could reason that stick A must also be longer than stick C. Andrews and Halford (1998) found that around 50% of 6-year-olds performed well on transitive inference problems.

Class inclusion – distinguishing between superordinate and subordinate categories.

STUDY

Aim

Piaget and Szeminska (1941) tested children's understanding of superordinate (whole) classes and subordinate (part) classes.

Method

Children were shown 20 wooden beads, 18 brown and 2 white. The researchers then asked:

1. Are the beads all wooden? Here the child has to think about a single class of objects at the superordinate level of 'beads'.
2. Are there more brown beads or white beads? Here the child has to think at the subordinate level of colour in which there are two subclasses, brown and white.
3. Are there more brown beads or more wooden beads? Here the child has to think at both the subordinate level of colour (brown) and at the superordinate level of the whole class, beads.

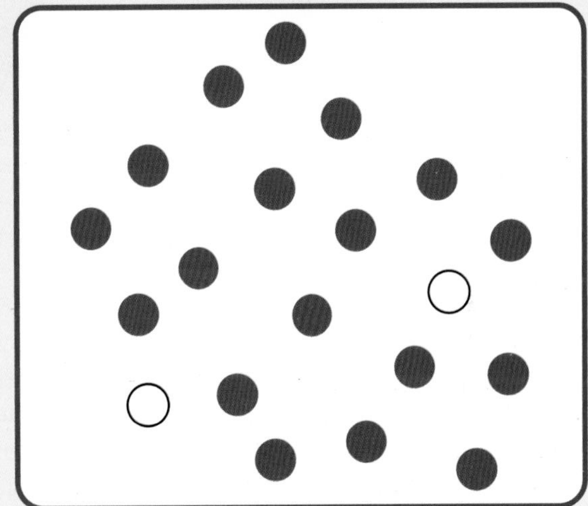

Figure 2.8

Result

Children under 7 years usually gave correct answers to the first two questions, but then gave an incorrect answer to Question 3, saying that there were more brown beads than wooden beads. Older children in the concrete operational stage usually gave the correct answer to all three questions. Questions 2 and 3 both require the child to consider two classes, but in Question 3 the two classes are not separate – they overlap. The subclass 'brown beads' is included in the whole class 'wooden beads' (class inclusion).

Conclusion

Children are unable to understand the difference between whole classes and part classes until they reach the concrete operational stage.

Evaluation of Piaget's class inclusion experiment

- Piaget's class inclusion test has been criticised because the questions are very unusual (even adults will say that there is something weird about Question 3) and may have made the task more difficult.
- Varying the question slightly has produced rather different results. Donaldson (1978) describes McGarrigle's cow study which is a variation on the class inclusion test. The child was presented with four toy cows, three black and one white. All the cows were lying down as if they were sleeping. Children aged 6 years were then asked the following questions: a) Are there more black cows or more cows? (the equivalent of Piaget's third question) and b) Are there more black cows or more sleeping cows? (a variation on Piaget's third question). Children answered the first question correctly 25% of the time and the second question correctly 48% of the time. This finding suggests that even 6-year-olds can understand class inclusion if the wording of the question is more accessible.

STAGE 4 The formal operational stage: 12 years +

In the formal operational stage adolescents can understand and use **abstract concepts**. An abstract concept is one which refers to things that are not real or tangible. Examples of abstract concepts include ideas such as obsession, calm, horror and boredom. Although we know what these concepts mean, we cannot see or touch them because they do not exist as real things. Formal operational thinkers can now apply operations to concrete situations and to abstract concepts.

STUDY

Aim

Inhelder and Piaget (1958) used the pendulum problem to study systematic reasoning in the formal operational stage (see figure 2.10).

Method

Participants were given a length of string and weights which could be attached to the string. The task was to discover what factor(s) affect the rate at which the pendulum swings. Possible factors are the length of the string, the weight, the height of release and the force of the push. Participants measure the rate of the pendulum swing by counting the number of swings per minute. They can adjust the length of the string and attach the various weights. To find the correct answer it is necessary to understand the principle of systematically changing one variable at a time, which is essentially the experimental method. Only in this way can cause and effect be determined.

Results

Children who are not yet in the formal operational stage change more than one variable at a time and cannot come to any firm conclusion. Formal operational thinkers change one variable at a time (e.g. changing the length of the string only) and can correctly identify factors affecting the rate of the swing.

Conclusion

Systematic logical reasoning is a feature of formal operational thinking.

Figure 2.9 *Formal operational thinkers are more able think hypothetically, offering more innovative and unusual suggestions to the 'third eye problem'.*

Algebra is a useful example of the application of formal operations. In algebra, symbols are used to represent unknown variables. Arithmetical operations can then be performed – for example, the value of 'a' can be calculated if we are told that 4a = 20 (the answer is a = 5). Transitivity tasks can also be performed with unknown variables: if P is two times older than Q and Q is two times older than R, how many times older is P than R?

Formal operational thinking can also be **hypothetical**, meaning that thinking is not constrained to the real and actual but can be speculative. In other words, a person in the formal operational stage can imagine situations that have never happened and can imagine what it would be like 'if' something were to happen. For example, what it would be like if the school leaving age was raised to 21 years.

One simple test of hypothetical thinking as a feature of formal operational thought was the 'third eye problem' proposed by Piaget. Children were asked where would be a good place to have an extra eye if it were possible. Schaffer (1988) found that 9-year-olds made fairly conventional suggestions like 'on the forehead'. Eleven-year-olds were more capable of hypothetical thinking, making more innovative suggestions, for example, proposing that the extra eye could go on a hand so that we could spy around corners.

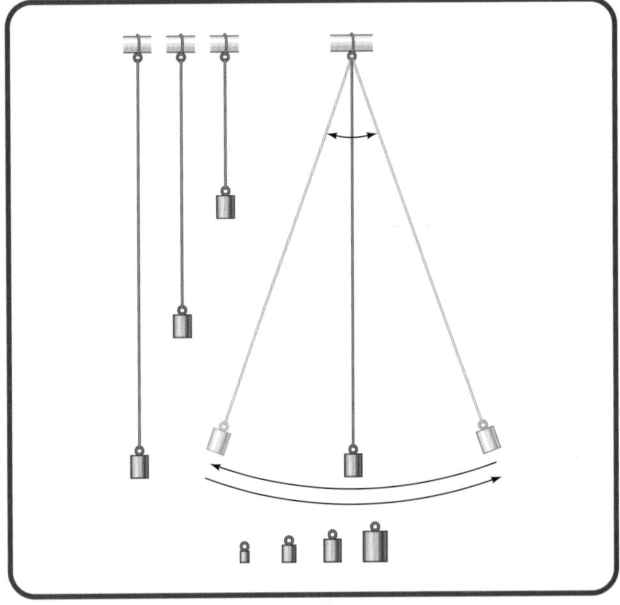

Figure 2.10 *Formal operational thinkers approach the pendulum problem in a logical systematic way when asked to figure out what factors will affect the speed of the swing.*

Formal operational thinkers can be much more **flexible** in their approach to problem solving than children in the concrete operational stage. If one method of solving a problem does not meet with success, a range of different strategies can be applied to find a solution. Formal operational thinkers use **hypothetico-deductive reasoning**, testing hypotheses in a **systematic** way to arrive at a solution to a problem.

Stage	Sensorimotor stage	Pre-operational stage	Concrete operational stage	Formal operational stage
Age	Age 0–2 years	Age 2–7 years	Age 7–11 years	12 years +
Key characteristics	Knowledge is action/sensation based Egocentrism Object permanence develops General symbolic function develops	Animism Centration Egocentrism Development of symbolic thought and language Lack of conservation Cannot perform operations like reversibility and compensation	Not egocentric Conservation Seriation Transitive inference Class inclusion Logical thinking with concrete problems	Abstract reasoning Hypothetical thinking Hypothetico-deductive, systematic problem solving

Figure 2.11 *Piaget's stages and the key characteristics of each stage.*

Evaluation of Piaget's theory – criticisms

- Piaget's concepts have been criticised for being too vague.
- Piaget's stage-based approach was considered too rigid; as a consequence he introduced the idea of **horizontal décalage**. According to the concept of horizontal décalage, a child could show characteristics of more than one stage at a time – for example, a child might be able to conserve number but not volume. Despite criticism of the stages, Piaget's general point about a sequential shift and qualitative differences in thinking at different ages does seem to be supported.
- Cultural specificity may be an issue as Piaget's theory was based on observations of a very limited sample of Swiss children. However, the same sequence of cognitive development has been noted in cross-cultural studies using large samples of children from the USA, Britain, Africa and China (Goodnow 1969), supporting Piaget's idea of universality. Other cross-cultural evidence does not entirely support Piaget's age-related stages. Dasen (1975) found that children from non-industrialised societies where state education is less common reached the stages later than Piaget proposed.
- The formal operational stage has proved especially controversial, mainly because few adults demonstrate the thinking required for scientific reasoning even in industrialised societies. Martorano (1977) tested 12- to 18-year-old females on ten of Piaget's formal operational science problems (such as the pendulum problem). Only 2 of the 20 participants succeeded on all of the problems, and success rates for the 18-year-olds varied between 15% and 95%.
- Other developmental psychologists have argued against Piaget's view that cognitive development occurs as a result of the child's independent discovery learning. Instead, they suggest that guidance from adults is an essential factor in the development of cognition (see Vygotsky page 48). However, in support of Piaget, Gelman (1969) found it was extremely difficult to teach the concept of conservation to children aged 4 and 5 years. Only after two days of repetition and 192 trials were they able to succeed, supporting Piaget's view that teaching and support cannot accelerate the process of cognitive development.

Evaluation of Piaget's methods – criticisms

- Piaget studied a small and unrepresentative sample, often using his own children.
- Piaget's reporting was less than rigorous; he often failed to record the number and ages of his participants and did not carry out any statistical analysis.
- Using the clinical interview, Piaget did not adhere to the normal scientific procedures of standardisation and control. His interactions with participants were quite informal and each participant was treated slightly differently. This meant that the results gained on any one occasion may have been partly due to the way in which the interview was conducted rather than to the age of the child.
- Some of Piaget's tests were confusing. In failing to consider how test performance might be affected by factors such as language ability, memory, context, motivation and perceived intention, Piaget may have seriously underestimated children's ability.
- Piaget assumed that if a child did not succeed at a task it was because they lacked ability. In fact there may have been many reasons why children did not give the correct answer in Piaget's tests. It is wrong to assume that task failure equals lack of ability.

Evaluation of Piaget's work – positive points

- Piaget's extensive work paved the way for further research and he made cognitive development a core aspect of developmental psychology. Numerous others have conducted studies to explore aspects of his theory and to see whether his findings are supported.
- Piaget's extensive clinical observations, in which he paid such close attention to how children behaved and what they said, have provided us with a rich and detailed account of cognitive development.
- Piaget's tests were innovative and creative, yet incredibly simple.
- His proposal that there is a universal sequence of cognitive development is generally supported by cross-cultural research.
- Piaget's findings have had an enormous influence on early years education.

2.1.3 Piaget and education

Piaget was instrumental in the shift from traditional classroom instruction to a more **child-centred approach** to learning involving active discovery and learning through experience. As such, the role of the teacher should be one of providing the necessary materials and tasks to enable children to solve problems and discover new concepts for themselves. His belief that cognitive development was largely dependent on maturation led to the conclusion that children will be able to acquire new concepts only when they are ready. According to Piaget, the teacher should take a **readiness** approach in the classroom, presenting opportunities for the learning of new concepts when the individual child is ready. This means that each child should progress at a pace that suits the individual.

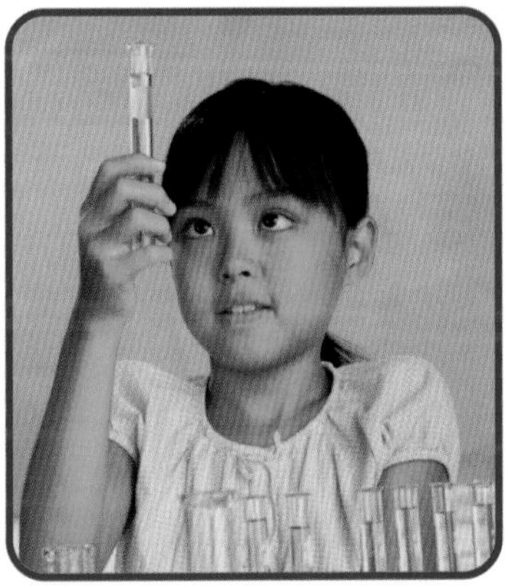

Figure 2.12 *Piaget's theory led to an emphasis on active discovery and learning through experience.*

Burman (1994) analysed the implications of applying Piaget's ideas in the classroom. She suggested how, taken to extremes, as it has been in some cases, the child-centred approach might result in the following problems:

- It makes the teacher's position ambiguous; the teacher is responsible for learning but is supposed to let the child progress at their own pace.
- The emphasis on readiness may perpetuate and even exaggerate social inequalities; children from advantaged social backgrounds are 'ready' before those from less advantaged backgrounds and therefore progress more rapidly.
- The child-centred approach has led to an assumption that failure must always be due to a problem with the child (lack of ability, poor motivation, etc.) rather than the fault of the teaching.
- Emphasis on individual programmes of learning may mean that social skills like cooperation and empathy, which would be gained through working with others, are not encouraged or valued sufficiently.

2.2 Alternative approaches to children's cognition

2.2.1 Vygotsky

The work of the Russian developmental psychologist Lev Vygotsky (1896–1934) contrasts with Piaget's notion of the child as an active constructor of his or her own knowledge. Vygotsky proposed a **sociocultural** theory of cognitive development, according to which culture plays a critical part in the development of cognition. He believed that cognitive development could only be fully understood by taking account of the context in which that development occurs, that is, the child's social world and the culture in which the child lives. Vygotsky suggested that the acquisition of the cognitive tools of a culture such as language, number systems and scientific concepts was a key aspect of cognitive development. He recognised that the cognitive skills that a child acquires are ones which are necessary for the child's culture. In the case of developed societies, examples of necessary cognitive skills are reading, writing, being able to recall and use large amounts of information in examinations and being able to use information technology. Because these skills are largely culture specific, their development is likely to be influenced more by social factors than by biological processes.

Internalisation is a key aspect of Vygotsky's theory. He believed that children learn through social experiences. The example of pointing can be used to illustrate this point. Initially a baby will reach for an object by extending arm and fingers towards it. When the parent sees this the parent will point towards the object and perhaps ask, 'Do you want teddy?' Through observing the parent's behaviour and understanding the meaning of the action, the child will then acquire the pointing behaviour, imitating the parent's action and using the newly acquired behaviour as a deliberate communication in other similar contexts.

The zone of proximal development

The zone of proximal development was a term used by Vygotsky to refer to the distance between what a child can achieve alone, and what the same child can achieve with guidance from another person. According to Vygotsky (1978), '...what is the zone of proximal development today will be the actual developmental level tomorrow...' By this he meant that what a child can achieve with help today, he or she will be able to do independently tomorrow. The word 'proximal' means 'next' or 'close'. A child being assisted to perform a task in his or her zone of proximal development is close to managing it alone; it will be the next thing they are able to achieve independently.

The significance of the zone of proximal development is evident if we consider two children, Frank and Jack. Frank can achieve a certain level of performance on his own but can achieve much more with help. Jack may have the same level of actual ability as Frank, but he is not able to achieve much more, even with help. Although the two children have the same level of ability at the present time, we can conclude that Frank is somehow more capable than Jack because he has the potential to achieve more, as seen in his performance with some assistance. Thus, the zone of proximal development takes account of a child's **potential** ability and not just their present ability.

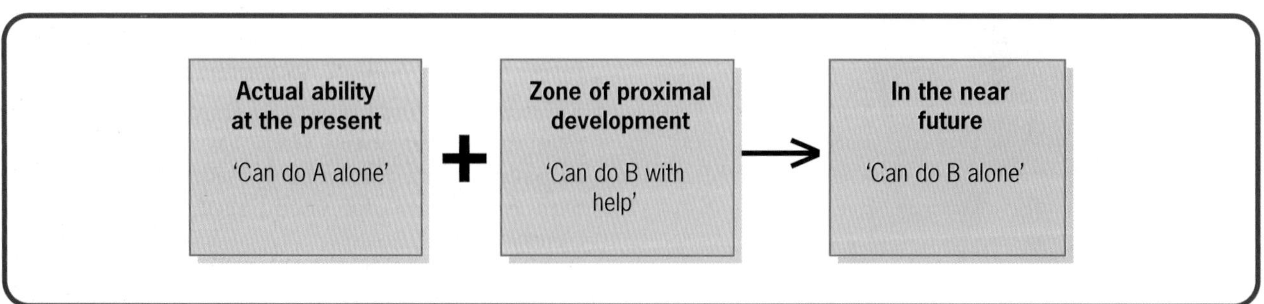

Figure 2.13 *Vygotsky proposed that the zone of proximal development was the distance between what a child can achieve unaided and what can be achieved with help.*

STUDY

Aim

Hedegaard (1996) investigated a teaching method which involved deliberately working within the zone of proximal development in a whole-class situation.

Method

A special programme of instruction was used with Danish primary school children in a longitudinal study. The three interrelated topics were the evolution of species, the origin of human beings and historical change in societies. These topics were presented separately through a range of learning and research activities, including the following: shared concrete activities; whole-class discussion; group work; collective problem solving. Although the topics were presented separately, children had to answer questions that required an integrated understanding of the three areas.

Results

The children were successfully able to answer the questions. They could identify problems and solutions and shifted from an interest in particular species (concrete) to the formulation of theories and models of species adaptation (general). Fast learners found the new approach to learning stimulating, whilst less able children also showed interest and motivation.

Conclusion

By carefully structuring class activities teachers can successfully work with the zone of proximal development in a whole-class teaching environment.

Figure 2.14 *Vygotsky emphasised the role of adult intervention and assistance in the development of cognition.*

Scaffolding

Vygotsky emphasised the role of adult intervention and assistance in the development of cognition. One such intervention that reflects Vygotsky's ideas is **scaffolding** (Wood *et al.*, 1976). Scaffolding is a form of instruction in which the child is given a level of help and support which is gradually reduced as the child becomes more competent, until finally the child can manage to complete the task unaided. For example, a child who is beginning to carry out additions and subtractions in mathematics lessons will be shown, helped and prompted. Later the child will attempt simple problems with the teacher watching and making suggestions. Later still there will be occasional help, and eventually problems can be solved alone. Thus the support structure, or scaffolding, is gradually withdrawn as the child becomes more able to work independently.

The following study provides some support for the existence of scaffolding.

STUDY

Aim

Wood and Middleton (1975) investigated the type of parental assistance offered in a block-building activity.

Method

The interactions between children (aged 4 years) and their parents were observed. Each was allowed to play individually with a set of wooden blocks with a parent looking on. The task, which involved assembling the blocks by fitting them together, was purposely too difficult for the child to complete alone.

Results

Initially parents showed their child how to assemble the blocks, and then, as the child became more capable of managing alone, the parent would stop helping directly but still give verbal suggestions and encouragement.

Various levels of parental support were noted:
Demonstration e.g. fitting blocks together
Preparation e.g. lining blocks up correctly
Indication e.g. pointing to the block needed next
Specific instruction e.g. 'You need a big block next'
Verbal prompt (general) e.g. 'See if you can make something'

Wood and Middleton found that the level of assistance declined as the activity progressed, with the greatest help (demonstration) given at the start and less and less help given later as the child's own skill develops.

Conclusion

Children's understanding is supported by adults in various ways other than by formal instruction.

Evaluation

- Wood and Middleton showed that as the child becomes more skilled they are given less specific support. This finding supports the notion of scaffolding.
- The study involves the development of a single specific skill rather than general cognitive development. More usually cognitive development involves the acquisition of general concepts such as conservation which can be used or applied in many different circumstances. In that sense Wood and Middleton's experimental task was not really a valid measure of cognitive development. Theories of cognitive development are really about explaining how children acquire conceptual rather than routine task-specific knowledge.

Scaffolding appears in many different forms. Parents will use scaffolding in their responses to a child's early attempts at speech and in helping children to understand their own feelings, 'You're a bit upset now, aren't you?' Nursery teachers will provide scaffolding for young children as they are introduced to formal learning activities, and in cultures where working life begins early adults will scaffold the skills of their young apprentices. As an example, Greenfield and Lave (1982) noted how young Mexican girls watched skilled women weavers, then worked with guidance from them, and finally worked alone.

Guided participation in sociocultural activity

Guided participation is a specific type of scaffolding studied by Rogoff *et al.* (1995). Guided participation refers particularly to the transmission of cultural practices, where children actively engage in cultural activities whilst adults model, encourage and regulate performance. It can be seen as a type of apprenticeship in which children actively take part in a practice of their culture whilst adults demonstrate and guide the child's performance. Over time the child will become more accomplished, eventually reconstructing the knowledge as their own. In this way the practices of a culture are maintained and reformulated through the generations.

Language

Vygotsky believed that cognitive development was heavily dependent on language since language affects and even shapes culture. It is through language that the ideas of a culture are expressed – for example, the language of children's playground rhymes and storybooks expresses the shared knowledge and values of the culture. Inevitably, then, the language of a culture affects the way that children think. Vygotsky suggested that cognitive development arises from the child's conversations with parents and others and that language provides a framework for thinking. Vygotsky was especially interested in the way that children use language. He noted how they talk to themselves as they play and believed that these monologues helped children to plan and direct their behaviour. Initially the

STUDY

Aim

Rogoff *et al.* (1995) investigated the process of guided participation in a study of a cultural practice in her local community.

Method

The researchers focused on the transmission of knowledge, understanding and skills during the annual Girl Scout Cookie Sale in the USA. The Cookie Sale is a highly organised, annual, national fund-raising event which has been in operation since the 1930s. Using qualitative methods of observation, interview and historical archive analysis, researchers focused on information at three different levels: the Community Level involved analysis of the cultural activity as guided by the values and goals of the culture; the Interpersonal Level involved analysis of face-to-face interaction and communication between the Girl Scouts and their mentors (mothers, sisters, friends, etc.) and the Personal Level involved analysis of how individual Girl Scouts changed as a result of their involvement in the Cookie Sale.

Results

Older members of the community passed on their knowledge and experiences of the event to the Girl Scouts, offering advice and practical help. The Girl Scouts then reshaped and extended this knowledge, developing new ways and innovations to be carried on into the future.

Conclusion

Individual cognitive development is inseparable from the external environment; understanding develops as a result of guided participation in shared activity.

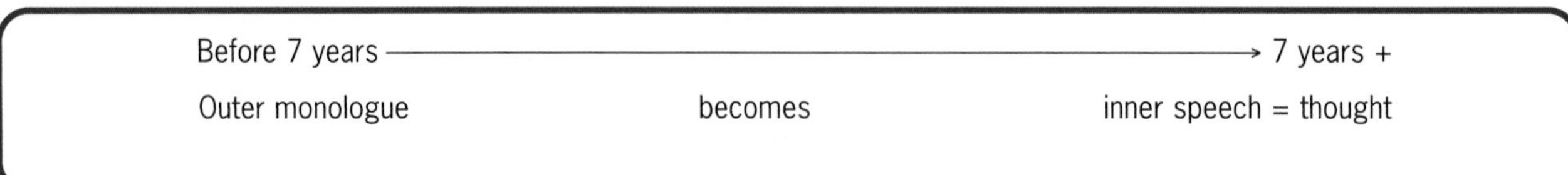

Figure 2.15 *Vygotsky's view of language and thought.*

monologues are outward, the child speaks out loud, and then, at around the age of 7 years, speech becomes internalised as 'inner speech', which is actually thought. As adults we generally do not use external monologues, but we do occasionally revert to thinking aloud when presented with an especially trying problem.

2.2.2 Vygotsky and education

Vygotsky's ideas have been extensively developed and applied in education. They were particularly in tune with the thinking of Jerome Bruner (1986), an American psychologist who also believed that socio-cultural influences and especially language were key influences on cognitive development. In addition to scaffolding, Smith *et al.* (2003) note other ways in which Vygotsky's (and Bruner's) ideas have been applied in education. These include:

Peer tutoring – where the child learns through interaction with another child who is slightly more able.

Collective argumentation – a structured approach to group discussion where individual viewpoints are presented and justified, different views are compared, a joint view is constructed and presented, and finally, the joint view is tested in the wider community.

Community of inquiry – proposed by Elbers and Streefland (2000). A community of inquiry involves pupils playing an active role, with lessons structured as a common enterprise in which teachers and learners both take the role of researcher and strive together to carry out tasks and find solutions to problems.

Evaluation of Vygotsky's theory

- According to Vygotsky's notion of the zone of proximal development, it should be possible to accelerate a child's development. This idea conflicts directly with Piaget's belief that development will only be possible when the child is cognitively ready. If Piaget is correct about 'readiness', then artificial acceleration would be pointless.
- Whilst some level of instruction may be beneficial, over-instruction might result in the child being less likely to learn independently and less inclined to show initiative in problem solving.
- Vygotsky's theory presupposes that adults will always have an enhancing effect on cognitive development. In fact, adults sometimes make it more difficult for children to understand the world by answering obscurely when asked about difficult topics such as death or sex.

STUDY

Aim

Elbers and Streefland (2000) tested the effectiveness of learning in a community of inquiry.

Method

Participants were children aged 11–13 years at state schools in Holland. A new mathematics curriculum was introduced using new learning community roles in the special 90-minute weekly lessons. The children were given the role of researcher, with the teacher in the role of senior researcher. At the start of each weekly lesson the new roles were defined explicitly, with the teacher announcing, 'We are researchers. Let us do research'. The children worked in either small groups or as a whole class.

Results

The 'researchers' adapted well to their roles. The children worked productively and collaborated positively to solve the mathematics problems. The teachers avoided instructing, instead paraphrasing and rephrasing the children's comments to correct errors and reminding them of their earlier findings.

Conclusion

The researchers concluded that a community of inquiry was highly productive; children learned to use evidence in a constructive way and developed a more critical understanding.

Vygotsky	Piaget
Cognitive development is driven by social interaction and experience within a culture	Cognitive development is driven by the child's inbuilt tendency to adapt to new experiences
Child learns through instruction and guidance	Child learns through active self-discovery
Knowledge is acquired through the internalisation of the adult's understanding	Knowledge is acquired through direct experience
Cognitive development can be accelerated	Child will only learn when ready
The ability to use language is the key to cognitive development. Outward monologues direct thinking and later become internalised as thought	Language develops as a result of cognitive development. Outward monologues are meaningless and egocentric speech is incidental to thought

Figure 2.16 *Table to compare the theories of Piaget and Vygotsky.*

2.2.3 Nativist explanations and early infant abilities

According to nativist explanations, we are born with **innate** cognitive structures which determine cognitive ability. Any developmental changes simply reflect genetic predispositions. In the 1960s and 1970s most nativist research focused on language and perception. Chomsky (1965) proposed that we are born with an innate ability to use and understand language. He pointed out that when young children are exposed to the language of their culture they internalise the grammatical rules of the language without explicit instruction. He therefore concluded that we are born with some kind of innate grammar device – he called it a Language Acquisition Device (LAD), which enables the capacity to learn language.

Knowledge of the physical world

Perception research in the 1970s revealed that certain perceptual abilities – for example, depth perception – seem to be present very early in infancy. In a study by Bower *et al.* (1970) infants aged 6–21 days were positioned facing an object suspended in front of them at a distance. The object was released from the start position and 'loomed' towards the infants' faces. As the object loomed closer, babies made a typical 'collision' response, pulling their heads upwards and away from the approaching object in an attempt to avoid collision. The researchers concluded that infants can perceive depth at just a few days old. This study appears to support a nativist explanation, that nature endows us with certain cognitive abilities, such as depth perception.

Nativist explanations apparently conflict with Piaget's views. Piaget proposed that the newborn infant's cognitive ability consisted of the basic organising principles of assimilation and accommodation and that, thereafter, cognitive development occurred as a result of the child's active experience in the environment. Piaget's theory is a constructivist theory as he states that knowledge is constructed through experience. According to nativist explanations, newborn infants are innately equipped with certain cognitive abilities and Piaget therefore underestimated young children's understanding of the physical world.

Baillargeon's work

Baillargeon developed new techniques that enabled her to challenge Piaget's views about the age at which infants develop object permanence. In a series of ingenious experiments she used a procedure in which infants are familiarised with a visual event sequence and then presented with a test event that either violates the expected sequence or conforms to the expected sequence. Infants' reactions to the test event are observed. If the test event does violate the expected sequence and the child shows surprise we can infer that the infant has a mental representation of the expected sequence. In other words, they have object permanence. Two of Baillargeon's experiments are described below.

STUDY

Aim

Baillargeon (1986) used an impossible event technique to test the age at which infants show evidence of object permanence.

Method

Infants saw a sequence of events in which a truck rolled down a ramp and behind a screen. After the infants had become familiar with this sequence the screen was raised and the infants watched as a block was positioned behind the screen. In the 'possible event' condition the block was to the rear of the track where it would not interfere with the passage of the truck. In the 'impossible event' condition the block was on the track, directly in the path of the truck. The screen was then lowered and the infants observed the truck being rolled down the track behind the screen and, in both cases, reappearing on the other side of the screen.

STUDY continued

Results

Infants aged 6–8 months showed more attention in the impossible event condition, looking for a longer time than in the possible event condition.

Conclusion

Infants of this age show object permanence; they are aware that the block continues to exist even when it is out of sight and can also memorise its precise location.

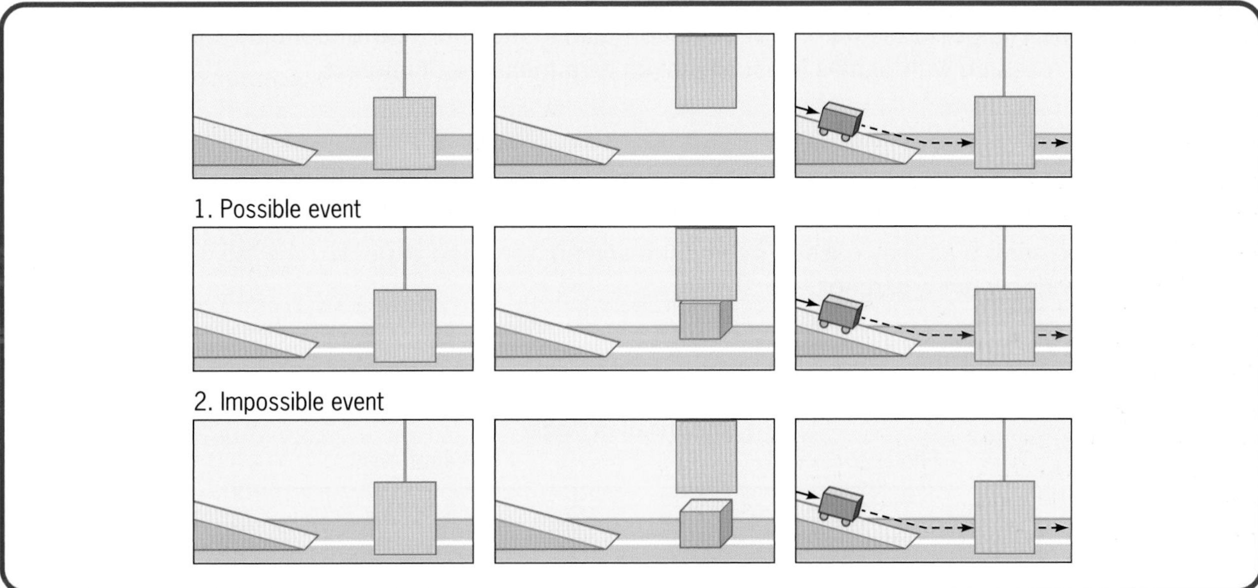

Figure 2.17 *Baillargeon (1986) showed how very young children were aware that the obstacle in the path of the truck continued to exist even when they could not see it.*

STUDY

Aim

Baillargeon and DeVos (1991) set up an ingenious 'impossible event' experiment to challenge Piaget's assumption that babies acquire object permanence at around 8 months.

Method

Three-month-old babies were placed in front of a screen. In the familiarisation stage they observed short and tall carrots move from left to right behind the screen to appear on the right-hand side.

STUDY continued

After familiarisation they were then tested with a screen that had a window in the top half. In the short-carrot condition babies saw a short carrot that moved from left to right behind the screen and then reappeared. The short carrot was not tall enough to have appeared in the window as it passed behind the screen, so this was a 'possible event'. In the tall-carrot condition babies saw a tall carrot move behind the screen and reappear on the right-hand side of the screen. The tall carrot was so tall that it ought to have been visible in the window as it passed behind the screen; however, the researchers created an 'impossible event' where the tall carrot was not visible in the window as it should have been.

Results

The babies looked longer in the tall-carrot condition than in the short-carrot condition. Longer looking time in research with babies is usually taken as a measure of interest.

Conclusion

Three-month-old babies show object permanence. The researchers reasoned that the 3-month-old babies were more interested in the tall-carrot event because they were aware of the continued existence of the carrots as they passed behind the screen; they had expected the tall carrot to appear in the window but it had not.

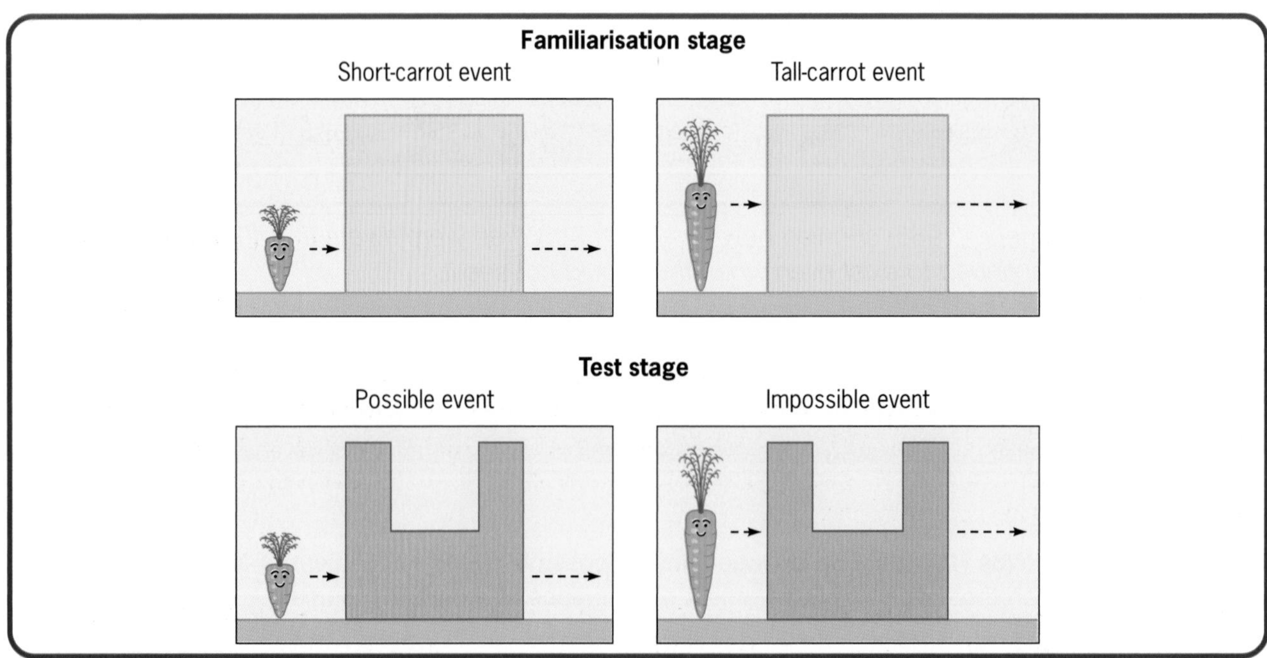

Figure 2.18 *Baillargeon and DeVos (1991) showed how babies could detect an impossible event at 3½ months of age, suggesting they have object permanence much younger than Piaget thought.*

Evaluation

- Baillargeon's research presents a challenge to Piaget's findings on object permanence and his theory that the child's knowledge is constructed through experience.
- Although the infants in Baillargeon's experiments demonstrate quite sophisticated understanding of object permanence, they are not as competent when tested on their understanding of other aspects of the physical world, such as gravity and how objects can support other objects.

2.2.4 The information-processing approach

The information-processing approach likens human processing to that of a computer, with the focus on the study of cognitive processes such as perception, attention, memory and problem solving. The information-processing approach to cognitive development is sometimes described as a neo-Piagetian approach because, in a similar way to Piaget, it specifies key changes in the way information is processed as children develop. However, information-processing theorists differ from Piaget as they do not agree that these changes reflect qualitatively different stages in the way that children think. Instead they see the changes as quantitative ones that lead to increased **cognitive efficiency** which affects the way that children approach cognitive tasks. Bee (1997) identifies four changes in information processing with age:

- increased processing capacity (including memory capacity)
- increased processing efficiency
- the development of rules for solving problems
- the development of **metacognition** (awareness of own cognitive abilities).

Since the 1960s, information-processing theorists have carried out many experiments to investigate children's cognitive abilities. One of the earliest observations of differences in the way in which adults and children use their memories was made by Flavell *et al.* (1966).

STUDY

Aim

Flavell *et al.* (1966) studied the spontaneous use of memory strategies in children aged 5, 7 and 10 years.

Method

Twenty children in each age group were tested individually. Each child was shown a set of seven pictures. The researcher pointed to some of the pictures and told the child to try to remember them. After a 15-second interval the child was asked to state out loud what they could recall. A lip-reader observed the child during the 15-second interval to see whether or not the child used verbal repetition as a strategy to aid recall.

Results

Only two of the 5-year-olds used verbal repetition, whereas over half the 7-year-olds and nearly all the 10-year-olds used this strategy. Flavell also found that those children who used repetition recalled more of the pictures.

Conclusion

Differences in memory performance with age appear to be due to the spontaneous use of mnemonic strategies such as rehearsal.

Evaluation

- In follow-up research it was found that younger children who were taught to use rehearsal could then recall as well as the older children (Keeney *et al*., 1967). This suggests that older children's memories are no better than the memories of younger children, but that they just use them more efficiently.
- Flavell's study has been criticised because the children may have been using rehearsal covertly without moving their lips. McGilly and Siegler (1990) carried out a similar experiment but interviewed the children afterwards. Many children who had not shown lip movements during the experiment reported that they had rehearsed when interviewed.
- Knowing a memory strategy does not necessarily mean that an individual will use it. Adults are often aware of memory-enhancing techniques such as organisation and elaboration, but do not always use them because they require effort and commitment.

STUDY

Aim

Siegler (1976) designed a task to investigate children's strategies when solving a balance-scale task. He wanted to know whether children approached the task differently according to age.

Method

The task involved showing children aged 5–17 years a balance scale with weights on either side of a fulcrum. All the weights were of the same value. The scale was held in place by a wedge that prevented either side moving up or down. On each trial different weights were positioned at different places on the balance scale. The task was to predict in each case whether or not the scale would tip and, if it would tip, which way.

Before testing began Siegler identified four increasingly sophisticated strategies that could be used.

I Choose the side that has more weights on it.

II Choose the side that has more weights on it, BUT if they have the same then choose the one where the weights are furthest from the fulcrum.

III Consider both the number of weights and the distance from the fulcrum, BUT if one has more weights and the other has weights that are further from the fulcrum, GUESS.

IV Multiply weights by distance from fulcrum. Choose the side that yields the biggest value in this calculation.

Results

Children aged 5 years used Strategy I while the 9-year-olds used Strategies II or III. Those above 9 years used Strategy III and very few children used Strategy IV.

Conclusion

Children's information-processing strategies become more complex with age and develop in a predictable sequence.

Siegler's research into problem-solving strategies

Siegler (1976) proposed that cognitive development involves the acquisition of a set of rules or strategies for solving problems. With age these rules become increasingly complex and can be applied to a range of different problems. He studied the different strategies that children used in a balance-scale task.

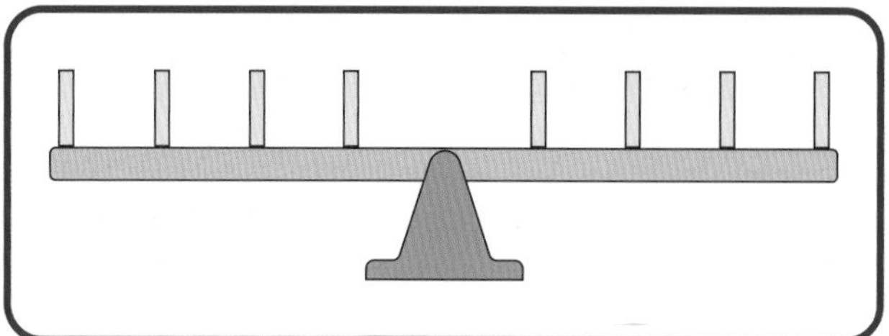

Figure 2.19 *Siegler (1976) used the balance-scale problem to show that children's problem-solving strategies become more complex with age.*

Siegler's (1996) **overlapping waves** theory of problem solving suggests that children have a selection of problem-solving strategies available to them, but will choose to use one in preference to another at any one time. These strategies compete against each other and some will prove more adaptive (useful) than others. Feedback is a very important element in this process as it enables the child to decide about the effectiveness of each strategy. Eventually the more adaptive strategies survive and the less adaptive ones die out, in a similar way to evolution. This view of problem solving has enabled computer simulations of the development of cognitive processes which have been tested and compared to children's performances on problem-solving tasks.

Evaluation of Siegler's research

- It is important to note how Siegler found that when children are given practice and feedback at the balance-scale task they will start to use more sophisticated strategies. Thus, although there is a sequence of change to cognitive development, this sequence depends on the individual child's experience rather than on age.
- Siegler's research involved the use of rigorous methods and systematic hypothesis testing, unlike the clinical interview procedure used by Piaget.

Evaluation of the information-processing approach to cognitive development

- Separate components of cognitive functioning, such as memory and attention, have been analysed in detail.
- Numerous experimental studies have yielded extensive insights into how cognitive processing changes with age.
- Findings from information-processing research have been used to develop new teaching techniques. For example, schools now encourage children to reflect on their own mental processing to enable the development of metacognitive awareness.
- There are opportunities for combining the findings from information-processing research with studies of the psychophysiological changes that occur with age – for example, exploring changes in the brain that might parallel increased memory capacity with age.

Evaluation – continued

- Findings from information-processing research are sometimes disparate and do not seem to offer a coherent, rounded theory of children's cognitive development in the same way as Piaget did.
- Use of the computer analogy means that information-processing researchers focus mostly on the logical aspects of cognitive processing and less on the emotional, creative and social aspects that also affect thinking.

How Psychology Works

A study of formal operational thinking

First read Inhelder and Piaget's pendulum study described on page 44. You are going to carry out a version of the pendulum test with a few participants. If your participants are over the age of 12 years (formal operational thinkers) they should be able to correctly determine the four factors that can affect the rate of the pendulum swing (weight, length of string, force of push and height of release). If they are under 12 years they should be able to identify some of the factors but not all. You should add the data that you collect to that in the table below.

- Photocopy Figure 2.10 onto a blank sheet of paper.
- Here is a set of instructions to use with your participants:

Standardised instructions

Please study the diagram of the pendulum. As you can see, weights of various sizes can be suspended on strings of different lengths. I would like you to tell me what factors will affect the **rate** at which the pendulum swings backwards and forwards. Take as long as you like to think about the problem before you answer.

- Write a suitable debrief to use with your participants after they have taken part. You should thank them and explain the purpose of the study in language that ordinary people could easily understand.
- Now carry out your study with a couple of participants. Record their answers on an answer sheet. Remember to also record their ages.
- Add the results obtained to the data in the table. Note that the numbers in the table refer to people in categories.
- Decide which statistical test should be used to analyse the data. Write a paragraph stating which test is appropriate and justifying your answer.

Task performance	Aged under 12 years	Aged 12 years +
Named all 4 factors	8	25
Did not name all 4 factors correctly	37	20

- Write a paragraph discussing how the method that you have used differs from that used in the original study. Refer to the concept of validity in your answer

Further Reading

Introductory texts

Bee, H. (1999) *The Developing Child*, 9th edn., New York: Longman.

Berk, L.E. (2003) *Child Development*, 6th edn., Boston: Allyn & Bacon.

Harris, M. and Butterworth, G. (2002) *Developmental Psychology: A Student's Handbook*, Hove: Psychology Press.

Messer, D. and Miller, S. (eds.) (1999) *Exploring Developmental Psychology: From Infancy to Adolescence*, London: Arnold.

Slater, A. and Bremner, G. (2003) *Introduction to Developmental Psychology*, Oxford: Blackwell.

Smith, P.K., Cowie, H. and Blades, M. (1998) *Understanding Children's Development*, 3rd edn., Oxford: Blackwell.

Specialist sources

Goswami, U. (2004) *Blackwell Handbook of Childhood Cognitive Development*, Oxford: Blackwell.

Meadows, S. (1996) *Parenting Behaviour and Children's Cognitive Development*, Hove: Psychology Press.

Rogoff, B. (1992) *Apprenticeship in Thinking: Cognitive Development in Social Context*, Oxford: Oxford University Press.

Siegler, R.S. (1996) *Emerging Minds: The Process of Change in Children's Thinking*, New York: Oxford University Press.

Sutherland, P. (1992) *Cognitive Development Today: Piaget and his Critics*, London: Paul Chapman Publishing.

Taylor, L. (2005) *Introducing Cognitive Psychology*, Hove: Psychology Press.

Van der Veer, R. and Valsiner, J. (eds.) (1994) *The Vygotsky Reader*, Oxford: Blackwell.

Moral development

Chapter 3

Most psychological research into moral development has tended to focus on children's understanding of right and wrong, that is, moral cognition, rather than on morally acceptable behaviour. In general, psychological findings suggest that children's level of understanding of moral issues increases with age and that there may be differences in understanding between males and females. Whether or not a child who has a sophisticated understanding of moral issues will behave in a morally acceptable way is something you might like to think about as you consider the various theories of moral development in this chapter.

3.1 Piaget and Kohlberg

3.1.1 Piaget's research into moral development

Jean Piaget (1896–1980) was a cognitive developmental psychologist who studied all aspects of the development of understanding, including the development of moral understanding. (See Chapter 2 for Piaget's general theory of cognitive development.) In his investigations of children's moral understanding Piaget (1932) studied the following:

- judgements of wrongdoing and punishment
- understanding of telling lies
- understanding of rules in the game of marbles.

Judgements of wrongdoing and punishment

STUDY

Aim

Piaget (1932) compared the moral judgements of children at different ages.

Method

Piaget read stories involving moral comparisons with children of different ages. In each story a child had done something wrong. In one of the stories the act was intentionally naughty but resulted in little damage; in the other story the act was not intentional but there was quite a lot of damage. Examples of the stories Piaget used:

STUDY continued

A little boy who is called John is in his room. He is called to dinner. He goes into the dining room. But behind the door there was a chair, and on the chair there was a tray with 15 cups on it. John couldn't have known that there was all this behind the door. He goes in, the door knocks against the tray, bang go the 15 cups and they all get broken!

Once there was a little boy whose name was Henry. One day when his mother was out he tried to get some jam out of the cupboard. He climbed up on to a chair and stretched out his arm. But the jam was too high up and he couldn't reach it and have any. But while he was trying to get it he knocked over a cup. The cup fell down and broke.

After reading both stories, Piaget asked which boy was naughtier, and why. He also asked about whether the children in the stories should be punished.

Results

Piaget found that children under 10 years reasoned according to the extent of the damage, stating that John was the naughtier of the two boys. They tended to recommend harsh punishments. Children 10 years and above considered intention and so decided that Henry was naughtier. They tended to suggest less severe punishments more appropriate for the situation.

Conclusion

From about 10 years old children's moral judgements are more sophisticated, taking into account not only the amount of damage but also whether the act was accidental or intentional.

Figure 3.1 *Piaget showed how young children would say that John was naughtier because in John's case there was more damage.*

Evaluation of Piaget's moral comparison experiment

- Recalling the details and mentally comparing two stories is cognitively demanding, making the task quite difficult, particularly for young children.
- Piaget may have underestimated the moral understanding of younger children. Other research has shown that where intention is clear, younger children can judge by motive rather than consequence (Imamoglu, 1975).
- Piaget's stories only used two stories but manipulated two different variables – amount of damage and intention. This means that it is impossible to say which factor was affecting the children's decisions about who was naughtier. Nelson (1980) used a similar technique to Piaget, but improved on his research by systematically varying the amount of damage and the intention of the actor.

STUDY

Aim

Nelson (1980) studied the effect of clear intention on the moral judgement of young children.

Method

Three-year-old children each heard one story. The story had four different versions in which the variables of intention and consequence were systematically varied. Each story involved a child throwing a ball to his friend. See below for the different stories. After listening to one of the stories, each child was asked to rate the actor's behaviour from good to bad on a scale.

Results

As expected, children tended to rate the actor whose behaviour had a negative consequence as more naughty than if there was a positive consequence. However, they also rated the actor whose intentions were good as better than an actor whose intentions were bad. In fact, despite the different consequences, the child in version 2 whose motive was good was judged to be better than the child in version 3 whose motive was bad. See Figure 3.2.

Conclusion

Where intention is made clear, even young children can take account of both intention and consequence when making moral judgements, and they sometimes consider intention to be more important than consequence. This goes against Piaget's findings that children only start to consider intention at approximately the age of 10 years.

Nelson's four versions of the stories

Bad intention + negative consequence
A child is angry with his friend and throws a ball towards the friend. The ball hits the friend on the head and makes the friend cry.

Good intention + negative consequence
A child sees that his friend has nothing to play with and throws a ball towards the friend. The ball hits the friend on the head and makes the friend cry.

Bad intention + positive consequence
A child is angry with his friend and throws a ball towards the friend. The friend catches the ball and plays with it.

Good intention + positive consequence
A child sees that his friend has nothing to play with and throws a ball towards the friend. The friend catches the ball and plays with it.

Understanding of telling lies

Piaget (1932) asked children to decide about how naughty different types of lies were. He found that younger children thought that lies which involved greater distortion from the truth were more naughty than lies which involved lesser distortion. In other words, young children would judge a 'big' lie to be naughty, even though it was obviously implausible and ridiculous. For example, the statement 'My bike goes faster than a space rocket' would be judged to be a naughtier lie than 'I have a new bike' (assuming this statement was false). For older children, the more significant the deception, the more naughty the lie was perceived to be. Thus the statement 'My bike goes faster than a space rocket' would be seen as insignificant, because nobody could possibly be deceived by it. However, the untrue statement that 'I have a new bike' would be seen as a lie, since there is a deliberate and plausible attempt to deceive. Piaget concluded that understanding of telling lies becomes more sophisticated as children get older. These findings are consistent with Piaget's work on moral comparisons in that older children could not only consider whether the statement was false, but also whether there was any deliberate and calculated intention to deceive.

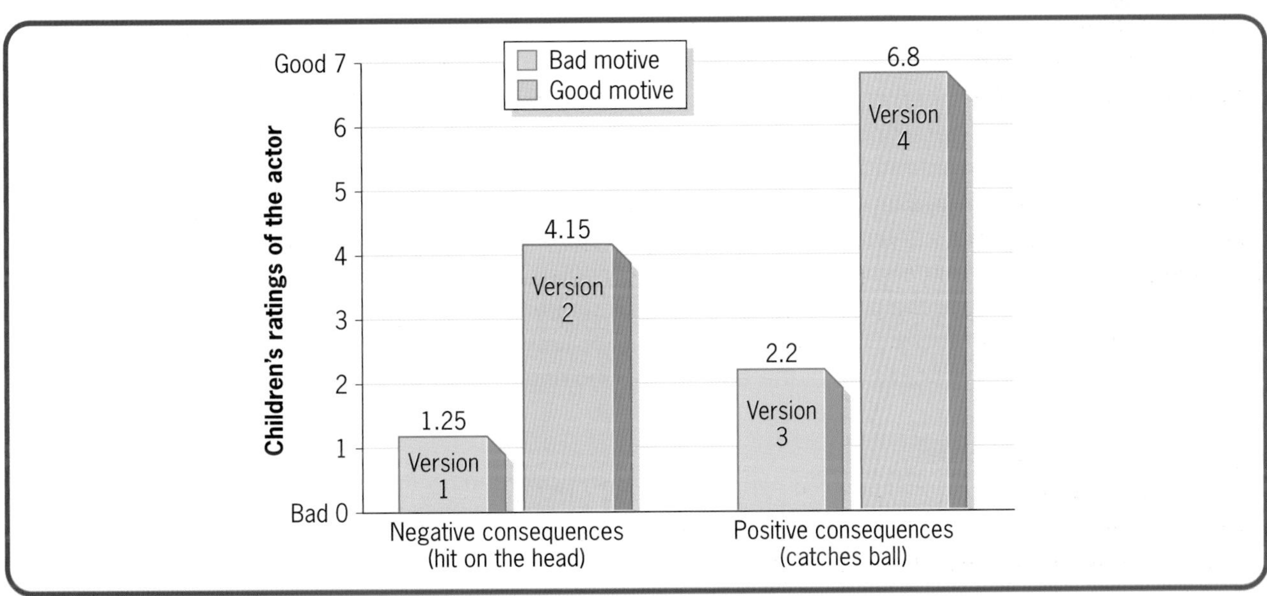

Figure 3.2 *Bar chart to show children's ratings of the actor on a scale of 0 (bad) to 7 (good) for each of the four versions of the story (Nelson 1980).*

Understanding of rules in a game of marbles

Piaget (1932) investigated children's understanding of the rules of the game of marbles in four ways:

- He asked the children to teach him the rules.
- He played the game pretending not to know the rules, so the children had to explain them.
- He observed the children playing marbles with each other.
- He interviewed the children about where the rules came from and whether or not the rules could be changed.

Piaget found that between 4 and 5 years, children did not really understand the rules. Between 6 and 9 years, they could follow rules, but did not always stick to them and would cheat to win. More interestingly, children at this age believed that rules were fixed and could not be changed, as if the rules were given by some higher authority (the marble God!). By about 10 years, children understood that rules existed because people had agreed to them, and that the rules of the game could be changed by common consent of the players. These findings seem to suggest that younger children rely on external authority to know what is allowable and see rules as moral absolutes, whereas older children understand that they can exercise their own judgement about the appropriateness of rules. In a large-scale study of English and Spanish children, Linaza (1984) confirmed Piaget's sequence of stages in the understanding of rules. There were no notable cross-cultural differences and the understanding of both boys and girls appeared to follow the same pattern.

Piaget's stages of moral development

The pre-moral stage

Before the age of 5 years the child is unaware of moral issues and so cannot make meaningful moral judgements. From the age of 4–5 years the child starts to adhere to rules, but those rules will be ones imposed by other people.

The moral realism stage

Between the ages of 5 and 9 years the child's moral understanding is based on parental views of right and wrong and parental control. The child's morality is not self-chosen but simply reflects the moral codes of others: **heteronomous morality.** Judgement is based on **consequence** – the amount of damage – and not on intention. The child sees rules as moral absolutes, believing they are inflexible and cannot be broken. The term moral 'realism' reflects the fact that the child at this stage sees right and wrong as real and objective rather than as a matter of subjective opinion. At this stage, the child believes in **expiatory punishment**, meaning that a person has to pay heavily for their wrongdoing. At this stage the child also believes that unpleasant events which happen by chance after wrongdoing are actually punishments – **immanent justice.** So if a child steals his friend's chocolate bar and then chokes on it, the accidental choking is seen as punishment.

The moral relativism stage

Aged 10 years and over a child's judgment is no longer governed by constraint of others but is rather based on a personal internalised moral code – **autonomous morality.** The child can see things from another's point of view, and can consider both **intention** and consequence when judging wrongdoing. The child can also understand that rules exist only because people have invented them and that they can be changed by common consent. The term moral 'relativism' reflects the fact that moral judgement is often a matter of subjective opinion, and an act is judged in relation to several factors such as intention, outcome, circumstances. The child now believes that punishment should reflect the nature of the wrongdoing – **reciprocal punishment.**

3.1.2 Piaget's stages of moral development

Piaget used the findings from his research to propose three stages of moral development. According to Piaget, progression through the stages involves a general shift from externally controlled morality, where parents govern ideas of right and wrong, to internally controlled morality, where the child's ideas of right and wrong are internalised. There is also a general shift from judgements based on consequences to judgements based on intention.

Piaget believed that progression through these stages depended on a child's level of cognitive understanding. According to Piaget's theory of cognitive development (see Chapter 2), two significant changes in thinking occur at approximately 7 years. First, the child starts to be able to take account of other people's points of view. In Piaget's terms the child is no longer **egocentric.** This lessening egocentrism enables a child to consider another person's intentions when making moral judgements, rather than just looking at the consequences. Second, at around the age of 7 years, the child becomes able to **de-centre**, meaning the child is able to consider more than just one factor at a time when making cognitive judgements. Thus, a child at this age can consider and evaluate multiple factors such as consequence, intention and circumstances all at the same time.

Piaget also believed that moral development was influenced by the change in the nature of the child's relationships with others as the child gets older. When the child is very young, the key relationships will be ones of **unilateral respect**, with the child respecting parents' views and adhering to parents' ideas of right and wrong. At this point, the child's most significant relationship will be with the parents – relationships with peers will have little influence. As the child gets older, relationships tend to be based more on **equal-status contact**, with the increasing importance of relationships with peers who are of equal status. Peer relationships often involve disagreements about right and wrong where the child has to solve the disagreement without parental guidance. In resolving these conflicts, the child learns to make independent decisions about moral issues. This change in the nature of the relationships as the child gets older would therefore explain the shift from heteronomous to autonomous morality. Although they become less influential as peer relationships become more dominant, parents are especially important in helping the child to achieve the moral realism stage because they provide authority and impose rules. However, parents who continue to enforce their view of right and wrong may make it harder for the child to achieve moral relativism.

Evaluation of Piaget's theory of moral development

- Much evidence supports Piaget's general view that moral understanding becomes more subtle with age and that older children focus more on intention than younger children (Berk, 2003).
- Social psychological research into attribution (that is, how we explain a person's actions) has shown that even adults tend to assume that a person is somehow to blame if his or her actions result in a negative consequence (Walster, 1966). This would suggest that Piaget was incorrect to assume that after the age of around 10 years people always judge by intention rather than consequence.
- Piaget's research was based mostly on a small sample of his own and his friends' children. The results should therefore be generalised with caution.
- Piaget may have underestimated children's moral understanding. His method of moral comparison required a crude judgement which may not have allowed children to show the full extent of their understanding.
- The work of other researchers has refined and in some cases contradicted Piaget's findings:

Evaluation – continued

- Nelson (1980) found that even 3-year-olds could take intention into account, showing that children can make meaningful moral judgements in Piaget's pre-moral stage, and that children can consider intention much earlier than Piaget suggested.
- Similarly, Helwig *et al.* (2001) showed that children as young as 3 years would judge ill-intentioned actors as more deserving of punishment than those who had good intentions.
- Laupa and Turiel (1986) found that children aged 6–10 years sometimes question rules imposed by parents, particularly conventional rules – for example, about tidying toys and helping around the house. This contradicts Piaget's idea that children in the moral realism stage have unilateral respect for parental rules and values.

- Piaget's theory does not allow for any advancement in moral understanding beyond the age of around 10 years. Other researchers, particularly Kohlberg (1963), have proposed a view of moral development that indicated increased sophistication in moral understanding beyond the ages studied by Piaget.

3.1.3 Kohlberg's theory of moral development

Lawrence Kohlberg (1969) carried out extensive research into moral development and moral reasoning, elaborating on the work of Piaget by using a more rigorous standardised procedure and exploring moral development in older participants. Kohlberg used the moral dilemma technique where participants heard a story in which a person is faced with a choice between two courses of action. It is called a dilemma because whichever course of action the person chooses, they have to do something which could be considered wrong. Kohlberg and his associates used different dilemmas over the years, the most famous of which was the 'Heinz' dilemma. Heinz has the dilemma of choosing between two unacceptable behaviours – stealing or failing to try to help his wife.

The Heinz dilemma

In Europe, a woman was near death from a special kind of cancer. There was one drug that the doctor thought might save her. It was a form of radium that a druggist in the same town had recently discovered. The drug was expensive to make, but the druggist was charging ten times what the drug cost him to make. He paid $200 for the radium and charged $2,000 for a small dose of the drug. The sick woman's husband, Heinz, went to everyone he knew to borrow the money, but he could only get together about $1,000 which is half what it cost. He told the druggist that his wife was dying and asked him to sell it cheaper or let him pay later. But the druggist said, 'No, I discovered the drug and I'm going to make money from it.' So Heinz got desperate and broke into the man's store to steal the drug for his wife. Should the husband have done that? Why or why not? (Kohlberg, 1969)

Examples of follow-up questions used in the moral dilemma interview (Kohlberg, 1984):

- If Heinz doesn't love his wife, should he steal the drug for her? (Why or why not?)
- Is it important for people to do everything they can to save another's life? (Why or why not?)
- Should people try to do everything they can to obey the law? (Why or why not?)
- Is it against the law for Heinz to steal? Does that make it morally wrong? Why or why not?

Figure 3.3 *Kohlberg (1969) used the Heinz dilemma to investigate moral reasoning. Should Heinz have stolen the drug?*

STUDY

Aim

Kohlberg (1963) wanted to know whether moral reasoning changes with age.

Method

He studied 72 middle-class and lower-class boys in Chicago. The participants were aged 10–16 years. Each boy heard a moral dilemma and was then asked a series of questions about the actions described in the story. Their responses during the hour-long interviews were recorded. Kohlberg was interested in the reasoning behind the participants' decisions, rather than in the decision about whether or not Heinz should steal the drug. Working with Colby *et al.* (1983), Kohlberg went on to interview 58 of the original participants every 3 years for the next 20 years.

Results

Kohlberg found that younger participants tended to reason on the basis of likely punishment or personal gain, whereas older participants were more concerned with issues such as care, the law and the views of society.

Conclusion

Analysis of the responses led Kohlberg to propose a six-stage theory of moral development. According to this theory, moral reasoning becomes increasingly complex with age as individuals progress through an invariant sequence of stages.

Kohlberg's three levels and six stages of moral reasoning

The Pre-conventional level:
Punishment stage
Reward stage

The Conventional level:
Good-Boy, Good-Girl stage
Law-and-Order stage

The Post-conventional level:
Social Contract stage
Ethical Principle stage

Kohlberg proposed that these stages occurred in an **invariant** and **irreversible** sequence, with no skipping of stages, and that an individual would show **stage unity**, meaning that a person's moral reasoning will be consistent across a range of different moral problems. He believed that progression through the stages was determined by a person's experience of thinking about moral problems and situations, similar to the way in which Piaget thought that moral and cognitive development resulted from active self-discovery. However, Kohlberg also thought that advances in moral reasoning were influenced by aspects of the social environment, such as what other people might say about the situation, and by experience of taking a variety of social roles which would encourage appreciation of other people's viewpoints. Kohlberg also believed that a child's moral reasoning would be enhanced if he or she grew up in a democratic environment where discussion was encouraged and disagreement was tolerated.

The Pre-conventional level

At this level moral reasoning is externally controlled, similar to the heteronomous stage proposed by Piaget.

Stage 1: Punishment
Reasoning is based on whether or not an action would result in punishment. Thus something that would result in punishment would be considered to be morally wrong, whereas an action that does not result in punishment would be considered to be morally acceptable. A possible response to the Heinz dilemma at this stage might be, 'He shouldn't steal the drug because he'll get caught and be sent to prison.'

Stage 2: Reward
Reasoning is based on what the individual has to gain from the various options. Whatever course of action benefits the individual is assumed to be morally correct, so people choose what to do according to **instrumental gain**. A possible response at this stage might be, 'He might steal the drug if he wanted his wife to live, but he does not have to if he wants to marry someone younger and better-looking' (Kohlberg, 1963).

The Conventional level

Conventional morality involves the active maintenance of a socially agreed system of behaving.

Stage 3: Good-Boy, Good-Girl
Moral decisions are made on the basis of what other people would think. Thus, an action that other people would approve of (Oh! What a good boy!) would be considered to be morally correct and an action that other people might disapprove of would be considered to be morally wrong. Kohlberg (1969) reported the following as an example of a typical response at this stage: 'Your family will think you're an inhuman husband if you don't (steal the drug).'

Stage 4: Law and Order
At this stage moral decisions are based on obedience to authority and conforming to the law. The morally correct decision involves consideration of the law as necessary to maintain social order. A typical response would be: '. . . if everyone did as he wanted to do, set up his own beliefs as right and wrong, then I think you would have chaos' (Colby *et al*., 1987b).

The Post-conventional level

Individuals at this level question the moral values of society and develop their own views about right and wrong. Morality is internally rather than externally governed.

Stage 5: Social Contract
There is an understanding that laws are part of a social contract between members of society which may sometimes need to be changed by democratic procedures. Individuals' rights are recognised and there is an understanding that those rights sometimes conflict with the existing law. Decisions about right and wrong are made according to unique circumstances and involve the recognition that law may not always be fair or appropriate, although basic rights like life and liberty must be upheld. At this stage a typical response might be, 'Stealing is against the law but it is justified in this case. The legal system should take account of how Heinz's wife has the right to life.'

Stage 6: Ethical Principle
Decisions about right and wrong are determined by an individual's self-chosen ethical principles. These principles are deemed to be more important than the law and can therefore bring the individual into conflict with the law. Strongly held self-chosen principles may result in demonstration and civil disobedience, such as antiwar demonstrations or refusal to pay what is believed to be an unjust tax.

Figure 3.4 *Reasoning at Kohlberg's Ethical Principle stage may bring individuals into conflict with the law to uphold their self-chosen ethical principles.*

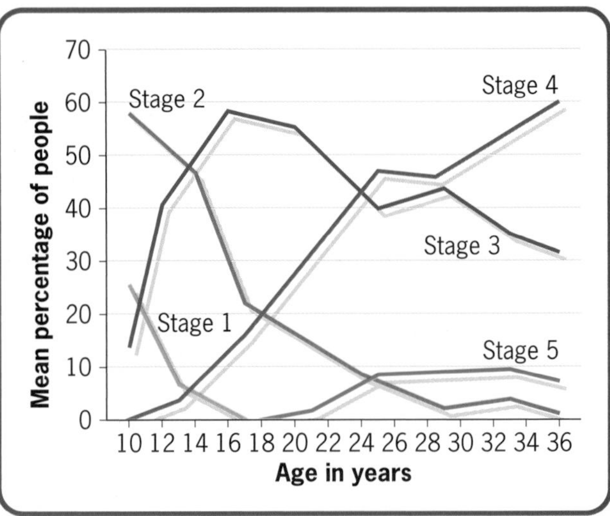

Figure 3.5 *Graph to show the percentage of people reasoning at each of Kohlberg's stages at different ages.*

STUDY

Aim

To investigate Kohlberg's theory that moral reasoning develops in an invariant and irreversible sequence of stages.

Method

Walker (1989) tested 233 male and female participants aged between 5 and 63 years over a period of two years. Using structured interviews, participants were given hypothetical dilemmas and their responses were scored and categorised at the appropriate Kohlberg stage.

Results

Over the two-year period, 37% of participants (62% for child participants) progressed to the next stage. A minimal number (6%) of participants had gone back to an earlier stage and no participants had skipped a stage altogether.

Conclusion

The findings generally supported Kohlberg's theory that there is an invariant and irreversible sequence of stages.

Evaluation of Kohlberg's stage theory

- Most research has confirmed the sequence of stages proposed by Kohlberg. Kohlberg and Kramer (1969) tested a group of teenagers with dilemmas at 3-year intervals. The majority of participants either stayed at the same stage as they had been at the previous testing or had moved on one stage, supporting Kohlberg's theory of an invariant and sequential progression. However, some participants missed a stage altogether and 20% even regressed to a previous stage.

- Turiel (1978, 1983) argued against Kohlberg's idea of distinct stages and the assumption that moral reasoning is a single, unitary phenomenon. He argued that there are different **moral domains** and that an individual's moral reasoning may be at different stages at the same time, depending on the domain. He identified the following three domains and suggested that moral understanding in each domain develops independently:
  - moral transgressions – for example, hitting and stealing
  - breaches of social convention – for example, omitting to say 'please' and 'thank you'
  - breaking of personal rules – for example, forgetting to send a birthday card to a friend.

- Nucci (1996) found that by the age of about 3 years children could understand that moral transgressions are more serious than breaches of social convention.

- Critics argued that stage 6 so rarely applied that it might not exist. Stage 6 was abandoned in 1975 and does not feature in the scoring manual (Colby *et al.*, 1987a).

- Kohlberg's theory seems to assume that moral understanding is linked to moral behaviour. However, Hartshorne and May (1928) found that children's moral beliefs were often inconsistent with behaviour – for example, some children who cheated said that they thought cheating was wrong. They also discovered that individuals would cheat in some situations but not in others. However, there does appear to be increasing consistency between moral beliefs and moral behaviour as children get older (Kohlberg, 1975; Blasi, 1980).

- Although much cross-cultural evidence supports Kohlberg's sequence of stages, people from technologically advanced urban cultures seem to advance through the stages more rapidly (Berk, 2003). Cultural differences in moral reasoning may be related to different years of compulsory schooling in different cultures (Snarey, 1995) and different values. Kohlberg's scoring system has been criticised for reflecting western values of individual freedom and choice. As a result, individuals from non-western cultures, where the social group is seen as more important than the individual, may score at lower stages using the Kohlberg scoring system. For example, Tietjen and Walker (1985) found that participants from New Guinea blamed the Heinz problem on the whole community who had not helped rather than on the individual. Many cultures have concepts of morality which cannot be accommodated in Kohlberg's theory at all – for example, the Hindu and Buddhist notions of karma, the Japanese notion of honour and the Indian ethic of duty.

- Gilligan (1982) noted that Kohlberg's stages were based on his early interviews with male participants and thought that they did not take account of female moral development. She believed that women tended to be placed at Kohlberg's stage 3 because their answers focused on empathy, whereas men tended to be placed at stage 4 because their answers focused on rights and the law. In her own theory,

Evaluation – continued

Gilligan tried to correct what she saw as an imbalance between the relative importance of care and justice. However, Walker *et al*. (1987) and Jadack *et al*. (1995) (see below) found no sex differences in responses to dilemmas using Kohlberg's scoring system.

- There are several methodological problems with the dilemma technique that Kohlberg used. See 3.1.4 below.

STUDY

Aim

Jadack *et al*. (1995) investigated three aspects of moral reasoning related to sexual attitudes and behaviour:

i) age differences in moral reasoning
ii) differences in moral reasoning across different dilemmas
iii) gender differences in moral reasoning.

Method

Male and female college students were given a number of hypothetical dilemmas about situations in which sexually transmitted diseases could be transmitted. They were asked about whether or not characters should take part in risk behaviour. Responses were scored using Kohlberg's stage theory.

Results

Significant age differences were noted, with older students scoring at a higher stage of moral reasoning than younger students. There were also significant differences in moral stage between dilemmas, indicating that it is possible to score at different stages in different situations. There were no significant gender differences.

Conclusion

The data support Kohlberg's stages and the notion of increasing sophistication in moral reasoning with age. They also suggest that criticisms that Kohlberg's theory is sex biased are unfounded. Finally, they suggest that the stages are not necessarily structured wholes, since it appears that the same person can reason at one stage in one situation and a different stage in another situation.

3.1.4 Ways of investigating moral development: moral comparisons and moral dilemmas

Moral comparison (used by Piaget)

A participant is given two short stories. In one story the act is intentionally naughty but there is little damage. In the other story the act was unintentional but there is a lot of damage (see the John and Henry stories in 3.1.1).

After reading both stories, the participant is asked which was naughtier, and why.

Figure 3.6 *Young children may find it difficult to recall the detail of Piaget's moral comparison stories.*

Examples of other moral comparison stories used by Piaget:

Alfred meets a little friend of his who is very poor. This friend tells him that he has had no dinner that day because there was nothing to eat in his home. Then Alfred goes into a baker's shop, and as he has no money, he waits till the baker's back is turned and steals a roll. Then he runs out and gives the roll to his friend.

Henriette goes into a shop. She sees a pretty piece of ribbon on a table and thinks to herself that it would look very nice on her dress. So while the shop lady's back is turned she steals the ribbon and runs away at once.

Evaluation of the moral comparison technique

- **Cognitive demand:** particularly with younger participants, there is the possibility that the task of remembering the detail of the two stories places too great a demand on memory. This may mean that participants are giving an answer based on an incomplete recollection of the details of the stories.
- **Demand characteristics:** children particularly are inclined to try to please the experimenter and it is likely they will give any response, even when they are unsure or do not understand, simply because they feel that the situation demands it.
- **Intention is only implied:** it is not explicit in the stories that one of the actors had a bad intention and the other had a good intention. Research by Nelson (1980) took account of this problem by making the intention clear.
- **Two variables are manipulated at the same time:** the two options are 'large damage, good intention' or 'small damage, bad intention'. This means that it is impossible for Piaget to say which variable is influencing the child's reasoning. Later work by Imamoglu (1975) and Nelson (1980) took account of this problem and showed that very young children can base judgements on motives rather than consequences.

Moral dilemma (initially used by Kohlberg)

A participant hears a story about what someone does in a situation where there is a choice between two courses of action. Both options involve doing something that could be considered wrong (see the 'Heinz' dilemma in 3.1.2).

In a structured interview, the participant is asked whether the action was wrong or not and then is asked to explain the reasons for their answer. There are a number of follow-up questions.

These responses are categorised or scored to indicate the level and stage of moral reasoning.

Eisenberg (1983) used the same technique, but instead of wrongdoing, her dilemmas involved the opportunity to do a good deed (pro-social dilemmas).

Other moral dilemmas used by Kohlberg:

Judy was a 12-year-old girl. Her mother promised her that she could go to a special rock concert coming to their town if she saved up from babysitting and lunch money to buy a ticket to the concert. She managed to save up the $15 the ticket cost plus another $5. But then her mother changed her mind and told Judy that she had to spend the money on new clothes for school. Judy was disappointed and decided to go to the concert anyway. She bought a ticket and told her mother that she had only been able to save $5. That Saturday she went to the performance and told her mother that she was spending the day with a friend. A week passed without her mother finding out. Judy then told her older sister, Louise, that she had gone to the performance and had lied to her mother about it. Louise wonders whether to tell their mother what Judy did.

Should Louise, the older sister, tell their mother that Judy lied about the money, or should she keep quiet? Why?

In a country in Europe, a poor man named Valjean could find no work, nor could his sister and brother. Without money, he stole food and medicine that they needed. He was captured and sentenced to prison for six years. After a couple of years he escaped from prison and went to live in another part of the country under a new name. He saved money and slowly built up a factory. He gave his workers the highest wages and used most of his profits to build a hospital for people who couldn't afford good medical care. Twenty years had passed when a tailor recognised the factory owner as being Valjean, the escaped convict who the police had been looking for back in his hometown.

Should the tailor report Valjean to the police? Why or why not?

Evaluation of the moral dilemma technique

i) Cognitive load
Particularly with younger participants, there is the possibility that the task of remembering the detail of the dilemma places large demands on memory. As a result, participants' answers may based on an incomplete recollection of the situation. This would mean that the results have little validity.

ii) Validity
A key issue in relation to the moral dilemma technique is **validity**. In other words, does the dilemma technique measure what it is supposed to measure, that is, moral reasoning?

- Kohlberg's participants were questioned about hypothetical situations which they were most unlikely ever to have experienced themselves. This means that responses may not reflect the participants' real-life moral reasoning and therefore may not be valid. Because it is highly artificial, Kohlberg's method might be said to lack **ecological validity**. Contrast this with the work of Gilligan (1977), who interviewed pregnant women who were contemplating abortions about their real dilemma. However, Walker *et al.* (1987) concluded that the technique did not lack validity (see study on page 78).

- Kohlberg's aim was to investigate and measure moral reasoning rather than moral judgement about right and wrong. To take account of this, the scoring system was revised so that the focus was more on the reasoning behind the judgement rather than on the judgement itself (Colby *et al.*, 1983).

- Critics argue that the dilemma technique does not have **predictive validity**, in other words, responses to the dilemma do not predict how participants would act in a real-life dilemma situation. However, Kohlberg (1975) studied whether or not participants would cheat and found that consistency between hypothetical reasoning and real-life reasoning increased with progression through the stages. For example, he found that 70% of people categorised at the Pre-conventional level cheated when given the opportunity to do so, compared with 55% of those in the Conventional level and only 15% of those in the Post-conventional level. These findings led Kohlberg to suggest that the dilemma technique does have predictive validity, at least for those at the more advanced level.

- Responses that are scored at the higher levels may be more sophisticated simply because the respondent is more educated and has the language ability to produce more complex arguments. Perhaps the moral dilemma technique measures level of education rather than moral reasoning.

Evaluation of the moral dilemma technique continued

iii) Reliability

Another key issue for the dilemma technique is that of **reliability**. In other words, can the responses be scored in a consistent way between different researchers and also by the same researcher on more than one occasion?

- It is important that dilemma responses can be scored reliably. Participants often produce long and rambling responses which can be hard to analyse objectively. The researcher has to make a fairly subjective decision – for example, whether a statement indicates stage 3 or stage 4 reasoning. This is often difficult to do consistently. Researchers using the technique need to be highly trained; Kohlberg has shown there to be a high degree of inter-rater reliability by asking a number of trained researchers to rate sample statements and then cross-checking the ratings for consistency.
- A detailed manual for coding of responses was produced (Colby *et al*., 1987a, 1987b) but Gibbs *et al*. (2002) have suggested that the scoring system is the most complex of any interview scoring system. A more simplified system has recently been proposed (Gibbs *et al*. 1992) and the results of this simplified interview scoring system appear to correlate well with the Colby *et al*. version.
- There is also the problem that participants themselves do not always show reliability. In other words, their responses sometimes indicate reasoning at one stage and later in the same interview they may indicate reasoning at another stage. This inconsistent responding on the part of the participant calls into question the whole possibility of reliable coding.

STUDY

Aim

To compare hypothetical and real-life moral reasoning.

Method

Walker *et al*. (1987) interviewed a large sample of adults and children about three of Kohlberg's moral dilemmas and one real-life dilemma the participant had experienced for themselves. The responses on each dilemma were scored according to Kohlberg's stages.

Results

The majority of participants (62%) reasoned at the same stage in the hypothetical dilemmas and the real-life dilemma. Approximately half of the remaining participants reasoned at a higher level when discussing the real-life dilemma, with the other half reasoning at a lower level.

Conclusion

Responses to hypothetical dilemmas are a fair reflection of real-life moral reasoning, suggesting ecological validity is not a problem.

3.2 Alternatives to Piaget and Kohlberg

3.2.1 Eisenberg's model of pro-social reasoning

Nancy Eisenberg (1983) used a dilemma technique similar to that used by Kohlberg, but instead of studying responses to dilemmas about wrongdoing, she looked at how participants reasoned in circumstances where there was an option to do good. For this reason, her dilemmas are known as **pro-social dilemmas.** In Eisenberg's dilemmas the participant has to choose between helping another person (behaving in an altruistic way) and looking after their own interests. The most famous of Eisenberg's dilemmas is 'the birthday party' dilemma described below.

Figure 3.7 *Eisenberg's birthday party dilemma. Should Mary carry on to the birthday party or should she help the girl who has hurt herself?*

STUDY

Aim

Eisenberg *et al.* (1987) carried out a longitudinal study to investigate changes in responses to pro-social dilemmas with age.

Method

American children were interviewed at 2-year intervals from the age of 4 years to the age of 12 years. The children were presented with dilemmas like the one below:

'One day a girl named Mary was going to a friend's birthday party. On her way she saw a girl who had fallen down and hurt her leg. The girl asked Mary to go to her house and get her parents so that they could come and take her to a doctor. But if Mary did, she would be late to the party and miss the ice cream, cake and all the games. What should Mary do?'

Responses to the dilemmas were recorded and analysed according to a scoring system where the minimum score was 4 and the maximum score was 16.

Results

Preschool and nursery-age children tended to score lower, giving self-oriented or **hedonistic**

STUDY continued

answers in which they put their own interest and pleasure before the needs of others. For example, they would say that it was more important that they get to the party in time and have all the treats. Older children scored more highly, giving **empathic** answers in which they placed more importance on the feelings and needs of others.

Conclusion

Pro-social reasoning changes with age from reasoning based on hedonism towards reasoning based on empathy.

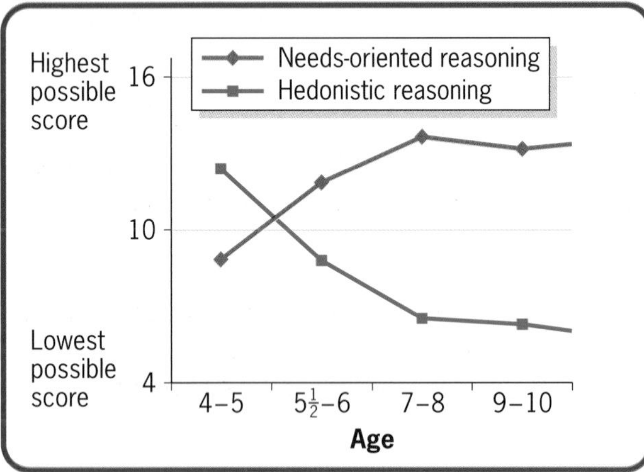

Figure 3.8 *Graph to show how Eisenberg's participants showed a gradual shift from hedonistic to needs-oriented reasoning with age (Eisenberg* et al.*, 1987).*

Eisenberg's levels or orientations of pro-social reasoning

Following extensive research during the 1980s, Eisenberg identified five stages in the development of pro-social moral reasoning which can be seen below. It is noticeable that the gradual shift from self-oriented reasoning to reasoning based on consideration for other individuals and broader society in many ways parallels the stages identified by Kohlberg.

Level or orientation	Description	Typical response to the birthday party dilemma
Hedonistic	Reasoning based on own interest	Mary can't help because she'd miss the party and get no cake.
Needs-oriented	Reasoning based on recognition of another's needs without sympathy or reference to moral values	The girl would feel better if Mary did help.
Approval-oriented	Reasoning based on what is expected or what is praiseworthy	It's nice to help. Mary's mummy would be pleased with her for doing something nice.
Empathic/ self-reflective	Reasoning based on sympathy and role-taking	Mary would feel sorry for the girl and think about how much it hurts.
Strongly internalised	Reasoning based on clear values, dignity and rights.	Mary should help. It's everyone's responsibility to care for other people.

Figure 3.9 *Eisenberg's five stages in the development of pro-social moral reasoning.*

Evaluation of Eisenberg's theory

- Eisenberg's view of a general shift from self-oriented reasoning towards concern for others and consideration of values and principles reflects the changes in moral reasoning identified by Kohlberg. As an example, there is an obvious parallel between Eisenberg's hedonistic stage and the punishment and reward stages identified by Kohlberg. There is also a clear similarity between Eisenberg's approval-oriented stage and Kohlberg's Good-Boy, Good-Girl stage. Both theories suggest that children in the later stages develop their own internalised norms as their reasoning becomes more sophisticated. These similarities indicate that Eisenberg's theory has validity.
- Despite the general similarity between Eisenberg's and Kohlberg's stages, it has been noted that reasoning about pro-social dilemmas is often slightly more advanced than reasoning about wrongdoing (Berk, 2003). This might be because Eisenberg's dilemmas focus on situations that are directly relevant to children and are therefore more appropriate for use with young children than those used by Kohlberg.
- Eisenberg focused on reasoning about pro-social issues, an area that had previously been neglected by researchers, even though many of the moral decisions that we make on a daily basis are about pro-social behaviour rather than wrongdoing. For example, we are faced with the decision about whether or not to give money to charity street collectors far more often than we are required to decide whether or not someone should be punished for stealing.
- The personal dilemmas used by Eisenberg are a better test of an individual's moral reasoning than those involving legal wrongdoing. For example, in the birthday party dilemma there is no law that says we should help another person, so reasoning is based on the individual's own moral understanding rather than a legal constraint.
- Eisenberg's stages are supported by cross-cultural studies in western societies – for example, Boehnke *et al.* (1989) found a similar pattern of development in German, Italian and Polish children. In non-western cultures the pattern of development has been found to differ – for example, Tietjen (1986) found that individuals in Papua New Guinea used needs-oriented reasoning into adolescence and adulthood.

3.2.2 Gilligan's ethic of care: differences between boys and girls

Carol Gilligan (1977, 1982) was a former student of Kohlberg and one of his fiercest critics. She argued that his view of moral reasoning emphasised justice rather than care, with the result that his scoring system was biased in favour of male reasoning. As a consequence of this bias, findings tended to show that females reasoned at a lower stage than males. For example, Holstein (1976) found that responses of female adolescents tended to be scored at Kohlberg's stage 3, whereas male responses were most frequently scored at stage 4. According to Gilligan, Kohlberg's descriptions of stage 4 reasoning (the Law and Order stage) focused on justice and authority, and his descriptions of stage 3 reasoning (the Good-Boy, Good-Girl stage) focused on empathy and care. This would explain why female participants tend to score lower on Kohlberg's stages. Gilligan criticised Kohlberg because his research, and therefore his theory, was based mostly on male participants.

Gilligan argued that the sexes think differently about morality, and that female moral reasoning is no less advanced than that of males. She proposed that women tend to have a greater interest in relationships and caring, which leads them to develop a morality of care and responsibility. Men, on the other hand, have more interest in rights and the law, which leads them to develop a morality of justice. Note how this idea tallies with traditional gender stereotypes of women as caring and men as tough and assertive. She proposed different moral orientations for males and females.

Gilligan's moral orientations

The morality of care: A tendency to consider how actions will affect the feelings and needs of others, to focus on relationships and on the prevention of harm.

The morality of justice: A tendency to consider whether or not the rules of society have been broken, and to focus on appropriate punishment.

STUDY

Aim

Gilligan (1977) wanted to see whether women's moral reasoning was equally sophisticated as the level of moral reasoning Kohlberg had identified in men.

Method

In a short-term longitudinal study, Gilligan used unstructured interviews with 29 pregnant women, aged 15–33 years. The women were all attending pregnancy/counselling services and were faced with the real-life dilemma of whether or not to have an abortion. She asked each woman about her situation and recorded the responses. These were then analysed for content.

Results

The women's thoughts about whether or not they should have an abortion tended to focus on issues of responsibility rather than on justice. Rather than use abstract, principled judgements typical of Kohlberg's stages 5 and 6, the women made judgements based on feeling for others which would typically put them at stage 3 according to Kohlberg's scoring system.

Conclusion

Gilligan concluded that women's moral reasoning was just as sophisticated as that of men, but different. She used this evidence to propose three levels in the development of a morality of care in women.

Figure 3.10 *Gilligan interviewed women who were considering whether or not to have an abortion.*

Gilligan's levels of moral development

Level 1 – Self-interest
Women focused on what was best for them and did not consider the needs of others.
Example response: *I can't have the baby, it would ruin my life.*

Level 2 – Self-sacrifice
Women tended to put the welfare of others before their own needs.
Example response: *My partner really wants another baby so I have to keep it.*

Level 3 – Non-violence or universal care
Women emphasised the importance of not hurting other people.
Example response: *It's not the baby's fault, but I worry about the effect that it will have on my whole family. I want to go to university and know that my parents would feel obliged to look after the baby, but they shouldn't have to at their age. My boyfriend thinks that we are too young to be good parents, and every child deserves to be well looked after.*

Gilligan concluded from her work that some of the statements made at the self-sacrifice and non-violence stages could involve the kind of principles which Kohlberg identified as typical of post-conventional reasoning, suggesting that women's moral reasoning could be at least as sophisticated as men's. According to Smith *et al.* (2003), Gilligan's research seems to show that women tend to put people before principles, as opposed to men who tend to put principles before people.

Evaluation of Gilligan's theory

- Gilligan has been accused of overemphasising sex differences. Many studies using Kohlberg's dilemma method show no difference in the sophistication of moral judgements made by women and men. Walker (1984) reviewed the results from 54 studies in the USA and found sex differences in only 8 of them.
- Gilligan interviewed only women in her research. Had she interviewed the partners of the women she might have found that men also have an ethic of care and produce similar care-based arguments. Walker's (1989) study shows that the type of reasoning shown may depend more on the type of dilemma than whether the participant is male or female.

STUDY

Aim

Walker (1989) set out to see whether there were any sex differences in moral reasoning.

Method

A large sample of participants aged 5–63 years were tested on hypothetical and self-generated real-life dilemmas. Their responses were scored according to both Kohlberg's stage theory and Gilligan's levels.

STUDY continued

Results

No significant sex differences in moral reasoning were found. Indeed, participants of both sexes used both orientations. However, it was also found that women's self-generated dilemmas tended to focus on personal relationships (e.g. telling a friend something that might be upsetting), whereas men's tended to focus on situations involving strangers (e.g. not owning up to bumping another car in a car park). When tested on personal relationship dilemmas, both males and females used the ethic of care orientation. Walker also found that personal relationship dilemmas (those where participants reasoned according to the ethic of care) tended to yield more sophisticated reasoning than other dilemmas. This directly conflicts with Gilligan's criticism of Kohlberg, that care-based reasoning results in a lower stage than justice-based reasoning.

Conclusion

There are no notable sex differences in moral reasoning between males and females. Both males and females reason according to both justice and care.

3.2.3 Damon's research into distributive justice

Children's real-life moral reasoning is often about whether or not something is 'fair'. Damon pointed out that reasoning about fairness frequently occurs when something is to be shared out between members of a group – for example, sharing of food or sharing of a toy that everyone wants to play with. Such ideas about how material goods ought to be fairly divided is sometimes referred to as **distributive justice**. Damon's research showed how ideas about distributive justice became more sophisticated with age (Damon, 1977, 1988). Although these changes in understanding are influenced to some degree by interactions with parents, it is the 'give-and-take' of peer interaction that seems to be especially important (Kruger, 1993).

- Young children understand that sharing is important, but only in as much as it might involve some **personal gain**. For example, a child under the age of 5 years might agree to share a toy with a friend who is visiting, but only because it means that they get to play with the other child's toys when they visit their house next week.
- By about 5 years, judgements about what is fair rely on the idea of **equality**, that everyone should have an equal share, irrespective of need or individual effort. At this point there is a clear rule about distribution, but it is inflexible. This is similar in some ways to Piaget's findings about rules in the game of marbles – the rules cannot be changed and appear to come from on high.
- By the age of about 7 years, decisions about fair distribution start to be based on notions of **merit**. For example, a child at this age might argue that someone should get more money from a cake sale because they worked the hardest.
- Finally, at around the age of 8–9 years, children base their reasoning on **benevolence**, understanding that some individuals should have special consideration, perhaps because of their disadvantage. For example, a child at this age might suggest that the smallest person in the class should have the best seat at the school concert so that they can get a better view.

Recent research into distributive justice (McGillicuddy-De Lisi *et al.*, 1994) has shown that benevolence is of key importance in reasoning about interactions with friends, whereas merit is more likely to be used in interactions with strangers. It has also been shown that reasoning about distributive justice continues to develop through adolescence and that gender differences in adult justice reasoning arise in adolescence; male students are more likely to reason by equity, whereas female students show more complex reasoning considering issues such as relationships and context (McGillicuddy-De Lisi *et al.*, 2008).

STUDY

Aim

To investigate age-related changes in reasoning about distributive justice.

Method

Damon (1977) gave children the dilemma of choosing how to distribute money from a sale of pictures drawn by their class.

'A classroom of children spent a day drawing pictures. Some children made a lot of drawings, some made fewer. Some children drew well, others did not draw as well. Some children were well-behaved and worked hard, others fooled around. Some children were poor, some were boys; some were girls and so on. The class then sold the drawings at a school bazaar. How should the proceeds from the sale of the drawings be fairly distributed?'

Children aged between 4 and 10 years were interviewed and their responses recorded.

Results

Children aged 4–5 years tended to focus on what they wanted, or tried to justify having more for themselves on the basis of some arbitrary characteristic such as gender: 'We should have more because we are girls'. Between 5 and 7 years, children thought that everyone should have an equal share of the profits. From the age of about 7 years children's responses showed consideration of individual merit: 'Those who worked hard should get the most', and individual need: 'The poor children should get more'.

Conclusion

As children get older, reasoning about distributive justice moves from emphasis on self-gratification to focus on individual merit and other's needs.

Evaluation of Damon's work

- Damon's work, based on justice and fairness, provides a different perspective to the body of research into moral development.
- The findings generally parallel the shift in emphasis from reasoning based on self-interest to reasoning based on the needs of others, as seen in the research of Kohlberg, Eisenberg and others.
- These findings have been replicated in other cultures, including Israel, Puerto Rico and Europe.
- The research is based on dilemmas that are within children's everyday experience and so has high ecological validity.
- The paintings dilemma is hypothetical and so may not reflect how children would really go about sharing, in other words, the findings may have little predictive validity. In later research, Gerson and

Evaluation – continued

Damon (1978) investigated children's real-life reasoning in a similar dilemma. The children were put into groups of four and were given the task of making bracelets with beads. They carefully manipulated the composition of each group in terms of age, ability and so on, so that some members of the group were more productive than others. At the end of the task, each group was given ten candy bars to share out between the group members. The children were also interviewed individually about how they thought the candy should be shared. It was found that 10% of the children showed more advanced reasoning in the actual sharing compared to what they said in their hypothetical interview, whereas 40% showed less advanced reasoning in real life. This suggests that real-life reasoning may be less sophisticated than hypothetical reasoning.

Figure 3.11 *Damon (1977) showed how reasoning about how to distribute money from a sale of class drawings changes with age.*

3.2.4 Psychodynamic explanations of moral development

Psychodynamic theory can be used to explain a variety of behaviours including moral development. Freud's theory differs from those already covered because it focuses on the feelings attached to doing good deeds (pride) or to wrongdoing (guilt) rather than on moral understanding. Freud (1961) believed that ideas of right and wrong are acquired at approximately 4–6 years of age, in the phallic stage of psychosexual development when the child acquires the superego.

The role of the superego

According to Freud there are three parts to the personality, the id, the ego and the superego. The superego is the part of the personality responsible for morality; it develops through the successful resolution of either the Oedipus or Electra complex in what is known as the phallic stage of Freud's psychosexual stages of development. Only when the superego has developed can the demands of the self-serving id can be controlled.

The three-part personality (Freud)

Id – *an unconscious aspect of the self*
Self-serving, demanding and unreasonable; – operates according to the pleasure principle and demands instant satisfaction, much like a spoilt, tantruming child.

Ego – *the conscious self*
Operates according to the reality principle; balances the unreasonable demands of the id with the opposing demands of the strict, punitive superego.

Superego – *an unconscious aspect of the self*
The morality principle comprised the internal parent or conscience and the ego-ideal. The conscience punishes us with guilt for wrongdoing. The ego-ideal indicates high moral standards and makes us feel proud when we have done something good. The superego is just as unreasonable as the id and can be extremely harsh, causing feelings of guilt even when we have done nothing wrong. It is the superego that influences us to act in morally acceptable ways. The superego normally represents the values and moral standards of the child's parents which have been internalised when the child goes through either the Oedipus or Electra complex. Freud likened this internal parent to a 'homonculus', or 'little man', living within us, continually threatening and chastising.

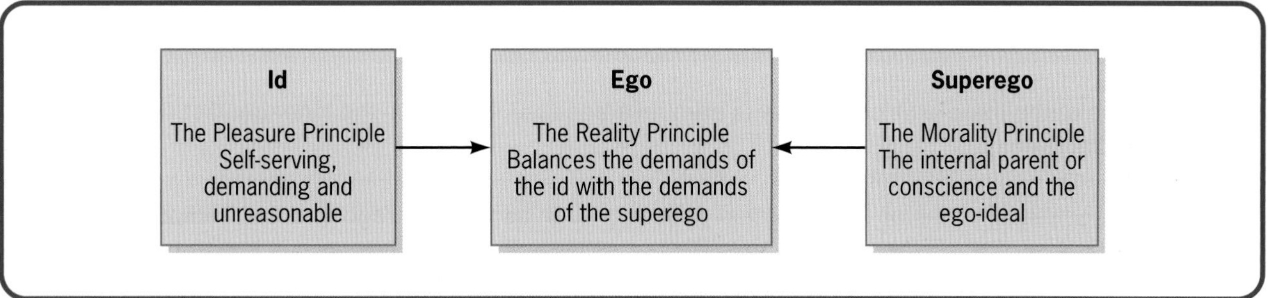

Figure 3.12 *Freud's three-part personality.*

Figure 3.13 *The superego acts like an internal parent or conscience, influencing us to act in morally acceptable ways.*

The Oedipus complex

In the phallic stage of development at around the age of 5 years the boy develops a sexual interest in his mother. The boy recognises his father as a powerful rival for the mother's affections and begins to fear that his father might castrate him if he discovers his desire for his mother. This is known as *castration anxiety*. To resolve the conflict between the love for his mother and the fear of castration the boy gives up the love for his mother and identifies with his father. This is referred to as *identifying with the aggressor*. It is this process of **identification** with the father that results in the boy internalising his father's moral values in the form of the superego. Freud would predict that a boy that has not satisfactorily resolved his Oedipus complex, perhaps because of the absence of a father, will not have successfully internalised moral standards.

The Electra complex

Freud believed that in the phallic stage the girl, becoming aware that she does not have a penis, believes she has already been castrated. Seeing that the mother also has no penis, the girl blames the mother for her lack of a penis. She sees both herself and her mother as powerless. The girl desires a penis, the symbol of male power. This *penis envy* leads her to desire the father because he possesses what she wants. As the girl cannot have a penis of her own, she converts her 'penis envy' into a desire for a baby, the 'penis-baby' project. Having resolved the conflict, the girl **identifies** with the mother, internalising her moral standards in the form of a superego. According to Freud's explanation, female identification is not as strong as male identification because the girl thinks she has already been castrated and therefore is not as fearful as the boy. This means that the girl does not identify with the mother as strongly as the boy identifies with the father, leading psychodynamic theorists to suggest that women are morally inferior to men.

Evaluation of Freud's theory of moral development

- Freud's idea of the three-part personality is attractive because it explains the inner conflict people feel in real-life moral dilemmas.
- There is no empirical evidence that Freudian concepts such as the superego and the Oedipus and Electra complexes actually exist.
- Freud's theory that moral understanding, in the form of the superego, is acquired suddenly at around 5 years is not supported. According to Freud, prior to this age, a child should have no understanding of right and wrong, and after this age, there should be no further development in moral understanding. Observations show that even very young children can understand right and wrong (Nelson, 1980), and many researchers, including Piaget and Kohlberg, have shown that moral development continues well beyond the age of 5 years.
- Freud's theory predicts that children who fear their parents will develop stronger superegos and so have a stronger conscience. However, evidence suggests that strict, punitive parents tend to have children who are naughtier and show less guilt (Brody and Shaffer, 1982).
- Freud's assertion that women are morally inferior to men is not strongly supported. Hoffman (1975) reviewed research from studies where children were given the opportunity to break rules. Few sex differences in rule-breaking were found, although girls did appear to be more able to resist temptation.
- Freud's theory about development of the superego rests on the assumption that children grow up with both parents, yet many children aged 4–6 years live with only one parent. There is no evidence that children in such circumstances fail to develop a conscience.
- Freud believed that the development of a conscience was determined solely by the resolution of the Oedipus and Electra complexes, yet there are much simpler explanations. Social learning theorists would argue that children's moral behaviour is influenced by much wider society, including adult role models and peers. For example, Bandura *et al.* (1963) found that children would imitate the aggressive behaviour of other adults.

How Psychology Works

Analysing moral dilemma responses: qualitative to quantitative

- **You are going to carry out an exercise in converting qualitative data to quantitative data. Find a friend who would be willing to act as a participant in a study of responses to one of Kohlberg's moral dilemmas. Tell them that you would like to interview them and ask if you can tape-record their responses.**
- **Select one of Kohlberg's dilemmas – for example, the Heinz dilemma – and photocopy it onto a sheet for your participant to read.**
- **Decide on a set of prompt questions for you to use during the interview and type them onto a sheet. Eight to ten questions is probably enough. Examples of some of the prompts used with the Heinz dilemma are on page 68.**

- Before you start the interview, brief your participant as to the nature of the study and assure them of confidentiality. Explain that they have the right to withdraw at any time.
- Carry out a structured interview with your participant and record the responses.
- At the end of the interview debrief your participant by explaining the purpose of your study and asking if it is still alright to analyse the data from the recording.
- Now you need to transcribe the responses. This must be done word for word, making a note of any hesitations.
- For the qualitative analysis you should read carefully through the transcribed interview and note any themes or issues that can be identified. Your understanding of the content should be used to form the basis of a written analysis of the interview content. Consider the meaning of the responses and the feelings of the respondent. You might also include something on your feelings about the interview. Aim to write about one side of A4. This written summary is the qualitative analysis.
- For the quantitative analysis you will need to set up a category system to code the responses. Identify target themes, issues or key words and then work through the content of the interview, tallying every time the target content appears. Ideally you should work with another researcher here and check for inter-researcher reliability. The numerical data from the tally sheets can then be presented in the form of bar charts.
- When you have completed both forms of analysis, consider how well each meets the criteria of validity and reliability. Validity – have you measured what you set out to measure, and how meaningful is the data? Reliability – is the measure consistent?

Further Reading

Introductory texts

Bee, H. (1999) *The Developing Child*, 8th edn., New York: Longman.

Berk, L.E. (2003) *Child Development*, 6th edn., Boston: Allyn & Bacon.

Schaffer, D.R. (1993) *Developmental Psychology: Childhood and Adolescence*, 3rd edn., Pacific Grove, CA: Brooks/Cole.

Smith, P.K., Cowie, H. and Blades, M. (1998) *Understanding Children's Development*, 3rd edn., Oxford: Blackwell.

Specialist sources

Durkin, K. (1995) *Developmental Social Psychology*, Oxford: Blackwell.

Eisenberg, N. and Mussen, P.H. (1989) *The Roots of Prosocial Behaviour in Children*, Cambridge: Cambridge University Press.

Gilligan, C. (1982) *In a Different Voice: Psychological Theory and Development*, Cambridge, MA: Harvard University Press.

Messer, D. and Miller, S. (eds.) (1999) *Exploring Developmental Psychology*, London: Arnold.

Thomas, R.M. (2000) *Comparing Theories of Child Development*, 5th edn., London: Wadsworth.

Vasta, R., Haith, M.M. and Miller, S.A. (1999) *Child Psychology: The Modern Science*, Chichester: John Wiley & Sons.

Cognition and law

Chapter 4

We all experience everyday memory problems, such as not being able to remember someone's name or not recognising someone out of their usual context. We often disagree with friends about the detail of an event and sometimes it is hard to decide whether something you thought you remembered actually ever happened at all. While annoying, these everyday memory problems are mostly of little importance; however, in some circumstances, for legal reasons, it really matters whether we recognise and remember faces accurately and can recall accurately the detail of events that we have witnessed. Cognition and law is an area of applied psychology concerned with how aspects of cognitive psychology relate to real life. The topic area is divided into two subsections: recognising and remembering faces and recalling events.

4.1 Recognising and remembering faces

4.1.1 Processes involved in recognition of faces

Cohen (1989) distinguishes between

- face identification: looking at a person's face and knowing who it is
- face recognition: knowing the face is one we have seen before
- face recall: when, from memory, we try to verbally describe a face, draw a face or form a 'mental image' of the face. Putting the stored mental image of a face into words for the description shows how difficult it is to convert the stored 'whole' into a list of 'features'.

	Time period between exposure and identification		
Type of task	11 days	1 year	8 years
Recognised task	69	47.5	26
Identification task	35.5	6	0

Figure 4.1 *Bahrick (1984) showed how it is easier to recognise a face than recall it, and that memory for faces deteriorates over time.*

Two fairly consistent findings from studies of face recognition are that people are better at recognition than identification, and that the ability to recognise faces deteriorates over time. Bahrick (1984) used a sample of teachers to investigate differences in recognition and identification at various time intervals. Teachers were asked to recognise/identify faces of present and former students when they were shown sets of five faces, four of which were distracters. Their tasks were to a) identify the known student from the set (recognition task), and b) name the student (identification task). As shown in Figure 4.1, recognition was better than identification, but in general, memory for faces deteriorated over time.

4.1.2 Explanations for face recognition

Feature analysis theory

It seems fairly obvious to say that a person's facial features are important for recognition, because without features, there would be no face. Indeed when people are asked to describe a face, the verbal description is inevitably a list of features (blue eyes, long nose, etc.). There may be other information too – for example, 'it's a friendly face' – but mostly the description will consist of features. Feature analysis theory is an example of a **bottom-up theory** in which it is suggested that analysing individual features is the key to face recognition. According to bottom-up theory, the visual cues from the face we are currently viewing are the most important information for recognition, and so we would need to focus on the detail of the face, analysing the separate features closely. Visual cues would include the way the light and shade appear on the face and the texture of the hair and skin. All these visual cues combine to enable us to perceive the broader features of the face, like the shape of the nose and mouth.

Shepherd *et al.* (1981) investigated how features are used in free-recall descriptions by showing participants some faces of people they had never seen before for a brief period of time. Participants were then asked to describe from memory the faces they had been shown. In describing these unfamiliar faces, the features most often referred to were: hair, eyes, nose, mouth, eyebrows, chin and forehead (in that order). This research suggests that faces of people we do not know very well tend to be recalled using the main features of the face. Ellis *et al.* (1979) discovered that descriptions of less familiar faces focus more on external facial features such as hair and face shape, etc., whereas we tend to use internal features when recalling faces of more familiar people. Obviously external features are more noticeable, particularly from a distance. However, they are also more likely to change, as when people dye or cut their hair, so internal features are probably more reliable for long-term recognition.

Consideration of how eyewitnesses help police to identify suspects illustrates the problems of using features for recognition. One method is to produce a list of features from a verbal description, and then use the description to make up a likeness which traditionally comprises five features – hair, eyes, nose, mouth and jawline. Davies *et al.* (1978) found most participants had difficulty producing a good likeness even when the real face was in front of them!

STUDY

Aim

Woodhead *et al.* (1979) evaluated the use of component features in face recognition by looking at the effectiveness of a feature-based face recognition training course. If faces are stored as features, then training in feature recognition should help recognition of whole faces.

Method

Participants spent 3 days learning to recognise features like 'full mouth', 'thin mouth', etc., and then took part in recognition tests of full faces. In one task, participants had to identify a 'wanted criminal' from 240 other faces.

Results

Participants who had undergone the feature training course were less able to identify the 'wanted criminal' than control participants.

Conclusion

This research seems to indicate that individual facial features are less important for face recognition, suggesting perhaps that faces are stored as wholes rather than as a collection of features.

Figure 4.2 *Features alone are not very helpful for face recognition.*

Evaluation of feature analysis theory

- There is some empirical evidence to show that features are used in the process of face recognition.
- Although visual cues and facial features are important in describing faces and must have a role in face recognition, relying just on bottom-up processing for such a complex activity is unlikely.
- Feature analysis theory neglects the importance of other information for recognition – for example, facial expression.
- Studies have shown that single facial features are not very easily recognised at all and that features need to be processed in the context of the whole face (see Study on page 98, Tanaka and Farah, 1993).
- Feature analysis theory does not explain why altering the configuration of a face interferes with recognition. If the features are all still there, and recognition depends on features, then why does recognition take longer?

Holistic form theory

Holistic form theory is an alternative to the feature analysis approach. Bruce and Young (1986) proposed a **top-down approach**, suggesting that recognising a face requires stored semantic and emotional information, and is more complex than simply adding together a set of features. For example, when we see someone in the street, we would need to refer back to previously stored information about where we know the person from in order to say that we have recognised them fully.

According to the holistic approach, a face is recognised as a whole, analysing the relationship between features, feelings aroused by the face and semantic information about the person. Ellis (1975) suggests we have a stored template or pattern for the face of each person we know, and when presented with a face, we try to match this stimulus to our mental pattern.

STUDY

Aim

Young and Hay (1986) demonstrated the importance of layout or configuration in the processing of faces.

Method

Pictures of famous faces were cut in half horizontally, and participants' recognition times for the people in the two separate halves were recorded. These halves were then combined together in non-matching pairs (composites) and participants were asked to name the two people. Again the time was recorded.

Results

It was found that recognition time from the halves was much longer when two were put together as a composite.

Conclusion

Recognition was difficult because the two halves combined seemed to produce an entirely new holistic face, making it harder to recognise the separate halves. This demonstrates that visual cues and features are not the only important information for recognition, as the overall layout of the face is equally, if not more important.

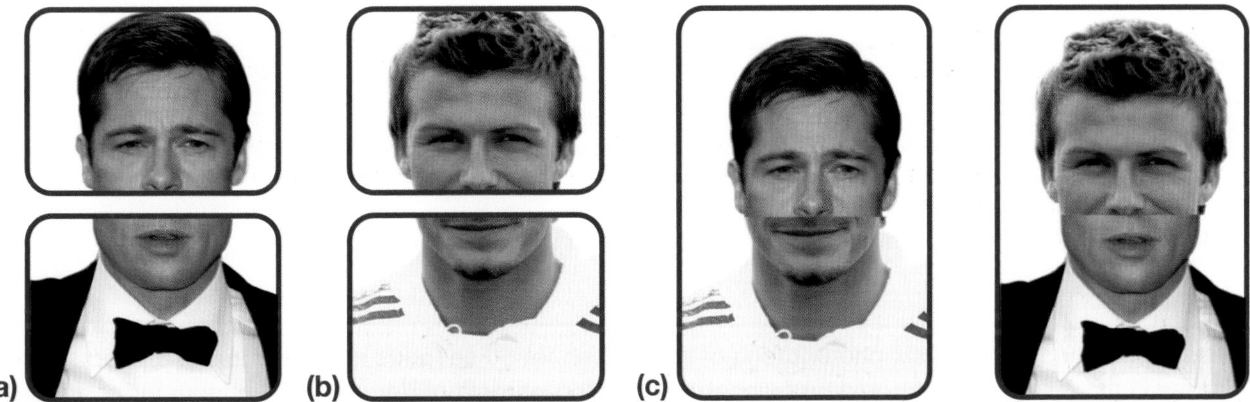

Figure 4.3 *It is more difficult to recognise the people in the two halves of face* **(c)** *than it is to recognise the two halves shown independently* **(a and b)** *(after Young and Hay, 1986).*

Similar research involves changing the layout of faces in other ways, either by altering the spacing between the facial features or by inverting the face, as shown in Figure 4.4.

Haig (1984) showed how recognition times increased for faces of famous people where the spacing between features was altered, and Yin (1969) found that upside-down or inverted faces are much harder to recognise. Cohen (1989) suggests this shows that faces 'are normally recognised holistically, and inversion destroys the global pattern relationships between features.' Such findings seem to support the holistic approach to face recognition.

Further support for a holistic model of face recognition comes from studies comparing recognition and recall. People are usually better at recognising faces seen before than they are at recalling them.

Figure 4.4 *Upside-down or inverted faces are much harder to recognise (Yin, 1969). Recognition is more difficult when the spacing between features is altered (Haig, 1984).*

Clinical studies of people with recognition disorders provide insights into the processes involved in face recognition (Ellis and Shepherd, 1992). **Prosopagnosia** is a rare disorder where patients cannot recognise familiar human faces. In extreme cases, they cannot even recognise their own reflection. Sufferers describe how they get the emotional feeling of recognition, but have no conscious awareness of knowing the person.

People with **Capgras syndrome** experience the delusion that 'doubles' have replaced people they know; they experience cognitive recognition, but have no feeling of emotional recognition. Hirstein and Ramachandran (1997) reported the case of a Capgras patient (DS) who was shown pictures of strangers and of his mother whilst he was attached to GSR machine (a device which records minute changes in surface moisture of the skin). Normally, when we see someone we recognise the surface moisture of our skin increases. Although the patient stated that the picture looked exactly like his mother, he was quite certain that it was not her and did not show the usual sweat response that comes with emotional recognition. In fact, his response to the photograph of his mother was just the same as his response to the pictures of strangers.

Clinical evidence such as this suggests that face recognition is an extremely complex activity involving both cognitive and emotional processes. Cases show how face recognition cannot rely just on features, as prosopagnosics and Capgras sufferers can name and describe individual features of familiar faces. This and other evidence points to a more holistic model of face recognition.

Bruce and Young (1986) put forward a holistic model

STUDY

Aim

Ellis *et al.* (1975) aimed to show the difficulties involved in verbally recalling faces.

Method

Participants were shown six photographs of male faces for 10 seconds and were asked immediately to recall the face so that it could be reconstructed using photofit materials. Independent judges then attempted to pick out the target face from the photofit reconstructions.

Results

Only 12.5% of identifications were correct, indicating that the reconstructed faces were not much like the original stimulus.

Conclusion

To describe a face, we must convert our stored mental image of it into words, i.e. features, which is a difficult and not very effective process, as this study shows, suggesting that we probably store faces as wholes rather than as sets of features.

of face recognition, proposing a sequence of stages as follows:

i The face is **structurally encoded**, meaning we take in the visual information, processing the physical appearance of the face, independent of the expression. Facial expression is analysed quite separately at the same time – we can tell whether someone is happy or sad even though we don't know them. At this point we also engage in actively scanning the face, perhaps focusing on specific features more than others and analysing what is referred to as 'facial speech' or lip-reading.

ii If the physical appearance matches an existing **face recognition unit (FRU)**, then this will be activated. The FRU contains physical information and might be thought of as a **template**. According to Bruce and Young, we have a FRU for every face we know.

iii Activation of the FRU triggers activation of the **person identity node (PIN)**, giving personal information such as occupation, interests, where we normally meet the person and whether we like them or not. Effectively, the face is recognised when the PIN is activated.

iv The final stage in the process is **name generation**. According to Bruce and Young, names are stored separately to the FRUs and PINs, but can only be accessed via the PIN. This would explain why we know things about a person we meet but cannot think of their name.

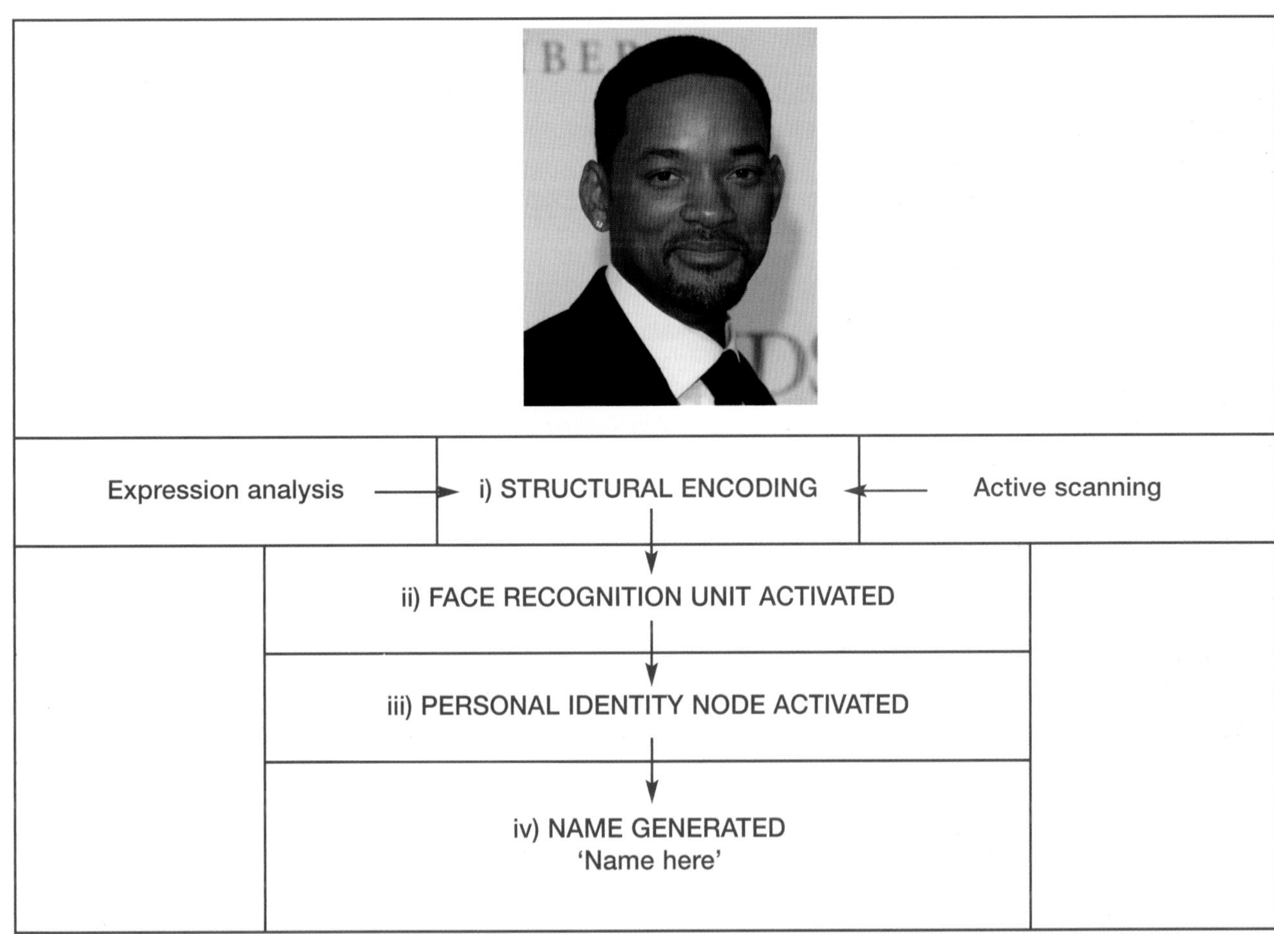

Figure 4.5 *Simplified version of the Bruce and Young holistic model of face recognition.*

STUDY

Aim

Young *et al*. (1985) set out to confirm the sequence of events proposed in the holistic model.

Method

Twenty participants kept a daily diary of problems in face recognition. These were then analysed for content.

Results

Out of 1,008 incidents, there were no reports of naming someone without knowing other information about them. In 190 cases, the opposite occurred – for example, occupation was known, but not the person's name. In 233 cases, participants reported experiencing familiarity, but nothing else.

Conclusion

The findings support the sequence proposed by the holistic model whereby names can only be accessed if semantic information has been accessed first. In the 233 cases where familiarity was experienced without full recognition, a FRU had been triggered, but the PIN had failed to activate, again supporting the sequence proposed by Bruce and Young.

Evaluation of the holistic form theory

- Evidence from diary studies and laboratory research supports the Bruce and Young model, suggesting that information about familiar faces is accessed in a sequence and that faces are analysed as wholes rather than as separate features.
- The theory takes account of the fact that face recognition is complex and involves emotion and semantic information.
- The model can predict and explain many everyday observations.
- The model does not explain why patients with prosopagnosia can show unconscious (or covert) recognition. Even though they do not consciously recognise familiar people, they can show unconscious recognition in their bodily responses, as measured by a galvanic skin response (GSR) meter. Presumably this unconscious response occurs because the patient knows something about the person's PIN – for example, whether they like them or not – yet no conscious match has been made via the FRU.
- The theory has been criticised, particularly over the lack of information about how we recognise less familiar faces (Estgate and Groome, 2005).
- The model was revised by Burton *et al.* (1990) using computer modelling to further investigate the face recognition process.

The revised Burton *et al.* model allows for semantic links between PINS for different individuals. Although each of us has a unique PIN, different people may have certain elements of their PINs in common. For example, your PIN includes information about where you went to primary school, in common with all the other people who went to the same primary school. This explains why we find it easier to recognise someone if we have been primed with an associated face beforehand. For example, we would be quicker to recognise Victoria Beckham if we were shown the face of her husband David Beckham beforehand. This semantic priming effect (Bruce and Valentine, 1988) can be explained by the Burton *et al.* model, which uses a computer programme to simulate the multiple associations made by neurons in the brain.

4.1.3 Construction of likenesses using composite systems

Eyewitnesses to a crime are usually asked to describe the offender. The description the witness gives can then be used to build a likeness that might aid the police in catching the offender. Most likenesses today are constructed using a composite system of separate facial features. Originally these were called identikit, and then photofit, likenesses. Using this type of system the witness selects features from a bank of noses, mouths and so on, and these are then combined to produce a face. These early paper-based systems are referred to as first-generation composite systems and had very limited success.

Computer-based, second-generation composite systems were invented in the 1980s and involved large databases of features. These second-generation systems were superior to the original composite systems in three ways:

- They allowed for the separate features to be combined into a face without the distracting lines on the face that had been so evident in the early systems.
- The software editing systems allowed for artistic enhancement so that features could be blended and altered to the witness's individual requirements.
- Features can be moved to a slightly different position on the face and exaggerated or minimised according to the needs of the witness. This is an important enhancement since studies have shown that configuration or spacing of features is a crucial factor in face recognition (Kemp *et al.*, 1990).

STUDY

Aim

Ellis *et al.* (1978) set out to investigate the usefulness of early composite systems.

Method

Participants observed a person on a video and then had to produce two versions of the person's face. One was a hand-drawn sketch and the other was constructed using the British photofit kit. There were two different conditions – in one condition the witness produced the face from memory; in the other condition the face was produced with the target person present.

Results

When producing the images from memory, the composite system was slightly better than the drawing. However, the composite images produced with the target person present were no better than those constructed from memory. Indeed, with the target person present, the hand-drawn images were assessed to be better likenesses than the composites.

Conclusion

Early composite systems are no more useful than verbal descriptions.

A key problem with many composite systems is that the witness is required to select features in isolation from the rest of the face before these can be combined to give the full composite face. It is not surprising that many composites are less than successful, since studies such as Tanaka and Farah (1993) have shown that we find it extremely difficult to recognise individual features in isolation. This ability to recognise faces more easily than separate features is known as the '**facial superiority effect**'.

To address the problem of using separate features to build a composite, the e-fit system is now used by UK police. Witnesses describe the person to the system operator, who inputs the information into the computer. The programme draws up a composite, inserting an 'average' component where there are any gaps in the description. Finally, the witness views the whole face and makes any necessary amendments. E-fit systems have over a thousand examples of each facial feature and have been shown to be an improvement on photofit likenesses under certain conditions, particularly where the target face is familiar to the witness.

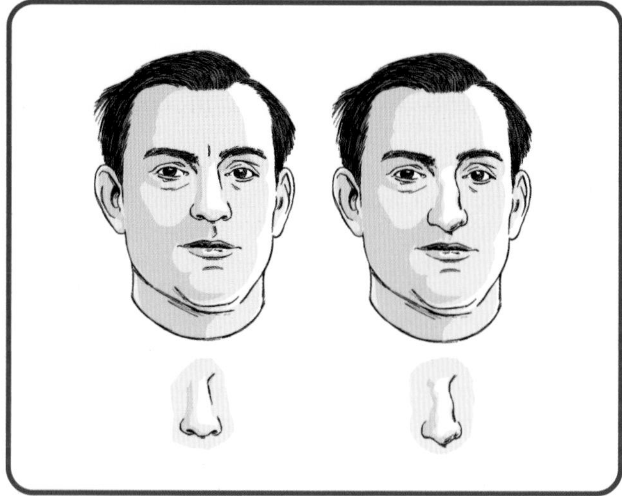

Figure 4.6 *Tanaka and Farah (1993) showed how participants could recognise Larry's whole face, but found it much harder to recognise Larry's nose on its own. This is known as the facial superiority effect.*

STUDY

Aim

Tanaka and Farah (1993) set out to investigate the ability to recognise single facial features in isolation.

Method

Participants were trained until they could name a series of composite faces correctly. After initial training, participants were presented with pairs of faces: one, the original 'Larry', and one that differed from the original only by a single feature like the nose. In a further condition, participants were required to look just at the two noses and identify which of them was 'Larry's' nose.

Results

In the whole-face condition, where the two faces differed only because they had different noses, participants could still tell the two faces apart and could identify the original 'Larry' correctly. In the isolated feature condition, participants had great difficulty identifying 'Larry's' nose.

Conclusion

Isolated facial features are very difficult to recognise, which supports the holistic theory of face recognition and perhaps explains why composite systems, which require witnesses to select from features in isolation, are of limited use.

Evaluation of composite systems

- Early systems had a limited number of features and were especially lacking in distinctive or unusual features.
- The new generation e-fit systems seem to be more effective than earlier versions (Davies *et al*., 2000).
- Police surveys generally suggest that composite systems are useful in a small but significant number of cases. For example, Kapardis (1997) notes that the FACE composite system used in Australia resulted in an individual being charged in 19% of cases and enabled the police to confirm a suspect in 23% of cases.
- Laboratory studies often require participants to recognise composite likenesses of people never seen prior to the study. However, real composites are normally used so that members of the public can recognise someone they are familiar with – for example, a work colleague or a neighbour. Brace *et al*. (2000) found that student judges could successfully identify composite faces of famous people (e.g. Paul McCartney and Sean Connery) that had been constructed by 'witnesses' working with e-fit operators. This study seems to show that composites can be useful, although in real life witnesses would not already be familiar with the offender beforehand.

4.1.4 Identification procedures: simultaneous and sequential line-ups

Identification procedures are used by the police to enable witnesses to make a positive identification of a suspect. In the UK these procedures are regulated by the Police and Criminal Evidence Act (PACE) 1984. UK identity parades typically involve nine possible suspects, usually the real suspect and eight volunteers known as 'foils'. In the past, identifications have been carried out using photographs, but these days most identifications involve real-life or corporeal line-ups. The unreliability of identifications made using the line-up procedure has been highlighted with the increased use of DNA evidence, which has frequently shown that suspects identified by eyewitnesses could not possibly be guilty. Estgate and Groome (2005) note how a significant number of suspects in murder or rape cases, who had been positively identified by witnesses, were later exonerated on the basis of DNA evidence.

Psychological research suggests that the way line-up procedures are carried out can have a crucial influence on the reliability of identifications made. A key debate centres on the controversy about whether line-ups should be simultaneous or sequential.

The simultaneous line-up

The witness is presented with all members of the line-up at one time. Simultaneous line-ups implicitly allow the witness to compare the available options, and thus involve the possibility of a relative judgement, where the witness chooses the person from the line-up that they think is most like their memory of the perpetrator.

Figure 4.7 *In a simultaneous line-up the witness views all members of the line-up at the same time.*

The sequential line-up

Members of the line-up are presented to the witness one at a time, with a separate judgement to be made about how each one compares with memory. Sequential line-ups do not allow for comparison and thus involve an **absolute judgement** for each individual, where the witness confirms whether or not each person in the line-up matches with their memory of the perpetrator.

Allowing witnesses the opportunity to make a relative judgement tends to lead to a greater chance of false identifications. Wells *et al.* (1998) have proposed a '**relative judgement theory**', suggesting that witnesses faced with a simultaneous line-up will naturally assume that one person in the line-up must be the suspect, and thus, even a very uncertain witness will tend to choose someone as the perpetrator. Steblay (1997) conducted a meta-analysis of laboratory studies to show that where witnesses were told that the culprit 'might or might not' be present in the line-up, the number of false identifications was significantly reduced.

Following Malpass and Devine's research (see below), PACE now requires that witnesses are informed at the

STUDY

Aim

Malpass and Devine (1981b) set out to investigate the effect of giving different instructions to witnesses in line-up procedures.

Method

Participants witnessed a staged act of vandalism and then were asked to identify the offender from a line-up. In the experimental condition the witnesses were asked 'which of these is the person you saw?', implying that the culprit was definitely present in the line-up. In the control condition, the witnesses were told that the culprit may or may not be present.

Results

In culprit-absent line-ups, the rate of false identifications in the experimental condition was 78%, compared with 33% in the control condition.

Conclusion

Unless they are explicitly informed that a culprit may not be present in a line-up, witnesses will tend to use a relative judgement strategy, increasing the risk of false identification.

time of the line-up procedure that 'the person you saw may or may not be in the parade'.

Lindsay and Wells (1985) devised the sequential line-up procedure to avoid the problem of relative judgements and encourage witnesses to make an absolute judgement about whether or not each person in the line-up matches their memory of the perpetrator. In a sequential line-up, the witness sees each person in the line-up one at a time and is asked to say whether or not each is the culprit.

Figure 4.8 *It is necessary for police officers to inform witnesses that the suspect may not be in the line-up.*

STUDY

Aim

Steblay *et al.* (2001) compared eyewitness performance using simultaneous and sequential line-up procedures.

Method

Findings from 30 experimental studies, involving 4,145 participants, were collated to look for the pattern of findings. This type of study is known as a meta-analysis.

Results

i) Across all 30 studies witnesses were less likely to identify a suspect in sequential line-ups than in simultaneous line-ups. Where culprits were present in the line-up, this meant that correct identification was less likely. Where culprits were not present in the line-up, this meant that false identification was less likely.

ii) Using data from only the most realistic of these studies, it was found that sequential line-ups led to a similar number of correct identifications, with fewer false identifications than occurred in simultaneous line-ups.

Conclusion

Initial findings suggested that sequential line-ups appear to reduce the number of false identifications, but also make it more likely that real culprits will escape conviction. However, the ultimate conclusion was that sequential line-ups lead to more reliable identification in more realistic circumstances.

Other factors affecting the outcome of line-up procedures

Appearance of the foils
Ideally, the foils and the real suspect should look at least similar in terms of race, build, hair colour and so on. Only in this way could the identification be said to have any validity. At any one time, police stations have only a limited selection of volunteers from which to choose the foils. On occasions, therefore, it is quite likely that some of the foils bear little resemblance to the real suspect.

Demand characteristics
Whether or not the police officer conducting the identification procedure knows the identity of the real suspect is likely to have an effect on a witness's ability to make an unbiased identification. Although PACE recommends that line-ups are supervised by an officer who has no direct involvement with the case, it is still likely that he or she will know which member of the line-up is the real suspect. The witness may pick up unintentional cues as to the identity of the suspect from the police officer's non-verbal behaviour.

Feedback
If witnesses believe they have made a correct identification, they are more likely to have greater confidence in their judgement. This can affect the outcome of a trial, since juries are more likely to believe the evidence if a witness appears confident. Wells and Bradfield (1998) showed how witnesses who were told that their identification was correct showed significantly higher confidence ratings in their judgement than participants who were told that their identification was incorrect or were given no feedback.

Recent developments in identification procedures – VIPER

A system of video line-ups (VIPER – video identity parade electronic recording) has been developed by West Yorkshire police (Kemp *et al.*, 2001), primarily because many of the traditional line-ups had to be cancelled because suspects failed to turn up at the appointed time. Using VIPER, a short video is made of the suspect turning his or her head from side to side. Suitable foil videos are then selected from a central database of short videos of volunteers showing the same head movements. The suspect is able to choose where in the sequence his or her video appears and the suspect's video is then recorded in sequence with the eight foil videos. The witness then watches the sequence of nine videos.

4.2 Recalling events

In 1932 Bartlett showed that we do not recall exactly what has occurred, but that we make '**effort after meaning**', which means that we try to fit what we remember with what we already know and understand about the world. Bartlett was especially interested in how memories could be distorted by existing knowledge about the world or schemas. His participants heard a story and had to tell the story to another person and so on, like a game of 'Chinese whispers'. The story was a North American folk tale entitled 'The War of the Ghosts'. When asked to recount the detail of the story, each person seemed to recall it in their own individual way, although there were consistent tendencies. With repeated telling, the passages became shorter, puzzling ideas were rationalised or omitted altogether and details were changed to become more familiar and conventional. For example, information about the ghosts was often omitted, whilst participants frequently recalled the more familiar idea that someone did not go on the trip because 'he hadn't told his parents'. From this research, Bartlett concluded that

Weapon focus

A factor that is partly related to emotion and stress is weapon focus. According to Loftus (1979), where a witness's attention is drawn to the weapon in a crime scene, they recall few other details. It is not surprising that a real-life witness will focus on a weapon rather than any other details because it is the weapon that poses the most obvious threat.

Context

In most cases, the surroundings at the time of testimony are different to the surroundings in which the initial event was witnessed. Much laboratory research on memory indicates that recall is better if participants are in the same context as when the information was encoded, and specific eyewitness research seems to show the same effect.

STUDY

Aim

Loftus *et al.* (1987) investigated the effect of the presence of a weapon on recall of an event.

Method

Participants watched a video of a robbery in a fast-food restaurant. Their eye movements were monitored as they watched the video. In one version of the video the customer pointed a gun at the checkout cashier. In the other version, the customer gave the cashier the bill. After viewing the video, participants were asked to recall details about the event – for example, the appearance of the customer-robber.

Results

Participants who saw the 'gun' video spent significantly longer fixating the item and had poorer recall of the event than witnesses in the 'bill' condition.

Conclusion

Where a weapon is present, attentional resources are directed towards the weapon, resulting in an adverse effect on recall for peripheral information.

STUDY

Aim

Malpass and Devine (1981a) set out to investigate the role of context in recall of events.

Method

Participants were shown an act of vandalism and interviewed 5 months later. Participants in one group were given cues, including information about the day, details about the room and reactions of people at the time. A control group received no contextual information.

Results

The group given information about the context had significantly better recall than the control group.

Conclusion

Context aids recall of events. This finding could be linked to the retrieval failure explanation for forgetting, according to which information is stored but not always accessible without the relevant cues.

Expectations and stereotypes

Studies show that eyewitness accounts often reflect commonly held stereotypes. The influence of racial stereotyping on memory for events was demonstrated by Howitt (1991), who presented participants with a story as follows:

> The time was 5.30 p.m., the underground train was overcrowded as usual ... Two men of different ethnic origins were standing up facing each other; one of them had an open, double-edged knife and a newspaper in his hand ... In the struggle to get in and out of the train, a passenger stepped on the foot of one of the men. A fight ensued ...

Howitt found that participants' recollections revealed distortions based on stereotypical racist assumptions. For example, one report stated 'there were two black men there. One was carrying a rolled-up newspaper with a knife partly hidden ...' In this case, it seems that memory was distorted by racial stereotypes.

Gender stereotyping also affects memory, as demonstrated by Gruneberg (1992), who found witnesses to a bag-snatch incident frequently reported that the thief was male, even though it had been a female who had snatched the bag.

4.2.2 Improving eyewitness recall

The cognitive interview

Findings concerning the reliability of eyewitness accounts have led researchers to devise methods for improving retrieval. One of these is the cognitive interview, proposed by Fisher and Geiselman (1992). This involves four procedures which have been found to enhance eyewitness accounts of events:

The four features of the cognitive interview

- The interviewer mentally **reinstates the context** of the crime for the witness by asking them about their general activities and feelings on the day.
- Witnesses are encouraged to **report every detail** of the event, however unimportant the information might seem. In this way, apparently unimportant detail might act as a trigger for key information about the event.
- Witnesses are asked to recount the incident in a **different order**. For example, the person might be asked 'What happened just before the robber shouted at the bank cashier?'
- Witnesses are asked to report from **different perspectives**, describing what they think other witnesses might have seen.

Figure 4.10 *In the cognitive interview, witnesses are encouraged to report every detail in the hope that it might trigger important information.*

The cognitive interview is now the preferred technique for police interviews with witnesses, although not all police interviewers are trained in the technique. Informal investigations reveal that officers generally attach more importance to the first two features of the cognitive interview, 'reinstating the context' and 'reporting every detail', and less significance to the other two features.

Geiselman's work suggested that the most superior recall of events will be produced when the four features of the cognitive interview are used in combination. More recent experimental evidence comparing the effectiveness of the four different features showed that, when each individual feature was used alone, it was more effective than the standard interview (Milne and Bull, 2002). However, the study also showed that recall is superior when the two features 'reinstating the context' and 'report every detail' are used in combination.

STUDY

Aim

Geiselman *et al.* (1985) investigated the effectiveness of the cognitive interview.

Method

Participants viewed a film of a violent crime. After 48 hours they were interviewed using either the cognitive interview, a standard interview used by the Los Angeles police or an interview using hypnosis. The number of facts accurately recalled and the number of errors were recorded.

Results

The mean number of correctly recalled facts for each condition was as follows: the cognitive interview, 41.2; the hypnosis condition, 38.0; the standard interview, 29.4. No significant differences in the number of incorrect responses were found.

Conclusion

The cognitive interview improves memory for events. A follow-up study also showed that participants were less likely to be misled by false information when the cognitive interview was being used.

Evaluation of the cognitive interview

- Studies show that the cognitive interview improves recall in many circumstances.
- The cognitive interview is less effective and may even lead to poorer recall in young children under 6 years (Geiselman, 1999).
- The enhancing effect of the cognitive interview appears to be significantly reduced as the time between the event and the interview increases.
- The cognitive interview does not appear to improve person identification – descriptions of criminals using this method are no better than those produced following a standard interview.

4.2.3 Children as eyewitnesses

For a long time it was assumed that young children's recall of events was altogether unreliable and that children's evidence should not be admissible in court. Nowadays children's evidence is accepted as valuable and video interviews can be presented as part of court proceedings. Over recent years there has been a great deal of research into the reliability of child witnesses, the findings of which might be summarised as follows:

- Preschool children are capable of giving accurate, detailed accounts of personal experiences even after extended periods of time (Fivush and Shukat, 1995), but in general have been found to make less reliable eyewitnesses than adults (Estgate and Groome, 2005).
- Children are more likely to make errors because of suggestion, and are more susceptible to post-event contamination and distortion.

- Deterioration of memory over time affects young children more than other age groups.
- Children are less able to distinguish between memory for events they have experienced and memories from other sources.

A specific area of interest involves children's ability to identify the origin of a memory. Studies like that of Poole and Lindsay (2001) indicate that very young children have particular difficulty in **source monitoring**, in other words, identifying whether memory of an event originates from first-hand experience of the event or from some other source.

Studies like the one below indicate that children's memories can be contaminated by suggestions from adults; other researchers have shown that young children's memories for events can also be influenced by peer discussions.

Figure 4.11 *Poole and Lindsay (2001) investigated young children's ability to recall details of science demonstrations and distinguish between events they had witnessed and events they had merely heard about.*

STUDY

Aim

Poole and Lindsay (2001) investigated children's ability to recall science demonstrations.

Method

Children aged 3–8 years participated in two science demonstrations with 'Mr Science'. They were then interviewed about the demonstrations. Three months later, the parents of the children read them a story describing the demonstrations they had experienced and two other science demonstrations they had not witnessed. The children were then interviewed to see what they recalled of the original demonstrations.

Results

When tested immediately, all age groups reported some correct information about the demonstrations with Mr Science, although for the youngest children recall was only 9%. After the story, 35% of the children recalled a total of 58 fictitious events, describing events from the story demonstrations rather than from the demonstrations they had experienced. At this point the researchers reminded children that they had seen two demonstrations and only heard about the other two in a story. This reminder about the source of their memories decreased false reports in the 5- to 8-year-olds, but not in the younger children.

Conclusion

Post-event contamination has a significant effect on young children, and very young children find it especially difficult to monitor the source of their memories.

STUDY

Aim

Candel *et al*. (2007) compared peer influences on memory in 6- to 7-year-olds and 11- to 12-year-olds.

Method

Children watched a video either alone or as a member of a pair (in fact, each member of the pair saw a different version of the video). The video showed a girl entering an office. In one version, there was some Coca-Cola on the desk; in the other, there was no Coca-Cola. After watching the video, the paired children discussed the video with each other. All children were then tested individually for recall.

Results

Using structured questions, 60% of the paired children recalled an event from the alternate video, whereas only 23% of the children in the individual condition reported a detail they had not seen. Comparison of age groups in free recall showed that the older children were more likely to be affected by peer contamination.

Conclusion

Child witnesses are vulnerable to contamination from peer discussion. Children aged 11–12 years may be more susceptible than younger children because their discussions are fuller and they have more extensive world knowledge, which may lead them to have more fixed expectations.

STUDY

Aim

Baker-Ward *et al.* (1993) investigated recall of detail of a medical examination in 187 children.

Method

Children aged 3–7 years experienced a medical examination and were later tested on their recall of 27 features of the procedure. They were asked specific questions – for example, ‘Did the doctor shine a light in your mouth?’ – and more open-ended questions.

Results

Recall improved with age, although initial analysis did not show large age differences. However, when the data were analysed using a more cautious scoring procedure, discounting items where the witnesses contradicted themselves or elaborated with incorrect detail, the 3-year-olds performed significantly less well than the other age groups.

Conclusion

The findings from child witness research may vary substantially according to the scoring procedures used in the particular study.

In studies that most closely parallel real-life child witness cases, participant witnesses are asked to recall details of medical examinations. One such study was conducted by Baker-Ward *et al.* (1993).

Despite evidence that children's eyewitness accounts can often be unreliable, some evidence shows that they can be remarkably accurate. For example, Marin *et al.* (1979) tested children of primary-school age, junior-school age, senior-school age and college students on recall of a 15-second scene where an adult male in a distressed state entered the room. They found that recall of both correct and incorrect material increased with age, but, crucially, there was no significant difference in accuracy of identification, ability to answer specific questions and influence of leading questions.

Evaluation

- Whilst research indicates that the recall of child witnesses may not always be accurate, the data are complex, with the results depending on many factors, such as age, context, time lapse, interview procedure, scoring of responses.
- Most laboratory studies involve recall of emotionally positive events, such as holidays and birthdays, or neutral events, such as science demonstrations, rather than the traumatic event a child witness may have to recall.
- In real-life witness events there are many potential sources of contamination that cannot be controlled.
- Inaccuracy in child witnesses can partly be explained by the way in which some experiments have been conducted. Young children assume they are expected to be able to answer questions that they are asked. In fact, many early studies of children as witnesses failed to take account of this, and as a consequence, child participants would sometimes give inaccurate accounts simply because they felt obliged to give any answer

Evaluation – continued

rather than admit that they did not remember (Ceci and Bruck, 1993).

- Interviewers should take special care when interviewing child witnesses, in particular avoiding any suggestion by using free recall and open questions.

4.2.4 Flashbulb memory: memory for shocking events

Estgate and Groome (2005) define flashbulb memories as 'the capacity of an important and shocking event to illuminate trivial aspects of the observer's current activities and surroundings.'

People often remember what they were doing when they heard about a shocking event, as if the moment was frozen in time and exactly preserved, just as if it had been photographed. Brown and Kulik (1977) proposed that the vividness and durability of such memories may have a survival advantage as they would lead us to be alert to such dangers in the future. In recent history, events like the death of Princess Diana and the terrorist attack on the World Trade Center have been the subject of flashbulb memories for many people. Most of us can recall exactly what we were doing when we first learned of these events. Flashbulb memories are not simply recollections of the event, but rather a vivid recollection of the context in which the memory occurred. It has been proposed that they are a particular type of source memory which can be tied to the time and place at which they were encoded.

Early work suggested that flashbulb memories may be specially preserved in neural mechanisms in the temporal or frontal lobes, and that they were largely immune to normal forgetting. It has since been demonstrated that the detail of flashbulb memories can be forgotten. For example, Neisser and Harsch (1992) interviewed people the day after the Challenger space shuttle exploded and 3 years later. Comparison of data from the two tests showed that participants were able to recall fewer details 3 years later, and that there were inconsistencies between the content of the initial and later recollections.

Figure 4.12 *Most of us will have a flashbulb memory of the attack on the World Trade Center on 11 September 2001.*

Research into the neural mechanisms responsible for flashbulb memories has not yielded firm links with the temporal or frontal lobe areas. However, a study by Sharot *et al.* (2007) indicates that the amygdala, a part of the brain normally associated with emotion, may be involved.

STUDY

Aim

Sharot *et al.* (2007) investigated the role of the amygdala in recall for the attack on the World Trade Center.

Method

Twenty-four participants were asked to recount their experiences of the attack 3 years after the event, whilst their brain activity was monitored using an MRI scanner. They were also asked to recall two other personally selected events from the same year (2001). Some of the participants were within 5 miles of the World Trade Center at the time of the attack; others were further away. Participants were also asked to rate their memories for vividness.

Results

Participants close to the scene showed selective activation of the amygdala when recalling the terrorist attack, but not when recalling other events. The more distant participants showed no differences. Participants close to the scene also rated their memory for the attack as more vivid than the distant participants.

Conclusion

For individuals closely involved with a shocking event, the flashbulb memory involves a special neural mechanism. Furthermore, direct observation of, or participation in, a highly arousing event leads to exceptionally vivid memories.

Evaluation

- Flashbulb memories may or may not be a special kind of memory.
  - There is little evidence to show that the neural mechanisms normally involved in memory are involved in flashbulb memories.
  - Flashbulb memories have not been found to be especially resistant to forgetting.
  - Strength of flashbulb memories may be a product of repeated retrieval rather than a consequence of any special property.
- The amygdala has been implicated in flashbulb memories. This link with the emotional centre of the brain may explain why sufferers of post-traumatic stress disorder (PTSD) experience vivid intrusive memories.

4.2.5 The false memory debate

Definitions

Recovered memory: the emergence of a memory for an event of which the person had no previous conscious knowledge. Most controversially, this would be a memory of childhood sexual abuse.
A false memory: memory for an event which did not take place, but which is believed by the individual to have happened.

False memory syndrome (FMS) is described by Khilstrom (1998) as:

> a condition in which a person's identity and interpersonal relationships are centred around a memory of a traumatic experience which is objectively false, but in which the person strongly believes. The memory often rules the individual's entire personality and lifestyle and disrupts all sorts of other adaptive behaviours. The memory tends to take on a life of its own, encapsulated and resistant to correction. The individual avoids confrontation with any evidence that might challenge the memory and may be effectively distracted from coping with the real problems of living.

The key questions in relation to the debate are whether real memories can be repressed, so that we are completely unaware of them, and then later be recovered; and whether false memories of events that never took place can be either deliberately or accidentally implanted so that people think they really happened.

4.2.6 Controversy surrounding the recovery of repressed memories

The theoretical basis for recovered memories rests on the Freudian defence mechanism of **repression**. According to Freud, memories of unpleasant events, particularly childhood events, can be unconsciously repressed to protect the conscious self. These memories might remain forever repressed, although they could affect behaviour in later life. According to Freud, many of his women patients were suffering anxieties due to repression of childhood memories of sexual encounters with parents or other adults. In extraordinarily severe cases, repression is said to result in **fugue amnesia**, where the patient shuts out all memories of their life, possibly taking on a new identity.

Certainly, most people remember little from before the age of 5 years. This infantile amnesia appears strongest before the age of 3 years. However, contrary to Freud's predictions, the lost memories of childhood are for all types of experience and not just unpleasant events.

Some experimental studies, such as the study below, have provided support for the concept of repression, although many studies do not.

STUDY

Aim

Levinger and Clark (1961) studied repression experimentally.

Method

Participants were given a set of emotionally negative words like 'argument' and 'unhappiness' and a set of neutral words. They had to provide an associated word for each stimulus word. For example, if given the word 'star', the participant might say 'moon'. Later on, participants had to say the word that went with the cue word.

Results

Fewer associated words for the emotionally negative set were recalled than for the neutral set; thus, for example, participants could not recall associated words like 'cry' or 'hurt'.

Conclusion

The difficulty recalling the negative word associations was taken as an indication of repression.

STUDY

Aim

Williams (1994) studied recollection of childhood abuse.

Method

Interviews were conducted with 129 women aged 18–31 years. Hospital records showed they had been abused between the ages of 10 months and 12 years.

Results

In interviews about their sexual histories, 38% of the women failed to report the abusive episode, although some reported more general experience of having been abused.

Conclusion

Failure to recall specific incidents of abuse could be due to repression.

Other studies have investigated repression as a possible explanation for forgetting of real-life events.

Case studies can also be used to determine the existence of recovered memories. However, it is necessary to show, first, that the event did occur; second, that for a time the individual had no memory of the event; and third, that the individual could not have received any information about the event from another source. Wright *et al.* (2006), summarising a number of cases, suggest that many are not as watertight as they might appear. The case of 'Jane Doe' was reported by Corwin and Olafson (1997).

The case of 'Jane Doe'

An interview with Jane as a young child was videotaped. In this session she reported that she had been abused by her mother. This report tallied with medical evidence and Jane was put in the care of her father. After her father died, Jane was brought up by foster parents. During her teenage years she had no conscious memory of the abuse and was considering re-establishing contact with her mother. At this time, Jane contacted Corwin and viewed the tape of the original interview. A further recording was made of Jane's reaction to the original tape. Immediately before recording began, Jane spontaneously recalled the abuse in some detail. Since it was published, the case has become very controversial, not least because Jane's true identity has been revealed.

Evaluation

- Repression is an unconscious mechanism and, as such, is not open to empirical study.
- Findings from studies showing poorer recall of words with negative associations tell us little about recall of real-life traumatic events.
- Williams' participants may have had other reasons for choosing not to talk about past events: wanting to get on with their lives; embarrassment; desire to protect others; not wanting to disclose to the interviewer (Femina *et al.*, 1990).
- Evidence from cases of flashbulb memory suggests that memory for upsetting events is often more vivid than memory for other events.
- Even if we accept that traumatic memories can be repressed in the first place, can we further be sure that such memories, when recovered, are accurate? Recovered memories often arise after hypnosis and dream analysis. In these circumstances, clients are particularly open to suggestion.
- Some clinical evidence suggests that event-specific amnesia can occur in people who have committed serious crimes, but the same memory loss is not usually found in victims (Parkin, 1993).
- Case studies of victims of child sexual abuse do not generally present convincing evidence for recovered memories.
- Dissociation amnesia theory provides an alternative explanation for recovered memory. Brown *et al.* (1998) suggests that people sometimes cope with unpleasant events by dissociating or mentally distancing themselves from the event.

4.2.7 The existence of false memories

The theoretical basis of false memory syndrome (FMS) relies on the reconstructive nature of memory. The role of reconstruction has been studied extensively by Loftus (2001). She argues that asking people to imagine events that never happened can lead to a belief that these non-existent events actually took place. According to Loftus, guided imagination used by therapists may be a prime factor in false memories. One early study of how memories could be implanted was the 'Lost in the Shopping Mall' study.

STUDY

Aim

Loftus and Ketcham (1994) studied whether a false memory of an unpleasant event could be implanted into a person's memory.

Method

The idea of having been lost in a shopping mall was casually introduced into conversation with five participants. With the assistance of family members, the topic was reintroduced into conversation several times and participants were asked questions about the event.

Results

Memories of the event were initially uncertain, but each time the incident was mentioned, participants became more confident. Finally they were able to provide extra details they had not been told.

Conclusion

Memories can be implanted using suggestion. Note that two of Loftus and Ketcham's participants were adults, so it is not just children who experience false memories.

Since the mid-1990s there have been many experimental studies showing that it is possible to deliberately implant false memories of events such as fictitious medical procedures (Mazzoni and Memon, 2003) and being attacked by a dog (Porter *et al.*, 1999), although not all participants have been shown to be equally susceptible to the effect.

Evaluation –

- Laboratory studies show that it is possible to implant memories of events that never happened. Thus it is also possible that cases of recovered memory following therapy are, in fact, false memories.
- For ethical reasons, the supposed events in these studies are not like the traumatic experiences that are the subject of real cases – for example, cases of child abuse.
- Personality factors such as suggestibility mean that some people are more susceptible to false memory than others.
- Merckelbach et al. (2006) found that people reporting recovered memories of child abuse had poor awareness of their own memories (meta-memory), leading to doubts about how and when they first became aware of the event.

STUDY

Aim

Lindsay *et al.* (2004) studied the effect of using a photograph on false memory.

Method

Forty-five college students were told three stories about what happened to them in school. Two of the stories were real, as recounted by parents, and one was fictitious. The fictitious story involved the participant and a friend putting gelatinous 'slime' into the teacher's desk. The researchers used guided imagery and context reinstatement to encourage recall. Half of the participants were also shown a photograph of their school class.

Results

Without the photograph, approximately 25% of participants had some memory of the 'slime' event. With the photograph, 67% recalled the event.

Conclusion

False memories can be created using suggestion and can be facilitated using photographs.

Figure 4.13 *Lindsay* et al. *(2004) showed how a false memory for a childhood event could be created.*

4.2.8 Ethical and theoretical implications of the false memory debate

The growth in the USA of therapy for recovered memories has caused widespread public and professional concern. In the 1980s, many women and children who had recently undergone therapy spoke out about their memories of early childhood abuse. In many cases, there were direct accusations against elderly parents, causing widespread family disruption. Some accusations led to legal proceedings, with parents accused of offences against their own children, sometimes dating back decades. Since the early 1980s, many people have retracted their accusations against the parent, instead accusing their therapist of implanting false memories. Accused families have formed themselves into self-help and pressure groups to expose the therapists they accuse of ruining their lives.

Implications of the false memory debate

Ethical implications
Someone may be wrongly accused.

The family may be split up.

The individual may be more unhappy after the memory is recovered than they were before.

Therapists may be tempted to let their own beliefs affect their interpretation of the case.

Implications of the false memory debate continued

Theoretical implications

If lost memories can be recovered, this would be consistent with Freud's repression theory.

If such memories are false, this would be consistent with the reconstructive view of memory.

The two largest societies for the families of accusers are the False Memory Syndrome Foundation (FMSF), formed in Philadelphia in 1992, and the British False Memory Society (BFMS), set up in 1993. Gudjonsson (1997) analysed the background of members of the BFMS and found:

- 87% of accusers were female
- most accused the biological father
- many had recently been receiving therapy
- many had been suffering from depression or eating disorders
- many had a history of relationship problems
- 59% of cases led to broken contact with family
- 14% of cases involved legal proceedings.

Figure 4.14 *Most cases of recovered memory involve women.*

Brandon *et al.* (1998) reviewed the literature for the Royal College of Psychiatrists to consider the issues surrounding recovered memories of childhood sexual abuse and the circumstances in which such memories arise. Although many cases involve therapy, some instances appear to have been triggered by popular therapy books that suggest child sexual abuse is the root of many adult problems. Where therapy is involved, some of the techniques used by therapists to enhance memory recovery include drugs, hypnosis, age regression, dream interpretation and imagery. Following the Brandon review, the following guidelines were proposed for psychologists:

Guidelines for psychologists (Frankland and Cohen, 1999)

Whilst practitioners should be open to the idea that memories of real events may be recovered, they should also be alert to the possibility that such memories may be 'literally/historically true or false, or may be partly true, thematically true, or metaphorically true, or may derive from fantasy or dream material.' Psychologists should guard against actively seeking for memories of abuse and should avoid suggestion.

Summary of the false/recovered memory debate

The argument about recovered/false memories and the existence of FMS continues. Wright *et al.* (2006), reviewing recent work, conclude that some claims of recovered memory are based on real events and some are not; others may be a combination of the two. They also conclude that certain factors, such as suggestibility and meta-memory (a person's awareness of their own memory), will have an influence in such cases.

How Psychology Works

An experiment to investigate the effect of post-event contamination on recall

Work in pairs or threes to design an independent design experiment to investigate the effect of post-event information on participants' recall for detail of a picture.

There will be two conditions. In the control condition, participants see a photograph of a fairly busy scene with lots of people in it. After viewing the photograph, participants are asked a number of questions about the detail contained in the picture. Only one of the questions is crucial – this is the target question. An example of a suitable target question would be: 'How many people were in the scene?' In the experimental condition, participants look at the same photograph for the same amount of time. After viewing the photo, they are then asked the same questions, but this time the target question is a leading question, for example: 'How many people were in the crowded scene?' According to previous research, participants in the experimental condition should recall more people on average than participants in the control condition because the question includes the word 'crowded'.

- Select a suitable photograph.
- Write a set of eight questions about the content of the photo. One of these should be a question that can be changed into a leading question for the experimental condition. Type up the two sets of questions, leaving spaces for participants to write the response to each question.
- Write a set of standardised instructions to explain to participants what they have to do, and a debrief to use at the end of the study. Check pages 381–383 for important ethical considerations.
- Carry out your experiment using an opportunity sample of participants. Try to use at least six participants in each condition.
- Collate the data and calculate the appropriate measure of central tendency and measure of dispersion (see page 366). Display these statistics in a table and write a short summary of what the stats show.
- Decide which inferential statistical test would be used with the data you have collected. Each person in your group should do this individually and then you can cross-check the outcome with each other. Write a paragraph explaining why the test is appropriate.

Further Reading

Introductory texts

Dwyer, D. (2001) *Angles on Criminal Psychology*, Cheltenham: Nelson Thornes.
Gross, R. (2005) *Psychology, the Science of Mind and Behaviour*, 5th edn., London: Hodder & Stoughton.

Specialist sources

Ainsworth, P.B. (1998) *Psychology, Law and Eye-witness Testimony*, Chichester: Wiley.
Bruce, V. and Young, A. (1998) *In the Eye of the Beholder: The Science of Face Perception*, Oxford: Oxford University Press.
Conway, M. (ed.) (1997) *Recovered Memories and False Memories*, Oxford: Oxford University Press.
Cutler, B. and Penrod, S. (1995) *Mistaken Identity*, Cambridge: Cambridge University Press.
Estgate, A. and Groome, D. (2005) *An Introduction to Applied Cognitive Psychology,* Hove: Psychology Press.
Gruneberg, M. and Morris, P. (eds.) (1992) *Aspects of Memory (Volume 1: Practical Aspects)*, 2nd edn., London: Routledge.
Loftus, E.F. (1996) *Eye-witness Testimony*, Cambridge, MA: Harvard University Press.
Loftus, E. and Ketcham, K. (1994) *The Myth of Repressed Memory*, New York: St Martin's Press.
Zaragoza, M.S., Graham, J.R., Hall, G.C.N., Hirschman, R. and Ben-Yorath, Y.S. (1995) *Memory and Testimony in the Child Witness*, London: Sage Publications.

Schizophrenia and mood disorders

Chapter 5

5.1 Introduction

Schizophrenia is primarily to do with thought disturbance. Mood disorders (types of depression) are primarily to do with disturbances of emotions and mood. Both of these disorders are major categories in abnormal psychology. Both disorders present the individual with difficulties in everyday living and professionals with difficulties of knowing what treatments are most effective. Both disorders have been known to exist for thousands of years. In ancient Greek times, for example, Hippocrates (460–377 BC), often called the 'father of modern medicine', used the term 'melancholia' to describe depression, and the terms 'delusions' and 'hallucinations' to describe schizophrenia. In the fifteenth and sixteenth centuries in Europe, people (largely women) showing thought disturbances and hallucinations were thought to be possessed by the devil and were tortured and burned at the stake in order to exorcise the devil. In the 1800s, sufferers were treated more humanely, with 'moral treatment' consisting of social care, and mental asylums were introduced.

Today, treatments for major disorders like schizophrenia and depression consist of a combination of drug therapies and psychological therapies. Whilst we may think we have an informed and enlightened approach to mental disorder, the stigma associated with such disorders seems to be as strong today as it was in past times. Generally, negative attitudes are held towards people who suffer from such disorders; people with schizophrenia are perceived as 'mad' and dangerous, depressives are seen as weak and cowardly. Sufferers often fear admitting their condition because of such prejudices.

5.2 Schizophrenia

The film *A Beautiful Mind*, starring Russell Crowe, tells the story of a real-life mathematical genius called John

Figure 5.1 *In the Middle Ages, women who reported hallucinations were seen as being possessed by the devil and were burned at the stake.*

Figure 5.2 *The film* A Beautiful Mind *portrays the delusions experienced by a person with schizophrenia.*

Nash, who, in 1959, had delusions that aliens from outer space and foreign governments were communicating with him. He became distant and hostile towards his wife and colleagues. He was hospitalised in a mental institution a number of times in the 1960s and subjected to what are now regarded as ineffective and harmful treatments. He went on to win the Nobel Prize in Economics and managed to live with the delusions, which never left him. The film illustrates the difficulties for people with schizophrenia and those around them. It also shows how a person can succeed and, to a certain degree, manage the condition.

Schizophrenia is not, as commonly depicted, a split personality. The word has Greek origins – *skhizien* for split and *phren* for mind. Where the 'split' occurs for the person is between reality and delusion. The schizophrenic believes their hallucinations and delusions to be real; by contrast, other people see them as not real and symptoms of a person who is ill. Schizophrenia is a **psychotic disorder**. A psychotic disorder is one where the person loses touch with reality and has a distorted view of the world. Some research suggests that it is more common in men than women (Goldstein, 2002), but this may vary depending on the criteria used to diagnose the disorder. The onset of schizophrenia is earlier in men – typically in late teens and early twenties – than in women, where onset is typically in the late twenties or early thirties (Goldstein and Lewine, 2000).

People with schizophrenia suffer the greatest social stigma of any disorder, probably because the behaviour and mental processes of the schizophrenic most closely match our stereotype of 'madness'. Schizophrenia conjures up fear and prejudice. Torrey (2001) showed that nearly 80% of schizophrenics live with a family member, under supervised living or independently. By contrast, in the 1950s and 1960s, many schizophrenics spent most of their life in psychiatric hospitals.

5.2.1 Classification of schizophrenia

Schizophrenia is a complex disorder. To classify someone as suffering from schizophrenia requires distinguishing the symptoms from other psychotic disorders and then determining the type of schizophrenia. The Diagnostic and Statistical Manual of Mental Disorders (DSM) provides guidelines and categories for the classification of psychological disorders. The DSM requires some symptoms to have been present for at least a month and others for 6 months before a diagnosis of schizophrenia can confidently be made.

The five categories for classifying schizophrenia (DSM)

Disorganised – symptoms include disorganised and unintelligible speech, bizarre behaviour, absence of emotion (flat affect), social withdrawal and apparent loss of interest in everyday life.

Catatonic – either excessive motor activity (grimacing, repeating again and again what another says, copying movements of others) or fixed, rigid posture for hours on end (catatonic stupor).

Paranoid – delusions and hallucinations are common. Typically the delusions are of grandeur and/or persecution. No disorganised speech or catatonic behaviour. Cognitive and emotional responses not affected.

Undifferentiated – a mixture of symptoms of the above categories, but without the main symptoms in one of the above three categories. Symptoms may be from all of these categories.

Residual – people who have once suffered from extreme and major symptoms of schizophrenia but who now display few/mild symptoms. Residual symptoms may include social withdrawal, bizarre thoughts and flat emotional affect.

Evaluation

- The catatonic type is relatively rare and may be due to certain types of drugs used to treat the disorder (McGlashan and Fenton, 1991). Some claim that it is not a true category of schizophrenia and should be dropped as a classification.
- The undifferentiated category is also controversial because it is said to be too vague and ill-defined. Many clinicians believe it is overused and sometimes confused with other psychotic DSM categories.
- The DSM distinguishes between a number of psychotic disorders, as shown in Figure 5.3. As can be seen from this table, it is difficult to distinguish between schizophrenia and a schizoaffective disorder.

Psychotic disorder	Main symptoms	Duration
Schizophrenia	Delusions, hallucinations, flat affect, disorganised speech, catatonic behaviour	6 months or longer
Schizoaffective disorder	Similar symptoms to schizophrenia as well as a major mood disorder	6 months or longer
Delusional disorder	Delusions that are not bizarre and not associated with schizophrenia, most commonly delusions of grandeur, jealousy and persecution	1 month or longer
Brief psychotic disorder	Delusions, hallucinations, disorganised speech and flat affect	1 month or less

Figure 5.3 *Some classifications of psychotic disorders made by the DSM.*

5.2.2 Symptoms of schizophrenia

There are two main categories of symptoms of schizophrenia. **Positive symptoms** (Type I) are those to do with the presence of hallucinations, delusions, thought and speech disturbances, and disorganised or catatonic behaviour. **Negative symptoms** (Type II) are to do with the absence, loss or deficit of cognitive, emotional, social and general life functions.

Positive symptoms

Hallucinations are perceptions that occur without stimuli from the external world. Hallucinations can be visual, auditory, tactile or somatic (about the body). The most common hallucinations found in schizophrenics are auditory, usually hearing voices. Women with schizophrenia report more auditory hallucinations than men. The voices are usually of someone persecuting, threatening or criticising. They are often described as coming from outside of the sufferer's head and the sufferer often talks back to them. Visual hallucinations are the second most common – for example, the devil or someone evil. When auditory and visual hallucinations occur together, the imagined person is usually the source of the voices. Somatic (body) hallucinations – for example, of insects eating away inside the body – are less common.

Delusions are ideas, beliefs or values that the schizophrenic thinks are true but are impossible or highly unlikely to be true. Common types of delusions are:

- Delusions of persecution – false belief that friends, family or work colleagues are plotting against them.
- Delusions of reference – false belief that random events are really a meaningful pattern of events.

- Delusions of grandeur – false belief that one has special power or is a famous person – for example, Jesus Christ.
- Delusions of being controlled – false belief that thoughts, feelings and behaviours are controlled by an external force – for example, aliens.
- Delusions of guilt – false belief that one has done something terribly wrong – for example, that one has killed somebody.

Thought and speech disturbances are shown by illogical thinking and speech which is difficult to understand or is incoherent. The thought and speech often jumps from one topic to another in an unconnected and incoherent way. It is extremely difficult or impossible to keep up with what is being said and make sense of the flow of thought. Incoherent speech is described as a *word salad*, which may make sense to the sufferer but appears as a 'salad' of unconnected words to the listener. Language deficits appear to be worse in men than in women (Goldstein *et al.*, 2002).

Disorganised behaviour appears as unpredictable, sudden and unexpected. It is this aspect of schizophrenic symptoms that is most likely to make others afraid of a person with schizophrenia. Disorganised behaviour also includes problems in organising the basics of daily life, such as eating and washing. Very excited or wild behaviour by a person is referred to as *catatonic excitement*.

Negative symptoms

Avolition is a general loss of energy, resulting in lack of goal-directed behaviour, inability to complete tasks and a general loss of interest in life. The sufferer may sit all day without showing any interest or wish to do anything. Such behaviour may well result in social isolation and withdrawal from society.

Absence of emotion or affective flattening involves almost total absence of emotional responses which would be considered normal or appropriate. The sufferer does not make eye contact when speaking and has an emotionless, monotonous voice. Research suggests that affective flattening may not really represent the sufferer's experience.

Absence of social functions is shown by poor social skills and interactions with other people. The sufferer may be unable to hold down a job, keep friends and

STUDY

Aim

Kring and Neale (1996) conducted a study to show that lack of appropriate facial expressions in people with schizophrenia does not mean emotions are not being felt and experienced.

Method

People diagnosed as schizophrenic and non-sufferers watched films with strong emotional content. During the films, the facial expressions of both groups were observed. After watching the film, participants were asked about their emotional experiences.

Results

Schizophrenia sufferers displayed less facial emotion whilst watching the film than normal people. However, both groups reported similar high levels of emotional experiences whilst watching the film.

Conclusions

People with schizophrenia experience similar, appropriate and intense emotions to people who are not schizophrenic. However, the schizophrenic group do not show these emotions in their facial expressions.

maintain intimate relationships, and generally becomes socially isolated as consequence.

Evaluation

The negative symptoms of schizophrenia are most important in explaining why such people have difficulties functioning in everyday life and society more generally. Eaton *et al.* (1998) have shown that people with schizophrenia who have many negative symptoms do less well in education, work and social functioning than those with few negative symptoms.

Secondary symptoms

Secondary symptoms occur as a result of having the disorder. The most common secondary symptoms are depression, anxiety, alcohol and drug abuse, and social isolation. Sufferers are also more likely to be unemployed due to unreliability and inappropriate behaviours. The presence and severity of secondary symptoms is related to the amount of ongoing medical, social and therapeutic support; high levels of support generally reduce the frequency and severity of secondary symptoms.

5.2.3 Diagnosis of schizophrenia

In the 1950s and 1960s, a diagnosis of schizophrenia was much more common than today. These days the DSM (in the USA) and the International Classification of Diseases (in the UK) have much more stringent criteria for a diagnosis of schizophrenia. Certain symptoms have to be present for at least 1 month and other symptoms have to be present for at least 6 months.

Symptoms and diagnosis

Core symptoms
Two or more must be present for at least 1 month:

- **delusions**
- **hallucinations**
- **disorganised speech**
- **disorganised behaviour**
- **negative symptoms.**

Other symptoms
Must be present for at least 6 months:

- **functioning poorly with respect to life skills – for example, interpersonal relationships and/or ability to work at a job effectively**
- **signs of continuous mental and behavioural disturbance over a 6-month period, with symptoms from the first category above clearly present for at least a month.**

Evaluation

- Diagnosing schizophrenia accurately and with reliability is not straightforward. The criteria for diagnosis do not specify a precise set of symptoms, but indicate that some from each category need to be present. This lack of precision means that misdiagnosis may happen. Empirical research has indicated that certain ethnic groups may be diagnosed with schizophrenia more often than other groups.

STUDY

Aim

Goater *et al.* (1999) investigated different rates of diagnosis of schizophrenia in ethnic groups in London.

Method

A 5-year study of schizophrenia in different ethnic groups in London was undertaken. People from different ethnic groups were followed for a 5-year period to see how many from each group were diagnosed with schizophrenia. This is called a *prospective study*.

Results

People from black ethnic minority groups were found to be more likely to be detained by the police, taken to hospital by the police and given emergency injections. They were also more likely to be diagnosed as schizophrenic.

Conclusions

Misdiagnosis of schizophrenia is more likely to occur amongst black ethnic minority groups.

Schizophrenia is regarded as a developmental psychological disorder that goes through three phases. It rarely starts before the age of 15 years, and in the early stages it is often difficult to detect because only a few symptoms may be present and these only in a mild form. Over time the symptoms become both more numerous and more severe.

Three phases in the development of schizophrenia

Prodomal phase – Work and leisure activities are present, positive symptoms are mild.

Active phase – Positive symptoms are strong and there is a range of positive symptoms. This phase can last for months or, if untreated, for years.

Residual phase – The highly obvious and active symptoms subside, with a return to what seems like the prodomal phase. Negative symptoms persist, with the person unable to function adequately, both socially and at work.

Evaluation

- The transition from one stage to another is often difficult to determine. Schizophrenia is only clearly diagnosed in the active phase where the symptoms are full-blown and numerous.
- Each phase may last for months or even years. Most sufferers show a degree of residual impairment for many years, if not the rest of their life, after the active phase (Putnam *et al.*, 1996).
- Some people remain in the active phase for many years. In such cases, the positive symptoms in the early years are replaced by negative symptoms in later years (Lieberman, 1995).

Overall, the diagnosis of schizophrenia is fraught with problems and challenges, ranging from misdiagnosis to incorrect identification of symptoms. The prodomal stage does not allow for a diagnosis of schizophrenia, but provides an indication that the full-blown positive symptoms may follow. Here a more confident diagnosis of schizophrenia can be made.

5.2.4 Explanations of schizophrenia

Explanations of schizophrenia include biological, cognitive and sociocultural theories. The biological explanation is the dominant one and has received the greatest empirical support, although it may not be sufficient on its own. Cognitive and sociocultural factors also need to be taken into account. The contemporary view is that stressful events in a person's life can 'trigger' the onset of the disorder in people who are biologically vulnerable. This is known as a **diathesis-stress model**, diathesis referring to biological vulnerability. The most well-researched and supported biological explanation is the genetic explanation. However, brain damage in early childhood is another possible biological cause.

Biological explanations

(i) Genetics

Genetic inheritance plays a major role in the cause of schizophrenia. Contemporary views suggest that heritability explains at least 50% of the cause, possibly more. Research evidence has come primarily from twin studies, but also family and adoption studies (see Chapter 2 of *AQA(B) Psychology for AS* by Pennington and McLoughlin, 2008). Gottesman (1991) looked at more than 40 studies, conducted over a period of 60 years, and found that concordance rates (where both twins are schizophrenic) for schizophrenia increase between people as the genetic similarity increases. Figure 5.4 shows that identical twins are almost 50% likely to be concordant, compared with a probability of less than 20% for fraternal twins.

Having a biological relative with schizophrenia does increase the chances that a person will develop the disorder, but it does not mean that this will always happen. For example, a child who has one parent with schizophrenia has a risk of just one in eight of becoming schizophrenic (Gottesman and Erlenmeyer-Kimling, 2001).

Adoption studies have supported the genetic explanation for schizophrenia. Here, biological mothers who are diagnosed with schizophrenia have been tracked, and their offspring, who have been adopted, followed to see if they develop schizophrenia. The rate of schizophrenia in adopted children is then compared with adopted children whose mothers do not have schizophrenia.

Relationship to person with schizophrenia	Percentage concordance
Identical twin	48%
Offspring of two schizophrenic parents	46%
Fraternal twins	17%
Offspring of one schizophrenic parent	13%
Sibling (brother or sister)	9%
Parent	6%
Grandchild	5%
Nephew/niece	4%
Uncle/aunt	2%
General population	1%

Figure 5.4 *Percentage of people with schizophrenia in relation to biological relatedness (adapted from Gottesman, 2001).*

STUDY

Aim

Tienara (1991) conducted an adoption study assessing the frequency of schizophrenia in the children of mothers who were and were not diagnosed as schizophrenic.

Method

One hundred and fifty-five children of mothers diagnosed as schizophrenic and 185 children of mothers who were not schizophrenic were traced. All the children of both types of mothers were adopted at an early age.

Results

Approximately 10% (15) of the adopted children of schizophrenic mothers were found to be schizophrenic. In comparison, just 1% (2) of the adopted children of non-schizophrenic mothers had the disorder.

Conclusions

The researchers concluded that there is a genetic basis to schizophrenia.

Gottesman and Shields (1982) found evidence that concordance rates for schizophrenia in identical twins were highest when they looked at twins with only the most severe form of the disorder. Here concordance rates were over 80%, compared with just below 50% for twins with all forms of schizophrenia.

Evaluation

- Twin studies show that there may be a genetic predisposition to develop schizophrenia. However, the fact that both identical twins do not always develop schizophrenia when one twin develops the disorder means that environmental factors also play a part.
- No single gene for schizophrenia has been identified. The present view is that multiple genes located in different places on the chromosome are involved.
- Evidence of concordance for schizophrenia based on older twin studies is less reliable due to changes in diagnostic criteria. These days, diagnosis is much more rigorous than it was 40 years ago. In consequence, some people diagnosed as schizophrenic 40 years ago may not be diagnosed in this way today.

(ii) Biochemical explanations

The most common and enduring biochemical explanation for schizophrenia is the **dopamine hypothesis**. This explanation is based on the claim that people with schizophrenia have excess levels of dopamine in the brain. You will recall from the biological approach in Chapter 2 of *AQA(B) Psychology for AS* (Pennington and McLoughlin, 2008) that dopamine is a neurotransmitter. Neurotransmitters serve to either increase or decrease the communication (rate of 'firing') between neurons and are released from synaptic vesicles (see Figure 5.5).

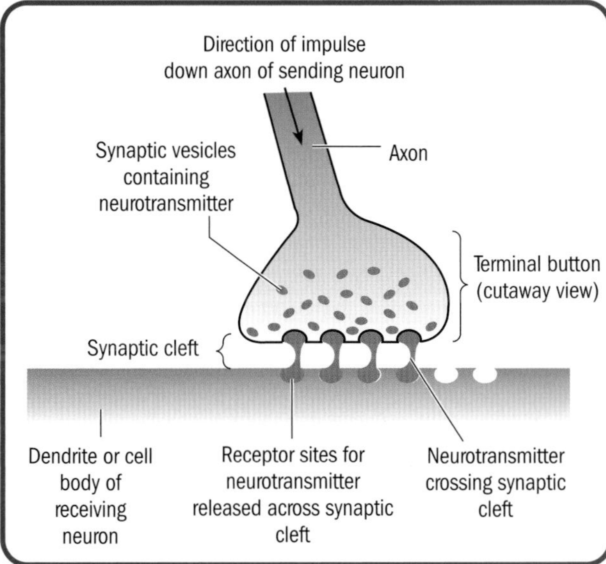

Figure 5.5 *The neurotransmitter dopamine acts to increase the 'firing' rate or communication between neurons.*

Dopamine acts to increase the rate of firing at the synapse, enhancing communication between neurons. Excess of dopamine has been found to cause greater neural activity associated with the positive symptoms of schizophrenia, such as delusions and hallucinations. Indirect support for this biochemical explanation has come from:

- Drugs such as amphetamines and cocaine can cause the positive schizophrenic symptoms, and also exaggerate them in people with the disorder.
- Post-mortems have shown that schizophrenics have unusually high levels of dopamine in their brain (Iversen, 1979).
- Antipsychotic drugs, such as Chlorpromazine, are

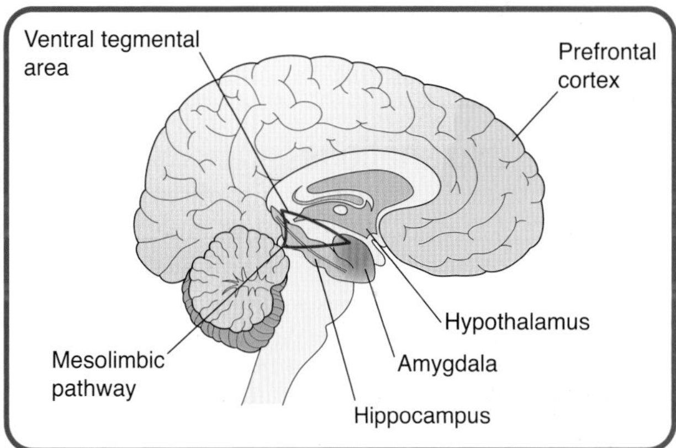

Figure 5.6 *People with schizophrenia have been found to have higher than normal levels of dopamine in the central parts of the brain (hypothalamus and amygdala) and lower than normal levels in the prefrontal cortex of the brain.*

Evaluation

- The dopamine hypothesis has been investigated through research correlating dopamine levels with symptoms of schizophrenia. As with any condition, it is impossible to establish whether high levels of dopamine are a cause or an effect of the disorder.
- The dopamine hypothesis is now regarded as too simple. Other neurotransmitters, such as serotonin, have also been associated with schizophrenia (Breier, 1995).
- Dopamine levels in people with schizophrenia vary in different parts of the brain. In the central areas of the brain, around the hypothalamus and amygdala, dopamine levels have been found to be abnormally high. By contrast, schizophrenics seem to have lower than normal levels in the prefrontal cortex.
- Recent views suggest that excess dopamine is responsible for the positive symptoms only.

known to reduce dopamine levels in the brain. Such drugs can greatly reduce the number and severity of the positive symptoms of schizophrenia.

(iii) Other biological explanations

Other biological explanations include abnormal structures in the brain, complications at birth and exposure of the mother whilst pregnant to viral infection which has then damaged the brain of the prenatal child.

Abnormal brain structures have focused on enlarged ventricles (Lieberman *et al.*, 2001). The ventricles are areas of the brain that are filled with fluids. Enlarged ventricles are associated with damage to other areas of the brain, particularly the central areas and prefrontal cortex (see Figure 5.6). Weyandt (2006) used advanced brain-scanning techniques to show that enlarged ventricles in schizophrenics may be strongly associated with negative symptoms of the disorder.

Cognitive explanations

The cognitive explanation for schizophrenia focuses on the faulty and erroneous thinking that occurs with the positive symptoms of disturbed language, attention, thought and perception. Beck and Rector (2005) produced a cognitive theory of schizophrenia in which abnormalities at a neurological (brain) level cause cognitive difficulties in attention, communication and dealing with potentially overwhelming amounts of information that result from, for example, hallucinations. Beck and Rector claim that schizophrenics have different perceptions and ways of interpreting mental experiences. For example, they say that hearing voices is perceived as someone trying to talk to them instead of a more realistic perception, such as 'I think I am hearing voices'. Frith (1992) suggested that schizophrenics do not monitor their thoughts correctly, and attribute them to someone or something in the external world communicating with them. Hearing voices is seen as a misperception of one's 'inner speech'.

Such processing problems in people with schizophrenia are sometimes referred to as **alien control symptoms**, because the sufferer feels as if external forces are influencing their thoughts and actions. Some ingenious experimental research has been conducted to test the hypothesis of alien control. Typically, the researchers ask a participant to perform a task and then ask the participant to identify their own response from a set of several responses. This enables the researchers to check whether or not patients with schizophrenia are aware of their own output and can distinguish it from other similar outputs.

STUDY

Aim

Stirling *et al.* (1998) investigated the ability of schizophrenia patients to monitor their own output.

Method

Three groups of participants were tested: a group of schizophrenia patients with reality distortion symptoms (hallucinations and delusions), a group of schizophrenia patients without reality distortion symptoms, and a control group of people without schizophrenia. Participants had to produce simple drawings of geometric shapes on paper. In some trials the participant could not see the drawing as they completed it because their arm was hidden behind a screen. After completing the drawing, the participant had to choose the picture they had drawn from a selection of four drawings. One of the four was the correct drawing and the other three were the same drawing but with the angle rotated through 90°, 180° or 270°.

STUDY continued

Results

Schizophrenia patients with reality distortion symptoms made more incorrect identifications than the two other groups of participants. The poor performance was found to be unrelated to the patients' general cognitive ability, the duration of their illness or their medication.

Conclusion

Schizophrenia patients suffering from reality distortion symptoms are poor at monitoring their own output. This finding suggests that schizophrenic experiences could be the result of faulty information processing.

Figure 5.7 *Schizophrenia patients with reality distortion symptoms find it difficult to monitor their own output.*

The cognitive explanation further suggests that the negative symptoms of schizophrenia may be a result of cognitive strategies used by the person to keep the level of mental stimulation to a manageable level. This happens when people experience potentially overwhelming levels of information from the external world and their inner world. Heinrichs and Zakzanis (1998) found that patients showed a variety of cognitive deficits, including problems with visual and auditory attention. As reported earlier, Kring and Neale (1996) showed that schizophrenics experience more emotions than they reveal in their facial expressions. Not sharing emotion may be a way to control the internal levels of emotion being experienced.

Evaluation

- There is evidence that cognitive processes in people with schizophrenia are different to those of non-schizophrenics.
- The cognitive explanation can explain both positive and negative symptoms.
- The cognitive explanation is compatible with the biological explanation and explains the symptoms, but it does not tell us about the initial cause.

Sociocultural explanations

There are two main sociocultural explanations of schizophrenia: labelling and family dysfunction.

(i) Labelling

Sociocultural theorists, such as Szasz (1962) and Modrow (1992), state that when a person is labelled as schizophrenic, this influences that person's behaviour in the future. Once the person has been labelled, this becomes a **self-fulfilling prophecy**, with the person then taking on more fully the characteristics of the label in the future. Rosenhan (1973) demonstrated labelling in a vivid way.

STUDY

Aim

Rosenhan (1973) conducted a field study to demonstrate the effect of labelling.

Method

Eight healthy people were asked to make appointments at different hospitals. At the appointment they complained of hearing voices and spoke strangely, often using the words 'thud', 'hollow' and 'empty'.

Results

All eight were diagnosed with schizophrenia. Once in hospital they behaved normally and showed no schizophrenic symptoms. They were ignored by professional staff and felt that staff created a sense of powerless and fear in them. The average hospital stay was 17 days. Other patients realised that they were normal and not mentally disturbed. When they were finally discharged, they left with a diagnosis of schizophrenia in remission.

Conclusion

The label 'schizophrenia' meant that normal behaviour in hospital was seen as abnormal or disturbed. Also the label remained – on being discharged they were said to be 'in remission', suggesting they might well revert to being sufferers in the future.

Evaluation

- Rosenhan was criticised for being unethical and for deliberately misleading professionals.
- The diagnosis of schizophrenia in those times was less well defined and much more commonly used as a catch-all category.
- The study shows how a label can be difficult to change and does result in other people having expectations that we will behave in ways consistent with the label. Perhaps schizophrenia is partly self-fulfilling as a result of the expectations of others.
- Generally, as argued by Scheff (1966), knowing somebody suffers from a psychiatric or psychological disorder creates a stigma or feeling of social inadequacy in the person.

(ii) Family dysfunction

The relationships and patterns of communication within a family have been identified as possible stress factors responsible for causing or contributing to the development of schizophrenia (Schiffman *et al.*, 2002). Research has shown that the parents of schizophrenics show three dysfunctional characteristics:

- high levels of interpersonal conflict (family arguments)
- difficulties in communicating with each other
- highly critical and controlling of their children.

As long ago as 1956, Bateson (Bateson *et al.*, 1956) identified faulty communication within families as a possible cause of schizophrenia. Bateson introduced the term **double bind** to describe the 'no win' situation that children were often put in by one or both parents. A double bind is when a parent verbally gives one message and non-verbally conveys the opposite message. For example, the mother might ask for a cuddle, but non-verbally 'push' the child away by avoiding eye contact and holding the child at arm's length. As a result, the child becomes confused, doubtful and uncertain about how best to respond. Negative symptoms of social withdrawal and flat affect may be an appropriate and logical response to double bind situations.

Nomura *et al.* (2005) found that when a person recovering from the active phase of schizophrenia goes back into a family context where criticism, hostility and disapproval are common features of communication, the person is likely to relapse. Relapse takes the person back to the highly active phase, with severe positive symptoms of persecution and hallucinations. Families where communications are commonly to do with criticism, hostility and disapproval are said to have high **expressed emotion**. Butzlaff and Hooley (1998) reviewed over 20 studies of expressed emotion. They found that 70% of schizophrenics in such families relapsed within a year, compared with just 30% relapse in families with low levels of expressed emotion.

STUDY

Aim

Brown *et al.* (1966) investigated the impact of expressed emotion in the family on the recovery of schizophrenics.

Method

People recovering from schizophrenia and discharged from hospital were followed up over a 9-month period. Interviews with family members were conducted to determine the level of expressed emotion.

Results

Families where expressed emotion levels were high resulted in 58% of the people with schizophrenia returning to hospital, compared to only 10% where expressed emotion was low.

Conclusion

Expressed emotion as a pattern of family communication is an important factor in determining how well people recover from schizophrenia.

Evaluation

- It is difficult to say that expressed emotion in a family is a cause of schizophrenia rather than a consequence of having a schizophrenic person in the family. People with schizophrenia are very disruptive to normal family life.
- The diathesis-stress model of schizophrenia is where biological factors cause a predisposition to develop schizophrenia. The stress factors in the environment may well be to do with family dysfunction and expressed emotion.
- Treatments that are focused on reducing the level of expressed emotion in families, where successful, result in lower relapse rates (Doane *et al.*, 1985).

5.2.5 Treatments of schizophrenia

Generally speaking, the most effective treatment is a combination of drug therapy, psychotherapy and social or community support. Unfortunately, it is not always possible to provide such a comprehensive treatment package for everybody diagnosed with schizophrenia.

Antipsychotic drugs

There are two main categories of antipsychotic drugs that are used to treat schizophrenia. These are called **conventional antipsychotic** drugs and **atypical antipsychotic drugs.**

(i) Conventional antipsychotic drugs

Conventional antipsychotic drugs are also called **neuroleptic drugs** because they often cause unwanted side effects of physical movements – for example, muscle tremors similar to those found in Parkinson's disease. Phenothiazines were the first antipsychotic drug to be used in the treatment of schizophrenia in the 1950s. These are a type of antihistamine and the name of the drug used to treat the disorder is called **Chlorpromazine.** Chlorpromazine reduces the frequency and strength of hallucinations and other positive symptoms and acts by blocking the receptors for dopamine that are located in the synapses of the neuron. This results in reduced levels of dopamine.

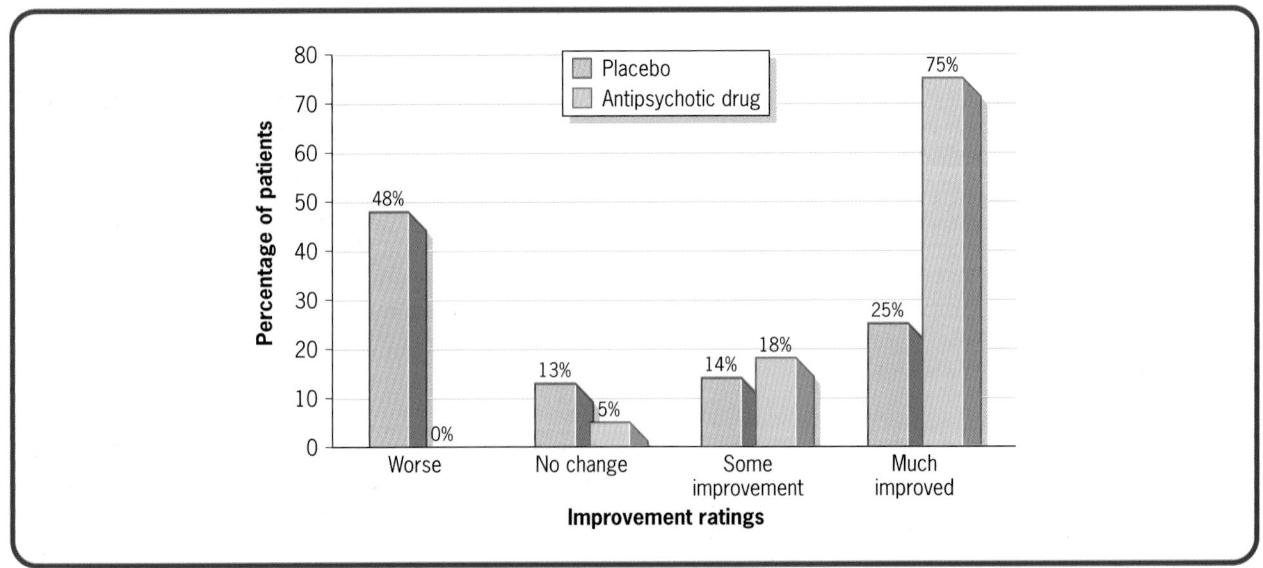

Figure 5.8 *Cole* et al. *(1964) found that 75% of schizophrenics treated with antipsychotic drugs showed much improvement.*

Chlorpromazine must be taken regularly and all the time or the hallucinations, delusions and thought disturbances return, often with great severity. The drug must be taken even if none of the positive symptoms are being experienced at the time. Long-term hospitalisation for people with schizophrenia was dramatically reduced when Chlorpromazine was introduced in the 1950s and 1960s.

Throughout the 1970s and 1980s, other types of antipsychotic drugs were developed. These include thioxanthenes such as Navane. All these conventional antipsychotic drugs reduce dopamine levels in the brain and reduce the severity and number of positive symptoms. An early study by Cole *et al.* (1964) found that after just 6 weeks of treatment with antipsychotic drugs, people with schizophrenia showed significant improvement compared to those given a placebo. Schizophrenics given a placebo were found to improve only a little (see Figure 5.8).

Side effects of conventional antipsychotic drugs

Severe muscle tremors, similar to those experienced with Parkinson's disease; these are known as **extrapyramidal effects** because the drugs affect the extrapyramidal parts of the brain

Shuffling of feet when walking, moving slowly and rigid facial expressions

Restlessness and limb discomfort accompanied by bizarre face and tongue movements

Tardive dyskinesia, characterised by jerky movements of the face, tongue or whole body, involuntary chewing, sucking and smacking of the lips. Around 10% of people develop this with long-term use.

Some side effects of the neuroleptic drugs can be reduced or eliminated if the person is also prescribed anti-Parkinsonian drugs at the same time. However, tardive dyskinesia has proved difficult to eliminate.

(ii) Atypical antipsychotic drugs

Over the past 10 years a new generation of antipsychotic drugs, which reduce both positive and negative symptoms, have been introduced. The most effective and commonly used are *clozapine* and *risperidone.* They are called atypical drugs because their action is different to the conventional drugs; they work less to reduce levels of dopamine but do change the levels of serotonin, another neurotransmitter. Clozapine is effective with schizophrenics who have not responded to conventional antipsychotic drugs. Whilst these new drugs do not have the same side effects as the conventional antipsychotic drugs, other side effects have been observed. These include nausea, weight gain, irregular heartbeat and excessive salivation. A few patients also develop a possibly life-threatening disorder in which the level of white blood cells drops dramatically.

Treatment effectiveness of antipsychotic drugs

- Conventional and atypical antipsychotic drugs reduce the positive symptoms of schizophrenia, often to the extent that the person can live a relatively normal life and not require hospitalisation. Atypical antipsychotic drugs also reduce the negative symptoms and so help even more with everyday living.
- Both types of drugs have undesirable, bizarre and significant side effects.
- The drugs make a dramatic difference to the lives of sufferers and families.
- About 25% of sufferers do not respond to the conventional antipsychotic drugs. However, these people do respond to the atypical drugs.
- If either type of drug is not taken, the positive symptoms return quite quickly, requiring urgent hospitalisation as a consequence.

Behavioural treatments

The behavioural treatment of schizophrenia is based on the assumption that schizophrenic behaviour has been learned through inappropriate conditioning and observational learning. The attention given to the bizarre or strange behaviour of people with schizophrenia may, in itself, be rewarding, and the behaviour is therefore reinforced.

Behavioural treatments based on operant conditioning or social learning theory have some effect on reducing

STUDY

Aim

Paul and Lentz (1977) investigated the effectiveness of a token economy in a hospital ward setting.

Method

Tokens or rewards were given to patients for appropriate behaviours. The tokens could be exchanged for meals, cigarettes and other items. Appropriate behaviours included making the bed, joining in social events and so on. The token economy was maintained over 6 years and the progress of patients was monitored.

Results

Both positive and negative symptoms of schizophrenia reduced over time. Many people were discharged from hospital as a result of the token economy.

Conclusions

Token systems based on operant conditioning can be successful in changing the behaviour of people with schizophrenia. However, when behaviour was no longer reinforced some patients relapsed.

bizarre behaviours. However, such treatment has little or no effect on disturbed thought processes such as hallucinations or delusions. In psychiatric hospital settings, **token economies** (Paul and Lentz, 1977) have been used. Here patients receive rewards for behaving appropriately and punishment or no reward for behaving in inappropriate or disruptive ways. Token economies, if taken to the extreme where basics like food, water and other essential needs are used as rewards have proved effective, but are sometimes regarded as inappropriate now and a breach of basic human rights.

Whilst behavioural treatments may modify extreme and bizarre behaviour, they do little if anything to treat the underlying psychological and thought disturbances that are central to schizophrenia. Behavioural treatments may be used as part of a wider package of treatment, especially with drug treatment and the newly emerging cognitive approach to treatment. On their own, behavioural treatments are of limited value.

Psychotherapy

A range of different types of psychotherapy have been used to treat people with schizophrenia. These include psychotherapy based on psychodynamics, insight therapy and family therapy.

(i) Psychoanalytic therapy

Freud viewed schizophrenia as a result of the ego being overwhelmed by demands of both the id and the superego. Hearing voices is the result of critical 'superego voices' criticising the person's inadequacies. Delusion of grandeur is a device the ego uses to satisfy the superego but has no basis in reality (for more on the psychodynamic approach, see Chapter 13). Generally, psychoanalytic therapy is of little value in treating people with schizophrenia. For psychoanalytic therapy to be effective, the individual must have insight into their condition and be able to talk rationally about themselves, which schizophrenics cannot do. Furthermore, using psychotherapy based on a Freudian approach with people who have partially recovered from the extremes of schizophrenia (people in the residual phase) may result in the return of severe positive and negative symptoms. This is because the ego may feel unable to cope with talking about the condition directly. So to protect itself, it may retreat into delusion, hallucination and social withdrawal, to reduce feelings of being overwhelmed.

(ii) Insight therapy

Insight therapy is based on the idea that people with schizophrenia can be helped to have greater insight and understanding of their symptoms. Treatment requires one-to-one therapy, with the therapist attempting to gain the trust of the person so that he or she feels safe to discuss their disturbing thoughts.

More recently, **cognitive therapy** has been developed to treat people with schizophrenia. This is based on the diathesis-stress model. Cognitive therapy attempts to help change negative attitudes that the person may have and get them to seek help when symptoms become severe, rather than withdraw from society. Cognitive therapy also works on symptoms such as hearing voices. Here the cognitive therapist tries to change the patient's perception from one of feeling out of control (hearing things) to being in control, regarding the voices as someone trying to talk to them. This approach to treatment tries to help the person to adjust and challenge their delusions and hallucinations, rather than deny or hide them away. The cognitive approach also helps people to identify situations that are found to be stressful and to develop better coping strategies (Beck and Rector, 2005).

Beck and Rector view the negative symptoms of schizophrenia as resulting from the person having low expectations for success and few feelings of pleasure in life. Cognitive therapies help the person to recognise success and take pleasure in success when it occurs. The cognitive approach is a new and emerging approach to explaining and treating schizophrenia. As such, it is too early to fully assess the effectiveness of cognitive treatment.

(iii) Family therapy

We have seen that communication patterns and high expressed emotion in families may contribute towards schizophrenia. It is therefore not surprising that considerable efforts have been directed at changing communications through family therapy. The main objectives of family therapy are:

- to get members of the family to be more tolerant and less critical
- to help all members of the family feel less guilt and feel less responsible for causing the illness
- to improve positive communication and decrease negative types of communication.

STUDY

Aim

Hogarty *et al.* (1986) investigated the effectiveness of family therapy in comparison to three other types of treatment for schizophrenia.

Method

People with schizophrenia received either medication only, medication plus social skills training, medication plus family therapy or medication plus both social skills training and family therapy. Patients were followed up over a 1-year period and the frequency of relapse for each type of treatment measured.

Results

It was found that 40% of those in the medication-only treatment relapsed, compared with 20% relapse in the medication plus social skill training or family therapy treatments. The combination of medication plus social skills training and family therapy resulted in no cases of relapse.

Conclusion

Family therapy helps prevent relapse in schizophrenia. When combined with social skills training and medication relapse is very low indeed.

Help groups for family members also exist. Here, families meet with each other to provide support, learn about what works for other families and maintain high motivation to continue with new communication patterns and support for the member with schizophrenia (Chien *et al.*, 2004).

Hogarty *et al.* (1986) followed up the people with schizophrenia into a second year after family therapy and social skills training had ceased. They found higher levels of relapse, emphasising the need to maintain treatment even when the person may be in the recovery phase.

Community care

Care in the community is an essential and broad approach to the treatment of schizophrenia. Thirty years ago, people with schizophrenia spent long periods of time, many years in some cases, in psychiatric hospitals. Fifty years ago, some schizophrenics had spent most of their life in institutional care. The present approach is to minimise hospital stays and provide support in the community, so that sufferers can live as normal a life as possible and hold down paid employment.

Ideally, community care should provide for a wide range of support and treatments, including sheltered/supported living arrangements, ongoing psychotherapy matched to needs and circumstances of the person, an environment where social skills can be enhanced and friendships developed to prevent isolation, and monitored medication. It has long been recognised that proper community care is more beneficial than long-term hospitalisation.

Community care is a highly effective treatment for schizophrenia. However, if the support is withdrawn then relapse will occur. One of the main issues with providing a full range of community care is the ongoing cost. It is expensive, and if costs are cut and some services withdrawn, then the effect on the people with schizophrenia is negative. Both positive and negative symptoms are likely to recur and cause a return to the active phase of schizophrenia.

STUDY

Aim

Stein and Test (1980) compared the effectiveness of community care and hospitalisation in people with schizophrenia.

Method

Two groups of 65 people suffering from schizophrenia were compared. One group received hospital treatment with medication and were then discharged without support. The other group were given community care to support them living in the community. Community care consisted of food and shelter, training in social and community skills, educational support and help with developing a social network of friends. The study lasted for 12 months.

Results

The unsupported discharged patients showed high levels of relapse – 58 out of the 65 were readmitted to hospital within the 1-year period. By contrast, 53 of the people given community care remained living in the community over the year.

Conclusion

Community care provides successful support to people with schizophrenia and helps prevent relapse and future hospitalisation.

Evaluation

- From considering the different range of treatments available to people with schizophrenia, from drug therapy to community care, one common theme emerges. Whichever treatment or combination of treatments, is used, it is important that they are maintained and are ongoing. Stopping medication, community care or psychotherapy may cause a relapse and result in hospitalisation.
- The most effective approach to treatment is a combination of drugs, psychotherapy and community care. It is not always possible to provide this due to the high cost.
- Individuals differ in the extent to which they respond to different treatments and their willingness to undergo some types of treatment. Unpleasant side effects may affect the likelihood of adherence to drug treatment.
- Generally, treatment of schizophrenia is much more effective now than it was 10 years ago. New drugs have fewer undesirable side effects and with the development of new therapies, such as cognitive therapy, the future looks good for helping people with one of the most debilitating and difficult mental disorders.

5.3 Mood disorders

Mood disorders are disturbances of emotion. Although we all experience feelings of being down at times and may even say that we are feeling a bit depressed, normal fluctuations in mood can be very clearly distinguished from those in a case of clinical depression. Clinical depression has a severe and debilitating effect on the individual and others around them, and affects the sufferer's ability to maintain employment. Clinical depression is also difficult to treat. In this section we will look at three types of depression: unipolar depression, bipolar depression and seasonal affective disorder (SAD).

5.3.1 Unipolar and bipolar depression: symptoms and diagnosis

The most common form of depression is **unipolar depression.** Here a person experiences an extremely depressed or sad mood state that may last for weeks or months if left untreated. Unipolar depression is where the person suffers just from deep depressive periods. **Bipolar depression** is where the person experiences two quite different emotional states: periods of depression followed by periods of mania (euphoria, high levels of energy, etc). People with bipolar depression experience extreme mood swings. People with unipolar depression do not experience or show signs of manic episodes and do not have extreme mood swings.

Unipolar depression

In any one year, 5–7% of adults suffer from unipolar depression. These rates are similar in most western countries such as the UK, USA and Canada (WHO, 2004).

Symptoms of unipolar depression

Emotional – sadness, depressed mood, loss of pleasure in life, short temper or irritability, feelings of guilt and worthlessness

Cognitive – poor concentration, poor memory, low self-esteem, hopelessness, suicidal thoughts

Physiological – sleep disturbances, fidgeting or agitation, palpitations, headaches, stomach upsets, lack of energy

Behavioural – withdrawal from social life, poor performance at work, poor personal hygiene, loss of interest in sex and intimate relationships, catatonia

With extreme unipolar depression, symptoms may include delusions and hallucinations. Delusions are negative and usually to do with the person having done something wrong for which they are being punished. Hallucinations may be auditory, where the person hears voices telling them to commit suicide or telling them they have done something terribly wrong, such as murdered somebody. Unipolar depression is an emotional disorder; however, extreme feelings of sadness and depression strongly affect other psychological functions and behaviour.

The DSM and ICD state that a clinical diagnosis of depression requires at least five of the above symptoms to be present for at least two weeks. Also, diagnosis of unipolar depression or a major depressive disorder requires that there has been no history or presence of mania. Comer (2008) provides the following definition of unipolar or major depression:

> a severe pattern of depression that is disabling and is not caused by factors such as drugs or a general medical condition. (Comer, 2008: 192).

Many people diagnosed with unipolar depression also have other psychological problems, including substance abuse (such as alcoholism), eating disorders and panic attacks (Blazer *et al.*, 1994).

Unipolar depression may have a gradual onset or appear suddenly. It occurs in all social classes and at all ages, from childhood to old age, but is most common in middle and old age. It is also recognised more frequently in childhood and adolescence nowadays; around one in six adolescents will experience a major depressive episode. Feelings of depression are often high with adolescents but do not last long, and most cases do not meet the diagnostic criteria to be classified as a unipolar depression (Saluja *et al.*, 2004). Unipolar depression can be a recurring disorder and people who have had one major depressive episode are at risk of having other depressive episodes. People who have numerous depressive episodes are more likely to have these episodes for longer periods of time compared to people who have only one major depressive episode. Blazer *et al.* showed that the percentage of people with depression in different age groups varied. The highest incidence is between 15 and 24 years and between 35 and 44 years of age (see Figure 5.9)

The rates of depression for people in their sixties, seventies and later years are not shown in Figure 5.9. However, rates are likely to be high, but this is often complicated by other medical disorders and social isolation. Depression in women is about twice as frequent as in men (Nolen-Hoeksema, 2002). This difference has been recorded across different age groups, different countries and amongst people of different ethnic origins.

Bipolar depression

With bipolar depression, periods of major depression occur with periods of mania.

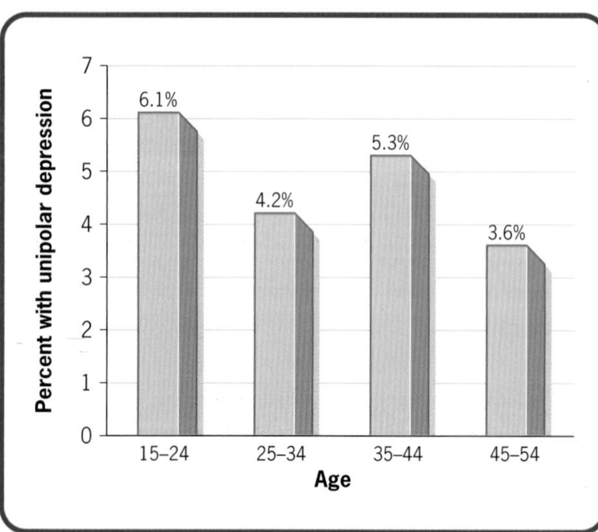

Figure 5.9 *Percentage figures for unipolar depression according to age group (adapted from Blazer, 1994).*

The symptoms of mania

Emotional – feelings of euphoria and highly elevated mood states, irritability due to not getting own way or frustration by others, lack of feelings of guilt and social inhibition

Cognitive – delusional ideas, grandiose plans, thinking that other people are persecuting them or 'out to get them', reckless and irrational decision making.

Behavioural and physiological – high energy, increased work activity, increased social and sexual activity, talkative with fast speech, little sleep, reckless and dangerous behaviours.

For an episode to be classified as mania, the above symptoms should be present for at least 1 week, along with distress or impairment of mental function. In a manic episode the person shows poor judgement and does not listen to advice from others. It is very difficult to dissuade them from embarking on a grand plan. At the extreme, they may be incoherent and have lost touch with reality. The person is full of energy and may go for days without sleep. During the manic phase they may stop taking the drugs which control bipolar depression, leading to further deterioration.

Following a manic episode the person may fall into major depression, feel exhausted and sleep for a long time.

Diagnosis of bipolar disorder requires that both a major depressive episode and a manic episode be present. The duration of each of these extremes may vary. For example, each depressive and manic episode may last for weeks at a time, or swing between each in the period of just 1 day.

Between 1% and 2% of adults suffer from bipolar depression at any one time and the disorder has the same rates of occurrence in women and men, different social classes and different ethnic groups (Shastry, 2005). The average age of onset varies between 15 and 40 years of age, with the average age being around 20 years. After the age of 40 years it is rare for bipolar depression to first occur; when it does it is usually very serious and long lasting. Suicide rates amongst people with bipolar depression are high, at around 12–15% (Rihmer and Pestality, 1999).

5.3.2 Seasonal affective disorder (SAD): symptoms and diagnosis

Seasonal affective disorder (SAD) is a mood disorder that typically occurs during the months of winter when days are short and nights long. The weather during the day in winter is also typically dull, gloomy and overcast. People with SAD recover when daylight hours are longer and the sun is shining – typically in the summer months of the year. The most common form of SAD is winter depression without manic episodes. More rarely it has been observed that some people show major depression in the winter and mania during the summer. The symptoms of depression during the winter are typically those we looked at with unipolar depression. In addition, the following symptoms are common:

- excessive periods of sleep
- increase in appetite
- weight gain.

Rates of SAD are higher in countries closer to the North and South Poles (for example, Finland, Sweden and Norway) and lower in countries closer to the equator. In the depths of winter, countries like Finland have very short hours of daylight (less than 2 hours) and, if overcast, can be like twilight, even in the middle of the day, for days on end.

STUDY

Aim

Terman (1988) set out to show that SAD occurs more often in areas of the USA that have short hours of daylight in the winter.

Method

Terman gained official figures for the incidence of depression in New Hampshire (where daylight hours are short in the winter) and Florida (where daylight hours are long all year round).

Results

It was found that around 10% of people living in New Hampshire suffered from depression in the winter months. By contrast, just 2% of those living in Florida suffered from depression in the same winter months.

Conclusion

Short daylight hours in the winter are a major cause of SAD.

For someone to be diagnosed with SAD, the following criteria are required:

- The person must have experienced depression for at least two years during the winter months.
- The symptoms of depression are those identified with unipolar depression.
- There should be an absence of obvious external causes of depression that may typically occur during winter months – for example, unemployment due to being a seasonal worker.

5.3.3 Explanations of mood disorders

Biological, cognitive, behavioural and psychodynamic explanations have all been put forward to explain mood disorders. For unipolar depression the explanations receiving the most research support are biological and cognitive. For bipolar depression and the manic stage the biological explanation is most strongly supported.

Biological explanations

Biological explanations for mood disorders include genetics, biochemical influences in the form of neurotransmitters, the endocrine system and hormones, and brain abnormalities.

(i) Genetics

Family history and twin studies suggest that mood disorders, particularly bipolar depression, have a genetic basis, with the risk of developing a mood disorder at least double that where there is no family history (Wallace *et al.*, 2002). Twin studies show that concordance rates for identical twins for bipolar depression are much higher than for dizygotic twins or other relatives (see Figure 5.10)

Some twin studies have also shown that concordance rates for mood disorders are higher in women than men (Kendler *et al.*, 2001). However, other studies show no difference in depression between men and women.

So far it has not been possible to pinpoint a single gene responsible for mood disorders. However, Wilhelm *et al.* (2006) suggested that an abnormal serotonin transporter (SERT) gene could play a key role. The present view is that mood disorders result from multi-gene rather than single-gene action.

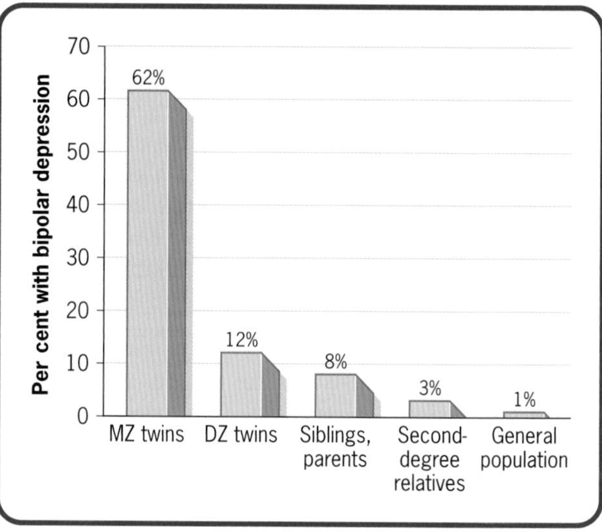

Figure 5.10 *Monozygotic twins have a much higher concordance rate for bipolar depression than dizygotic twins and other relatives (adapted from McKinnon* et al.*, 1997).*

(ii) Biochemical factors

The neurotransmitters **serotonin** and **norepinephrine** have been identified as being involved in both unipolar and bipolar mood disorders. Both affect energy levels, sleep patterns, hunger and activity levels. Both are found in high levels in the **limbic system** which controls sleep, appetite and emotions. Imbalance of these neurotransmitters in one direction (lower levels) may cause depression, and in the other direction (higher levels) may cause mania. It is known that the drug called Reserpine, which is used to reduce high blood pressure, can also cause depression. Reserpine reduces the levels of both serotonin and norepinephrine in the brain.

The role of neurotransmitters in the manic phase of bipolar depression is important. Recent research suggests that in the manic phase levels of the neurotransmitter serotonin are low and levels of norepinephrine are high (Shastry, 2005). In the depressive phase of bipolar depression the levels of both these neurotransmitters are low.

(iii) The endocrine system and hormones

The endocrine system is made up of a number of glands in the body that secrete hormones and is controlled by central parts of the brain called the hypothalamus and the pituitary gland.

When a person is stressed, an increase in the levels of certain hormones is a common physiological response.

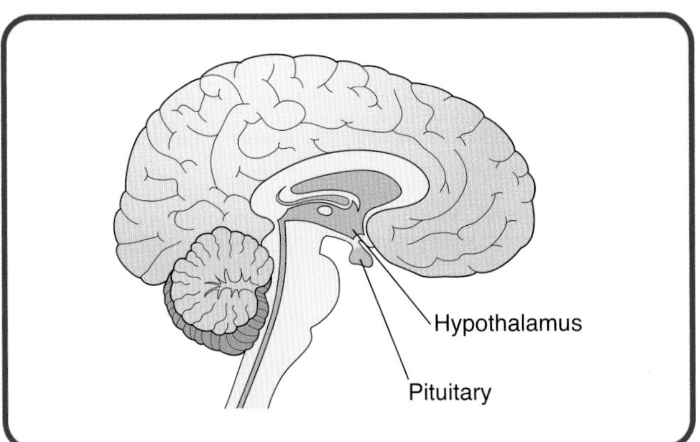

Figure 5.11 *Location of the hypothalamus and pituitary gland in the brain. These two parts of the brain stimulate the endocrine system to release hormones such as cortisol, which has been associated with depression.*

One of these hormones is **cortisol**, which helps to respond to stress during the flight-or-fight response. People with unipolar depression have unusually high levels of cortisol in their body. Sometimes people respond to stressful events by becoming depressed, especially when they feel unable to cope with the level of stress. People with depression have been found to maintain the high level of cortisol released by the endocrine system when the immediate stressful event has disappeared (Southwick *et al.*, 2005). This means that the depressive episode continues in the absence of any obvious external stressful event.

Evidence that depression in women is linked to the menstrual cycle, the post-partum period (immediately after birth) and the menopause has not strongly supported the idea that the hormones oestrogen and progesterone are the cause. With respect to premenstrual depression, the research indicates that whilst a higher percentage of women may experience depression at this time, it is usually the case that they have a history of depression not related to the menstrual cycle. Around one in ten women experience post-partum depression, but this has not been linked to levels of hormones such as oestrogen. Research has focused on life events such as stress, marital problems and 'difficult' babies rather than a biological explanation (Hendrick *et al.*, 1998).

Seasonal affective disorder is associated with the level of **melatonin** in the brain. Melatonin is secreted by the pineal gland in the absence of daylight. The short hours of daylight and long hours of darkness result in higher levels of melatonin in the brain than during summer months, especially when the sun is shining.

(iv) Brain abnormalities

Brain scans using techniques such as positron-emission tomography (PET) have identified four areas of the brain that show abnormalities associated with depression. These are:

- prefrontal cortex
- hippocampus
- anterior cingulated cortex
- amygdala.

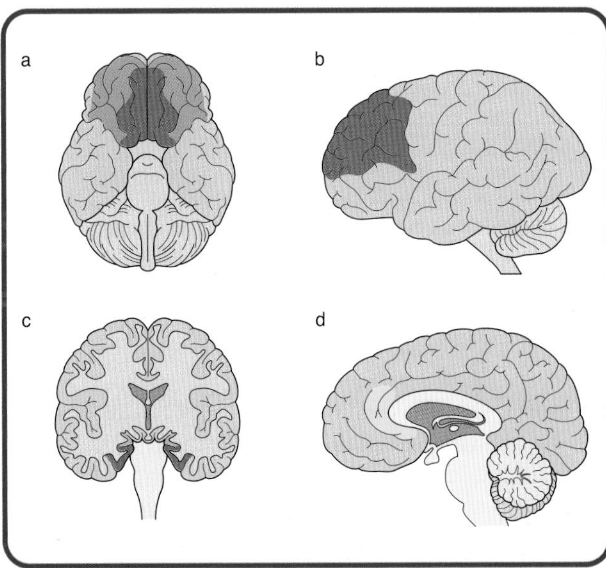

Figure 5.12 *The areas of the brain which show abnormalities from brain scans.*

The prefrontal cortex is involved in goal-related behaviour, the hippocampus with memory, the anterior cingulated cortex with the body's response to stress, and the amygdala with mood. Clearly all these feature in the symptoms of depression. What is less clear is whether or not these brain abnormalities are a cause of depression or result from the person being depressed.

Behavioural explanations for depression

Generally, the behaviourist explanation for depression is based around the idea that people with depression gain rewards for behaving in negative ways. Research has shown that depressed people prefer and seek out friends or partners who view them in negative ways

STUDY

Aim

McGuffin et al. (1996) studied the contribution of genes and shared family environment in unipolar depression.

Method

177 people (all twins of the same sex) with unipolar depression were recruited through the Maudsley Hospital Twin Register. For each person with depression their twin was assessed for symptoms of depression. The assessments were done blind.

Results

The concordance rate for the 68 pairs of identical twins was 46%. For the 109 pairs of non-identical twins the rate was 20%. Analysis revealed no evidence of an effect of shared family environment.

Conclusion

Unipolar depression has a substantial genetic component.

and behave negatively towards them (Swann *et al*; 1992).

The most influential behavioural theory for depression is that of **learned helplessness** (Seligman, 1975). This states that uncontrollable negative events in a person's life can lead to depression. Frequent experiences of not being in control lead a person to think that they cannot control events in their life. This leads to feelings of helplessness resulting in depression. Learned helplessness results in the following:

- thinking that you cannot control the rewards and punishments in your life
- thinking that you are responsible for this state of affairs.

Seligman (1975) developed his theory of learned helplessness from laboratory experiments with dogs.

Evaluation of biomedical explanations

- In twin studies the concordance rate for identical twins is not 100% suggesting the environment also has a role.
- Higher rates for identical pairs than non-identical pairs would also be predicted by environmentalists as identical pairs usually have a more shared environment than non-identical pairs.
- No single gene for mood disorders has been identified although several have been linked with bipolar disorder.
- Brain abnormalities and high or low levels of brain chemicals may be a consequence of the disorder rather than a cause.
- Some evidence suggests mood disorders are caused, or at least triggered, by social factors. Reducing such a complex disorder down to the level of genes and chemicals may be an oversimplification.

STUDY

Aim

Swann *et al.* (1992) conducted a study to show that depressed people choose to be with others who view them negatively.

Method

College students who were depressed and students who were not depressed were allowed to select a partner to interact with. The students were informed that one potential partner viewed them negatively, another positively and another in a neutral way.

Results

Depressed college students showed greater desire to interact with a partner where that partner viewed them negatively. By contrast, students who were not depressed preferred to interact with a partner who viewed them positively.

Conclusion

Depressed people prefer to interact with others who see them negatively, reinforcing the negative behaviour of the depressed person (see Figure 5.13).

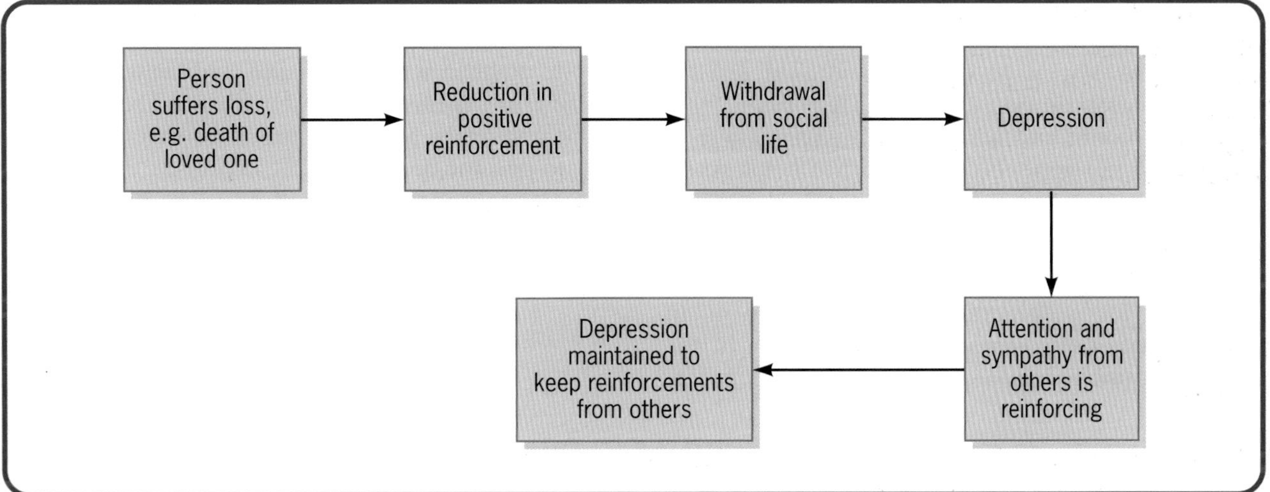

Figure 5.13 *Process of development and maintenance of depression due to loss and behavioural response of others, Lewinsohn (1974).*

STUDY

Aim

Seligman (1974) used a classical conditioning technique to show how learned helplessness develops in dogs.

Method

In the training period, dogs were placed in an apparatus where they could not escape painful electric shocks. At first the dogs tried to escape, but without success. After a while, the dogs gave up and no longer tried to escape the shocks. Later the dogs were placed in an apparatus where they could escape the shocks by jumping to the other side of a box.

Results

Dogs that had previously been unable to escape the shocks did not attempt to escape when they later could do – they had become helpless.

Conclusion

Having no control over unpleasant events leads to learned helplessness. Seligman likened this to how people with depression respond in their lives.

Miller and Seligman (1975) showed that when people were exposed to negative events over which they had no control they scored high on a depressive mood questionnaire. Wu *et al.* (1999) conducted learned helplessness experiments on rats. They found that levels of serotonin and norepinephrine were lower in rats that had not gone through a learned helplessness schedule.

Lewinsohn (1974) offered a behavioural explanation for depression based on **operant conditioning.** He argued that loss – for example, the break-up of an intimate relationship – results in a reduction in the amount of positive reinforcement that is experienced. As a result, the person withdraws from social life and interaction with others, leading to further reduction in positive experiences (positive reinforcement). This leads to further withdrawal and a downward spiral resulting in depression. Those with poor social skills in the first place are more prone to this and more likely to become depressed. The depressive response is maintained through reinforcement from others in the form of sympathy and attention. Depression then becomes rewarding for the person and to remain this way maintains the attention and sympathy (see Figure 5.13).

Evaluation

- Behavioural explanations for depression have largely been based on experiments conducted on animals, such as dogs. These findings are then generalised to humans.
- The behavioural explanations based on classical conditioning (learned helplessness) and operant conditioning (Lewinsohn) both require an understanding of cognitive processes and so are not pure behavioural explanations.
- Learned helplessness theory was reformulated as **attribution-helplessness** to take account of cognitive factors.

Cognitive explanations for depression

Cognitive explanations for depression state that people become depressed because they think in negative and self-defeating ways. Beck (1987) suggested that in childhood **negative schemas** develop, providing a cognitive framework for viewing events pessimistically. Negative schemas can develop in childhood and adolescence, when parents and authority figures such as teachers have unrealistic demands and are overly critical. These negative schemas continue into adult life, resulting in a distinctive way of thinking, including:

- overgeneralisation – believing that one negative event means that everything is negative
- magnification – blowing things up out of all proportion
- selective perception – perceiving only bad events and ignoring good things
- absolutist thinking – believing everything must be perfect or else it is a disaster.

STUDY

Aim

Beck (1976) investigated the schemas used by people with depression.

Method

Beck administered the dysfunctional attitude scale (DAS) to a group of people diagnosed with depression and a group of people who were not depressed. The DAS consists of a number of statements which the person is asked to agree or disagree with – for example, 'People will think less of me if I make a mistake'.

Results

People with depression scored higher on the DAS, indicating that they thought more negatively about events and situations than people who were not depressed.

Conclusion

People diagnosed as depressed think more negatively and use negative schemas.

Beck (2002) has identified a **cognitive triad** of negative thinking whereby depressed people consistently think negatively about the self, the world and the future.

Beck's cognitive triad

Self – I am not good enough to go to university.

World – School's horrible. Life is horrible.

Future – Nothing good will ever happen to me.

Beck's cognitive triad model of depression resulted in him developing the most commonly used and most successful psychological treatment for the disorder, cognitive behavioural therapy, which we shall consider later in this chapter.

The learned helplessness explanation of depression, considered in the previous section, was revised to place cognitions at the centre of depression. The revision is called the **attribution-helplessness model** (Peterson and Seligman, 1984; Abramson *et al.*, 2002). This model is based on the way in which people attribute or make causes to events. People who think that they have little control over their lives and what happens to them are seen to have a particular pattern of attributing causes to negative events, as follows:

- Internal attribution for the cause – It is my fault and I am responsible.
- Stable attribution – That's the way I am and will always be.
- Global attribution – That's how I am with everybody and all events in my life.

This pattern of attributions results in a lowering of self-esteem and a lack of motivation to change leading to a state of depression (see Figure 5.14).

Seligman *et al.* (1974) developed a questionnaire to assess a person's attributional style. This questionnaire presents people with 12 hypothetical situations for

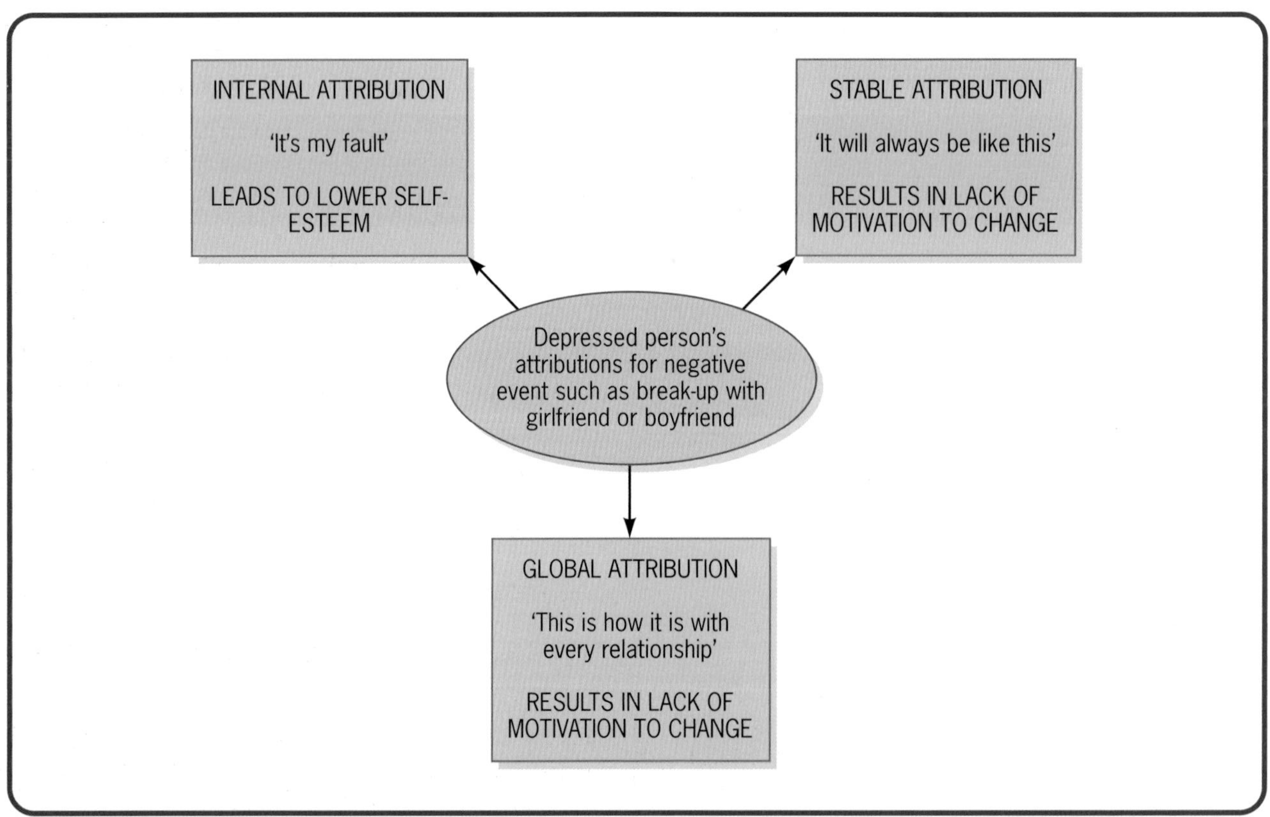

Figure 5.14 *Depressed people make internal, stable, global attributions for negative events such as the breakdown of a relationship.*

Evaluation

- Cognitive explanations of depression are based on sound experimental research using people and have enjoyed widespread acceptance.
- The cognitive approach is less successful in explaining the manic phase in bipolar disorder.
- Cognitive explanations have resulted in effective cognitive therapies for the treatment of depression.

which a cause has to be indicated. The hypothetical situations are categorised into positive and negative achievements and positive and negative interpersonal matters. An example of each is as follows:

- Positive achievement – you apply for a job that you badly want and get it.
- Negative achievement – you cannot get all the work done that is expected of you.
- Positive interpersonal – you meet a friend who compliments you on your appearance.
- Negative interpersonal – you meet a friend who acts hostilely towards you.

For each event you are asked to write down one major cause. Depressed people show an attributional style where positive events are seen as caused by other people and negative events are caused by themselves.

Psychodynamic explanations for depression

Freud (1917) and Karl Abraham (1916) based their psychoanalytic explanation of depression on grief (loss) and dependency. How the child deals with and responds to loss and dependency in childhood sets the pattern for how the adult responds to similar experiences later in life. Grief as a result of loss in early childhood is often followed by feelings of desertion and rejection. Because the child's ego is highly self-centred, the child interprets, irrationally, these feelings as resulting from something the child has done, making them feel alone, abandoned and unlovable. Unable to express anger and rage at others for this loss, these feeling are turned inwards to the self, resulting in self-blame and self-punishment for the loss. Freud called this the **introjection of hostility** theory of depression. When loss happens in adulthood the person is likely to regress or return to an early childhood stage of psychosexual development called the **oral stage** (see Chapter 13). If the child was not able to come through the feelings of desertion and rejection as a child, then regression to this stage as an adult means that the adult is not able to deal appropriately with grief and loss. The outcome is depression.

Whilst most people feel depressed for a while when they experience a significant loss in their life (such as the death of a loved one), they come through this and return to normal once the loss has been grieved. However, some people maintain their depression after loss. The psychodynamic explanation for this is to do with childhood experiences and regression back to the high dependency period of the oral stage.

Another explanation is based on feelings of inadequacy which result from failure to meet the standards and expectations of parents (or caregivers) in the first 5 years. If the child has overbearing, critical and authoritarian parents, it is likely that whatever the child does to please will never be enough. In adulthood this may cause depression because such a person will always be setting themselves goals and standards that they cannot achieve. Failure then leads to depression and lack of motivation to even try any more.

Klein *et al.* (2002) identified a small number of personality traits that are commonly shown by people with depression:

> Dependency on others; belief that they must be perfect in all respects; low self-esteem and an inability to express anger openly, especially to those close to you.

Research has offered some support for the psychodynamic description of parents of people with depression as cold, moralistic, demanding perfection and asking for total devotion.

Psychodynamic explanations of depression have led to

the development of interpersonal theories of depression. These are concerned with how people interact, seek for and maintain close and intimate relationships in their adult lives. Such theories draw heavily on attachment theory (Bowlby, 1951), with the basic claim that unsatisfactory or poor attachments to parents in early childhood may lead to adult depression. This is because the person attempts to seek approval from others to compensate for the feelings of rejection caused by poor childhood attachments.

Psychodynamic explanation for mania in bipolar depression

Freud suggested that bipolar depression can be explained by how the three components of personality (the id, ego and superego) interact with each other. During the depressive phase the superego dominates the ego. Since the superego is made up of a person's ego-ideal and conscience, the result is that the ego experiences extreme feelings of guilt and inadequacy, resulting in depression. The ego tries to take control away from the superego and in doing so overreacts and the individual enters the manic phase. The cycle is repeated, with the superego and ego alternately taking control.

Evaluation

- It is difficult to establish good scientific evidence for the claims about the influence of early childhood experience. However, Bowlby's work on attachment and loss has enjoyed support and has been based on empirical observations.
- The early theories of Freud and Abraham led to the development of an interpersonal theory of depression which resulted in an effective treatment for depression.

5.3.4 Treatment of mood disorders

The most successful treatments for unipolar depression and seasonal affective disorder (SAD) are through a combination of drugs and some form of psychological therapy, usually cognitive therapy. For bipolar depression, psychological therapies have been less successful and the treatment is predominantly drug therapy, especially to control the manic phase of the disorder.

Biological treatments of mood disorders

(i) Drug therapy

Three main categories of antidepressant drugs have been used to treat clinical depression.

- **Tricyclic antidepressants:** Initially used in 1958, these drugs prevent noradrenalin and serotonin being taken back into the neuron after it has been released. The effect of this is to increase the activity levels of these neurotransmitters.
- **Monoamine oxidase inhibitors (MAOIs):** MAOIs work by stopping the breakdown of the monoamine oxidase chemical in the presynaptic neuron. Stopping the activity of MAO means that higher levels of neurotransmitters are active in the brain.
- **Selective serotonin reuptake inhibitors (SSRIs):** These are the most recent types of antidepressants, with the most well known being Prozac (fluoxetine). These allow serotonin to remain active for longer at the synapse.

Tricyclic antidepressants have a number of undesirable side effects, including dry mouth, excessive perspiration, constipation, blurring of vision and sexual dysfunction. They are effective in alleviating depression for about 60% of people treated. However, they can take a long time to have a positive effect – typically 6–8 weeks. Tricyclics can also be fatal if an overdose is taken, here an overdose may be only five times the prescription level.

Monoamine oxidase inhibitors (MAOIs) have potentially more serious and undesirable side effects than tricyclics. These include an interaction with certain foods, such as red wine or chocolate, increase in blood pressure, liver damage and weight gain.

Selective serotonin reuptake inhibitors (SSRIs) are fast-acting, bringing relief from depression relatively quickly, usually after just 2 weeks. They also have less severe side effects, but do increase a person's feelings of anxiety and agitation. On the negative side, there does appear to be an increased risk of suicide with people taking these drugs.

For **bipolar disorder** the most common and widely used drug is **lithium.** Lithium returns the levels of neurotransmitters such as serotonin and dopamine to normal. It is most effective for treating mania rather than depression. People who suffer from bipolar disorder must take lithium for the rest of their life if they are to prevent the reccurrence of a manic episode. Each person differs in their uptake of lithium and has to be regularly monitored to maintain the correct level. There are also undesirable side effects, which include blurred vision, difficulty in concentration and kidney dysfunction. The main problem with lithium is that many people with bipolar disorder do not like taking the drug and often stop taking it despite the advice of their doctor. Since the drug has to be taken in the absence of mania, many people feel they can cope at this time and stop their medication. Lithium remains the main and preferred drug treatment for bipolar disorder.

Evaluation

- Tricyclics, MAOIs and SSRIs all help to reduce depression but have undesirable side effects and not everybody responds to drug treatment.
- They all take time to work. Someone who is severely depressed may find it difficult waiting for the drug to 'kick in' and may feel that they are not being helped during this period.
- These drugs are used for unipolar depression and seasonal affective disorder, but are not effective for bipolar depression, especially the relief of mania.

(ii) Electroconvulsive therapy (ECT) for depression

Electroconvulsive therapy (ECT) has been used to treat people with depression for at least 50 years. It is a highly controversial treatment, since it induces a brain seizure by passing electricity through the brain. The person is first anaesthetised and then given a muscle relaxant; electrodes are placed on the head and an electric shock is given. This induces a seizure which lasts for about 1 minute. Typically between 6 and 12 sessions are administered.

ECT is generally used as a treatment of last resort when a severely depressed person does not respond to drug treatment. It has been found to help around 50% of people treated (Fink, 2001) and is therefore seen as an effective treatment for severe depression.

How ECT alleviates depression is unclear. There are common and undesirable side effects, most notably memory loss, which may be permanent. People who have ECT experience disorientation following treatment and are often fearful before the next treatment. Relapse rates for people who have had ECT are high, approximately 80%. ECT may be effective in relieving depression, but it only does so for short periods, meaning that a second or further series of treatments is required.

(iii) Light therapy

Exposing people to bright light for 1 or 2 hours a day during the winter months has been shown to alleviate SAD (Wileman *et al.*, 2001), with benefits felt within a few days. Light therapy seems to work by increasing the

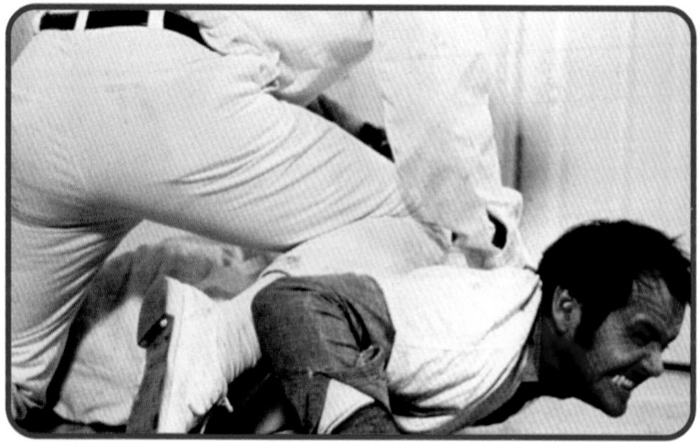

Figure 5.15 *The famous film 'One Flew Over the Cuckoo's Nest' starring Jack Nicolson depicts the use of ECT in a psychiatric hospital set in the 1960s.*

level of melatonin, which is lower than normal in people with SAD.

Cognitive treatments of depression

Cognitive therapy aims to treat depression by challenging and removing the negative thoughts. Cognitive therapy also aims to help people solve practical problems in their lives in a positive way. Cognitive therapy is meant to be brief – for example, over 3 months. It involves techniques to help change the way a person thinks and behavioural techniques to help change negative behaviours into positive ones. There are two main types of cognitive therapy commonly used to treat depression. These are **rational-emotive therapy** (Ellis, 1984) and **Beck's cognitive therapy** (Beck, 1993).

(i) Rational-emotive therapy

This type of cognitive therapy attempts to replace a person's irrational thoughts with rational thoughts. Negative thoughts or self-defeating ways of thinking are regarded as irrational. The therapist's task is first to make the sufferer aware of their self-defeating and irrational thoughts – for example, 'I must be perfect at everything I do.' The therapist then challenges the person's irrational belief through confrontation and argument. Finally, the irrational belief is replaced by a more rational belief – for example, 'I try to do things to the best of my ability but accept that I cannot do this all the time.' Self-esteem will increase as a result of success.

(ii) Beck's cognitive therapy

Beck's cognitive therapy is aimed at changing the cognitive triad of thoughts that is shown by people with depression. There are four phases, as follows:

- Phase 1 – increasing confidence and elevating mood
- Phase 2 – challenging automatic negative thoughts
- Phase 3 – identifying negative thoughts
- Phase 4 – changing key attitudes and beliefs. [end]

Beck's therapy involves 'the patient as scientist', with the patient and therapist together setting hypotheses to test the patient's negative thoughts. The patient then gathers evidence to refute the negative thoughts. This form of therapy usually lasts for 20 sessions over a 10-week period. Between sessions the person keeps a diary to monitor thoughts and identify situations where they think negatively. The person is also asked to change behaviour in specific ways between sessions and report back on this at the next session.

STUDY

Aim

Hollon *et al.* (2006) compared the effectiveness of cognitive therapy and drug therapy.

Method

People with moderate to severe depression were given either drug therapy or cognitive therapy. Those given cognitive therapy received treatment for 16 weeks and then treatment was terminated. Both groups were followed up over a period of one year.

Results

Relapse rates for people who had cognitive therapy were around 40%. Those on drug therapy showed a relapse rate of about 45%. People given a placebo instead of a drug showed relapse rates of around 80%.

Conclusion

Cognitive therapy is as effective as drug therapy for treating people with moderate to severe depression.

Evaluation of cognitive therapy

- Cognitive therapy has been shown to be a highly effective treatment for depression. Recovery rates are typically 60–70% after a 10–12 week programme.
- Cognitive therapy can be used in both one-to-one settings and small-group settings and is very cost-effective.
- A combination of both drug therapy and cognitive therapy has been shown to be highly effective and is very commonly used.
- Cognitive therapy is also successful in preventing mild depression from developing into severe depression.
- Cognitive therapy is not useful for people in the manic phase of bipolar disorder.

Other treatments for depression

Bipolar disorder has proved difficult to treat effectively with any type of psychological therapy. The main treatment is drug therapy using lithium. By contrast, unipolar depression and SAD have been treated with a range of different therapies, including psychodynamic therapy and interpersonal therapy.

Psychodynamic therapy

This involves a major commitment since sessions are usually three times a week or more and may last for a number of years. Psychodynamic therapies require that the person has insight into their condition and so are not effective in the treatment of bipolar disorders, especially when the person is in the manic phase. The techniques of free association and analysis of childhood memories are commonly used (see Chapter 13). Some evidence of effectiveness has come from people who have suffered traumatic loss in childhood (Blatt, 1999).

Interpersonal psychotherapy (IPT)

IPT aims to address the key ways in which the person with depression interacts with other people, including friends, colleagues, relatives and partners. Four aspects of interpersonal dysfunction are treated (Klerman and Weissman, 1992):

- Grief due to interpersonal loss – for example, loss of a loved one. IPT helps a person come to terms with the loss and develop new relationships.
- Interpersonal role disputes – for example, different expectations in a relationship. IPT helps to resolve such disputes.
- Role transitions resulting from major life changes – for example, divorce. IPT provides support and helps the person to identify those who can provide social support.
- Interpersonal skills deficits – for example, shyness or being socially awkward. IPT helps to overcome these, leading to improved social interactions.

Research on the effectiveness of IPT has shown it to be almost as effective as cognitive therapy. It is of real value when it is clear that the cause of the depression is to do with interpersonal aspects of life, such as divorce, death of a spouse or sudden unemployment.

Evaluation of treatments for mood disorders

- Clinical depression responds well to treatment, with many people getting over depression and not relapsing.
- Drug therapies have proved effective in the treatment of depression, but do have undesirable side effects. The modern drugs, such as Prozac, have been shown to help in about 75% of cases. Newer drugs have fewer side effects but may still cause problems.
- Bipolar depression, especially the treatment of mania, seems only to respond to drug treatment using lithium.
- Cognitive therapy and interpersonal therapy are effective in about 60% of cases. Combined with drug therapy the effectiveness may be even higher.
- There are ethical issues involved in research using a placebo condition, where participants in the placebo group are led to believe they are taking medication when in fact they are not.

How Psychology Works

An experiment to test the ability to monitor one's own output

The ability to monitor one's own output is impaired in some people with schizophrenia, but not normally impaired in non-schizophrenics (Stirling *et al.*, 1998). See pages 130–131 for details of the experiment Stirling used to investigate this.

- Your task is to devise a different experimental procedure that could be used to test a friend's ability to monitor his or her own output. In the case of the Stirling study, the output was simple line drawings of geometric shapes.
- Your task should involve production of some form of simple output – for example, a drawing, the finished version of an incomplete sentence, a piece of artwork, a moulded piece of plasticine or play dough.
- Decide on a suitable task. Remember to consider any timing restrictions. It is also important that you are clear about how you determine whether or not your friend has successfully identified his or her own output. In order to do this you will need to present your friend with a number of options, only one of which will be their own output. How many options would be appropriate? In the Stirling study there were three bogus options and one correct one, so the chance of guessing correctly was 1 in 4 or 25%.
- Make a list of the materials you would need to carry out the procedure and then gather the materials together.
- Write a set of instructions that will explain to your friend exactly what he or she has to do.
- Write a suitable debrief. Note – you are not going to carry out the study with anyone suffering from a psychological disorder. The debrief should just explain in simple everyday language what the task is designed to test.
- Carry out the procedure five times with your friend as a participant. For each of the five trials, record the outcome on a simple record sheet.
- Write a short report of your activity, explaining what the task involved and justifying your choice of task and materials. Explain what happened when you carried out the task.

Further Reading

Introductory texts

Beck, A.T. (2004) *Madness Explained: Psychosis and Human Nature*, Harmondsworth: Penguin.
Carr, A. (2001) *Abnormal Psychology*, Hove: Psychology Press Limited.
Frith, C. and Johnstone, E. (2003) *Schizophrenia: A Very Short Introduction*, Oxford: Oxford University Press.
Gross, R. and McIlveen, R. (2000) *Psychopathology*, London: Hodder & Stoughton.

Specialist sources

Barlow, D. (2008) *Abnormal Psychology: An Integrated Approach*, 4th edn,. Belmont, CA: Wadsworth Publishers.
Comer, R.J. (2008) *Fundamentals of Abnormal Psychology*, 5th edn., New York: Worth Publishers.

Stress and stress management

Chapter 6

6.1 Introduction

We all experience stress at some time or another, and find certain situations and events in our lives highly stressful. We often say that we are feeling 'stressed out' when, for example, we are facing an examination or required to make a presentation at an interview for a job. What is stressful to one person may not be stressful for another person. Stress, therefore, has a very important psychological component that should always be taken into account. This is very much a layperson's view of stress.

Psychologists distinguish between stress that harms and damages the individual, which is called *distress*, and stress that may be beneficial to helping a person perform at their best. This positive aspect of stress is called *eustress*. The theory and research that we shall be considering in this chapter is mostly to do with the harmful, undesirable aspects and consequences of stress.

Figure 6.1 *A very stressful situation for a person may mean that they are not able to perform at their best and in consequence do poorly at an interview for a job.*

Stress can be seen as both a stimulus in the environment and a response by the individual to a specific situation. Stress as an environmental stimulus is where something is seen to be stressful – for example, an examination, job interview or presentation to a large audience. Stress as a response is where a person says he or she is 'stressed out'. This involves both a physiological aspect (dry mouth, butterflies in the stomach and sweating), and a psychological component (anxiety, fear and nervous laughter). Some health psychologists like to make a distinction between stress as a stimulus, which is called a *stressor,* and stress as a response, which is called *strain.*

Given the above, a very useful model of stress is that of Lazarus (1993), called the **transactional model**. Lazarus stated that stress involves a transaction between the person and their external world. The person is stressed if he or she perceives the external event or stimulus to be stressful. For example, if John loves to speak in front of an audience (he may be an extrovert) then he is unlikely to feel stressed when told that he has to make a presentation to his classmates the next day. By contrast, if Ian dislikes speaking in front of an audience (he may be an introvert), then being told he has to make a presentation to his classmates the next day may well cause him to feel highly stressed and he may have a sleepless night. With the transactional model of stress the individual has to appraise the external event, and if it is perceived to be harmful, threatening or challenging then it will be stressful to the person. This is where the person appraises the event itself and decides whether or not it is potentially stressful to the person. This is called *primary appraisal.*

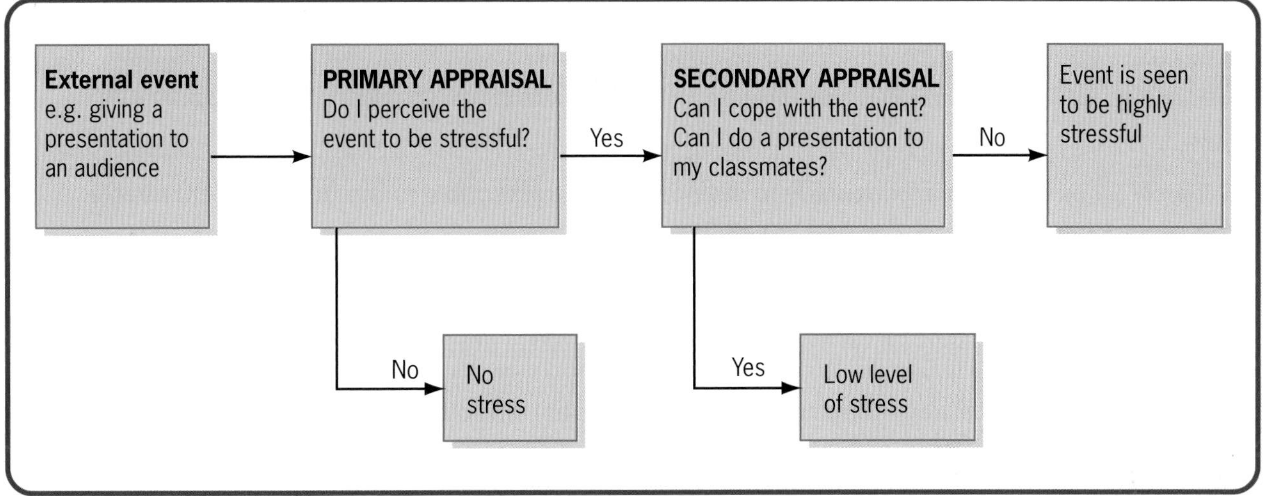

Figure 6.2 *The transactional model of stress, where both the situation and the person's ability to cope with the situation are appraised.*

Next a *secondary appraisal* takes place, in which the person decides how well they can cope with the event. If the person feels unable to cope with the stressful event then it is likely to cause the person to be highly stressed.

Stress may also have a negative effect on an existing medical condition that a person has. A stressed person will make high demands on our health care system and the resources that it offers. Stress both causes ill health and causes a person to worry about their health. Minor ailments may be blown up out of all proportion for the stressed person and may evoke little sympathy from others because they are seen as minor and not things to worry about.

In what follows we will look at both stress and illness, and how stress may be effectively managed.

6.2 Stress and illness

Stress is known to be linked to illness and ill health. For example, high blood pressure, or hypertension, is more commonly found in people who have jobs which are known to be highly stressful (for example, air traffic controllers; Cobb and Rose, 1973) than in people with low-stress jobs (such as being a nun in a convent). People who experience a lot of stress from the style of life they lead (high-pressure job, competitive approach to relationships, etc.) are likely to have a much increased risk of coronary heart disease (Kimvaki *et al.*, 2002).

From the experiment on the following page you will note that some participants scored on the questionnaire as being stressed but did not catch a cold, whilst others who were not regarded as stressed did catch a cold. This relates to the general observation that what appear to be the same environmental stressors may lead to illness in one person but not another person. One explanation for this comes from the diathesis-stress model (see Chapter 5 on schizophrenia for a fuller explanation). This model states that a person's biological or genetic disposition needs to be taken into account as well as their psychological reaction to a situation. In the Cohen experiment people not stressed and who caught a cold may have a greater biological predisposition to catching a cold. This may apply to stress-related illnesses, such as hypertension and coronary heart disease, and other illnesses associated with stress, including psychological disorders such as schizophrenia.

Links between stress and illness have also been studied in the context of cancer, diabetes and how quickly somebody recovers from a surgical operation. Stress may also affect the diet of people. For example, people who are highly stressed have been found to eat a higher-fat diet, eat less fruit and vegetables and consume more alcohol (Ng and Jeffery, 2003). This pattern of poor diet and high alcohol consumption is known to cause illness.

Psychologists have made a distinction between chronic and acute stress (Johnston, 2002) in attempting to understand how stress may cause illness. Chronic stress is where the person is continually stressed over a long

STUDY

Aim

Cohen *et al.* (1991) conducted a study to determine how susceptible to the common cold people who were stressed and not stressed would be.

Method

Participants were recruited for an experiment and given nasal drops. For half the participants the nasal drops contained a common cold virus. For the other half the drops were a placebo solution of water. Before the drops were administered each participant completed a questionnaire designed to measure their level of stress.

Results

Forty-seven per cent of participants who were given nasal drops containing the common cold and were found to be stressed developed a cold. In contrast, just 27% given the common cold virus and found to be low in stress developed the common cold.

Conclusion

High levels of stress are likely to make a person more susceptible to catching an illness such as the common cold. People with low stress levels are less likely to catch a common illness from other people.

period. Acute stress is where a stressor appears for a short period – for example, intense exercise or a sudden shock or traumatic event (death of a loved one). Johnston sees chronic and acute stress as interrelated. Someone who is chronically stressed may be even more susceptible to being ill when an acute stressor suddenly comes along. Chronic stress has an adverse effect on a number of bodily systems, including the autonomic system. We will now look at the role of biological systems, including the autonomic nervous system, in stress.

6.2.1 Biological systems and stress

Stress results in numerous physiological changes to the body. The overall reaction of the body to stress is determined by the central nervous system. However, the two main biological systems that change when a person is stressed are the *autonomic nervous system* and the *endocrine system*.

- The **autonomic nervous system** is made up of the *sympathetic* and *parasympathetic nervous systems*. It is the sympathetic system that responds to stress by preparing the body for flight or fight. The parasympathetic system returns the body to normal when the stress has been removed or lessened.
- The **endocrine system** releases hormones, particularly catecholamines and corticosteroids, in response to stress. Change in hormone levels may lead to illnesses such as hypertension, lowering of the effectiveness of the immune system and, more controversially, cancer.

Later in this section we will look at each of these biological systems and how both respond to and mediate stress. It will help if you read Section 9.3 of Chapter 9 before proceeding further.

People differ in their physiological response to stress. The physiological changes that result from stress are called *stress reactivity*. Some people are more reactive to stress than others. High stress reactivity is shown by sweating, raised blood pressure and raised heart rate.

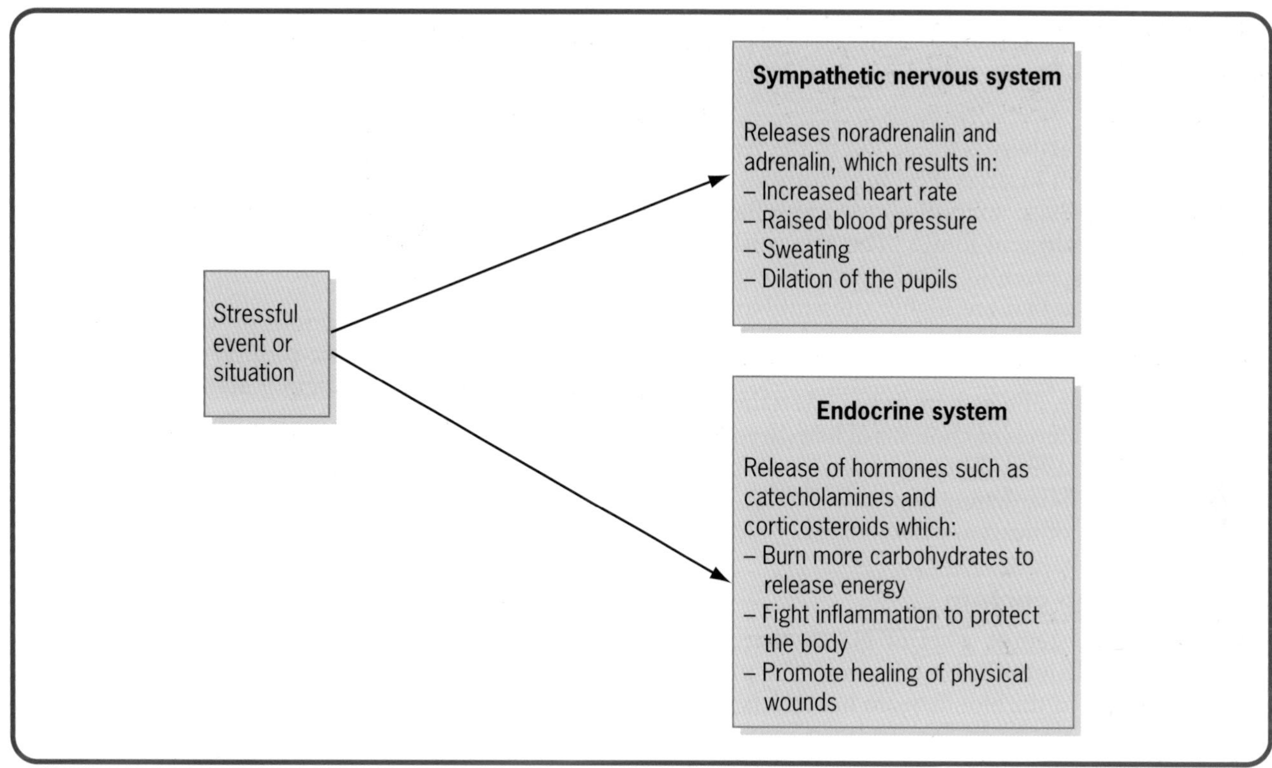

Figure 6.3 *Summary of the key effects of stress on the autonomic (sympathetic) nervous system and the endocrine system.*

Low stress reactivity does not result in these physiological changes, or the changes are only minimal. Whilst stress reactivity may vary between people on a physiological level, the psychological response may not vary between people. Stress reactivity is seen as genetic in origin. There is also some evidence that men show more high stress reactivity than women (Stoney *et al.*, 1990).

Once the stress has passed, the body attempts to recover to its normal levels of physiological functioning. This varies both between people, where some recover faster than others, and over the lifespan of a person. With the latter, an individual may recover from stress faster when young than when older.

The autonomic nervous system

The sympathetic and parasympathetic nervous systems are often seen as working in opposition to each other. For example, the sympathetic nervous system increases heart rate when the person is faced with a stressful situation. The parasympathetic system helps return the body to normal by reducing heart rate when the stressor is no longer present. The physiologist Walter Cannon first described the action of the sympathetic nervous system as a response to stress in preparing the person for **fight or flight**. If the stressor only lasts a short while, the parasympathetic nervous system returns physiological functions to normal. However, when the stressor lasts for a long time – for example, many months – the body is in a state of perpetual arousal in its readiness for fight or flight. This perpetual state of arousal of bodily functions resulting from the action of the sympathetic nervous system can have extremely negative effects on the physical and mental health of the individual. Selye (1976) proposed the general adaptation syndrome to understand the stages that the body goes through under prolonged or very intense stress (see Chapter 9 for more detail).

The sympathetic nervous system affects cardiovascular activity (network of organs that circulates blood to supply oxygen etc. to the body) by:

- increasing heartbeat
- constricting blood vessels

- allowing the lungs to take in more air
- preparing muscles for action by increasing blood flow to them.

Cardiovascular reactivity is the action of the sympathetic nervous system to stress. Prolonged cardiovascular reactivity in response to prolonged stress has been shown to cause physical illness. The typical illnesses that occur are hypertension and stroke (Dougall and Baum, 2001). Jobs that are highly stressful have been linked to high blood pressure and enlarged hearts (Schnall *et al.*, 1990). The composition of blood has been found to be affected by stress. Certain blood platelets and high levels of cholesterol have been found (Patterson *et al.*, 1995). These changes contribute to the narrowing and hardening of arteries, which in turn increases the risk of heart attack or stroke.

The endocrine system

The endocrine system is a set of glands that secrete hormones directly into the bloodstream. The presence of the hormones in the bloodstream has effects on different organs in the body. In stressful situations the endocrine system and the sympathetic nervous system work together to prepare the body to respond to the stressor. For example, both release the hormones epinephrine (adrenalin) and norepinephrine (noradrenalin). Whilst the parasympathetic nervous system quickly returns the body to normal, the body takes longer to recover from the release of hormones by the endocrine system. This explains why you feel uptight and nervous for a long time, a number of hours maybe, after the stressor has gone away.

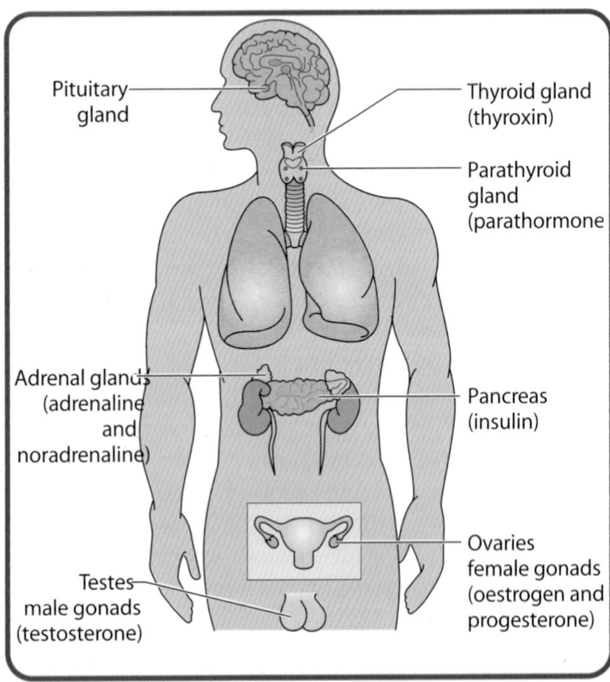

Figure 6.4 *The major glands of the endocrine system.*

The endocrine system responds to stress through what is called the **hypothalamic-pituitary-andrenocortical system,** or HPAC. This system is activated by messages from the central nervous system to the hypothalamus (a small organ in the centre of the brain – see Chapter 2 of *AQA(B) Psychology for AS* by Pennington and McLoughlin, 2008). When activated in response to stress the hypothalamus secretes corticosteroids. These are steroid hormones which fight inflammation in the body, promote healing and draw on body resources to supply more energy. The HPAC system responds more slowly to stress than the action of the endocrine system identified above (release of epinephrine and norepinephrine).

Corticosteriods have been found to impair the functioning of the immune system. Lowering the effectiveness of the immune system exposes the person to an increased risk of picking up infections (colds, influenza and other infectious diseases) from other people. Lowering of the immune system may expose the person to an increased risk of developing a chronic condition such as cancer (Vedhara *et al.*, 1999).

The endocrine system also has a way of countering the effects of corticosteroids. Corticosteroids may be damaging to the body if these hormones are present at high levels in the body for a prolonged period of time. The adrenal gland can stop the response of the body to stress by releasing another hormone called *cortisol*. One effect of cortisol is to instruct the hypothalamus and pituitary gland to stop secreting corticosteroids into the bloodstream. The presence of too much cortisol over a prolonged period of time may also lead to ill health. For example, research has found that high levels of cortisol can lead to hypertension and a lowering of the body's ability to ward off infections.

The endocrine system can, therefore, be seen both to help the body respond to stress and to mediate the physiological effects of stress through the release of the hormone cortisol.

STUDY

Aim

Willis *et al.* (1987) conducted a longitudinal study with elderly people to study the process of ageing. As part of the study they investigated how stress affected the level of cortisol in the body.

Method

Healthy elderly males and females were recruited for a longitudinal study. They were asked to contact the researchers should a crisis occur in their life. Fifteen elderly people contacted the researchers, reporting a crisis such as death of a loved one or diagnosis of serious illness. The level of cortisol on their bodies was measured both during the crisis and after it had passed.

Results

Levels of cortisol rose during the crisis and fell when it had passed.

Conclusions

The researchers assumed that a crisis caused the participants to be highly stressed at the time it happened, with stress reducing as the crisis passed. High stress, therefore, was found to result in high levels of cortisol in the body. The level of cortisol returned to normal when the stress ceased.

Evaluation

- The response to and mediation to stress of the autonomic nervous system and the endocrine system need to be considered alongside the psychological response of the person. The psychological response can affect the physiological response and vice versa.
- An emerging area of stress research is psychoneuroimmunology. This recognises the interaction between the body and the mind. The research investigates both the nervous system and the immune system and how they interact with mental (psychological) processes and experience.
- Low levels or short periods of stress may be of benefit to the individual. This is because the cardiovascular system and the respiratory system receive exercise from the physiological stress response. Positive stress is known as eustress.

6.2.2 Measuring stress

Attempts to obtain objective, valid and reliable measures of stress have not proved easy to achieve for psychologists. What is regarded as stressful varies from person to person. Also, the experience of stress differs from person to person. Given this, it is not surprising that psychologists use a range of different measurement approaches in their attempt to measure stress. The main methods used to measure stress are:

- Physiological measures that measure some aspect of bodily activity. If valid and accurate, these are likely to be the most objective.
- Behavioural measures which involve seeing how well a person performs at a given task or measures some

aspect of everyday behaviour, such as speed at which a person talks.

- Self-report measures which usually involve completion of a questionnaire or some other kind of self-report on how a person thinks and feels.

We will look at each of these approaches to measuring stress in turn.

Physiological measures

Stress affects many different systems of the body. Potentially, changes in bodily functions offer an objective way to measure stress. Blood and urine samples can be analysed to assess the levels of hormones in the body that are associated with stress. There are two main types of hormones here; these are corticosteroids and catecholamines (which include epinephrine and norepinephrine). These are secreted by the adrenal glands. We have seen above how stress affects the autonomic nervous system and the levels of hormones associated with stress.

Measures of bodily activity through more mechanical means include measuring blood pressure (high when stressed), heart rate (fast when stressed), rate of breathing (fast and shallow when stressed) and galvanic skin responses (GSR). These measures are often combined and all measured at the same time through the use of a *polygraph*.

The GSR measures the skin's resistance to electricity. A person who is stressed is likely to perspire. This has the effect of increasing the skin's ability to conduct electricity. A person who is highly stressed will, therefore, show increased electrical conductivity of their skin compared to when not stressed, or in comparison to other people who are not stressed. For this measure to be useful, it is best to obtain GSR measures from the same person when he or she is both stressed and not stressed.

Figure 6.5 *The polygraph measures a number of different body activities, such as blood pressure, heart rate and galvanic skin response. It may provide objective measures of the level of stress a person is experiencing.*

The polygraph measures a number of body activities. To obtain accurate and reliable measures, the person is asked to sit quietly and relax for a short period, usually 30 minutes, before any measures are taken. This allows a baseline to be established against the measures to be taken. An experiment to measure stress levels would then present something stressful to the person – for example, a difficult problem to solve or watching a distressing film clip. The polygraph would then produce measures in the person's stressed state and allow comparison of changes from the baseline in the relaxed state.

Evaluation

- Physiological measures offer the prospect of being objective. However, the body becomes aroused for a variety of reasons and it may not be possible to link any particular event with specific physiological changes.
- Physiological measures require expensive equipment, a high level of technical training to use the equipment, and the readings produced are not easy to interpret.
- Subjecting somebody to such measures, and wiring them up to a polygraph, may in itself be stressful for the person. This could then affect measures instead of the experimental conditions themselves.
- Physiological measures are affected by gender, body weight, prior activity and prior intake of substances such as caffeine or alcohol.

Behavioural measures

Behavioural or performance measures also offer the potential for objective measurement of stress. These measures fall into two main types, as follows:

(a) Measures of behaviours occurring naturally in everyday life – for example, rate, tone and loudness of speech, aggressive behaviours, behaving in a helpless or confused manner.

(b) Performance measures taken in more controlled, laboratory conditions where a person is presented with a task and behavioural measures associated with performing the task are taken – for example, performing a task under conditions of very loud noise, in a crowd of people, or in a very hot or very cold room.

Stress can affect a person's behaviour in a number of ways. For example, a person may become more aggressive, which may be manifested in both the way the person speaks and their body behaviour (body language) to others. If stress is prolonged the individual may experience a 'breakdown', which may involve the need for medical treatment and hospitalisation. Behavioural measures of speech, for example, require that the psychologist has information about the speech of the person when not stressed. This is so that it can be compared to speech behaviour of the person when in a stressed state. With respect to speech, measures not only of the rate of speech and tone of voice may be taken, but also the number of speech errors that a person makes. Speech errors include 'ums' and 'ahs' as well as using inappropriate words.

Performance measures allow for controlled laboratory experiments to be conducted so that the effect of stress on behaviour can be carefully measured. Typical stressors used in laboratory experiments include loud noise (for example, very loud rap music or white noise), being in a confined space with other people, administering electric shocks and extreme room temperature (hot or cold).

Generally, it is thought that stress has a negative impact on performance. However, certain levels of stress, as long as the level is not too high, can have a positive effect and improve performance.

STUDY

Aim

Glass and Singer (1972) conducted an experiment to investigate the effect of noise on a cognitive task.

Method

Students were recruited to an experiment in which they had to attempt to solve a number of problems using paper and pencil. Half the participants were exposed to loud, random bursts of noise over a 25-minute period. The other half of the participants formed the control group and worked in quiet conditions. At the end of the 25-minute period, both groups were given a number of cognitive tasks to perform. These included proofreading an article and solving difficult problems.

Results

Students who worked in quiet conditions prior to doing the cognitive tasks performed the task more accurately and solved more of the difficult problems than the group who worked in noisy conditions.

Conclusions

Environmental noise reduced the speed and accuracy with which people were able to perform cognitive tasks. This indicates that stress resulting from working in difficult conditions adversely affects performance.

Evaluation

- To compare the effect of stress on the behaviour of a person requires measures of the behaviours both when the person is stressed and when the person is not stressed. This may not always be possible to obtain since it is often not known in advance whether or not a person will become stressed.
- Performance measures on the effects of stress induced in the laboratory provide objective behavioural measures. However, the stress in the laboratory is often short-term and artificial.
- Comparing the behaviours of different people when they are stressed may result in different measures of the same behaviour because different people react to stress in different ways. For example, with speech, one person may talk more rapidly and another person may use more aggressive language.
- Behavioural measures do offer the potential for obtaining reliable and objective measures of stress, but it is not the level of stress itself that is being measured but the consequences of stress for behaviour.

Self-report measures

Psychologists have developed a wide range of self-report techniques to measure both acute and chronic stress. Self-report measures fall into two broad categories:

(a) Self-report measures that ask people to indicate how they think, feel and behave in relation to their self-perceived stress levels.

(b) Self-report measures that ask a person to identify stressful events in their life at any one time. These self-reported stressful events are then compared to an established scale of stressful events to determine level of stress of the person.

One of the earliest and most widely used self-report measures is that of Holmes and Rahe (1967). This is a questionnaire that asks people to report on significant events in their life, such as death of someone close, loss of employment, moving house.

Figure 6.6 identifies the main stressful events in our lives and ranks them, with a score, according to the level of stress the event typically causes for a person. So, for example, if you have just moved house, lost your job and got divorced, you would be expected to be very highly stressed indeed!

Holmes and Rahe (1967) gave a score to these events by first asking a large number of people to rate, on a 100-point scale, how difficult they thought it would be to adjust to each of the different life events. It was assumed that the more difficult it is thought to adjust to a life event, the more stressful it will be for a person. Responses were averaged to arrive at a scale of increasingly stressful life events.

Life event	Value
Death of spouse	100
Divorce	73
Marital separation	65
Death of close family member	63
Personal injury or illness	53
Marriage	50
Loss of job	47
Retirement	45
Sex difficulties	39

Figure 6.6 *List of life stressors and scores for each, with a high value indicating a more stressful event. Adapted from Holmes and Rahe (1967).*

Figure 6.7 *Stressful life events can accumulate to make someone highly stressed!*

Evaluation

- The Holmes and Rahe scale has been criticised because it made no attempt to account for differences between people, and took no account of a person's age, gender and ability to cope with stress (hardiness).
- The additive nature of the points scale implies that two less stressful events (such as changing eating habits and moving to a smaller house) are the same in terms of stress as one major event. Such a quantitative approach oversimplifies matters.
- The scale does not acknowledge that one event can be both positive and stressful for the individual at the same time. For example, going on holiday is supposed to be relaxing and to take you away from everyday hassles; however, it can also be stressful. For example, there may be delays at the airport, the hotel may not be finished or the weather may be poor.

One of the most commonly used self-report measures to assess a person's perceived level of stress is the Perceived Stress Scale (PSS) developed by Cohen *et al.* (1983). This asks questions such as, 'In the past month how often have you been upset by something that has happened unexpectedly?' Peacock and Wong (1990) developed the Stress Appraisal Measure (SAM), which asks people to think of a stressful event in their life or think of a potential stressful event and then rate it against a number of questions on a five-point scale. For example:

Event: failing your Psychology A level examination

Questions: Does this situation create tension in me?
Does this situation make me feel anxious?
Does this situation have serious implications for me?
Will I be able to overcome the problem?

The SAM measures stress or likely future stress from an event by giving scores on three different scales: potential for harm or loss (threat), challenge from the situation, and perceived importance of the event for the person (centrality). These measures allow for a programme of support to be developed for the person.

Kanner *et al.* (1981) developed a **hassles scale.** This scale attempts to measure the stress we associate with everyday, small hassles in life. Whilst each may be minor in terms of stress, a combination of minor hassles may be cumulative and create a high level of stress.

Evaluation

- Self-report measures of perceived stress rely on the person having insight into the stressors operating on them in their daily lives. This insight may not always be present, since people do often report after recovering from being highly stressed just what it was that was causing it.
- Self-report measures attempt to quantify what people think and feel, so comparison of numbers or scales may be problematic.
- Self-report measures are cheap and easy to administer and require much less training for the administrator than physiological measures.
- Self-report measures tell us what the person may be experiencing, but do not give an accurate assessment of what is going on within the person's body.

General comments

The three different approaches to measuring stress that we have considered above each have strengths and weaknesses. Where possible, a combination of two or all three measures may provide the best measure of the stress a person is under and also help with devising a support programme to help the person manage their stress.

6.2.3 The role of personal variables in mediating stress

A number of psychological characteristics or personality factors have been found to mediate or reduce stress. The most important personality factors are Type A, B and C behaviours, locus of control and hardiness. Interpersonal factors, such as social support, can also mediate stress. We will look at this later in the chapter.

Type A, B and C behaviours

Friedman and Rosenman (1974) produced evidence to show that people with a certain type of personality are more likely to experience stress than other personality types. This they called the **Type A personality**, which they said was shown in three types of behaviour:

- *Competitive achievement orientation*. Type A people are very competitive, self-critical and focused on achieving goals and targets. When achieving goals they seem not to be satisfied and do not show joy or happiness.
- *Time urgency*. Everything has to be done as soon as possible, and people working with a Type A person feel that life is a constant race against the clock. Type A people are impatient, try to do many things at the same time and set deadlines that are difficult to achieve.
- *Anger and hostility*. Type A people quickly become angry and show hostility to other people. At times,

STUDY

Aim

Friedman and Rosenman (1959) conducted an investigation to see whether or not there is a link between Type A behaviours and coronary heart disease. Previous research had suggested that high levels of stress and competitiveness were related to heart disease.

Method

Two groups of men were interviewed about their work patterns, exercise, diet, alcohol consumption and sleep patterns. Measures of their cardiovascular function were also taken; these included cholesterol levels and electrocardiogram readings of the heart. Group 1 consisted of men identified by their work colleagues as showing Type A behaviours. Group 2 consisted of men matched with Group A for physical characteristics but identified by their colleagues as relaxed and easygoing (Type B behaviours).

Results

Men in Group 1 were judged to be five times more likely than men in Group 2 to be at risk of developing heart disease. Group 1 were found to work longer hours, be more active generally and have a family history of heart disease.

Conclusions

Men displaying Type A behaviour patterns are more at risk of developing heart disease than men with Type B behaviour patterns. It was also found that Type A behaviours may be inherited.

this may be expressed to another person or may not expressed openly.

In contrast, the **Type B personality** has the opposite set of personality characteristics and behaviours, making the person generally more easygoing. The Type B personality consists of the following behaviours:

- low level of competitiveness
- low level of time urgency
- friendly and positive approach to people.

Friedman and Rosenman (1959) began their research with the Type A personality by suggesting that there was a link with coronary heart disease (heart attacks). Type A people, they suggested, were more likely to suffer coronary disease than Type B personality types. They made the further link between high levels of stress (especially prolonged periods of stress) and heart problems. Recent research has focused on the anger and hostility component of the Type A personality and coronary heart disease (Kop and Krantz, 1997).

There has been extensive research into the relationship between Type A behaviour, stress and stress-related illness. Type A people show a stronger physiological response or 'reactivity' to stress. This involves increased blood pressure, increased heart rate and increased catecholamine levels, all of which are related to risk for heart disease. Krantz *et al.* (1982) found that Type A people prescribed beta blockers showed less of the typical behaviours compared to Type A people not on this drug.

More recently, psychologists have identified **Type C behaviours** and personality type. This has been related to individuals who might be more at risk of developing cancer. The behaviours associated with Type C are:

- passive
- uncomplaining
- compliant.

Denial of emotions and emotional reactions is thought to underly these behaviours (Holland and Lewis, 1996). The suggestion here is that suppressing emotions may itself be stressful for the person and so lead to being prone to illness. Links with Type C and depression have also been suggested (Cohen and Herbert, 1996). However, research has not found a strong link between Type C behaviours and cancer. The present view is that the idea is worth researching more, but a firm conclusion has yet to be reached.

Evaluation

- The most common method to measure Type A behaviour has been through a structured interview.
  Here, predetermined questions are asked about behaviours and emotions to do with competitiveness, impatience and hostility. At the same time, the style of interaction of the person with the interviewer is assessed and Type A behaviours identified in this way also. Assessment looks at interruptions, challenges, signs of impatience and so on from the person. Having two approaches to assess Type A behaviour is a strength since it allows comparison of findings with each approach. The weakness is that it is time-consuming and relies on using highly trained interviewers and then ratings of the behaviours by a number of other people.
- Recent research has focused on hostility rather than the other two Type A behavioural components. Hostility and stress reactivity are now thought to be closely linked.
- There is a danger that Type B and Type C behaviours and personality types may have a degree of overlap. Clear separation of each is needed for each to be valid on its own.

Locus of control

The effect of perceived control on stress and illness has been extensively investigated. Rotter (1966) introduced the idea of **locus of control.** This is the extent to which an individual thinks and feels that they are able to control what happens to them. Locus of control can be internal or external:

(a) *Internal locus of control* is where the person believes they are able to control what happens to them and to control success in their life.

(b) *External locus of control* is where the person believes that they have no or little control over what happens to them and regards success as due to external, uncontrollable events.

The internal–external locus of control is on a scale from very high internal control to very high external control. At the extreme of external control, the person may feel helpless, which may result in the person feeling highly stressed and lead to illness such as depression. A person who is at the extreme of internal locus of control may also experience stress, since it is not possible or realistic to think that you can control everything in your life and control what other people do.

One area of intensive research on locus of control has been to do with stress and illness at work. People who have a high internal locus of control will attempt to be highly organised at work, control what other people do, and want other people to do things their way. This may result in the person becoming stressed since it is not possible to control work so much and other people want to do things in the ways they think are best and do not like to be controlled by other people.

STUDY

Aim

Frankenhauser (1975) investigated control and stress in workers at a sawmill factory. The work was boring and repetitive where the same routines were repeated again and again.

Method

A number of physiological measures of the sawmill workers were taken. These included levels of catecholamines (associated with stress) and blood pressure. Self-report measures of headaches and stomach disorders were also recorded.

Results

It was found that these workers had high levels of catecholamines and high blood pressure. The workers also reported frequent headaches and stomach disorders.

Conclusions

The sawmill workers did not have any say in the work they had to do and hence felt that the locus of control was totally external. The findings indicated that the workers were very stressed as a result of their dull and monotonous work.

Evaluation

- People who are high on internal control or high in the perception of external locus of control are likely to become stressed. A balanced perception of locus of control leads to low stress levels.
- High internal locus of control (but not at an extreme) is associated with people being more fit than those with external control. People who perceive themselves to be in control cope better with illness and experience less mental disorder.
- At the extreme, internal control can lead to obsessive-compulsive behaviours and such people are labelled as 'control freaks'. They also tend to experience higher levels of guilt and shame, which may be maladaptive for them.
- The most commonly used method to assess internal or external locus of control is the questionnaire. Self-report measures may be misleading. Actual behaviour needs to be assessed as well.

Hardiness

The personality characteristic of **hardiness** was first put forward by Kobasa (1979) to describe a set of traits that seems to protect or help a person cope with stress. Kobasa identified three main traits of hardiness that seem to buffer or protect the person from stress:

(a) **Commitment**: Commitment to family, job and career, the community lived in and other significant groups of people in their lives.

(b) **Challenges**: Such people view everyday life as a series of challenges and opportunities, rather than threats and ways of failing.

(c) **Control**: Such people feel that they have a sense of control over their lives and that they can make important decisions in their lives rather than other people making such decisions for them.

Hardiness does seem to affect how people view things. For example, hardy people may cope with stress better because they see themselves leading a challenging life and actively seek out challenges. In a sense, such people seem to thrive on continual challenge as long as they feel in control. Such people also see stressful situations or events in a positive way and may generally be optimistic in their outlook on life. Being optimistic may help to feel in control of things. Closely related to the concept of hardiness is that of resilience and stamina.

STUDY

Aim

Kobasa *et al.* (1982) investigated how hardiness affected managers to deal with stress in the workplace.

Method

Six hundred and seventy middle and senior managers were assessed as either high or low level for the personality factor of hardiness. Stress at work was assessed using the Social Readjustment Rating Scale. The latter assesses stress over a range of work events.

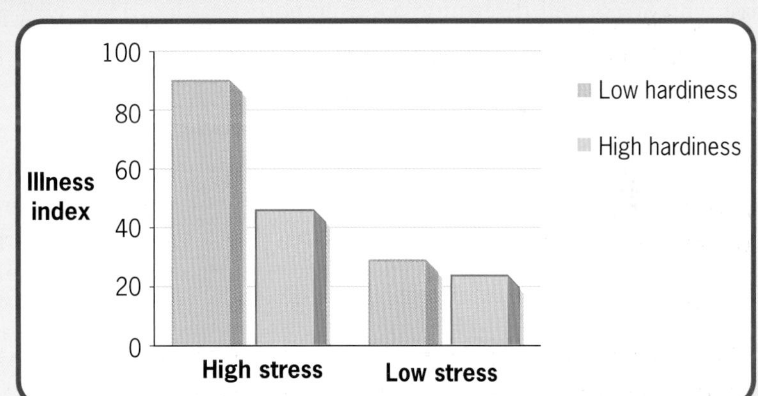

Figure 6.8 *People high in hardiness under stress show lower levels of illness than people low in hardiness under stress (adapted from Kobasa* et al., *1982).*

Results

As can be seen from Figure 6.8, managers who scored high in hardiness and high in stress experienced less illness than managers who scored low in hardiness and high in stress. Level of hardiness with people who were low in stress did not show high illness levels.

Conclusions

The personality characteristic of hardiness appears to help a person cope with stress, with the result that illness levels are low compared to people who are not hardy.

Evaluation

- Research has suggested that hardiness applies more to men than women and that this personality characteristic may reflect more of a male approach to work.
- Hardiness does not seem to protect a person from 'burnout' in jobs that are very demanding and continually stressful – for example, social workers and nurses working with cancer patients (Rowe, 1997).
- Research on hardiness has placed an over-reliance on self-report questionnaires both for measuring this personality factor and for assessing levels of stress and ill-health. More behavioural and objective measures are needed.

6.3 Stress management

At one time or another we all experience some level of stress in our lives. How well we are able to manage or **cope** with stress will determine good or poor health. People who are able to manage or cope with stress well experience less ill health and adjust and adapt well to the demands of everyday life. Good stress management, resulting in good adjustment to changes in our life, will have a positive impact upon our work (career), family, friendships and intimate relationships.

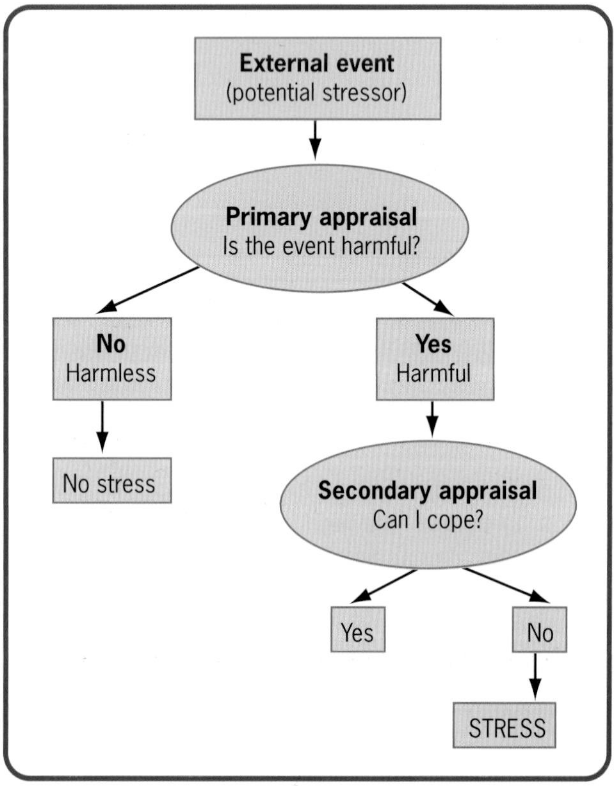

Figure 6.9 *Two-stage stress appraisal process developed by Lazarus (1999).*

How well a person manages stress depends on many factors. Coping with stress may be described as 'how well a person can manage the discrepancy between the demands of the situation and the resources the person thinks they have to deal with the situation'. If the demands of the situation are high and potentially stressful, and the person does not think they have the resources (personal ability, skills, social support, etc.) to cope, then the person will be stressed, and will remain stressed until something changes (situation or person). Lazarus (1999) developed a two-stage model where stress is appraised in two stages. This is shown in Figure 6.9.

The first appraisal carried out is called *primary appraisal*. Here the event external to the person is perceived as either harmful (potentially stressful) or harmless. *Secondary appraisal* is where the person judges whether or not they have the ability (personal resources) to deal with the event. This is often called **self-efficacy** by psychologists and is a very important area of research in health psychology. When an event is perceived to be harmful and the person thinks they are unable to cope with it, the person will become stressed. If the external event can be changed or avoided then the stress will reduce for the person. However, all too often the event cannot be changed and the person has to find ways to cope with the situation and manage their stress.

Lazarus distinguishes between three types of stress as follows:

(a) *Loss.* This is when a person loses, for example, a loved one or their job, or a relationship breaks down and ends.

(b) *Threat.* This is when the person thinks that something in the environment will cause harm, either physically or psychologically.

(c) *Challenge.* This is where there is an opportunity presented to the person but with it comes change, uncertainty and very hard work.

From these three types you can see that challenge has both positive and negative aspects, showing that stress is not always negative.

In what follows we will look at different approaches to helping people manage stress and ways in which people help themselves.

6.3.1 Problem-focused and emotion-focused strategies

Lazarus (1999) suggested that strategies for coping with stress may serve one or both of two main functions for the person.

1 *Problem-focused.* Coping by attempting to change the problem or event causing the stress.

2 *Emotion-focused.* Coping by the person dealing with their emotional reaction to stress

Effective coping has two beneficial effects for the individual. First, it reduces the intensity and duration of the stressor. Second, it reduces the risk that stress will lead to mental and/or physical illness.

Skinner *et al.* (2003) identified over 30 different coping strategies that people use and classified them into

STUDY

Aim

Billings and Moos (1981) conducted a study to find out the factors which cause a person to use either a problem-focused or emotion-focused strategy to cope with stress.

Method

Two hundred married couples completed a questionnaire asking them about how they coped with a recent crisis in their life. They were asked, for example, about use of friends, past experience.

Results

Generally, both husbands and wives more often used problem-focused instead of emotion-focused strategies. However, women did use emotion-focused to a greater extent than problem-focused compared to men. All participants used emotion-focused strategies when coping with personal loss such as bereavement.

Conclusion

Use of the two strategies varies according to gender of the person and the type of stressful event.

Emotion-focused coping strategies	Problem-focused coping strategies
Avoidance Denial Distraction Hiding feelings Humour Physical exercise Praying Worry Wishful thinking	Seeking assistance from others Confrontive assertion Direct action Information seeking Logical analysis Problem solving

Figure 6.10 *Examples of emotion-focused and problem-focused coping strategies that people commonly use to deal with stress (adapted from Skinner* et al., *2003).*

problem-focused, emotion-focused and both strategies of coping styles. Some of these are listed in Figure 6.10.

Below we describe in more detail two of each type of coping category. The most important example of a strategy that serves both problem-focused and emotion-focused function is that of **social support.** This is considered in more detail in the next section of this chapter.

(a) **Problem-focused strategies**
Planful problem solving: This concerns developing and implementing plans to deal with the event. This may seem an obvious approach to take. However, many people do not do this and often seek to avoid or not recognise the problem in the first place. Planning means that you acknowledge and understand the stressful event.

Confronting: This involves tackling the problem 'head-on'. If a bank is threatening to reclaim a person's house for non-payment of the mortgage, it is best to go and talk to the bank rather than thinking the problem will go away. Confronting is not to be confused with *confrontational.* The latter is an aggressive response, the former a problem-solving response.

(b) **Emotion-focused strategies**
Positive appraisal: This is where the person tries to identify positive aspects from the negative stressful situation. This is often difficult since the event may seem totally negative. For example, a person whose husband or wife dies may not see anything positive. However, the person may be able to identify something they could now do which they were unable to do when the other person was alive.

Accepting responsibility: People often find it a relief to move from denial of a problem to accepting that there is a problem and that other people are not going to sort it out for you. However, this is only a successful strategy when it is appropriate for the person to accept responsibility. It is counterproductive if the person is accepting responsibility for another person's problem.

Evaluation

- It is important to take the nature of the stressor into account. Different stressors may require different strategies for coping to be successful. Confronting and accepting responsibility are most successful in situations where the person is able to do something about the stressful situation.
- One behavioural response to stress may involve more than one coping strategy. For example, reading up about an illness may be seen as an example of confronting the problem. However, becoming too technically knowledgeable may result in the person avoiding the real impact of the illness due to *over-intellectualisation*. This helps the person distance themselves emotionally from the illness.
- Much of the research on coping strategies has sought to identify different types of problem-focused and emotion-focused strategies. More research is needed on the effectiveness of different strategies and the best combination of strategies for different types of stress.

6.3.2 Defence mechanisms

The psychodynamic approach (see Chapter 13), especially Freudian theory, claims that the ego uses a number of coping mechanisms to deal with stress and conflict called **defence mechanisms.** These operate at an unconscious level within the mind of the person. Generally, defence mechanisms work by defending the person against the full force of reality by distorting or denying what is going on in the real world. Figure 6.11 identifies and describes the most common defence mechanisms used in response to stress.

Defence mechanism	Description	Example
Denial	Refusing to acknowledge a stressful, unpleasant event is happening.	Not thinking about a close friend who has cancer.
Regression	The person responds to stress by regressing or returning to a childhood period, which gives them comfort.	Having a tantrum outburst.
Rationalisation	Also known as intellectualisation. The emotional feelings are replaced with logical analysis and a desire to know all about the problem, especially knowledge of technical/medical details.	Reading medical textbooks about a disorder.
Repression	Person unconsciously pushes memory of an unpleasant stressful event from conscious awareness.	Forgetting about an argument with friend that was very upsetting at the time.
Projection	The problem is projected or attributed to belong to another person. This means that the person does not think the problem is his or hers and so does not attempt to deal with it.	Focusing on another person's alcohol problem instead of one's own.

Figure 6.11 *Defence mechanisms commonly used to cope with stress.*

Psychologists have researched how people react to and cope with the initial diagnosis of having a life-threatening illness, such as cancer. Shontz (1975) suggested that people typically go through three stages following diagnosis of a life-threatening and chronic illness. These are:

1 **Shock**: The person is stunned and bewildered.

2 **Encounter reaction**: The person shows disorganised thinking, feelings of loss, grief, helplessness and despair.

3 **Retreat**: The person typically denies that he or she has a problem and retreats into themselves.

Use of denial in the retreat stage is seen as an emotion-focused strategy that helps the individual gradually to get used to the reality of their illness and its implications. Retreat, therefore, should be a temporary stage in the process of the individual adapting to changed circumstances. However, if denial continues for a long period it will not help the person cope with the stress of the diagnosis and the reality of the situation. This may result in the person not taking appropriate treatments and measures to deal with the illness. Intellectualisation and rationalisation may have the same negative effects if these defence mechanisms are used for too long a period.

Evaluation

- Defence mechanisms, such as denial, repression and rationalisation, can be seen as examples of emotion-focused strategies. Each of the defence mechanisms has the effect of reducing the intensity and strength of the emotional response to the stressor.
- The use of defence mechanisms when dealing with stress may be of value in the short-term and help the person adjust to the problem. However, longterm use will work against the individual and not assist in, for example, confronting the problem.
- Defence mechanisms are said to operate at an unconscious level in the mind. This makes them difficult to study scientifically and difficult to establish the effectiveness of each type of defence mechanism

6.3.3 Behavioural and cognitive techniques of stress management

There are very many different ways in which people can be helped to manage their stress. The two most successful and effective are *behavioural* and *cognitive* approaches.

- Behavioural approaches aim to change a person's behaviour to help reduce levels of stress.
- Cognitive approaches aim to change the way a person perceives and thinks about stressful situations and their ability to cope with stress.

A combination of behavioural and cognitive techniques is often the most successful and effective for the individual. Relaxation is an example of a combined technique. *Progressive muscle relaxation* is where the person focuses on different muscles in the body and tries to relax them. The technique involves systematically going round all the major body muscles, from foot to head, and relaxing each in turn (Sarafino, 2001). A combination of selecting different muscles and then mentally trying to relax them has been shown to be successful in reducing stress (Carlson and Hoyle, 1993). Physiological benefits have also been reported. These include benefits to the immune system and cardiovascular activity (Lucini *et al.*, 1997).

Biofeedback

Biofeedback is a technique for stress management which involves 'wiring up' a person to an instrument which measures physiological functions such as muscle activity, heart rate, blood pressure and skin temperature. The recordings of these physiological functions are fed back to the person. Information is provided to the person about what are the normal levels for each of these functions. Ideally, levels for each function should be obtained from the same person when they are not stressed; however, this is not always possible. The person receives either visual or auditory feedback about these functions. For example, feedback may be in the form of light or a tone. If the person's physiological function is not at a normal level – for example, heart rate or blood pressure is high, a tone will sound. The person is then helped by the psychologist to try to reduce their physiological function to a normal level. Biofeedback training first takes place in a laboratory and then the person uses the technique at home. Biofeedback machines can be readily purchased to help the person at home.

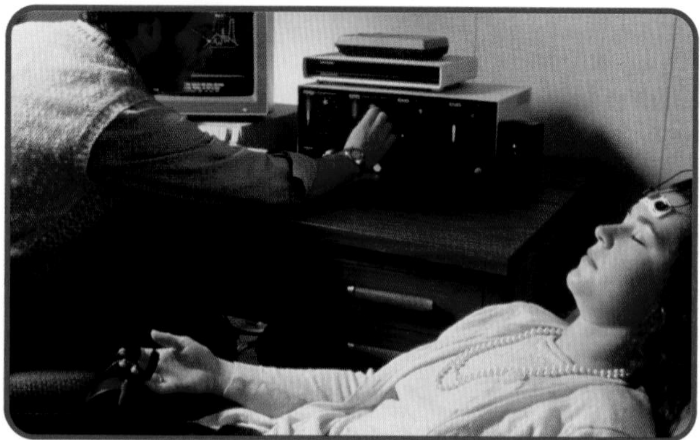

Figure 6.12 *Biofeedback is a technique for helping a person control physiological functions such as heart rate and blood pressure. It aids relaxation and has proved effective in the management of pain with certain disorders. Managing pain helps reduce stress for the individual.*

Thermal biofeedback is based on the idea that skin temperature is affected by stress. A highly stressed person typically shows lower skin temperature than a person who is not stressed.

Thermal biofeedback has been successfully used to help people with disorders such as Raynaud's disease (cardiovascular disease resulting in cold hands and feet due to poor circulation). It has also, as the study below shows, been used to help people who suffer from migraine and stress-related headaches.

STUDY

Aim

Scharff *et al.* (2002) conducted an experiment to evaluate the effectiveness of hand-warming biofeedback and stress management for children with migraine.

Method

Thirty-six children, with a mean age of 13 years, together with their mothers/fathers, were randomly assigned to one of three groups. Group 1 were trained in the use of thermal feedback from the hand to increase hand temperature. Group 2 were trained to cool their hand. Group 3 were the control group who were simply put on a waiting list.

Results

Children in the hand-warming group (Group 1) showed a greater reduction in their reported migraine than children in the other two groups. These improvements remained for up to 6 months in a follow-up study of the same children.

Conclusions

Migraine in children may be effectively treated with hand-warming biofeedback. This form of biofeedback training has long-lasting benefits for the individual.

Evaluation

- Research on the effectiveness of biofeedback in reducing stress levels is very mixed. It does seem to work for anxiety, hypertension and headaches (Gatchel *et al.,* 1989). However, this may be due to the technique of biofeedback resulting in general relaxation rather than the specific physiological function being controlled.
- Lehrer *et al.* (1994) reviewed numerous studies and concluded that biofeedback offers no advantage over other techniques such as simple relaxation. Other techniques are also cheaper for the person to use.
- The positive effects of biofeedback may result from the general relaxation that occurs, a placebo effect and suggestion rather than direct control of physiological function(s).
- A person typically learns the technique of biofeedback in a laboratory wired up to a monitoring device. In real life, stress occurs in situations that are not like this at all! This means that biofeedback techniques cannot be used easily when a stressful situation suddenly occurs.

Systematic desensitisation

Systematic desensitisation is a highly successful behavioural technique that has been widely used in the treatment of anxiety and phobic disorders (see Chapter 9 of *AQA(B) Psychology for AS* by Pennington and McLoughlin, 2008). This technique has also been successfully applied to stress. The idea is the same as with anxiety disorders. Treatment of stress using systematic desensitisation involves gradual exposure to the stressor. For example, if a person gets easily stressed by minor hassles in life (for example, waiting in a queue or sitting next to someone on a train who is speaking loudly into a mobile phone), exposure on a systematic basis to each minor hassle helps the person cope better with the hassle.

Wolpe (1958) was the originator and he said that the counter-conditioning of a calm response to replace a fear response in a stressful situation is a highly effective way to help a person manage stress. Systematic desensitisation uses a *stimulus hierarchy* to help the person deal with the situation which stresses them. A stimulus hierarchy is a graded sequence of approximations to the real situation. For example, suppose a person gets very stressed (fear, sweating, panic attacks) by going in a lift. Systematic desensitisation may use the following graded hierarchy to help the person cope and reduce their stress:

1 Think about going into a lift and the lift moving.

2 Look at a photograph of people in a lift.

3 The person imagines that they are in a lift with other people.

4 The person actually goes into a building with a lift and watches others using the lift.

5 The person arranges to enter a lift when there are no other people around, to try to stay calm when in the lift.

6 The person goes with another that they trust to use a lift.

7 The person uses a lift on their own.

STUDY

Aim

Morrow *et al.* (1992) investigated the effectiveness of systematic desensitisation on cancer patients for stress associated with chemotherapy treatment.

Method

Cancer patients were randomly assigned to a treatment group (given systematic desensitisation by nurses or doctors) or a control group that did not receive the systematic desensitisation. Both groups were assessed for the length of time each person felt nauseous following chemotherapy treatment.

Results

Those in the control group reported feeling nauseous for 15 hours longer on average than those in the treatment group.

Conclusion

Systematic desensitisation reduces a cancer patient's stress levels when anticipating chemotherapy and its side effects. This results in feeling nauseous for less time than those people who do not have systematic desensitisation.

Evaluation

- Systematic desensitisation has been shown by research evidence to be effective in helping people manage their level of stress. It works through a combination of both behavioural and cognitive techniques.
- The technique can be used when the person knows that particular situations will cause them stress. However, when a stressful situation is not expected and the person has to cope with it immediately, the technique cannot be easily used. This is especially the case if the stressful situation is unlikely to arise again.
- Systematic desensitisation works because it counter-conditions the person to feel calm instead of fearing an object or situation. Another explanation is that it works because it extinguishes the fear response.

Cognitive therapy

The use of cognitive therapy to help with stress management involves changing how a person thinks about the stressful situation and their own ability to cope with the stress. People do generally use their own self-taught techniques when faced with a stressful situation. For example, they may 'talk to themselves', by mentally telling themselves to keep calm, count to ten before reacting or think about something they associate with relaxation. Psychological techniques using cognitive therapy most commonly use *cognitive restructuring* to replace negative and self-esteem lowering thoughts the person may have when faced with stress.

One of the most effective cognitive therapies for helping a person manage stress is *rational-emotive therapy (RET)*. RET was first developed by Ellis (1962). Ellis said that people often *catastrophise* about events. This is where something is blown out of all proportion and is seen by the individual to be catastrophic or extremely harmful to them. This has the consequence of making the person feel totally unable to cope and manage the stressor because it is perceived as so overwhelming and unmanageable. For example, somebody who has just been told by their husband or wife that they are leaving them and want a divorce may think that they cannot live without them and that they are a total failure in a relationship. These thoughts may render the person helpless to deal with the stress of relationship breakdown.

Rational-emotive therapy helps the person by replacing negative thoughts with positive ones, and catastrophic thoughts with more realistic ones.

Faulty cognition (emotional response)	Healthy cognition (rational response)
Oh no, it's spoiled now	One thing has gone wrong. One is not all.
There is no point.	There is always some point.
I'm sick of it all.	I'm sick of this particular thing.
Everyone hates me.	Some people dislike me, but most like me.
Why is it always like this?	It isn't always like this.
It always happens to me.	This kind of thing happens to everyone now and then.
I am jinxed.	Everyone is unlucky sometimes.

Figure 6.13 *Faulty cognitions are replaced with more rational and realistic ones.*

Another cognitive approach is that of *stress inoculation training* (SIT). This integrates both cognitive and emotional (affective) aspects of stress (Meichenbaum, 1996). SIT involves three phases as follows:

1 Conceptualisation. The nature of the stress is understood and the person is helped to think about it and how to cope with it.

2 Skills acquisition and rehearsal. The person is helped to learn cognitive and behavioural skills to manage both the stressor and their emotional reaction to the stress.

3 Application and follow-through. The person practices and implements the skills learned from the previous stage.

Stress inoculation therapy has been used in a wide range of situations – for example, preparing patients for surgery, people with chronic medical conditions, pain management and teachers with classroom stress (Meichenbaum, 1996).

Other techniques

Other approaches to stress management that are

STUDY

Aim

Jaremko (2006) assessed the effectiveness of stress inoculation training in the reduction of public-speaking anxiety.

Method

Sixty-two students who said that they experienced high levels of anxiety when speaking in public were recruited to the study. Students were given SIT and then asked to report on their anxiety levels immediately after giving a public speech.

Results

Students reported experiencing less anxiety when speaking in public after being given SIT.

Conclusion

Stress inoculation training reduces the stress of public speaking for people who find the task stressful.

Evaluation

- Cognitive therapies to help people manage their stress are most successful when combined with behavioural techniques. The latter may include relaxation or more formal psychological therapies.
- Stress inoculation training has been used effectively with individuals, couples and small groups. The length of intervention using this technique varies from 20 minutes to 1-hour sessions over 40 weeks. The technique is flexible and can be inexpensive.
- Cognitive therapies recognise that stress causes people to think illogically and in a distorted way, and these maladaptive thoughts have effects on both behaviour (which may become irrational) and emotions (which may become extreme and lead to panic and feeling out of control).

commonly used include hypnosis, exercise and time management. Hypnosis can help a person relax whilst being open to suggestion. Behaviours that are suggested to the person whilst hypnotised will often be performed for some time after the hypnosis has ceased. Generally, hypnosis does seem to help manage pain and stress (Jacobs *et al.*, 1995). Self-hypnosis has been found to help with the management of examination stress (Gruzelier *et al.*, 2001). There is a vast amount of research on hypnosis and stress management; some supports the claim that it is effective and other research finds little supporting evidence.

6.4 Social factors and coping with stress

Support from work colleagues, friends, family and those who occupy a more intimate place in our life is very important for helping us to cope with stress. Conversely, lack of such support when life is stressful makes us feel isolated, unable to cope with stress and may lead to mental illness, such as depression. **Social support** includes support from those identified above, but can also be extended to include support from professionals – for example, psychotherapists. Stroebe (2000) has identified five types of social support as follows:

1 **Appraisal support**: This is where others help the person to better understand and evaluate the stressors and any effects on health. This helps the person contextualise what is going on.

2 **Emotional support**: This is where others demonstrate that they care for you and, where appropriate, that they love you. Emotional support is also shown by the person knowing that he or she is being listened to and has empathy. Having a 'shoulder to cry on' often helps and comforts.

3 **Esteem support**: Is feeling that others value you and hold you in high esteem. This helps strengthen your feelings of self-worth and self-esteem when stressful situations may bring them into question by yourself. Feeling worthwhile and competent makes the person feel that they can cope with the stress.

4 **Informational support**: This may come from the

STUDY

Aim

Sosa *et al.* (1980) conducted a field experiment to look at the effects of instrumental support on the experience of childbirth.

Method

Pregnant mothers were allocated, on a random basis, to either an experimental or control group. In the experimental group, the pregnant women were accompanied throughout labour by a helper who provided social support. Social support was in the form of general care and talking, but not professional nursing. The control group did not receive this additional social support.

Results

The mothers in the experimental group reported having a better labour period and birth than the control group. Also, the experimental group had an average labour period of 8.8 hours, compared to 19.3 hours in the control group.

Conclusions

Instrumental social support helped the pregnant women to cope with the stress of labour, making them less anxious and resulting in spending less time in labour.

medical profession if stress is making the person ill. It also includes advice and guidance that others may give. Informational support includes feedback from other people so that the person can see how they are doing.

5 **Instrumental support:** Here, practical help is provided by other people. This may be, for example, to help with other daily matters to free the person up to deal with the stressful situation or to provide direct help in dealing with the stressful situation.

The type of social support available depends on the social network of the person, whether they are male or female, and various culture-specific factors. In different cultures the role of family and friends differs. For example, in India the extended family is a very important source of support, especially instrumental support, esteem support and emotional support. However, if too many different people are offering different types of social support, the person may feel overwhelmed and this may add to stress levels! Dakof and Taylor (1990) produced research evidence to show that when support is offered but the person does not see it as support, it does not help with coping with stress.

Figure 6.14 *Social support can help a person cope with stress. However, too much social support may only add to the already existing stress!*

A classic study by Berkman and Syme (1979) showed how social support over a period of years benefited individuals in relation to their health. Thousands of people were followed over a 9-year period. Assessment of each person's level of social support was obtained from questionnaires asking about marital status, attendance at church, contact with friends, membership of organisations and self-reports on health, and tobacco and alcohol intake. It was found that there was a direct relationship between level of social support and death rates of people in the study. Those receiving high levels of social support were less likely to die over the period of the study. This was especially true with older people. The research found a clear and strong link between good social support and good health.

The accepted hypothesis of how social support helps a person cope is that it acts as a *buffer* against stress (Cohen and Wills, 1985). This explanation says that the link between social support and coping with stress is indirect. Research has also shown that social support works best when stress is high rather than at low levels for the individual. How social support actually works has been more difficult to explain. It seems that a combination of raising self-esteem to help the person feel able to cope better and minimising the impact of the stressor may offer an explanation.

Cohen *et al.* (1986) found some evidence that certain people may benefit more from social support than others. They found that people with good social skills (people who interact and relate well with others) have much more extensive and stronger networks with other people. This in turn means that they can potentially draw on high levels of social support. Generally, it seems that a large social network provides better social support and helps a person cope with stress better. In consequence, large social networks also have a positive effect on a person's health.

Evaluation

- Social support has been found to be unhelpful if the person receiving the support does not see it as beneficial, and where it is the wrong type of support at a particular time. An example of the latter is where a part-time female student with a family has examinations coming up. The most useful support would be instrumental support – someone taking the children off her hands whilst she revises – however, only emotional support may be available. This will not give her the time she needs for revision.
- What is seen to be social support varies between people and according to the situation. This makes it difficult to assess the impact and value of social support.
- Measuring social support relies heavily on self-report measures from the person experiencing or under stress. Highly stressed people may not recognise or be able to accept social support when it is offered to them.

How Psychology Works

Stress: a study of problem-focused and emotion-focused strategies in males and females

You are going to carry out a study to investigate differences in coping strategies preferred by males and females. You should read the background information on page 171 before you start.

- Write a questionnaire to find out about how much people prefer different kinds of coping strategies. Aim to have at least three items about problem-focused strategies and at least three items about emotion-focused strategies. Examples of suitable items for the questionnaire would include:
  - **Problem-focused:** If I was worried about pressure at work I would talk to my boss about reducing my workload.
  - **Emotion-focused:** If I was anxious about an argument with my parents I would try to forget about it by going out and having a laugh with friends.
- Type up your statements, with a scale for people to indicate how likely they would be to use the strategy in that situation. A five-point scale will probably be appropriate where 1 = I would be very unlikely to use this strategy and 5 = I would be very likely to use this strategy. You will need to include brief instructions at the top of the page so respondents know what to do.
- Write a short debrief so you can explain what the study was about.
- Try out your questionnaire with a small sample of male and female friends. Remember to comply with ethical guidelines by asking for informed consent before you start and debriefing them at the end.
- Score the completed questionnaires for each person by totalling up the overall score for the emotion-focused items and the overall score for the problem-focused items. Use the overall scores to calculate average scores for males and females which can then be displayed on a bar chart.
- Write a few short paragraphs, as follows:
  a) Summarise the outcome of the activity and compare the results with previous findings in this area. Are there any differences in male and female coping strategies?
  b) Comment on the design of the questionnaire and suggest at least two improvements you would make if you were carrying out a full-scale study.
  c) Describe how you could test the questionnaire for validity and reliability.
  d) Briefly discuss any ethical considerations in relation to this study.

Further Reading

Introductory texts
Morrison, L. and Bennet, P. (2005) *An Introduction to Health Psychology*, Englewood Cliffs, NJ: Prentice Hall Publishers.
Ogden, J. (2007) *Health Psychology: A Textbook*, Milton Keynes: Open University Press.
Sarafino, E. (2006) *Health Psychology: Biosocial Interactions*, 5th edn., New York: John Wiley and Sons.

Specialist sources
Forshaw, M. (2001) *Essential Health Psychology*, London: Arnold.
Stranks, J. (2005) *Stress at Work*, Oxford: Butterworth-Heinemann Publishers.
Straub, R.O. (2007) *Health Psychology*, 2nd edn., New York: Worth Publishers.

Substance abuse

Chapter 7

7.1 Introduction

Most of us start the day with a cup of coffee or tea. Both these drinks contain caffeine and help 'kick-start' us into action. When people say they cannot start the day without a strong cup of coffee, does that make them an addict or a substance abuser? Most of us would say not; however, if you asked someone who is used to starting the day with a strong cup of coffee to give it up for a month and drink water instead, how difficult would they find it?

Tobacco and alcohol are the most widely used drugs all over the world. It is estimated that one in three people globally over the age of 15 years smokes (World Health Organization, 2000) – more than 1 billion people! Alcohol is the next most commonly used drug, and one that is socially acceptable in many countries. Alcohol usage has increased in Great Britain over the past 10–15 years, with reports of 'binge drinking' among young people. Would you regard binge drinkers as drug-dependent and alcoholic?

Figure 7.1 *Binge drinking has become a common feature of city life on Saturday nights. Alcohol abuse damages health. Would you regard binge drinkers as alcoholics?*

The use of illegal substances or drugs is a continuing problem for most western countries, including the United Kingdom. Marijuana or cannabis is the most widely used illegal drug, with estimates that over 140 million people worldwide regularly use this drug (World Health Organization, 2000).

In this chapter we will look at why so many people use drugs. We will also consider programmes aimed at preventing substance abuse in the first place and treating drug addiction.

7.2 Use and abuse

It is important to make a distinction between *use* and *abuse*. In making this distinction it is also useful to talk about substance misuse as well (see Figure 7.2).

- *Substance use* is where people do not experience harm from taking a substance. For example, drinking a cup of strong coffee first thing in the morning is not usually harmful; however, drinking five cups of very strong coffee in succession could be harmful, especially if this happens every morning for months or years.
- *Substance misuse* is where use of the substance results in some kind of problem. In the case of the person who drinks five cups of strong coffee each morning, there are likely to be harmful physiological and mental effects. Being on such a 'high' from excess caffeine may interfere with concentration at work.
- *Substance abuse* is where the person (and indirectly others) will be harmed in some way from taking the drug. The harm may be physical, mental or social, or a combination of all three. Use of the word 'abuse'

Term	Definition
Substance use	The use of substance without any immediate harm to the person
Substance misuse	The use of a substance in a way that results in the person experiencing social, psychological, physical or legal problems
Substance abuse	The use of a substance in a way that causes harm

Figure 7.2 *Definitions of use, misuse and abuse of substances. Adapted from Drugscope (2001).*

has judgemental overtones since it implies some kind of wrongdoing. Care should therefore be taken over when it is best to use the term 'substance abuse' and when best to use the term 'substance misuse' (Drugscope, 2001).

Substance use, misuse and abuse may vary between different societies. For example, in most Muslim countries, selling and drinking alcohol is against the law. In the United Kingdom it is not illegal to buy alcohol if you are over the age of 18 years, and there are laws controlling the sale of alcohol.

7.2.1 Addiction and physical dependence

Definitions

Addiction: where a substance, natural or synthetic, has been used repeatedly, resulting in the user being preoccupied with the substance (drug), maintaining a supply and likely to relapse if attempts are made to stop taking the drug. The user is likely to be both physically and psychologically dependent on the drug.
Physical dependence: where the body has got used to the substance and continued usage is needed to maintain the body in what is now its normal state. 'Normal' in this context means not having withdrawal symptoms or unpleasant feelings as a result of not taking the drug.

To highlight this distinction, consider a person who takes a psychoactive drug, such as cannabis or LSD. Psychoactive drugs are often used for recreational purposes. They affect chemical and neural processes in the brain, affecting mood, behaviour and thought processes (for example, hallucinations or altered perceptions of reality). Over time, use of psychoactive drugs changes the way neurons operate and the presence of such drugs in the body becomes a normal state. Reducing or stopping the drug altogether usually results in a very unpleasant experience. Taking the drug again will return to body to its now 'normal' state, remove the unpleasant experience and bring about a pleasant experience. *Dependence* can be defined as a compulsion to continue taking a substance (drug) to avoid unpleasant experiences and to feel good (Drugscope, 2001).

Many drugs that cause addiction and physical dependence act at the level of the neuron, resulting in increased levels of dopamine in the brain. Dopamine is a neurotransmitter (see Chapter 2 of *AQA(B) Psychology for AS* by Pennington and McLoughlin, 2008) which is affected by drug addiction. Research has shown that the release of dopamine in the brain results in a pleasant experience and one that the individual desires to experience again. Olds and Milner (1954) were the first researchers to investigate the role of certain areas of the brain as 'pleasure centres'.

STUDY

Aim

Olds and Milner (1954) investigated the role of the septal area of the brain (part of the limbic system in the middle of the brain) in addictive behaviour.

Method

Electrodes were implanted into the septal brain area of rats. The electrode supplied a small electric current when the rat pressed a lever. This is called 'self-stimulation'.

Results

Rats pressed the bar very rapidly and for long periods to maintain the mild electrical stimulation into the brain. Some rats continued to press the lever until exhausted and unable to press the lever any more.

Conclusions

Stimulation of the septal area of the brain was highly rewarding for rats and may be seen as pleasurable.

More recent research has shown that self-stimulation of this area of the brain increases the level of dopamine in the brain (Phillips *et al.*, 1992).

There are two types of dependence: physical dependence and psychological dependence. It was thought that physical dependence was the main reason for a person's addiction to a drug. However, people who come off drugs and go through the physical withdrawal effects sometimes go back on the drug because the psychological addiction is more difficult to overcome.

Figure 7.3 *'Hard drugs' are usually both physically and psychologically addictive.*

Six main components of addictive behaviour can be identified:

1. The activity associated with the addiction is central and of high importance in a person's life.
2. The experience of carrying out the addictive behaviour results in a 'rush' and a feeling of high which is pleasant.
3. Physical tolerance to the drug means higher levels have to be taken to maintain the pleasant feeling.
4. Withdrawal occurs when the drug has not been taken for a long period.
5. Relationships with other people are often characterised by conflict and hostility.
6. Risk of relapse after having come off the drug is high.

Evaluation

- The use of the word 'addiction' carries with it stereotypes and a set of judgements about the person who is a drug addict. The British Medical Association discourages doctors from using this term and recommends the phrase 'problem drug users' instead.

Psychological dependence

Psychological dependence may be defined as 'the emotional and cognitive compulsion to use a drug' (Straub, 2007). This definition emphasises the psychological component of 'compulsion', which is an uncontrollable urge or desire to repeat a behaviour or action (similar to an obsessive-compulsive disorder – see Chapter 9 of *AQA(B) Psychology for AS* by Pennington and McLoughlin, 2008). This definition also emphasises that psychological dependence is manifested at both emotional and conscious thought levels. With psychological dependence, the drug becomes the centre of a person's life and will determine many daily activities. People who are alcoholic may not talk about their drink problem, and when asked how much they drink will normally underestimate their daily intake (both to others and themselves). Alcoholics will often become anxious if there is no alcohol in the house and may take to storing large quantities in strange places, out of sight of others. Here there is a mixture of psychological insecurity and self-denial about the extent of their alcohol problem.

Figure 7.4 *This is just in case we have friends round for dinner!*

Psychological dependence is also evidenced by a *craving* for the drug when going without for a long period or during withdrawal from the drug. Craving is a motivational state that involves want and desire, often overwhelming, for the drug. With some drugs, psychological dependence may take longer to develop than physical dependence. Also, drug users often have less insight into the fact that they are psychologically dependent as well as physically dependent. For example, a smoker may say, 'I can stop smoking anytime I like'. But when it actually comes to it the person will find it very hard to stop smoking cigarettes.

The extent to which drugs cause psychological dependence differs. Heroin and cocaine result in rapid psychological dependence; cannabis, or marijuana, is moderate and LSD lower for this type of dependence (Schuster and Kilbey, 1992).

Psychological dependence affects not only the individual but also family, friends and work. Relationships may be negatively affected and work performance may suffer, possibly leading to job loss. Users of hard drugs, such as heroin and crack cocaine, may turn to crime to get money to feed their addiction.

Evaluation

- The term 'dependence' is now used to refer to both psychological and physical dependence. Pinel (2003) argues against distinguishing between physical and psychological dependence because both types of dependence are involved with addiction.

Tolerance

Tolerance to a substance may be defined as 'a state of progressively decreasing responsiveness to a frequently used drug' (Straub, 2001). This definition highlights the fact that most drugs taken over a prolonged period of time result in the body adapting to the drug and requiring more of the drug to have the same physical and psychological effects. For example, a person who first takes a drink of alcohol needs very little to feel the effects and may become drunk very easily. A 'hardened' drinker or alcoholic requires large amounts of alcohol to achieve a similar effect to that of a person who drinks infrequently.

Somebody who drinks a lot of alcohol on a daily basis over a period of years usually finds that the effects level

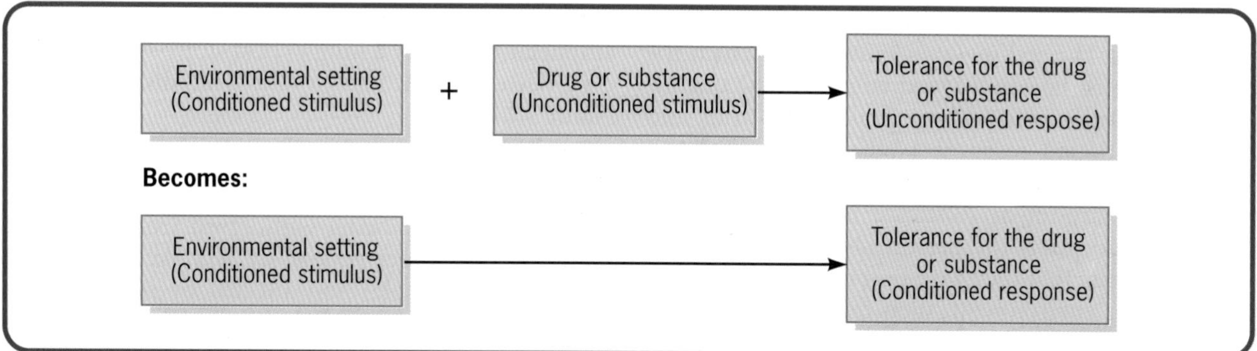

Figure 7.5 *Siegel* et al., *(1982) theory of conditioned drug tolerance resulting from classical conditioning.*

off or reach a plateau, even when more and more alcohol is drunk (Sarafino, 2006). Tolerance to a drug is shown in two ways:

1 A certain amount of the substance has less effect than when the person first started taking or using the substance.

2 More of the substance or drug is needed to produce a similar effect to when it was first taken.

Tolerance does not mean that a regular, heavy drug user can continue to increase the intake level of the drug over and over again. At some point the body cannot take any more and the result is an *overdose*. An overdose may result in death or irreversible damage due to continued high usage of a substance. Alcohol causes cirrhosis of the liver and damages the neurons in the brain.

Siegal *et al.* (1982) produced a theory of *conditioned drug tolerance* to explain how the same level of drug usage, but in different settings, can result in drug overdose. This was explained by classical conditioning (see Chapter 10) and is shown in Figure 7.5. Each time the

STUDY

Aim

Siegel *et al.* (1982) investigated how drug tolerance may be situationally dependent.

Method

Rats were injected with heroin in their normal place of living for a period of 80 days. Following this, half the rats were put in a new environment and the other half remained in their normal place. The rats were then given a potentially lethal dose of heroin.

Results

Sixty-five per cent of rats in placed a new environment died of the heroin injection. By contrast, just 30% of the rats who remained in their normal environment died of the heroin overdose.

Conclusion

Drug tolerance is related to the normal environment in which the drug is taken.

person takes the substance is seen as a trial in classical conditioning. The setting (environment) in which the drug is taken is the conditioned stimulus. The unconditioned stimulus is the effect of taking the drug, and the unconditioned response is the tolerance to the drug. After taking the drug many times (trials) and in the same environment tolerance becomes the conditioned response. If the person now takes the same amount of drug that they have become tolerant to, but in a different environment, then their tolerance level will be less. This explains how some drug users die when taking a level of the drug that they have become used to (tolerant of) in an unfamiliar setting.

Evaluation

- Not all drugs result in a tolerance being built up, Alcohol, nicotine and heroin do result in tolerance, whereas cannabis and LSD do not appear to lead to tolerance.

Withdrawal

Withdrawal may be defined as 'the unpleasant physical and psychological side symptoms that occur when a person abruptly ceases using certain drugs' (Straub, 2001). This definition emphasises the fact that withdrawal symptoms occur when a drug that someone has became tolerant of, and has used consistently over a significant period of time, is suddenly and totally stopped. Withdrawal effects are usually the opposite of the initial and pleasant effects of a drug. For example, amphetamines create feelings of happiness, euphoria and well-being. If a person who has regularly used amphetamines over a long period stops, they typically experience anxiety, nausea and sleep disruption (see Figure 7.6).

A person trying to 'kick' a drug habit or stop using a drug altogether will suffer withdrawal symptoms. The risk of relapse following withdrawal from a drug is related to age (older people are less likely to relapse than younger people) and affected by stressful situations. A person may respond to a stressful event by taking the drug again as a way of avoiding conflict or in an attempt to deny the situation. For this reason, withdrawal from a drug should be carefully managed, with social support for the person during the withdrawal period (and after, to keep the person off the drug).

7.2.2 Types of substance abuse

Abused substances range from those that are often referred to as 'soft' drugs, such as cannabis, to 'hard' drugs, which include heroin and cocaine. Here we will consider several commonly abused substances, including prescription drugs such as antidepressants. According to a Drugscope (www.drugscope.org.uk) survey of school pupils in 2007 (Drug use, smoking and drinking among young people in England 2007):

- cannabis usage has fallen among 11- to 15-year-olds since 2001
- illicit drug use among 16- to 24-year-olds is at its lowest level since 1995
- most young people think that drug use is an unacceptable behaviour in their age group.

Effects of heroin	Heroin withdrawal symptoms
Feeling elated and happy Constipaton Feeling relaxed	Feeling down and unhappy Diarrhoea and stomach cramps Feeling agitated

Figure 7.6 *The effects of heroin and symptoms of withdrawal.*

This provides a positive picture; however, the survey also reports that abuse of solvents and glues appears to be on the increase.

Solvent abuse

Solvents are widely used in everyday products such as glues, paints, nail varnish and nail varnish removers, aerosols and cigarette lighter fuel. They evaporate at room temperature, allowing the fumes or vapours to be inhaled through the mouth or, more commonly, the nose. Solvent abuse is most frequent amongst young teenagers, with up to 20% of 15- to 16-year-olds claiming that they have tried inhaling solvents (Drugscope, 2001). Products containing solvents are relatively easy to purchase, although there are now age restrictions operating on many products for sale in shops. This ease of availability explains their widespread use.

Inhaling solvents provides a similar experience to that of being drunk on alcohol, typically dizziness, poor motor co-ordination and a sense of unreality.

Males and females appear to be equally involved in solvent abuse, although more males are reported as dying from solvent abuse (Chadwick *et al.*, 1991). Between 1983 and 2000, males accounted for around 80% of solvent abuse deaths (Field-Smith *et al.*, 2002). Glues and solvents are highly toxic and can result in brain damage and lung disorders as well as damage to the nose.

Tobacco and nicotine

It is estimated that about 35% of men and 22% of women in the world smoke (National Statistics, 2005).The General Household Survey (2004) for Great Britain shows that smoking:

- is generally in decline, with a greater decrease in men than women
- the highest percentage of smokers is in the unskilled manual group
- the highest rate of smoking is in the 20- to 34-year-old age group.

Tobacco contains an addictive drug called *nicotine.* Nicotine is a mild stimulant and turns into vapour when burnt. Nicotine, as well as other gases, including carbon monoxide, are quickly absorbed by the lungs and, in consequence, enter the bloodstream quickly. However, nicotine levels in the bloodstream decline rapidly, and over a 30-minute period the level of nicotine is reduced by half. In consequence, a person has to smoke regularly to maintain nicotine at a certain level in the bloodstream. Although the sale of tobacco to under-16-year-olds is illegal, young people find it easy to obtain cigarettes.

Smoking cigarettes and other tobacco-based products is known to be bad for a person's health. For over 50 years, a link between smoking and lung cancer, has been established. Smoking has also been related to

STUDY

Aim

Field-Smith *et al.* (2002) investigated the trend in deaths from solvent abuse in the United Kingdom.

Method

Data for the period 1971–2000 was collected from a number of different sources, including the Press and Coroners' reports.

Results

In 1990 there were 152 recorded deaths as a result of solvent abuse. This fell to 64 in the year 2000.

Conclusions

Death rates from solvent abuse have fallen from 1990 to 2000, possibly due to an advertising campaign by the Department of Health which took place in 1992.

Type of smoker	Description
Habitual	Continues smoking as a matter of habit; they derive little pleasure from the activity and are often unaware that they are smoking
Positive emotion	Smoking provides a way of relaxing and feeling good
Negative smoking	Smoking provides a way of reducing anxiety and stress
Addictive	Are aware of their smoking and are also aware of the times when they are not smoking

Figure 7.7 *Four main types of smokers identified by Tomkins (1968).*

coronary heart disease, other cancers such as throat and bowel cancer, bronchitis, emphysema and shortened life expectancy. Passive smoking has also received a great deal of attention in recent years. The ban on smoking in public places across Great Britain was in response to health risks for non-smokers exposed to cigarette smoke.

Tomkins (1968) identified four main types of smokers, as shown in Figure 7.7. Habitual smokers, according to Tomkins, are not really aware of their smoking and smoke out of habit. By contrast, addictive smokers are acutely aware of when they are and are not smoking.

A number of social and personality characteristics have been found to help explain why people start smoking:

- peer pressure and role models who smoke
- teenagers are more likely to start smoking if their parents and friends smoke
- teenagers who are rebellious and risk-takers are more likely to smoke.

STUDY

Aim

Schachter (1977) conducted an experiment to provide evidence for the nicotine regulation model of smoking.

Method

Smokers were asked to smoke low-nicotine cigarettes for a week, then high-nicotine cigarettes for another week.

Results

Participants smoked more low-nicotine than high-nicotine cigarettes. Heavy smokers showed this more strongly by smoking 25% more low-nicotine cigarettes.

Conclusion

Smokers maintain a certain nicotine level in their body, as predicted by the nicotine regulation model.

Robinson and Klesges (1997) state that teenagers are attracted to smoking because they think being a smoker conveys a grown-up image of being tough, cool and independent to their peer group.

There are biological, social and cultural explanations offered for both why people start smoking and why they continue to smoke when they know it is bad for their health. One biological explanation is the *nicotine regulation model*, according to which people continue to smoke to maintain a certain level of nicotine in their bodies and avoid symptoms of withdrawal.

Alcohol

Alcohol is commonly used as a form of relaxation when drunk in moderation. It is used in social settings and much of our culture is built round it through pubs, wine bars and restaurants. The General Household Survey (2004) reported that on average men drink 16 units a week and women about 5.5 units per week. Alcohol is made up of ethyl alcohol, which is absorbed very quickly into the bloodstream. Alcohol is both an addictive drug and one for which a person builds a tolerance when it is drunk consistently every day. Alcohol also creates both physical and psychological dependence, which explains why alcoholics find it so hard to give up drinking. Alcoholics who stop drinking experience severe withdrawal symptoms. *Binge drinking* has become common amongst teenagers in this country and is defined as:

> Drinking eight or more units for men and six or more units for women on at least one day of the week (www.drugscope.org.uk).

The recommended weekly 'safe' levels are 21 units a week for men and 14 units a week for women. Research has shown that nearly 60% of 15 to 16-year-olds have drunk more than five units of alcohol in a single session in the past month.

Alcohol has both positive and negative effects on health.

> **Negative effects:** An increased risk of developing liver cirrhosis, some cancers, hypertension and memory deficits (Korsakoff's syndrome, where people find it difficult to retain information in memory and learn new things). Alcohol can affect a person's ability to drive a car and other skilled behaviour. Alcohol-related deaths have more than doubled over the past decade.
>
> **Positive effects:** Light and moderate drinking has been shown to reduce coronary heart disease by protecting blood vessels from the build-up of cholesterol and lowering blood pressure.

Light to moderate drinkers report that alcohol relaxes them, helping them to be more sociable and talkative. On the negative side, alcohol has been linked to aggression and domestic violence. The relationship between alcohol and aggression is not straightforward. Brannon and Feist (1992) suggest that alcohol-related aggression depends on both the personality of the individual and the situation. Zucker *et al.* (1996) suggested that some alcoholics have antisocial personalities. Such people find it difficult to stop drinking or reduce their intake, and abuse other substances. Alcoholics who do not have this type of personality are able to give up drinking more easily and do not usually take other drugs.

Stage	Symptoms
1	Shaking, sweating, feelings of anxiety, nausea and stomach cramps
2	Convulsions and seizures
3	Hallucinations (DTs), fever and irregular heart beat may develop

Figure 7.8 *The three-stage model of alcohol withdrawal proposed by Winger* et al. *(1992).*

Winger *et al.* (1992) proposed a three-stage model of withdrawal from alcohol dependence (see Figure 7.8). The first stage usually starts 2 or 3 hours after the last drink of alcohol. The second stage occurs 2 or 3 days later, and the third stage is where the person has *delirium tremens* (the 'DTs'). People who have become highly dependent on alcohol and drink excessive amounts each day usually experience all three stages during withdrawal.

Stimulants

Stimulants are substances that stimulate the central nervous system and result in feelings of happiness, euphoria and being full of energy. The most commonly used stimulants, often called *recreational drugs*, include amphetamines (ecstasy is a synthetic amphetamine), cocaine, alkyl nitrites (sometimes called *poppers*, such as butyl nitrite).

Amphetamines have street names such as 'uppers', 'speed' and 'whizz'. They produce feelings of well-being, euphoria and self-confidence and are relatively long-lasting (4–8 hours plus) compared with cocaine. They lead to an increase in heart rate, increased blood supply to the muscles and greater levels of dopamine in the brain. Tolerance develops quickly, meaning more has to be taken to achieve the same effect. Withdrawal symptoms include exhaustion, depression and sleeplessness.

Ecstasy (or MDMA) is a hallucinogenic amphetamine taken as a pill, with the effects felt after about an hour or so. Ecstasy causes the person to feel calm, and friendly towards other people. Animal studies show that MDMA causes damage to the endings of nerve cells. There is some evidence that MDMA causes memory impairment, but the evidence is not compelling.

Cocaine comes from the leaves of the coca plant and is usually sniffed through the nose. The effects are immediate, peaking after about 20 minutes, but are relatively short-lived, so repeated doses have to be taken to maintain the effect. Cocaine produces feelings of well-being, exhilaration and self-confidence. People do not build up a tolerance to cocaine and the withdrawal effects are not as severe as with alcohol and heroin. Cocaine dependence is characterised by periods of heavy use followed by periods of recovery and no use. During recovery periods individuals often use alcohol and cannabis to relax and offset the withdrawal symptoms. Caan (2002) states that people who have become dependent on cocaine do not experience too much difficulty in stopping taking the drug, but are likely to relapse to regain the euphoric feelings.

Alkyl nitrites or poppers are often called the 'sex drug'. They are often sold in sex shops and gay bars. They act to dilate blood vessels and enhance the erection of the penis. They are supposed to make an orgasm more intense and last longer. They come in small bottles labelled as 'thrust', 'ram' and 'hard rock'. Alkyl nitrites are not illegal and seem not to produce either psychological or physical dependence. After-effects include severe headaches, nausea and faintness. They should not be taken by people with heart problems or those taking medication for hypertension.

Depressants

Depressants slow down the activity of the central nervous system and have the opposite effect to stimulants. Taking a low dose of a depressant may make a person feel calm and relaxed. However, high doses are dangerous and may lead to unconsciousness. Alcohol and solvents, which we have already considered, are depressants. Here we will look at two other depressants:

- opiates or narcotics; this category includes heroin, morphine and codeine
- tranquillisers such as diazepam (valium) and temazepam, which are prescribed drugs for certain mental disorders; and barbiturates, which are sleeping pills.

Heroin, a Class A drug, is an opiate which comes from the poppy plant. Heroin can be injected or smoked and quickly results in dependence (it is highly addictive) and tolerance. Opiates are used by the medical profession as sedatives and to reduce pain. Opiates such as heroin produce feelings of euphoria, but once a tolerance has been developed these positive feelings disappear and people have to keep taking the drug just to feel normal. The general view is that heroin is certain to lead to addiction from repeated use. However, research on American soldiers during and after the Vietnam War in the 1960s indicates differently. Many American soldiers used heroin to cope with stressful situations on the front line. Yet Bourne (1974) found that most stopped using heroin when they returned home and the immediate stress of war was absent. Note, though, that some soldiers did become addicts and required treatment.

Tranquillisers such as diazepam and temazepam, which are benzodiazepines, are Class B drugs. They are prescribed by GPs for anxiety disorders and panic attacks. Tranquilliser and barbiturate abuse occurs where the drug has been acquired legally through prescription or stolen from a pharmacy. Benzodiazepines work by acting on the neurotransmitter receptors in the nerve cells in the brain, causing the release of a neurotransmitter called GABA. This acts to 'calm nerves' by reducing high levels of activity, resulting in calmness and sleepiness. The effects are exaggerated by alcohol and may prove fatal. Normally these drugs are prescribed for short-term use only, because a tolerance quickly builds up and dependence is common. Unpleasant withdrawal symptoms include insomnia, sweating, tremors, loss of appetite and irritability.

Benzodiazepines are typically used in combination with other drugs such as alcohol and heroin – this is called *polysubstance abuse.* Users say the benzodiazepines enhance the desired effects of the other drugs (Ashton, 2002).

7.2.3 Explanations for substance abuse

Explanations for why people abuse substances include: personality and mental illness, genetics, family environment, peer group pressure, socio-economic factors, ease of availability and pleasure seeking. In this section we will consider hereditary factors, personality characteristics and social factors.

Hereditary factors

The role of genetics in explaining why some people abuse substances has gained interest from researchers in recent years. For example, Melo *et al.* (1996) conducted experiments where animals that preferred alcohol to other non-alcoholic beverages were selected and then mated with one another. It was found that the offspring of these animals also showed a preference for alcohol over other types of beverages. Research on identical human twins has suggested that some people may be predisposed to substance abuse and dependence on drugs (Kendler *et al.*, 1994).

STUDY

Aim

A classic study by Kaij (1960) investigated the rates of alcohol abuse in identical and fraternal twins.

Method

Identical and fraternal twin pairs, where one of the twins was known to abuse alcohol, were recruited to the study. The concordance rates for alcohol abuse with both twins were recorded.

Results

For identical twin pairs the concordance rate was 54%. With fraternal twins the concordance rate was just 28%.

Conclusion

The higher concordance rates for identical twins points to a genetic explanation for alcohol abuse.

Evaluation

- Care should be taken not to over-interpret the data as conclusive evidence for a genetic explanation for substance abuse. Twins are usually brought up in the same environment and identical twins often treated in the same way.
- Nearly half of the identical twins in the study did not show concordance for alcohol abuse. An explanation of why one identical twin abused alcohol and the other did not is needed.
- Identical twins where at least one of the twins abuses alcohol or other substances are rare and may have special characteristics that set them apart from identical twins where neither twin abuses alcohol. For example, the latter may have had a more stable and nurturing home environment as children.

Another approach to investigating the genetic basis for substance abuse is research conducted on people who were adopted shortly after being born. These studies look at the alcohol abuse in adopted children when they are adults and compare this to whether or not one or both of the biological parents abuses alcohol. Goldstein (1994) found that adopted children who abused alcohol as adults were significantly more likely to have biological parents where at least one was an abuser of alcohol. It has also been found that the biological parents of adoptees with an alcohol problem are more likely to have an alcohol problem themselves than the adopted parents. Peters and Preedy (2002) noted that 18% of adoptees where one biological parent abused alcohol went on to abuse alcohol themselves. In comparison, only 5% of adoptees where neither parent abused alcohol went on to abuse alcohol.

A more recent technique used to investigate the role of genes in substance abuse is *gene mapping*. Research has suggested links between abnormal genes and substance disorders (Melo *et al.*, 1996). Dopamine-linked genes have been investigated, leading to findings that over 60% of people with alcohol dependence and 50% of people who regularly use cocaine have an abnormal form of a dopamine receptor gene. Some of these findings are regarded as controversial and more research is needed before a genetic explanation for substance abuse can be accepted. However, research to date does seem to indicate that genes play a role in substance abuse and the development of drug dependency.

Evaluation

- A genetic predisposition to substance abuse does not inevitably mean that the person would become dependent on a drug such as alcohol. Other factors are also important.
- Plomin (1990) suggests that it is unlikely that some people possess a gene that drives them to drink alcohol. Hereditary effects are more likely to be to do with an 'absence of brakes' to control alcohol intake. Psychological and physiological factors that stop people drinking after taking a certain amount may be inhibited or absent in those who abuse alcohol.

Personality factors

It has been suggested that certain personality types are more likely to be associated with substance abuse than other personality types. Much of the research in this area has been with the abuse of alcohol. A number of different personality types have been researched, as follows:

- **Extroversion:** Flory et al. (2002) found alcohol abuse was associated with high levels of extroversion. Extroverts are outgoing, sociable and easily bored.
- **Conscientiousness:** McAdams (2000) found that low conscientiousness was associated with alcohol abuse. Low conscientiousness is shown by a person being disorganised, careless and unreliable.

Figure 7.9 *Are extroverts more likely to develop an alcohol problem than introverts?*

Research has also investigated the link between *antisocial personality disorder* (APD) and alcohol abuse. APD is one of the most common personality disorders, with around 3% of the population being diagnosed with this disorder at some point in their lives. A person with APD disregards rules, has little concern for the rights of others, lacks regard for truth, shows physical aggression inappropriately and may be extremely irritable. APD occurs more in males than females. People with APD have been found to be at risk of substance abuse generally. For example, Fabrega *et al.* (1991) found that 40% of people seeking therapy for APD were engaged in some kind of substance abuse. Binge drinking has been linked to APD because of the antisocial behaviour that often results from such a drinking pattern.

The psychodynamic approach (see Chapter 13) proposes that people who abuse substances have strong dependency needs which can be traced back to early childhood (Shedler and Block, 1990). Psychodynamic psychologists suggest that there is a personality dimension to do with dependency, with some people high in dependency (on other people and material objects) and other people low in dependency. Thus, if parents fail to satisfy a child's needs, the child will grow up to be a person who is over-reliant on others to provide comfort, nurture and reassurance. If others fail to provide this, drugs may act to provide substitute comfort and reassurance and so create dependency and addiction.

STUDY

Aim

Morgenstern *et al.* (1997) investigated the relationship between antisocial personality disorder (APD) and alcohol abuse.

Method

A structured interview to identify personality characteristics and patterns of alcohol abuse was carried out with 336 alcohol abusers attending for treatment.

Results

Antisocial personality disorder was found to be associated with alcohol abuse.

Conclusion

Certain types or personality, especially APD, are more associated with alcohol abuse than other types of personality.

Evaluation

- One problem with trying to explain substance abuse as a result of certain types of personality is that a wide range of personality factors have been linked to substance abuse. Different studies may link opposite traits to substance abuse. No one personality type has been found to offer a significant explanation for substance abuse.
- Establishing cause and effect is impossible in correlation studies. Perhaps the personality type causes a person to abuse substances, or perhaps the personality type develops as a result of substance abuse.
- Most research on personality and substance abuse has been with alcohol abuse rather than the full range of different types of substance abuse. This is probably because participants for alcohol abuse studies are more readily available as there are more of them.

Social factors and peer influence

Substance abuse often takes place in a social setting and an individual often starts taking a drug as a result of the influence of other people. In this section we will consider the following social factors that explain how substance abuse first starts and is subsequently maintained:

- social learning theory and the influence of role models
- peer influence and peer pressure
- social norms and sociocultural factors.

Social learning theory (see Chapter 11) is based on observational learning where the person being observed acts as a model for the observer. If the person being observed is perceived by the observer to be rewarded for behaving in a certain way, then it is likely that the observer will imitate or copy the behaviour. With smoking, for example, the mildly stimulating properties of nicotine, together with pleasurable social situations in which smoking takes place (socialising with friends, over dinner at a friend's house, etc.), are potentially strong social influences on the individual to smoke. The characteristics of the model are important to take into account when explaining substance abuse. For example, people we perceive to be like ourselves are more influential on our behaviour than people we see as very different to ourselves. Characteristics such as gender, age, status (especially celebrity status) all influence substance abuse. However, this varies according to the type of substance abuse. Stein *et al.* (1987) found that alcohol abuse was influenced more by role models such as parents, whereas other forms of substance abuse (cannabis and cocaine) were more likely to be influenced by the behaviour of peers.

Peer influence is very important in explaining substance abuse. Social pressure and the encouragement of others play a role in both starting and continuing to abuse substances. Teenagers spend more time with their peers and less time with their families in social interaction than younger children.

The relationship between peer influence and behaviour is complex. The teenager often makes a choice about which group of friends they want to socialise with. With this often comes a subculture (chavs, goths, hippies, etc.). This *social selection* (Reed and Rowntree, 1997) means that some teenagers associate with groups known to abuse substances and so are at risk of becoming substance abusers themselves.

Figure 7.10 *Peer influence is an important factor explaining why some teenagers start and continue to abuse substances.*

STUDY

Aim

Garnier and Stein (2002) investigated the role of peer influence in predicting adolescent substance abuse.

Method

One hundred and ninety-eight families took part in a longitudinal study. Data were collected from mothers when they were pregnant, and, 18 years later, from their children as teenagers. Information about peer substance abuse and the teenagers' own substance abuse was recorded.

Results

Substance abuse by the teenagers was significantly associated with peers abusing substances.

Conclusion

Teenagers modelled themselves on their peers. Peer pressure in the form of peer encouragement explained why teenagers started to abuse substances. There was also some evidence that those teenagers who abuse substances actively sought friends with similar interests to themselves.

Social norms are important sociocultural factors that operate both within subcultures and across different cultures. Cross-cultural studies of substance abuse show there to be different levels of alcohol abuse in different cultures. In Taiwan the level of alcohol abuse is low, whilst in South Korea it is four times higher (Helzer and Canino, 1992). Different social norms operate in each country. In Taiwan it is socially acceptable to drink alcohol with an evening meal and on special occasions. However, getting drunk is socially unacceptable. In South Korea drinking after work with colleagues is normal and heavy drinking is socially acceptable.

Evaluation

- Social influence and peer pressure may be offset by the extent to which the teenager is involved with religion, school/college activities and conventional social institutions. *Social control theory* states that the stronger the attachment to these aspects of life, the less likely the person is to abuse substances.
- Personality factors are also known to counter social and peer influences. People with high self-efficacy who believe in their ability to determine their own behaviour are less influenced by peers (Bandura, 1997).
- Moving from drug use to drug abuse may be more to do with personal characteristics than social influence and peer pressure. Heavy substance abuse may be best explained through a cumulative effect of social influence and personality.

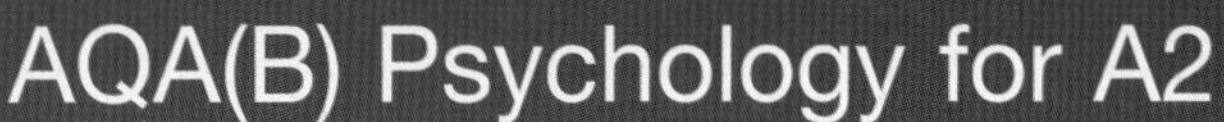

7.3 Treatment and prevention

7.3.1 Psychological treatments and effectiveness

Treatments such as aversion therapy and self-management are most effective when the individual is motivated to want to reduce or stop taking a drug. Relapse is also a problem and most likely in the first weeks or months of a treatment programme. For example, most people who stop smoking start again within a year, usually within the first three months (Ockene *et al.*, 2000).

Aversion therapy

Aversion therapy is based on the principles of classical conditioning (see Chapter 10). Here the abused substance is paired with an unpleasant stimulus, such as an electric shock or drug that makes the person sick when they take the abused substance. After a number of pairings, being sick or fear of an electric shock becomes the conditioned response. Eventually the individual avoids the substance so as not to be sick or to avoid the unpleasant feelings associated with the expectation of an electric shock (see Figure 7.11).

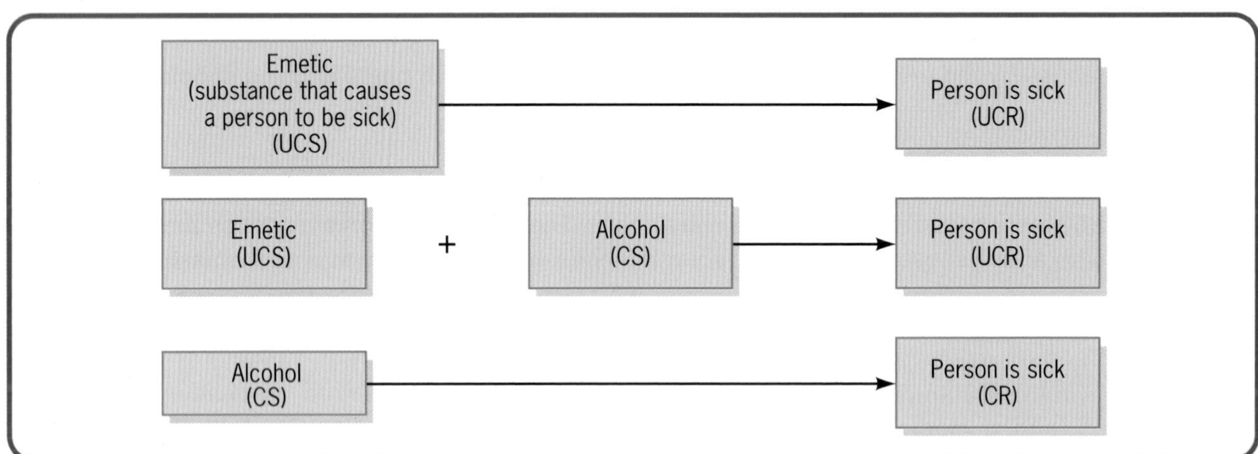

Figure 7.11 *How aversion therapy for alcohol abuse works on the principles of classical conditioning.*

STUDY

Aim

Wiens and Menustik (1983) investigated the effectiveness of aversion therapy on alcohol abusers using an emetic.

Method

Several hundred people with a drink problem were treated using an emetic, according to the principles of aversion therapy and classical conditioning.

Results

Over 60% of men and women ceased taking alcohol altogether over the 12-month period following aversion therapy. Half of these remained free of alcohol 2 years later.

Conclusion

Aversion therapy is effective in the treatment of alcohol abuse, but the success rate is not very high and some people relapse following the termination of the treatment programme.

Evaluation

- Aversion therapy treatments for substance abuse are rarely offered as the sole form of treatment these days and have limited success. For aversion therapy to be effective the person needs to be motivated to give up their substance abuse and there needs to be good social support when the person experiences withdrawal symptoms.
- Aversion therapy is most effective as a treatment for substance abuse if it is used in conjunction with biological therapy and/or cognitive therapy. Biological therapies include carefully managed detoxification in a hospital setting and antagonist drugs which block the effect of the abused substance. For example, narcotic antagonists such as *naxolone* attach to receptor sites in the brain and block the effects of drugs such as heroin. However, narcotic antagonists must be administered carefully and under full medical supervision because they can rapidly cause severe withdrawal symptoms. Narcotic antagonists have also been found to be effective with alcohol abuse and cocaine users (O'Malley et al., 1996).
- There are ethical issues with some forms of aversion therapy. For example, giving electric shocks as part of a treatment programme may be painful and unpleasant for the individual. The recipient should have the procedure fully explained and should give fully informed consent.
- Aversion therapy has been used most with alcohol abuse and smoking. There is less evidence that it is an effective treatment for other types of substance abuse.
- Aversion therapy for alcohol abuse using an emetic may not be effective because the person has become classically conditioned to aspects of their environment. For example, alcohol abusers may report a desire to drink when they see their favourite drink or are in the social environment (public house, wine bar) where they usually drink. Rankin et al. (1983) developed a technique called cue exposure and response prevention to extinguish these conditioned responses – for example, drinking a soft drink in their favourite drinking place or holding their favourite alcohol drink but not drinking it.

STUDY

Aim

Higgins *et al.* (1993) used an alternative to aversion therapy to treat cocaine abusers.

Method

Cocaine abusers were recruited to the study and given contingency training over a 6-month period.

Results

Sixty-eight per cent of cocaine users who completed the 6-month therapy programme achieved at least 8 weeks without taking the drug.

Conclusion

Incentives and monitoring can be effective in treating cocaine abusers. Therapy based on operant conditioning can be an effective alternative to aversion therapy.

Another form of aversion therapy which has been found to be successful to help stop people smoking is called *rapid smoking* (Danaher, 1977). Here smokers sit in a closed room and take a drag on a cigarette every 6 seconds until they cannot smoke any more. The intention is to make the experience of smoking itself unpleasant. Rapid smoking has a degree of success; however, the risks include increased heart rate and increased level of carbon monoxide (a poison) in the bloodstream.

Another type of aversion therapy is called *covert sensitisation therapy*. Here the aim is to get the person to associate unpleasant and negative thoughts with the substance abuse. For example, a cigarette smoker might be asked to imagine some of the most unpleasant effects of smoking, such as accelerated ageing of the face (wrinkles, grey and saggy skin, etc.), the painful consequences of having lung cancer, and losing both legs because of emphysema. Covert sensitisation therapy seems to be effective for alcohol abuse and to help a person stop smoking (Emmelkamp, 1996).

An alternative behavioural therapy to aversion has been used for cocaine abuse. *Contingency training* is based on operant conditioning and involves giving incentives (reinforcement) to abusers whose urine samples show they have not taken cocaine.

Self-management

Self-management approaches provide a structured and evidence-based means of helping an individual to help themselves with managing their substance abuse. Self-management usually revolves around a self-help group made up of other people who abuse the same substance. It may involve the person ceasing to take the substance altogether or controlling intake to an agreed level. Self-management groups are usually conducted under the supervision and facilitation of a trained health-care professional – for example, a health psychologist. Self-management often involves one or all of the following activities:

1. *Monitoring* the intake of the substance, perhaps by keeping a written record of the frequency and amount of the substance taken and where this happens.
2. *Awareness* of the reasons for taking the abused substance and insight into what causes the person to abuse the substance. Causes may be immediate stressors in the environment or relate to childhood problems and unhappiness.
3. *Consequences* of the substance abuse, both for the individual and other people such as family, friends and work colleagues.

Perhaps the most widely known self-management group is Alcoholics Anonymous (AA). This group operates according to two basic principles. First, people who abuse alcohol are alcoholics for life, even when not drinking alcohol. Second, taking just one drink after a period of abstinence will cause a person to binge drink, hence even one drink must be avoided. AA has deep religious roots and emphasises public confession, contrition and admitting wrongdoing to God. Part of being in AA is that the alcohol abuser meets people who have given up drink, hears about their struggles and gets social and emotional support to see them through their own difficulties with stopping drinking.

How effective is Alcoholics Anonymous in helping people both give up drinking alcohol and stay 'dry'? Research has shown that the more regularly and longer a person goes to AA meetings, the more likely they are to stop drinking and the better their intimate and social relationships become (Moos and Moos, 2004). However, for people who do not believe in God (such as atheists and agnostics), research shows that they are less likely to keep going to AA meetings and as a result can be unsuccessful in giving up alcohol (Tonigan *et al.*, 2002).

Self-management of substance abuse can also be assisted through *community-based programmes*. Here all members of a large community (for example, a town or county) are offered a facility for obtaining

Figure 7.12 *Self-help groups help a person self-manage their substance abuse whilst providing social and emotional support.*

advice on how to cease their substance abuse and are exposed to an advertising campaign. One community-based programme, called the North Australia Coast Study, resulted in a 15% reduction in smoking over 3 years. Such programmes are expensive to run and rely on individuals responding to what is offered. This may not always reach long-term substance abusers.

The most successful self-management approach for the treatment of substance abuse is the use of cognitive

STUDY

Aim

Botvin *et al.* (2001) conducted a community programme about binge drinking with teenagers attending inner-city schools in New York.

Method

A group of over 1,700 teenagers received a programme about the negative effects of binge drinking and information about norms of drinking among teenagers generally. A control group of more than 1,300 teenagers did not receive the programme.

Results

Binge drinking was over 50% lower among the teenagers who received the programme.

Conclusion

Community programmes which provide information and practical guidance on how to stop binge drinking help individuals to manage alcohol abuse.

Evaluation

- The effectiveness of self-management approaches are difficult to verify scientifically, since many groups do not keep appropriate records, and other groups, such as Alcoholics Anonymous, do not disclose who is attending their meetings. Self-help groups may be suspicious of requests to conduct scientific research and often refuse to participate.
- Self-management techniques do seem to enjoy a degree of success equal to that of other single treatments. However, better success rates are found when self-management is based on a structured approach and is supplemented by, for example, cognitive behavioural therapy. This combination offers the best of both worlds – social and emotional support from a self-help group and evidence-based therapy from a trained psychologist.
- The biggest problem is relapse. Budney and Higgins (1998) state that about one-third of substance abusers relapse as a direct result of peer pressure and pressure from friends. Attending self-help groups brings the person into contact with others who are trying to stop their substance abuse. However, outside of the self-help group, the person comes into contact with friends who are still engaged in substance abuse. Some self-management programmes provide help to resist relapse when with others who are still abusing substances. This is called *refusal training* and involves role play and developing ways of saying 'no'. Self-management which incorporates refusal training is successful.

behavioural therapy to help the individual manage the problem in their daily life. One example of cognitive behavioural therapy for the treatment of alcohol abuse is *behavioural self-control training* (Miller *et al.*, 1992). There are two main aspects to this therapy.

1 People monitor their alcohol abuse, recording times, location, emotions and bodily changes that accompany drinking. This helps them understand the factors that put them at risk of drinking.

2 The therapist then teaches them coping strategies – for example, to limit drinking and use relaxation techniques when feeling the need to drink.

With this insight and set of practical techniques to use, they are then asked to self-manage their drink problem. Research using this training technique reported 70% improvement by clients (Miller *et al.*, 1992). Behavioural self-control training seems to be more effective for people who abuse alcohol and less effective for those who are physically dependent on alcohol. The approach has also been successful with people who abuse cannabis and cocaine (Carrol and Rounsaville, 1995).

7.3.2 Prevention techniques

Prevention techniques can be classified into three types: primary prevention, secondary prevention and tertiary prevention:

- **Primary prevention** is concerned with when substance abuse starts and aims at preventing substance abuse in the first place. This is often aimed at children and teenagers.
- **Secondary prevention** is aimed at preventing people or groups who may be at risk of becoming substance abusers.
- **Tertiary prevention** is aimed at people who are already abusing substances and to prevent them from developing further problems whilst trying to reduce their substance abuse.

Two or even all three techniques can be used at the same time.

Risk groups

One approach to preventing substance abuse or targeting limited resources to treat substance abuse is to identify groups of people that are most at risk of becoming substance abusers. The main issue is how best to identify at-risk groups of people. Groups such as teenagers come to mind as an at-risk group, but does this apply to all teenagers or just certain subgroups? Naidoo and Wills (1998) identified three factors to consider in risk assessment of groups of people for substance abuse:

1 **Psychosocial factors**: These include employment status, level of social support, degree of social isolation and access to appropriate living accommodation.

2 **Cultural factors**: Certain ethnic groups seem to be at greater risk of substance abuse than other ethnic groups.

3 **Biological factors**: Where a parent or both parents have a history of substance abuse. As noted earlier, some types of substance abuse may have a hereditary influence.

With respect to psychosocial factors, people who are unemployed, have low levels of social support and are homeless are at risk of being involved in substance abuse (alcohol, solvent abuse and heroin). With respect to cultural factors, Aboriginal Australians who do drink alcohol, which is not the majority, seem to drink to excess (Gray *et al.*, 2000).

Figure 7.13 *Some ethnic groups may be at greater risk for substance abuse than others.*

Another way of identifying people who are at risk of substance abuse is through people who come into contact with health care professionals. For example, many people who abuse substances go to see their family doctor or general practitioner (GP). Anderson (1993) produced evidence to show that early intervention by GPs is successful in reducing substance abuse amongst their patients, and Wallace *et al.* (1988) found

STUDY

Aim

Drummond (2002) investigated the effectiveness of helping people identified at accident and emergency (A & E) departments who abused alcohol.

Method

People with an alcohol problem were identified from those attending A & E. They were invited to attend a clinic where advice and help for alcohol abuse was given.

Results

About 50% of those identified with an alcohol problem at A & E attended the clinic the following day to discuss their alcohol abuse with a health care professional.

Conclusion

Identifying substance abusers in a general medical setting can help with treatment for the substance abuse.

Evaluation

- Interventions aimed at high-risk groups have focused too much on the individual and not enough on the social and cultural factors that are impinging on these high-risk groups.
- Treatments for substance abuse with high-risk groups of people need to develop culturally sensitive programmes. Understanding the plight of someone who lives in poverty, is homeless and unemployed is essential if such people are to engage and continue with a treatment programme.
- Prevention techniques with groups identified as at high-risk of substance abuse require a range of approaches and co-ordination of services to support the individuals.

that GPs provided effective help with people who abused alcohol.

The UK Government set up Drug Action Teams (DATs) round the country in an attempt to target young people at risk of becoming substance abusers (see www.drugs.homeoffice.gov.uk). DATs bring together a range of services from different organisations, including social services, the police, education services, health authority, housing, probation and voluntary services. One of the targets for DATs is to work with groups of young people identified as being at high risk of substance abuse.

Fear-arousing appeals

Fear-arousing appeals are commonly used to present in stark and often upsetting terms the effects of substance abuse for both the individual abuser and other people. Around Christmas, fear-arousing appeals are used by the police in various advertising media to persuade people not to drink and drive. Fear-arousing appeals are also common to discourage smoking and drug abuse.

Social psychological research on the effect of fear appeals as attempts to persuade people to change their attitudes and behaviours dates back to the classic

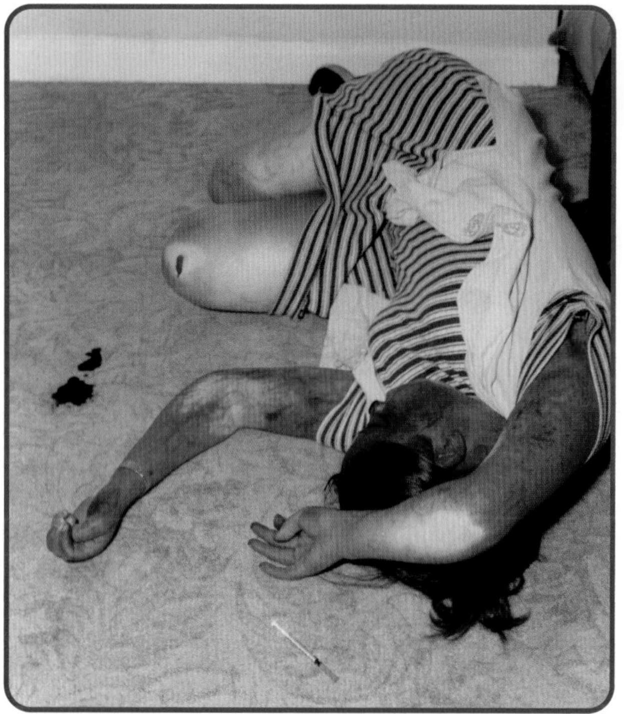

Figure 7.14 *Fear-arousing appeals are assumed to frighten people so much that they will not abuse substances because of the potentially horrific consequences.*

studies by Janis and Hovland (1959). This research, known as the Yale Studies, identified three main factors that need to be taken into consideration when using fear appeals:

1 **Source factors** such as expertise, trustworthiness and status of the source of the communication. For example, a fear appeal using the police as the source is using the factors of expertise and status. If a celebrity such as David Beckham was used as the source of the message, the factors would be status and trustworthiness.

2 **Message factors** include type of appeal (here it is fear appeal), conclusion made and type of arguments used. The most important aspect of the message is that it is comprehensible and saying what it is intended to say.

3 **Audience factors** include consideration of how persuadable the audience is, intelligence, self-esteem and the initial views held by the target audience. For example, people with high self-esteem are likely to be influenced by a fear appeal for a long time after the appeal itself (Baumeister and Covington, 1985).

These findings are important when applied to the use of fear appeals to prevent people engaging in substance abuse. Generally, it would seem that 'shocking' people

STUDY

Aim

Janis and Feshbach (1953) investigated the effect of different levels of fear appeal on health behaviour.

Method

Three lectures on tooth decay were designed to vary the level of fear caused in the audience. The lectures were strong, medium or weak in fear appeal.

Results

The strong fear appeal lecture created the highest level of anxiety in the audience and was rated as interesting by the audience. However, in follow-up research it was found to lead to the least change in dental health behaviour. The low fear appeal lecture created the least anxiety in the audience but resulted in the greatest change in health behaviour.

Conclusion

High fear appeals create high anxiety but least behavioural change. Low fear appeals seem to change behaviour more.

with highly dramatic or visually disturbing images may not be the most effective method of prevention of substance abuse. Flay (1985) reviewed a large number of studies on prevention of smoking and found that fear appeals were not that effective at preventing people from starting to smoke. The assumption that if people know that a substance like tobacco is bad for their health, and for the health of others, it will prevent them from engaging in substance abuse seems to be incorrect.

Evaluation

- Fear-arousing appeals may not be effective in preventing substance abuse because it may be too threatening for some people and mean that the ego-defensive function of holding an attitude is emphasised (see Chapter 6 in AQA(B) *Psychology for AS* by Pennington and McLoughlin, 2008). High fear appeals may be so threatening that people 'switch off' because it makes them too anxious. For this reason, low fear appeals may be more effective in persuading people not to engage in substance abuse.
- Fear-arousing appeals do not usually take into account the reasons for engaging in substance abuse in the first place.
- Fear-arousing appeals are addressed to a wide audience and not often targeted at specific groups – for example, groups known to be at high risk.
- Fear appeals may be offset by advertising campaigns which encourage people to smoke cigarettes or drink alcohol. In the USA, anti-smoking campaigns targeted at ethnic groups such as African Americans have been found not to be effective because the tobacco companies have spent large sums of money advertising cigarettes to these ethnic groups (Borum, 2000).

STUDY

Aim

Cuijpers *et al.* (2002) evaluated the effectiveness of a school-based social inoculation programme in Holland designed to prevent substance abuse.

Method

Some schools delivered the social inoculation programme and others did not. Pupils from both categories of schools reported on their own behaviour with respect to substance abuse. Rates of substance abuse were compared.

Results

Pupils from schools with the social inoculation programme reported drinking less alcohol than pupils from schools that did not use the programme. However, they were also found to have higher rates of cannabis use.

Conclusion

Social inoculation programmes can influence levels of substance abuse in school-aged teenagers.

Social inoculation

Social inoculation is a way of making people resistant to persuasion, changing their attitudes and their behaviour. With respect to substance abuse, social inoculation is to do with protecting people from social pressures, advertising and other factors that might encourage them to abuse substances. Flay *et al.* (1985) identified four factors that are important for social inoculation to be effective.

1. **Knowledge:** The programme should convey knowledge and facts about the negative effects for health and social, economic and other consequences of substance abuse.
2. **Discussion:** The programme should allow for discussion about how a person's substance abuse may be affected by peers, family and the media.
3. **Skill development:** People should be helped to develop communication skills, arguments and social skills to resist the influence of others.
4. **Public commitment:** People make a commitment in public that they will not take or abuse a certain substance.

McGuire (1964) suggested that an important way of inoculating people to resist persuasion by others is to rehearse arguments against the persuasive appeal. McAlister *et al.* (1980) used social inoculation techniques with young teenagers to help them resist the social pressure of their peers to smoke. The young teenagers were presented with and asked to learn arguments about why they should not smoke. For example, 'I would be a real chicken if I smoked just to impress you.' The researchers followed these young teenagers over a number of years and found that they were much less likely to smoke compared to a similar-aged group of teenagers who had not received social inoculation. Social inoculation has also been found to be successful in reducing teenage smoking (Flay *et al.*, 1985). Social inoculation in young teenagers is most effective if they learn arguments to refute peer pressure and peer criticism for not taking the substance.

7.3.3 Health promotion and health education

Health promotion and health education can be regarded as a system for helping people to lead a healthier life and develop attitudes and engage in behaviours that will result in good health. There are three main factors to health promotion (Sarafino, 2006):

1. **Individual factors**, including habits, behaviours, attitudes and beliefs held by the individual. Habitual and addictive behaviours are resistant to change and people must have incentives to change. One possible incentive might be knowledge of the benefits of a healthy lifestyle from health educationalists.
2. **Interpersonal factors** are the social factors that we considered earlier in this chapter. Family and friends act as models for behaviour. It may be that for a person to change their behaviour they will have to change their friends!
3. **Community factors:** Health promotion and education which takes place within a person's own

Evaluation

- People tend to underestimate the ease with which they can be persuaded and influenced by others. At the same time they overestimate how easily they can produce counter-arguments to attempts to persuade them to take a substance. Social inoculation helps people in these circumstances.
- For social inoculation to work well, the characteristics of the person inoculating others is important. Ethnic teenage groups at risk of substance abuse may listen to social inoculation delivered by someone of the same ethnic group or of celebrity status that they look up to.
- Most research on the effectiveness of social inoculation has been with teenagers who may be at risk of substance abuse. Less is known about the effectiveness of social inoculation with older people and those who are on the verge of becoming substance abusers (for example, people who drink over the weekly recommended limit of alcohol and may be at risk of becoming alcoholics).

community are likely to be more effective than national health campaigns. Communities may have specific values and established patterns of behaviour on which the campaign should focus.

Health promotion can take the form of specific interventions which encourage a healthy lifestyle. People who abuse substances such as solvents and alcohol and take hard drugs usually have an unhealthy lifestyle – they eat badly, lack exercise and have poor accommodation. Health promotion for both prevention and reduction of substance abuse uses four main methods:

1 **Information giving** – about healthy diet, exercise and medical conditions associated with specific substance abuse. The information may come from the media, the internet and the medical profession.
2 **Information to motivate** – certain types of information motivate the person to want to be healthy. This may be how the message is framed (fear appeals) and personalised advice.
3 **Motivational interviewing** – usually on a one-to-one basis, where the resistances and motives of the individual are explored to identify what needs to change for the person to lead a healthier life.
4 **Behavioural techniques** – aimed at changing unhealthy behaviours and replacing them with healthy behaviours. These techniques usually involve the use of rewards, especially ones that are important for the individual.

Health promotion campaigns may take place in school,

STUDY

Aim

Moher *et al.* (2005) reviewed the effectiveness of work-based attempts to help employees stop smoking.

Method

The outcomes of different types of programme were reviewed. Some programmes focused on individuals (counselling, group therapy, nicotine replacement, self-help materials, etc.). Others were aimed at the workforce as a whole (bans, competition, incentive schemes, etc.).

Results

Group therapy, counselling and nicotine replacement therapy increased cessation rates in comparison to controls. Self-help materials had little effect. Whole workforce programmes did not reduce smoking, although competition and incentive-based schemes did increase attempts to stop. Bans decreased consumption during the working day but had little effect on total consumption.

Conclusion

The most effective workplace programmes to help employees stop smoking are those which focus on individuals.

at the person's place of work or in the community. They may target specific types of substance abuse and the associated health issues that are typically found with people who abuse such substances.

The Prochaska model of behaviour change

A model of behaviour change related specifically to substance abuse was developed by Prochaska *et al.* (1992). This model proposes that behaviour change takes place through a six-stage process (see Figure 7.15).

Stage 1 **Pre-contemplation:** The person is not aware that they have a substance abuse problem and have no intention of changing their behaviour.

Stage 2 **Contemplation:** The person has become aware that they have a problem and starts to think about changing their behaviour. As yet no commitment has been made to change; people may stay in this stage for a long time, perhaps years.

Stage 3 **Preparation:** The person has made a decision to change their behaviour in the near future. Substance abuse level may have been reduced in preparation for ceasing to take the substance.

Stage 4 **Action:** Here behaviour actually changes. Once behaviour has changed for at least 1 day the person is in the action stage.

Stage 5 **Maintenance:** The behaviour change, either reduction or cessation of substance abuse, is maintained. If a person has not abused the substance for at least 6 months then they are in the maintenance stage. The main danger in this stage is relapse.

Stage 6 **Termination:** The new behaviour has become established and is now 'normal' for the person. Danger of relapse has passed.

An important feature of this model is that it recognises that people who abuse substances may not be able to change their behaviour on their first attempt. Seeing the model as a spiral shows how substance abusers may have to go through some of the stages, especially the action stage, a number of times before they successfully change their behaviour.

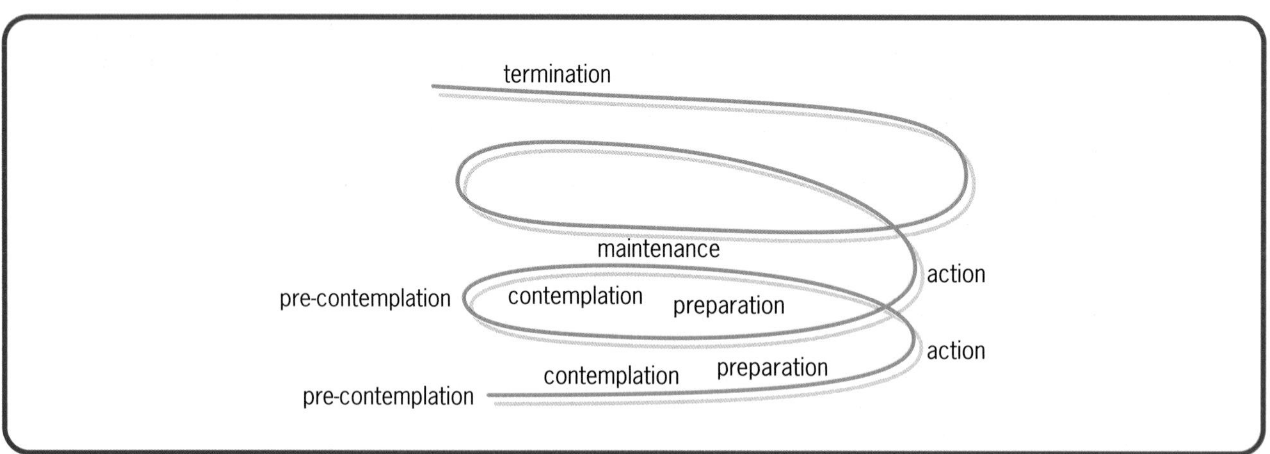

Figure 7.15 *Diagrammatic representation of Prochaska* et al.*'s model of behaviour change for substance abuse.*

Evaluation

- Participants in programmes that use this model report high completion rates with high success – for example, people stopping smoking.
- Smokers who try to stop smoking when in the early stages of the model are less successful than if they try to stop smoking when prepared (preparation stage) and go into the action stage. The period of abstinence from smoking is also longer.
- Use of a stage model for health promotion and cessation of substance abuse presents the person with a structured programme that they can manage and they can plan how to tackle each stage. When the task of stopping substance abuse is not broken down into stages, it can appear overwhelming and impossible to achieve.

How Psychology Works

A content analysis of health promotion/education literature

You are going to analyse the content of health promotion/education literature aimed at preventing substance abuse. Any form of substance would be appropriate, although most of the literature will probably relate to smoking and alcohol.

- Gather together a selection of leaflets from your local health centre, library, community centre or youth centre.
- Working in pairs, analyse each leaflet for content, using categories and rating scales. Before you start, discuss the criteria with your partner, then analyse the material separately. When you have finished you can do a reliability check with each other to see whether or not your findings are consistent.
- Category analysis, examples:
  source of the message (expert, celebrity, peer, etc.)
  target audience (age, sex, background)
  type of message (factual, emotive, fear-arousing, one- or two-sided argument)
  references to motivation
  references to specific techniques
  references to sources of social support.
- Rating analysis (using a 1–5 scale), examples:
  fear-arousal appeal
  raising awareness of the role of social factors (peers, family, etc.)
  references to social inoculation
  overall effectiveness of the message.
- Write a few paragraphs summarising your findings and discussing the outcome of the reliability check.

Further Reading

Introductory texts

Ogden, J. (2007) *Health Psychology: A Textbook*, Milton Keynes: Open University Press.

Sarafino, E. (2006) *Health Psychology: Biosocial Interactions*, 5th edn., New York: John Wiley and Sons.

Specialist sources

Miller, W.R. and Carroll, K.M. (eds.) (2006) *Rethinking Substance Abuse*, New York: Guilford Press.

Straub, R.O. (2007) *Health Psychology*, 2nd edn., New York: Worth Publishers.

Forensic psychology

Chapter 8

Forensic psychology is an example of an area where psychologists apply their knowledge of psychological approaches, methods and treatments to a specific problem. This chapter includes the contributions of forensic or criminological psychologists to the problems of explaining and treating offending behaviour. There is also discussion about how crime can be measured and about the way in which forensic psychologists carry out offender profiling.

8.1 Offending behaviour

8.1.1 Problems in defining crime

Crime might simply be defined as 'breaking the laws of society', in which case, deciding what constitutes criminal behaviour is a **legalistic** decision and should be quite straightforward. However, crime is rather more difficult to define because a number of factors need to be taken into account. Here the following factors are considered:

- historical context
- culture
- age
- specific circumstances.

Historical context

What is defined as a crime at one point in time might not be considered to be a crime at a different point in time. For example, homosexual acts between consenting adults were a criminal offence in the UK before 1967, but they are not now. Conversely, physically punishing a child by smacking hard enough to leave a mark did not used to be regarded as a crime in England, but was legally prohibited in the Children Act 2004.

Figure 8.1 *Smacking a child was not against the law before 2004, but is now a criminal offence.*

Culture

The situation is further complicated when we consider differences in cultural acceptability. In some cultures it is quite acceptable to have more than one wife, whereas in the UK this constitutes the crime of bigamy. Particular problems arise where a group of people who have their origins in one cultural background live in a different culture, but prefer to retain their own cultural ideals of what is right and wrong. For example, in some ethnic minority groups in the UK forced marriage is acceptable, yet the law dictates that it is unacceptable.

Age

Age is clearly an important factor in determining whether or not a person is a criminal. Although stealing is against the law, a 3-year-old child who picks up a toy or a packet of sweets in a store and wanders out of the shop with it is hardly a criminal. In contrast, a group of teenagers who go on a shoplifting spree, deliberately distracting security officers whilst another member of the group steals CDs and DVDs, are clearly offending. Here the issue is centred on the level of understanding and whether or not the person has reached the age of criminal responsibility. In England this is 10 years, but it varies in other countries.

Specific circumstances

Individual circumstances might also determine whether or not a particular behaviour could be defined as a crime. For example, although stealing is against the law, we would probably not want to say that a mother who steals food because her child is hungry is a criminal.

The above problems arise when using a legalistic definition of crime. An alternative way to define crime would be to take a **deviance** approach, classifying behaviour as a crime if it breaches codes of socially acceptable behaviour. This would mean that antisocial behaviours that are not necessarily against the law, such as hanging around bus shelters in a big threatening group, or spitting in the street, might be considered to be a crime. However, this fails to take account of the intention behind the act; it is unlikely that teenagers in a large group intend to be threatening, although they are often perceived to be so by outsiders. For this reason, Blackburn (1993) suggested that crimes should involve conscious rule-breaking.

8.1.2 Measuring crime

Traditionally, crime has been measured by taking official crime figures, but these are now widely believed to underestimate actual crime figures (Putwain and Sammons, 2002). For this reason, other ways of measuring crime have been developed. Here we shall consider the use of official statistics, victim surveys such as the British Crime Survey, and offender surveys.

Official statistics

The official crime rate is based on crimes that are reported to the police and recorded in the official figures. Whilst these might be expected to be reasonably accurate, there are many reasons why they might not reflect the true extent of crime. Indeed, Hollin (1992) suggested that the official statistics account for only 25% of actual crime. Criminologists refer to a 'dark figure' of crime, which is all the offences that are unreported or do not appear in the official statistics for other reasons. See Figure 8.2 for some of the reasons why crimes may be unreported or not recorded by the authorities.

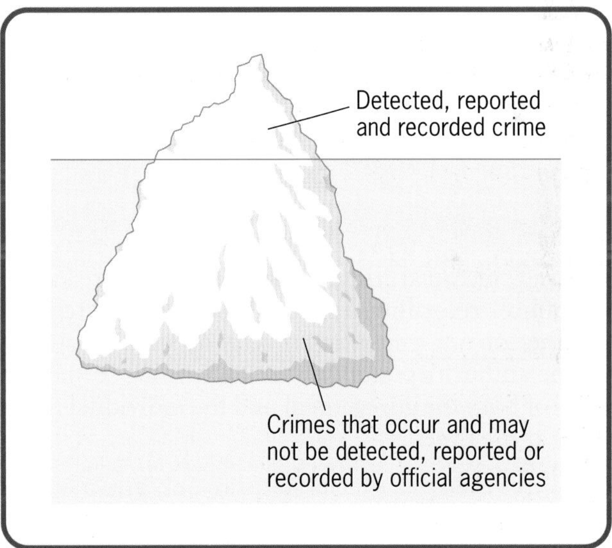

Figure 8.3 *Official statistics mask the 'dark figure' of crime, crimes that are unreported or unrecorded.*

Reasons why crimes are not reported	Reasons why crimes are not recorded
There is no victim e.g. speeding Victim too afraid Too trivial Can't be bothered/inconvenient Mistrust police Perpetrator is friend/family member	Insufficient time Crime too trivial One of several similar offences Not a priority Victim withdraws charge Lack of evidence Police recording rules (see next page)

Figure 8.2 *Reasons why crimes are not reported and recorded.*

STUDY

Aim

Farrington and Dowds (1985) investigated apparent differences in crime figures between counties in the UK.

Method

The researchers analysed a random sample of police records of crimes in Nottinghamshire, Staffordshire and Leicestershire.

Results

Nottinghamshire police were more likely to record thefts of less than £10 value, although this was an informal policy rather than an officially stated policy. Crimes below this value were regarded as minor and were not recorded by the two neighbouring police forces. Thus the official crime rate in Nottinghamshire was higher than for the other two counties.

Conclusion

Police recording procedures can create distortions in the official statistics.

Officially recorded crime is affected by what are known as **police recording rules**. These rules determine whether or not a specific crime is deemed recordable by the authorities, and can vary according to the priority of both the government and the individual police force at the time.

It appears then that official statistics only give a limited picture of the amount of actual crime. As a consequence, other methods of measuring crime have been developed by criminological researchers. In recognition of the limitations of the official statistics, the Home Office presents two sets of crime figures on its website, the official statistics and the British Crime Survey statistics (see below).

Figure 8.4 *Official statistics of reported and recorded crime often hide the 'dark figure' of crime.*

Victim surveys

Victim (or victimisation) surveys involve asking people whether they have been a victim of crime over a specified time period. The most comprehensive and well-known victim survey in the UK is the British Crime Survey (BCS), which is carried out roughly every 2 years and involves interviews with a huge sample. Participants are people aged over 16 years from randomly selected households.

In 2006/7 the BCS data were based on a sample of over 47,000 people, plus a booster sample of 4,000 people aged between 16 and 24 years. The additional booster sample was thought to be necessary because many of the original randomly selected people from this age group had declined to take part. Participants were asked whether they or a member of their household had been a victim of crime in the last year. Interviews were heavily structured, with pre-set questions and

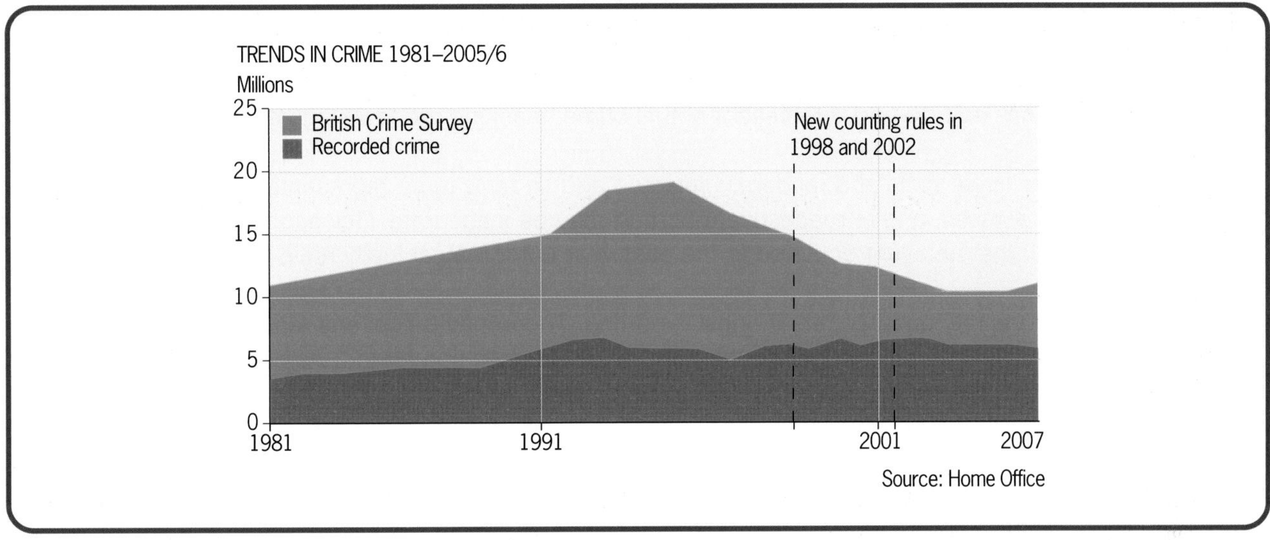

Figure 8.5 *Official statistics of recorded crime are consistently lower than the British Crime Survey figures.*

optional responses for respondents to choose from. The 2006/7 survey showed that victim reports were greater than police recorded crime. For example, the official figures for overall crime showed a 2% decrease whilst the BCS showed a 3% increase. For violent crime, the official statistics showed a decrease of 1% for violent robbery and a 7% decrease in sexual offences. In contrast, the BCS figures showed there to be an increase of 5% in violent offences overall.

In addition to collecting crime statistics, the BCS also collects information about fear of crime and attitudes to crime. The 2006 report carried a recommendation that the survey should be extended to cover under-16s by also conducting interviews with 10- to 15-year-olds from the randomly selected households.

Whilst the BCS is the largest and most influential of the victim surveys carried out in the UK, there are other more specific surveys. One example is the Commercial Victimisation Survey, which is a survey of small and medium-sized retail and manufacturing businesses in England and Wales.

Self-report measures

Offender self-reports or offender surveys ask people about their offending behaviour. As Putwain and Sammons (2002) point out, if these figures are accurate, they can provide additional useful information, not only about the number of crimes being committed, but also about how many people are responsible. This takes account of the fact that although there are many individual crimes, there are rather fewer offenders, since many offenders commit several crimes. Offender surveys tend to focus on groups that might be likely to commit offences, such as people who have previously been convicted, or people from specific age ranges or social backgrounds.

One example of a self-report offender survey is the Offending, Crime and Justice Survey (OCJS), in which young people in England and Wales are interviewed about their attitudes towards and experiences of offending. Due to the sensitive nature of the questions, responses are gathered using a computer, hopefully increasing the validity of the data. The aim of the survey is to assess the extent of offending, antisocial behaviour and drug use among young people aged 10–25 years. This is a random selection, national, longitudinal survey and therefore does not focus specifically on 'serious' offenders. The survey covers offences such as burglary, shoplifting, assault and fraud. It is focused on 10- to 25-year-olds, with the same young people being re-interviewed each year. In addition to the continuing respondents, new respondents are brought into the sample each year, to ensure the total sample remains at around 5,000. The longitudinal information allows for investigation of patterns of delinquency in individuals.

In 2006, OCJS data from 1,669 young people revealed that much crime was alcohol-related, with the most

Evaluation – measuring crime

- The official statistics tend to under-represent actual crime, masking the 'dark figure' of crime.
- Victim surveys are large-scale and randomly selected and so tend to be representative. However, they rely on accuracy of recall, and retrospective reporting may be inaccurate. 'Telescoping' may occur where respondents think that an event occurred in the past year but it may actually have been longer ago.
- Offender self-reports rely on offenders' honest reporting. There may be several reasons why offenders fail to report truthfully or even exaggerate the number of offences committed. As only certain age/social groups are targeted, the sample could be said to be biased.
- Each set of data should be interpreted with caution in the light of its methodological limitations, with particular regard to validity and reliability. A combination of measures perhaps yields the best overview of offending behaviour.

common offences amongst male binge drinkers being violent crime (16%) and theft (14%). The figures also showed that 27% of binge drinkers had offended in the past 12 months, as opposed to only 13% of those classified as regular drinkers. In all categories of offence, the figures were higher for males than females.

8.2 Offender profiling

Definition and background

Douglas and Burgess (1986) define offender profiling as 'an investigative technique by which to identify the major personality and behavioural characteristics of the offender based upon an analysis of the crime(s) he or she has committed'. Profiling began in the USA in the 1960s/1970s, when FBI specialists were trained to infer personality and behavioural traits of an offender by detailed analysis of the way he or she committed the crime. The technique was initially devised to help narrow down the search for serial offenders in apparently motiveless cases of murder and rape. Offender profiling is also known as **crime scene analysis**, or **criminal investigative analysis**, as it involves forming hypotheses about an offender based on analysis of the crime scene, victim and existing knowledge about offender behaviour.

Organised offender	Disorganised offender
Crime scene characteristics	**Crime scene characteristics**
Evidence of planning Victim is a stranger Controlled conversation Use of restraints Removes weapon from scene Body hidden	Little evidence of planning Victim is known Little conversation Leaves evidence–semen, blood, etc. Little use of restraint Body in open view
Likely personality and behaviour	**Likely personality and behaviour**
Average to high intelligence Socially competent Skilled employment Sexually competent Living with partner	Below-average intelligence Socially inadequate Unskilled employment Sexually incompetent Lives alone and close to scene

Figure 8.6 *The typology approach: Personality traits of organised and disorganised offenders and crime scene characteristics.*

The typology approach

Early work on offender profiling by the FBI indicated a broad distinction between **organised offenders** and **disorganised offenders**. This distinction was based on interviews and case details of 36 serial sex offenders who volunteered to be interviewed about their crimes. Since its first appearance, the organised/disorganised distinction has been widely cited in academic literature and used as a model by professional investigators. According to the Crime Classification Manual (Douglas *et al.*, 1992), the organised/disorganised typology can be applied to all sexually motivated murders and some cases of arson.

In 1992, Douglas suggested that a third category of 'mixed' offender be added to the twofold category system, to accommodate those offenders who cannot easily be categorised as either organised or disorganised.

Evaluation – the typology approach

- Although the organised/disorganised distinction is widely cited, its validity has not been established. See Alison *et al.* (2002), page 216.
- The interviews conducted to establish the two types were conducted with a very limited sample.
- The distinction is an oversimplification and the addition of a third catch-all category bring into question the original notion of only two types of offender.
- There are other classification systems: Jenkins (1988) suggested two different categories of serial murderer, the respectable type and the predictable type; Holmes and De Burger (1988) proposed six types that could be defined according to the combination of 14 characteristics.
- Canter *et al.* (2004) questioned the organised/disorganised distinction, arguing that whilst there is some evidence for a subset of 'organised' features being typical of most serial killers, there is no evidence for a distinct disorganised type.

STUDY

Aim

Canter *et al.* (2004) set out to test the validity of the organised/disorganised distinction.

Method

The researchers used information from 100 murders by 100 serial killers in the USA. Each case was assessed for the presence of 39 characteristics identified in literature as typical of either organised or disorganised offenders. A statistical technique known as smallest space analysis was used to test for the co-occurrence of the 39 variables across the 100 cases.

Results

A subset of organised characteristics was found to be typical of most serial killers, including body being left in an isolated spot and the use of restraint. Disorganised characteristics were much rarer and did not occur together often enough to be considered a type.

Conclusion

There is no clear distinction between organised and disorganised offenders. Being organised is a core characteristic of serial killers as whole.

Alison *et al.* (2002) reviewed the processes involved in offender profiling and noted that these are based on two assumptions – first, that there is consistency in an offender's behaviour at their different offences, and second, that aspects of the offender's behaviour at the scene of the crime will tally with their normal everyday behaviour. For example, if the offender is violent at the crime scene, then he or she will be violent in everyday life. Alison *et al.* concluded that whilst the first assumption is supported, the second is not. They referred to contemporary personality theory which states that interactions between the person and the situation will lead a person to behave differently in different situations – the **Person X Situation effect**. According to Alison *et al.*, current profiling methods rely on an outdated understanding of personality and should be used with extreme caution until such time as there is evidence that the technique has predictive validity.

Geographical approaches

The geographical approach to profiling involves generalising from the locations of linked crime scenes to the likely home or operational base of the offender (Rossmo, 1997). The basic assumption is that offenders prefer to operate in areas they know well, close to either home or places visited regularly. Many offenders have been found to have a crime range of as little as 2 miles (Canter and Gregory, 1994). Canter and Gregory distinguish between offenders who commit crime in their own neighbourhood, marauders, and those who travel to commit their crimes, commuters. In either case, knowledge about the location of related crimes enables the investigator to narrow down the search and surveillance area. In the case of Peter Sutcliffe, the Yorkshire Ripper, who attacked and murdered several female victims in the Leeds area in the 1970s, investigators were able to determine roughly where Sutcliffe lived by studying the locations of his crimes. Kind (2008) explained how analysis of the locations in this case identified a 'centre of gravity', which enabled inferences about Sutcliffe's base and occupation.

David Canter is the main exponent of geographical profiling in the UK. Canter and Youngs (2008) explain how geographical profiling is built on accepted psychological theory about how people represent or conceptualise information. Bartlett (1932) proposed that information is stored in mental schemas, which are organised units of knowledge. A specific type of schema is a **mental map**, an organised set of information about spatial information. According to Canter, information about location of crime scenes reflects the offender's mental map of the area. Since each person's mental map is highly individual and reflects their personal experience of their environment, the location of crime scenes can be used to infer not only where an offender is based, but also other aspects of their experiences, such as interests, employment and relationships.

Lundrigan and Canter (2001) argue that all criminal spatial decision making is influenced by social, cognitive and economic factors. Examples of relevant factors include age, intelligence, marital and job status, motive, method of transport and when in the series the crime is being committed.

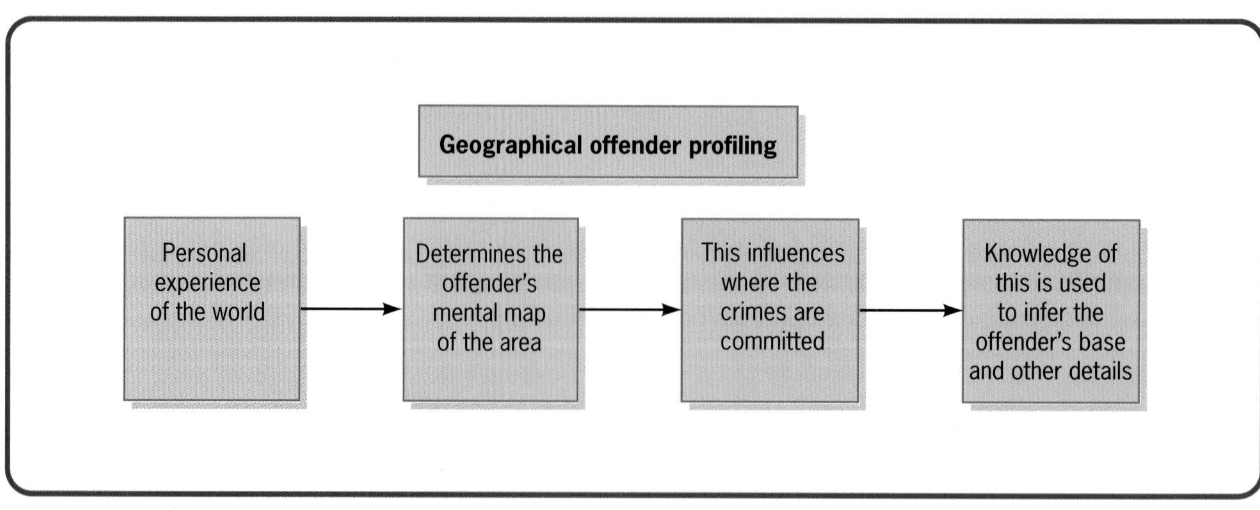

Figure 8.7 *Geographical offender profiling.*

The case of John Duffy

The case of John Duffy, the Railway Rapist, is probably the most well known of all British profiling cases (Canter, 1994).

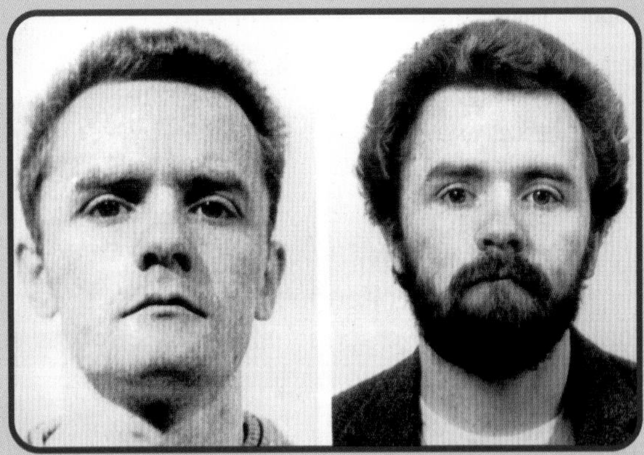

Figure 8.8a *John Duffy – the Railway Rapist.*

Between 1982 and 1986, a total of 24 sexual assaults and three murders occurred in London. David Canter, a psychologist, was asked by the police to produce of a profile of the likely offender. Geographical information about the scene of the crimes was an important aspect of the investigation, along with witness reports of behaviour at the scene of the crimes. Canter's profile led to the arrest of John Duffy in November 1986. The profile was found to be accurate in many respects: he lived in Kilburn, was separated from his wife to whom he had been violent, and had a job as a carpenter on the railways.

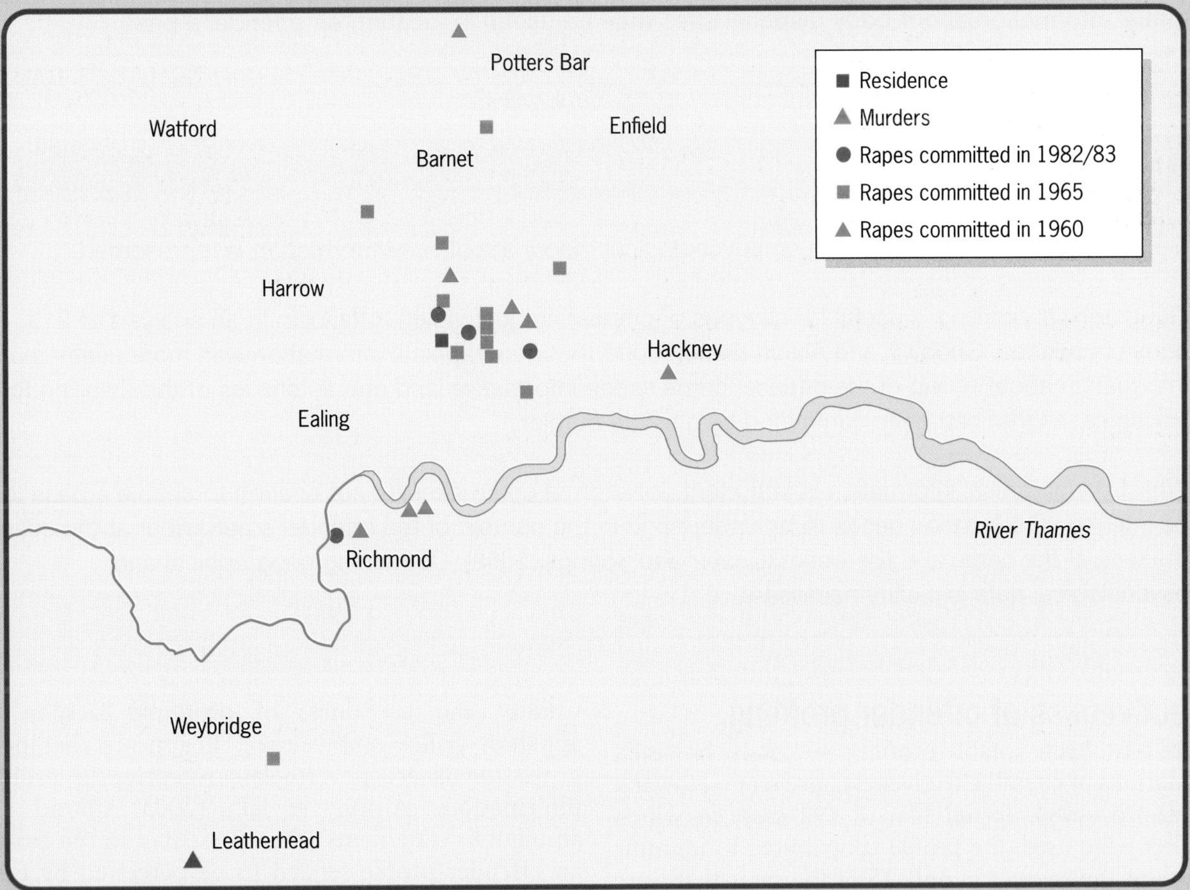

Figure 8.8b *Map of Duffy's offences.*

STUDY

Aim

Lundrigan and Canter (2001) studied the spatial behaviour of 120 serial murderers in the USA.

Method

Information from solved murder cases was obtained. Each murderer had committed a series of murders. For each offender, the researchers analysed distances between the offender's home location and body disposal sites used for the series. A statistical technique (smallest space analysis) was used to determine patterns of disposal.

Results

Three key findings emerged: 1) The offender's home was geographically central in the pattern. 2) The location of each disposal site tended to be in a different direction to the previous disposal site. 3) This effect was most evident for offenders who travelled shorter distances (less than 10 km).

Conclusion

Spatial information about body disposal sites may be useful in locating an offender's base.

Evaluation – geographical profiling

- Geographical profiling is founded on psychological theory about how information is represented.
- Geographical profiling is useful for all types of crimes, not just violent offences. In an analysis of 215 house burglaries, Goodwill and Alison (2006) found that geographical information was more useful than information about timing of the offence, crime scene information and characteristics of the dwelling for linking cases that had been committed by a single burglar.
- Whilst geographical information is important, location of crime alone is not enough to enable a base to be inferred. The location needs to be understood in the context of the offender's behaviour at the scene, the time of the crime and the victim (Canter and Youngs, 2008). Combining geographical and psychological data is clearly necessary.

Effectiveness of offender profiling

There have been notable profiling successes; however, evaluations of overall effectiveness have tended to vary. Pinizzotto (1984) found that of 192 cases in which profiles were used, the profile contributed to identification of the suspect in only 15 of the cases that were solved. Bartol (1996) surveyed 152 police psychologists and found that 70% of them were unsure about the validity and usefulness of profiling. Despite this apparent police ambivalence, it appears that police professionals are nevertheless receptive to profiling information. Alison *et al.* (2003) found that ambiguous statements when presented in the guise of an offender profile tended to be perceived by police officers as accurate descriptions of the offender, even when the profile included contradictory statements.

STUDY

Aim

Pinizzotto and Finkel (1990) carried out an evaluation of the effectiveness of offender profiler training.

Method

Five groups of participants were compared on their ability to construct two profiles of real (previously solved) cases. They were given information about the crime scene, method and victim and asked to describe the likely offender. One case was a murder and the other a sex offence. The participants were four trained FBI officers, six trained police detectives, six experienced detectives who had not received profiling training, six clinical psychologists naive to profiling and six students. The profiles were compared with the actual details of the offender and assessed for accuracy. Participants were also assessed on the types of cognitive strategies they employed during the task.

Results

The trained experts produced better, more accurate profiles of the sex offender, but were not significantly better than the other groups with the murder case. There were no differences between trained profilers and other participants in the cognitive strategies used.

Conclusion

Profiling training appears to be of some use.

8.3 Theories of offending

Several theories for offending have been proposed. Here we shall consider some traditional and now outdated physiological explanations, along with more contemporary biological and psychological explanations.

8.3.1 Physiological approaches

Early theories of offending focused on aspects of the offenders' physical make-up or constitution – for example, their facial features and body type. The general belief was that certain physiological characteristics were commonly found amongst criminals and identify a criminal type.

Lombroso's theory of atavistic form

Lombroso was an Italian physician whose theory of criminal types is thought to be at the foundation of modern criminological theory. Lombroso (1876) proposed that offenders were a biologically distinct group of people exhibiting primitive characteristics, a separate species with a primitive genetic form (**atavistic**), whose features enabled them to survive in the wild but made them ill-suited to existence in civilised society. In his book *L'Uomo Delinquente* (*The Criminal Man*) he presented physical measurements taken from Italian convicts, showing that they had distinctive **physical anomalies** such as large jaws and large ears. Lombroso argued that the shape of the head and facial features determined the criminal type and that criminals were born, not made.

Lombroso's criminal characteristics
Large jaws Narrow sloping brow High cheekbones Large ears Extra nipples, fingers, toes Dark skin Hairiness Insensitivity to pain

Figure 8.9 *Lombroso proposed that criminals have distinctive physical features.*

Lombroso based his theory on survey data of criminal heads and bodies. He sampled the proportions of 383 skulls of dead criminals and the heads of 3,839 living ones. He did not suggest that all criminal acts were perpetrated by people with atavistic constitutions, but concluded that approximately 40% could be accounted for in this way. He later went further, attributing criminality to congenital illnesses – for example, stating that most born criminals suffer from epilepsy to some degree. The theory caused great controversy in the nineteenth century and, although Lombroso's conclusions are not really supported by his own data (Gould, 1981), was highly influential in promoting views about biological determinism.

Evaluation

- There is now thought to be no scientific foundation for Lombroso's theory. Goring (1913) compared the physical features of 3,000 convicts and a control group. He found little support for Lombroso's theory of distinctive facial and cranial characteristics.
- Lombroso's sample may have included people with learning difficulties.
- Criminality and certain facial characteristics may both be affected by confounding factors such as poverty and poor nutrition.
- The theory had significant racial undertones; criminals were defined as genetic throwbacks or primitive species and the facial characteristics identified were those typical of people of African origin. Even today similar views exist. For example, Rushton (Rushton, 1988); (Rushton and Jensen, 2005) argues that higher crime rates among black Afro-Caribbean people are due to genetic differences in intelligence and social disorganisation.
- Even if certain facial features occur more often in criminal types, it does not mean that there is a causal relationship. There may be other explanations: people with certain facial features may be stereotyped as 'hard' and picked on more often, leading to a self-fulfilling prophecy.
- In the face of opposition, Lombroso modified his theory of the born criminal, stating that criminality could also be due to environmental factors.
- One lasting consequence of the theory is the notion that criminals have a certain look or stereotype.

Type and physical description	Personality traits
Endomorph – soft, fat and rounded	Social, relaxed characters
Ectomorph – skinny and fragile	Shy and introverted characters
Mesomorph – hard and muscular	Aggressive and adventurous characters – the criminal type

Figure 8.10 *Sheldon's theory of body types or somatotypes.*

Sheldon's somatotype theory

Sheldon (1949) proposed a constitutional theory of crime based on body shape or **somatotype**. He argued that there were three basic body types: endomorphs, ectomorphs and mesomorphs, and that each had associated temperaments. Sheldon accepted that most people were a combination of somatotypes and that the extreme was rare. He did however believe that the degree of mesomorphy could predict the extent to which a person would show criminal tendencies.

Figure 8.11 *Sheldon (1949) argued that the mesomorph is the criminal type.*

STUDY

Aim

Sheldon (1949) investigated the link between body shape and criminality.

Method

Two hundred photographs of delinquents and 200 control photographs of non-delinquents (students) were rated for mesomorphy on a scale of 1–7 (1 = not at all mesomorphic and 7 = extremely mesomorphic). Sheldon rated the photographs himself.

Results

The average rating for the delinquent photos was 4.6, compared to an average rating for the non-delinquent control photos of 3.8.

Conclusion

Delinquency is associated with a mesomorphic body shape.

Evaluation

- Sheldon's research was criticised because he did not use the legal criteria for delinquency (Sutherland, 1951). When delinquency was defined according to the legal criteria, the association was no longer present.
- The theory established and reinforced the idea of the criminal stereotype.
- Even if there is a link between body type and criminality, it is not necessarily causal. Perhaps muscular people are treated as tougher and so become tougher – a self-fulfilling prophecy.
- High testosterone levels may affect both body shape and aggressive behaviour (Blackburn, 1993).
- Some research has supported the link between body shape and delinquency (Glueck and Glueck, 1956). Other studies have found no such association (West and Farrington, 1973).

Further analysis of Sheldon's data by Hartley *et al.* (1982) involved analysing the ratings for just the most serious offenders in the sample. This showed there to be an even greater difference in ratings for the delinquent and non-delinquent conditions.

8.3.2 Biological explanations

Lombroso and Sheldon were forerunners of modern biological psychologists, who look for biological explanations for offending. Three biological explanations are considered here: genetics, chromosomes and neurophysiology. Note that these are not mutually exclusive. It is quite possible that a behaviour determined initially by genetic inheritance in turn influences neurophysiology.

Genetic transmission

Twin and adoption studies have been carried out to investigate the heritability of offending behaviour. Concordance rates between identical or monozygotic (MZ) twin pairs and non-identical or dizygotic (DZ) twin pairs are compared. If offending behaviour is genetic, we would expect a greater degree of similarity for that trait between MZ pairs, who share 100% of their genes, than between DZ pairs, who share only 50% of their genes. The earliest twin study of criminality was carried out by Lange (1929). He found concordance rates of 77% for MZ pairs and 12% for DZ pairs. However, early twin studies tended to neglect the fact that MZ twins were more likely than DZ twins to have more similar shared environments. Subsequent studies that are better controlled have not tended to yield such markedly different concordance rates. For example, Christiansen (1977) found rates of 35% and 12% in MZ and DZ pairs respectively in a very large sample study in Denmark.

To properly assess the extent of genetic influences, the effect of inheritance should be disentangled from the effect of a shared environment by using twins who were separated at birth or very early in life. Finding such a sample is rarely possible; however, Grove *et al.* (1990) did manage to conduct a separated twin study.

Adoption studies

Adoption studies involve comparing the criminal futures of adopted children with the criminal history of a) their biological parents and b) their adoptive parents. The method assumes that if there is a greater degree of similarity in the criminal behaviours of adoptees and their biological parents than there is for the adoptees and their adoptive parents, criminality has a genetic component.

STUDY

Aim

Grove *et al.* (1990) investigated concordance rates of criminal behaviour in separated pairs of MZ twins.

Method

Thirty-one sets of MZ twins and one set of triplets were interviewed individually. All the interviewees had been reared apart from shortly after birth. The researchers assessed their behaviour at the average age of 43 years. The interviewers, who were blind to the purpose of the study, scored each interviewee for presence of DSM-III Axis I psychiatric disorders and antisocial personality. Scores for alcohol problems, drug problems, child and adult antisocial behaviour were calculated.

Results

The drug score and both antisocial scores showed significant heritability. The concordance rate for antisocial personality disorder was 29%.

Conclusion

The researchers concluded that these traits had a substantial genetic component.

STUDY

Aim

Mednick *et al.* (1984) studied the heritability of criminal behaviour is an adoption study.

Method

Using data from the Danish adoption data bank, which covers the social histories of more than 14,000 children, the criminal conviction rates of male adoptees were compared with those of their biological and adoptive parents.

Results

Twenty per cent of adoptees whose biological parents had convictions but who had been raised by non-criminal parents had convictions. For adoptees whose birth parents were not criminals and who had been raised by non-criminal adoptive parents the rate was 13.5%.

Conclusion

The results are consistent with a modest genetic effect.

In a review of six adoption studies, Carey and Goldman (1997) found a genetic effect for criminal behaviour.

Chromosomes

Although much is known about chromosomes and genetic disorders, no single criminal gene has been identified. However, there has been an attempt to link criminal behaviour to possession of an extra Y chromosome. You will recall that males have a Y sex chromosome as one of their 23rd pair of chromosomes. The Y chromosome is what determines maleness and is responsible for male sexual development and the male hormone testosterone. You will recall from your AS studies that testosterone has been linked to aggression (see Chapter 3 of *AQA(B) Psychology for AS* by Pennington and McLoughlin, 2008).

In 1965, Jacobs *et al.* claimed to have discovered an incidence of the atypical sex chromosome pattern XYY in 1.5% of the prison population, as opposed to the incidence rate of 0.1% in the normal population. There was great excitement that a cause of criminal behaviour had been identified, but this quickly abated when further studies failed to confirm the link. For example, Witkin *et al.* (1976) found that only 12 men in a sample of over 4,500 had the extra Y chromosome, and none of the XYY males was an offender. The XYY theory of offending is no longer accepted.

Neurophysiology

Animal research has identified structures in the brain, specifically the limbic system and amygdala, responsible for the modulation of aggressive behaviour. Even in animals however, the expression of aggression usually requires an environmental stimulus, such as the presence of another male of the species to trigger aggressive behaviour. Different regions of the brain have been implicated in different types of aggression. For example, Adams (1986) found that lesions to the ventral tegmental area of the midbrain of rats led to the disruption of offensive aggression but did not affect predatory and defensive aggression.

In humans, most neurophysiological investigation has been conducted with people diagnosed with antisocial personality disorder (APD). People with APD, sometimes referred to as psychopaths, show no emotion and no feeling for others. Studies using EEGs of brain activity in the 1950s and 1960s showed that people with APD had abnormal EEG patterns of slow-wave

STUDY

Aim

Raine *et al.* (2000) compared brain volume in people with APD and controls.

Method

Volume of prefrontal grey and white matter was measured using magnetic resonance imaging (MRI) in 21 people with APD and controls. Autonomic activity was also measured in response to a stressful situation during which participants had to give a videotaped speech about their faults. The autonomic measures were heart rate and skin conductance (GSR).

Results

There was a reduced volume of grey matter (11% reduction) in the prefrontal area for the APD group. They also showed reduced autonomic responses during the stressful situation.

Conclusion

There is a structural brain deficit in people with APD which might be the cause of APD behaviours such as poor arousal, lack of conscience and poor fear conditioning.

activity, which are typical of brain immaturity. This led Hare (1970) to propose the **maturation retardation hypothesis,** which proposed that the brain of the APD individual is immature and childlike – an appealing notion given that characteristics of APD include impulsivity, self-centredness and the inability to delay gratification (all childlike traits). Moffitt (2003) argued that adolescent delinquency may be a result of delayed brain development, although this would not explain persistent life-course offending.

Other neurophysiological anomalies have been noted in highly aggressive APD individuals. Kurland *et al.* (1963) found that 66% of APD individuals with a history of uncontrollable and violent episodes showed spontaneous bursts of rapid brain waves (positive spikes) during sleep. It has also been suggested that APD may be correlated with hemispheric dysfunction. The left hemisphere is usually responsible for language function and the right hemisphere for the understanding and communicating of emotion. Hare and Connolly (1987) suggested that criminals with APD show an abnormal balance in hemispheric activity, which might explain their inability to use language to regulate their impulsive behaviour and aggressive outbursts. More recently, Raine *et al.* (2000) have found that people with APD show abnormal brain structure.

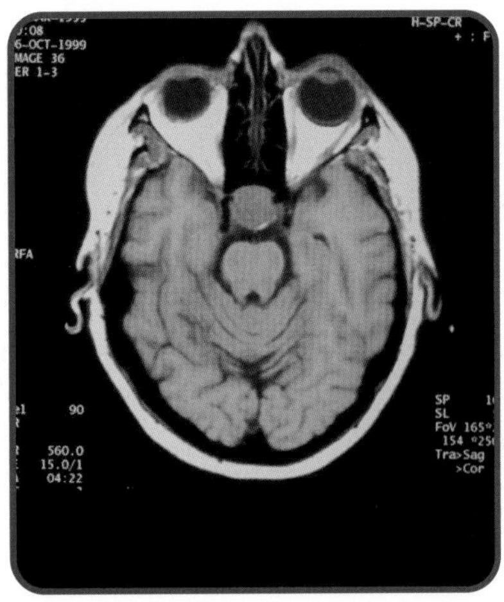

Figure 8.12 *Raine* et al. *(2000) found a reduced volume of grey matter in the prefrontal area in people with antisocial personality disorder.*

Evaluation of the biological explanation

- Although much is known about chromosomes and genetic disorders, no single criminal gene has been identified.
- Twin and adoption study evidence seems to support a genetic component, but does also indicate that the environment may have an influence; even MZ pairs do not show 100% concordance.
- Early twin studies were not well controlled: there was no definitive way to determine whether twin pairs were MZ or DZ, so the researchers often guessed. Twins who were supposedly separated at birth often attended the same school and visited each other regularly.
- Andrews and Bonta (2006) point out that the common criminality of biological parent and adopted child may be a side effect of inherited emotional instability and/or mental illness rather than directly inherited criminality.
- No direct causal link can be established between anomalies in neurological function and criminal behaviour. Evidence from animal studies cannot readily be generalised to explain human behaviour.
- Biological explanations are reductionist, attempting to explain complex offending behaviour at the level of chemicals and cells.

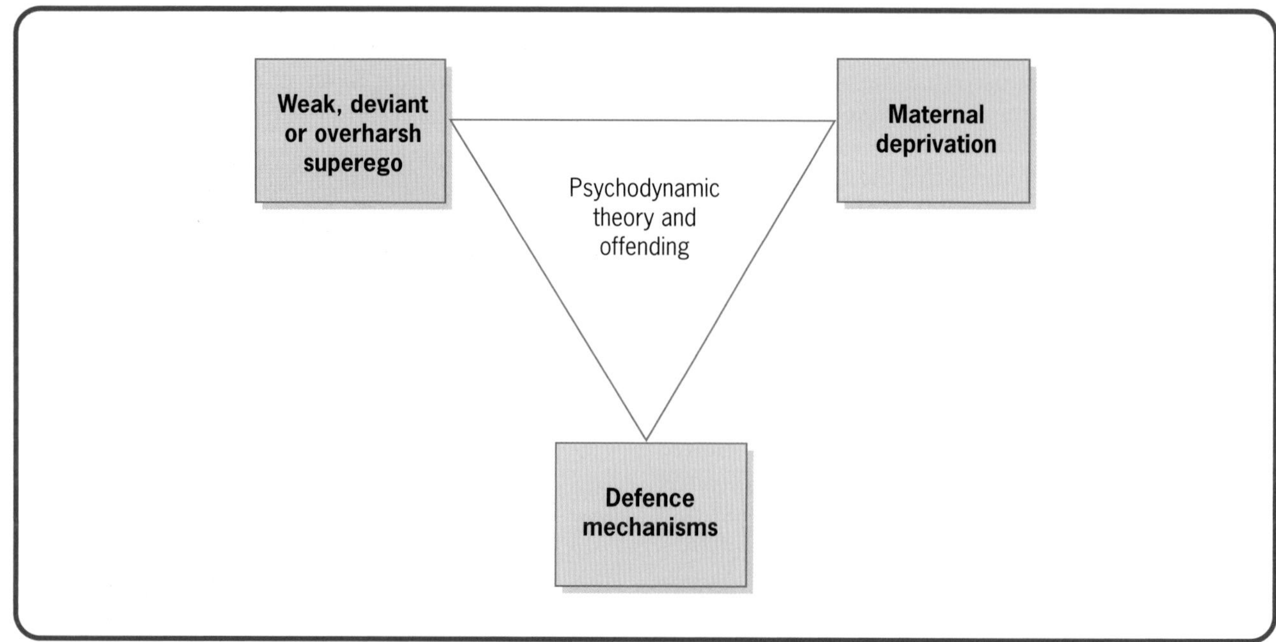

Figure 8.13 *Three ways in which psychodynamic theory can be used to explain offending.*

8.3.3 Psychodynamic explanations

Although Freud himself never attempted to explain offending behaviour, the following three aspects of psychodynamic theory can be used to explain crime: inadequate superego; defence mechanisms; maternal deprivation.

Inadequate superego

According to Freud, the personality has three components: the **id**, which is the demanding, self-gratifying instinct – the tantrumming child who seeks instant gratification; the **superego**, which is the conscience or internal parent, which develops through identification with same-sex parent in the phallic stage as part of the resolution of the Oedipus/Electra complex; and the **ego**, which acts to moderate the demands of the id and the harsh strictures of the superego, and responds to the demands and expectations of external society. Freudian theory would predict that offending behaviour is due to an imbalance between the three components of the personality, primarily because the id is not sufficiently controlled. Blackburn (1993) stated that three types of superego may result in a person demonstrating offending behaviour:

- **The weak superego** – There is an absence of a same-sex parent in the phallic stage. As a result, the child has no opportunity to identify with the same-sex parent and internalise the parent's moral code. The child grows up to have no firm idea of right and wrong. The superego is not sufficiently punitive, therefore does not cause guilt, meaning the person shows no inhibition.
- **The deviant superego** – The same-sex parent with whom the child identifies in the phallic stage is an immoral person. The child therefore internalises a moral code that is deviant, with what most people would perceive to be immoral values and standards. The person's views of right and wrong are at odds with those of the rest of society.
- **The over-harsh superego** – The child's superego is excessively punitive and demanding of guilt, leading the child to seek out opportunities to be chastised and punished to satisfy this need for punishment. The person engages in compulsive criminal behaviour because they have an unconscious desire to be punished. This is explained as a reaction to guilt from unconscious infantile desires.

Superego-based explanations for offending rely on the psychodynamic theory of psychosexual development, whereby internalisation of the parent's moral code takes place in the phallic stage at around 5 years. According to Freud, boys identify more strongly with their fathers than girls identify with their mothers because boys are more fearful (of castration). Thus according to Freud, girls are less morally developed because their moral code is less firmly internalised.

Defence mechanisms

Defence mechanisms are unconscious processes designed to defend the conscious self from unpleasant events in the world and unpleasant truths about the self. Whilst some defence mechanisms, like denial, operate to keep emotions hidden, others are **cathartic**, meaning that they operate through allowing the individual to release pent-up feelings. The concept of defence mechanisms can be used to explain crime in a number of ways. Here are some examples:

- **Denial** involves refusing to accept that an unpleasant event is happening because to acknowledge it consciously would be too disturbing. Thus a person who commits a series of murders might refuse to consciously acknowledge that they are taking place or refuse to recognise the severity of their actions.
- **Rationalisation** involves explaining unacceptable behaviour in a rational and acceptable way. Thus a person who attacks provocatively dressed young women might rationalise these actions by explaining that the women are a scourge on decent society and should be taught a lesson.
- **Displacement** involves the individual taking out anger and frustration on a substitute object. Thus a young man who is angry with his girlfriend might take that anger out on a substitute object, lashing out with a knife at a stranger in the street.
- **Sublimation** involves the redirection of normally primitive impulses into other more acceptable activities. Thus a person who wants to rape and murder might seek out the services of a prostitute to engage in violent sexual activity.

Maternal deprivation

According to the psychoanalyst John Bowlby (1951), being deprived of a continuous and loving relationship with the mother in first 2 years of a child's life results in irreversible, damaging consequences, including delinquency, affectionless psychopathy and intellectual retardation (see Chapter 1, page 15). Klein (1987) describes affectionless psychopathy as a permanent lack of feeling for others. Maternal deprivation might thus explain many types of offending, since most offenders appear to have no feeling for their victims, and some, although not all, have below-average intellectual ability. The evidence for Bowlby's theory came from studies carried out with infant animals deprived of their mothers and from Bowlby's own research with 44 juvenile delinquents (see pages 16–17 for details of the study and evaluation of the theory of maternal deprivation).

Evaluation of the psychodynamic explanation for offending

- Many people without a same-sex parent with whom they can identify grow up to be perfectly law-abiding.
- According to Freud, the greater fear in boys (of castration) leads to a stronger superego in boys than girls – so males should be more moral, but statistics show that males commit more crime.
- As defence mechanisms are unconscious they cannot be tested. This means that there is no real evidence for their existence.
- Bowlby's study has been criticised on a number of counts: the data were retrospective and therefore likely to be unreliable; even if maternal deprivation is a contributing factor in crime, there is no simple cause-and-effect relationship between maternal deprivation and delinquency; some of the delinquents in the study had not suffered maternal deprivation, therefore there must be other explanations for offending behaviour.

8.3.4 Learning theory explanations

According to traditional behaviourist theory, all behaviour is learnt through association, either between two stimuli that occur together in time (classical conditioning) or between response and consequence (operant conditioning). Traditional behaviourists would therefore argue that criminal behaviour is learnt. According to social learning theory (SLT), offending behaviour would be learned through the processes of observation, imitation, identification and direct and vicarious reinforcement (Bandura, 1977). Vicarious reinforcement operates through observation of the consequences for others of their actions, and hence is indirect reinforcement.

Sutherland (1939) proposed a learning theory of crime known as **differential association theory**, which can be summarised as follows:

- Offending behaviour is learnt in the same way as any other behaviour.
- This learning results from close association with other people (peers, family, etc.).
- From these people we learn our values and norms (in the case of the offender, these would be deviant ones).
- Everyone's associations are different (differential association), therefore everyone has different values and norms.
- If a person is exposed to more pro-criminal attitudes than anti-criminal attitudes then they will offend.
- The learning is of attitudes, motives and techniques for committing crime.

Figure 8.14 *Sutherland's differential association theory of offending stated that offending is learnt through exposure to criminal norms and values.*

Thus a person who is exposed to pro-criminal attitudes and norms in the family and amongst peers will be more likely to engage in criminal behaviour than a person who is exposed to anti-criminal norms and values. According to Sutherland's theory, criminal behaviour was not exclusive to those from deprived and uneducated backgrounds, but could also explain crime in the middle classes. For example, a person might cheat on a tax return or steal stationery from the office to use at home if such behaviour was always seen as acceptable in the family.

Later developments of Sutherland's theory focus on the effects of reinforcement and punishment; if the benefits of engaging in criminal behaviour are greater than the benefits of not engaging in criminal behaviour then a person will commit crime. The benefit would be reinforcement in the form of respect and approval of people with whom we associate. The theory can be further refined if observational learning is also taken into account. The norms and values demonstrated by influential role models can affect the aspirations and expectations of those who identify with them and are a powerful influence on behaviour.

It is extremely difficult to determine the extent to which socialisation affects criminal behaviour. Whilst snapshot studies can show that people from difficult or disaffected backgrounds tend to commit crime more frequently than those from less disadvantaged backgrounds, meaningful data tend to be infrequent. It is time-consuming to conduct well-controlled prospective studies, where at-risk individuals are identified and their criminal career is tracked into the future. An example of a large-scale prospective study of offending can be seen on the opposite page.

STUDY

Aim

Farrington *et al*. (2006) carried out the Cambridge Study of Delinquent Development, a longitudinal study.

Method

A group of 411 working-class boys and their families, from a deprived inner-city area of south London, were studied from the age of 8 years in 1961 to the age of 50 years. Researchers recorded details of family background, parenting styles and school behaviour. They also recorded the rate and type of convictions at various points.

Results

Forty-one per cent of the sample had criminal convictions between the ages of 10 and 50 years. At the age of 17 years, 50% of the convictions were attributable to a hard core of 5% of the sample. Key risk factors were family criminality, poverty, poor parenting, risk-taking and low school achievement.

Conclusion

Criminality develops in a context of inappropriate role models and dysfunctional systems of reward and punishment.

Evaluation of learning theory explanations

- This focus on socialisation as a key factor in criminal behaviour represented a dramatic shift from previous theories, which had viewed criminal behaviour as either innate, instinctive or due to individual weakness.
- Differential association theory can explain all types of offending, not just violent crime.
- A causal link between socialisation and criminality cannot be established.
- Studies like the Farrington *et al.* (2006) research could also be taken as evidence for a genetic theory of offending, since a high percentage of the sample had biological parents who were criminals. Indeed one analysis of the Cambridge data showed intergenerational criminality across three generations (Smith and Farrington, 2004).
- Learning theories do not explain why many offenders cease to offend as they get older.
- The theory is founded on sound scientific principles, but it is perhaps an oversimplification to apply these to such a complex behaviour.

8.3.5 Eysenck's theory of the criminal personality

Hans Eysenck was a key figure in personality theory and intelligence research in the 1950s and 1960s. He proposed that traits such as personality and intelligence are innate. As such, Eysenck's theory of offending (1964) is another biological theory. However, for Eysenck, offending behaviour is not directly inherited, but rather a consequence of the type of nervous system we inherit which determines our personality. His theory of personality initially stated that individuals vary across two dimensions, introvert-extravert (IE) and neurotic-stable (NS). Each of us varies in terms of the amount to which we are introvert (shy) or extravert (outgoing), and, similarly, the amount to which we are stable (not anxious) or neurotic (anxious). He later added a third dimension, psychoticism, typically cold, uncaring and aggressive.

Eysenck proposed that these personality dimensions were measurable using a personality questionnaire, the Eysenck Personality Inventory (EPI). The EPI consists of a large number of questions to which respondents must answer either yes or no. The total number of yes and no answers to certain questions reveals an E score (extraversion) and an N score (neuroticism), indicating the respondent's position in relation to the two dimensions. Responses to further items yielded a P score. The E and N scores can then be plotted on the two dimensions, as shown in Figure 8.15, allowing the respondent to be classified as a personality type.

Examples of items from the EPI

Do you worry too long after an embarrassing experience?

Are you rather lively?

Do you find it hard to fall asleep at bedtime?

Do you like working alone?

Do you nearly always have a 'ready answer' when people talk to you?

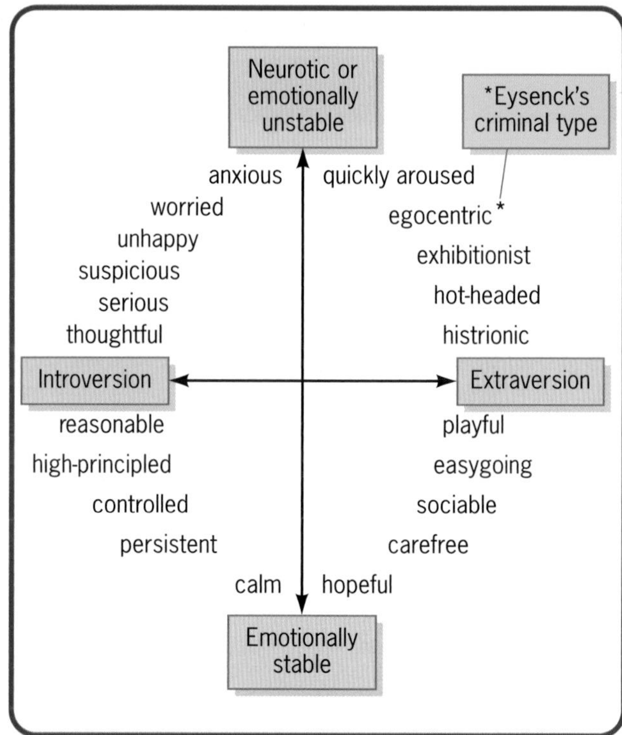

Figure 8.15 *Eysenck's theory of personality. Eysenck proposed that neurotic extravert was the criminal type.*

Based on this general theory of personality, Eysenck proposed that **neurotic-extravert** was the criminal type. He suggested that extraverts are sensation-seeking because their nervous system is chronically under-aroused. This leads them to seek out stimulation and excitement and engage in risk-taking behaviour. Extraverts also have a nervous system that does not condition easily, meaning that they do not learn from their mistakes. They find it difficult, therefore, to learn appropriate behaviour. Neurotic individuals are emotionally unstable and anxious; they react unpredictably. This combination of sensation-seeking, unpredictability and inability to learn leads the neurotic-extravert into criminal behaviours.

STUDY

Aim

McGurk and McDougall (1981) investigated the link between criminality and personality type.

Method

One hundred students defined as 'delinquent' and 100 control students who were not delinquent completed the EPI and their E and N scores were calculated.

Results

There were significant differences in scores on all three dimensions. The delinquent group had a combination of high P, E and N scores.

Conclusion

There is a relationship between personality type, as assessed using the EPI, and delinquent behaviour.

Evaluation of Eysenck's theory

- Several studies show that offenders have higher P and N scores (Farrington *et al.*, 1982), but the evidence for high E scores is not so convincing.
- Consideration of offending in terms of just two key dimensions is perhaps an oversimplification. Contemporary theories of personality such as the Five Factor Model (Digman, 1990) suggest that other personality dimensions are important. The Five Factor Model considers additional dimensions of openness to experience, agreeableness and conscientiousness. Thus a neurotic-extravert person, who is the criminal type according to Eysenck, need not necessarily become an offender, depending on the person's psychological make-up in relation to the other dimensions.
- Eysenck's theory proposes a single criminal type. Moffitt (1993) argued that there are four distinct types of young male offender, as differentiated on the basis of the timing and duration of the offending behaviour, the pattern of offending and the type of offence committed. She proposed four types as follows: stable early starters; adolescent-limited; adult starters; discontinuous offenders.
- Eysenck's theory lends itself to testing and the EPI is considered to be a reliable tool for measuring personality.

8.4 Treatment of offenders

8.4.1 The role and effectiveness of custodial sentencing

A custodial sentence involves the offender serving time in a prison or a young offenders' institution. Custodial sentencing might be considered to be effective to the extent to which it prevents **recidivism** or reoffending; however, statistics are not very encouraging. Cullen and Minchin (2000) tracked prisoners released in 1996 and found that 57% reoffended within two years. For young males the rate was much higher, at 76%. Rates of recidivism appear to vary according to the type of crime. Doherty (2001) cites the following figures: 77% for those convicted of burglary; 18% for those convicted of sex offences. Such raw figures must be interpreted with caution. For example, offenders who are sent to prison for more serious offences are likely to be older when they are released and therefore may be less likely to reoffend.

Custodial sentencing is generally seen as having four roles, although these four are not always satisfied each time an offender is sent to prison. The four roles are incapacitation, rehabilitation, retribution and deterrence.

- **Incapacitation** means that an offender is prevented from offending for the duration of the sentence. This is essential in cases of serious violent crime where the public needs to be protected from a dangerous individual, but not really necessary in cases where the criminal does not pose a threat. For example, an old lady who refuses to pay her council tax is not a threat to anyone else.
- **Rehabilitation** (reform) involves changing the offender for the better, such that they become law-abiding citizens upon release. Whilst in prison the offender might have the opportunity to attend treatment sessions to change attitudes and behaviours, although many prisons do not have the resources to provide treatment. The effectiveness of some treatments is discussed on pages 237–241. However, recidivism rates suggest that many people receiving a custodial sentence are not reformed by the experience.
- **Retribution** means that society 'gets its own back' on the offender by making the offender pay back to society in some way. Many argue that prison serves this function more than any other – see Davies and Raymond opposite.
- **Deterrence** occurs if a potential offender is 'put off' offending by the prospect of receiving a prison sentence. Deterrence acts as a vicarious negative reinforcer, preventing offending through observation of the negative consequences for others. Theoretically, those who have received a prison sentence in the past should be deterred from further offending; however, recidivism rates suggest prison is not an effective deterrent.

Figure 8.16 *Davies and Raymond (2000) concluded that custodial sentences do not deter others but are popular with the public because they are seen to make the offender pay for wrongdoing.*

Evaluation

- Davies and Raymond (2000) carried out a judicial review of custodial sentencing. They concluded that custodial sentences do not deter others and are often given to appease the public or for political reasons. They also noted that certain types of criminal – for example, those committing crimes to feed a drug addiction – are not deterred by the prospect of prison.
- **Recidivism** rates for those receiving custodial sentences suggest that prison is neither rehabilitative nor a sufficient deterrent.
- Prison may have several negative effects.
  - Inmates become institutionalised within the prison system and cannot function adequately on the outside. Zimbardo's famous prison study (Zimbardo *et al.*, 1973) showed how even in a role-play situation prisoners quickly adapted to their role, becoming helpless and pathetic.
  - The prison experience can have negative psychological effects on mental health, leading to greater psychological disturbance after a custodial sentence.
  - Prison is sometimes referred to as a 'school for crime'. Incarceration with hardened criminals gives younger inmates an opportunity to learn from the more experienced offenders (brutalisation).
  - Loss of contact with family and disruption of employment make it more difficult for the offender to stay out of trouble in the future.

STUDY

Aim

Zimbardo *et al.* (1973) investigated the psychological effects of imprisonment in a simulated prison environment.

Method

Basement rooms at Stanford University were converted into a mock prison. Student volunteers were screened for suitability and only those tested as emotionally stable and unaggressive were selected to take part in the 14-day study. None of the participants knew each other before the experiment began. They were randomly allocated to the role of either 'prisoner' or 'guard', with each participant equipped for the role. Prisoners wore prison uniforms and were called by their number, and the guards wore guard uniforms.

Results

Prisoners assumed their roles, becoming passive, submissive and miserable. The guards asserted their power, subjecting the prisoners to penalties for 'bad behaviour'. After 6 days the study was halted because of the severe negative effects on the prisoners.

Conclusion

The prison experience can have negative psychological effects on prisoners due to powerlessness and the de-individuation of the prison regime.

8.4.2 Alternatives to custodial sentencing

Alternatives to custodial sentencing include fines, anti-social behaviour orders (ASBOs), probation, electronic tagging, community service and restorative justice. Alternatives to prison have the benefit that family contacts and possibly employment can be maintained, hopefully making future reoffending less likely. Non-custodial alternatives are also much less expensive than sending offenders to prison, and some evidence suggests that they can be more effective. Two alternatives to custodial sentencing will now be considered in further detail: **restorative justice** and **electronic tagging**.

Restorative justice

Restorative justice involves the offender making amends directly in some way to their victim. At the heart of restorative justice are the concepts of **healing** and **collaboration** between offender and victim, which means it is fundamentally different to other forms of punishment. The first programme of restorative justice occurred in Ontario in 1974, where two teenage vandals were taken by their probation officer to meet their victims and see how the victims had been affected by the crime (Andrews and Bonta, 2006).

Meetings between offender and victim enable the offender to see the consequences of their action and allow the victim to have their say. Such programmes recognise that crime violates relationships between members of society and is not just a violation of the law, thus taking account of the very personal experience of being a victim. Anyone who has experienced a house burglary will understand the feeling of personal violation experienced by the householder, almost as if the attack had been a physical one against their person.

Restorative justice can be used as an alternative to prosecution, particularly with young offenders where it might serve as a final warning. It can also be used as an add-on to sentencing – for example, as a supplement to community service. It can also be used when imprisoned offenders are being prepared for release, to prevent further offending. The process may involve face-to-face encounters and practical reparation, such as repairing a damaged garden fence, or financial restitution.

Studies of effectiveness have been conducted, although it is difficult to come to firm conclusions given that programmes are so diverse. One recent report suggests that the outcomes are favourable when restorative justice schemes are compared with the conventional justice approach.

STUDY

Aim

Sherman and Strang (2007) set out to review evidence of the effect of restorative justice.

Method

Data from 36 studies (UK and abroad) comparing restorative and conventional justice were analysed. Some programmes involved face-to-face meetings between victim and offender, and others involved the offender paying financial restitution to their victim.

Results

Offender outcomes: repeat offending was substantially reduced for some offenders; in comparison to custodial sentencing, recidivism rates were reduced for adults and for young offenders. Victim outcomes: post-traumatic stress symptoms were reduced; desire for revenge was significantly lower; greater satisfaction with the process was reported.

Conclusion

The data provide extensive positive evidence in favour of restorative justice programmes, with a recommendation that they be 'put to far broader use'.

Evaluation

- Ideally, a conciliatory meeting between offender and victim should help to heal wounds and provide an opportunity for atonement. In practice, victims are often reluctant to meet the offender. It is also possible that the offender doesn't truly feel any remorse and opts for restorative justice as an easy way out.
- There is controversy about how much victim involvement is necessary. Some programmes identified as restorative justice schemes actually involve very little victim participation – for example, court-ordered restitution schemes.
- Many studies have very high rates of attrition because offenders and victims drop out before the programme is finished.
- Summarising evidence to date, Andrews and Bonta (2006) conclude that in some cases restorative justice schemes can lead to a significant reduction in rates of recidivism.

Electronic tagging

When an offender is tagged, an electronic device is strapped to the person's body, usually on the ankle. This enables continual monitoring of the offender's whereabouts by specialist contractors. The aim of the tagging system is to reduce opportunities for further offending. The tag is normally used to enforce a curfew order imposed by the court. Curfew orders differ according to circumstances. If the offender has been released early from prison, the curfew must last at least 9 hours per day. If used as a substitute for a custodial sentence, it may be imposed for up to 6 months, and the curfew can be between 2 and 12 hours per day, as directed by the court. During the hours of curfew, the offender is not allowed out of the home. Breaches of the curfew mean that the person will be re-arrested by the police and face further penalty, possibly prison. Since tagging of adult offenders began in England and Wales in 1999, over 225,000 people have been subject to electronic monitoring (National Audit Office, 2006). A scheme for the introduction of electronic monitoring of juveniles aged 12–16 years was introduced in 2002.

Figure 8.17 *Electronic tagging is an alternative to custodial sentencing.*

STUDY

Aim

Cassidy *et al.* (2005) studied the use and effectiveness of tagging in juvenile offenders aged 12–16 years.

Method

National statistics from Youth Offending Teams and monitoring contractors were analysed, yielding data on 315 tagged juvenile offenders. The researchers also conducted a literature review and interviews with a small sample of offenders remanded in local authority accommodation.

Results

Tagging was reserved for the most persistent offenders – each person had committed on average more than seven offences before they were tagged. Of those tagged, 88% were young males, and black males were over-represented in the population. Tagging resulted in a 7% decrease in the number of offenders breaching bail conditions, although those who continued to break bail conditions did so more frequently. Interviews with offenders revealed that tagging gave them an excuse they could use with their friends to help them stay out of trouble.

Conclusion

Tagging of young juveniles is reserved for the most persistent offenders and can be effective in some cases.

Evaluation

- Tagging is much less expensive than prison and helps to reduce pressure on the rapidly expanding prison population. Current Home Office estimates indicate that the average daily cost of prison is £75 per prisoner, whilst the average daily cost of tagging is approximately £15 (National Audit Office, 2006).
- Tagging is seen as an effective alternative to custodial sentencing. It provides the offender with order and structure, preventing them from slipping back into old lifestyles and habits, at the same time allowing family relationships to be maintained.
- Family relationships can be strained, as the curfew prevents the offender taking full part in family life and curtails joint activities outside the home.

8.4.3 Treatment programme: behaviour modification

Behaviour modification is based on operant conditioning principles. It involves reinforcing desirable behaviour and extinguishing undesirable behaviour. Secondary reinforcers, usually tokens (**token economy**), are exchanged for primary reinforcers. Typical primary reinforcers in a prison setting would be a telephone call home or watching a video. Most behaviour modification programmes take the following structure:

- The desired change in behaviour is clearly specified.
- A baseline rate is measured over a period of days.
- A reinforcement strategy is adopted (when to reinforce, what to reinforce).
- All those in contact with the offender should adhere to the programme.
- The offender's progress is carefully monitored.
- The target behaviour after treatment is compared with the baseline.

Although most studies show that the positive effects of a token system do not persist once the treatment stops, Cohen and Filipczak (1971) showed that the benefits extended beyond the duration of the programme. They compared two groups of young male prisoners: a token economy group that was reinforced with tokens exchangeable for phone calls, tobacco, family visits and so on, and a control group. The treatment group showed more desirable behaviour and was less likely to have re-offended 1 and 2 years later. However, by 3 years the reoffending rates were the same.

STUDY

Aim

Cullen and Seddon (1981) investigated the modification of behaviour in young offenders using a token economy.

Method

Boys in a young offenders' institution were reinforced using tokens to be exchanged at the 'shop' for sweets and so on. Positive behaviours, such as avoiding confrontation, were rewarded, whilst undesirable behaviours, such as hostility, were not reinforced, to bring about extinction.

Result

Those on the programme began to display more positive behaviours over the duration of the study.

Conclusion

Operant conditioning techniques can be used to modify antisocial behaviour.

Evaluation of behaviour modification

- Token economy systems are controversial because they often involve depriving the prisoner of all non-essential comforts and privileges at the start of the programme so that they are motivated to 'work' to gain the tokens.
- Token economies successfully control behaviour in the institution and for the duration of the programme, but the benefits seem fairly short-lived and do not tend to generalise beyond the institution.
- Several studies show improvement and occasional studies show that recidivism is delayed (Cohen and Filipczak, 1971).
- Blackburn (1993) suggests that systems of behaviour modification have 'little rehabilitative value' and simply facilitate management.
- A combination of behavioural and cognitive therapy is preferred as it seems to result in greater success long-term (Andrews and Bonta, 2006). Cognitive behavioural therapies give the offender an insight into their behaviour, enabling self-regulation of behaviour rather than external regulation.

8.4.4 Treatment programme: social skills training

Social skills training (SST) in the treatment of offenders assumes that many offenders commit crime because they lack social skills. This deficiency in social skills might cause an offender to have problems in reading other people's behaviour, leading to the mistaken assumption that people are being aggressive or insulting. Lack of social skill might also cause problems communicating thoughts and feelings, creating frustration which might lead to aggression. Dollard and Miller's (1950) **frustration-aggression hypothesis** stated that frustration often results in aggression.

Training involves equipping offenders with **micro-skills** – for example, non-verbal skills like eye contact and facial expression. More global **macro-skills** are also taught – for example, maintaining a conversation and negotiation. Techniques vary but are generally founded on social learning theory principles of observation, imitation and modelling, and the behavioural principle of reinforcement for desired behaviour. Social skills training also has a cognitive element, as it aims to change the offender's understanding of social situations. Typically, SST would involve the following:

- observation of the offender's normal behaviour in a role-play situation (for example, someone pushing in to a queue or a general conversation); this might be video-taped so the person can observe their own behaviour later
- instruction and demonstration of appropriate behaviour in that situation
- practice and rehearsal in role play
- feedback on performance and reinforcement for appropriate behaviour
- homework tasks to practise appropriate behaviour between sessions.

Figure 8.18 *Lack of social skills may lead people to misinterpret the behaviour of others as threatening or offensive.*

A checklist of behaviours is also sometimes used to encourage the offender to focus on what constitutes normal social skills, what they are good at and where they might have inadequacies.

Examples from a typical social skills checklist

I am bad (1), not very good (2), not bad (3), good (4) at the following:

Looking other people in the eye
Going into a room full of strangers
Initiating a conversation
Introducing myself to someone
Being criticised
Responding to praise

STUDY

Aim

Long and Sherer (1985) studied the effectiveness of SST with young male offenders.

Method

Thirty adolescent males convicted of various offences were assigned to either a social skills training group, an unstructured discussion group or a control group. Participants were classified as either high-frequency or low-frequency offenders.

Results

SST was more effective with high-frequency offenders and the discussion group was more effective with low-frequency offenders. The effect was noted immediately after training and also at a 2-week follow-up.

Conclusion

Social skills training can be effective with certain types of offender.

Evaluation of SST

- Some studies show improvement in overall competence and self-esteem. As such, the effect on offending may be indirect, enabling offenders to better resist peer pressure to commit offences.
- The treatment is based on an assumption that poor social skills are a cause of offending. However, certain types of offender, particularly non-violent offenders such as fraudsters, are extremely socially competent.

Evaluation of SST – continued

- Research by Spence and Marziller (1981) appeared to show that SST reduced recidivism 6 months after training. However, self-reports revealed that the group had actually engaged in more offending, suggesting that they had not been rehabilitated.
- Some studies – for example, Sarason (1978) – show that reoffending rates for SST groups are the same as for groups receiving general discussion-based therapy. This suggests that any type of therapy involving social interaction is just as effective.
- Goldstein (1986) reviewed the effectiveness of SST with delinquent teenagers. The data from 30 studies of SST were combined in a meta-analysis. The results showed that SST does lead to improvement in the short-term, but that the effects often did not generalise beyond the training situation.

8.4.5 Treatment programme: anger management

Anger management programmes for offenders assume that offenders commit crimes because they cannot control their anger and that cognition plays a key role in anger (Novaco, 1975). Anger management is a form of cognitive behaviour therapy that focuses on learning to control anger and respond in more appropriate ways. Most anger management programmes consist of three stages as set out below.

The three stages of anger management

Cognitive preparation: The offender learns to recognise feelings of anger and to recognise events and situations that trigger their anger response.

Skill acquisition: This stage involves teaching of techniques to control the anger response in difficult situations. For example, the person might use positive self-talk to keep calm, reciting phrases such as 'Be calm, be calm'. Relaxation techniques such as deep breathing can also be used.

Application practice: Formerly anger-provoking situations are re-enacted and the offender practises controlling anger using the newly acquired techniques in a non-threatening environment.

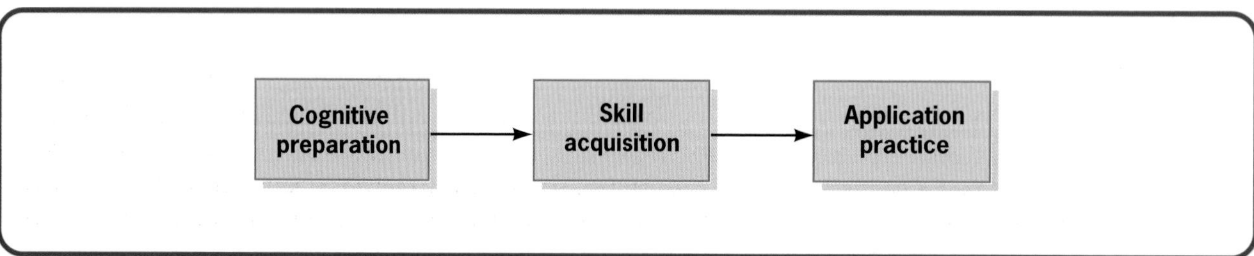

Figure 8.19 *The three stages of anger management.*

The National Anger Management Package was developed by the UK Prison Service in 1992, for use with young male offenders aged 17–21 years. The treatment involves increasing awareness of anger and of the need to monitor behaviour. It also provides education about the benefits of controlling anger. Offenders improve anger management techniques and practise these techniques in role play. Treatment is intensive, usually eight 2-hour sessions. Feedback indicates that participants have increased awareness of their difficulties with managing anger and increased self-control (Keen, 2000).

STUDY

Aim

Ireland (2000) studied the usefulness of a group-based anger management programme with young male offenders.

Method

Pre- and post-programme anger scores for an experimental group of 50 prisoners were compared with scores taken at the same time intervals from a control group of 37 prisoners who had no treatment. The groups were matched for age, type of offence and anger level. The programme was a version of the national programme (see above), involving 12 one-hour sessions over 3 days. At the end of the programme anger levels were assessed using a checklist of 29 problem behaviours and a self-report measure.

Results

The experimental group showed significantly reduced anger, with 92% having improved on at least one measure, 48% improved on both and 8% deteriorated.

Conclusion

The programme successfully reduced anger and disruptive behaviour in prison.

Evaluation of anger management

- Studies suggests that programmes are effective in reducing anger in the short term, but there is no clear evidence that programmes affect long-term recidivism rates (Blackburn, 1993).
- Changing cognitions aids insight, enabling offenders to self-discover other ways of managing their problem.
- The treatment presupposes a link between anger and offending. Some researchers say there is no link between anger and crime (many crimes are committed in a cold, rational state). Loza and Loza-Fanous (1999) interviewed 271 Canadian male offenders and found no significant differences in anger measures between violent and non-violent offenders. They concluded that encouraging violent offenders to explain their offence as being due to uncontrollable anger may serve merely to offer an excuse for their behaviour.
- To be effective, anger management programmes require careful planning, a high level of staff commitment and offender motivation.

How Psychology Works

An experiment to investigate the criminal stereotype

One lasting consequence of the work of Lombroso (page 219) is that there is a stereotype of the criminal type. To investigate this you are going to plan and pilot an experiment.

- Use a facial composition website to construct two faces. One of these should include some of the criminal facial characteristics described by Lombroso. The other should be a control face which includes none of the criminal features identified by Lombroso.
- Now construct a rating scale so that participants can rate the face they see on a number of personality characteristics. A scale from 1–7 should be about right. Appropriate characteristics might include honest–dishonest, predictable–unpredictable, aggressive–gentle and so on. Arrange the characteristics so that the positive descriptor is sometimes on the right and sometimes on the left of the rating scale.
- Write a set of standardised instructions to use when you pilot your experiment with a few friends. The instructions should explain to them exactly what you want them to do.
- Write a debrief that can be used to explain the purpose of the study.
- Pilot your experiment by carrying it out with a few friends. Note that this will be an independent groups design because you have to use different participants in each condition.
- Collate the results. You can analyse the score for each characteristic separately or put them all together to give a single score. Remember you will need to reverse the scoring for some of the items because 1 will sometimes be the extreme negative response and sometimes the extreme positive, depending on which way round the adjective pair is.
- Write a few paragraphs summarising your activity. Refer to the following issues:
  - Has the independent variable – IV (presence of Lombroso's criminal features or not) affected the dependent variable – DV (the personality ratings)?
  - Discuss the use of the independent design and controls in this experiment. Explain why it was important to order the adjectives so that the positive response was sometimes on the left and sometimes on the right.
  - Discuss ethical considerations relevant in this case.

Further Reading

Introductory texts

Dwyer, D. (2001) *Angles on Criminal Psychology*, Cheltenham: Nelson Thornes.

Harrower, J. (2001) *Psychology in Practice: Crime*, London: Hodder & Stoughton.

McGuire, J. (2004) *Understanding Psychology and Crime: Perspectives on Theory and Action*, Buckingham: Open University Press.

Putwain, D. and Sammons, A. (2002) *Psychology and Crime*, Hove: Routledge.

Specialist sources

Andrews, D.A. and Bonta, J. (2006) *The Psychology of Criminal Conduct*, 4th edn., New York: Anderson Publishing/LexisNexis.

Bartol, C.R. and Bartol, A.M. (2008) *Introduction to Forensic Psychology: Research and Application*, 2nd edn., London: Sage.

Blackburn, R. (1993) *The Psychology of Criminal Conduct*, Chichester: John Wiley and Sons.

Canter, D. (1994) *Criminal Shadows*, London: Harper.

Canter, D. and Youngs, D. (2008) *Principles of Geographical Offender Profiling*, Aldershot: Ashgate.

Jackson, J.L. and Bekerian, D.A. (eds.) (1997) *Offender Profiling: Theory, Research and Practice*, Chichester: Wiley.

The biological approach

Chapter 9

9.1 Introduction

The biological approach is concerned with how our genetic inheritance, evolution of the human species and the nervous system (both central and peripheral) affect how we think, feel and behave. The biological approach, because of the influence of Darwin's theory of evolution and the idea of the 'survival of the fittest', looks at how well a person adapts and adjusts in life. An inability to adapt or adjust to the ups and downs of everyday life may result in a person suffering from psychological disorders such as schizophrenia or depression, or being aggressive towards other people. The biological approach seeks to discover how the genes we inherit from our parents may have a role to play in these and other types of maladaptive behaviours.

The biological approach is also concerned with understanding how our central and peripheral nervous systems, particularly the brain, affect how we think, feel and behave. Questions arise within the biological approach, such as how the brain, a physical organ, can produce the psychological experience of awareness of things around us and consciousness. These are matters that physiological psychologists find difficult to answer.

The biological approach also raises the issue of the relative contribution of nature (genetics, evolution, etc.) and nurture (experiences since birth) to mental abilities such as intelligence, and actual behaviours (such as schizophrenia and aggression). This is commonly called the **nature/nurture debate** or the debate about the relative contribution of heredity and environment (see Chapter 16).

A recent development in biological psychology is called **evolutionary psychology**, which is defined as follows:

> Evolutionary psychology is the study of the evolutionary origin of human behaviour patterns... that may influence everything from sexual attraction, infidelity and jealousy to divorce. (Coon, 2002: 519).

One area that has been extensively researched within the biological/evolutionary approach is that of human mating or sexual preferences. Buss (1994) studied attitudes and behaviours of men and women across 37 different cultures towards sexual behaviour. Buss found, for example, that compared to women, men are more interested in casual sex, prefer a younger partner and get more jealous over sexual infidelity on the part of the woman. By contrast, women prefer older partners, are less upset by sexual infidelity but more upset by a man becoming emotionally involved with another woman. Buss attributes these differences to mating preferences that have evolved in response to the reproductive demands placed on men and women. Generally, women are more involved in nurturing offspring and men in providing for the family, although this traditional pattern has changed dramatically in westernised societies. Evolutionary theory explains the male concern with sexual infidelity by the female partner as being related to concern over the paternity of offspring.

Evolutionary psychology presents and, to some extent, justifies a traditional male and female role in the family. It has to be noted that other explanations of the findings of Buss (1994) are possible – for example, that, generally speaking, the male controls money and resources.

In this chapter we look further into the biological approach in psychology. First we will consider the basic assumptions of the biological approach which we came across in AS psychology (see Chapter 1, pages 5–9 of

Figure 9.1 *The genes that are passed down from generation to generation play an important part in human behaviour.*

AQA(B) Psychology for AS by Pennington and McLoughlin, 2008). We will then look at the role of the central and autonomic nervous systems in behaviour, and the genetic basis of behaviour. In doing this we will build on Chapter 2, Biopsychology, of *AQA(B) Psychology for AS* by Pennington and McLoughlin. So it would be a good idea to refresh your memory and read that chapter now.

9.2 Assumptions of the biological approach

The biological approach has five main assumptions, as follows:

- Human behaviour is strongly determined by our genes and our genetic inheritance. Non-human animal behaviour is almost totally determined by genes.
- The central nervous system, especially the brain, plays an essential role in thought and behaviour. To explain human thought and behaviour, it is necessary to understand the functions and structure of the brain and the nervous system more generally.
- Chemical processes in the brain are responsible for many different aspects of psychological functioning. An imbalance of certain chemicals in the brain may cause abnormal behaviour and thought – for example, bipolar mood disorder (see Chapter 5).
- Humans and other animals have evolved biologically through Darwinian evolution. This means that animals 'high' on the evolutionary tree, such as monkeys and apes, are similar genetically to humans.
- Evolution has taken place over millions of years, and the 'flight-or-fight-response' is common across the animal kingdom and is important to understanding how humans react in threatening situations.

The biological approach in psychology uses highly scientific methods of research. Techniques such as single-cell recording of neuronal activity and scanning techniques using PET scanners are used to understand the activity of neurons in the central nervous system. The biological approach makes use of the natural occurrence of identical and fraternal twins to help determine the extent to which psychological characteristics, such as personality and intelligence, have a genetic basis. Case studies on people with brain damage are used to help understand the role of different parts of the brain in personality, higher thought processes and intelligence.

The most common methods of investigation used by the biological approach are:

- Laboratory experiments on both humans and other animals. Ethical guidelines strongly determine what can and cannot be done to humans and other animals. Testing animals for drugs and removing a part of the brain to see how behaviour is affected are common techniques.
- Observation of behaviour under strict laboratory conditions is used to investigate, for example, human sleep patterns and aggressive behaviours in animals.
- Studies of identical twins (who share exactly the same genetic make-up) brought up together or reared apart are used to help determine the contribution of genes to psychological characteristics.

Figure 9.2 *Animals are commonly used in laboratory experiments to help understand the function of different parts of the brain.*

9.3 The role of the central and autonomic nervous systems in human behaviour

In Chapter 2 of *AQA(B) for AS Psychology* by Pennington and McLoughlin (2008), we looked at the divisions of the nervous system (see Figure 9.3), localisation of function in the brain and the basic function of the autonomic nervous system. In what follows we will look in a little more detail at the role of each of these parts of the nervous system in human behaviour.

9.3.1 The central nervous system

(a) The cerebral cortex

The cerebral cortex is the most highly developed part of the brain in humans compared to other animals. In evolutionary terms, the cerebral cortex is the most recent structure of the central nervous system and is associated with higher mental functioning. This includes conscious awareness, personality, problem solving and creative thinking (intelligence in its widest sense). Fish and amphibians have no cerebral cortex. Reptiles and birds have only a very basic cerebral cortex. As you go up the evolutionary tree, the amount of cortex in comparison to the total size of the brain increases.

The cortex is divided into four different lobes, as shown in Figure 9.4. These are called the frontal, parietal, occipital and temporal lobes. Each of the lobes has different functions, as follows:

- **Occipital lobe** is primarily to do with the function of vision and is often referred to as the visual cortex.
- **Temporal lobe** is primarily to do with the function of hearing and is often referred to as the auditory cortex.
- **Parietal lobe** processes sensations from the skin and different muscles throughout the body.
- **Frontal lobe** is concerned with higher thought processes such as reasoning and abstract thinking.

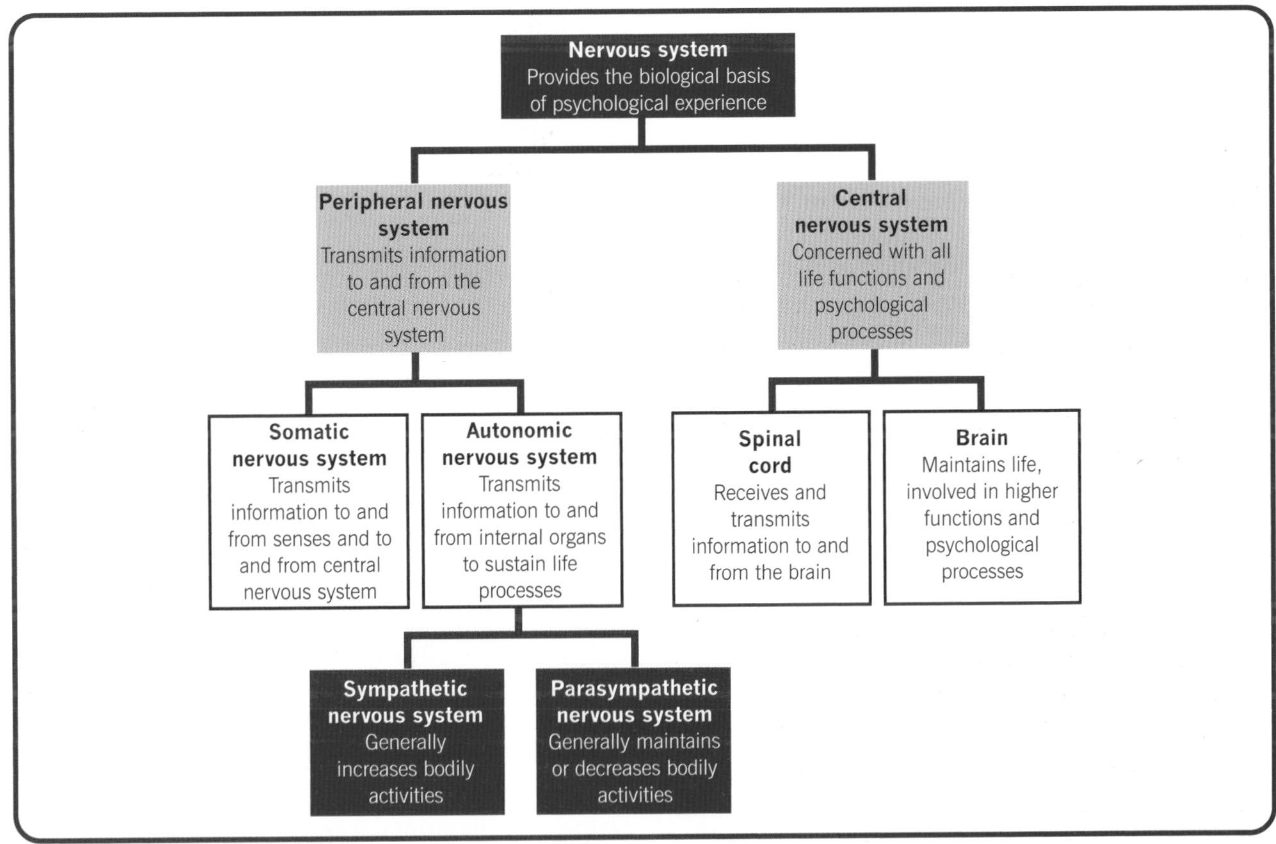

Figure 9.3 *Divisions of the nervous system, with an indication of the basic functions of each division.*

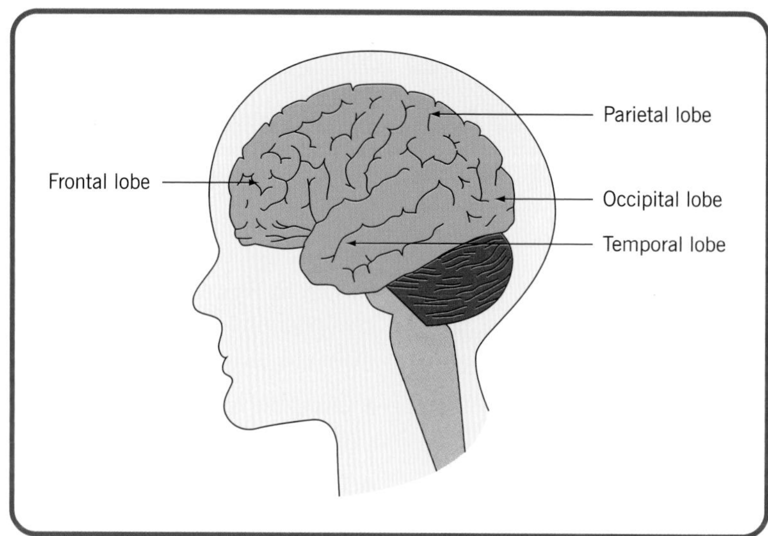

Figure 9.4 *The four main lobes of the cerebral cortex: frontal, parietal, occipital and temporal lobes of the brain.*

Each of these lobes has specific parts which are specialised for different functions, as identified above. Each of these lobes of the cortex can be divided into two areas, as follows:

1 **Primary areas.** These process incoming sensory information from our different senses. The occipital or visual cortex receives information from our eyes, and the temporal or auditory cortex receives information from our ears. The primary areas in each lobe also control motor functions to do with the senses. For example, the muscles of each eye are controlled by the visual cortex. The basic organisation of the primary areas in humans is very similar to that of other animals, such as the rat. This indicates that these areas are old in evolutionary terms.

2 **Association areas.** These areas are involved in complex mental processes and complex behaviours. The association areas are involved in perception, memory, language, creative thinking and planned behaviour. The association areas make use of information from the different senses for higher mental functions and complex behaviour. The higher up the evolutionary tree, the greater the proportion of association areas in the cerebral cortex. This is shown in Figure 9.5.

Damage to the visual and auditory cortex will usually result in a person being blind or deaf. If there is damage to the parietal lobe, the person will be clumsy and unco-ordinated in their movements. Significant damage to the whole cerebral cortex would reduce complex human behaviour to nothing more than primitive reflexes, similar to creatures at the bottom of the evolutionary tree.

The frontal lobes of the cortex are the parts of the brain that set humans apart from other animals. The frontal lobes can be divided into three main areas:

Motor cortex: This controls fine movement of the hands, feet, tongue and face. The motor cortex is responsible for voluntary behaviour – for example, lifting your arm or walking.

Sensory cortex: This receives sensory information from the nerve endings in different parts of the body.

Prefrontal cortex: This receives information from all the senses and different parts of the body. It is involved in the highest mental functions and complex, planned behaviours.

Both the motor cortex and the sensory cortex are organised to reflect the density of neurons in different parts of the body. For example, the lips and fingertips are highly sensitive parts of the body and each of these areas of the body has a high density of neurons. In the two cortexes, the lips and fingertips have a great deal of space devoted to them. By contrast, the upper legs, trunk and upper arms of the body have relatively low density of neurons and have only a little space devoted to them in the motor and sensory cortexes.

Damage to the frontal lobes can cause a range of different deficits. These include memory loss, loss of fine

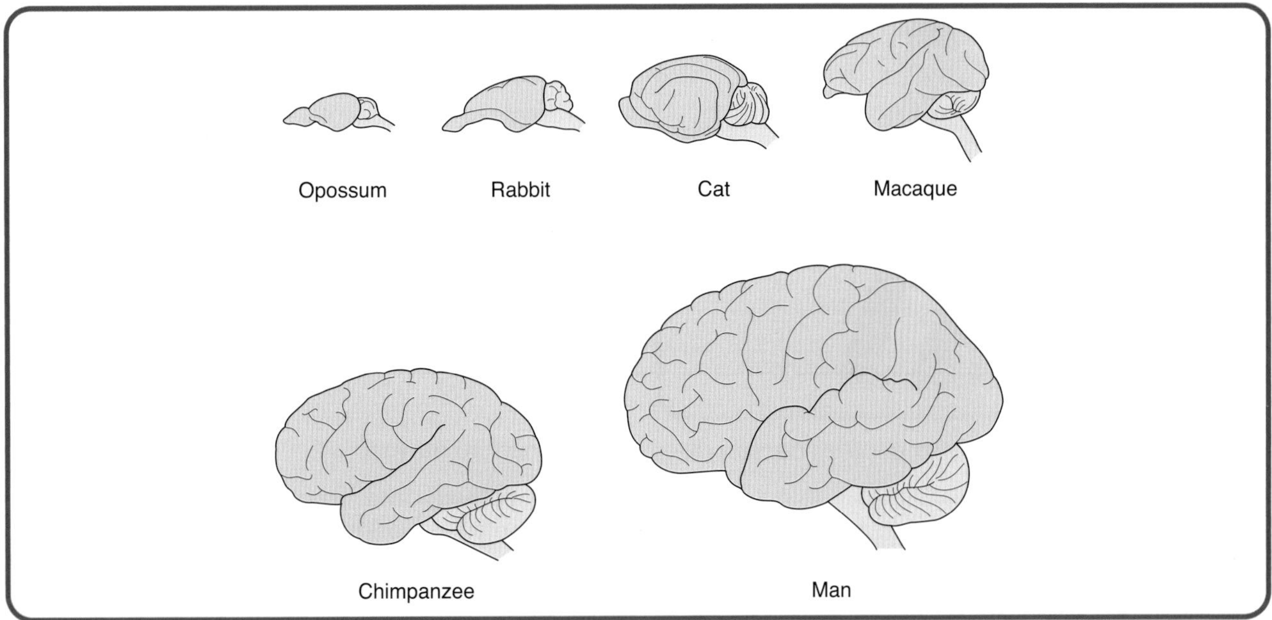

Figure 9.5 *The amount of association areas in the cortex increases the higher up the evolutionary tree of the animal. Humans have the greatest amount of association areas of all animals in their cerebral cortex.*

movement, personality change, inability to focus attention and inability to coordinate complex sequences of behaviour – for example, working at a computer.

(b) Limbic system

The limbic system is deep in the brain and is a set of structures that are around the top of the brainstem. The limbic system in humans is involved in emotions, motivation, learning and memory. It has also been identified as being involved in eating and sexual behaviour. This makes the limbic system fundamental to what we feel, think and do. The limbic system is made up of three main structures, called the septal area, amygdala and hippocampus.

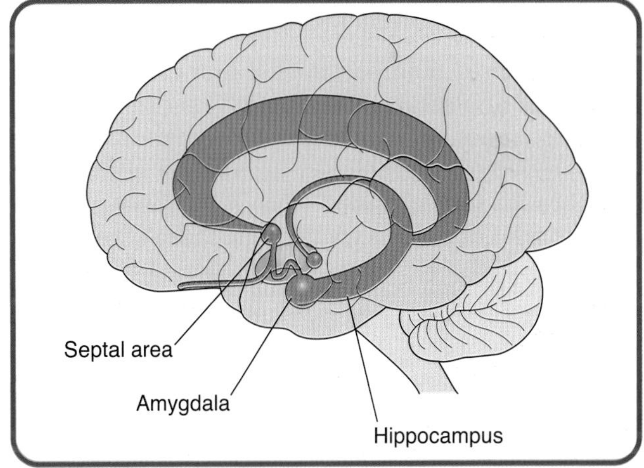

Figure 9.6 *The limbic system of the brain, consisting of the septal area, amygdala and hippocampus.*

The **amygdala** is involved in emotions, especially the attachment of emotional importance to events. For example, the amygdala is responsible for causing someone to cry when they see a picture or part of a film that has deep emotional significance for them. The amygdala is also involved in making us feel afraid or fearful. It is also involved in recognising that someone else is fearful or afraid. Morris *et al.* (1996) put people in a PET scanner and showed them pictures of fearful, happy and neutral faces of other people. They found from the PET scan that the amygdala showed high levels of neural activity when fearful faces were shown to the person. This may have an evolutionary explanation: recognition of fear in others may help to identify a dangerous situation early. The person can then respond appropriately by flight or fight. The advantage of being able to do this is that the person does not need to be in the dangerous situation themselves.

The **hippocampus** is involved in memory. In particular, it seems that it is specifically involved in recent

Figure 9.7 *Identifying fear in another person may help with survival.*

memories. People who have suffered damage to the hippocampus lose recent memories, whilst older memories are retained. The hippocampus has two main roles to do with memory:

- a temporary store for information immediately following an experience or event
- feeding recent memories to the prefrontal cortex for retention in long-term memory.

The **septal area** is important for motivation and the experience of pleasure. Milner (1991) showed that rats with electrodes implanted in the septal area would cross an electrified grid to get stimulation of the septal area through the electrodes – that is, the rats would put up with a lot of pain to get the septal area stimulated.

In terms of human behaviour, the limbic system seems to be involved in many of the defining features of what we regard as being human. These are to do with higher-level memories, the attachment of emotion to memories and feelings of pleasure and sexual satisfaction.

9.3.2 The autonomic nervous system

The autonomic nervous system is responsible for sending information to and receiving information from organs responsible for vital bodily functions such as the basic life processes of breathing and digestion. It would help if you refreshed your knowledge of the autonomic nervous system by reading Chapter 2, pages 53–5, of *AQA(B) Psychology for AS* by Pennington and McLoughlin (2008).

The autonomic nervous system is made up of two parts:

- The **sympathetic nervous system**: This prepares the person to deal with danger and threats in the external world. It does this by preparing the body for the flight- or fight-response to threat. In doing this the parasympathetic nervous system stops digestion, directs more blood to muscles, increases heart rate, dilates the pupils and causes the hairs on the body to stand on end.
- The **parasympathetic nervous system** supports normal and routine body functions. It does this by conserving energy expenditure, regulating heart rate, controlling blood sugar levels and secreting saliva. When danger has passed, the parasympathetic nervous system takes control and brings body functions back to normal.

The sympathetic and parasympathetic systems are often regarded as working in opposition to each other. However, a better way to see the interaction of the two systems is as balancing the bodily functions of the person so that the person is responding appropriately to what is going on in their immediate environment.

(a) The autonomic nervous system and stress

Stress can be seen as both a psychological and a biological response by the individual to difficult and demanding external pressures in life. External pressures or dangerous situations trigger a flight-or fight response from the sympathetic nervous system. The sympathetic nervous system also triggers the release of noradrenalin and adrenalin from glands in the body. This helps with the flight-or fight response by making more energy available to the person.

Stress is to do with the perception the person has of a situation and how able they deal successfully with the situation. The life events recognised as being most stressful for a person are death of spouse, divorce and loss of employment (Holmes and Rahe, 1967). Selye (1976) identified three stages in the physiology of stress that he called the **general adaptation syndrome**. He conducted a range of experiments on rats where they were exposed to different stressful situations – for example, fatigue and extreme cold. He found that the body responds to stress in three stages if the stressful situation is maintained.

1. **Alarm stage.** This is the body's initial response to the stress which has been described above, in relation to an external threat or dangerous situation. The sympathetic nervous system prepares the body for flight or fight. Blood pressure rises, heart rate increases,

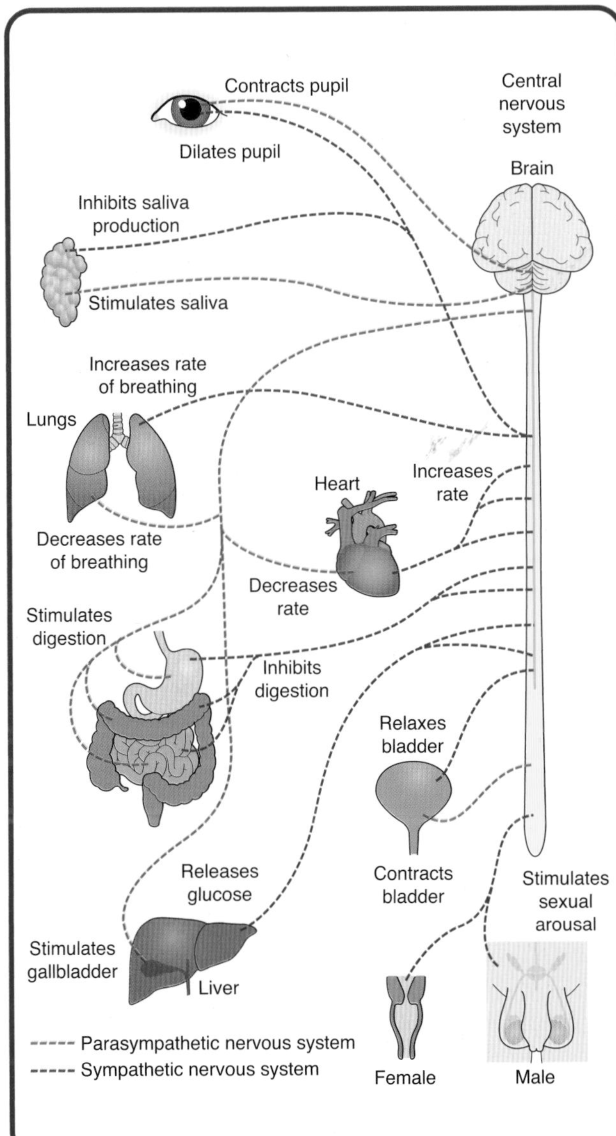

Figure 9.8 *The actions of the sympathetic and parasympathetic nervous systems.*

breathing gets faster, blood sugar levels rise. This high state of readiness of the body uses up a lot of energy and if continued for a long time would be dangerous for the person – for example, prolonged high blood pressure may have a negative effect on the heart.

2 **Resistance stage.** The alarm stage cannot continue for too long and the parasympathetic nervous system kicks in and returns some bodily functions to normal. However, the external stress has not gone away. The body still has high levels of adrenalin, high heart rate and so on, but the body is adapting to being like this over a prolonged period. The body is now susceptible to illness such as influenza and colds.

3 **Fatigue stage.** If the resistance stage lasts for a long period, the body becomes exhausted from being in a permanent state of alertness. The body defences are weakened and the person becomes vulnerable to serious illness such as a heart attack.

For the parasympathetic nervous system to return bodily function to normal, the perceived threat or stressor needs to be removed or the perception of the situation being stressful changed for the person. Only then can the person escape from general adaptation syndrome.

For more on the physiological and psychological aspects of stress, see Chapter 6 of this book.

(b) The autonomic nervous system and emotion

There are three important theories of emotion. These are the James-Lange theory, the Cannon-Bard theory, and Schachter and Singer's (1962) cognitive theory. Each of these is based on the experience of the individual of the action of the sympathetic nervous system. Here we will consider just the Schachter and Singer theory.

The Schachter and Singer theory proposes a two-factor theory of emotion. Here specific bodily sensations, caused by the action of the sympathetic nervous system, result from external situations that cause a general level of physiological arousal. The body sensations are, typically, increased heart rate, flushing, tremor and rapid breathing. These sensations have to be interpreted according to social and environmental factors and the general context in which the sensations occur. This allows the person to identify what emotion is being experienced – for example, fear or happiness. This is shown in Figure 9.9.

The Schachter and Singer theory implies that it is the context that determines the specific emotion and not bodily sensations. In effect, all emotions have similar bodily sensations.

9.4 The genetic basis of behaviour

The key concepts needed for an understanding of how genetics may influence behaviour are as follows:

- genetics and heredity
- genes and chromosomes
- genotype and phenotype.

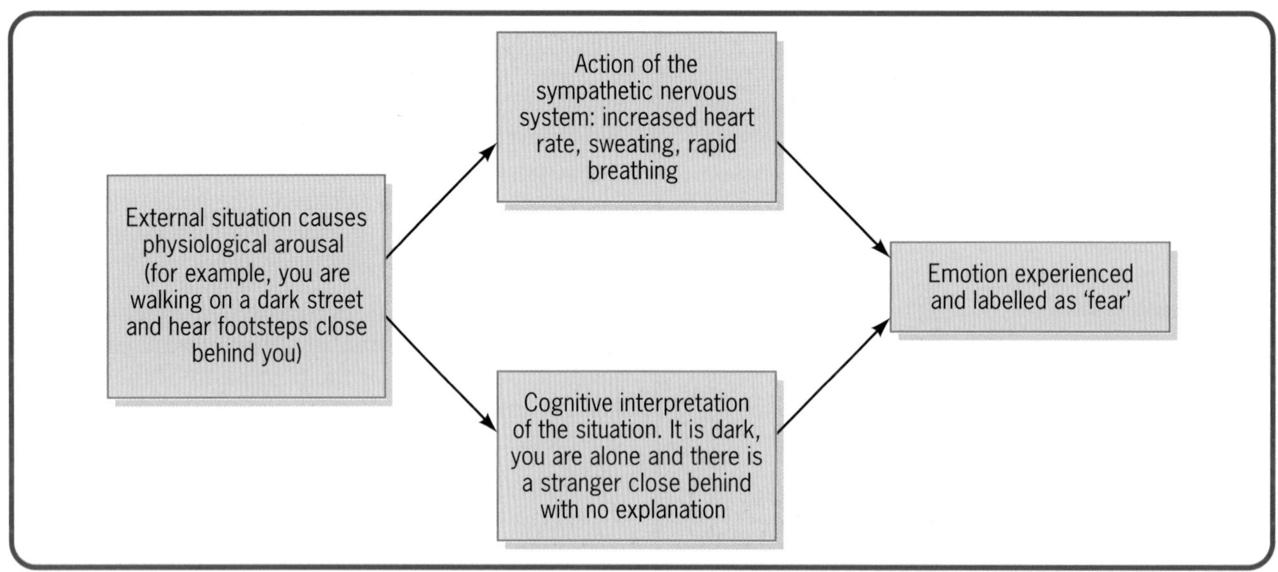

Figure 9.9 *The Schachter and Singer cognitive theory of emotion.*

Researchers rely on the use of the naturally occurring phenomenon of monozygotic and dizygotic twins to investigate heritability of behaviour and psychological characteristics. Of special interest is when identical twins are reared apart and how similar they are with respect to, for example, intelligence, personality and concordance for schizophrenia. Adoption studies are also used to help determine the extent to which characteristics and behaviours are most similar to natural or adopted parents. It would be useful to read Chapter 2, pages 57–67, of *AQA(B) Psychology for AS* by Pennington and McLoughlin (2008) at this point.

In what follows we will look at different areas of psychology and the extent to which behaviour may be genetically determined.

9.4.1 Anxiety, obesity and homosexuality

Anxiety

Anxiety disorders such as panic attacks, phobias and obsessive-compulsive disorder are thought to have a genetic basis (Kendler *et al.*, 1992). Some people are thought to have a genetic predisposition for developing an anxiety disorder. However, this will not usually happen unless there are trigger events in the environment. The chemical that has been identified as genetically determined is the neurotransmitter norepinephrine. A high level of neural activity in the amygdala is also associated with anxiety (Shin *et al.*, 1997). It is generally accepted that stressful life events are an essential component for triggering an anxiety attack. However, some people may be prone to developing an anxiety disorder as a result of their genetic make-up. A biological basis to anxiety does not seem to have a single-gene explanation, but a contribution from a number of genes (Plomin *et al.*, 1997) – see the study described on the next page.

A study has shown that there may be a biological link between smoking when a teenager and an increased risk of developing an anxiety disorder as an adult (Johnson *et al.*, 2000).

The reason that this research is mentioned here is that it is thought there is a biological mechanism linking smoking and anxiety. It has been suggested that high levels of nicotine from smoking may sensitise certain areas of the brain and increase vulnerability for anxiety.

Obesity

Twin studies have clearly demonstrated that both body weight and the amount of fat in the body have a strong genetic basis (Allison *et al.*, 1994). For monozygotic twins, the correlation for body fat is around 0.80; in contrast the correlation for dizygotic twins is low at about 0.40. Obesity is thought to be highly heritable, with a correlation for identical twins of about 0.70 (Borjeson, 1976).

In the case of obesity, there are two main biological components, as follows:

STUDY

Aim

Johnson *et al.* (2000) conducted a study to investigate the link between teenage smoking and anxiety in adulthood.

Method

A longitudinal study followed 700 teenagers through to adulthood. The number of cigarettes smoked a day as a teenager was recorded. As adults, the incidence of anxiety disorders was recorded.

Results

It was found that teenagers who smoked more than 20 cigarettes a day were 15 times more likely to have panic attacks as an adult. Such smokers were also five times more likely to have a general anxiety disorder as an adult.

Conclusions

Smoking as a teenager may cause anxiety disorders as an adult.

- The number of fat cells in the body. People who are obese have more fat cells than people who are about the right weight for their size.
- The body settles at a constant weight as an adult. This is regulated by a small but important area in the brain called the hypothalamus.

The number of fat cells in the body is genetically determined, as is the natural weight that the adult tends towards, which is regulated by the hypothalamus. This means that someone who wishes to lose a lot of weight when slightly overweight, which is also their 'natural weight', will find it very hard indeed! By contrast, someone who is overweight and over their 'natural weight' will find it relatively easy to lose weight. The ease with which someone can lose weight through dieting may also have a genetic basis.

Homosexuality

Evidence has been put forward to show that homosexuality among males may have a genetic basis. Buhrich *et al.* (1991) found that relatives of homosexual males showed a higher incidence for homosexuality than in the general population. Bailey *et al.* (1993) investigated homosexuality in twins. These researchers found that concordance rates for monozygotic twins was about 50%, compared with a concordance rate of about 20% for dizygotic twins. However, environmental factors play at least an equally important role in determining the sexual orientation of an individual. Given that concordance rates for monozygotic twins is just 50%, this means that half of the twins in Bailey's study were not both homosexual.

9.4.2 Chromosome anomalies

Individual genes are located on chromosomes in the nucleus of each cell in our body. For humans there are normally 23 pairs of chromosomes, where one of each pair comes from each parent. When the egg is fertilised by the sperm cell, 23 single chromosomes from the egg and 23 single chromosomes from the sperm come together to produce 23 pairs of chromosomes. Occasionally something happens to cause an abnormal number of chromosomes. When this happens most cases do not survive. However, some chromosome anomalies are viable in terms of life. Here we will look briefly at just three such anomalies: Down's syndrome, Turner's syndrome and Huntington's chorea.

Down's syndrome

Down's syndrome is a consequence of an extra chromosome on chromosome 21; this is known as trisomy. The extra chromosome usually comes from the mother's side. Generally, this syndrome affects about 1 in 700 children and occurs more frequently in women who get pregnant later in life. People with Down's syndrome have recognisable facial features and are of short stature. They often have heart defects, susceptibility to respiratory infections and have learning difficulties. Down's syndrome results in a wide range of physical and mental ability. With mental ability the range is from near normal mental functioning to quite extreme learning difficulties. Some people with Down's syndrome are able to live independently and have employment; others need constant nursing attention and cannot live without such continuous care.

Turner's syndrome

Turner's syndrome is an anomaly to do with the sex chromosomes. The normal female has two X chromosomes and the normal male an X and a Y chromosome. Turner's syndrome is where the female has only a single X chromosome. Women with this chromosome anomaly are usually sterile, and have other physical anomalies. Mental functioning is not affected generally, although some cognitive deficits have been identified. These include deficits in spatial ability and numerical ability.

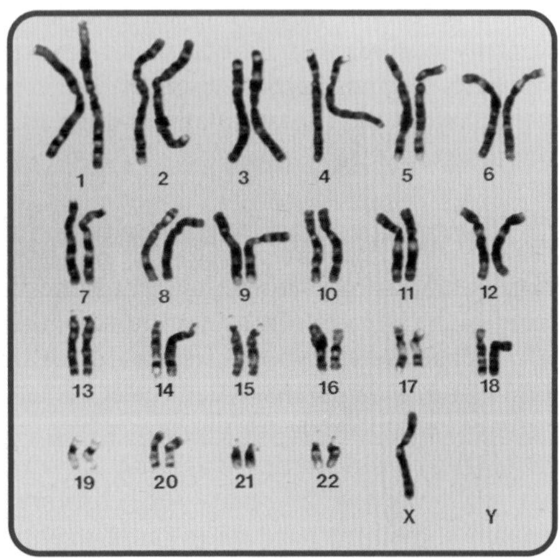

Figure 9.10 *Chromosome make-up of Turner's syndrome showing the single X chromosome instead of the normal XX chromosomes of the female.*

Huntington's chorea

Huntington's chorea is a disorder in which sufferers have severe memory impairment, personality change (both emotional and intellectual) and show uncontrollable body movements. The word 'chorea' means 'dance', and the body movements, particularly the arms and legs, resemble a bizarre type of whole-body dance. It is a rare disease affecting just 1 person in 10,000 and is more common in white people of European origin. The disorder is caused by an abnormal gene located on chromosome 4. This genetic defect causes certain areas in the brain, including the cerebral cortex, to degenerate more quickly than normal. The disorder can start early, or late in life. The faulty gene can be inherited from either the mother or the father, depending on who is the carrier for the gene. The chance of inheriting the disorder is about 50% if one of the parents has the disease.

9.4.3 Genetic engineering

Science has advanced enormously over the past 10 years with respect to understanding the structure and functions of genes. **Genetic engineering** is concerned with changing physical, behavioural or psychological characteristics by changing genes. The oldest means of manipulating genetic characteristics is through selective breeding. This has been practised for hundreds of years with the breeding of, for example, race horses and domestic dogs. Selective breeding is a bit of a hit-and-miss affair, since little or no understanding of the underlying genetics is known or required to be known. However, recent scientific advances have allowed for cloning to take place. The most famous example is that of Dolly the female sheep.

Figure 9.11 *Dolly the sheep was the first mammal to be artificially cloned.*

Advances in genetic technology are being used to study human genetic disorders. For example, researchers have used mice to help develop a treatment for Huntington's chorea. Lione *et al.* (1999) have conducted experiments on mice in which the human gene causing Huntington's chorea has been introduced. The mice show similar physical symptoms to those of humans. Researchers hope that from this research they can develop a gene which will knock out or replace the action of the faulty gene that is responsible for causing Huntington's chorea.

9.5 Strengths and limitations of the biological approach

Strengths

- The biological approach adopts highly scientific methods of investigation. It uses high technology in laboratory experiments and develops new methods of investigation.
- Because of the highly scientific approach, other researchers are able to replicate experiments quite precisely with the same laboratory conditions, to find out if the same results can be obtained through independent research. As a result, the biological approach is objective and open for all to see.
- The biological approach attempts to understand just how much of human behaviour, human characteristics and thought processes can be explained by genetics and inheritance.
- The use of twin studies and adoption studies has provided a way of estimating the heritability of a range of psychological characteristics, including intelligence, personality and certain types of mental disorders.
- Experiments can be conducted on non-human animals that cannot, for ethical reasons, be conducted on humans. Whilst experimenting on animals is controversial, many of the advances of science, especially the development of drugs, could not happen without studies taking place.

Limitations

- The biological approach adopts a reductionist explanation for human behaviour and thought. This means that psychological characteristics are reduced to biological processes, such as the action of parts of the brain and the action of genes. Reductionism ignores the whole person in ways that humanistic psychologists regard as essential (see Chapter 14).
- There are ethical issues with research conducted on animals. Also, with advances in areas such as cloning and genetic engineering, ethical considerations are both very important and divide people with different views.
- The biological approach comes down more in favour of the nature side of the nature–nurture debate (see Chapter 16). It overemphasises the importance of biological processes and heritability at the expense of environmental influences.
- With modern advances in technology and equipment, research can be very expensive to conduct. This may mean that some areas for research are prioritised over others, which may result in some important areas being overlooked or under-researched.

9.6 Applications of the biological approach

We have seen throughout this chapter that the biological approach enjoys a wide range of applications. Drugs that operate at the level of the neuron and affect neurotransmitters have been developed to treat severe mental disorders such as schizophrenia and unipolar depression (see Chapter 5).

Knowledge of the structure and function of the brain provides an understanding of how damage to the brain may affect thought and behaviour. In some circumstances, this allows for neurosurgery to treat abnormalities of the brain that may be caused by, for example, tumours or strokes.

Genetic engineering has resulted in cloning of animals and possible treatments for genetic disorders such as those we have considered above. Great advances are expected in this area in the future and such advances will be surrounded by ethical controversy. The futuristic novel by Margaret Atwood called *Oryx and Crake* depicts the use of body parts in cloned people to prolong the life of the person from whom the clones were made.

Further Reading

Introductory texts

Gross, R. (2005) *Psychology: The Science of Mind and Behaviour,* 5th edn., London: Hodder Education.

Kolb, B. and Whishaw, I.Q. (2001) *An Introduction to Brain and Behaviour,* New York: Worth Publishers.

Wagner, H. and Silber, K. (2004) *Physiological Psychology: Instant Notes,* London: Taylor and Francis.

Specialist sources

Kalat, J.W. (2007) *Biological Psychology,* San Francisco, CA: Thomson Wadsworth.

Toates, F. (2007) *Biological Psychology,* 2nd edn., London: Prentice Hall.

The behaviourist approach

10 Chapter

10.1 Introduction

> Give me a dozen healthy infants, well-formed, and my own specific world to bring them up in, and I'll guarantee to take any one at random and train him to become any type of specialist I may select – doctor, lawyer, artist, merchant, and yet, even beggar man and thief, regardless of his talents, penchants, tendencies, abilities, vocations, and race of his ancestors (Watson, 1930: 104).

This famous quotation was made by one of the most important founding fathers of the behaviourist approach in psychology. As you can see from the quotation, Watson took an extreme position, which is called **radical behaviourism.** This extreme position claims that all learning comes from experience. For the radical behaviourist, biology (or nature) has an insignificant influence on how people behave and what they do in their lives. Not all psychologists working within a behaviourist approach adopt such an extreme position, as we shall see later in this chapter. However, all seek to provide a theory of how learning, in both humans and other animals, takes place, and how behaviour can be changed.

Learning may be defined as follows: 'any relatively permanent change in the behaviour, thoughts and feelings of an organism that results from prior experience'. Note that this definition would not be acceptable to radical behaviourists such as Watson, since it refers to thoughts and feelings. Radical behaviourists were only concerned with what is observable, that is, behaviour. Since thoughts and feelings cannot be directly observed, the radical behaviourists did not regard them as a legitimate object of study by scientific psychology.

The behaviourist approach is made up of a number of different theories of learning. All seek to explain, understand and change human and animal behaviour. In this chapter we will consider two theoretical perspectives: classical conditioning and operant conditioning. In the following chapter we will consider social learning theory. This takes account of thoughts, cognitions and mental processes.

At this point it will help you to read Chapter 1, pages 9–15, of *AQA(B) Psychology for AS* by Pennington and McLoughlin (2008). This will refresh your memory about the basics of classical and operant conditioning.

10.2 Assumptions of the behaviourist approach

The behaviourist approach, especially that of radical behaviourism, is based on four main assumptions. These are determinism, empiricism, reductionism and environmentalism (see Figure 10.1). We shall consider determinism more fully in Chapter 16 of this book.

- **Determinism** represents the view that all behaviour is determined by past events. Within the behaviourist perspective this means that knowledge of the stimulus allows the prediction of the response, or behaviour. Conversely, given the response or behaviour, the cause or stimulus can be specified. Behaviour, whether human or other animal, is controlled by external forces in the environment.
- The second assumption of **empiricism** means only that which can be observed, recorded and measured is scientific. Thoughts and feelings cannot be observed, therefore they are not within the scope of behaviourism. To quote Watson: 'Psychology, as the behaviourist views it, is a purely objective,

experimental branch of natural science which needs introspection as little as do sciences of chemistry and physics. It is granted that the behaviour of animals can be investigated without appeal to consciousness' (Watson, 1919). This means that mental events of any kind cannot be the study of empirical psychology.

- The third assumption of **reductionism** is drawn from the natural sciences. For example, the workings of a clock can be understood by reducing it to the basic, physical components of which it is made. This applies to any machine, however complex, since its workings are no more than the collection of component parts. A lawnmower can be taken to bits, reassembled and, if properly done, will work the same as before it was taken apart. In a similar way, complex human behaviour is assumed, by behaviourists, to be reducible to simple components. In this case, the simple components are stimulus–response (S–R) associations which have been learned. For example, behaving in a friendly way to another person involves a cluster of behaviours, such as smiling, laughing and saying nice things. Each of these component behaviours of friendliness would, according to behaviourists, be learned from the reinforcement of the S–R links.
- The fourth assumption of **environmentalism** is that all behaviour comes from experience and that biology and genetics play a minimal role. In terms of the nurture/nature debate, the behaviourist perspective comes down clearly on the side of nurture (see Chapter 16 for a more detailed treatment of this issue). However, in explaining emotional reactions – the actual physical reactions of a person experiencing an intense emotion – Watson did acknowledge three innate emotions. These inherited or biologically given physical responses could be found in human infants and are those of rage, fear and love. Watson (1930) called these *basic pattern reactions* that are inherited. Any other emotion came through conditioning and learning. Watson also accepted that certain reflexes or instincts were innate and present in the newborn child – for example, the grasping reflex, as shown in Figure 10.2.

Assumption	Description	Comment
Determinism	All behaviours are determined by past events	All human behaviour is controlled by external events; this means that free will does not exist
Empiricism	Only that which can be observed, measured and recorded should be scientific psychology	Consciousness and mental processes cannot be observed, so cannot be part of the subject matter of psychology
Reductionism	Complex human behaviour can be reduced to simple, component parts	People are not like machines; people cannot be reduced to components without losing the sense of a person
Environmentalism	Extreme view that all learning comes from experience and that heredity has no role to play	Even radical behaviourists had to admit three innate emotions and certain reflexes occur as a result of heredity

Figure 10.1 *The four basic assumptions of the behaviourist approach.*

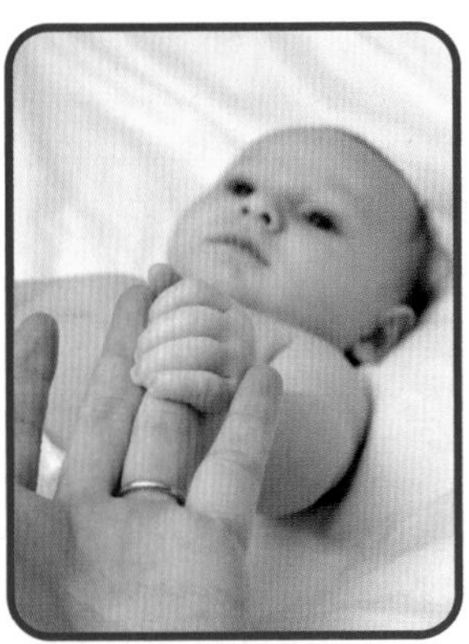

Figure 10.2 *The grasping instinct in the baby is inherited. Watson's radical behaviourist approach accepted a limited number of physical instincts in humans.*

Present status of behaviourism

Behaviourism as a method has been and continues to be highly influential in present-day psychology.

Behaviourism as a theory, as we shall see in Chapter 11, has had to modify its early, extreme, environmentalist and determinist position, to take account of consciousness and mental processes.

Evaluation

- If the extreme deterministic position were to be adopted today, then the cognitive approach (see Chapter 12) would not be regarded as scientific psychology. However, the cognitive approach is the main approach in modern psychology and adopts a highly scientific approach to investigating human thought and mental events through careful experimentation and measurement.
- In the early days of behaviourism, Edward Tolman used the term **purposive behaviour** to state that all behaviour is goal-directed. The use of the word 'purposive' was criticised by radical behaviourists because it seemed to acknowledge mental events as important. Tolman (1932) proposed a cognitive explanation for learning. For example, when rats learn to get food in a maze, they develop **cognitive maps**. This is similar to humans who know a town or neighbourhood well and can go from one point to another by various routes because they have a cognitive map of the area represented mentally. Therefore, even within the behaviourist perspective, early psychologists regarded mental events or processes as essential to explain human and animal learning.
- The idea that human behaviour can be reduced to simple component parts has been challenged by the humanistic approach (see Chapter 14). Humanistic psychologists argue that people are not like machines, and that the whole is greater than the sum of the parts. This means that reducing, for example, friendly behaviour to simpler, component parts will result in the general behaviour of friendliness being lost. A machine can be taken apart and reassembled without changing how it works and functions. In contrast, human behaviour does not have equivalent physical component parts that can be separated in such a way.
- In considering the four basic assumptions of behaviourism, summarised in Figure 10.1, it is possible to distinguish between behaviourism as a method of study in psychology and behaviourism as a theory of human behaviour. With the former, this approach advocates controlled experiments and objective observation. With the latter, behaviourism puts forward a rather mechanistic model of human behaviour. This mechanistic model pays little acknowledgement to heredity or consciousness, and explains all behaviour as resulting from conditioning.

10.3 Key concepts: stimulus, response and reinforcement

There are three key concepts that are needed to understand both classical and operant conditioning. These are stimulus, response and reinforcement. To have a full understanding of the behaviourist approach it is also important to understand the concepts of punishment, and extinction and spontaneous recovery.

10.3.1 Stimulus

In the behaviourist approach, the stimulus is an object or event in the environment that causes or elicits a response by a person or other animal. The concept of stimulus takes a number of forms. In Pavlov's original study of classical conditioning the food presented to the dog was an unconditioned stimulus; the bell was originaly a neutral stimulus and later became a conditioned stimulus after having been paired with the food several times. Note that in all these three types of stimuli in classical conditioning, the stimulus occurs, in time, before the response (salivation in Pavlov's dog experiments).

Stimulus generalisation is where the same response is caused or elicited by a number of stimuli that are all similar to each other but not identical. For example, a rat might have its behaviour conditioned to respond to a red circle. The stimulus could be varied to both different shades of red and to shapes that are oval rather than an exact circle. Variations of the stimulus in this way may elicit the same response in the rat. **Stimulus discrimination** is where the response occurs only to a very specific and narrow range of stimuli. For example, a dog may have been trained to respond only to a white circle. If the shape is even slightly oval and the dog has not been trained to respond to an oval shape, then the dog will show stimulus discrimination. Generally, the less the new stimulus resembles the original stimulus, the more stimulus discrimination will occur.

10.3.2 Response

In the behaviourist approach, a response is a behaviour that results from the presentation of a stimulus to a human or other animal. In both classical and operant conditioning, the response is the actual behaviour that takes place. In classical conditioning, the response is normally automatic and not under the control of the organism. For example, it is difficult not to salivate if you are hungry and see and smell nice food. Hence the behavioural response in classical conditioning is said to be **elicited** by the stimulus. In contrast, in operant conditioning the behaviour is under the control of the organism, is not normally automatic or involuntary, and may not be a behaviour that the organism has made before. In operant conditioning, then, the response is said to be **emitted.** For example, a rat will not press a bar to obtain food unless it is conditioned to do so.

Behaviourist experiments usually measure the response or behaviour of the animal that results from presenting a stimulus. In rats this may be, for example, the number of times a rat presses a bar to obtain pellets of food, or the number of times a pigeon pecks a coloured disc to obtain food. These are behaviours which can be observed and measured. However, it is also possible to use the behaviourist approach to condition an emotional response of, for example, fear. This is most relevant to understanding human behaviour, and how generalised fear, known as anxiety, may be acquired and treated.

10.3.3 Reinforcement

Reinforcement is something which strengthens, reinforces or makes it more likely that a behaviour will be repeated in future. For example, a hungry rat will continue to press a lever to obtain food. The food is called a reinforcer. Seen in another way, a reinforcer is an environmental consequence of behaving in a certain way. For a hungry rat it may be pressing the lever to get food; for a human it may be obtaining money or praise. Behaviourists distinguish between primary reinforcement and secondary reinforcement. **Primary reinforcement** is a reinforcer that is essential to the survival of the organism, such as food or water. **Secondary reinforcement** is a reinforcer that is not essential to survival but which aids survival or functioning. It is most important for humans, since money and praise help one live and provide self-confidence respectively. However, it might be argued that people can survive without either of these types of reinforcement.

Reinforcement can be of two types – positive reinforcement and negative reinforcement. A **positive reinforcement** occurs when a behaviour (response) is strengthened because it is followed by a rewarding stimulus. This is generally how people think of reinforcement – as positive, associated with reward and with inner mental states such as good, satisfying, pleasurable. By contrast, a **negative reinforcement** occurs when a behaviour (response) is strengthened because it is followed by the removal of a painful or an aversive stimulus. The word 'negative' is often a source of confusion and often associated with punishment. However, negative reinforcement increases the likelihood of a response and is reinforcing of a behaviour. By contrast, **punishment** stops a behaviour. Negative reinforcement strengthens a response, and punishment weakens or stops the response.

Skinner made an important distinction between reward and reinforcement. Whilst these two terms are often used interchangeably, they should not be used in this way. For Skinner, a reinforcement strengthens or makes more likely repetition in the future of the response or behaviour. A reward may or may not strengthen a response or behaviour. Rewards such as prizes, money and praise often do strengthen behaviour, but may not necessarily do so. Also, rewards often do not immediately follow behaviour, whereas for Skinner, reinforcement does immediately follow the response. **Reinforcers, by definition, always strengthen a response or behaviour.**

Schedules of reinforcement

Operant conditioning experiments for example, with rats, involve reinforcing the rat for pressing a lever to obtain food. Typically, the rat is rewarded with food after every single press of the lever or bar. However, it is possible to vary the reinforcement schedule, either through providing food after a certain number of lever presses or after a certain period of time. Four different **schedules of reinforcement** have been investigated: fixed ratio, variable ratio, fixed interval and variable interval.

A ratio schedule of reinforcement is where the rat must press the lever a certain number of times before food (the reinforcer) is given. A **fixed ratio** is where, for example, reinforcement would be given after every 10 or 20 presses of the lever. A **variable ratio** schedule of reinforcement is where reinforcement is given on a variable basis – for example, after 5, 10, 8, 12, 14 presses of a lever. With a variable ratio a regular pattern does not exist. An interval schedule reinforces behaviour according to time and not the number of lever presses that take place. A **fixed interval** schedule of reinforcement might be, for example, issuing a food pellet after every 20 seconds, regardless of how often the lever is pressed. A **variable interval** schedule of reinforcement is where a reinforcer is issued at variable times – for example, after 10, 20, 25, 15 and 30 seconds. The following examples may help to understand these different schedules of reinforcement better:

- In a factory, being paid £10 for every 10 items produced. This is a fixed ratio schedule.
- Playing a slot or fruit machine and winning sometimes. This is a variable ratio schedule.
- Surfers waiting for the 'big wave' to surf on. This is a variable interval schedule.
- Getting paid every week on Friday. This is a fixed interval schedule.

Given these four schedules of reinforcement, it is of interest to know which produces the strongest

	Fixed schedule	Variable schedule
Ratio schedule	Fixed ratio Reinforcement given every X times as behaviour is emitted. For example, every 10 lever presses.	Variable ratio Reinforcement given after variable times behaviour is emitted. For example, after 8, 12, 18, 15 lever presses.
Interval schedule	Fixed interval Reinforcement given after every fixed time period. For example, after every 20 seconds.	Variable interval Reinforcement given after variable periods of times. For example, after 20, 40, 35, 50, 30 seconds.

Figure 10.3 *Different schedules of reinforcement.*

response and most strengthens behaviour the most. Ratio schedules produce faster lever-pressing in rats than interval schedules, whilst variable schedules (either ratio or interval) usually result in the response or behaviour occurring in a more steady and enduring way.

Evaluation

- People who are addicted to gambling may become so because playing fruit machines, or playing roulette, provides reinforcements or rewards (winning) on a variable ratio schedule of reinforcement. However, not everybody who plays a fruit machine becomes a gambling addict. Hence, it would seem reasonable to infer that other factors also need to be present. For example, an addictive personality type may be more susceptible to becoming addicted to gambling than other personality types.

10.3.4 Punishment

Punishment acts to **decrease** the likelihood that a behavioural response will occur. Punishment occurs in many aspects of our lives – getting a fine for speeding, not being allowed out by parents as a child does after doing something wrong, being sacked from a job for being dishonest. Punishment can be divided into two basic types. One type is where something happens which is aversive – for example, a fine for speeding or not being allowed out. The other type is where something is taken away – for example, losing your job for being dishonest or having your clothes allowance (if you have one) taken away.

Punishment can be effective in decreasing the strength of a behaviour or the likelihood that it will be repeated in the future. However, when parents punish children for naughty behaviour, the child may not know which behaviour is being punished. This may especially be the case, in both humans and animals, if the punishment is delayed and does not immediately follow the naughty or incorrect behaviour.

10.3.5 Extinction and spontaneous recovery

Extinction of a behaviour occurs when the behaviour ceases to be emitted or the response to the stimulus no longer occurs (see the study on page 261). In operant conditioning, removal of the positive reinforcer usually results, after a period of time, in the behaviour being extinguished. However, with negative reinforcement, behaviour is less readily extinguished and may take a considerable period of time to become so. Spontaneous recovery can also occur. This is where a previously learned behaviour recurs, but in the absence of any new reinforcement.

10.4 Classical and operant conditioning

Classical and operant conditioning exemplify the basic principles of learning and have been applied equally to humans and other animals. Whilst modifications have been made with cognitive theories of learning (see Chapter 11), it is important to understand the concepts underlying operant and classical conditioning. It is worth defining what is meant by the term **conditioning**. Consider the following definition:

> Conditioning involves learning associations between events that occur in an organism's environment (Weiten, 2002: 167).

The association between events involves the stimulus and the response. A stimulus is that which causes us to do something and the response is the specific behaviour which takes place. So, for example, if you have been conditioned to run away when you see a very large spider, the stimulus is the spider and the response is running away. Events in the past have conditioned this response. Both classical and operant conditioning are able to explain a good deal of human behaviour, as we shall see.

10.4.1 Classical conditioning

Classical conditioning was the first type of learning to be studied systematically by Ivan Pavlov, a late nineteenth-century Russian psychologist. Classical conditioning is sometimes called Pavlovian or respondent conditioning. Classical conditioning is a form of learning in which a stimulus (the conditioned stimulus) acquires the ability to cause a behavioural response originally evoked by another stimulus (unconditioned stimulus). The basic process of classical conditioning is summarised in Figure 10.5.

Laboratory research on classical conditioning has

STUDY

Aim

Williams (1959) attempted to extinguish tantrum behaviour in a 21-month-old infant, using the principles of operant conditioning.

Method

Whenever the child threw a tantrum, the parents refused to respond to the screams and crying of the infant (previously they had sat with and comforted the child until he fell asleep, i.e. reinforcing the tantrum behaviour).

Results

As can be seen from Figure 10.4, the tantrum behaviour extinguished quickly over a number of nights when the child was put to bed (solid line). Figure 10.4 also shows spontaneous recovery of tantrums and that this was extinguished also.

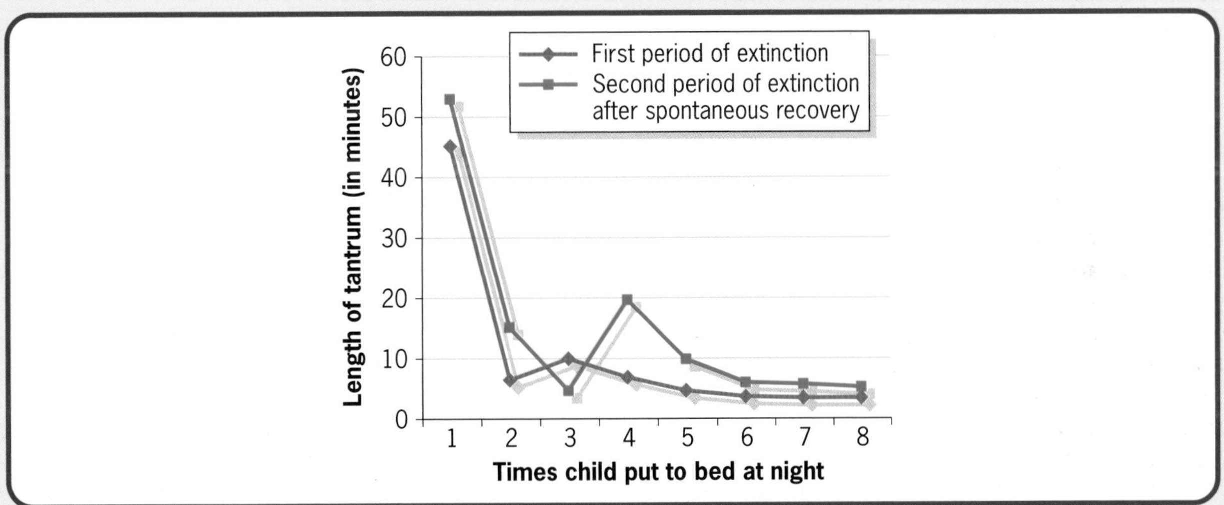

Figure 10.4 *Extinction of tantrum behaviour using operant conditioning principles. The green line shows spontaneous recovery after the initial extinction period (adapted from Williams, 1959).*

Conclusions

Operant conditioning techniques can be effective in changing unwanted and unnecessary behaviour in children. To do so, the reinforcers have to be recognised and then withdrawn.

tended to use simple behavioural responses. Besides salivation, behavioural responses of eye blinks (by putting air into the eye), knee jerks and limb flexing have been used. Conditioning of fear and fear responses have been widely studied in human behaviour. Emotional responses, including fear, have been studied when specific behavioural or physiological responses occur. In general, emotional responses appear to be very susceptible to classical conditioning, perhaps one of the most famous being the case of Little Albert, conducted by Watson and Raynor (1920), see page 263.

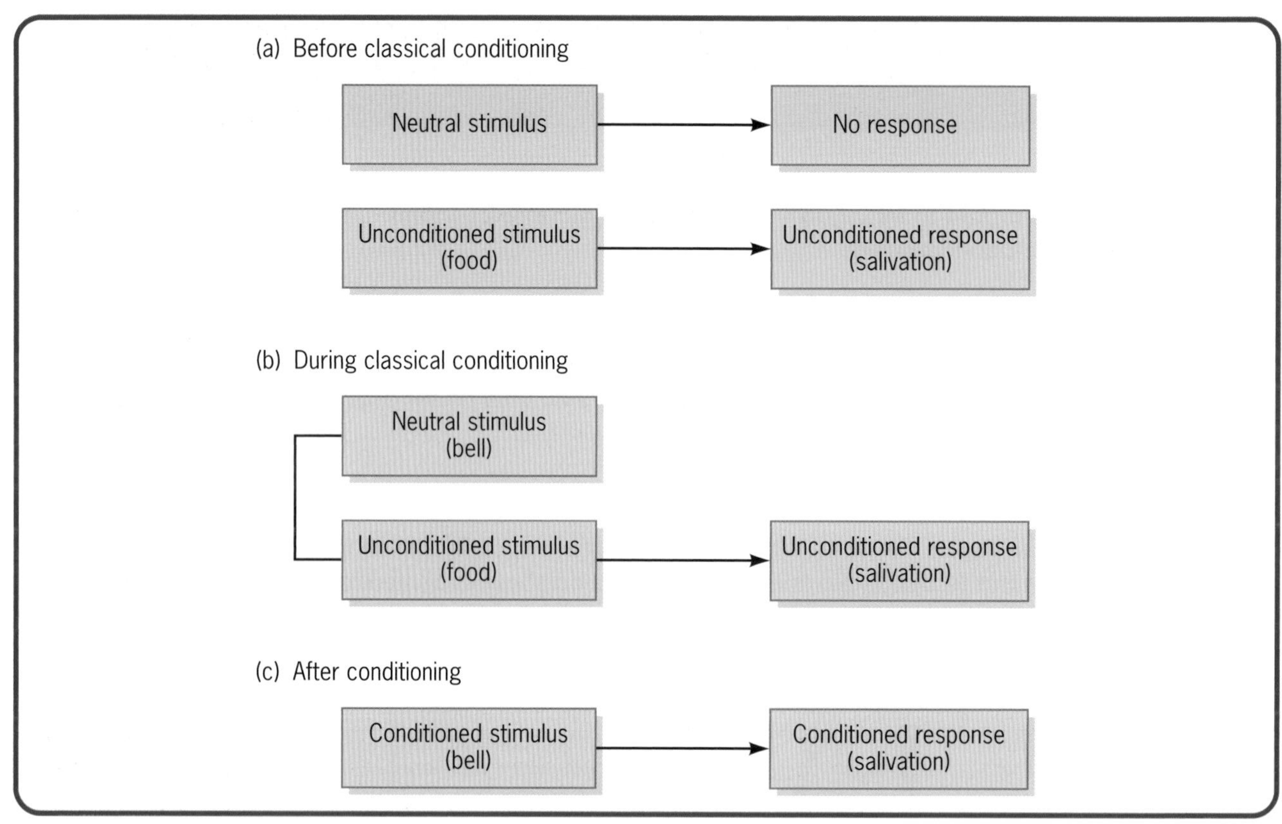

Figure 10.5 *The process of classical conditioning. (**a**) Initially, the UCS (food) elicits the UCR (salivation). The neutral stimulus (the bell) does not cause the response of salivation. (**b**) The neutral stimulus of the bell is paired with the UCS (food). (**c**) After conditioning, the bell becomes the conditioned stimulus which elicits the conditioned response of salivation in the absence of food being presented.*

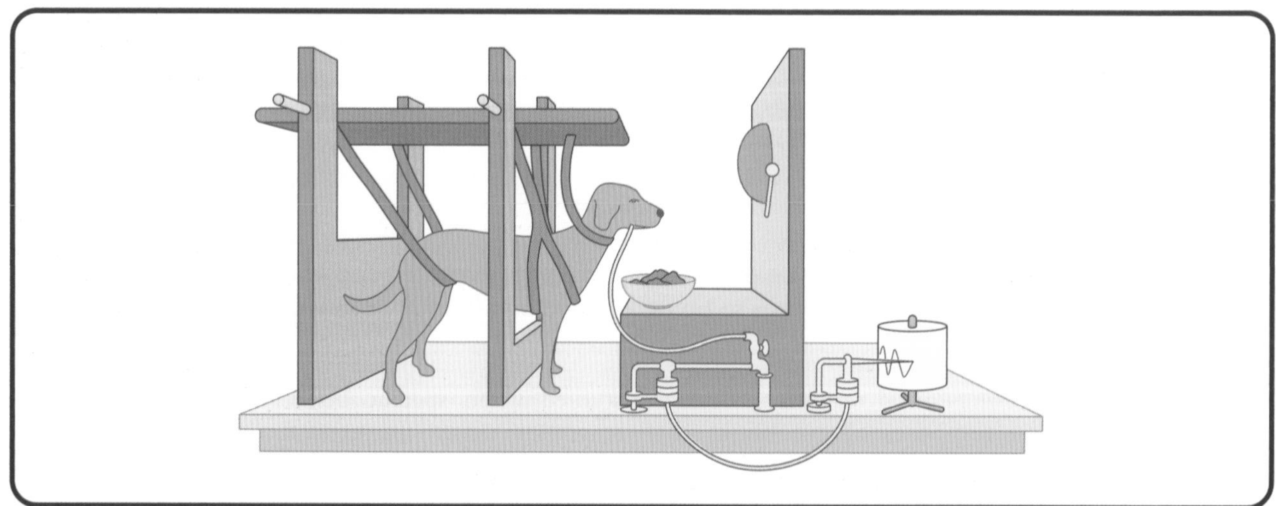

Figure 10.6 *Pavlov investigated classical conditioning using the salivation reflex action of a dog when presented with food.*

STUDY

Aim

Watson and Raynor (1920) conducted a study to demonstrate how classical conditioning could result in a young infant developing a fear of white rats.

Method

An 11-year-old boy, called Little Albert, was presented with a white rat and at the same time a very loud noise was made by striking a steel bar with a hammer. This was repeated a number of times. Eventually the white rat was put in front of Little Albert, but in the absence of the loud noise.

Results

Initially Little Albert was unafraid of white rats. After the pairing of the loud noise with the presentation of the white rat, Little Albert showed fear of the rat. In the absence of the loud noise, the white rat alone elicited a fear response in Little Albert.

Conclusions

Fear can be conditioned in a young child by pairing an initially neutral stimulus (the white rat) with an unpleasant stimulus (UCS) of a very loud noise. Five days later, Watson and Raynor found that Little Albert had generalised his fear to any small white object, such as a small rabbit and a white dog.

In what follows two aspects of classical conditioning will be discussed: first, application to human behaviour, and second, whether or not some pairings of stimuli and response are formed more easily than others.

Application of classical conditioning to human behaviour

Classical conditioning has been proposed as a good explanation for many human phobias or irrational fears (Merckelbach *et al.*, 1991; Ost, 1991). For example, a person may develop a phobia about driving a car because as a teenager one parent may have been a bad driver and scared the teenager on many occasions when they went out in the car. Munjack (1984) studied people with a phobia about driving cars and found that about half of the phobics traced their phobia back to experiences of poor driving or a car accident.

Joseph Wolpe (1958) pioneered the treatment of phobias and anxiety disorders using a therapeutic technique called **systematic desensitisation**. This may be seen as the use of classical conditioning as a behaviour therapy to reduce a person's anxiety through counter-conditioning. The goal of systematic desensitisation is to weaken the association between the conditioned stimulus and the conditioned response of anxiety. If you have a phobia of dogs, for example, the association between the stimulus of a dog (CS) and fear (CR) would be weakened by first showing pictures of dogs, then real dogs at a distance, then the dogs on a lead with the owner and so on. In a sense, the association between dog and fear is unlearned through counter-conditioning.

Ease of pairing of stimulus and response

The second point of discussion is whether or not some pairs of stimuli and response are formed more easily than other pairings. Until research by Garcia and Koelling (1966), it was thought that any conditioned stimulus (CS) could be paired with an unconditioned stimulus (UCS) to produce a conditioned response. For example, in Pavlov's experiments with dogs, it was found that a bell, or a piece of music, or another sound could be presented with the unconditioned stimulus and produce the conditioned response. Garcia and Koelling (1966) found that taste was more effective as a conditioned stimulus for learning a conditioned response to mild poisoning in rats. By contrast, pairing a bright light and a noise was more effective as conditioned stimuli for learning a conditioned response to an electric shock. From this, the originally neutral stimulus, which becomes the conditioned stimulus, is not entirely neutral. Some stimuli will pair more quickly with a response than others.

Evaluation

- Pavlov's research into classical conditioning helped psychology to become more scientific and objective. Pavlov regarded animal and human behaviour like the workings of a machine. For Pavlov, humans were complicated machines, but machines that could be broken down to the simple components of stimulus, response and association.
- Classical conditioning has provided an understanding of how phobias and anxiety disorders may arise in humans and has provided effective treatment through the use of systematic desensitisation therapy.
- Pavlov did recognise that other forms of conditioning took place and were not based on pairing a conditioned stimulus with an unconditioned stimulus. The most important alternative form of conditioning is where responses are conditioned by their consequences. This is called *operant conditioning.*

10.5 Operant conditioning

Imagine that you have just handed in a psychology essay and that you worked very hard on it, to the extent that you gave up going out on Friday and Saturday nights to complete the essay. A week later you are given your essay back by your teacher and to your delight you have been given an A+ grade. You are very pleased with this mark and say to yourself that you will work just as hard at the next essay assignment. This is a good example of operant conditioning – your hard work has been rewarded and you will continue to work hard in the future. Operant conditioning is a type of learning

Figure 10.7 *A typical example of a Skinner Box. In this version, both positive reinforcement (food) and negative reinforcement (avoidance of electric shock to the floor) can be studied.*

in which voluntary behaviour is controlled or conditioned by its consequences. In our example, being prepared to work hard at an essay in the future has been conditioned by the rewarding consequence of getting a high mark for an essay you have recently worked hard on.

B.F. Skinner (1953) developed research methods for the experimental analysis of behaviour, and stated that the principles of operant conditioning could be applied to both human and animal behaviour. To study behaviour experimentally, Skinner developed the **Skinner Box**, an example of which is shown in Figure 10.7. Typically, a hungry rat would be placed in the box and the experimenter would condition the animal to press a bar or lever. Because lever-pressing is not normal behaviour for a rat, the first step is to **shape the behaviour.** To do this, the experimenter would reward (issue food from the dispenser) if the rat came close to or touched the lever. Once this had been done a few times the rat would have to actually press the lever to obtain food. Once the rat had learned that food appeared as a consequence of pressing the lever, the rat would continue to press the lever to receive food. Here the rat has operated on its environment to obtain a reward. As a consequence, lever-pressing has been learned or conditioned as an operant behaviour.

Skinner brought a scientific approach to every aspect of his work. How then, might you define a 'hungry rat'? How would you know it was hungry? A hungry rat (or any other animal) is motivated to find food to reduce sensations of hunger. Skinner would not refer to internal mental terms like motivation. Instead he would define a hungry rat as a rat that had not, for example, had any food for 24 hours.

Reinforcement of an operant behaviour is the key to conditioning taking place. Without a reinforcement, the rat may only press the lever by accident and not again. If you had not gained an A+ grade for your essay, in our imaginary example, you would not have been reinforced and may, as a consequence, not work so hard in the future. Skinner derived the **law of acquisition** from his basic experiment. This states:

> that the strength of an operant behaviour increases when it is followed by a reinforcing stimulus (Schultz and Schultz, 2000: 234).

Negative reinforcement occurs in two ways:

- by escape learning: here behaviour is reinforced through escape from an aversive situation
- by avoidance learning: here a potentially aversive situation (being nagged by parents) is avoided by behaving in a certain way (tidying up your bedroom).

Evaluation

- In this definition of the law of acquisition, no mention is made of any type of inner event such as motivation or inner state such as pleasure or satisfaction. You might feel joy or pleasure in our imaginary essay example when getting a high grade. However, Skinner only wanted to make reference to observables, and inner feelings or states are not observable. In this sense, Skinner carried on the radical behaviourist tradition established by Watson.
- Also in this definition, the reinforcer is also called a stimulus. So whilst behaviourists talk about the strength or conditioning of a stimulus–response (S–R) link, with operant conditioning the stimulus (reinforcer) comes after the response. In classical conditioning, the reinforcer comes before the response.

Figure 10.8 summarises the two types of reinforcement and punishment in operant conditioning.

Evaluation

- Skinner (1974) regarded operant conditioning as applying to all animals, including humans. However, recent research has shown that there are biological limitations imposed on conditioning (Shettleworth, 1998). The present view is that the basic laws of learning are universal across species. However, specific instincts, resulting from evolution, may affect the learning of a particular type of animal. For example, some animals have an instinctive aversion to certain kinds of taste. Animals must quickly learn what food is poisonous and what is safe to eat. Evolution will favour animals that quickly learn what not to eat (Garcia, 1989). Therefore both biology and evolution need to be taken account of in the operant conditioning of animals.

10.6 Strengths and limitations of the behaviourist approach

Strengths

- One very important strength of the behaviourist approach is that it is highly scientific. The approach applies the rigour of observation, measurement and replication of experiments to the study of human and animal behaviour. This has had a profound influence on psychology being an evidence-based scientific discipline of study.
- Another strength is that similarities between humans and other animals are highlighted and findings from non-human animal studies have been generalised to help understand how humans learn and how their behaviour can be changed through reinforcement and punishment.
- The principles of operant and classical conditioning have been used to train animals such as guide dogs for use by people who are blind or partially sighted.

Limitations

- The behaviourist perspective consists of a number of different theories of learning. On their own, neither classical conditioning nor operant conditioning can

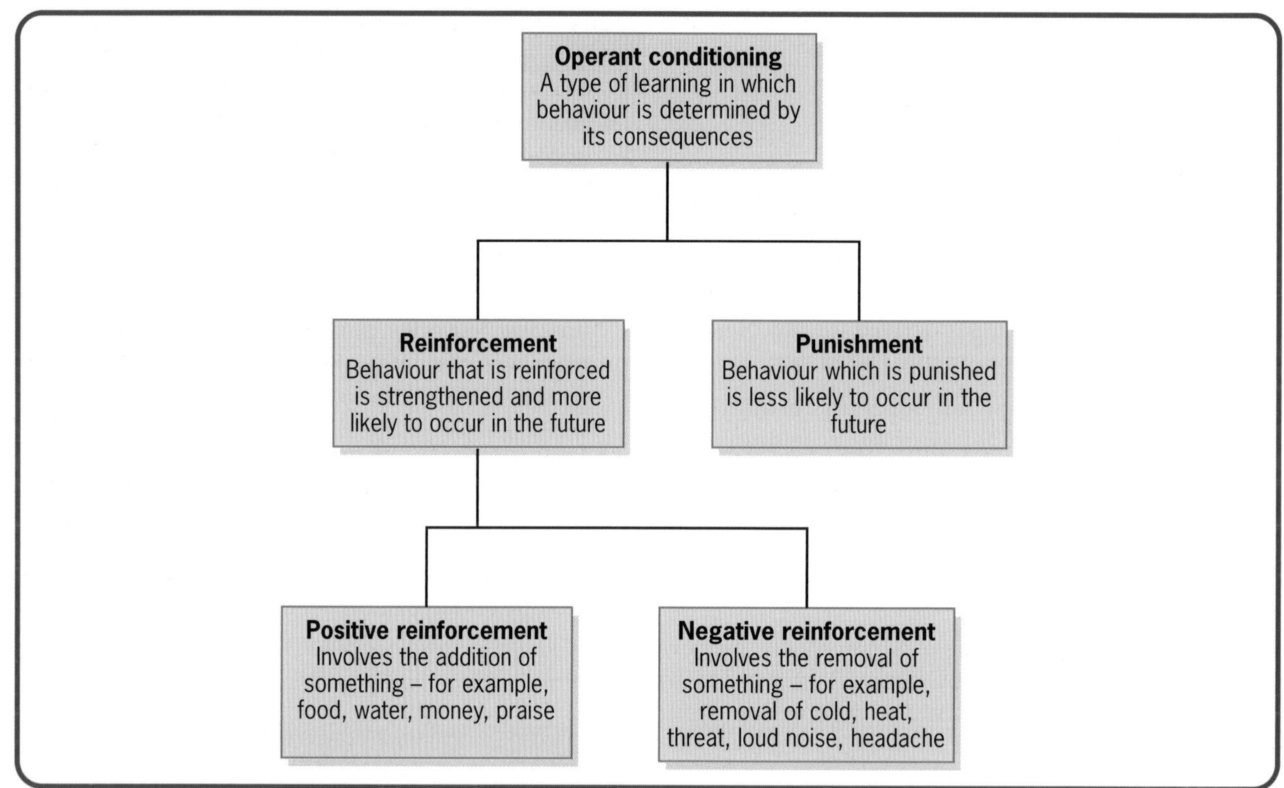

Figure 10.8 *The key concepts of reinforcement and punishment in Skinner's operant conditioning.*

explain all aspects of human learning and behaviour. Supporters of classical and operant conditioning have attempted to apply principles to both animal and human behaviour. However, it does seem clear that animal behaviour can be better explained than human behaviour by this approach.

- The limitations of operant conditioning are that mental and emotional events are ignored as an object of study. This is a major shortcoming, since we often regard the difference between humans and other animals as being to do with consciousness, reflective thought and recognition of how emotions affect how we behave. Skinner regarded emotions as responses to behaviour and not causes of behaviour. As such, Skinner thought that behaviour could only be changed by reinforcement or punishment, and not by analysing emotions as in the 'psychodynamic approach'.
- Another limitation of the behaviourist approach (both classical and operant conditioning) is that most of the research has been conducted on animals such as rats, pigeons and dogs. It is assumed that the principles of learning identified in these animals can be equally applied or generalised to humans. This is a mistake for two reasons. First, human behaviour is more complex. Second, humans are conscious beings who can think about how to behave, rather than mechanically responding to a stimulus or reinforcement or punishment.
- There are philosophical limitations of the behaviourist approach. The main one is that the approach is deterministic and allows little or no free will for humans (see Chapter 16 for a detailed treatment of the free will–determinism debate).
- Another limitation is that it ignores or undervalues the contribution of heredity to explaining and understanding behaviour. Behaviourists do not regard instinctive or inherited behaviour as featuring in any important way in human behaviour.

10.7 Applications of the behaviourist approach

Classical conditioning and operant conditioning have enjoyed a wide range of applications. These have been in most areas of psychology, but most importantly in the areas of abnormal or atypical behaviour, forensic or criminological psychology, health psychology and organisational or occupational psychology.

Behaviour therapy, based on classical and operant conditioning, has been used with great success to treat phobias and anxiety disorders. (For a detailed description and the disorders treated, please read Chapter 9 of *AQA(B) Psychology for AS* by Pennington and McLoughlin, 2008.) Behaviour therapy is conducted over a short timescale, with the objective of seeking change in a person's behaviour. Behaviour therapy includes the techniques of counter-conditioning, aversion therapy and systematic desensitisation. Counter-conditioning is where the learned response to a stimulus is replaced by another, adaptive response. For example, an alcoholic may not be able to resist drinking alcohol whenever he sees it. Counter-conditioning would get the person to resist drinking alcohol using the technique of aversion therapy.

The technique of systematic desensitisation is widely used by health psychologists. For example, over 50 years ago, Wolpe (1958) used this technique to treat people with gastric ulcers. Wolpe found that often people with gastric ulcers suffer from intense social anxiety. Over a 2-month period, Wolpe reduced social anxiety using this technique. Whilst this form of behaviour therapy did not get rid of the ulcer, being less anxious caused the ulcer to be less painful and debilitating for the person.

Behaviour modification techniques have been used with some success in forensic psychology in the area of offender rehabilitation. The most successful techniques seem to be with medium- to high-risk offenders. With these categories of people, the treatments used need to be based on changing specific behaviours and very structured programmes. It is also beneficial to conduct such treatments in the community in which the offender lives. Greater success is also achieved if behaviour modification is extended to the immediate family of the offender as well (Andrews *et al.*, 1990).

Further Reading

Introductory texts

Hill, G. (2001) *A Level Psychology Through Diagrams,* Oxford: Oxford University Press.
Pennington, D.C. (2003) *Essential Personality,* Chapter 7, London: Hodder & Stoughton.
Weiten, W. (2001) *Psychology: Themes and Variations,* 5th edn., Chapter 6, London: Wadsworth.

Specialist sources

Nye, R.D. (2000) *Three Psychologies: Perspectives from Freud, Skinner and Rogers,* 6th edn., Chapter 2, London: Wadsworth.
Ryckman, R. (2007) *Theories of Personality,* Chapters 15, 16 and 17, London: Wadsworth.
Schultz, D.P. and Schultz, S.E. (2000) *A Modern History of Psychology,* 7th edn., Chapters 9, 10 and 11, Fort Worth, TX: Harcourt College Publishers.

The social learning theory approach

Chapter 11

11.1 Introduction

The social learning theory approach developed out of the traditional behaviourist approach by acknowledging the importance of learning but at the same time recognising that cognitions need to be taken into account. One of the major issues in understanding and explaining learning in humans is the extent to which inner or outer forces control our behaviour. The behaviourist approach claims that environmental or outer forces are all that need to be taken into account, specifically reinforcement and punishment. Social learning theory claims that both inner and outer forces have to be taken into account, especially for human behaviour. By contrast, and at the other extreme, both the psychoanalytic and humanistic approaches claim that inner forces are the most important to helping understand and explain human behaviour. The social learning approach acts as a bridge between the traditional behaviourist approach and the cognitive approach.

Social learning theorists such as Bandura (1971) and Rotter (1982) observed from experiments on learning by other psychologists that cognitive factors played an essential and central role. This applied to both humans and non-human animals. Evidence for the role of cognition in learning came from early research by Köhler on insight learning and by Tolman on cognitive maps.

Köhler (1929) investigated learning which seems to occur in a flash, which he called **insight learning**. For example, Köhler conducted experiments with chimpanzees who were placed in a large cage where bananas were out of their immediate reach (see figure 11.1). In the cage were boxes and long sticks. Köhler found that some chimpanzees used the long stick to pull bananas into the cage to eat. In another situation some chimpanzees stacked the boxes on top of each other to reach the bananas. The point here is that the chimpanzees had no prior experience or reinforcement for behaving in such a way. It was almost as if the chimpanzees had studied the problem of how to get the bananas and then come up with a solution. It would be difficult to ascribe thought processes like this to chimpanzees; nevertheless they did show insight, reflecting cognition of some sort, to get the bananas.

Tolman (1948) showed that animals such as rats held a

Figure 11.1 *The chimpanzee showed insight learning by being able to use items in the environment to get the bananas.*

mental representation of their spatial environment. This was demonstrated in a classic study (see below) by Tolman and Honzik (1930).

These two very different types of experiments with animals demonstrate that cognitions have to be taken into account to explain how learning takes place. Humans are both conscious and have awareness of many of their thought processes. Given this, cognitions are even more important to human learning.

11.2 Assumptions of the social learning theory approach

The social learning theory approach is built upon five main assumptions, as follows:

(i) Human learning of behaviour takes place in a social context and needs to take account of the importance of other people in the learning process.

(ii) The most important way in which we learn from other people is from our observations of how people behave in social situations, together with the rewards and punishments received for behaving in certain ways.

(iii) Other people act as 'models' for the observer, and characteristics of the model influence whether or not the behaviour of the model is imitated by the observer.

(iv) People learn how to behave by observing other people; however, this does not always result in the performance of that behaviour. Social conditions

STUDY

Aim

Tolman and Honzik (1930) conducted an experiment with rats to show that learning took place in the absence of behavioural conditioning.

Method

Three groups of rats were placed in mazes and their behaviour observed over a 3-week period.

- Group 1 always found food at the end of the maze.
- Group 2 were not provided with food at the end of the maze.
- Group 3 were not provided with food at the end of the maze for 10 days, and then were provided with food for the remaining 4 days of the experiment.

Results

The Group 1 rats quickly learned to run the maze correctly to obtain the food. Group 2 rats often did not go to the end of the maze. Group 3 rats did not often go to the end of the maze on the first 10 days. However, when food was placed at the end of the maze on day 11 they very quickly learned to run the maze to get to the food. In fact, Group 3 rats ran the maze faster than Group 1 rats on the final days of the experiment.

Conclusion

Group 3 rats demonstrated latent learning on the first 10 days when no food was present. Over this period they formed a 'mental map' of the layout of the maze. This mental spatial representation meant that they were able to run the maze correctly and with speed to get to the food.

have to be right for the learned behaviour to be performed.

(v) Language and other forms of symbolism allow people to turn experience into conscious thought, reflect and plan future behaviour.

Bandura (1991) claims that because of our ability to be reflective and have self-consciousness we are able to decide what behaviour to perform in a specific social situation. To quote Bandura:

> People form beliefs about what they can do, they anticipate the likely consequences of prospective actions, they set goals for themselves and they otherwise plan courses of action that are likely to produce desired outcomes (page 248).

Using the terms 'belief', 'anticipation', 'goals', 'plan' and 'desired outcomes' emphasises the central role of conscious cognitions in human behaviour. Bandura, therefore, takes account of the person's social environment, cognition and actual behaviour performed. Bandura (1977) called the interaction of these three factors **reciprocal determinism** (see figure 11.3).

While Bandura used the term 'determinism' in his reciprocal determinism model, he believes that people are able to exercise a degree of free will in deciding how to behave. Our cognitions do allow us to decide what to do in many situations. For example, we may have to work to earn money in order to live and survive; however, we can choose the work we do and the career we follow in life. Bandura (1997) called this **personal agency**. This is the basic belief we have that we are able to change things and make life better for ourselves. Bandura also introduced the term **collective agency**. By this he means that a group of people with shared beliefs can come together with the object of changing all their lives for the better. For example, a person may join a religious group or environmental group to make changes to both their own and other people's behaviour.

Evaluation

- The relative influence of each of these factors will vary from person to person (thus acknowledging personality differences between people) and from social situation to social situation.
- The use of the term 'determinism' means, for social learning theorists, that behaviour is determined by previous experience, cognitions and environmental factors. The social learning theory approach adopts a 'soft' deterministic model (see Chapter 16) of human behaviour, which is in contrast to the humanistic approach (see Chapter 14). Bandura adopts a halfway position with free will and determinism, and recognises that both play a role in human behaviour.
- The reciprocal determinism model, as shown in Figure 11.2, also acknowledges that feedback from behaviour and environmental experience (whether the behaviour was rewarded or punished) will confirm or change a person's beliefs. For example, an extrovert may believe that his or her friends are also extrovert. This means that the person will behave in extrovert ways when in the presence of friends. This acts to confirm extroversion as positive and makes it likely that the person will behave in extrovert ways to friends in the future.

Figure 11.2 *Bandura's concept of 'collective agency' helps to explain why people come together in groups to change their own and other people's lives for the better.*

The social learning approach has become the dominant approach to human learning since it takes account of the role of cognitive processes to explain how and why we behave as we do.

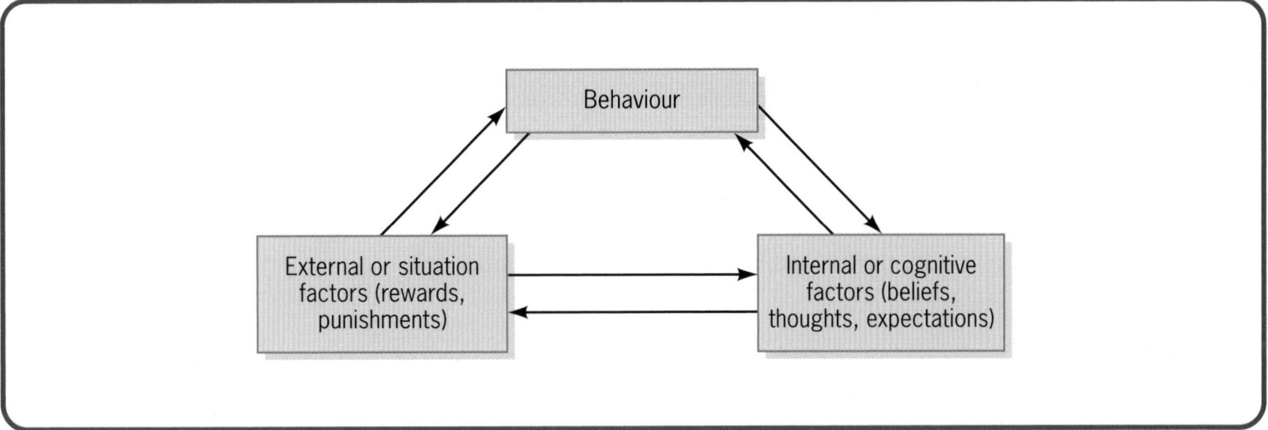

Figure 11.3 *Bandura's reciprocal determinism model in which the three elements interact and influence each other in determining actual behaviour.*

11.3 Mediational processes in learning, motivation and performance

The social learning theory approach of Bandura makes an important distinction between learning a behaviour and performing that behaviour. According to social learning theory, a person may learn a behaviour but not perform or enact the behaviour unless the appropriate social situation comes along. For example, a person may learn that it is necessary to curtsey when meeting the Queen, however, the person will only have to do this when actually meeting the Queen. Most people have learned this but never had to curtsey since they have never met the Queen! For Bandura, the main determinant of whether or not a behaviour that has been learned will actually be performed depends on the perceived rewards or punishment for the person in a specific social situation. The person has to believe that the performance of the learned behaviour will lead to desired outcomes and be rewarded (as given in the reciprocal determinism model shown in Figure 11.2). Bandura's (1989) concept of **self-efficacy**, which we will look at later in this section, develops these ideas more fully.

11.3.1 Learning and performance

Bandura (1965) demonstrated, in a classic study, that young children learn to be aggressive by observing another person being aggressive, but only perform the aggressive behaviour in an appropriate situation.

From this experiment Bandura drew the conclusion that learning takes place from watching or observing other people behave, and that behaviour results from imitation of the observed behaviour. However, the learned behaviour is only performed when the person has seen another rewarded for behaving in such a way. By imitating an observed behaviour which has been rewarded, the person imitating the behaviour also expects to be rewarded for behaving in a similar way. Bandura (1977) regarded observational learning to be a four-stage process, as shown in Figure 11.4.

Stage 1 is to do with attention and the requirement that the observer is watching the model and is aware of the consequences for the model of behaving in certain ways. Certain features of the model may gain greater attention from the observer (see Section 11.4). The observer must also be motivated to observe the model.

Stage 2 is to do with remembering the behaviour observed by encoding in language, visual and other kinds of imagery. Retention of what is observed is where the learning of the behaviour takes place.

Stage 3 is the motor reproduction process. Here the observer must feel able to perform the behaviour observed. If a person observes a world class tennis player and has only occasionally played tennis, then it is very unlikely the person can perform to the same world-class standard. Bandura's concept of **self-efficacy** has been developed from the motor reproduction stage.

STUDY

Aim

Bandura (1965) conducted a laboratory experiment with children to demonstrate that learning an aggressive behaviour takes place from observing another person behave aggressively. The learned aggressive behaviour is only performed in an appropriate situation.

Method

Children watched a 5-minute film of an adult behaving aggressively to a life-size doll, called a Bobo doll. The adult punched the doll, hit it with a hammer and kicked it round the room. At the same time, the adult used aggressive language towards the Bobo doll.

The children were then divided into three groups. Group 1 were shown a second film where the adult was praised and rewarded for behaving aggressively to the doll. Group 2 were shown another film in which the adult was punished and told off for behaving aggressively to the doll. Group 3, the control group, were not shown any sort of second film.

Each child was then put in a room with the Bobo doll, and the behaviour of the child observed and recorded.

Results

Group 1, who saw the adult or model reinforced or praised for behaving aggressively, were most likely to behave aggressively themselves towards the doll. Group 2, who saw the adult or model punished and told off for behaving aggressively, were least likely to behave aggressively themselves towards the model. The control group, Group 3, were between the other two groups.

Conclusion

Children had learned how to behave aggressively towards a life-size doll from observing an adult. However, children were most likely to perform aggressive behaviour when they saw the adult rewarded and praised for behaving aggressively.

Stage 4 is the final stage and is to do with the motivation of the person to perform the observed behaviour. The main influence on motivation is whether or not the observer has perceived the model to be punished or rewarded for his or her behaviour in that situation.

Reinforcement (or rewards) and punishment play a major role in determining whether or not the observer imitates the observed behaviour. If the observer expects to obtain a reward for performing the behaviour then the behaviour is likely to be imitated and performed. If the observer expects to be punished for performing the observed behaviour then the behaviour is unlikely to be performed, even though it has been learned. Performance of a behaviour is mediated by the perceived consequences of performing the behaviour.

11.3.2 Self-efficacy

Self-efficacy is concerned with the belief about the behaviour a person is able to perform, together with the perceived consequences of actually performing the learned behaviour. Bandura (1989) defined self-efficacy as follows:

> people's belief about their capabilities to exercise control over events which affect their lives.

Self-efficacy has become a very important area of study, both theoretically and empirically, in psychology over

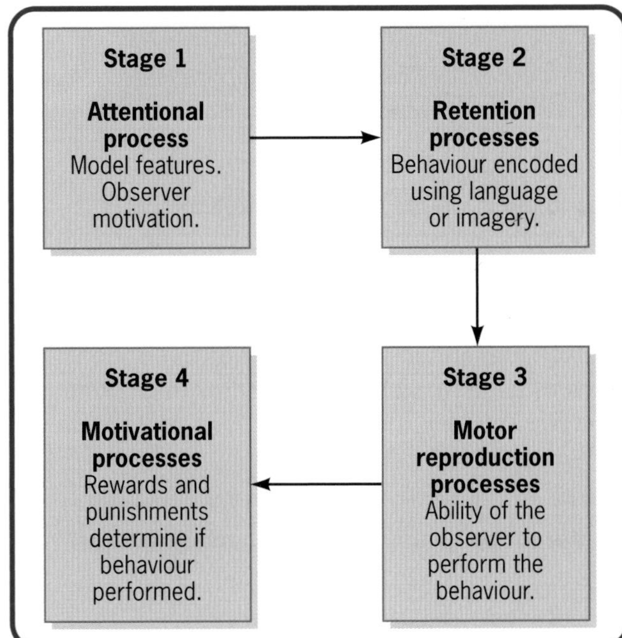

Figure 11.4 *The four-stage process of observational learning suggested by Bandura (1977).*

the past 10 years or so. One of the most important applications of the concept has been in health psychology (see Section 11.6 of this chapter on applications).

Self-efficacy is on a continuum from high to low. People who are regarded as having a high level of self-efficacy believe they can perform behaviours that will allow them to achieve the goals they set themselves. For example, a person who smokes and wants to give up smoking will think about the behaviours he or she has to perform in order to achieve this goal. A person with high self-efficacy will believe that he or she can control behaviour and do what is necessary to give up smoking. A person with low self-efficacy will regard him or herself as unable to perform behaviours to achieve the desired goal. The smoker with low self-efficacy will know what behaviours to perform but be unable to actually behave in these ways. Self-efficacy is about how you perceive yourself and the confidence you have that you can behave in certain ways to achieve goals and desired outcomes.

Perceived self-efficacy has been widely researched by psychologists, with evidence showing that it is related to:

- achieving significant weight loss through dieting
- academic performance – getting high grades at A level
- job satisfaction and performance at work
- ability to cope with trauma and crisis in one's personal life
- performance at sports and athletics.

Bandura (1995) has researched the characteristics of people with high levels of self-efficacy and found that those with high self-efficacy:

- set themselves challenging goals and high standards of achievement
- are adventurous
- overcome setbacks and frustration quickly
- are less likely to suffer from anxiety or depressive disorders.

A person's level of self-efficacy (high to low) is a product of past experience, comparison of self with the performance of others, and social influence (other

Factors	Description	Level of self-efficacy
1. Performance Accomplishments	Past experience of success	High
2. Vicarious experience	Seeing other people being successful	High
3. Verbal persuasion	Other people telling us that we cannot do something	Low
4. Emotional arousal	Very high level of anxiety	Low

Figure 11.5 *Factors affecting the level (high to low) of a person's self-efficacy.*

STUDY

Aim

McCormick and McPherson (2003) conducted a study to investigate the role of self-efficacy in a music performance examination.

Method

Three hundred instrumental music players studying for examinations at a music college in London were measured for level of self-efficacy. The performance of each musician in graded examinations was taken and compared with levels of self-efficacy.

Results

Musicians with high levels of self-efficacy performed better in the examinations than musicians with low levels of self-efficacy.

Conclusion

The researchers acknowledged that practice plays a very important part in the development of a musician's ability to play an instrument well. However, perceived level of self-efficacy does predict performance in an examination situation.

people telling us that we can perform a behaviour well). Figure 11.5 shows four factors which affect a person's level of self-efficacy.

Bandura (1977) has suggested that self-efficacy develops and changes over the lifespan of an individual. For example, in childhood, the infant learns that behaviours can result in good or bad outcomes (rewards or punishments). In adolescence, high self-efficacy makes the transition from teenager to adult less stressful and 'stormy'. In old age, high self-efficacy causes a person to seek new challenges and to see the benefits of life experiences.

Evaluation

- The social learning theory approach makes an important distinction between what a person learns and the actual performance of behaviour. This distinction can only be made on the assumption that people use conscious thought processes to decide when to enact a learned behaviour and when not to.
- The concept of self-efficacy has enjoyed great success in psychology and has been applied to the areas of personality differences, health psychology, performance at sport and many other applied areas of psychology.

11.4 Observational learning and vicarious reinforcement

As we have seen, Bandura makes an important distinction between learning and behaviour, and the actual performance of that behaviour. The social learning theory approach, as its name implies, regards most learning as taking place by observing other people. Observing how other people behave in specific social situations and learning behaviour in this way is called **observational learning**. With this approach, the person observed is called the **model** since the observer attempts to copy or imitate the behaviour of the model in the future and when appropriate. As we shall see shortly, there are certain features of the model that encourage the observer to imitate behaviour and other features which result in the behaviour of the model not being imitated.

Figure 11.6 *Here learning takes place from the observer watching how another (the model) performs a behaviour. This is called observational learning.*

11.4.1 Vicarious reinforcement and vicarious punishment

Matters are a little more complex however, since the observer also notices the consequences for the model of behaving in a certain way. For example, if the model in Figure 11.6 gave a good speech that was well-received by the audience, then the observer will perceive that the person giving the speech has been rewarded or reinforced for behaving in this way. The observer will think that if he or she gives a speech in such a way on a future occasion, then reward or reinforcement will also follow. This is called **vicarious reinforcement**. Simply stated, vicarious reinforcement is when an observer perceives another person being rewarded or reinforced for performing a behaviour. It is worth recognising that there are a number of

STUDY

Aim

Bandura *et al.* (1961) conducted an experiment to investigate the effects of exposure to aggressive and non-aggressive models and where the model was not given any reward or punishment.

Method

Two groups of children were used in the experiment. Group 1 were put in a room, one at a time, where an adult was acting aggressively to a life-size doll called a Bobo doll. Children in Group 2 were put in a room, again one at a time, where an adult was behaving in a subdued and non-aggressive manner.

Following this initial exposure, each child was then put in a room on his or her own where there were both 'aggressive toys' (Bobo doll, hammer, etc.) and 'non-aggressive toys' (tea set, crayons, etc.). The researchers recorded the number of aggressive acts performed by each child.

Results

The researchers found that children in Group 1, who were exposed to an aggressive model hit and punched the Bobo doll significantly more often than children in Group 2, who were exposed to a non-aggressive model.

Conclusion

Observation of a model behaving aggressively is likely to result in the observer behaving aggressively. This happened in the absence of any obvious reward to the model for behaving in such a way – although it may be argued that for the child the adult behaviour was thought to be appropriate because the model was an adult.

cognitive processes taking place here, and these include:

- the observer's perception that the model is getting a reward for behaving in such a way
- the observer remembering the social situation in which the model behaves and being able to match a future social situation as being similar
- the expectation on the part of the observer that if he or she copies or imitates the same behaviour in the future in a similar social situation, that he or she will also be rewarded
- that the observer values the reward gained by the model and wishes to receive that type of reward themselves.

Suppose that the model delivered the speech very poorly and got a very negative response from the audience, which included 'boos' and 'hisses' of disapproval. The observer is not likely to copy or imitate the model, since the expectation has been created that delivering a speech in the same way as the model would have negative consequences. This is called **vicarious punishment**. With vicarious punishment, the likelihood that the observer will imitate the behaviour of the model is reduced. Similar cognitive processes as identified above are operating, except that reward is replaced by punishment. However, what is different is that the observer may have learned the behaviour of the model (how to give a poor speech), but is unlikely ever to actually speak in such a way should the opportunity arise! The study described on page 275 demonstrates the effects of vicarious reinforcement and vicarious punishment on subsequent behaviour of the observer.

11.4.2 Characteristics of the model and the observer

There are characteristics of both the model and the observer which influence whether or not the observer will copy or imitate the behaviour in the future. We will deal with each in turn.

Characteristics of the model

Bandura (1977) identified three main characteristics of the model which have an influence on the observer:

- The more similar the model is seen to be by the observer, the higher the likelihood that the observer will imitate the behaviour of the model. Similarity is commonly to do with age and sex of the model. High-status people are also likely to influence the observer to behave in the same way. By contrast, if the observer perceives the model to be different to themselves it is less likely that the observer will imitate the behaviour of the model.
- Simple and easy-to-imitate behaviour is more likely to be copied by the observer. Complex or very highly skilled behaviour is less likely to be copied or imitation attempted by the observer. The observer may think that he or she will fail to imitate complex behaviour and hence not attempt it in the first place.
- Aggressive and antisocial behaviour by a model is more likely to be imitated by the observer than non-aggressive and altruistic behaviour.

Characteristics of the observer

We have already seen that one of the most important characteristics of the observer influencing performance of an observed behaviour in the future is the level of self-efficacy of the observer. According to Bandura (1989), a person with a high level of self-efficacy believes they can 'exercise control over events which affect their lives'. This means that people with high self-efficacy are confident that they can imitate the behaviour of a model in an appropriate social situation. People with high self-efficacy will also feel more confident about imitating complex behaviours. The reverse is the case for people with low self-efficacy.

Other characteristics of the observer which result in imitation of a model's behaviour are low self-confidence (which is different, since it is more general, than self-efficacy) and low self-esteem. On first sight, this may seem the wrong way round. However, people who have low self-esteem are more likely to do what other people do rather than be different and behave differently in a social situation. People with low self-esteem would not have the self-confidence to be different and therefore stick out in a crowd. Finally, people with a conforming personality or who have been rewarded for conforming in the past are more likely to imitate a model.

11.4.3 Imitation of behaviour

Throughout this chapter we have talked about 'copying or imitation' of the behaviour of a model by the observer. It is important to recognise that in Bandura's social learning theory approach this is not passive or 'blind' imitation of behaviour. We saw when considering the four-stage process of observational learning (see Figure 11.4), that learning through observation is

Figure 11.7 *If you see yourself as similar to another person then you are more likely to behave in a similar way.*

an active process. It is a process that requires higher order cognitions such as consciousness and perception. The observer creates a mental image of the behaviour and stores it in memory so that it can be reproduced in an appropriate situation in the future. Knowing what is an appropriate situation in which to perform the learned behaviour also requires high-level cognitive judgements. Bandura uses the term **forethought** to refer to the fact that people anticipate reinforcements for behaving in a certain way. This anticipation of reward also serves to motivate the person in their behaviour.

11.5 Strengths and limitations

Strengths

- Bandura recognised that neither classical conditioning nor operant conditioning could adequately account for learning in humans. The social learning theory approach places cognitions and thought processes at the centre of learning. One consequence of this is the recognition that people learn much more than is represented in the behaviour that they perform.
- The social learning theory approach employs carefully controlled scientific experiments to investigate observational learning and imitation of the behaviour of a model.
- The concept of self-efficacy has been widely adopted by psychologists and used in many applied areas, such as health psychology, sport psychology and other areas of human performance. As we shall see in the next section, therapeutic techniques have been developed to raise levels of self-efficacy in people who lack confidence to behave in certain ways.
- The social learning theory approach regards human behaviour as complex but rational, and able to be explained and understood. There are no hidden, unconscious conflicts as with the psychodynamic approach.
- Bandura adopts a compromise position with respect to free will and determinism. For Bandura, people are rational and capable of some degree of free choice; at the same time they are also controlled to some extent by environmental forces. In consequence, people are seen as responsible for their own behaviour.

Limitations

- The social learning theory approach does not pay much attention to the role of biology and heredity in human behaviour, particularly with respect to aggressive behaviour, where there is a large amount of research in biological psychology (see Chapter 9).
- The approach does not deal very fully with aspects of human development, particularly child development. Little reference is made to biological processes involved in maturation, or the influences of hormones on behaviour.
- The social learning theory approach, whilst recognising the importance of cognition and thought, does not deal with internal mental conflicts that people have and regularly experience. This is in contrast to the psychodynamic approach (see Chapter 13), which places both conscious and, most importantly, unconscious mental conflict at the heart of its theories.
- Some of the early experiments investigating aggression in children (the Bobo doll experiments) would be deemed unethical by modern standards. It is very doubtful if the British Psychological Society's Code of Conduct would permit such experiments to be carried out now. Also, it does seem very strange to think of adults acting aggressively to a large, inflatable, life-size doll!

11.6 Applications

The social learning theory approach has enjoyed a wide range of applications. These include a focus on important behaviours such as aggression, moral behaviour and dysfunctional behaviour. Also, application has been made to applied areas in psychology, such as health psychology, sport and performance psychology, abnormal or atypical psychology and education.

Health psychology

The concept of self-efficacy is regarded as important to how well people will perform behaviours beneficial to their health. Behaviours such as regular exercise, eating a balanced and healthy diet, drinking alcohol in moderation and using relaxation techniques to reduce stress all seem to be affected by self-efficacy. People with high levels of self-efficacy see themselves as able to control their health behaviours and keep themselves fit and healthy.

Self-efficacy has also been found to be an important factor in how well people cope with chronic diseases such as arthritis, diabetes and hypertension (high blood pressure). High self-efficacy increases healthy behaviour in two ways:

- It helps people to persist in their behaviours – for example, high self-efficacy is related to success at staying on a healthy diet. People with low self-efficacy tend to give up a diet quickly.
- People with high self-efficacy experience lower levels of anxiety whilst doing difficult things. It has also been shown that high self-efficacy has a positive effect on the immune system (Wiedenfeld *et al.*, 1990).

In a sense, high self-efficacy is like a self-fulfilling prophecy. If you think and believe you can do something then you will most likely do it!

Atypical psychology

In the area of atypical psychology, techniques that have helped people increase their levels of self-efficacy have helped with coping with phobic and anxiety disorders. For example, Bandura *et al.* (1982) showed that people

STUDY

Aim

Manning and Wright (1983) investigated how high and low levels of self-efficacy in pregnant women affected their ability to master pain and delivery at birth without taking pain-relieving drugs.

Method

Fifty-two pregnant women attending childbirth classes were assessed in terms of self-efficacy, using a questionnaire. The women were also asked how well they thought that they could cope with the pain of childbirth without using drugs to relieve pain.

After giving birth, the women were interviewed and asked about medication used during childbirth.

Results

It was found that women who had high levels of self-efficacy before giving birth were able to cope with the pain of childbirth well and did not make much use of pain-relieving drugs. By contrast, women who scored low on self-efficacy coped less well with the pain and used more drugs.

Conclusion

High self-efficacy is an important factor in managing pain control when giving birth.

with a spider phobia were able to overcome their fear after having their self-efficacy level enhanced. Wiedenfeld *et al.* (1990) helped people overcome their phobia of snakes through enhancing self-efficacy by exposure to a harmless snake.

From the above examples of applications of the social learning theory approach, it can be seen that the most important aspect has been the application of the concept of self-efficacy.

Further Reading

Introductory texts

Maltby, J., Day, I. and Macaskill, A. (2007) *Personality, Individual Differences and Intelligence,* Chapter 5, London: Prentice Hall.

Pennington, D.C. (2003) *Essential Personality,* Chapter 7, London: Arnold.

Specialist sources

Allen, B. (2006) *Personality: Theory, Development, Growth and Diversity,* Chapter 13, Boston: Pearson.

Bandura, A. (2001) 'Social cognitive theory: an agentic perspective', *Annual Review of Psychology,* 52, 1–26.

The cognitive approach

Chapter 12

12.1 Introduction

Pause from your studies for a moment. What thoughts are you conscious of? In looking round where you are, what are you paying attention to? It may be that you are recalling something from memory, perhaps some exciting event you were involved in a few days ago. From this it is evident that you have thoughts and that you are conscious about what you are thinking. In many ways, this characteristic of people to be conscious and aware of their thoughts distinguishes us from other animals. Given this, it is hardly surprising that psychologists regard our thoughts, or more generally our mental processes, as a legitimate area of study. Such psychologists are called cognitive psychologists and work within the **cognitive approach**.

Refresh your knowledge and understanding of cognitive psychology which you studied at AS level by reading Chapter 1, pages 19–24, of *AQA(B) Psychology for AS* by Pennington and McLoughlin (2008). Additionally, you will have studied at least one topic in cognitive psychology at AS level. Look through the rel-

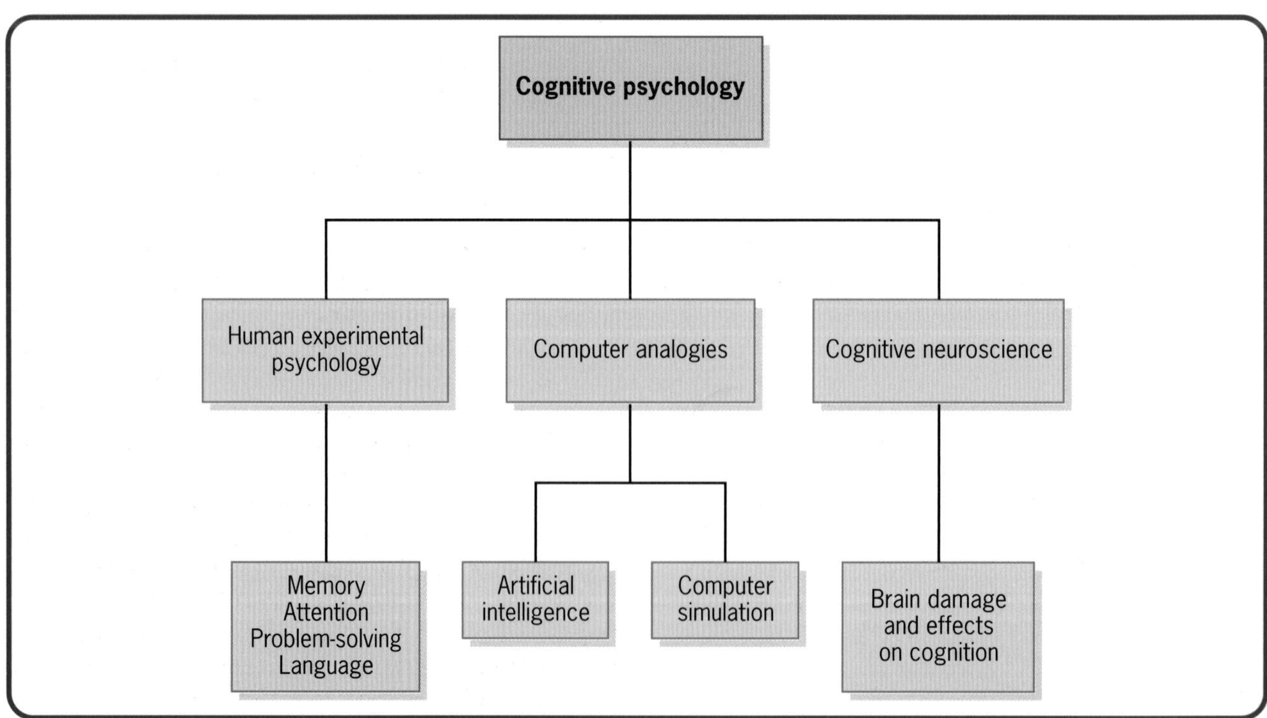

Figure 12.1 *Cognitive psychology is made up of three related areas: human experimental psychology, computer analogies and cognitive neuroscience.*

evant chapters (Chapters 7 and 8) of *AQA(B) Psychology for AS* to refresh your memory about remembering and perceptual processes.

Cognitive psychology has been the dominant perspective in psychology for over 40 years. The use of a computer metaphor applied to human mental processes provides a model for investigating human mental functioning. The word *cognition* comes from the Latin *cognoscere*, which means 'to apprehend' in the sense of getting the meaning of, understanding and recognising (not to catch, as in 'the police apprehended a criminal'). However, as we shall see in this chapter, cognitive psychologists also need to take motivation, emotion and other human aspects into account in developing theories of cognition.

Cognitive psychology may be seen as being made up of three different but interlinking areas, as shown in Figure 12.1. These are human experimental psychology, which investigates and develops theories about memory, attention, problem-solving and language; the use of the computer analogy in terms of artificial intelligence and computer simulation; and cognitive neuroscience, which looks at how damage to the brain affects cognitive processes. These three areas are all related because they all are concerned with human (and sometimes animal) **cognitive processes**.

12.2 Development of cognitive psychology

The seeds of cognitive psychology date back to the times of the ancient Greeks, over 3,000 years ago. The ancient Greeks were interested in how we gained knowledge of the world. Later, the seventeenth-century philosopher René Descartes defined human existence through his famous phrase *cogito ergo sum*, which means 'I think, therefore I am'. For Descartes, thinking or thought was the defining aspect of being human. Later, the empiricist philosopher John Locke proposed that simple ideas came from observation and experience, and that complex ideas result from mental manipulation of simple ideas. However, it was not until the late 1900s that attempts were made to investigate human thoughts and feelings scientifically.

12.2.1 Early introspection

> If we are to study consciousness we must use introspection and introspective reports (Farthing, 1992).

This quotation, from a relatively recent book on consciousness, applies as strongly today as it did over 100 years ago when Wilhelm Wundt established the first scientific laboratory in psychology. **Introspection** is a method of investigating conscious thought and mental processes by asking people to report verbally on what they are conscious of thinking and feeling. Wundt trained his assistants to introspect in a particular way and to analyse sensations, images and emotional reactions into component parts. Essentially, Wundt tried to break down conscious thoughts and feelings into smaller and smaller parts or elements. From this you can see that Wundt may be regarded as an early cognitive psychologist. However, because his method of introspection was subjective and not scientific, the use of introspection in scientific psychology did not re-emerge until the 1960s.

The shortcomings of Wundt's version of introspection are that:

- there is no objective way of resolving differences between different observers
- disagreements cannot be resolved by repeated introspections, as Wundt had hoped
- Wundt claimed that higher mental processes could not be investigated by introspection – only simple sensations and feelings; as a result, Wundt limited the scope of psychology.

Modern cognitive psychology regards all mental processes as a legitimate area of study.

12.2.2 The influence of early cognitive psychologists

Edward Tolman (1932) was a behaviourist who proposed a cognitive explanation for learning based on **purposive behaviour**. Tolman rejected Thorndike's law of effect and hence rejected one of the key principles of behaviourism (see Chapter 10) that learning resulted from the reinforcement of responses. Tolman conducted much of his research on rats running in simple mazes to get food. Tolman showed that rats, after running the same maze a number of times, develop **cognitive maps** of the maze. This is much the same as a person knowing the roads and streets of the town or city in which he or she lives. People with a cognitive map of where they live can use a number of routes to get to the same destination. Tolman is regarded as a forerunner of modern cognitive psychology, introducing the idea of an **intervening variable** (in this case cognitive processes) between stimulus and response.

In 1960 George Miller founded the Center for Cognitive Studies at Harvard University. Miller rejected behaviourism and instead seized upon similarities between computers and how the mind works. Miller did not regard the shift to cognition as representing a revolution in psychology, but a process of gradual change which was taking place in psychology. Researchers at the Center for Cognitive Studies studied aspects of human mental processes, now commonly associated with cognitive psychology. These included language, memory, attention, thinking and cognitive development in children.

Finally, Ulric Neisser published a highly influential book in 1967 called *Cognitive Psychology* which attempted to define this new field of psychology. As a result, Neisser became known as the 'father' of cognitive psychology. Just 19 years later, Neisser was critical of the way cognitive psychology had developed. He thought it should be applied to practical problems and not be obsessed with laboratory experiments which have questionable ecological validity. Together, Miller and Neisser were of great importance in the development of modern cognitive psychology.

12.3 Assumptions of the cognitive approach

Seven main assumptions can be seen to underlie or provide the foundations for the cognitive approach in psychology. These are as follows:

1 That thought, both conscious and unconscious, can influence behaviour. Thought acts as mediational processes between stimulus and behavioural response.

2 That mental processes can be regarded as information processing.

3 That mental processes can be scientifically studied.

4 That the mind operates in a similar way to a computer. This means that a computer analogy can throw light on cognition.

5 That introspection is a valid scientific method for studying cognitive processes.

6 That the brain, particularly damage to parts of the brain, affects cognitions and cognitive processes.

7 That the findings and methods of cognitive psychology can be applied to other areas of psychology, such as child development, abnormal psychology and applied areas such as sport and the law.

12.3.1 The influence of thought on behaviour

The behaviourist approach (see Chapter 10) is only interested in observable behaviour and objectivity. The emphasis on reinforcement of stimulus–response links ignores mental processes taking place within the organism. Cognitive psychologists, and cognitive behaviourists such as Tolman, regarded it as essential to look at mental processes of the organism and how these influence behaviour. Instead of a simple S–R linkage, the **mediational processes** or thoughts of the organism are of central importance (see figure 12.2). Without an understanding of the mediational processes that occur in the mind of the person, it is argued, psychologists cannot have a proper understanding of behaviour. In this chapter we will consider conscious and unconscious human thought processes as well as individual differences. We will also consider the question of whether or not animals can think.

Conscious and unconscious processes: thought

Consciousness is still regarded as one of the great mysteries of mind (Young and Block, 1996). This is because it is not clear how the physical brain causes us

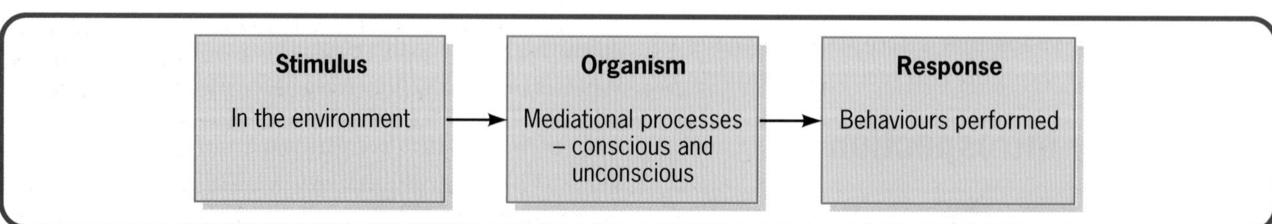

Figure 12.2 *Cognitive psychologists place thought or mediational processes as central to understanding and explaining human behaviour.*

to be conscious. **Consciousness** is the awareness we have of both stimuli in the environment and stimuli from our body and our states of mind. Consciousness may also be seen to involve different levels:

- alert and awake, asleep
- altered states of consciousness, hypnotic states.

Some people, when experiencing an altered state of consciousness, describe being overwhelmed by stimuli – internal and external – and being conscious of too much at once. Attentional processes, which you may have studied at AS level, limit the amount of information that we are conscious of at any one time. In a different way, memory allows vast amounts of information to be stored so that at any one time we are conscious of only a limited amount of information and few feelings.

Research has shown that if a person is aware that attempts are being made to condition certain aspects of his or her behaviour, conscious awareness of this can prevent conditioning taking place. This means that thoughts have to be taken into account to understand how humans learn and behave. This also sets human beings apart from other animals. Conscious thought mediates between stimulus and behavioural response, and may at times prevent the stimulus from resulting in the behaviour.

Consciousness serves two main purposes in relation to cognition (Kilstrom, 1984):

- **Monitoring:** The monitoring function allows the person to keep track of the environment, their behaviour and internal mental and emotional states.
- **Controlling:** The controlling function allows the person to plan and control their behaviour, based on the information received from the environment and internally.

Conscious thought mediates behaviour through controlling how to behave and ensuring (and monitoring) that the behaviour is appropriate for the particular social situation or context. At a conscious level, your perceptions, thoughts, memories of previous experiences, feelings and even mood at that particular time, are all aspects of cognition that mediate between stimuli and responses.

Cognitive psychologists have also shown interest in unconscious thought processes. These are not the irrational, instinctive unconscious processes of Freud (see Chapter 13). Instead it may be better to use the term **non-conscious** (Kilstrom *et al.*, 1992). Most human mental processes – for example, memory, attention – occur at a non-conscious level.

Research in the area of **subliminal perception**, which may be regarded as non-conscious information processing, shows that we can be influenced by stimuli we cannot see or hear consciously. While the effects of subliminal perception studies have been shown to be small (Krosnick *et al.*, 1992; Greenwald *et al.*, 1991), they do show that thought processes can and do operate at a non-conscious or unconscious level.

Individual differences

Perhaps the most important individual difference with respect to cognition and thought processes is that of intelligence. Sternberg (2001) characterises intelligence as how well people learn from experience and adapt to the world in which they live. Additionally, and importantly, Sternberg links intelligence to people's understanding and control of their thought processes, in particular the processes of problem solving, reasoning and decision making.

A cognitive and information-processing view of intelligence has been put forward by Deary (2000). In this view, individual differences in intelligence are seen as differences between people in the rate of processing of simple information. For example, consider two lines, where it is obvious that one line is longer than the other. Cognitive psychologists have found that highly intelligent people need to see the picture of the two lines for a shorter period than less intelligent people to judge which is the longer line.

Intelligence, however it is determined and measured, may act as a mediational process because of its influence on the speed with which information is taken in and processed by the person. Highly intelligent people seem to process information more quickly and hence will respond more rapidly to a stimulus.

Other types of individual differences that affect thought processes include **need for cognition** (Cacioppo and Petty, 1982). Need for cognition refers to the level of thought a person gives to a task, message or problem. People who score high on the need for cognition scale think deeply about a problem and have a need to understand the world around them more than those who score low on the scale. People who score high on the need for cognition enjoy thinking and reasoning and have good access, through introspection, to their cognitive processes. Need for

cognition is a mediational process because it influences how fully a person may or may not process information in forming a response. Figure 12.3 gives some items from the Need for Cognition scale of Cacioppo and Petty (1982).

Can animals think?

Dog lovers often use the phrase 'he understands every word I say' to indicate that their pet is conscious of what is being said. Research by Kemp and Strangman (1994) showed that around 40% of the general population regard animals as possessing consciousness. Animal psychologists have attempted to look at the cognitive capabilities of the organism in the stimulus-organism-response (S-O-R) model of cognition. Research has shown that:

- some animals do respond to colour photographs of familiar objects (Cook, 1993)
- laboratory animals display thought or mediational processes such as the coding and organisation of abstract symbols (Wasserman, 1993)

However, psychologists sometimes argue that whilst animals may show evidence, on the basis of behavioural responses, of cognitive processes, these are not similar to those operating in human beings (Baum, 1994).

How do we know that we think? Probably because we say so and are conscious of having thoughts and can communicate this using language. Animals cannot do this, therefore any inference about animal thought can only come from observing behaviour. Therefore, we can probably never really know if animals think, and whilst pet owners may believe their dog understands every word said, this is highly unlikely to be the case.

12.3.2 The scientific study of mental processes

Mental processes, such as memory, attention, problem solving and reasoning, are studied by cognitive psychologists through the use of laboratory experiments. The extensive use of laboratory experiments in cognitive psychology is similar to the behaviourist approach. However, there are two important differences:

- First, the vast majority of laboratory experiments in cognitive psychology use people as participants. In the behaviourist approach, animals such as rats and pigeons are commonly used.
- Second, cognitive psychologists use the findings of experiments to *infer* mental processes. The use of the word *infer* here reflects the fact that mental processes cannot be observed, but measures can be taken that allow cognitive psychologists to be confident of what is going on mentally. An experiment by Sternberg (1966) illustrates this.

1. I really enjoy a task that involves coming up with new solutions to a problem.	Agree/disagree
2. I only think as hard as I have to.*	Agree/disagree
3. I find little satisfaction in deliberating hard and for long hours.*	Agree/disagree
4. I would prefer a task that is intellectual, difficult and important to one that is somewhat important but does not require much thought.	Agree/disagree
5. I prefer to think about small, daily projects rather than long-term ones.	Agree/disagree
6. Learning new ways to think does not excite me very much.*	Agree/disagree

Figure 12.3 *Agreement with 1, 4 and 5 scores towards the need for cognition; disagreement with (those with an asterisk) 2, 3 and 6 scores towards need for cognition. If you score 5 or 6 points you are likely to have a high need for cognition.*

Modern introspection

Farthing (1992) regards the use of introspection and introspective reports by people as essential to the study of thought and consciousness. Contemporary cognitive psychology remains uncertain about the value of introspection for shedding light on cognitive processes.

Modern introspection falls into two categories:

- First, methods that ask people to reflect and report on their experiences (thoughts and feelings). This is called **retrospective phenomenological assessment** because of the focus on reporting experiences (phenomenology).
- Second, methods which ask people to 'think aloud' whilst solving a problem (Ericsson and Simon, 1980). This approach regards verbalisations as the product of mental processes and therefore capable of being scientifically interpreted.

Have a go at each type of introspection. For the 'think aloud' approach, select a problem to solve (this may be a crossword clue or other type of puzzle). Get a tape recorder and attempt to solve the problem by verbalising everything that comes into your head. For the phenomenological approach, look at something in your surroundings – for example, a picture or another person – and try to report into a tape recorder what you think and feel. With the phenomenological type of introspection, attempts have been made to quantify the reports and conduct statistical analysis. This is an attempt to make the reports more objective and appropriate for scientific analysis.

However, some psychologists have questioned whether or not a person can have access to higher mental processes, particularly those to do with making judgements and decisions. An influential paper by Nisbett and Wilson (1977), entitled 'Telling more than we can know', stated, with evidence, that we do not have access to our thought processes. Nisbett and Wilson showed that often introspective reports do not reflect mental processes but a person's beliefs about something.

Modern introspection employs different methods of achieving introspective reports from people. However, there is still controversy over the scientific value of such reports, and whether they really do reflect our actual mental cognitive processes.

STUDY

Aim

Sternberg (1966) conducted a study to determine whether or not people retrieve information from a list by scanning all information, in sequence, until they come across the piece of information they are looking for.

Method

Participants were asked to memorise a list of words of different lengths. Following this, participants were asked to say whether or not the words they had learned were on two other lists of words. With these two lists, one was twice as long as the other.

Results

Participants took longer to identify words they had learned from the longer list compared to the shorter list.

Conclusions

Because participants take longer to recognise words on the longer list, they must be scanning the list in a sequential rather than a random way.

12.3.3 Cognitive neuropsychology

Over the past 20 years cognitive psychologists have become interested in how damage to different parts of the brain affects both behaviour and cognitive (thought) processes. It was found that people who suffered cognitive deficits, such as loss of speech or inability to read the printed word, could provide insights into the cognitive processes of normal people. One of the most well-researched areas in **cognitive neuropsychology** is around reading and writing. For example, cognitive psychologists state that there are a number of different pathways in the brain by which the written word becomes translated into speech. This is evidenced by some brain-damaged patients reading aloud the written word by translating each letter of the word into an appropriate sound. Patients with damage to different parts of the brain can only read aloud the whole word, and have difficulty pronouncing non-words. In this case it seems that reading takes place because the whole word is recognised rather than trying to pronounce the whole word from its constituent letters (Ellis, 1973). This is shown in Figure 12.4.

Cognitive neuropsychology makes the assumption that any cognitive system (reading, writing, speaking, etc.) is made up of a number of component parts that are called *modules* (Marr, 1982). Each module, it is claimed, has a distinct function, and together these modules perform a larger-scale function. Another assumption is that these modules are located in different parts of the brain. This means that damage to a specific part of the brain will not destroy the larger scale function of, for example, reading or speaking or writing, but will destroy some of the component modules that make up the function of, for example, reading aloud. Hence the example given in Figure 12.4 of two different brain-damaged patients is understood in terms of different modules having been destroyed by the damage to the brain.

Evaluation

- Cognitive neuropsychology is a complex area of study and one requiring psychologists with high levels of skills and knowledge about the brain. The idea of 'modules' in the brain is useful, but in reality brain damage can be quite extensive, and it is not always clear exactly which parts of the brain have been damaged. Hence, it is difficult to be certain about damage to specific areas of the brain and the resultant deficit in cognitive functioning for the person.

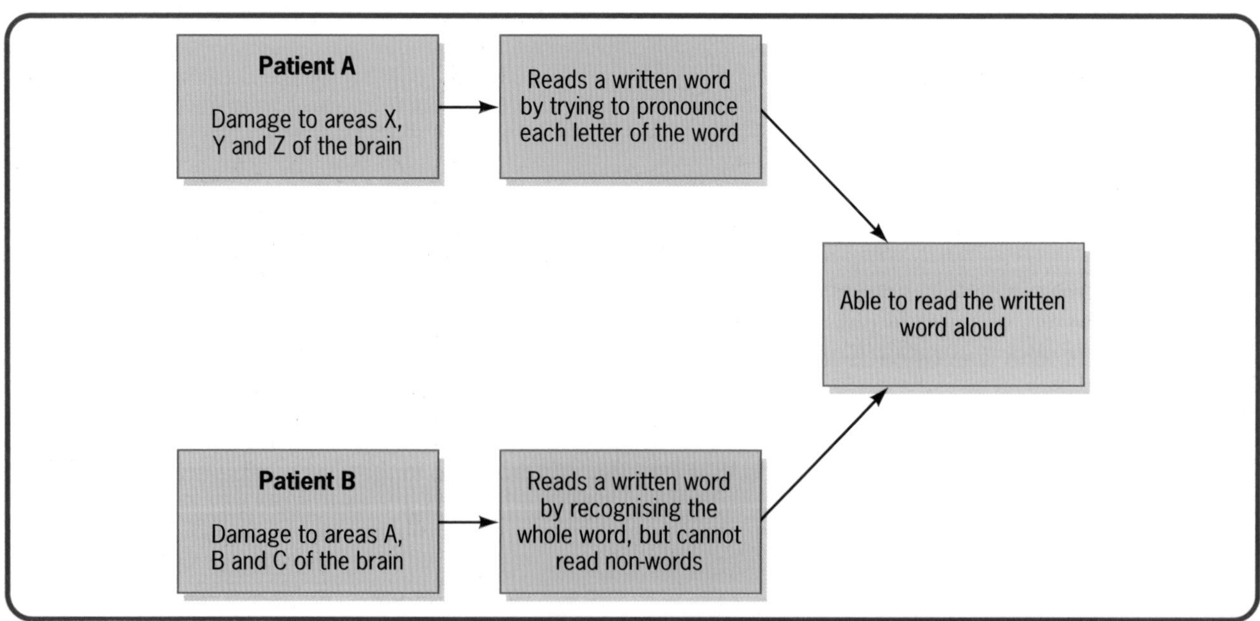

Figure 12.4 *Two different ways in which people with damage to different areas of the brain read aloud the written word.*

12.4 Information processing

Central to the cognitive approach is the idea of information processing. This characterises the cognitive approach and makes it different from other approaches such as behaviourism and humanism. Information processing is based on:

- transforming information
- storing information.
- retrieving information from memory.

The environment (external or internal to the person) provides stimuli through the senses. These stimuli are inputs which can be transformed, stored and retrieved using various mental or cognitive processes. Information is stored in and retrieved from memory. It is transformed through thinking and reasoning to solve a problem. This information-processing model is depicted in Figure 12.5.

The information-processing model of cognitive psychology presents a mechanistic view of the mind. This is because it is seen to be governed by rules and likened to a computer. We will look at the computer analogy in more detail in Section 12.5. Information-processing models of cognitive processes, such as memory and attention, are usually represented by flow charts. The use of flow charts, such as that of memory given in Figure 12.6, assumes that mental or cognitive processes follow clear sequences. There are two views about this – the **serial processing** view of early cognitive psychology, and the more recent **parallel processing** or connectionist view of contemporary cognitive psychology.

12.4.1 The classical view: serial processing of information

Cognitive psychologists first used the idea of information processing as a model to explain human cognitive processes. In the early days it was assumed that each of the stages in a flow diagram, such as that shown in Figure 12.6, had to be completed before moving on to another stage. This classical view, known as the **serial processing** model, also assumes the stimulus or information impinging on the person is processed in an automatic way by that person. This rather passive view of information processing is conceptualised as *bottom-up* information processing – that is, information processing is entirely dependent on the stimulus input of information through the senses. However, it is easy to show that the knowledge a person holds and the expectations a person has influence perception and what is attended to and remembered. This is called *top-down* processing. The well-known psychological example of the young woman/old woman ambiguous figure demonstrates top-down processing. Look at Figure 12.7 – what do you see? If you look for an old woman you can see one, and if you look for a young woman you can see one. Hence, with an ambiguous picture, what you expect to see or are looking for, you usually do see. Translating this idea more widely to interpreting human behaviour, it is often the case that an example of behaviour is ambiguous and needs interpreting. Hence, expecta-

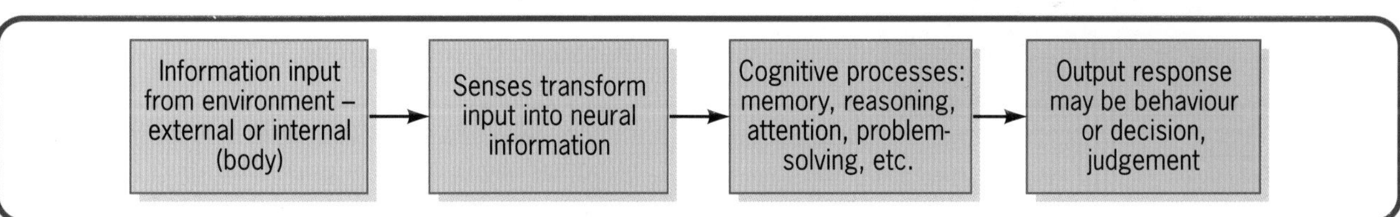

Figure 12.5 *The information processing approach which is central to cognitive psychology.*

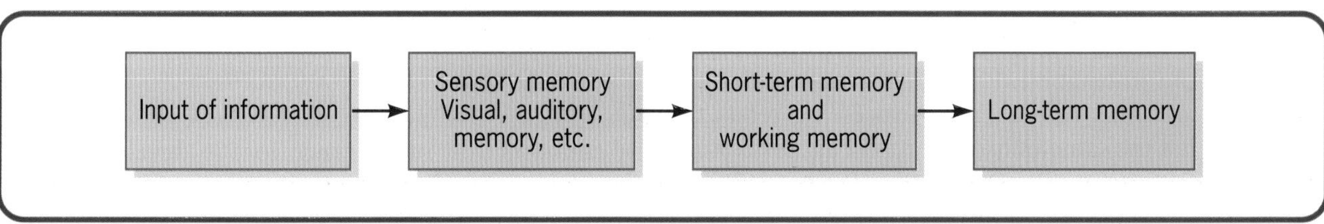

Figure 12.6 *An information-processing model of memory (adapted from Atkinson and Shriffin, 1971).*

tions and pre-judgements often strongly influence the meaning you give to what somebody has done.

12.4.2 The connectionist view: parallel processing of information

A number of problems have been identified with the classical or serial information-processing view.

- First, serial processing is too slow to account adequately for human information processing. The one-step-at-a-time approach of serial information processing does not reflect how the brain and interconnection of neurons seem to work (Dawson, 1998). For example, Posner (1978) showed that people can perform extremely complicated information-processing tasks in a fraction of second. This does not seem to square with a serial-processing explanation.
- Second, studying how the brain works and how networks of neurons in the brain operate does not show step-by-step serial processing of information.

Figure 12.7 *The young woman/old woman ambiguous figure. You can see either, depending on what you are looking for.*

Instead, it is much more likely that **parallel processing** of information is taking place. Parallel processing means that a number of steps or operations in an information flow diagram are operating at the same time. Also, parallel processing refers to the idea that the same information is being processed at the same time in different parts of the brain.

The parallel processing model has been developed into a *connectionist network* which, at its simplest, has three types of information-processing units:

(a) input units

(b) hidden units

(c) output units.

An example of a simple connectionist network is shown in Figure 12.8. Input units receive stimuli or information from the environment. Hidden units detect and process patterns and features of the input units. Finally, output units encode information for the response. Notice in Figure 12.8 that there are many interconnections between all three types of units, hence the name connectionist networks.

Evaluation

The connectionist view of information processing has a number of advantages over the serial-processing view:

- First, connectionist networks represent better what goes on at a physical level in the brain between neurons.
- Second, connectionists assumed that the architecture of cognition, how cognitive processes are structured, is like that of the brain.
- Third, connectionist networks explain how people can perform complex information-processing tasks in very short periods of time measured by milliseconds.
- Finally, connectionist networks have been successfully applied in understanding how knowledge is represented in the mind and how information is organised in long-term memory (Smolensky, 1995).

12.5 Computer analogies

Of fundamental importance to the development of cognitive psychology has been the use of the computer as an analogy for the human brain. The computer was being developed at about the same time

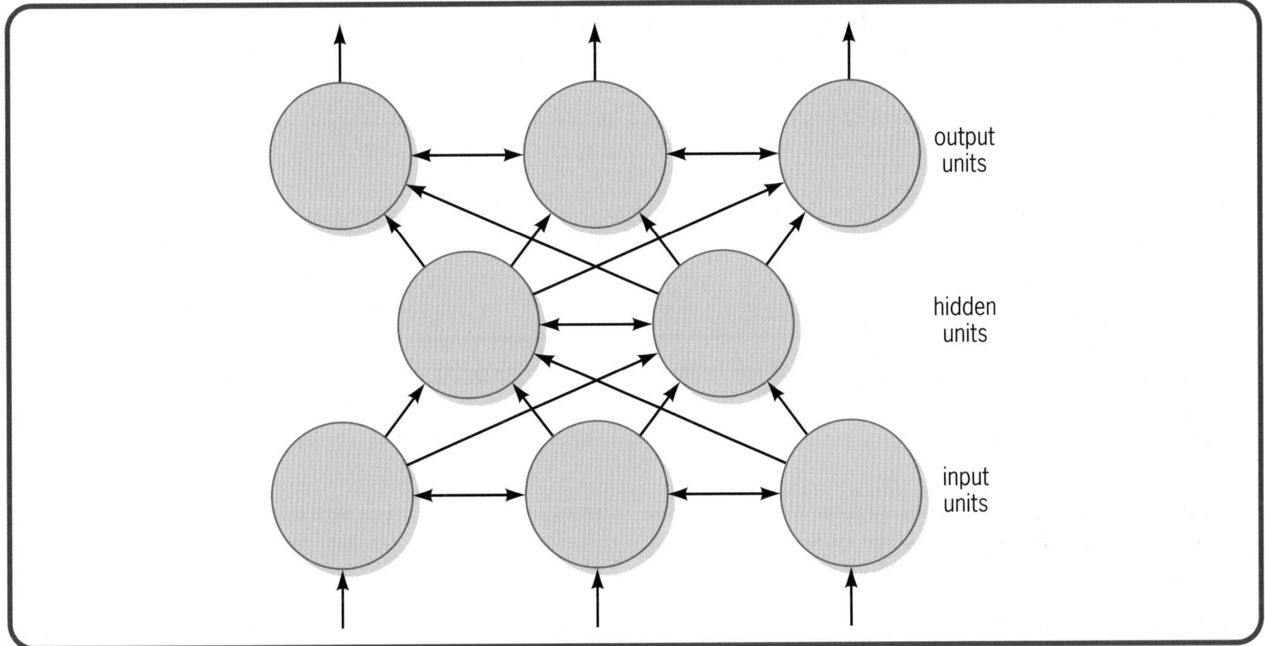

Figure 12.8 *A simple connectionist network showing the three types of units: input, hidden and output. The direction of the arrow indicates the flow of information.*

that cognitive psychology was becoming established as a legitimate area of scientific psychological inquiry. Likening the human mind and its operations to a computer and how it works through information processing has been and remains, a powerful analogy for cognitive psychology. In what follows we shall explore the computer analogy more fully, then look at how psychologists have used the computer to simulate human mental abilities, in artificial intelligence and areas of application.

12.5.1 The computer as human mind

The parallels between how computers process information and how humans process information are very compelling, as the following quotation demonstrates:

> Computers take a symbolic input, recode it, make decisions about the recoded input, make new expressions from it, store some or all of the input, and give back a symbolic input (Lachmann *et al.*, 1979).

This is very similar to how the human mind processes information. Humans code information, remember it, make decisions based on it, change their internal levels of knowledge and turn all this into a behavioural output. This is shown in Figure 12.9.

The computer analogy of human cognitive processes can be seen to work because of five key areas of similarity. Both computers and humans as information processors have the following in common:

- coding
- channel capacity
- span of apprehension
- central processing unit
- information store.

Coding is fundamental to both how computers work and human information processing. All communication systems use some form of *coding*. For example, a telephone translates our voice into an electrical signal and transmits it to another telephone, where it is decoded back into a voice. How the brain represents a picture, for example, is through coding the information into electrical impulses. The ancient Greeks, such as Aristotle and Plato, believed that a picture was literally copied into our mind and not coded.

Channel capacity is the idea that any system which channels or communicates information has an upper limit on the amount of information it can deal with at any one time. Even with fibre optics, there is a limit to

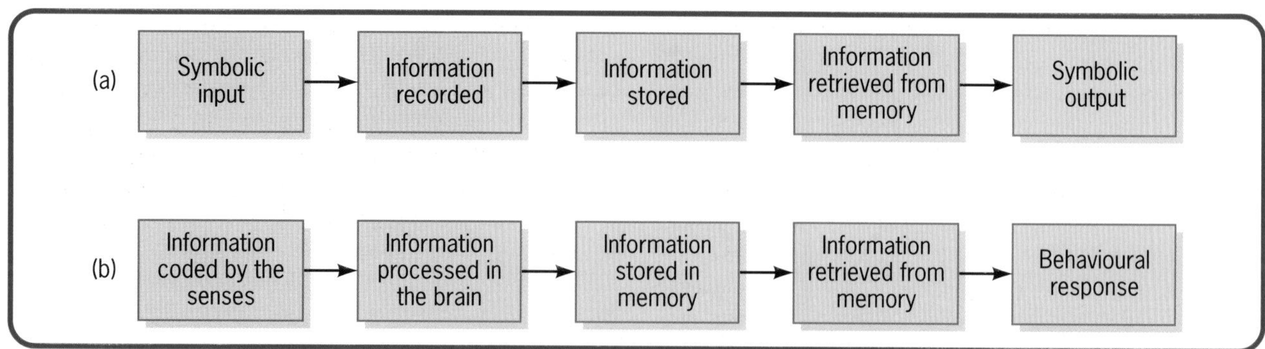

Figure 12.9 *Simplified flow diagrams of (**a**) how a computer processes information and (**b**) how humans process information.*

the amount of information that can be transmitted at any one time, but this is very large indeed. In human attention, people seem able only to attend properly to one message at a time. Channel capacity in humans is, it seems, much less than in computer systems.

Span of apprehension refers to how much information can be taken in at any one time. This depends on how the information is arranged. The span of apprehension can be increased if information is organised in ways which make it easy to apprehend. This is the same with computers, but there are fewer constraints here.

A **central processing unit** manipulates information, which is what both computer systems and mental processes do.

Evaluation

There are shortcomings with the computer analogy, which are as follows:

- Representing humans as just mechanical devices which operate in an entirely predictable way.
- Information stored in the memory of a computer can be transferred to another computer. By contrast, human memory, built up over a lifespan, cannot be 'downloaded' to another person (or computer) in the same way.
- Finally, in what sense can a computer be said to be aware and conscious in the way people are conscious beings?

Finally, **information is stored** in memory. With computers, a random access memory (RAM) system is used. In humans, information is stored in the memory in an associative or network form. Both computers and humans store information and retrieve information from memory. One important difference is that computers do not 'forget' in ways that people do. If a computer stores information it can be retrieved, and this only fails if the computer is faulty or the memory capacity has been exceeded. In humans, forgetting is a common occurrence, for which there are numerous explanations (see *AQA(B) Psychology for AS*, Chapter 7, by Pennington and McLoughlin, 2008).

12.5.2 Computer simulation and artificial intelligence

Computer simulation and artificial intelligence are different. Computer simulation is concerned with attempting to simulate human cognitive processes on a computer. The aim of computer simulation is to make computers perform in the same way as humans. To do this, a psychological theory is first needed about how humans perform a cognitive task. If a computer performs in indistinguishable ways from humans, including making the same types of errors, then it can be said that a computer simulation has been achieved. Attempts to simulate human cognitive processes, such as making judgements and decisions, may help psychologists understand the shortcomings of a theory. A computer simulation may differ from how a human works and this may provide valuable insights into shortcomings of a psychological theory.

Artificial intelligence (AI) is about getting computers to perform tasks that we regard as requiring intelligence. Here, there is not necessarily an attempt to simulate human intelligence. Artificial intelligence has as one of its aims an attempt to understand human intelligence, but it is primarily concerned with producing machines that behave intelligently, regardless of whether this reflects human intelligence. One area of AI that has developed greatly over recent years is that of *expert systems*. Expert systems, such as systems for medical diagnosis, are attempts to develop intelligent systems dealing with complex problems that exist in the world. Artificial intelligence has also produced computers that play chess to grand master (international) standards. AI also has a key role to play in the development of robots, where vision, movement and three-dimensional perception are all programmed into the computer in order for the robot to 'see' and move around in its environment.

12.6 Strengths and limitations of the cognitive approach

The cognitive approach in psychology has both strengths and limitations; overall the strengths outweigh the limitations and make it one of the dominant perspectives in psychology, both today and for the foreseeable future.

Strengths

- The cognitive approach is scientific and objective. This means that carefully controlled experiments can be conducted and confidence placed in the findings. Also, experiments are replicable by other cognitive psychologists.
- The approach investigates mental processes, mental functioning and mental characteristics of people. In doing this, the cognitive approach does take as its subject matter what we regard as essential human characteristics.
- The cognitive approach has practical applications – for example, in helping people improve their memory, cognitive treatments for mental disorders and to sports psychology.
- The cognitive approach solves the long-standing debate about the brain and mind being different, and the problem of how they interact. This debate is around how the physical (the brain) interacts with the mental (the mind). For cognitive psychologists, the brain and the mind are one and the same thing.
- The behaviourists refused to study mental events because they regarded behaviour as objective and measurable because only overt behaviour is observable. Cognitive psychologists have clearly demonstrated that a scientific, mainly experimental laboratory approach, can be applied to cognitive processes. Theory, hypotheses and empirical investigation all characterise the scientific approach of the cognitive psychologist (see Chapter 15 for more on the scientific approach in psychology).

Limitations

- The approach is mechanical, is often more interested in mental processes than behaviour, tends to be theoretical and abstract, involves experiments that lack ecological validity, and has until recently ignored affect and human emotion. Because of the use of the computer analogy, human beings are depicted as little more than machines (hardware and software), with the result that the image of people is rather mechanical and lacking in essential humanity. Human attributes, like consciousness and self-awareness, which distinguish people from animals, remain major problems or mysteries for cognitive psychologists.
- Some critics accuse cognitive psychologists of being too narrow in their theoretical and empirical treatment of people. There is too much focus on detailing and understanding mental processes, such as memory and attention, and not enough on behaviour. Ironically, this criticism is almost exactly the opposite of that made of the behaviourist perspective. This leads on to the limitation that cognitive psychology tends to be seen as highly theoretical and abstract, and in some ways loses sight of the whole person, whilst theories of memory and attention are developed and tested.
- The dominant empirical approach in cognitive psychology is the laboratory experiment. The danger here is that abstract or technical experiments are conducted that do not readily generalise or relate to how people think and act in the 'real' world.
- Finally, until recently, cognitive psychologists had paid little attention to emotions and how emotions can affect cognitive processes such as memory and attention. Recently research has turned to look at how cognitions and emotions interact in everyday life – for example, how cognitions play a role in stress and emotional responses (Lazarus, 1991).

12.7 Applications of the cognitive approach

The cognitive approach is now central to psychology and is commonly applied to many areas of relevance to psychology. This is shown in Figure 12.10.

Therapeutic applications. Practical applications have been made in the treatment of people suffering certain mental disorders, such as anxiety and depression, using for example, Ellis's (1989) rational-emotive therapy. Rational-emotive therapy requires people to think logically and rationally and attempts to minimise irrational and illogical thinking. Another therapeutic approach is that of cognitive therapy (Beck, 1991). In a similar way to rational-emotive therapy, attention is given to the way a person's cognitions about themselves and the world are distorted. Cognitive therapy has been used successfully to treat depression, anxiety disorders and eating disorders (Beck, 1991). With anxiety disorders, attempts are made to get the person to believe that they are overemphasising the feared event, and underemphasising their abilities to cope and adjust to life.

Applications to criminology. The cognitive interview (Geiselman *et al.*, 1985) is built upon certain basics of what is known about human memory. Attempts are made in the cognitive interview to provide cues and the context of the crime to help trigger memories of the event. Also, the person interviewed is asked to state everything that he or she can remember about the event and to attempt to describe the event from the point of view of another person. Research has demonstrated that the cognitive interview produces more correct detail than other interview techniques (Geiselman *et al.*, 1986).

The theories, concepts and research methods of cognitive psychology have been readily applied to other areas of psychology. For example, in child development, how a child comes to know about and understand the world around them has been extensively investigated by psychologists such as Piaget, Vygotsky and Bruner. In looking at exceptional child development, we can see how cognitive processing occurs in children with autism.

Another application of the cognitive approach is in the area of ageing. Here psychologists are interested in, for example, how memory may differ in very old age, and

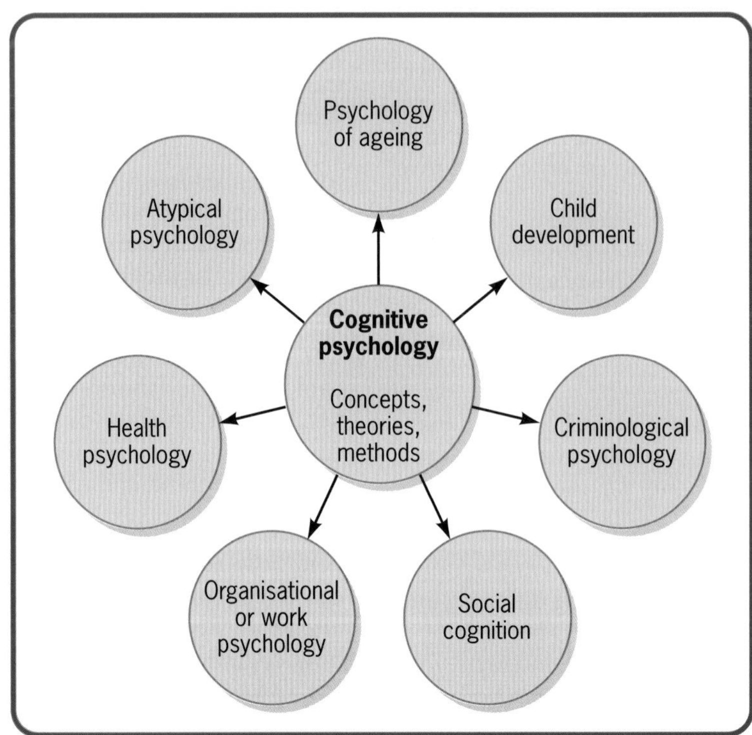

Figure 12.10 *Cognitive psychology as a central or core area which influences other areas and applications in psychology.*

how attention in the elderly differs from that in younger people. Knowing about normal human memory helps in understanding memory impairments that may come from degenerative diseases associated with old age, such as dementia and Alzheimer's disease.

Further Reading

Introductory texts

Groome, D., Brace, N., Edgar, H. and Esgate, A. (2006) *An Introduction to Cognitive Psychology,* 2nd edn., Hove: Psychology Press.

Parkin, A. (2000) *Essential Cognitive Psychology,* Chapter 1, Hove: Psychology Press.

Specialist sources

Eysenck, M.W. and Keane, M.T. (2005) *Cognitive Psychology: A Student's Handbook.,* 5th edn., Hove: Psychology Press.

Schultz, D.P. and Schultz, S.E. (2000) *A History of Modern Psychology,* 7th edn., Chapter 15, Fort Worth, TX: Harcourt College Publishers.

Sternberg, R.J. (2005) *Cognitive Psychology,* London: Wadsworth Publishing.

The psychodynamic approach

Chapter 13

13.1 Introduction

The psychodynamic approach in psychology includes a number of different theories, resulting in numerous applications. In this chapter we will consider the theories of Sigmund Freud, Erik Erikson and Melanie Klein. These have three important assumptions in common.

(a) Mental processes or thought processes occur at conscious, preconscious and unconscious levels. Unconscious mental processes are not directly accessible to consciousness. Techniques such as dream analysis and free association are used in an attempt to understand the unconscious. Preconscious thoughts are those which are held in memory and which we are capable of bringing to consciousness.

(b) Psychodynamic theories regard early childhood experiences, particularly parent–child relationships and interactions, as important and vital influences on the adult personality. In particular, how the young child copes with and responds to conflict and unpleasant experiences will be repeated by the adult when he or she faces periods of stress and traumatic situations.

(c) These theories are concerned with how the adult is able to adjust to changes in life and the difficulties and challenges in everyday life. People who are able to adjust well to changing circumstances will function effectively. People who do not adjust to change may experience anxiety and suffer from, for example, depression. This means that the psychodynamic approach is applied to treat and help people recover from mental disorder.

Following consideration of the theories of Freud, Erikson and Klein, we will look at applications of each of these psychodynamic theories.

13.2 Freud's approach to personality structure and dynamics

Sigmund Freud's theories and therapy have had a profound influence on the development of psychology, particularly in the treatment of various types of abnormal behaviours. Sigmund Freud regarded himself as a scientist; however, psychologists today would not agree with this since he did not conduct empirical research or controlled experiments. Furthermore, most of his concepts and ideas refer to unobservable mental events.

Id, ego and superego

Freud's model of the mind consists of three types of mental processes or structures, the id, ego and superego. How these three personality structures interact is called the dynamics of personality. The **id** is the most primitive part of the mind; to quote Freud:

> It contains everything that is inherited, that is present at birth, that is laid down in the constitution. (Freud, 1933/1973).

The id operates according to the **pleasure principle** and has no concept of reality or anything to do with the real world. The id's most important driving forces are the sex (life) instinct and the aggressive (death) instinct. These instincts create wishes and desires at an unconscious level, which result in tension or anxiety if they are not fulfilled. For the id, the ideal state is absence of any tension or anxiety. This is achieved through wish fulfilment. The fulfilment of a wish reduces tension and this tension reduction is experienced as pleasurable. So, for Freud, the pleasure principle is concerned with the absence of tension, rather than the receiving of something pleasurable. This is shown in Figure 13.2.

Figure 13.1 *For Freud, pleasure results in the reduction of tension for the individual.*

The **ego** operates according to the **reality principle**. It operates at conscious, preconscious and unconscious levels. The ego is in touch with the outside world (reality). This means that it guides the behaviours of a person by determining what is possible and practical. The ego, in contrast to the id, uses logical reasoning and common sense. The ego also employs various defence mechanisms (see the next section) to cope with the unreasonable and instinctive demands of the id. The ego gives a person a sense of their own identity and needs to be strong to cope with both id and superego demands.

The **superego**, according to Freudian theory, develops around the age of 4–5 years, which is during the phallic stage of psychosexual development (see Section 13.4.3). The superego is made up of two systems: a person's conscience and the ideal self. The conscience can punish the ego through causing feelings of guilt. If the ego gives in to id demands, the superego may make the person feel bad through guilt. The ideal self is an imaginary image of how you ought to be or how you would like to be. The ideal self represents career aspirations, how to treat other people, and how to behave

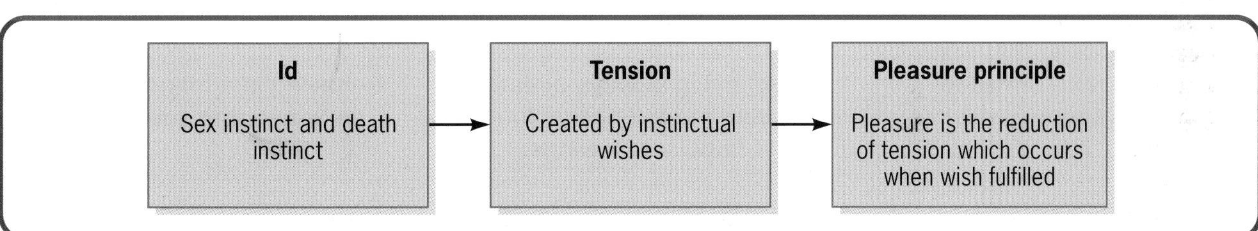

Figure 13.2 *The id and how the pleasure principle works.*

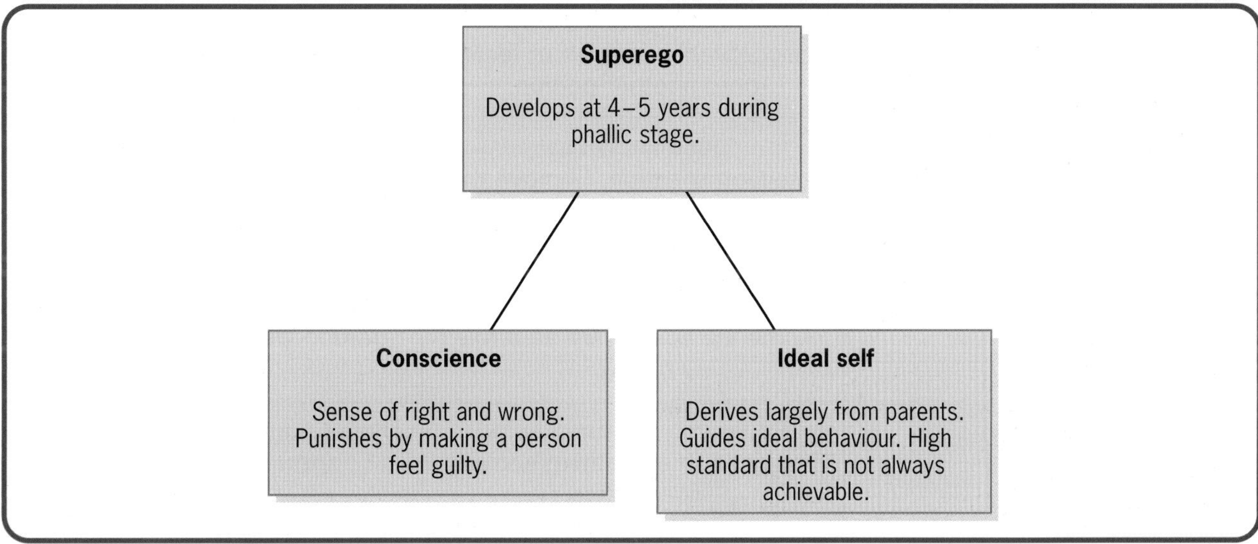

Figure 13.3 *The two components within Freud's concept of the superego.*

Evaluation

- The ideal self and the conscience of a person can be seen to come about through both classical and operant conditioning (see Chapter 10). The rewards and punishments that parents give to a child when the superego is developing will have long-lasting effects for the individual. This may be why a person's sense of guilt and ideal self do not change much throughout life.
- The ego has to manage the unreasonable demands of both the id and the superego. If the ego is weak it will give in to id and superego demands. This may result in a person not being able to adapt and adjust effectively to changes in the real world.

as a member of society. Behaviour which falls short of the ideal self may be punished by the superego through guilt. If a person's ideal self sets too high a standard for the person, then whatever the person does will represent failure because it will never be good enough. The ideal self and conscience are, according to Freud, largely determined in childhood from parental values and how you were brought up. Figure 13.3 summarises Freud's concept of the superego.

Defence mechanism	Description	Example
Repression	Unconscious forgetting. Disturbing thoughts not allowed to become conscious.	Aggressive thoughts from the id remain unconscious.
Reaction formation	Behaving in ways directly opposite to unconscious impulses, feelings.	Behaving in a friendly way to someone that you dislike.
Displacement	Transferring impulses and feelings to an originally neutral or innocent target.	Scapegoating where a social group is wrongly blamed, e.g. the Jews.
Projection	Attributing one's own unacceptable impulse or feeling onto another person.	Saying somebody else is frightened of the dark when actually you are.
Rationalisation	Also known as intellectualisation. Remove the emotional content of an idea or event by logical analysis.	Coping with the death of someone close to you by intellectual analysis.
Identification	Behaving in a similar way to someone you regard as a role model.	Son imitating father in the garden with toy wheelbarrow.
Sublimation	Redirection of threatening impulses to something socially acceptable.	Use of aggressive impulses in a sport such as boxing.

Figure 13.4 *Examples of defence mechanisms commonly used by the ego.*

Ego defence mechanisms

To deal with conflict (which may be internal or with other people and hence external) and problems in life, Freud stated that the ego employs a range of **defence mechanisms**. Defence mechanisms are used by the ego and operate at an unconscious level. They help ward off unpleasant feelings or make good things feel better for the individual. There are a large number of defence mechanisms. The main ones are summarised in Figure 13.4. We shall consider four in more detail: repression, projection, reaction formation and sublimation.

The defence mechanism of **repression** is of fundamental importance within Freud's theory of personality. Repression is an unconscious mechanism employed by the ego to keep disturbing or threatening thoughts from becoming conscious. Repression is a widely used defence mechanism and one used by everybody, according to Freud. Thoughts that are commonly repressed are those that would result in feelings of guilt from the superego. Examples include thoughts of aggression or hostility against another, or sexual fantasies and childhood memories from the psychosexual stages of development. Memories resulting from the Oedipal complex (see Section 13.4.3) are strongly repressed because the thoughts and desires would be very disturbing to the person if they became conscious. In the Oedipal complex, aggressive thoughts about the same-sex parent for the 4- to 5-year-old child are repressed. There has been recent research on repression.

Projection is when an individual attributes or places their own thoughts, feelings or motives onto another person. Thoughts most commonly projected onto another person are ones that would cause guilt – for example, aggressive and sexual fantasies or thoughts. Newman *et al.* (1997) have shown that individuals actively suppress thoughts that have undesirable characteristics and see other people as possessing such characteristics rather than themselves.

Reaction formation is where a person behaves in the opposite way to how he or she thinks or feels. For example, Freud claimed that men who are prejudiced against homosexuals are making a defence against their own homosexual feelings. Adams *et al.* (1996) demonstrated reaction formation when homophobic men showed sexual arousal to viewing homosexual behaviour between two men.

Sublimation was regarded by Freud as a very positive and productive mechanism of defence and one which benefited society. In sublimation, sexual and aggressive thoughts and feelings are channelled or redirected in socially acceptable behaviour. For example, id energies could be sublimated by the ego into work and become dedicated to career ambitions. Freud thought that all art and literature resulted from sublimation of the sexual instinct. Here, instinctual sexual energy is converted into love of beauty and expression.

13.3 Unconscious mental processes

Unconscious mental processes take place without our being directly aware of them. For Freud, unconscious thoughts have the greatest influence on how we consciously think and feel, and how we behave. The **preconscious** contains thoughts and feelings that a

Figure 13.5 *The defence mechanism of projection may mean that what the woman is really saying is that 'I am very selfish!'*

Figure 13.6 *Repressed desires and conflicts can be transformed or sublimated by the ego into works of art.*

STUDY

Aim

Boden and Baumeister (1997) used a questionnaire to investigate individual differences in memory for emotional events.

Method

The Repressive Coping Style questionnaire (Weinberger *et al.*, 1990) was given to a large number of people; at the same time, participants were asked to recall details about emotional events in their lives.

Results

Participants scoring as 'repressors' (i.e. use the defence mechanism of repression) were less able to recall details of emotional events than non-repressors.

Conclusions

Use of a repressive coping style in everyday life has the consequence that both positive and negative emotions are less well remembered.

Evaluation

- Defence mechanisms operate at an unconscious level in the mind. As such they are not observable. They cannot be studied scientifically as is the case with behaviour. Therefore, a link has to be made between behaviour and defence mechanisms to provide evidence of a defence mechanism. Recent research by experimental psychologists has seen a renewed interest in defence mechanisms, especially repression, and their measurable effects.

person is not currently aware of, but which can easily be brought to consciousness. This is what we mean in our everyday usage of the word 'memory'. For example, you are presently not thinking about your mobile telephone number, but now it is mentioned you can recall it with ease. Mild emotional experiences may be in the preconscious, but sometimes traumatic and powerful negative emotions are repressed and hence not available in the preconscious. The **conscious** is that which you are aware of at any one time and this is your

Evaluation

- By definition the unconscious is hidden. This makes it a difficult concept for many psychologists to accept because it is not possible directly to investigate the unconscious and its claimed effects on our conscious thoughts and awareness of feelings.
- The unconscious is the irrational side of being human. For Freud, all people are basically irrational; this goes against our view of people as logical and rational.

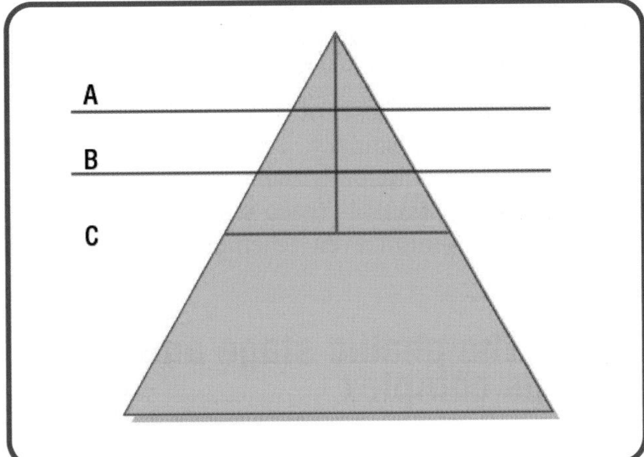

Figure 13.7 *The id, ego and superego in relation to conscious, preconscious and unconscious mental systems.*

thoughts and feelings. For example, you may be feeling thirsty at this moment and decide to get a drink.

Freud applied these three systems to the id, ego and superego. Here the id is regarded as entirely unconscious, while the ego and superego have conscious, preconscious and unconscious aspects. Freud also regarded the mind to be like an iceberg, where the greatest part is hidden beneath the water or unconscious. This is shown in Figure 13.7.

13.4 Freud's psychosexual stages of development

One of Sigmund Freud's lasting contributions to psychology was the recognition that early childhood (the first 5 years of life) strongly influences and determine the adult personality. Positive childhood experiences have ego-strengthening effects, whilst negative experiences play a role in psychological disorders in older teenage and adult life. Freud proposed that all children go through five stages of development, three of which occur before the age of 5–6 years. These are called **psychosexual stages** of development, since they represent how the sexual instinct results in strong sexual urges and unconscious desires in the young child.

13.4.1 The oral stage

The **oral stage** of psychosexual development occurs in the first year of life. Here, the areas of the mouth (lips, tongue, mouth) become associated with pleasure due to feeding. The mother's breast (or bottle) becomes the first object of desire for the infant, since feeding reduces uncomfortable feelings of hunger. Feelings of hunger create tension in the infant; removal of tension, as we saw earlier, is experienced as pleasure by the id. For Freud, the mother becomes the first emotional attachment for the child because of the pleasure from feeding she gives the infant. As the first person and love object of the infant, the mother becomes a model for all future love relationships, both as a teenager and as an adult.

Evaluation

- Freud's concept of sexual urges in the young child needs to be taken in the wider context of the life instinct, rather than the more narrow interpretation that we, as adults, may place on the idea of sexual urges. It may be more appropriate to think of pleasurable bodily experiences in the young child as what Freud meant by sexual urges. However interpreted, these do originate from the sexual instinct and impulses from the id.

The oral stage is subdivided into two sub-stages: oral passive and oral aggressive. The oral-passive stage occurs first and pleasure is gained from sucking at the breast. The oral-aggressive stage is marked by biting or grabbing at the breast. Oral-passive personality characteristics and behaviours are, for example, being accepting of others, being gullible and speaking kindly of people. Oral-aggressive behaviours are, for example, having a 'biting wit', being sarcastic and being overcritical of others.

Freud thought that the infant could become *fixated* at the oral stage. By fixation he meant that the infant does not move on properly to the next psychosexual stage, but instead remains 'stuck' or unable to 'give up' the oral stage. This may happen, according to Freud, because of very negative experiences of breastfeeding or discomfort associated with feeding. Someone fixated at the oral stage may be very clingy and overdependent on others as an adult. Such a person may also have a need for approval and love from others all the time.

13.4.2 The anal stage

The **anal stage** typically occurs during the second year

of life as the child gains control of anal muscles during toilet-training. Freud said that in the anal stage the child gains pleasure from retention and expulsion of faeces. The child learns that he or she can please or defy the parents. The parents are trying to toilet-train the child and the child can comply and use the toilet instead of defecating in the nappy, or the child can defy the parent by either retention of faeces or defecating in the nappy.

As with the oral stage, the anal stage was seen to fall into two sub-stages: the anal-expulsive and anal-retentive stages. In the former, which comes first, the child enjoys expulsion or elimination. Symbolically, Freud regarded this as not caring for the parents – trying to 'eliminate' them. In the second sub-stage, the retention and then expulsion symbolically represent the child giving the parents a gift. Towards the end of the anal stage, retention outweighs elimination pleasure and the child is then toilet-trained.

Evaluation

- Most people find these claims ridiculous upon first reading. However, if you observe children of this age, the experience of defecating does seem to be emotionally very powerful. A rare, but recognised, abnormality in young children is the hoarding of their faeces or stools in their bedroom drawers, for example. After this stage, the anal region is associated with dirtiness and disgust rather than pleasure.
- Fisher and Greenberg (1977) looked at numerous correlational studies of the three characteristics of the anal personality. The evidence does show that these three characteristics go together and are present in some adult personalities. The strongest pairing was found to be between orderliness and meanness. However, studies reviewed by Fisher and Greenberg (1977) have failed to support the claim that the anal personality results from difficulties during toilet-training. Freud's observation that the characteristics of orderliness, parsimony and obstinacy go together seems to be correct, but the claim that the anal personality results from fixation at the anal stage has not been supported empirically.

Fixation at the anal stage may come about because of conflict-ridden or inconsistent toilet-training. The personality characteristics resulting from fixation at this stage include those of orderliness, parsimony (miserliness) and obstinacy. The **anal personality** is characterised by somebody who is excessively tidy, does not give to others, is mean with money and will stick to their opinion even when it is obvious it is wrong to do so.

13.4.3 The phallic stage and Oedipus complex

Between the ages of 3 and 6 years, the main object of the sexual instinct moves from the anal region to the genital region. In boys it is the penis and in girls the clitoris that becomes the source of pleasure. Because the superego has yet to develop, according to Freud, boys and girls discover that playing with their genitals is pleasurable. This is what Freud called 'childhood masturbation'. Also, children do not feel inhibited from playing with their genitals in front of other people. Adults may find this embarrassing, but young children seem to find this good fun!

The most important aspect of the phallic stage is the **Oedipus complex**. This is one of Freud's most contro-

Evaluation

- The Oedipus complex for girls has been heavily criticised because it is based on the absence of something that the male possesses – a penis. In Freudian theory, women are regarded as having a weak superego. This lack of a balanced view of male and female psychosexual development has, rightly, been regarded as chauvinistic and reflecting the male-dominated and patriarchal society in which Freud lived. Karen Honey, a psychoanalyst, has suggested that men suffer from 'womb envy' and the inability to bear children. (See also the film *What Women Want.*)
- Freud's theory of psychosexual development was regarded as sexist because the stage was named after the male sexual organ – the phallus – when it covered both males and females. Notice that the next section of this chapter deals with the genital stage which has no connotations of gender.

versial ideas and one that many people reject outright. The name of the Oedipus complex derives from Greek mythology, where Oedipus, a young man, killed his father and married his mother. Upon discovering this, Oedipus poked out his own eyes and became blind.

In the young boy, the Oedipus complex, or more correctly Oedipal conflict, arises because the boy develops sexual (pleasurable) desires for his mother. He wants to possess his mother exclusively and get rid of his father to enable him to do so. Irrationally, the boy thinks that if his father were to find out about all this, his father would take away what he loves the most. In the phallic stage, what the boy loves most is his penis. Hence the boy develops castration anxiety. This is the Oedipal (generic term for both Oedipus and Electra complexes) conflict. The Oedipal conflict is resolved in the young boy by repressing or 'giving up' his desire for his mother and identifying with his father. The consequence of this is that the boy takes on the male gender role, and adopts an ego ideal and values of the male role in society. This becomes the superego.

For girls, the Oedipus or Electra complex is less than satisfactory. Briefly, the girl desires the father, but realises that she does not have a penis. This leads to the development of penis envy and the wish to be a boy. The girl resolves this by repressing her desire for her father and substituting the wish for a penis with the wish for a baby. The girl blames her mother for her 'castrated state', represses her feelings and identifies with the mother to take on the female gender role.

13.4.4 Latent and genital stages

Following the phallic stage and the 'resolution' of the Oedipal complex, the child enters a latency period through to the onset of puberty. It is called a latency period because no further psychosexual development takes place. The sexual drive does not develop, but it is present during this stage. Freud thought that all or most sexual impulses and urges were heavily repressed during the latent stage and sexual energy could be sublimated towards school work, hobbies and friendships.

The final stage of psychosexual development is the **genital stage**. The genital stage starts at puberty and the sexual instinct is directed to heterosexual pleasure, rather than the self-pleasure during the phallic stage. For Freud, the proper outlet of the sexual instinct in adults was through heterosexual intercourse. Fixation and conflict might prevent this, with the consequence

Psychosexual stage	Age	Primary concerns	Conflicts
Oral	0–18 months	Feeding and dependency	Feeling hungry and poor feeding experiences
Anal	2–3 years	Toilet-training – expulsion and retention of faeces	With authority – parents – anal personality – orderliness, parsimony, obstinacy
Phallic	4–6 years	Oedipus/Electra complex – desire for opposite sex	Conflict with same-sex parent until identification takes place
Latency	7–11 years	Repression of sexual instinct and urges	Sublimation of sexual instinct to schoolwork, hobbies, friends
Genital	12+ years	Heterosexual intercourse as adult	Sexual perversions may develop if fixated at earlier stage

Figure 13.8 *The five psychosexual stages of development suggested by Freud.*

Evaluation

- Freud's emphasis on psychosexual development was too narrow, since other forms of development, such as social, emotional and intellectual, are also important during childhood. Developmental psychologists do not regard psychosexual development as of prime importance.
- The mother–child attachment, in terms of providing trust and security, is seen as critical to child development. Difficulties in interpersonal relationships in adult life may come from insecurity of attachment to the mother. In turn, difficulties in interpersonal relationships may result in sexual problems, rather than the other way round with Freud.

that sexual perversions may develop. For example, fixation at the oral stage may result in a person gaining sexual pleasure primarily from kissing and oral sex, rather than normal sexual intercourse.

13.5 Freud's use of case studies

Freud pioneered the use of case studies in psychology and demonstrated how detailed accounts of a person's mental life could illuminate Freudian concepts and ideas. It is incorrect to criticise Freud for selecting middle-class Victorian women for his case studies and psychoanalytic treatment. Throughout Freud's 20 volumes of writing, 133 cases are mentioned (Storr, 2002). However, only six are developed into full accounts; seven if you include Freud's self-analysis, which appears in his book *The Interpretation of Dreams*. The six case studies he writes about at length are as follows:

- Judge Schreber
- Dora
- Rat Man
- Little Hans
- Wolf Man
- Unnamed female of 18.

Of these, Judge Schreber was dead, and Freud used his autobiography to make psychoanalytic interpretations. With Little Hans, Freud conducted the analysis through the father, and Freud only ever met Little Hans once during the course of this study. Freud saw the other four people personally over varying lengths of time. Freud did not use case studies in an attempt to prove his theories and concepts of psychoanalysis. His case studies were written for three main reasons.

- First, he wanted to show how psychodynamic concepts applied to a real person's mental life – that is, to give practical demonstrations of his theories and ideas.
- Second, he aimed to appeal to a wider audience than other psychoanalysts in an attempt to spread the word about psychoanalysis and make it accessible to interested people.
- Third, he wanted to show how psychoanalysis could help treat and, to some extent, 'cure' a person suffering from some kind of mental disorder or struggling to deal with the difficulties of everyday life.

Evaluation

- Case studies can be of scientific value if conducted in certain ways – see Chapter 4 of *AQA(B) Psychology from AS* by Pennington and McLoughlin (2008). Freud did not take notes at the time he was seeing a client; instead he made notes in the evening of the day he had seen the client. Freud usually saw five to six clients a day. He wrote up his notes in the evening, which may have meant that he selected only those things he could recall that suited his theories. Selective memory might have been a problem, since Freud may only have recalled material consistent with his theory and concepts.
- Case studies provide valuable insight into the person and the problems they face. Case studies may highlight a Freudian concept, but cannot be used to generalise to claim this is true of all people.
- Case studies should be written in such a way as to preserve the anonymity of the person, and permission from the person should be gained in advance. Freud did neither of these, and after publication the actual people were identified and in some cases followed up by other psychologists.

In what follows we shall look at three of Freud's case studies: Little Hans, Dora and the Rat Man.

Little Hans

The case of Little Hans (Freud, 1909/1977a) was called 'Analysis of a phobia in a five-year-old boy'. Hans suffered from a phobia of horses: he feared they would bite him or fall down in the street and 'make a row'. Freud interpreted the horses as symbolising Hans' father, and the fear of being bitten as representing the Oedipal complex that Little Hans was going through. The fear of being bitten Freud interpreted as representing the castration anxiety resulting from Little Hans' sexual desire for his mother. The castration anxiety comes about because Little Hans thinks his father would castrate him if he found out about Little Hans' sexual desire for his mother. Little Hans' father, whose name in real life was Max Graf, acted as his son's analyst, and interpreted, following Freud's instructions, the boy's sexual interests, beliefs about where babies come from, and his feelings for his parents. These interpretations were all made in relation to the Oedipal complex and the conflicts this produces.

Evaluation

- Whilst Freud used the Little Hans case to highlight his theory of the Oedipal complex, other simpler explanations for Little Hans' phobia exist. His parents did not get on and his mother threatened him with castration and abandonment. All this must have been deeply unsettling for Little Hans. What does need explaining is why Little Hans feared horses. One account is that his mother was cruel to his baby sister and Little Hans associated the screams of his sister with horses 'making a row' when they fall down. Little Hans had witnessed a horse falling down next to him in the street.
- In reading the case study, what Little Hans is reported as saying does not confirm these Oedipal interpretations. In fact, Little Hans was more frightened of his mother, who, for example, threatened to have his 'widdler' (penis) cut off if he kept touching it. She also threatened to abandon him.
- Shortly after the time Freud spent with Little Hans' father on the case, Little Hans's parents got divorced. Freud failed to mention this important fact.
- Try to imagine yourself as this 5-year-old boy. Your father is talking to you about sex, sexual desires for your mother and hostile feelings to the father. Just how much sense do you think that Little Hans could make of all this? How much might Little Hans have accepted because of lack of understanding?

Dora

Dora (Freud, 1905/1977) was an 18-year-old woman referred to Freud by her father following a suicide note that Dora had written. Dora suffered from a number of 'hysterical' or neurotic symptoms, including headaches, shortness of breath, a nervous, persistent cough that led to loss of voice and depression. Dora's father said to Freud that her symptoms could be traced back to an incident when she was 16 years of age. Dora's parents were friendly with another family, called the 'Ks' in Freud's case study. In fact, at the time, Dora's father was having an affair with Frau K. The incident when Dora was 16 was, according to Dora, when the two families were on holiday in the Alps. Dora was out walking by a lake with Herr K when he made sexual advances towards her. Dora said that she slapped his face and ran away. Herr K denied the event and Dora's father believed him.

When in psychotherapy with Freud, Dora said that Herr K had made another sexual advance to her recently, and this seemed to precipitate the suicide note. Dora felt in some way she had not been believed by her father about Herr K's advances because of his own guilt at the affair he was having. Freud was forceful in his interpretations to Dora. For example, her rejection of Herr K's advances Freud interpreted as a reaction formation (see Section 13.2), where in fact Dora is really in love with Herr K. Freud also interprets some of Dora's symptoms as love for Herr K. For example, Freud establishes that her loss of voice only occurs when Herr K is away on business. Since he is away her voice is of no use since she is not able to speak to the man she really loves. At one point Freud also says that Dora has sexual (lesbian) desires for Frau K and is in love with Freud as well!

Evaluation

- In some ways it is a mystery why Freud published this case study since it seems to be a failure – he did not cure Dora. He used it to highlight the ego's use of defence mechanisms and how Oedipal conflicts from the age of 5 years were present in an 18-year-old woman. Freud in a sense betrayed Dora, just as her father had failed to believe her, because he assumed that 18-year-old women would respond to an older man's sexual advances.
- Dora took control. Finding the relentless sexual interpretations unacceptable she broke off the psychoanalysis. Critics have regarded Freud's approach to this young woman as unsympathetic and overly aggressive.

The Rat Man

The Rat Man (Freud, 1909/1977b) whose real name was Ernst Lanzer, came to see Freud when he was 29 years of age. He displayed numerous obsessive-compulsive behaviours and had obsessive and fearful thoughts about rats. The onset of these obsessive thoughts about rats seemed to be when he was on military training and heard an officer describe a particularly nasty torture using rats. This consisted of putting hungry rats into a bucket and tying this to the buttocks of a person. The torture consisted of the rats eating into the person through the anus. To ward off this image and thoughts that it might happen to his father, girlfriend and other people he was fond of, the Rat Man engaged in obsessive-compulsive rituals.

Freud interpreted these thoughts and obsessive behaviours as resulting from the mixture of love and hate that he felt for his father. Unconsciously, Freud said, the Rat Man hated his father and wished to torture him with rats. Any thought of this would cause the Rat Man to experience unbearable feelings of guilt and fear. The obsessive-compulsive behaviours helped to reduce the fear and feelings of guilt. Freud treated the Rat Man for about a year, after which he said that the treatment had 'led to the complete restoration of the patient's personality, and to the removal of his inhibitions'. In short, Freud claimed to have cured him of his phobia of rats and obsessive-compulsive tendencies.

Evaluation

- Freud made no mention of the Rat Man's mother throughout the case study. As with the other two case studies we have considered, Freud focused on the father and the Oedipal complex, and omitted the mother. With the Rat Man, the mother was a dominating and controlling figure in his life. For example, even at the age of 29 years, he had to get her permission to see Freud, and she controlled all his money.
- Freud did not mention the fact that the Rat Man had experienced the death of his older sister when he was 4 years old. Hence, a domineering mother and childhood feelings of abandonment might offer a simpler explanation for his phobia and compulsive behaviours.

13.6 Post-Freudian theories

Numerous theories within the psychodynamic approach have been developed since Freud's original ideas. Some theories developed the idea of unconscious mental processes more fully. For example, Carl Jung (Storr, 2002) thought that each person had two types of unconscious – the personal and the collective. The collective unconscious contains memories from our ancestors (see Steven, 2001, for an introduction to Jung). Other theories developed the idea of the ego and became known as **ego theories** – in what follows we shall consider the ego psychology of Erik Erikson. Other theories were broadly within the Freudian tradition, most notably Freud's youngest daughter, Anna, and Melanie Klein. We shall consider Melanie Klein since she developed the idea of the death instinct more fully and centrally in her theory. Other psychologists rejected the overwhelming importance of the unconscious and sex instinct and focused on conscious thought and experiences. These became known as the humanistic psychologists (see Chapter 14).

13.6.1 Erik Erikson

Erikson adhered to the Freudian structure of the personality in terms of id, ego and superego, as well as the existence of strong instinctual forces. He also regarded development as occurring in stages, but instead of Freud's childhood psychosexual stages, Erikson (1963) proposed that development takes place over the lifespan of the person. Erikson regarded **psychosocial development** as the most important aspect of human development – more important than psychosexual development. By using the term 'psychosocial development', Erikson saw the greatest influence on psychological development to be the interactions of the person (child, teenager and adult) with other people. These are parents, brothers and sisters, friends and peers, teachers and other significant people in a person's life. Erikson's view of psychosocial development over the lifespan of an individual was also concerned with the development of the ego and different strengths that the ego gains, or should gain, from each of the developmental stages. Erikson also emphasised the importance of culture and society on a person's development.

According to Erikson (1968), psychosocial development takes place in eight stages. The first occurs in the first year of life and the last in old age. For Erikson, each stage is marked by a critical point or **crisis** that the individual has to experience and resolve. Successful resolution of the crisis provides the ego with a basic strength. Failure to resolve the crisis means that the ego lacks the strength associated with any one stage. Figure 13.9 identifies each stage, the age at which it occurs, the nature of the crisis and ego strength gained from successful resolution of the crisis.

From Figure 13.9 you will see that the first psychosocial stage of development is that of **trust versus mistrust** and that the important relationship is with the mother. The ego strength of hope results from a basic feeling of trust from this stage. Hence, for Erikson, the mother–child relationship is of fundamental importance to whether or not the child will trust others and the world in which he or she lives (see Chapter 1 of this book for more on social development and mother–child attachment).

Erikson's theory differs from Freud's in three important ways:

- First, Erikson focuses on relationships between people, whilst Freud's main concern is with unconscious effects of the sex instinct.
- Second, Erikson considers what factors can strengthen and weaken the ego. By comparison, Freudian theory is more concerned with the conflicts the ego has to resolve between the id and superego.
- Third, Erikson's theory presents a much more positive and optimistic view of the human condition. By contrast, Freud presents a negative view of human beings locked in perpetual conflict.

Erikson studied other cultures and individuals to provide evidence for his theory. For example, he studied the Sioux and Yurok American Indians (Erikson, 1963), and analysed Ghandi, a leader of the Indian Congress movement, from a psychosocial perspective (Erikson, 1969).

13.6.2 Melanie Klein

Melanie Klein developed a psychodynamic approach called **object relations theory** (Klein, 1964). This theory regards close and intimate relationships of central importance, in particular how young children develop relationships with important (mother, father, etc.) people as they develop. The term **object** comes from Freud's claim that an instinct has an aim and an object – the object is usually a person, but not always. Hence object relations theory is about how the two most important instincts, life (sex) and death (aggression), affect psychological development and how a person interacts with other people (external objects). Klein's (1932) theory pays particular regard to the death or aggressive instinct and its consequences. Klein held to Freud's ideas of the id, ego and superego, and to the importance of unconscious mental processes.

Klein differed from Freud in that she thought that the newborn was not pure id (as Freud thought), but contained a primitive ego. This primitive ego also has a number of primitive defence mechanisms that it can use – the most important being that of **splitting.** Klein said that in order for the baby to cope with feeding at the breast as a positive experience on one occasion and a negative experience at another time, the breast is 'split'. The 'good breast' exists when there is a positive experience, and the 'bad breast' whenever there is a negative experience. Therefore, one-part object, of the mother, the breast, is split into two objects, one good, one bad. Klein claimed that the young baby does this with many things, and one of the early developmental tasks is to combine the good and bad into one object (Klein, 1975).

Klein also differed from Freud by stating that the child goes through two **developmental positions** (she did not like the word '*stages*') in the first year of life. The first is called the 'paranoid-schizoid position', and the second the 'depressive position'. In contrast to Freud,

Stage	Rough age	Psychological crises	Description of the crisis	Ego strength	Important relationship
1	0–1 yr	Trust vs mistrust	Learns to feel comfortable and trust parents' care; or develops distrust of the world	Hope	Maternal person
2	1–3 yrs	Autonomy vs shame	Learns sense of competence by learning to feed oneself, play alone, use toilet; or feels ashamed and doubts own abilities	Will	Parents
3	3–5 yrs	Initiative vs guilt	Learns to use own initiative in planning behaviour; or develops sense of guilt over misbehaviour	Purpose	Basic family
4	5–11 yrs	Industry vs inferiority	Learns to meet demands imposed by school and home responsibility; or comes to believe he or she is inferior to other people	Competence	Family neighbours, teachers
5	11–18 yrs	Identity vs identity diffusion	Acquires sense of identity in terms of beliefs, vocation, etc.; or fails to achieve identity	Fidelity	Peers, ingroups and outgroups
6	18–40 yrs	Intimacy vs isolation	Engages in successful intimate relationship, joint identity with partner; or becomes isolated	Love	Friends, lovers
7	40–65 yrs	Generativity vs stagnation	Helping others, allowing independence to children; or self-centred and stagnant	Care	Spouse, children
8	65 onwards	Integrity vs despair	Reaps benefits of earlier stages and develops acceptance of temporary nature of life; or despairs over ever being able to find meaning in life	Wisdom	Spouse children, grandchildren

Figure 13.9 *The eight stages of psychosocial development proposed by Erikson. The figure shows the crisis associated with each stage, the ego strength gained from successful resolution of the crisis, and the main social relationship.*

Klein claimed that the superego was formed at the end of the second position. That is, at about 1 year of age. Freud claimed the superego is not formed until around the fifth year of life.

Klein also developed and pioneered a form of psychoanalysis for young children. This she achieved through analysis of a child's play. Klein would give a young child a box of toys to play with. These included little people, cars, lorries and so on. At each session Klein would ask the child to play with the toys. She would note down the play and make interpretations. For example, if the child repeatedly ran over a toy person with a lorry, Klein might interpret this as the child symbolically hating or wanting to get rid of a parent.

In many ways, Klein's object relations theory adheres closely to most of Freud's theory. Whilst Freud recognised the death or aggressive instinct later in his theoretical development, Klein saw it as central from the outset. In Klein's theory, the life and death instincts produce unconscious conflict in the individual. This is then reflected in the nature of relationships with other people.

13.7 Strengths and limitations of the psychodynamic approach

Strengths

- The psychoanalytic approach has, and continues to be, a major influence in psychology. In particular, its influence has been most profound in the clinical area, and with the development of therapies to treat psychological disorders. The psychodynamic approach has also provided unique insights into human psychological functioning, particularly showing that people have internal conflicts, at both conscious and unconscious levels, that may result in psychological distress.
- The psychodynamic approach regards early childhood experiences as an important basis for later adult psychological functioning. This is now accepted in psychology and professional areas such as social work and psychiatry. When Freud was first writing and proposing this idea there was not common acceptance, and indeed at times there was hostile rejection of such a claim.
- The psychodynamic approach provides insight into the deeper psychological motives and drives of a person. By comparison, the behaviourist approach (see Chapter 10) only looks to behaviour and more superficial thought processes in its attempt to understand people.

Limitations

- Psychoanalysis, particularly Freudian theory, has been likened by some psychologists to a religion (Fine, 1990). This means that it depends on whether or not a person believes in the fundamentals: unconscious, repression, sex instinct and so on. A religion is not built upon scientific facts and testability of hypotheses derived from theory. Therefore, likening psychoanalysis to a religion means that some regard it as not scientific. This is a major limitation of psychoanalysis, as many critics have pointed out (Eysenck, 1990; Fisher and Greenberg, 1996). Concepts such as repression, the Oedipal complex and psychosexual stages of development are difficult to subject to scientific examination because testable hypotheses cannot be derived. If a testable hypothesis cannot be derived from a theory, then according to Popper (1963), a theory is not scientific.
- Another limitation is that one behaviour can have numerous Freudian interpretations – some of which are directly opposite to each other. For example, imagine someone saying that they strongly dislike another person. With Freudian interpretation, this could mean either that they do dislike the person or that the defence mechanism of reaction formation is operating, in which case, the expressed emotion is really the opposite at an unconscious level – that is, the person really likes the other person! In the world of Freudian interpretations, both may be equally valid, but how would you go about deciding scientifically which is the true interpretation?
- Another limitation of the psychodynamic approach is that case studies are open to numerous different interpretations. Different interpretations may result from a different theoretical perspective (for example, Freudian and Erikson's ego psychology) or differences within one perspective. The latter is possibly more problematic, since if two Freudian psychologists disagree over interpretation of the same case, there is not an objective way of supporting one and rejecting the other interpretation. Interpretations in psychoanalysis are, in the end, subjective, and may depend on what behaviours and thoughts of the person are selected to interpret in the first place (Powell and Boer, 1995).

- Eysenck (1952) examined thousands of case histories of people who underwent psychoanalytic therapy. He concluded that psychoanalytic therapy did not significantly help people suffering from neurotic disorders to recover. Eysenck found that over 70% of people who suffered from neurotic disorders but received no treatment of any kind recovered. In contrast, two-thirds of those treated to completion by psychoanalysts were cured or much improved. It may be that psychoanalytic therapy is effective for some types of people and not others, but recent research has not demonstrated the effectiveness of the therapy (Stunkard, 1991).
- Psychoanalysis is regarded as too deterministic and fatalistic when explaining human behaviour (see Chapter 16 for more on determinism). This means that the theory provides a sequence of psychosexual stages that is predetermined.
- Freudian theory of female psychosexual development has not been carefully worked out and is based on male development. Finally, Freudian theory regards the sexual instinct and its psychological effects as central and of overriding importance to psychological functioning. This has been at the expense of other importance influences, such as social and other people, particularly the mother.

13.8 Applications

By far the most important application of the psychodynamic approach has been the development of therapeutic techniques to help people overcome psychological disorders such as anxiety, depression and obsessive-compulsive behaviours. The original approach to treatment developed by Freud was called psychoanalysis. This involved daily sessions lasting an hour, which continued for many months or even years. These days, shorter psychodynamic therapies are available. However, to train as a psychoanalyst requires the person to undergo analysis for a number of years.

The psychodynamic approach also tried to make sense of seemingly irrational aspects of human mental life, such as dreams, slips of the tongue, jokes and why we forget things that have a strong emotional importance for the individual.

Erikson developed an application which he called **psychohistory**. This allows for the intensive study of an individual over that person's lifespan and focuses on a person's ego development. For example, Erikson's psychohistory of Ghandi showed how the ego strengths of this Indian leader helped him to resolve difficult political conflicts that faced his country. With Ghandi, Erikson looked at all eight psychosocial stages of development, but emphasised the achievement of identity from the teenage stage of psychosocial development.

Melanie Klein was one of the first Freudian psychoanalysts to develop a technique of child psychoanalysis. Klein interpreted the play of children with toys as representative of their unconscious thoughts and the relationship of the child with his or her mother and father.

Further Reading

Introductory texts

Hill, G. (2001) *A Level Psychology Through Diagrams,* pages 16, 158–9, 161, 216, Oxford: Oxford University Press.

Pennington, D.C. (2003) *Essential Personality,* Chapters 3, 4 and 5, London: Arnold.

Storr, A. (2002) *Freud: A Very Short Introduction,* Oxford: Oxford University Press.

Specialist sources

Breger, L. (2000) *Freud: Darkness in the Midst of Vision,* New York: John Wiley and Sons.

Freud, A. 1986) *The Essentials of Psychoanalysis: The Definitive Collection of Sigmund Freud's Writing,* Harmondsworth: Penguin Books.

Nye, R.D. (2000) *Three Psychologies: Perspectives from Freud, Skinner and Rogers,* 6th edn., Chapter 2, London: Wadsworth.

Ryckman, R.M. (2007) *Theories of Personality,* 8th edn., Chapters 2, 3, 4, 6 and 7, London: Wadsworth.

The humanistic approach

Chapter 14

14.1 Introduction

Humanistic psychology, or humanism, places central and overriding importance on the unique aspects of individual human experience. It values the subjective feelings and conscious thoughts of the person.

Refresh your knowledge and understanding of humanistic psychology, which you studied at AS level, by reading Chapter 1, pages 30 to 35 of *AQA(B) Psychology for AS* by Pennington and McLoughlin (2008).

Humanistic psychology makes three key assumptions about human beings:

- First, that each person can exercise free will and has control over what they think and feel, and how they behave.
- Second, that each person is a rational and conscious being, and not dominated by unconscious, primitive instincts.
- Third, that a person's subjective view and experience of the world is of greater importance to understanding the person than objective reality.

These three assumptions characterise the humanistic approach in psychology and are the foundations for numerous different theories within this approach. In what follows we shall consider the person-centred approaches of Carl Rogers and Abraham Maslow.

14.2 The person-centred approaches of Rogers and Maslow

Two of the most influential and enduring theories in humanistic psychology that emerged in the 1950s and 1960s are those of Carl Rogers (1951, 1961) and Abraham Maslow (1962, 1970). Both theories regard people as essentially good and view human nature as positive, not bad or evil. Both theories view people as active, creative and constantly seeking to express themselves. Additionally, and most importantly, people seek personal growth and may suffer psychologically if they are not able to grow and change psychologically in a positive way throughout their life. Because of this focus on the person, and his or her personal experiences and subjective perception of the world, the humanists regarded scientific methods as inappropriate for understanding and studying people.

Figure 14.1 *Humanistic psychologists, such as Carl Rogers and Abraham Maslow, regard each person as unique and focus on the subjective experiences of the person.*

Humanistic psychology is called the 'third force' in psychology after psychoanalysis and behaviourism. Humanistic psychology rejected the behaviourist approach, which is characterised as deterministic, focused on reinforcement of stimulus–response contingencies and heavily dependent on animal research (see Chapter 10). Humanistic psychology also rejected the psychodynamic approach (see Chapter 13) because it is also deterministic, with unconscious, irrational and instinctive forces determining human thought and behaviour. Both behaviourism and psychoanalysis are regarded as dehumanising by humanistic psychologists (De Carvalho, 1991).

14.2.1 The person-centred approach

The person-centred approach is so called because, as we have seen above, humanistic psychologists place a person's subjective experience and subjective point of view at the very centre of their theories. This approach to understanding people can be traced back over 200 years to philosophers such as Jean-Jacques Rousseau, Friedrich Nietzsche and Søren Kierkegaard. Broadly speaking, these philosophers developed a type of philosophy called **existential philosophy**. Existential philosophers ask very fundamental questions about what it is to be human, such as 'What is the meaning of life?' Existential philosophers are concerned with personal responsibility for actions, and the need people have to exert free individual choice. In the twentieth century, Martin Heidegger developed **phenomenology**. This is a method used to examine human experience and how people should live their lives (Heidegger, 1927). Basically, these philosophers state that each person has to find the meaning of his or her life from within the self rather than from the external world. This is very much the basic idea within humanistic psychology, particularly the theories of Rogers and Maslow.

Both Rogers and Maslow regarded personal growth and fulfilment in life as a basic human motive. This means that each person, in different ways, seeks to grow psychologically and continually develop themselves. This has been captured by the term **actualisation**, or **self-actualisation**, which is about psychological growth, fulfilment and satisfaction in life.

14.2.2 Carl Rogers

Carl Rogers originally entered religious training in his early twenties, and as a result developed an interest in psychology. He qualified as a clinical psychologist and throughout his life was committed to both psychotherapy and the development of psychological theory. In 1963 he founded the Center for the Studies of the Person, in California.

In considering the work of Carl Rogers, we will look at **person-centred theory** (Rogers 1951, 1961, 1980), both in terms of the key theoretical ideas and his approach to therapy. The key ideas are those of:

- the fully functioning person
- self-worth and positive regard
- the self-concept
- and congruence/incongruence.

The fully functioning person

In common with other humanistic psychologists, Rogers believed that every person could achieve their goals, wishes and desires in life. This is self-actualisation or self-fulfilment. For Rogers (1961), people who are able to self-actualise, and that is not all of us, are called **fully functioning persons**. This means that the person is in touch with the here and now, his or her subjective experiences and feelings, and continually growing and changing. In many ways, Rogers regarded the fully functioning person as an ideal and one that people do not ultimately achieve. It is wrong to think of this as an end or completion of life's journey; rather it is a process of always becoming and changing. Rogers identified five characteristics of the fully functioning person which are shown in Figure 14.2.

For Rogers, fully functioning people are well-adjusted, well-balanced and interesting to talk to and be acquainted with. Often such people are high achievers in society, business and social life. In many ways, western society values and prizes such people. The fully functioning person, as conceived by Rogers, represents an ideal state, and probably one that is never achieved by any person. Critics claim that the fully functioning person is a product of western culture and represents an individualistic and selfish approach to understanding what human beings are about. In other cultures, such as eastern cultures, the achievement of a group of people may be valued more highly than the achievement of an individual.

Self-worth and positive regard

How we think and feel about ourselves, our feelings of **self-worth**, are of fundamental importance both to psychological health and to the likelihood that we can achieve goals and ambitions in life. Self-worth may be seen as a continuum from very high to very low. For Rogers (1959), a person who has high self-worth has confidence and positive feelings about him or herself,

Characteristic of fully functioning person	Description
1. Open to experience	Both positive and negative emotions accepted. Negative feelings are not denied, but worked through.
2. Existential living	In touch with different experiences as they occur in life; avoiding prejudging and preconceptions.
3. Trust feelings	Feelings, instincts and gut reactions are paid attention to and trusted.
4. Creativity	Creative thinking and risk taking are features of a person's life. Person does not play safe all the time.
5. Fulfilled	Person is happy and satisfied with life, and always looking for new challenges and experiences.

Figure 14.2 *Five characteristics of the fully functioning person as seen by Rogers (1961).*

faces challenges in life, accepts failure and unhappiness at times, and is open with people. A person with low self-worth may avoid challenges in life, not accept that life can be painful and unhappy at times, and will be defensive and guarded with other people.

Rogers believed feelings of self-worth developed in early childhood and were formed from the interaction of the child with the mother and father. As the child grows to be a teenager and adult, interactions with significant others affect feelings of self-worth. Significant others include teachers, friends, family and more intimate relationships. Early influences on a child's feelings of self-worth can influence how future interactions with people and achievements are perceived. For example, a teenager with low self-worth who does well in an examination may say that it is due to the questions being easy rather than to do with the teenager's ability and the fact that he or she studied hard for the examination. The consequence of this subjective perception is that feelings of low self-worth are perpetuated.

Rogers viewed the young child as having two basic needs: positive regard from other people and positive self-worth. **Positive regard** is to do with how other people evaluate and judge us in social interaction. Rogers made a distinction between unconditional positive regard and conditional positive regard.

- **Unconditional positive regard** is where parents and significant others (including the humanistic therapist, as we shall see later) accept and love the person for what he or she is. Positive regard is not withdrawn when the person does something wrong or makes a mistake. The consequences of unconditional positive regard are that the person feels free to try new things out and make mistakes, even though this may lead to getting it wrong at times. People who are able to self-actualise are more likely to have received unconditional positive regard from others, especially their parents in childhood.
- **Conditional positive regard** is where positive regard, praise and approval depend upon the child, for example, behaving in ways that the parents think correct. Here the child is not loved for the person he or she is, but on condition that he or she behaves only in ways approved by the parent(s). At the extreme, a person who constantly seeks approval from other people is likely only to have experienced conditional positive regard as a child.

In most people's lives, and early childhood, both types of positive regard are likely to be experienced. It is the relative balance between the two that determines the extent of a person's positive or negative feelings of self-worth. Also, either type of positive regard is preferential to negative regard. **Negative regard** is where the person can do nothing right from another person's view. If a person has experienced considerable unconditional positive regard, he or she may avoid and not wish to develop a friendship with someone showing only conditional positive regard.

		Person A	
		Unconditional positive regard	Conditional positive regard
Person B	Unconditional positive regard	1. Unconditional–unconditional relationship	2. Unconditional–conditional relationship
	Conditional positive regard	3. Unconditional–conditional relationship	4. Conditional–conditional relationship

Figure 14.3 *Different types of positive regard – conditional and unconditional – in a relationship between two people.*

Self-concept and congruence/incongruence

For Rogers, the **self-concept** has two aspects.

- The first is self-worth, which we have already considered.
- The second is our *ideal self*, which is our idea of how we should be in all aspects of our life, work, relationships, feelings of fulfilment and so on. A person's ideal self may not be consistent with what actually happens in life and the experiences of the person. Hence, a discrepancy or difference may exist between a person's ideal self and actual experience. This is called **incongruence**. Where a person's ideal self and actual experience are consistent or very closely aligned, a state of **congruence** exists. Rarely, if ever, does a total state of congruence exist; all people experience a certain amount of incongruence, as shown in Figure 14.4.

When incongruence is high, the person may find it difficult to adjust to change and live a happy life. High incongruence will be reflected in many aspects of a person's life and there will be a large difference from their ideal. When incongruence is low, or congruence is high, then a person is likely to be satisfied and fulfilled with life. A person with a high level of incongruence may suffer psychological distress, and may find it difficult to adjust and live effectively in society.

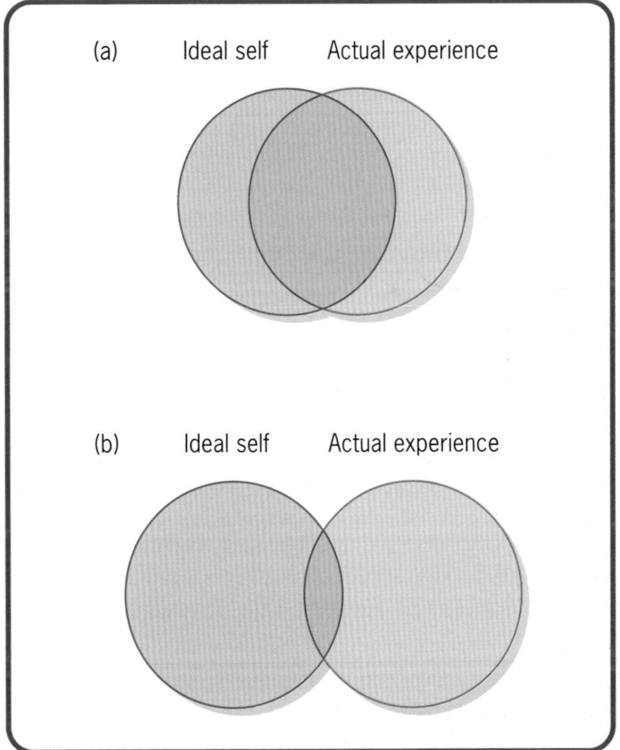

Figure 14.4 *Different levels of incongruence between a person's ideal self and actual self. In (**a**) incongruence is low, and in (**b**) it is high.*

Client-centred and person-centred therapy

Having looked at Rogers' concepts of the fully functioning person, self-worth and positive regard, the self-concept and congruence/incongruence, you may begin to see what Rogerian therapy tries to achieve.

Someone with low self-worth and a high degree of incongruence may have developed this state of mind because of the absence of unconditional positive regard. Rogers (1959) called his therapeutic approach **client-centred** or **person-centred therapy** because of the focus on the person's subjective view of the world. Person-centred therapy operates according to three basic principles that reflect the attitude of the therapist to the client; these are:

- The therapist is congruent with the client.
- The therapist provides the client with unconditional positive regard.
- The therapist shows empathetic understanding to the client.

The purpose of Rogers' humanistic therapy is to increase a person's feelings of self-worth, reduce the level of incongruence between ideal and actual self, and help a person become more of a fully functioning person. The three principles given above, and described in more detail in Figure 14.5, are designed to help achieve the goals of humanistic therapy.

Later in his career, Rogers moved away from one-to-one therapy and became more involved with group counselling. He developed what he called **encounter groups** in which people could feel safe and free to express feelings and explore problems in their lives. An encounter group would be facilitated by a Rogerian therapist and operate according to the three principles described in Figure 14.5.

Principle of client-centred therapy	Description
1. Therapist congruent with the client	The therapist is real, genuine and non-defensive towards the client. Genuineness reflects harmony and trust towards the client.
2. Therapist provides unconditional positive regard	The client is valued and accepted in all ways for what he or she thinks, feels or says. This makes the client feel safe to be open to the therapist.
3. The therapist shows empathy towards the client	The therapist does his or her best to understand the subjective experiences and perceptions from the point of view of the client. At the same time, the therapist should not get bound up in the emotions of the client.

Figure 14.5 *The three principles of genuineness (congruence), unconditional positive regard and empathy on which Rogerian therapy or counselling is based.*

Evaluation of Rogerian therapy

- Sexton and Whiston (1994) reviewed a large number of research studies to find out just how effective Rogerian therapy or counselling is for people. They found that generally the three principles of therapy did result in positive personality changes and successful outcomes for clients. However, they also reported that success was not inevitable and that much may depend on the personality of the client. It was found that clients who became very involved in the therapeutic process saw their therapists as more helpful than clients who were more detached from the process.

- The problem with most of these studies is that effectiveness is based on what clients say rather than any objective measure of better functioning and adjustment to life. Another criticism of these studies is that there is not usually a long-term follow-up of clients.

14.2.3 Abraham Maslow

Abraham Maslow was born in 1908 in New York. As a child and teenager he was shy and socially introverted. Initially he studied law, but psychology interested him more and he undertook a PhD with Harlow (who conducted the famous research on attachment in monkeys). Maslow rose to fame later in his career, in the 1960s and 1970s, when his theory of human needs and the concept of self-actualisation became highly influential. Maslow remained shy with people throughout his life and disliked public speaking. He died in 1970 after suffering poor health for a number of years.

In what follows we shall consider Maslow's theory of motivation and hierarchy of needs and his concept of self-actualisation. We shall also look at Maslow's research on the healthy personality and research measuring potential for self-actualisation.

Human motivation and hierarchy of needs

Maslow (1970) stated that human motivation is based on people seeking fulfilment and change through personal growth. Maslow characterised the human condition as one of 'wanting' – meaning we are always seeking and desiring something. Maslow conceptualised these 'wantings' or needs into a hierarchy of five needs. These five needs are made up of basic or **deficiency needs** and **growth needs.**

Maslow's hierarchy of needs contrasts with the psychodynamic approach which characterises people as avoiding conflict and wanting absence of tension (see Chapter 13). Maslow's theory also contrasts with the behaviourist approach (see Chapter 10), which ignores drives or needs and explains behaviour as a result of external (reinforcement and punishment) and not internal forces.

Maslow (1970) conceptualised needs as of five types: physiological needs, safety needs, belonging and love needs, self-esteem needs, and self-actualisation needs. These are traditionally represented as a pyramid, where the basic needs must be met before moving upwards to the top of the pyramid. This is shown in Figure 14.6.

- Physiological needs are strong, basic needs deriving from biology that relate directly to the survival of the individual.
- Safety needs include needs for security, protection and stability, and, more importantly, freedom from fear.
- Belongingness and love needs reflect the assumption that we are social animals and need to be with people and be loved by someone.

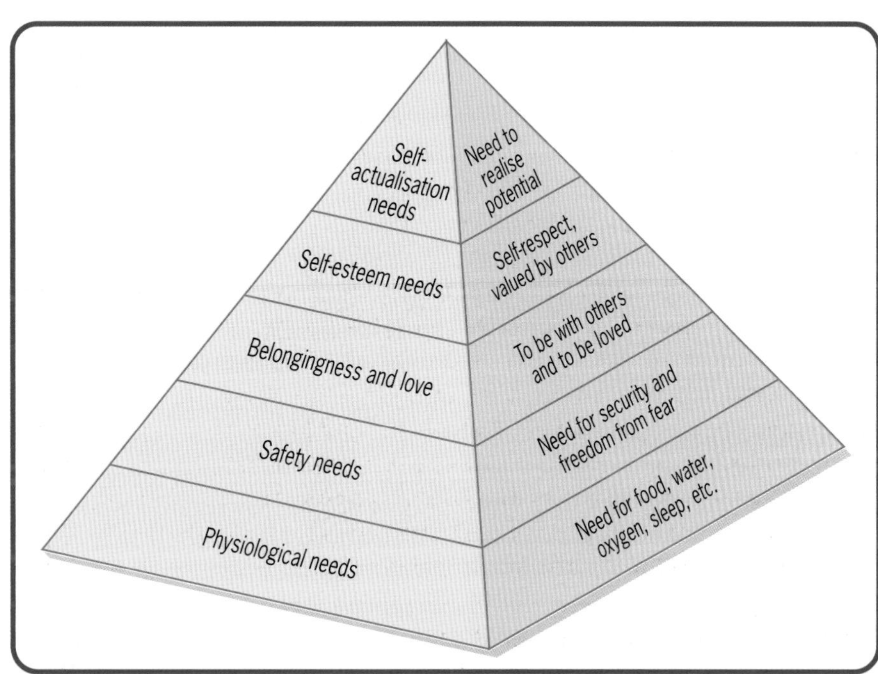

Figure 14.6 *Maslow's hierarchy of five human needs. Progression to the top of the pyramid can only be achieved by the fulfilment of lower needs.*

Evaluation

- Maslow's hierarchy of needs oversimplifies human needs and behaviour. The four deficiency needs do not have to be fully satisfied before moving to self-actualisation needs. If this were the case, just what level of satisfaction of a need is required before moving up to the next need?
- Human behaviour may be partially satisfying a number of needs at the same time. Only in conditions of extreme poverty and deprivation is a person motivated solely by physiological needs.

- Self-esteem needs are to do with self-respect and regard from other people.
- Self-actualisation needs are to do with realising full potential.

The first four needs are deficiency needs, and it is only when these are satisfied, according to Maslow, that the person can attempt to satisfy their self-actualisation needs.

Self-actualisation

The growth need of self-actualisation (Maslow, 1962) refers to the need for personal growth that is present throughout a person's life. For Maslow, a person is always 'becoming' and does not remain static. With self-actualisation a person comes to find a meaning to life that is important to them. The growth needs include those of:

- striving for goodness
- helping others
- seeking truth and justice
- striving to create beauty and order.

Notice that these needs are not solely to do with personal satisfaction resulting from a positive contribution to the development of the society in which we live, and support and help for others.

Maslow (1962) believed that some people actually fear self-actualisation since it brings about duties and responsibilities for the individual. The idea that some people fear being their best or reaching their potential Maslow called the **Jonah complex**. For males, the Jonah complex shows itself as a wish to avoid responsibility or a belief that success does not bring social recognition (Hoffman, 1974). For females, the Jonah complex is said to show itself as a reluctance to use intellectual abilities and fear of being successful in a career. Crawford and Maracek (1989) have criticised the idea that females fear success. They say that females are often, wrongly, judged against male norms of competition and winning. Hyland (1989) argues that females do not display a Jonah complex if judged against female norms. These norms include making friends and socialisation.

Maslow's research on the healthy personality

Maslow (1970) conducted extensive, but not very scientific, research on people he categorised as self-actualisers. Maslow defined self-actualisers as people who are fulfilled and use their abilities to the fullest. This is subjective and does not guarantee that a person Maslow categorises as a self-actualiser would be so categorised by another psychologist. Maslow stated there were three preconditions for a person to self-actualise. These are:

- absence of restraints
- no or little distraction from deficiency needs
- good knowledge of yourself.

From this, Maslow identified what he claimed were characteristics of self-actualisers. These are summarised in Figure 14.7.

Maslow also introduced the idea of **peak experiences**. These are feelings of ecstasy or a deep and satisfying sense of fulfilment that causes a feeling of timelessness. Some people may regard a peak experience as religious or mystical; other people may regard it as an event of major significance in their life. Peak experiences often happen spontaneously and are not that frequent in life. Generally, during a peak experience the person experiences an absence of deficiency needs. Peak experiences may change a person's life.

Maslow did not adopt a rigorous, scientific approach

Characteristic	Explanation
Accurate perceptions	Correct and realistic understanding of reality. Able to tolerate uncertainty and ambiguity.
Accepting of others	Accept own strengths and shortcomings and those in other people. Not threatened by others.
Spontaneous and simple	Straightforward, but often unconventional. High ethical and moral standards.
Problem-centred	Oriented to tasks and challenges in the world rather than dealing with their own problems.
Autonomous	Able to be independent of the social context and culture in which they live. Self-contained.
Creative	Able to think in new ways and produce original ideas, works of art, etc.
Sense of humour	Spontaneous sense of humour that does not get a laugh at someone else's expense.
Democratic	Friendly and considerate of other people regardless of sex, race, colour, age, etc.
Detached	Similar to autonomous, but able to put aside own feelings and emotions.
Private	Have a need to spend times in solitude, reflection and privacy.

Figure 14.7 *Ten characteristics that Maslow (1970) identified with self-actualisation.*

to identifying self-actualisers in his research into the healthy personality. He interviewed people he thought were self-actualisers and made his own judgements on the characteristics of these people. More objective measures of personality were not used, and self-actualisers were not compared with non-self-actualisers. Maslow's research ignored people with psychological disorders and hence did not really identify what prevents people from self-actualisation. Nevertheless, the research has provided valuable insights into the higher achievements of people.

Measuring self-actualisation

Shostrum (1963, 1977) developed a standardised personality questionnaire to measure self-actualisation. This is called the Personal Orientation Inventory (or POI for short). This consists of 150 fixed-choice items, some of which are shown in Figure 14.8.

The results of scoring the questionnaire reveal the extent (high or low) to which a person self-actualises in their life. Research has shown, for example, that people who score low on self-actualisation experience poor interpersonal relationships (Sheffield *et al.*, 1995). Also, creative thinking has been shown to be associated more with high self-actualisers (Runco *et al.*, 1991).

14.3 Rejection of the scientific approach

The humanistic theories of Carl Rogers and Abraham Maslow give key importance to the subjective, conscious experiences of the individual. Humanistic psychologists argue that objective reality is less important than a person's subjective experience and subjective understanding of the world. Because of this, Rogers and Maslow placed little value on scientific psychology, especially the use of the psychology

Evaluation of Maslow

- Maslow's theory of motivation, hierarchy of needs, and concept of self-actualisation have been highly influential in psychology. Maslow's ideas have been applied to the field of organisational psychology in an attempt to understand what motivates people to work (apart from money) and what gives satisfaction at work.
- The concept of self-actualisation has enjoyed widespread acceptance and more rigorous scientific research has been conducted. Self-actualisation has also been applied to atypical or abnormal behaviour to help understand people's fears and anxieties.
- On a more critical note, Maslow's theories have been criticised as culture-specific, representing white, middle-class North American values.
- Maslow has been criticised for paying too much attention to healthy people and not enough to those who have psychological disorders or do not function well in society.

laboratory to investigate both human and other animal behaviour.

The humanists view human beings as fundamentally different from other animals. This is mainly because humans are conscious beings capable of thought, reason and language. For humanistic psychologists, research on animals, such as rats, pigeons or monkeys, has little value. Research on non-human animals can tell us, so they argue, very little about human thought, behaviour and experience.

Humanistic psychologists rejected a rigorous scientific approach to psychology because they saw it as dehumanising and unable to capture the richness of subjective conscious experience. In many ways the rejection of scientific psychology in the 1950s, 1960s and 1970s was a backlash to the dominance of the

Sample items from Shostrum's Personal Orientation Inventory		
Time competence scale		
1.	(a)	I strive always to predict what will happen in the future.
	(b)	I do not feel it necessary always to predict what will happen in the future.*
2.	(a)	I prefer to save good things for future use.
	(b)	I prefer to use good things now.*
3.	(a)	I worry about the future.
	(b)	I do not worry about the future.*
Self-oriented scale		
4.	(a)	My moral values are dictated by society.
	(b)	My moral values are self-determined.*
5.	(a)	I feel guilty when I am selfish.
	(b)	I do not feel guilty when I am selfish.*
6.	(a)	I am bound by the principles of fairness.
	(b)	I an not absolutely bound by the principles of fairness.*
7.	(a)	I feel I must always tell the truth.
	(b)	I do not always tell the truth.*

Figure 14.8 *Sample items from Shostrum's (1963, 1977) Personal Orientation Inventory. Select one of the two statements. The starred (*) statement scores for high self-actualisation.*

behaviourist approach in North American psychology. Today, many of the ideas and concepts of humanistic psychology have been scientifically investigated by psychologists. We saw this earlier in this chapter with the measurement of self-actualisation. Many of the insights of Rogers and Maslow have been put on a more scientific footing over the past 20 years or so.

14.4 Key concepts in humanistic psychology

When considering the person-centred approaches of Carl Rogers and Abraham Maslow, a number of key themes or concepts are present in both theories. These are the concepts of:

- individual experience
- promoting personal growth
- free will
- holism.

These four key concepts are defining features of humanistic psychology. In what follows we will look at each more closely.

14.4.1 Individual experience

William James (1890) was one of the founders of modern psychology and put forward the view that the correct study of human beings should be to do with how people adapt to their environment and how conscious experience helps with this. James regarded conscious experience as an essential feature of what it is to be human. It allows people to adapt to a complex environment. For James, consciousness is a continual flow of thoughts, feelings and sensations that cannot be divided up or broken down into component parts. He coined the phrase 'stream of consciousness' to encapsulate this idea.

The development of humanistic psychology in the mid-twentieth century retained William James' idea of consciousness. However, it went further by considering the uniqueness of each person's experiences. This focus on individual experience was underpinned by three important principles:

1 Individual experience is unique to each person and cannot be repeated. Attempts can be made to reconstruct an experience, but the reconstruction can never be the same as the original experience.

2 To understand a person and in what ways a person is well-adjusted and poorly adjusted to life, humanistic psychologists needs to try to see things from that person's perspective. This is called being **empathetic** with another. It entails trying to experience things as if you were the other person. Whilst it is impossible to experience fully as another person does, attempts can be made to enter into another person's way of thinking or feeling.

3 The individual experience of a person, which involves subjective perceptions and feelings, is to be seen as valid. This means that experience is valued for what it is and how the person reports it. For humanistic psychologists, the experience of a person is not questioned or challenged, but attempts are made to understand it.

The focus on the uniqueness of individual experience led to a 'counterculture' in the 1960s (the hippies). Here, eastern religions and meditation became popular because of the centrality of awareness of your experiences, as well as 'mind-altering' drugs such as LSD, which gave a person an altered or different experience of the world.

Figure 14.9 *The hippy movement in the 1960s reflected many of the ideas of humanistic psychology.*

14.4.2 Promoting personal growth

Our consideration of Rogers and Maslow has shown that both these humanistic psychologists regard personal growth as an essential part of what it is to be human. Personal growth with Rogers occurs with the fully functioning person (see Section 14.2.2). With Maslow it is through satisfaction of deficiency needs to allow for growth needs to be satisfied. Both theories talk about self-actualisation, which is the realisation of a person's full potential. In looking at what may help promote personal growth, it will be instructive to consider the other side of the coin – what prevents self-actualisation?

Rogers (1959) used the word **threat** to represent a person's perception of conflict and incongruity within a person's self-concept. Conflict may threaten how we think of ourselves because our sense of continuity and wholeness as a person may be threatened. This may come about due to a relationship breakdown, death of a loved one, or loss of job or career. In such circumstances, Rogers said that defensive processes such as denial and distortion are employed by the person. These defences ward off the anxiety resulting from the threat to our self-concept, and feelings of self-worth and self-esteem. When this happens to a normally well-adjusted person, we may say that they are 'not themselves'. In such circumstances, a fragmented self-concept, supported by defence mechanisms, will prevent personal growth. The attention of the individual is inwards and towards the threat and conflicts – dealing with the negative – rather than outwards and dealing with the positive.

On the other side of the coin, we may ask what events, circumstances or situations actually promote personal growth. For Maslow and the hierarchy of needs, the four deficiency needs (see Figure 14.7) would need to be satisfied to allow self-actualisation. Research using standardised measures of self-actualisation has shown, for example, that absence of psychological disorders, relationship difficulties and drug dependence fosters self-actualisation and hence personal growth (Daniels, 1988). Self-actualisers are more likely to be open to experiences and accepting of those experiences. They are also more likely to recognise a peak experience and use such experiences to enhance personal growth (Thomas and Cooper, 1980).

Csikszentmihalyi (1990) developed a **theory of flow**. Flow is where a person becomes so involved in an activity that nothing else matters or intrudes on consciousness. Flow experiences occur in a wide range of situations – during both physical and mental activities. Stein *et al.* (1995) showed that students who played sport and were in a flow experience showed more enjoyment, concentration and satisfaction than students who were in bored or anxiety states. Flow experiences lead to personal growth because the person will want to improve at the activity, and increase the challenges. So if you have feelings of intense involvement with an activity, this helps with other activities and means that you grow through setting more and more challenges for yourself.

Figure 14.10 *Total involvement and absorption in an activity is called 'flow' by humanistic psychologists.*

14.4.3 Free will

The humanistic theories of Rogers and Maslow rejected the deterministic approaches of psychoanalysis and behaviourism. In part, this rejection was because the humanists regarded individuals as possessing **free will**. We will consider the free will–determinism debate more fully and generally in Chapter 16, but now we will consider the idea of free will in relation to humanistic psychology.

Free will does not mean that an individual has the freedom to do anything that he or she pleases or wishes to do. Free will has to be considered alongside personal responsibility and the rules (laws and unwritten rules) of the society in which a person lives. Whilst you are, in a sense, free to behave antisocially and break laws, there are consequences for behaving in such ways. The consequences may be seen to be of two types:

- **External consequences** include punishment (imprisonment, etc.) by the law for acting illegally.
- **Internal consequences** are to do with the self-punishment or guilt that may follow from behaving in antisocial or illegal ways.

While a person may be free to think about engaging in any kind of behaviour (whether good or bad), there are strong constraints operating internally and externally which stop most people behaving in these undesirable ways. Humanistic psychologists place great emphasis on making people accept and take responsibility for their actions. Rogers (1977), for example, states that the person-centred approach raises potential issues to do with power, control and decision making. The person-centred approach places control and free will in the hands of the individual and expects responsible behaviour of individuals, groups and organisations.

Should a person be held responsible for all actions that he or she engages in? Should it be assumed that a person exercises free will in every aspect of life? These are difficult questions that do not have clear-cut answers. For example, a murderer may be judged insane and hence not be held accountable for the dreadful deed of killing another person.

14.4.4 Holism

'The whole is greater than the sum of the parts'. This statement sums up the gestalt approach to psychology. gestalt psychology developed during the 1930s and 1940s through the work of psychologists such as Köhler and Wertheimer. This approach to psychology argued that perceptions, problem solving and learning could not be broken down into parts or 'actions', as with physics or chemistry. Humanistic psychology adopts a holistic approach to personality and behaviour and was influenced by the gestalt school of psychology in this respect.

Humanistic psychologists saw the behaviourists as attempting to break down or reduce behaviour to 'elemental' stimulus–response (S–R) contingencies. They saw psychoanalysts, such as Sigmund Freud, attempting to break down personality into parts such as the id, ego and superego, and conscious, preconscious and unconscious (see Chapter 13). This analytic approach of behaviourism and psychoanalysis borrowed the reductionist or atomistic theme (reducing matter to its constituent atoms) of physical and biological science. Humanistic psychologists adopted **holism** as a fundamental principle in their approach. Holism avoids attempts to reduce personality to smaller elements and regards it as essential to consider the person and behaviours in a holistic way.

An important influence on the development of the person-centred approaches of Rogers and Maslow was **organismic theory** (Goldstein, 1939). The organismic or holistic viewpoint treats the individual, in terms of both mind and body, as a unified and organised whole. This means that to understand a person, both biological and mental processes have to be taken together in a holistic way. The main proponent of organismic theory was Kurt Goldstein, who was an eminent neuropsychiatrist in the first half of the twentieth century. Goldstein worked with brain-injured soldiers during World War I. He said that to understand and help soldiers with physical brain damage, the psychological consequences also had to be considered. Hence, the soldier has to be understood as a whole, with both mind and body (in this case the brain) unified. Goldstein stated that the person is a single entity and what happens in any part, psychologically or physically, affects the whole.

- Organismic theory attempts to discover the principles by which the whole person functions, and assumes that each person is motivated by one overriding drive: that of self-actualisation. This single drive provides purpose and unity to the total or whole life of the person.
- Organismic theory studies one person in detail and in a holistic way, rather than studying a large number of people from only selected perspectives.

Abraham Maslow, as we have seen, studied healthy people from a holistic perspective, and attempted to show that peak experiences help people feel more integrated and complete or whole as a person. Carl Rogers used person-centred or client-centred therapy to treat the whole person using the approach of unconditional positive regard.

14.5 Strengths and limitations of the humanistic approach

The humanistic approach to understanding the person provides an optimistic and positive view of human nature. Critics, however, have argued that this optimism has been unrealistic since human behaviour can be very negative and destructive.

Strengths

- One of the key strengths of the humanistic approach is that it promotes a positive image of human beings and the human condition. The concepts of personal growth and self-actualisation demonstrate ways in which each person can grow and change throughout their life. Also, achievements and interactions with other people are highly enjoyable and rewarding to the individual.
- Another strength is the focus on subjective experience. We all know this is important in our everyday lives and that psychology should in some way attempt to understand and study the subjective as well as the objective.

- A third strength of this approach is that each person is seen as being in control of their lives, experiences and relationships with other people. For the humanistic psychologist, people are said to have free will and be able to determine what happens to them in their lives. This contrasts very much with the behaviourist and psychodynamic approaches in psychology.

Limitations

There are three main limitations: lack of empirical research, lack of comprehensiveness and vagueness of key concepts or terms.

- **Lack of empirical research.** Whilst humanistic psychologists reject the scientific approach, it is nevertheless important to find out the extent to which key concepts and claims are supported by empirical evidence. One criticism is that humanistic psychology has not generated a great deal of empirical evidence to support its claims. However, there have been, as we have seen, recent attempts to measure concepts such as self-actualisation through standardised questionnaires. The empirical research that does exist has been conducted by psychologists who are often not humanistic in their outlook, but wish to put some of the valuable insights of humanistic theories onto a more scientific footing.
- **Lack of comprehensiveness.** Some critics argue that the humanistic approach is not as comprehensive as, for example, that of psychoanalysis or behaviourism. In some ways this may seem like a strange criticism to make since, as we have seen, humanistic psychology deals with the whole person. The criticism about comprehensiveness is to do with the strong emphasis and focus on one main drive, motive or need: that of self-actualisation. This focus on self-actualisation is regarded as a limitation because other drives, particularly biological and instinctive ones, play a much less central role than may be considered appropriate.
- **Vagueness of concepts.** Some of the key concepts and terms have been seen as vague or poorly defined. Terms such as self-actualisation, the fully functioning person and peak experiences, whilst providing valuable insight into human behaviour, need precise definition. Precise definition allows empirical research to be undertaken so that human thought and behaviour can be investigated. It may be because of the vagueness of these terms that little empirical research has been generated from the humanistic approach.

14.6 Applications

The humanistic approach has made valuable applications in the areas of:

- **Therapy and counselling:** The humanistic focus on subjective experience and the 'here and now' has proved successful in helping people cope with and adjust to changes in their lives. Humanistic counselling tries to get a person to understand how he or she thinks about and structures their perception of the world.
- **Education and learning:** Here, for example, unconditional positive regard by the teacher helps the pupil or student to realise their full potential and use their abilities to the full.
- **Understanding relationships between people:** For many people, a satisfying and rewarding intimate relationship is one of the most important things in life. An intimate and successful relationship is fulfilling for people and may lead to self-actualisation.
- **Maslow's idea of a hierarchy of needs** has been widely applied outside of humanistic psychology. It has been an important concept in organisational psychology. The motives of a person to work have been investigated according to the different needs in the hierarchy. Application has been made to help understand and predict what gives people job satisfaction and why some people are driven to be successful in their career. A person who thinks that he or she has a highly successful career is more likely to achieve and experience self-actualisation.

Figure 14.11 *A loving and intimate relationship may lead to self-actualisation for many people.*

Further Reading

Introductory texts

Maltby, J., Day, L. and Macaskill, A. (2007) *Personality, Individual Differences and Intelligence,* Chapter 6, London: Prentice Hall.

Pennington, D.C. (2003) *Essential Personality,* Chapter 8, London: Hodder.

Specialist sources

Maslow, A.H. (1970) *Motivation and Personality,* 2nd edn., New York: Harper and Row.

Nye, R.D. (2000) *Three Psychologies: Perspectives from Freud, Skinner and Rogers,* 6th edn., Chapter 4, London: Wadsworth.

Rogers, C.R. (1961) *On Becoming a Person,* Boston: Houghton Mifflin.

Ryckman, R.M. (2000) *Theories of Personality,* 7th edn., Chapters, 11, 12, 13 and 14, London: Thompson Learning, Wadsworth.

Comparison of approaches

Chapter 15

15.1 Introduction

You should now be familiar with the six main approaches in psychology – biological, behaviourist, social learning, cognitive, psychodynamic and humanistic. You may, rightly, be asking yourself why there are so many different approaches in psychology, whether other approaches than these six exist, and how coherent different theories are within any one approach. The range of approaches in psychology reflects how complex it is to capture a full understanding of human thought, feelings and behaviour within a single approach. As we shall see later in this chapter, in Section 15.4, there is value in accepting and working with a range of approaches – or theories representing different approaches – at the same time.

Figure 15.1 *Each person is a unique individual with unique experiences. Can one approach in psychology capture all this?*

As you will have seen from reading the previous six chapters, each approach has both limitations and strengths. For psychology to adopt a single approach would, it may be argued, result in too narrow and simplistic a view of human nature. Adopting just one approach would miss important aspects of what it is to be a human being. For example, the cognitive approach is overly concerned with human thought and pays relatively less attention to emotions and actual behaviour. By contrast, the psychodynamic approach is overly concerned with a person's unconscious, emotional life and childhood experiences. The behaviourist approach is overly concerned with overt behaviour and pays less attention to thoughts and feelings which may be important determinants of behaviour. The social learning theory approach has little to say about heredity and the role of biology in human behaviour. The humanistic approach focuses on the individual's subjective experiences and is less concerned with attempting to discover rules or laws that may govern human behaviour.

In what follows we will compare the six different approaches, and consider the extent to which they overlap and complement each other. Finally, we will look at the value of using multiple approaches in psychology – that is, an **eclectic approach** to understanding human thought and behaviour.

15.2 Comparison of approaches

In what follows we will compare the different approaches in psychology in six different ways:

- view of human nature
- personality development
- atypical behaviour
- role of society/culture
- views on aggression
- methods of studying human behaviour.

Approach	View on human nature	Similar to other approach
Biological	Human characteristics and behaviour determined by genetic inheritance. Physiological determinants of human behaviour.	Psychoanalytic in terms of instincts.
Behaviourist	Sees people as machines responding to reinforcements or punishments in environment. Little free will.	None with radical behaviourism, but cognitive with social learning theories.
Social learning theory	Behaviour takes place in a social context, and is learned from observing how others behave.	Both behaviourist and cognitive.
Cognitive	People as conscious, logical thinkers, with memory as defining human characteristic.	Psychoanalytic at a conscious level. Behaviourist with social learning theories.
Psychodynamic	Negative, conflict-ridden, at mercy of instincts, unconscious and childhood repressions.	Biological and cognitive approaches.
Humanistic	Positive image where a person grows and realises potential. Freedom to act and choose.	None really, but some elements of biological and cognitive.

Figure 15.2 *Views on human nature from the different approaches in psychology..*

15.2.1 View of human nature

The psychoanalytic approach of Freud presents the most negative view of human nature. This sees people as conflict-ridden, dominated by instinctual demands, operating at a largely unconscious and irrational level, and consistently coping with childhood repressions. By contrast, the humanistic approach presents a positive view of human nature, where personal growth and the need for each person to reach their potential are the key motivating forces. With humanistic psychology, people are seen to have free will (see Chapter 14) and human nature is to be trusted. The behaviourist approach views human nature rather like a machine. By this is meant that human behaviour is determined by reinforcement and punishment contingencies in the environment. These are not under the conscious control of people. The behaviourist approach regards biological and instinctual aspects of the person as unimportant. The social learning approach depicts people as copying the behaviour of others when that behaviour is observed to be rewarding for the other person. The social learning approach does not present a view of human nature in which people have free will and choice over how to behave. The biological approach puts human nature too much in control of genetic and physiological forces over which the individual has little or no control. To some extent the biological approach is compatible with the psychodynamic approach because instincts are biological. Finally, the cognitive approach presents an image of human nature as logical, rational and thinking before behaving. People are seen as conscious thinking beings; however, the relationship between thought and behaviour is less clear.

In summary, each approach does present a different view or image of human nature. These range from the negative and pessimistic (psychodynamic) to the positive and recognition of the importance of free will

(humanistic). In many ways, the behavioural and biological approaches are negative in the sense that the person is seen to have little control over how to behave or freedom to make their own life choices.

15.2.2 Personality development

Both the psychodynamic and cognitive approaches put forward a 'stage' approach to personality development and child development. The psychodynamic approach typically deals with the psychosexual and emotional development of the personality. In contrast, the cognitive approach, through the work of such psychologists as Piaget, Bruner and Kohlberg (see Chapters 2 and 3), deals with cognitive development in terms of intellectual and moral development. Both approaches state that developmental stages take place in early childhood through to early teenage years, with development complete by early adulthood at the latest.

The behaviourist approach does not put forward any kind of stage theory of development, but sees development as a continual process resulting from the action of the environment (reinforcement contingencies and punishment) in a continuous way. Behaviour is emitted, shaped and changed in a gradual way by the action of the environment.

The social learning approach does not offer a staged approach to personality development. This approach sees learning and behaviour as resulting from observational learning at all ages of the person, from early childhood through to old age. The basic processes of observational learning, with significant models being influential on what the person learns and does, are the same at all ages.

Figure 15.3 *Realising your potential is one of the most rewarding experiences that you may have in your life.*

The humanistic approach sees personality development to do with personal growth and the realisation of life goals as taking place throughout a person's life. As such, the humanistic approach sees growth as continual and over the whole life of the person. Carl Rogers regarded development as taking place over the lifespan and proposed eight psychosocial stages of development. Finally, the biological approach sees personality development as a maturational process where predetermined genetic predispositions cause physical and psychological changes up to early adulthood. For example, the onset of puberty or adolescence is a predetermined maturational process caused by biological factors, but which has significant psychological consequences for the individual.

15.2.3 Atypical behaviour

The application of psychological theory, research and treatments to a range of atypical behaviours and abnormal psychological conditions has, by and large, been a success story over the past 50 years for psychology. The application of different approaches in psychology has improved people's lives and been of benefit to society. The different approaches attempt to explain psychological disorders and dysfunctions differently and offer different means of treating a range of disorders.

With the psychodynamic approach, psychological disorders, especially neurotic or anxiety disorders, are seen to result from unconscious conflict, childhood repressions and unreasonable demands of society upon the individual. Treatment is through the so-called 'talking cure' of psychoanalysis, although 'cure' is not the key objective. The objective of psychoanalytic therapy is to strengthen the ego to enable it better to deal with the conflicting demands of the id, superego and reality. Psychoanalytic therapy may take place over many years and it is difficult to assess its effectiveness objectively. Behaviourism, by contrast, attempts to change the actual behaviour of a person without delving into or even attempting to delve into the deeper, mental causes of the dysfunctional behaviour. Behaviourist treatments, such as systematic desensitisation, have been shown to be effective with anxiety disorders and phobias.

The social learning approach has been used to treat aggressive behaviour in children and teenagers (Webster-Stratton and Reid, 2003). Therapy based on

Approach	Personality development
Biological	Development as a maturational process resulting from inheritance and genetic predisposition.
Behaviourist	Development as a continual process resulting in environmental (reinforcement and punishment) contingencies.
Social Learning Theory	Observational learning takes place throughout life, with the same processes at all ages. No 'stage' approach to personality development.
Cognitive	In relation to child development – Piaget and Kohlberg – intellectual and moral development occur in stages.
Psychodynamic	Psychosexual stages of emotional development. Oral, anal and phallic stages take place in first 6/7 years of life.
Humanistic	Development throughout life, not in stages, through personal growth and realisation of potential.

Figure 15.4 *Views on personality development from the different approaches in psychology*

Evaluation

- Freud's theory of psychosexual development (oral, anal and phallic stages) and Piaget's theory of intellectual development (sensorimotor, pre-operational, concrete operations and formal operations stages) appear to be biologically determined. This is in the sense that the stages occur in a set sequence and the child enters the stages at certain ages in childhood. From this we can see that stage theories of development do seem to rely on a biological and genetic predisposition.

social learning theory involves trying to expose the child to correct models or changing the behaviour of parents to provide models with more appropriate behaviour for the child to observe and imitate. Success is long-lasting as long as the behaviour of the models is appropriate and remains so. If not, the child or teenager may relapse to their original, problematic behaviour pattern.

Cognitive approaches to the treatment of psychological disorders have adopted a more problem-solving approach which attempts to change the way a person thinks (Ellis, 1995; Beck and Weishaur, 1995). For example, with depressive disorders, attempts are made to change the way a person views the causes of behaviour. Typically, a person suffering depression sees factors in the environment, external to themselves, as causing negative thoughts and behaviour. This means the person thinks that he or she cannot control their behaviour. Cognitive therapy attempts to help the person feel more in control and to change his or her way of thinking from negative to positive. This results in changes to how the person behaves.

Humanistic psychology views psychological disorders as resulting from the stunting or prevention of personal growth. Psychological disorders also result from other people, and society more generally, stopping or preventing a person self-actualising or reaching their full potential. Humanistic therapy uses empathy, unconditional positive regard and acceptance towards the person in an attempt to promote

personal growth, self-worth and help a person self-actualise.

The biological approach uses drugs to treat psychological disorders and is more aligned with the medical model of mental illness. Drug treatments are particularly prevalent with major psychotic disorders such as schizophrenia and bipolar depression (see Chapter 5).

15.2.4 Role of society/culture

Psychology, almost by definition, focuses on the individual. However, the influence of the society and culture in which we live affects our beliefs, values, attitudes and behaviours. To some extent, the differing approaches in psychology take these influences into account.

The psychodynamic approach, especially Freudian theory, sees an inevitable conflict between the instinctual demands within the person and society/civilisation. The sexual urges and instinctual needs of the person, even if at an unconscious level, are often at odds and in opposition to the requirements of an ordered, civilised and moral culture or society in which the person lives. For civilisation to continue, individual needs are often ignored or repressed. At times, this may result in psychological disorder or the inability of an individual to adapt to the 'rules' or requirements of society.

Behaviourists, by contrast, view society, in the form of the external environment, as controlling the person, and controlling its citizens. Behaviourists see society as setting up planned contingencies of reinforcement to promote and maintain the desired and acceptable behaviours of a society. The environment, as the society, culture or civilisation, operates to control and determine the behaviours of a person.

The social learning theory approach explains learning through the influence of models. Society has clear rules and laws about acceptable and unacceptable behaviour in society. For example, society regards it as a problem that some teenagers have guns and knives. However, such young people can act as important models for other teenagers. This has the consequence that behaviour society deems undesirable may be imitated from these models. The goal here is to either change the models that other teenagers look up to or change the behaviour of the models so that they do not have weapons.

The humanistic approach regards society/culture as far

Approach	Explanation of atypical behaviour	Treatment of atypical behaviour
Biological	Chemical imbalances or deficiencies, mostly in central nervous system.	Use of drug therapies, as with the medical model.
Behaviourist	Incorrect or maladaptive reinforcements/punishment.	Change behaviour by changing reinforcement and punishment contingencies.
Social Learning Theory	Observational learning from behaviour of inappropriate models.	Change the models that the person observes, or change the behaviour of the models.
Cognitive	Inappropriate and negative way of thinking about self.	Change way of thinking about self, problem-solving approach.
Psychodynamic	Unconscious conflict, childhood repressions, weak ego.	Psychoanalysts to uncover repressions, and strengthen the ego.
Humanistic	Blocking of personal growth and self-actualisation.	Unconditional positive regard to remove these blocks.

Figure 15.5 *Explanations and treatment approaches to atypical behaviour according to different approaches in psychology.*

too restrictive upon the freedom and choices of an individual. Psychological growth and ability to self-actualise are threatened by the structures of society – education, employment and the institution of marriage, for example. From this it can be seen that there are similarities between the psychodynamic and humanistic perspectives on how society restricts and causes the individual to experience conflicts and unhappiness.

The cognitive and biological approaches have less to say and take less account of the influence of society upon the person, although, for example, the attitudes, beliefs and values that a person holds – personal cognitions we may call them – are heavily influenced by cultural or societal norms.

15.2.5 Views on aggression

Aggression can be seen from an interpersonal (between individuals), intergroup (between groups of people) and international level (between nations). Aggression is a major problem for humankind in the twenty-first century. Aggression even occurs when people try, and often succeed, in harming themselves (self-harm) – whether this be physical or psychological harm. Aggression may be defined as follows:

> Any form of behaviour directed toward the goal of harming or injuring another living being who is motivated to avoid such treatment (Baron and Richardson, 1994).

Because of the widespread occurrence of aggression across all cultures and societies in the world, each of the six approaches in psychology that we are considering offer an explanation of why aggression occurs.

Figure 15.6 *Aggression is better understood from a number of different approaches in psychology.*

The psychodynamic approach explains human aggression as resulting from an instinctual and destructive part of human nature in the unconscious. In Freud's later writings, admission was made of a death or destructive instinct that worked against the life or sex instinct. This leads to a pessimistic view about the future of humankind and society's ability to cope with human aggressive tendencies. For Freud, the one positive aspect was the ability that people have to use defence mechanisms to redirect or sublimate aggressive impulses towards socially positive and valuable activities such as work, art, literature, sport and relationships.

The behaviourist approach, even that of radical behaviourism as put forward by Skinner, acknowledges that an innate component may be present. However, the main explanations of why people engage in aggressive behaviour is explained as more to do with environmental factors such as upbringing; social circumstances such as poverty; and, more generally, reinforcement contingencies that have strengthened the aggressive behavioural response to certain stimuli in the environment. Behaviourism advocates changes in the environment at a societal level in order to change people and prevent aggression.

The social learning approach states that aggressive behaviour results from observational learning of aggressive models. The classic experiments of Bandura, using Bobo dolls to examine the learning of aggressive behaviour in children, clearly highlights the importance of this explanation. The research of Bandura and his colleagues also showed how learned aggressive behaviour could be reduced or changed (see Chapter 11).

The humanistic approach explains aggressive behaviour as resulting from people who are not fully functioning at a psychological level – not fully functioning means that personal growth is stunted and self-actualisation not realised. To combat aggression, humanistic psychologists advocate the creation of conditions, at both interpersonal and societal levels, which will allow people to become more fulfilled in their lives.

The biological approach is consistent with the psychodynamic view of aggression as being a result of inherited instincts and as behaviour that evolved to allow an individual to protect themselves, especially in

Approach	View on aggression
Biological	Aggression innate and instinctive resulting from benefits once provided to the individual and species for survival
Behaviourist	May be some innate component, but largely determined by the environment. Factors such as upbringing, social conditions, poverty play a major role.
Social Learning Theory	Aggression results from observational learning. An influential model who behaves in an aggressive way and is seen to be rewarded for such behaviour may be imitated by the observer.
Cognitive	Perceptions and cognitions about a situation will determine whether or not seen as threatening and hence requiring an aggressive response.
Psychodynamic	Aggression as instinctual and biologically given – death or destructive instinct. May be sublimated into socially constructive activities – work, art.
Humanistic	Aggression is a result of blocking of personal growth and prevention of self-actualisation. To remove aggression facilitates personal growth.

Figure 15.7 *Explanations of aggression from the six main approaches in psychology.*

the animal kingdom. The aggressive instinct, similar to the sex instinct, functions to ensure the survival of the species and the survival of the fittest.

The cognitive approach has been less concerned with emotions and specific behaviours such as aggression. Nevertheless, the cognitions or perceptions that a person has about a situation that confronts them will determine how it is interpreted. If a situation is perceived to be threatening in some way, then conscious thought will be given to how best to reduce the threat – this may be to remove oneself from the situation or attack (the classic 'flight-or-fight' response).

15.2.6 Study of human behaviour

Each of the six approaches adopts a range of methods by which to study, research and collect evidence about human thought and behaviour. Some methods – for example, the laboratory experiment – are common to a number of approaches. These include the behaviourist, cognitive and biological approaches. In general, the more

Approach	View on aggression
Biological	Laboratory experiments, often using animals to investigate functions of parts of the brains. Twin studies.
Behaviourist	Laboratory experiments, often using animals such as rats and pigeons.
Social Learning Theory	Laboratory experiments and field experiments, naturalistic observations.
Cognitive	Typically, laboratory experiments, sometimes single subject experiments and case studies.
Psychodynamic	Case studies. Interpretation of behaviour to unconscious motives.
Humanistic	Case studies, biographies (psycho-history), subjective conscious experience.

Figure 15.8 *Typical methods of studying human behaviour adopted by different approaches in psychology.*

quantitative methods are characteristic of these three approaches. Qualitative methods, such as case studies, are more likely to be used in the psychodynamic and humanistic approaches. Figure 15.9 summarises the main methods used by each of the six approaches in psychology. From your knowledge and understanding of research methods at both AS and A2 level psychology, you should be aware that both qualitative and quantitative methods are widely used in the more scientific areas of psychology, such as cognitive psychology, personality, social psychology, atypical psychology and health psychology.

15.3 Overlap and complementarity of approaches

The comparisons that have been made between the six approaches in relation to views of human nature, personality development, atypical behaviour, the role of culture/society, views on aggression and study of human behaviour have shown that each approach does not exist in isolation. There is overlap and a degree of complementarity with these different approaches. In what follows we will consider just a few ways in which this occurs. You are invited to think of other ways from your knowledge of psychology and each of the approaches.

The cognitive and biological approaches come together and overlap in the area of cognitive neuroscience (see Chapter 12). Cognitive neuroscience studies the physiological (central nervous system, especially the brain) basis of cognitive functions and processes such as memory, attention, perception and consciousness.

We have seen earlier in this chapter that the psychodynamic and biological approaches have a degree of overlap and complementarity in relation to the inheritance of instincts and evolution of psychological functions. Darwin's theory of evolution became an important factor in Freud's development of his theory about the sexual instinct, psychosexual development and unconscious, repressed conflicts. It is probably true to say that biological psychology has been influential in the development of the psychodynamic perspective. However, the reverse is much less the case in that psychoanalysis has had much less or little influence on the biological perspective.

It may seem strange to say, but the psychodynamic and behaviourist approaches also have a degree of overlap and complementarity. Psychoanalysis provides an explanation about what is going on in the human mind, often at a largely unconscious level. Behaviourism provides an account of how we learn from experience. Thus, for example, the first psychosexual stage of development, the oral stage, will be affected by the experience the baby has of (breast) feeding. In a similar way, during the anal stage of psychosexual development, toilet-training is deemed to be of vital significance. The actual experience itself, the approach used by parents and significant others can be couched in terms of learning theory.

The six different approaches in psychology that we have considered in this chapter do offer quite different views and models of human beings and how they think and behave. These different models or views of humans all exist together because people are complex psychologically. People cannot readily or adequately be represented by a single approach. Whilst modern psychology, especially in universities, adopts a strongly scientific approach (see Chapter 16), other approaches, such as the psychodynamic and humanistic, do exist and thrive as much now as they did 50 years ago. Groups of psychologists tend to adopt a particular approach and find it difficult to adopt or operate across a range of approaches, particularly when there are major differences, such as that between, for example, behaviourist and humanistic or biological and humanistic.

15.4 The value of an eclectic approach

An eclectic approach adopts ideas, theories, methods and points of view from a number of different approaches in an attempt to capture better and represent the subject matter under study, that is, human beings. In the case of psychology, taking aspects, ideas or methods from each of the six approaches we have considered in this chapter may provide a richer, fuller and more accurate picture of human nature and what it is to be human. A definition of an eclectic approach is as follows:

> An eclectic thinker is one who selectively adopts ideas from different sources and combines them in the development of a new theory (Mautner, 2000: 158).

Notice with this definition that an eclectic approach is not only about taking ideas and insights from different approaches, but also putting these together in such a way as to produce a new theory. This new theory should, eventually, replace two or more approaches to provide a broader, more widely applicable approach. (See Chapter 16 for a more general discussion on the nature of scientific theories and how science progresses.)

With your knowledge of psychology gained at AS and A2 levels, you should be in a position to realise that psychology has not progressed, theoretically, to combine ideas from different approaches into a new theory. The value of adopting an eclectic point of view in psychology is that human thought and behaviour do not readily lend themselves to explanation and understanding from within one approach. To some extent we have seen this in the previous section, when we considered some of the complementarity of the different approaches.

This is demonstrated in a more concrete way when considering explanations and treatments for atypical behaviour. If a treatment based upon one approach for schizophrenia, for example, were successful, it would be used to the exclusion of other therapeutic approaches. Clearly this is not the case with any of the major psychological disorders. In the case of unipolar depression, for example, both a biological and a cognitive approach to treatment is often used (see Chapter 5). Here drugs are commonly used with cognitive therapy to help treat depression, and this combined approach has been found to be more effective than using just a single approach. Drugs may help alleviate the symptoms of depression whilst cognitive therapy helps change thought patterns to prevent the person getting depressed in the future.

Further Reading

Glassman, W.E. and Hadad, M. (2004) *Approaches to Psychology,* Milton Keynes: Open University Press.

Krahé, B. (2001) *The Social Psychology of Aggression,* Hove: Psychology Press.

Nye, R.D. (2000) *Three Psychologies: Perspectives from Freud, Skinner and Rogers,* London: Wadsworth.

Schultz, D.P. and Schultz, S.E. (2000) *A History of Modern Psychology,* 7th edn., Fort Worth, TX: Harcourt College Publishers.

Debates in psychology

Chapter 16

16.1 Introduction

Psychology developed from philosophy over 100 years ago when Wilhelm Wundt established the first psychology laboratory. Modern psychology is a scientific discipline and uses a range of empirical methods, including the laboratory experiment, to investigate human and animal behaviour. Psychological researchers explore topic areas such as social, developmental and cognitive psychology, and areas of application such as sport, health and forensic psychology. Because of the range of methods and the importance of applications of psychology, a number of key philosophical debates are important.

The word **philosophy** comes from the Greek word *philosophia*, meaning love of wisdom, and the search for knowledge and truth. The philosophical method is rational inquiry, whereby logic, reasoned argument and theory are used to inquire into issues such as the nature of truth, whether or not God exists and the nature of science. Philosophy, as love of wisdom and truth, reflects the idea that the quest for knowledge and truth are undertaken for their own sake (for the 'love of') rather than for any obvious purpose.

Psychology developed out of philosophy, and because of this a number of philosophical debates remain of central importance to this day. These are debates concerned with free will and determinism, heredity and environment, holism and reductionism, idiographic and nomothetic approaches, and psychology as science. In this chapter these debates are considered in detail.

16.2 Free will and determinism

The free will–determinism debate revolves around whether or not people are free to choose how to think and behave or whether behaviour is determined and caused by factors outside of an individual's control. There are two extreme positions. First, that all thought and behaviour results from a person's free will with each person having complete freedom to control what he or she thinks or does. In a sense, the person determines, through free choice, his or her thoughts and behaviour. At the other extreme is the position that all human thought and behaviour is determined by forces outside of a person's individual control. These may be biological, environmental or psychic (unconscious).

Figure 16.1 *Just how much freedom to choose how to behave does a person have in certain situations? Here it would appear that behaviour is determined by what the gunman wants the person to do.*

16.2.1 Hard and soft determinism

An extreme or **hard determinism** position states that it should be possible, in principle, to identify all causes of a person's behaviour. As a consequence, this means that all behaviour should be predictable and able to be scientifically analysed. Hard determinism may be defined as follows: 'The view in psychology that all human behaviour is determined by external, environmental forces. The external forces are subject to scientific laws and can be investigated scientifically. This means that all human behaviour can be predicted once the scientific causal laws have been discovered.' However, some determinist psychologists think that such an extreme viewpoint is inappropriate and prefer the idea of 'soft' determinism. William James (1890), one of the founding fathers of psychology, believed that scientific principles should be employed in the study of human behaviour. This implies an extreme determinism position similar to that of sciences such as physics or biology. However, James also recognised that subjective experience is important and that our awareness of thoughts and ability to choose courses of action implies free will. This has been called the **soft determinism** position because it allows both for human behaviour to be determined, and for people to be able to exercise free will at the same time. Soft determinism may be defined as:

> The view in psychology that human behaviour is caused by conscious mental life rather than external, environmental events or situations.

Soft determinism allows for people to have conscious mental control over how they behave. Thus people have free will and are not coerced or forced to behave in certain ways (as shown in Figure 16.1). Hard determinism takes all internal, mental control away from the person and claims that all behaviour is determined by external, situational forces.

Consciousness and self-awareness are often regarded as the key distinguishing features which separate human beings from other animals. In consequence, psychologists are much more likely to apply a hard determinism position to non-human animals, such as rats, dogs, and monkeys, than to human beings.

The free will-determinism debate can be seen as a continuum rather than an either/or debate. Figure 16.2 shows the relative positions of five main approaches to psychology on this continuum. The behaviourist and biological approaches are at the deterministic extreme because they view all human behaviour as determined, either by the external forces of reward and punishment or by biological mechanisms. At the free will end of the continuum is the humanistic approach, which claims that people have the freedom to choose how to behave. The cognitive approach is towards the free will end of the spectrum because it allows for conscious mental control of behaviour. The psychoanalytic approach is towards the deterministic end because it claims that conscious thought and behaviour are determined by the unconscious, over which we have no control.

16.2.2 Types of determinism

At least three types of determinism apply to human beings. These are biological, environmental and psychic or mental determinism.

Biological determinism relates to the functioning of the brain, the hormone system and genetics or heritability. It is well established that different parts of the brain govern different behaviours and mental functions. This is what is meant by localisation of function in the brain (see Chapter 2 of *AQA(B) Psychology for AS* by Pennington and McLoughlin, 2008). For example, language is located primarily in the left hemi-

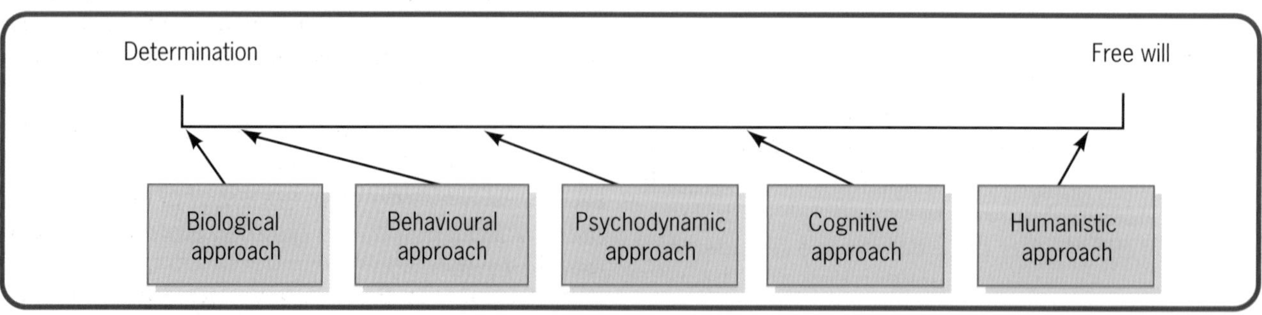

Figure 16.2 *Relative positions of five main approaches to psychology on a free will-determinism continuum.*

sphere, with Broca's area being responsible for speech production, and Wernicke's area for comprehension. The hypothalamus, a small structure in the middle of the brain, is involved in aggression and sex drive. Damage to Broca's or Wernicke's areas will affect language function, and no amount of willing or free will can restore speech production to normal if Broca's area is damaged. Similarly, an overactive hypothalamus may cause increased aggression or heightened sexual feelings. The individual may try to exert free will to control these feelings, but may not be completely successful. Hess (1957) found that when he stimulated certain areas of a cat's hypothalamus it behaved aggressively. By contrast, Vergnes (1975) has shown that another part of the brain, the amygdala, when stimulated, inhibits aggressive behaviour. Thus the brain does determine our behaviour, and disorders of the brain may result in uncontrollable effects, no matter how much we may try to exert our will.

Figure 16.3 *These twins are identical and have exactly the same genetic make-up. Genes determine physical characteristics. Genes may also play a key role in determining psychological characteristics such as personality and intelligence.*

Our genes are increasingly regarded by scientists as determining many aspects of human behaviour, personality and individual differences. Identical twins, who have exactly the same genetic make-up, have been found to have similar personality characteristics and levels of intelligence (see Chapter 2 of *AQA(B) Psychology for AS* by Pennington and McLoughlin, 2008).

Environmental determinism is most strongly associated with the radical behaviourist view put forward by Skinner and Watson (see Chapter 10), which states that all behaviour is under the control of just two features in the external environment: reinforcement and punishment. Environmental determinism is also a position that some social psychologists subscribe to. For example, Milgram's studies of obedience (1963), Zimbardo's (1969) prison study and Asch's (1955) line study on conformity all demonstrate the determining influence of external social forces (other people).

Psychic determinism is best represented by Sigmund Freud's theory of the causes of our conscious thought and behaviour. Freud regarded all thought and behaviour to come from the unconscious, and to be ultimately determined by two instincts: the sex (life) and aggression (death) instincts. Freud also regarded all behaviour as being **overdetermined**, meaning that each behaviour has multiple causes and that to understand the behaviour the numerous causes need to be identified. For example, Freud (1900) regarded all dreams as meaningful psychic events, caused by events of the previous day and unconscious childhood repressions (see Chapter 13).

16.2.3 Free will, determinism and other key concepts

The concepts of free will and determinism need to be considered in relation to the key concepts of personal responsibility, fatalism and fear of freedom.

Free will and personal responsibility

The free will position is not, at the extreme, a practical, ethical or morally acceptable position. For example, just because you do not like somebody does not allow you to go out and hit them or even murder them. Wanting to be rich does not allow you to exercise your free will and steal from a bank. Living in society and engaging in relationships (friendships, intimacy or work-related) brings with it certain responsibilities which limit a person's freedom to act and choose what to do. Of course, these responsibilities may not limit what you fantasise about!

The limits on individual freedom are dramatically highlighted in Luke Rhinehart's (1999) classic novel *The Dice Man*. In this book the main character decides (exercises his free will) to conduct his life according to the roll of a dice. He creates behaviours for each of the six numbers, rolls the dice, and then carries out the behaviour according to the number that comes up. Over a period of time, the Dice Man attaches more and more extreme behaviours to the numbers on the dice and ends up behaving in extreme, and illegal, antisocial ways.

Humanistic psychologists (see Chapter 14) subscribe to a free will view, yet also recognise that personal responsibility rightly constrains the extent to which free will can influence behaviour.

Determinism and fatalism

Fatalism is the idea that all human behaviour (and thought) is predetermined and that attempting to change things is futile. A hard determinism position supports a position of fatalism. Being fatalistic may mean that a person does not bother to consider options or influence outcomes, passively submitting to whatever fate has in store. Astrology is often seen as representing a fatalist position: the configuration of the stars and planets at birth determines your personality and events in your life. A soft determinism position does not support fatalism; neither of course, does the view that we have free will.

Fear of freedom

Erich Fromm, a psychoanalyst with humanistic sympathies, saw western society as causing an internal conflict for the person between freedom and helplessness. Fromm (1941) viewed people as moral beings who had to balance freedom of will with the constraints and requirements of modern society. Fromm (1941) saw this conflict as healthy and one that people deal with all the time. An unhealthy resolution of the conflict between freedom and moral obligation to society is the renunciation of personal freedom. Personal freedom may be relinquished to authority, destructiveness (of self or others) and what Fromm called **automation conformity** (blindly following others). These ways of relinquishing personal freedom led Fromm to analyse how people became alienated and detached from society. Fromm does not really fit into a position on the free will–determinism debate, since he talks about free will in the context of morality. Hence, the forces constraining behaviour are internal, rather than external to the person.

16.2.4 Science and causal explanations

The scientific approach (see Section 16.6) seeks to establish laws and theories in order to predict future events. In psychology, for example, the behaviourist approach claims that future behaviour can be predicted from knowledge of rewards and punishments experienced in the past. For example, knowing that someone has been rewarded in the past for doing charity work allows the behaviourist to predict that the person will continue to devote time to charity. Thus science attempts to establish causal explanations for behaviour based on a scientific approach, in this case linking rewards for past behaviour to predictions about future behaviour.

As another example of causal explanations, consider the idea of the extrovert personality. An extrovert person is outgoing and sociable, with good interpersonal skills. Suppose you have a friend called John who is an extrovert. Imagine John at a party, working on a project with four or five other students and at job interview. In all these situations you can imagine John to be talkative, friendly and energetic. Using the general personality characteristic of extroversion has allowed for a causal explanation of John's behaviour (see Figure 16.4).

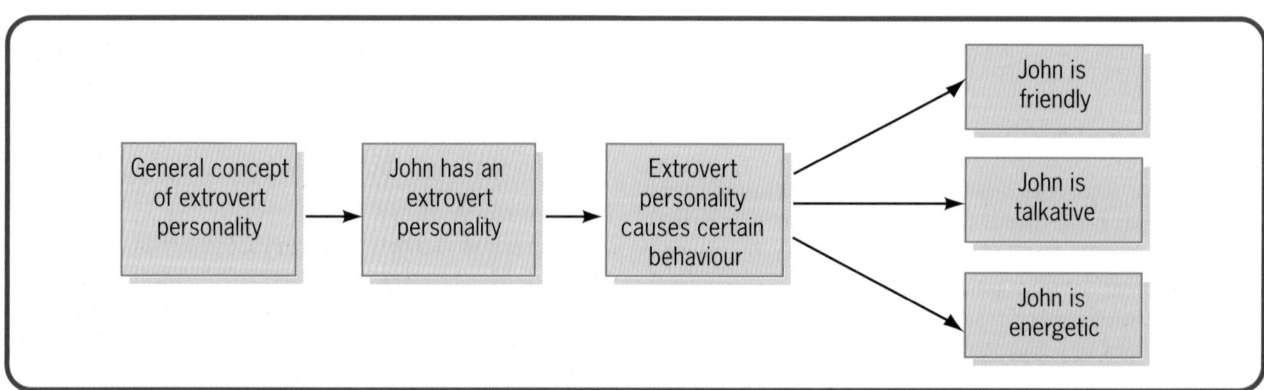

Figure 16.4 *Causal explanation of specific behaviours such as being friendly, talkative and energetic using the general personality concept of extroversion.*

16.3 The nature–nurture debate

The debate over whether **nature** (heredity) is more or less important than **nurture** (environment) in determining psychological characteristics, such as intelligence and personality, is of fundamental importance in psychology. As with the free will–determinism debate, the nature–nurture debate can be traced back to the philosophical roots of psychology. The French philosopher René Descartes (1596–1650) believed in what is called a **nativism** view. Nativism, or innatism, states that certain human characteristics are innate (result from nature or heredity). Descartes even claimed that some aspects of knowledge – for example, knowledge of God – are also innate. In the sixteenth and seventeenth centuries, the science of genetics and the idea of genes being passed from generation to generation did not exist. Hence to claim that human characteristics and types of knowledge were innate meant that these were simply part of being human and did not need any explanation.

At the other end of the philosophical spectrum is the nurture (environmentalism) or **empiricist** viewpoint. Philosophers such as John Locke (1632–1704), David Hume (1711–76) and John Stuart Mill (1806–73) proposed an empiricist position, stating that all knowledge comes from experience. Translated into the discipline of psychology, the empiricist view is that human characteristics (thought, behaviour, personality, etc.) result from social and other environmental forces that influence a person throughout their life.

Philosophically, therefore, two extreme positions can be seen. The extreme view of the empiricists is that the mind is like a **tabula rasa** or blank sheet on which experience is written. At the other extreme, all human characteristics result from genetic influences or the product of heredity. Research shows the truth to lie somewhere in between the two extremes; the **interactionist** position proposes that **both** nature and nurture are necessary to understand and explain human characteristics and behaviour. The challenge, then, is to show the relative contribution of both nature (genetics) and nurture (environment) to human psychological characteristics.

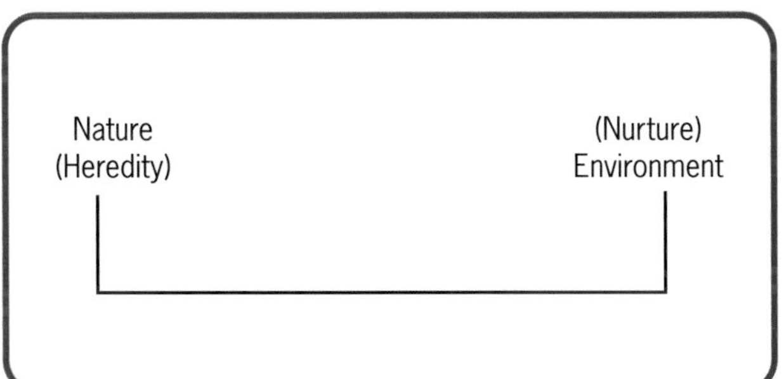

Figure 16.5 *The nature–nurture debate can be seen as two extreme positions. The reality is that both are needed to explain human psychological characteristics. The debate is about the relative importance or contribution of each.*

At this point you may find it useful to read Chapter 2 of *AQA(B) Psychology for AS* by Pennington and McLoughlin (2008). A summary of some of the key points covered at AS level is given below. Following this, we will move on to consider other types of human behaviour from a nature–nurture perspective, and take a more detailed look at the nature–nurture debate.

16.3.1 Heredity and environment

Heredity

The **heritability coefficient** provides a numerical figure, from 0 to 1.0, representing the extent to which a characteristic is genetic in origin. A value of 1.0 means that the trait or characteristic is determined totally by genetics, and a value of zero that genetics play no role at all and the environment is the sole determinant. Plomin *et al.* (1997) have shown that personality characteristics such as neuroticism and assertiveness have a heritability coefficient between 0.15 and 0.50, meaning that **both** genetics and environment play a role, thus representing the interactionist position.

The most common way of attempting to establish the contribution of nature and nurture is by using twin studies. Monozygotic or identical twins share exactly the same genetic make-up. Dizygotic or fraternal twins share 50% of genes, just like ordinary brothers and sisters. The degree of similarity (physical and/or psychological) between monozygotic compared to dizygotic twins is often taken as an indication of genetic influence. Twin studies of intelligence, temperament and schizophrenia have demonstrated clear genetic influence in each case (Gottesman, 1991; Sternberg and Grigorenko, 1997). However, knowing a characteristic has a genetic base tells us nothing about how environmental experience might modify the genetic potential. For example, height is a highly heritable characteristic, with a coefficient typically of around 0.9. However, the average height of Europeans and North Americans has increased by over 5 centimetres between 1920 and 1970 (van Wieringen, 1978).

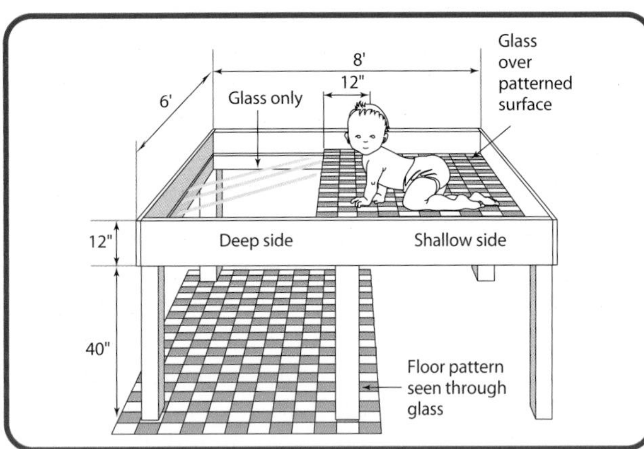

Figure 16.6 *The visual cliff used by Gibson and Walk (1960) in their classic laboratory demonstration of innate depth perception in young infants.*

This increase in height is due to environmental factors, such as diet, and not genetic factors.

Perception of depth in young infants has also been shown to be strongly influenced by nature. Gibson and Walk (1960) demonstrated that infants have an innate perception of depth in a laboratory experiment using a **visual cliff** (see Figure 16.6). Here, infants who had just begun to crawl and had no previous experience of falling off a flat surface into a deep space would crawl to the 'edge' of the cliff, but not onto the clear glass which gives the perception of a deep hole.

Evaluation

- Estimates of the heritability of intelligence are almost solely based on how people score on IQ tests. The use of standard tests of intelligence may only capture certain aspects of human intelligence. Also, practice at these tests improves performance, thus falsely indicating a higher level of intelligence compared to those who have never completed an intelligence test (Gould, 1981).

Environment

Twins have been used to assess the relative contribution of heredity and environment in psychological research for over 100 years. Identical twins reared together are assumed to share the same environment. However, this is a crude generalisation that does not take account of what is shared in a family environment between identical twins, fraternal twins and brothers and sisters, and what is not shared and unique. Plomin (1996) makes a distinction between **shared** and **non-shared environments.** It is the non-shared environments – that is, those environmental experiences unique to each sibling or each twin in the family – that explain differences between genetically related individuals. For example, research has shown that identical twins reared together in the same family environment yield a correlation coefficient of 0.86 for IQ, demonstrating a high degree of similarity (Henderson, 1982). However, this is not a perfect correlation, a coefficient of 1.0 is needed; hence identical twins also show differences in intelligence as well. Plomin (1996) argues that the relatively small differences in intelligence between identical twins are due to the unique experiences gained from each respective twin's non-shared environment. Essentially, two people cannot experience exactly the same environment as they grow from baby to toddler to teenager to adult.

16.3.2 Interactionist approach

The following three examples will demonstrate how nature and nurture interact and how both are vital to understanding and explaining human behaviour.

Phenylketonuria (PKU) is a rare genetic disorder in which the body is unable to convert phenylalanine (found in dairy products) into tyrosine. Without treatment, phenylalanine builds up in the blood and causes severe learning difficulties. PKU results from the inheritance of a recessive gene from each parent. If detected early enough, the young child can be given a low-phenylalanine diet, preventing any damage to intelligence and learning ability.

Chomsky's (1965) theory of **language acquisition** claimed that each person is born with an innate (genetic) potential to acquire language, with a brain that has evolved to become specialised for language. He stated that the ease with which each child learns a language, in whichever country or type of language, is evidence for a **language acquisition device** present at birth (nature or heredity). The particular language we learn and the fluency with which we command that language is due to environment (nurture).

Sexual motivation and behaviour is another example of the interaction of nature and nurture. Sexual motivation in humans is under hormonal control (nature).

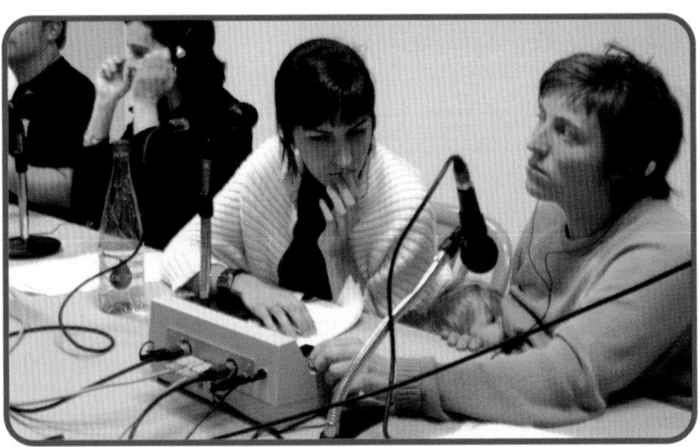

Figure 16.7 *The acquisition of language is an interaction between heredity and environment. Chomsky claims that all people are born with a language acquisition device. Which language we learn depends on nurture or the culture we are brought up in.*

Evaluation

- Psychologists no longer talk about whether or not heredity or environment explain human characteristics and behaviour. Instead, research is aimed at attempting to assess the relative contribution of nature and nature. Psychologists look to identify factors which can modify human characteristics and how enriched environmental experiences can help to realise the innate potential of many human traits.
- Some psychologists claim that nature accounts for 80% of many human characteristics, such as intelligence, personality, schizophrenia, whilst other psychologists claim it is the other way round, with nature only accounting for 20% and nurture 80% in the debate.

However, the release of hormones to create sexual arousal in men and women is often due to environmental factors such as clothing, smells from perfume and romantic music (nurture). In non-human animals, the sexual response results predominantly from nature, and is instinctual and almost 'automatic'.

The six different approaches that we have looked at in Chapters 9 to 14 can be placed between the two extremes of nature and nurture, as shown in Figure 16.8. The biological approach occupies the most extreme nature position, as you would expect, because of its focus on genetics and physical structures such as the brain and the hormone system. The traditional behaviourist approach of classical and operant conditioning occupies, the most extreme nurture position because this approach assumes that all human behaviour is learned as a result of rewards and punishments experienced. The psychodynamic approach claims that the basic inherited instincts of life (sex) and death are at the root of all human behaviour and thought. Cognitive psychology is placed – towards the middle on the nature–nurture debate because of the present interest in cognitive-neuropsychology and the interaction between emotions (nature) and thought (nurture).

16.4 Holism and reductionism

The holism–reductionism debate in psychology has important implications both for the nature of theories developed about human thought and behaviour, and the methods used for investigation. First we need to define each term.

16.4.1 Holism

Holism is the view that: 'to understand a person the whole person has to be considered and that a person cannot be broken down into different parts. Holism says that the whole is greater than the sum of the parts'.

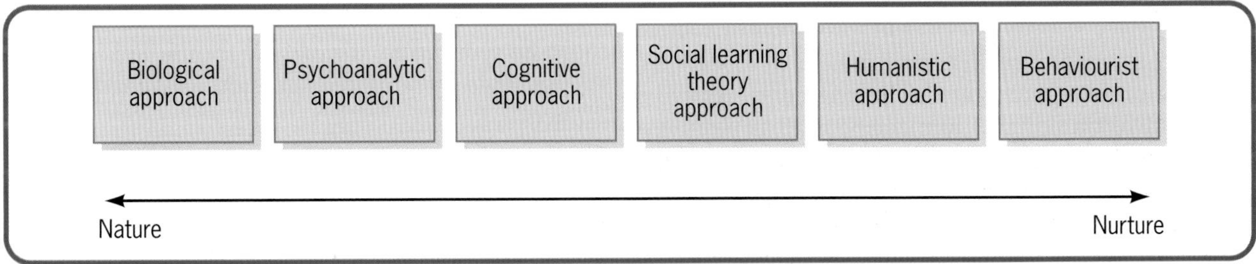

Figure 16.8 *The relative positions of the six approaches in psychology in the nature–nurture debate.*

In relation to human beings, this means that analysing component parts such as the brain, or specific cognitive processes such as memory, or specific personality traits such as aggression, does not properly capture or do justice to the whole person. Gestalt psychologists summed this up in the phrase 'the whole is greater than the sum of the parts'. Let us consider an everyday physical example such as a watch. A watch is made up of many component parts. However, how all these parts combine to tell the time (the purpose of the watch) is missed when the focus is on any one of the different components. An alien visiting earth would never have seen a wristwatch before, but may be able to understand how each component works. However, this would not tell the alien what the watch is for.

Figure 16.9 *Analysing the different parts of the watch will not tell you what the watch does.*

Gestalt psychologists stated that psychological phenomena need to be understood as a whole. The German word *gestalt* means something like a whole, single form. The phrase that 'the whole is greater than the sum of the parts' reflects the holistic approach. For example, Köhler (1929) applied the principles of gestalt psychology to problem solving in animals, such as cats and chimpanzees. Köhler argued that animal problem solving could not always be reduced to automatic responses to stimuli (the behaviourist view) or to elementary sensations. Instead, problems are often solved through **insight learning**, where new ways of solving a problem are created. This related to creativity and creative thinking in humans. Gestalt psychology lacked rigorous experimental approaches, but did influence the development of cognitive psychology.

16.4.2 Reductionism

Reductionism is the opposite view to holism, that: 'to understand human beings, psychologists must analyse and reduce the whole person into the simplest and smallest component parts'. To understand human consciousness, for example, consciousness should be reduced to component psychological parts. These, in turn, can be reduced to physical operations in the brain, which can then be reduced to the simplest parts – neurons (see Figure 16.10).

Reductionism was frequently debated in the mid-twentieth century in relation to sciences such as physics and biology. However, the debate over whether whole organisms or psychological characteristics could be meaningfully reduced to the simplest component parts dates back to the development of biology in the nineteenth century. Then it was thought that an organism could be reduced to a set of organs, such as the heart, brain, lungs, which in turn could be reduced to individual cells. Individual cells could then be reduced further to the cell wall and the cell nucleus. This is shown in Figure 16.11.

In a similar way, physics, especially with the discovery of atoms at the beginning of the twentieth century, reduced matter to component atomic particles. Modern physics reduces atoms to subatomic particles. The success science has enjoyed by adopting a reductionist approach was seized upon by early psychologists and adopted as a model to apply to human thought and behaviour, and animal behaviour. The reductionist approach of sciences such as physics and biology was highly influential in the development of psychology. For example, in the late 1800s, Wundt used introspection in the first psychology laboratory attempting to reduce experiences to component parts. The structuralist school of psychology, developed in North America after Wundt, was highly influential for many years, and reductionism influenced the development of the radical behaviourism of Watson and Skinner (see Chapter 10). For the behaviourists, reductionism meant that all human and animal behaviour could be reduced to stimulus–response links that are strengthened by reinforcement and weakened by punishment.

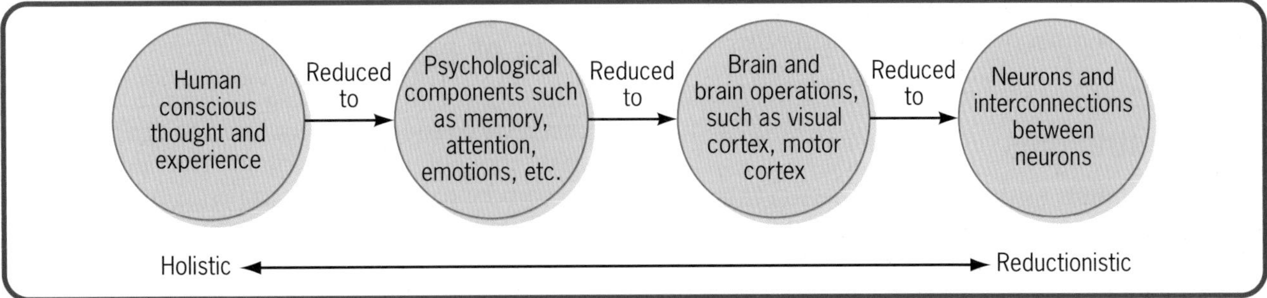

Figure 16.10 *The reductionist approach to understanding and explaining human consciousness. The reductionist approach is to reduce complexity to the very simplest and most basic components, in this case, neurons in the brain.*

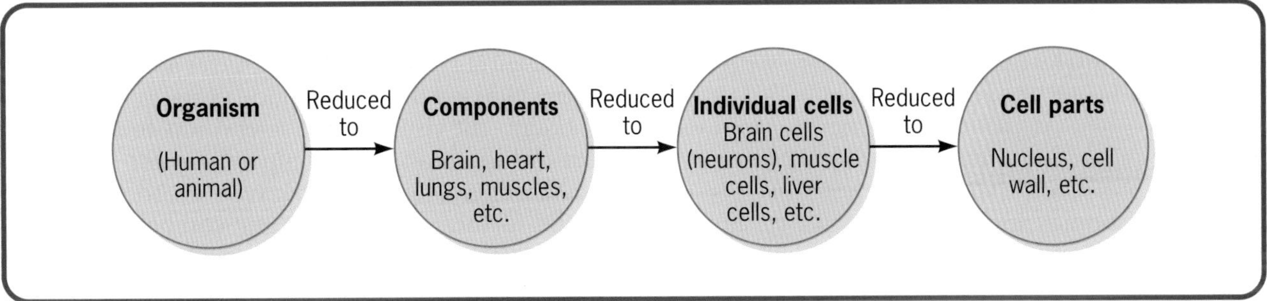

Figure 16.11 *Reductionist approach in biology to understanding organisms such as human and non-human animals.*

Reductionism and structuralism

Edward Titchener (1867–1927) developed what is known as a **structuralist approach** to the study of human consciousness. Titchener (1910) believed that all conscious experience could be reduced to elementary components or sensations. He stated that the subject matter of psychology is conscious experience and used a method of self-observation which he called *systematic experimental introspection*. This involved using highly trained psychologists to discover the 'actions of the mind'. Titchener stated that psychology had three general issues to explore:

1 To reduce conscious experience to the elementary components.

2 To discover the laws by which these elementary components come together to create consciousness.

3 To relate these elementary components to physiological and neural processes in the senses and nervous system.

Clearly this is reductionism, whereby the general state of human consciousness is reduced first to elementary sensations and then to physiological operations. Titchener's structuralist approach was influential for 20 years in the early twentieth century. However, it soon became apparent that an almost infinite number of elementary sensations could be produced. Also, the approach had little practical value outside the laboratory and introspectionist techniques are subjective. Titchener later recognised that structuralism did not help to understand thought processes; he stopped referring to mental elements or atoms and adopted a more holistic approach towards understanding human consciousness.

16.4.3 Strengths and limitations

Reductionism: strengths

- The reductionist approach in psychology has brought with it both an analytic and scientific way of attempting to understand and explain human and other animal behaviour.
- Scientific investigation of component parts, such as human memory, allows for empirical investigation and theory to be investigated and tested.
- The reductionist approach demonstrates how

important biology is for understanding and explaining human behaviour, especially the role of genes in thought and behaviour.

Holism: strengths

- Holism reminds us that the whole person is not just the sum of numerous component parts, but an entity to be considered in its own right.
- Holism seeks to integrate the different components, – for example, memory and consciousness – in order to understand the person as a whole.
- The holistic approach underpins the humanistic approach in psychology (see Chapter 14), which has introduced holistic therapies, helping people to develop themselves and cope with everyday psychological problems.

Reductionism: limitations

- The reductionist approach may lead to an over-simplistic view of human behaviour and mental functioning.
- Many different theories of aspects of human behaviour and thought have been developed and empirically investigated – for example, theories of memory, perception and language. However, little attempt is made to combine the various theories to provide a general theory of cognitive functioning as a whole.
- Some physicists (*Capra*, 1975) argue that a reductionist approach, in both physics and psychology, suffers from an infinite regress – that is, that one can go on reducing component parts to more basic and even more basic parts ad infinitum (endlessly).

Holism: limitations

- Holistic approaches in psychology do not generally lend themselves to scientific inquiry and empirical testing.
- The holistic approach tends to neglect the importance of biological explanations, especially the role of genes in human behaviour and mental disorders such as schizophrenia.
- The holistic approach has tended to shun the findings of scientific psychology. As a consequence, holism is seen as different from a scientific approach.

16.4.4 Interactionist approach: levels of explanation

Reductionism and holism can be seen to be interactionist if we consider different levels of explanation for human thought and behaviour. The idea that the whole can be reduced to its simplest component parts – that is, reductionism – when applied to human psychology, results in a number of different levels of explanation, as shown in Figure 16.12. The highest, most holistic level is the societal/political/sociological context of the individual. At the next level is a social-psychological level which reflects interactions and relationships between individuals. Below this is the psychological level of cognitive processes – personality, motivation and so on. At the next level are physical and physiological systems such as muscles and the nervous system. Next are the physiological units such as parts of the brain – the visual cortex, cerebellum, frontal cortex. Next are the individual component parts – neurons and the interconnections between neurons. Neurons can be further reduced to their component parts – axon, cell body, dendrites – which in turn can be reduced to molecules and then atoms.

Evaluation

- In this section we have considered the approaches of early psychologists, such as structuralism and gestalt psychology, and their positions with respect to holism and reductionism. Then, as now, psychologists generally adopt either a holistic or reductionist viewpoint. For example, the experimental and laboratory approach reflects a reductionist position. Qualitative methods and the experiential approaches of humanistic psychologists reflect a holistic position.

- With advancements in the identification of individual genes for different types of behaviour and psychological disorders, the reductionist approach is currently enjoying great favour and success. Perhaps a return to a more holistic view will dominate again in the future. There is no right or wrong in the holism–reductionism debate. It is a philosophical view on how best to think about a person and how best to conduct psychological inquiry.

Within each level it is possible to see how both a holistic and a reductionist approach apply. For example, at the social-psychological level of explanation, different components of social psychology can be investigated within a reductionist approach (interpersonal skills, social influence, etc). At the same time, the holistic view of the person as a social being can also be considered. To understand a person fully it may be useful to adopt both reductionist and holistic approaches.

16.5 Idiographic and nomothetic approaches

The idiographic and nomothetic approaches in psychology are often regarded as representing opposing and conflicting positions about how best to study people, especially intelligence and personality. However, the two may be seen as complementary, with both necessary to gain a fuller understanding of human beings. Allport (1937) introduced the idiographic and nomothetic distinction into psychology, borrowing the terms from a philosopher called Windelband (1894). Windelband distinguished between natural sciences and moral sciences, arguing that the humanities, social science and psychology are moral sciences.

16.5.1 The idiographic approach

The **idiographic approach** focuses on: 'the individual and recognises the uniqueness of the person in terms of their experiences, feelings, developmental history, aspirations and motivations in life, and the values and moral code by which they live'. The word idiograph comes from the Greek word *idios*, meaning 'own' or 'private'. Hence, the idiographic approach in psychology is concerned with the private, subjective and unique aspects of a person and employs methods of inquiry which provide information about subjective experiences. Most commonly, the idiographic approach is characterised by qualitative methods of investigation (see Chapter 17 in this book, and Chapter 4 of *AQA(B) Psychology for AS* by Pennington and McLoughlin, 2008). Qualitative methods include unstructured interviews, case studies, self-report measures, introspection and reflection, and the psychoanalytic techniques of free association and dream analysis (see Chapter 13). The idiographic approach is holistic and places great value on the individual's conscious experiences. The humanistic perspective in psychology perhaps best exemplifies the

	Level of explanation	Descriptions
Holistic ↑	Societal, political, sociological	Context in which a person lives and cultural context.
	Social psychological	Interactions and relationships between people.
	Psychological	Cognitive processes, emotions, motives, personality. Aspects internal to the person.
	Physical and physiological systems	Muscles, organs, skeleton, central and peripheral nervous system.
	Physiological units	Parts of the brain such as the visual cortex, frontal lobes, cerebellum.
↓ Reductionist	Basic physiological components	Neurons and interconnections between neurons.

Figure 16.12 *Levels of explanation of human beings: from holistic to reductionist levels.*

idiographic approach. However, Freudian psychoanalysis can also be said to adopt an idiographic approach. Traditionally, an idiographic approach has been regarded as non-scientific, although this is not really the case. Scientific principles can be applied to study the uniqueness of individuals, and the norms and rules by which a specific person operates can be identified.

16.5.2 The nomothetic approach

The **nomothetic approach** in psychology focuses on: 'similarities between people and attempts to establish general laws of behaviour and thought that can be applied to large populations of people, or indeed to all people'. The word nomothetic comes from the Greek word *nomos*, meaning 'law'. Hence, the nomothetic approach is most closely aligned with the scientific approach in psychology (see Section 16.6). This means that use is made of scientific methods of investigation, particularly experiments, to test hypotheses that are derived from theories about human behaviour and thought. The nomothetic approach adopts a reductionist viewpoint, placing great value on objectivity and replication. The behaviourist, cognitive and biological perspectives best exemplify the nomothetic approach. However, Freudian theory also attempts to establish laws or rules about human beings – for example, the psychosexual stages and the Oedipus complex. Freud believed these were applicable to all and the theory is nomothetic in this respect. However, Freud did not use the scientific method to test or find evidence for his theoretical claims.

16.5.3 Discussion of idiographic and nomothetic approaches

Traditionally, the idiographic and nomothetic approaches are seen as conflicting, with the implication that as a psychologist you can only operate from one of these positions – that is, a psychologist is either highly scientific, using laboratory experiments to test theories about people on the basis of hard evidence and empirical support for hypotheses – or not scientific and employs a range of methods, many subjective, to explore the uniqueness of the individual and his or her experience.

Cronbach (1957) identified this potential source of conflict between psychologists about how best to study the nature of what it is to be human. If the psychologist seeks to develop theories that apply to large populations then the nomothetic approach is preferable. If, however, the psychologist is interested in the uniqueness of a person, then the idiographic approach is the one to adopt.

In personality theory (see Pennington, 2003), both the nomothetic and idiographic approaches are used by different psychologists. Trait theories of personality, which look at individual traits, tend to adopt a nomothetic approach, as do behaviourist approaches to personality. In contrast, humanistic and certain aspects of psychoanalytic theories adopt a more idiographic approach. Whilst idiographic and nomothetic approaches are commonly seen as quite different, with individual psychologists in one camp or the other, it is

Approach	Key aspects
Idiographic	• recognises the uniqueness of the person • concerned with private, subjective and conscious experiences of the person • uses qualitative methods of investigation • exemplified by humanistic aspects of psychoanalytic approaches
Nomothetic	• attempts to establish laws and generalisations about people • concerned with objective knowledge through the use of scientific methods • uses quantitative methods of investigation • exemplified by trait approaches to personality, behaviourism and cognitive psychology

Figure 16.13 *Distinguishing features of the idiographic and nomothetic approaches in psychology.*

also possible to see how the two may interact and complement each other.

Evaluation

- The idiographic and nomothetic approaches are often seen as determining the methods psychologists use. Crudely, the idiographic approach employs qualitative methods and the nomothetic approach employs quantitative methods. This has consequences for the focus of research: either the unique, subjective aspects are of central interest (idiographic): or, the similarities between people and the laws that govern behaviour (nomothetic).
- In contemporary psychology, the idiographic–nomothetic debate is still an important distinction. Attempts have been made to bring the two approaches together in an interactionist model (Bandura, 1986), but no influential solution has been found.

16.5.4 Strengths and limitations

Idiographic: strengths

- The idiographic approach focuses on the subjective experiences of the person making the individual feeling valued and unique. Each person is valued as an individual rather than seen as one amongst many.
- The idiographic approach provides detailed psychohistories and attempts to understand the many influences on how they come to be as they are.
- Humanistic psychology uses an idiographic approach to enable people to develop to their full potential.

Idiographic: limitations

- It is difficult to generalise from detailed subjective knowledge about one person.
- The idiographic approach is often regarded as non-scientific, as subjective experience cannot be empirically tested.
- The idiographic approach largely neglects biological, especially genetic, influences.

Nomothetic: strengths

- The nomothetic approach has helped psychology to become scientific by developing laws and theories of human behaviour that can be empirically tested.
- The nomothetic approach attempts to determine laws and common characteristics for all people or large groups of people in a culture.
- The nomothetic approach helps to combine biological and social aspects of a person.

Nomothetic: limitations

- The focus on general laws and theories neglects the subjective and unique experiences of the person.
- The extensive use of controlled laboratory experiments means that there is a problem of generalisation to everyday life.
- The nomothetic approach overemphasises the similarities and underplays individual differences.

16.6 Psychology as science

We live in a constantly changing scientific and technological world, with cars, computers, drug treatments and many other benefits of scientific endeavour. The changes in the world and people's lives over the past 100 years have been far greater than the changes that took place over the previous 1,000 years. Many psychologists adopt a scientific approach to the study of human beings and other animals, in the belief that the degree of understanding, prediction and control enjoyed in physical sciences will also become a feature of psychology. Not all psychologists agree with applying scientific procedures to the study of people, as we have seen with the humanistic approach. Nevertheless, the scientific approach is dominant in modern psychology and an obvious feature of the cognitive approach, which is probably the dominant research area in present-day psychology.

16.6.1 The scientific approach

The word science comes from the Latin word *scienta*, meaning 'knowledge', and until the seventeenth century, science and philosophy were regarded as a single enterprise. This changed with the British empiricist philosophers – John Locke (1632–1704), David Hume (1711–76) and John Stuart Mill (1806–73) – who advocated an **empirical approach** to knowledge. Empiricists believed that the only source of knowledge was that received through our senses – sight, hearing, smell, taste and so on. This contrasted with the existing view that knowledge could be gained solely through the powers of reason and logical argument. Thus empiricism is the view that all knowledge is based on, or may be derived from, experience. This important change helped reject prevailing superstitions (for example, belief in witchcraft and demonic possession) and irrational beliefs. The empirical approach of gaining knowledge through experience became the scientific approach, greatly influencing the development of physics and chemistry in the seventeenth and eighteenth centuries. The idea that knowledge should be gained through experience (empirically) turned into a method of inquiry involving careful observation and experimentation to gather facts and evidence. By the late nineteenth century, psychology was adopting an empirical and scientific approach, with the first psychology laboratory being established by Wilhelm Wundt in 1879.

The subject matter of conscious experience that Wundt tried to examine in his laboratory was not really amenable to scientific methods. However, the novel and controversial idea of adopting scientific methods of inquiry in psychology was important, although nowadays it is viewed as a normal and necessary part of psychology.

Five main reasons why psychologists look to the scientific approach

1 The scientific study of human and animal behaviour and mental processes will provide greater understanding and knowledge at a theoretical level.

2 Evidence and facts gathered through scientific procedures are objective and can be used to support a theory or hypothetical statement.

3 Applications of a scientific approach to the study of people will bring benefits to people's lives and help them to adjust better to change and cope with trauma in their lives.

4 Scientific procedures used by one psychologist can be replicated by other psychologists.

5 The study of human beings is inherently interesting and fascinating in its own right.

Psychology and common sense

In some ways everybody is a psychologist; to successfully adjust to the demands, changes and traumas of life, people must operate as 'informal' or 'intuitive' psychologists (Heider, 1958). In short, people have common-sense views of themselves, the world and other people. These views come from personal experience, through socialisation, from cultural or subcultural beliefs and other sources. People have common-sense views about the causes of behaviour, about personality, about moral codes and how to raise children and so on.

This common-sense knowledge is gathered in a haphazard, anecdotal and non-scientific way and is often based on a single experience or observation. Racial or religious prejudices may reflect what seems like common sense within a group of people. However, prejudicial beliefs rarely reflect reality, even though they are notoriously difficult to change (Rokeach,

Figure 16.14 *Empiricism helped to get rid of superstitious beliefs by stating that knowledge should be gained through observation and scientific method.*

1960), especially when they reflect the culture in which a person has been raised.

Common sense, then, is an essential element of life. But because it is not based on systematic knowledge, or derived from scientific inquiry, it can be misleading and erroneous. Common sense has also been called **folk psychology**. Folk psychology is the beliefs, values, attitudes and morals that are held by a culture or subculture.

There are examples of psychology influencing and changing common-sense views. Perhaps the most influential has been Sigmund Freud, as indicated by the following quotation from an authority on Freud:

> Freud is often linked with Darwin and Marx as being one of the three original thinkers who have most altered man's view of himself in the twentieth century (Storr, 2002: 145).

Whilst there is debate about the scientific status of Freudian theory, there is little doubt that many Freudian concepts have entered everyday language. People commonly and regularly use words such as 'defensiveness', 'repression' and 'unconscious' when making common-sense interpretations of their own and other people's behaviour. These are all terms which Freud introduced to psychology.

Common sense, then, is something which everybody uses in their day-to-day life to guide decisions and influence interactions. Humanistic psychologists advocate that people should trust their intuition and common sense more, but in the context of having positive regard for other people. Psychology can therefore be seen to be split over the value and reliability of common sense. Scientific psychologists are sceptical about its value, and humanistic psychologists more positive about its worth and the trust that should be placed on common sense.

Commonsense psychology is not scientific. In what follows we look at different aspects of the nature of science and how it applies to psychology. The nature of scientific inquiry may be thought of at two levels:

- to do with theory and the derivation of hypotheses
- to do with the actual empirical methods of inquiry.

We will consider these in a later section of this chapter. Next we turn to consider the concept of **paradigms** in psychology and the criteria by which we can judge whether or not psychology is a science.

16.6.2 Paradigms

Is psychology a science? This simple question does not have a straightforward or simple answer. A number of different answers can be given, depending on which of the many different views of the philosophy of science is taken. It is generally agreed that a science consists of:

- agreement over the subject matter to be studied
- theories and hypotheses
- empirical, objective methods of data collection.

Thomas Kuhn (1970), a famous philosopher of science, characterised science as consisting of a unified and agreed-upon subject matter which constitutes what he calls a **paradigm**. A paradigm may be defined 'as a set of theoretical assumptions that are agreed upon by scientists. These assumptions provide a means of making sense of the world in which we live'.

Consider the science of astronomy. Astronomers adopt a model of the universe as an infinite space with millions of galaxies and stars, and the earth as a planet revolving around the sun. In ancient times, the earth was thought to be at the centre of the universe. This is a different model than the one adopted by modern astronomers. The metaphors used by astronomers liken planets and stars to spheres occupying different positions in the universe. The methods of scientific inquiry are objective observation using sophisticated telescopes and other devices. Astronomy, therefore, is a science and adopts a paradigm with agreed theory and research methods. An example of a paradigm in physics is Newton's laws of mechanics and electromagnetism.

How does psychology conform to this picture? The existence of the different approaches in psychology – psychodynamic, 'socal learning', behaviourist, cognitive, biological and humanistic – means that there is no agreement over general theoretical assumptions or methods. Different approaches adopt different models of human beings: the psychoanalytic model sees people suffering constant unconscious conflicts and driven by instincts, the behaviourist model sees people as machines responding to stimuli, and the humanistic model sees people as free to control their lives. Neither is there agreement over the methods adopted by the various approaches. The behaviourist method of

> **A paradigm in science – the three main factors**
>
> - A set of theoretical assumptions that provide a model of the world or object of study.
> - A set of metaphors that compare the object of study in a simple, understandable way.
> - A set of methods for empirical inquiry agreed upon by scientists working within the paradigm.

inquiry is experimental, whereas the method of inquiry in psychoanalysis is the case study.

Considering the five approaches in relation to the description of a paradigm, it is evident that there are few general assumptions in common. Also, that different approaches foster different methods of inquiry. Whilst each approach might qualify as a paradigm in its own right, this would not reflect what Kuhn meant by a paradigm. Kuhn (1970) did not regard psychology to be a mature science, but a **pre-science** without a dominant paradigm. In a pre-science there are numerous theoretical approaches, each with its own distinctive set of research methods. To become a mature science, Kuhn argued, would require the coming together of the different approaches into a paradigm. Psychology would need to have a set of shared general assumptions and agreement about the methods of empirical inquiry.

Whilst the cognitive approach is dominant in modern psychology, and therefore might be seen as the dominant paradigm, the other, very different, approaches of psychoanalysis and humanistic psychology remain important influences. Within each different approach, progress occurs through greater theoretical sophistication and rigorous and accepted methods of inquiry. It may be, therefore, that because of the very different ways in which human beings can be thought of, psychology cannot achieve the status of a mature science as defined by Kuhn. Nevertheless, psychology does adopt scientific methods in the form of theories, hypothesis testing and the collection of evidence, to achieve greater understanding of people and to make applications to help solve human problems.

Figure 16.15 *The psychoanalytic model of the person is one of unconscious conflict arising from id instincts.*

16.6.3 The role of theory, hypothesis testing, methods, replication and generalisation

The role of theory and hypothesis testing

A theory may be defined as:

> a set of propositions which provides principles of analysis or explanation of a subject matter (Mautner, 2000: 563).

Thus, the propositions that all people have an innate desire to fulfil their potential or that all men are naturally aggressive could be called theories. It should also be possible to generate a number of hypotheses from a theory, which can then be tested through empirical research. A hypothesis is a conjecture or premise that is tentatively proposed, requiring empirical inquiry to determine whether it is false or supported by evidence. Hence, from the proposition that men are aggressive, a number of hypotheses can be derived. For example, a man barred from a nightclub may pick a fight with the doorman; or, when shouted at by someone, he will fight rather than argue. Many more hypotheses can be generated from this theoretical statement.

Hypotheses can then be tested using scientific procedures or methods. The empirical findings may either support the hypothesis or refute it. If the former, the theory will be maintained. If the latter, the theory will not have been supported. However, whether the theory is rejected or maintained will depend on findings from testing other hypotheses derived from the theory (see Figure 16.16).

Karl Popper (1963) argued that for a theory to be classed as scientific it must, in principle, be capable of **falsification.** Popper argued that falsification had to be the criterion for science, rather than attempting to prove a theory to be true. As noted above, the findings of empirical research may support a hypothesis, providing support for the theory. However, we cannot say that a theory is true because a future hypothesis derived from the theory may not be supported. This would result in the theory being rejected. Hence, for Popper, a scientific theory is one that allows hypotheses to be derived and be capable of falsification. Theories that receive empirical support will be maintained. Theories that suffer many refutations will be rejected.

Consider the psychoanalytic and behaviourist approaches. It is clear that behaviourism does make testable hypotheses and produces objective evidence to support or refute the hypotheses, but it has often been argued that Freudian theory does not produce testable hypotheses. Kline (1984) has challenged this assertion and shown that testable hypotheses, can be drawn from Freudian theory. The problem is that whatever the findings, Freudian theory can offer an explanation and hence not be refuted. For example, consider the following hypothesis:

People with an anal personality will be miserly.

If it were found that some people were not, we would normally say the hypothesis has been refuted. However, a Freudian might argue that non-miserly people with an anal personality use the defence mechanism of reaction formation to turn a trait into its opposite. Thus non-miserly people do really possess an anal personality just like miserly people! Freudian explanations of behaviour typically fall into this pattern; as a consequence, it is difficult to see how Freudian theory can be seen to be scientific in the way Popper describes a scientific theory.

If we accept that for a theory to be classed as scientific it must produce hypotheses which are capable of being refuted, the question arises as to how a scientific theory is developed in the first place. Just how do scientists create or make up a theory?

Figure 16.17 shows the commonly held view concerning the development of a scientific theory. This depicts scientists first making careful observations of their object of study and then noticing some kind of regularity amongst these observations. This leads to the development of one or more hypotheses. These hypotheses are then confirmed by means of experiments or other scientific methods of inquiry. The hypotheses are then turned into a theory or scientific law. This is called the **inductive method** of scientific reasoning. Induction goes from the specific (observations about the world) to the general (theories and laws). However, philosophers of science such as Feyerabend (1975) have argued that science does not typically progress in such an orderly way and that human imagination and creativity have also to be taken into account. Feyerabend argues against seeing science and theory development as conforming to a prescribed order, and uses the phrase 'anything goes'. By this he means that science often progresses through adopting any methods, scientific or otherwise, and that creativity, insight and intuition play an

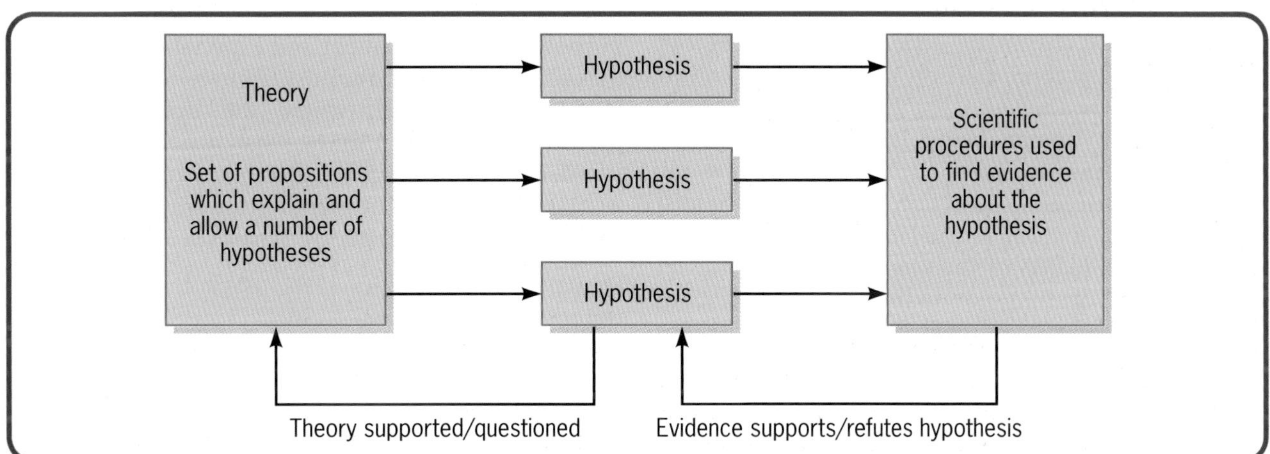

Figure 16.16 *The scientific method of using a theory to derive hypotheses which are then tested using scientific methods of inquiry. Evidence may support or refute a hypothesis, which in turn helps evaluate the value of the theory.*

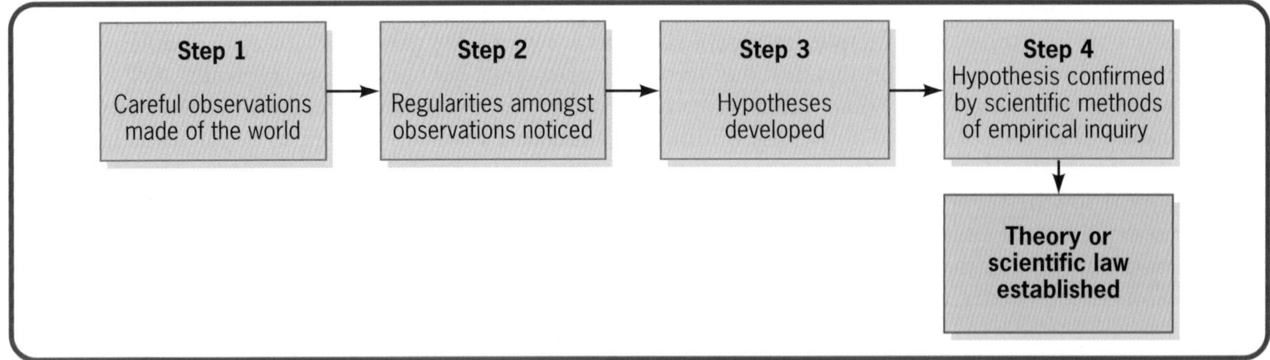

Figure 16.17 *Traditional or commonly held view of how a theory or a law is developed.*

important role in the development of scientific theories. In many ways, and because of the radically different perspectives and range of methods employed in psychology, Feyerabend's extreme views do seem to reflect what goes on in psychology. For example, what factors do you think might influence what type of psychologist a person decides to be in his or her academic career? Why do people who study the same or similar undergraduate degree in psychology – as approved by the British Psychological Society – prefer cognitive psychology or psychoanalysis or biological psychology?

Methods in psychology

The main method of inquiry in science is the experiment. The key features of the experiment are:

- control over variables (independent, dependent and extraneous)
- careful objective measurement
- establishing cause–effect relationships.

In physics and chemistry, experiments carried out under laboratory conditions provide objective knowledge that can be applied to the real world. In physics and chemistry, human beings as scientists conduct their experiments on inert matter. There is not, in any meaningful sense, any interaction between the scientist and the object of study in the laboratory experiment. The views and beliefs of the scientist do not interact with the object of study, nor do they affect or influence the outcome of the experiment. The scientist is said to be objective and not able to influence or bias the outcome of the experiment. This ideal position in sciences such as physics and chemistry does not, unfortunately, hold up that well in psychology.

A number of problems exist when psychologists attempt to adopt scientific methods of study, most notably the laboratory experiment, in the study of human beings. The two we shall consider here are those of **experimenter bias** and **demand characteristics** of the experimental situation.

Experimenter bias (Rosenthal, 1966) occurs when the beliefs, wishes, attitudes and even mere presence of the psychologist affect the experiment, or more precisely the participants (human or animal) taking part in the experiment.

Perhaps the best-known experiment demonstrating experimenter bias is that of *Pygmalion in the Classroom* by Rosenthal and Jacobson (1968). Teachers' expectations of their pupils were manipulated; they were told that one group of children would be likely to do well over the school year. Another group of children had no predictions made about them. One year later, intelligence tests showed that the expectations of the teachers came true. In fact, the two groups of children were randomly formed and with no known differences between the two groups. This has become known as a **self-fulfilling prophecy**.

Experimenter bias, in the form of knowledge about the purpose of the experiment and expectations, can affect the outcome. One way round this is to conduct the experiment **double blind**, where the experimenter or psychologist does not know what hypothesis is being tested. However, even in a double-blind study, the general attitude (friendly or unfriendly) towards a participant may influence how the person behaves in the experiment.

Demand characteristics of the psychology experiment were identified by Orne (1962). Orne said that it was wrong to regard the participant in the psychology experiment as passively responding to environmental stimuli and experimental changes. Instead, the participant plays an active role, trying to guess what the experiment is about and trying to respond in ways the participant thinks the psychologist desires. The participant may also try to guess the hypothesis (note that many research participants are psychology students)

STUDY

Aim

Rosenthal and Fode (1963) set out to see whether experimenter expectations could affect the results in an animal experiment.

Method

Researchers were told to train rats to run through a maze. The rats' performance on the maze was timed. One group of researchers were told their rats were specially bred to run round a maze fast (called 'maze bright' rats). The other group was told that their rats were specially bred to be slow ('maze dull' rats). In reality, both groups of rats were the same and had not been bred for any special maze running ability.

Results

At the end of the training period, the rats belonging to the researchers who had been told their rats were 'bright' ran faster times than the rats in the 'dull' group.

Conclusion

Researcher expectation can affect the outcome of research.

and behave in ways supporting the hypothesis. The above assumes that the participant wants to be helpful and please the psychologist, which is not always the case; sometimes participants may be deliberately unhelpful. Either way, this means that the measures taken and the findings may have little validity.

Consideration of experimenter bias and demand characteristics illustrates major differences between experiments in sciences, such as physics and chemistry, and experiments in psychology (see Figure 16.18).The important point to make is that there are limitations on adopting a scientific approach in psychology. These

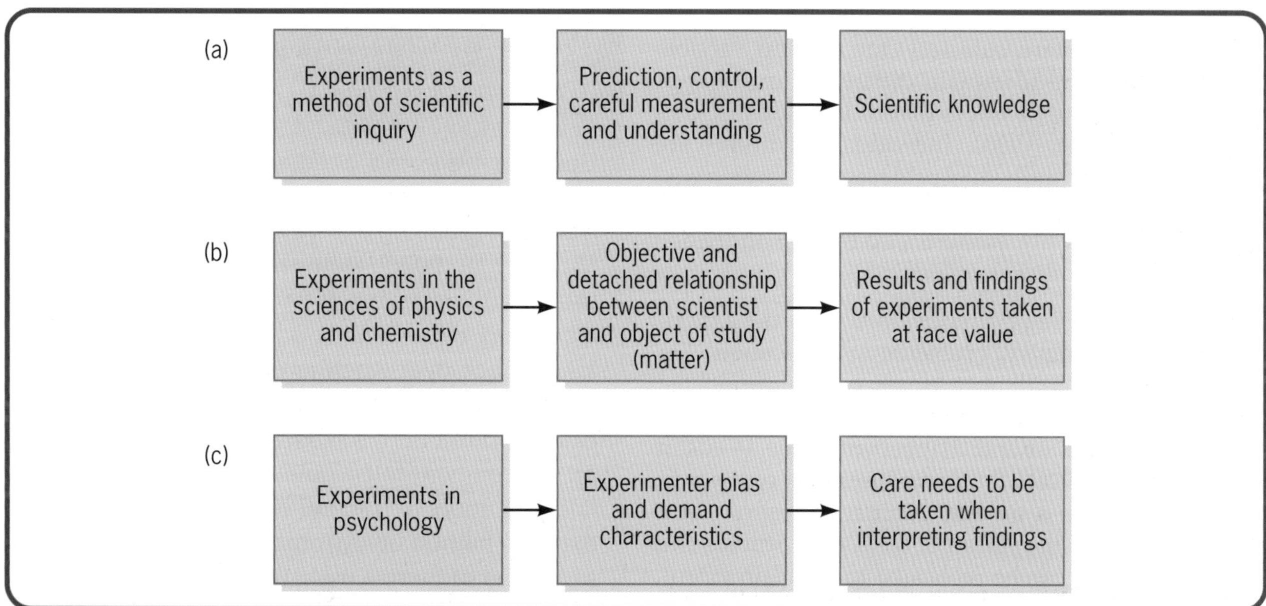

Figure 16.18 *Simplified view of the scientific method of the experiment (**a**), and how it translates in sciences such as chemistry and physics (**b**), and psychology as science (**c**).*

limitations need to be taken into account and considered in relation to any experiment using people as participants.

Replication

In psychology, **replication** is most often discussed in reference to laboratory experiments, but may apply to other empirical methods. For findings to be considered scientific, it must be *verifiable* by other psychologists. This means that other psychologists must be able to copy the original experiment, using the same methods and procedures, and producing the same results or similar patterns of data as in the original experiment. A psychology experiment is replicable to the extent that the method, procedure, materials used and method of gaining of participants are clearly and precisely described. This description may appear in a research journal in psychology or may be obtained directly from the psychologist who carried out the original experiment.

In principle, an experiment in psychology should be able to be replicated anywhere in the world and at any time. This is the criteria used in physics and chemistry. However, in psychology there is a limit to the extent to which this principle can be realised. One problem is the culture. Much of the experimental research in psychology has taken place in western cultures such as in North America and Europe. Smith and Harris Bond (1999) review psychological research conducted in numerous cultures, and show that quite different results are often obtained from replicating the same experiment in eastern cultures. One cultural variable that has been used to explain differences in findings from the same experiment is that of individualist-collectivist (Hofstede, 1980). Individualist cultures are those which value individual achievement. Collectivist cultures are where the welfare of the group is of greater importance. Typically, western cultures are individualist and eastern cultures collectivist.

Methods of gathering evidence, other than the experiment, present different problems of replication. For example, a case study on a single person conducted over a number of years is simply not replicable because each person is unique and changes with time. Whilst it is possible to replicate the procedures of a case study, each case study is a unique, qualitative analysis of a person over a specific period of time. Field studies and field experiments can be replicated to a certain extent, but the controlled conditions of the psychology laboratory cannot easily be translated to research undertaken in real-life settings.

Generalisation

For theories and findings from empirical research to be of value, it should be possible to generalise from a small or limited sample to a population as a whole. Generalisation is an important issue in psychology and occurs in three ways as set out in the boxes below:

Generalisation of results from an empirical study using a small or limited sample of people to a large population of people

With respect to generalisation from a sample of people in a study to the whole population, psychologists try ensure that the sample represents the population, taking account of factors such as age, social class, intelligence and level of education. However, it is often impossible to represent the many different factors that characterise a population in the sample; the psychologist should try to identify the most important factors in relation to the research being undertaken and ensure these are represented in the sample.

Generalisation of findings from a laboratory experiment to life in the 'real world'

Consider Milgram's obedience research and Asch's conformity research (see Chapter 5 of *AQA(B) Psychology for AS* by Pennington and McLoughlin, 2008). Both these psychologists produced controversial findings from laboratory experiments, and debates have taken place over whether or not people would behave in similar ways in their everyday lives. Some argue that the laboratory is too artificial an environment to be able to say that such findings apply to the real world. Others cite extreme human behaviours, such as historical examples of human massacres and 'ethnic cleansing' of one group by another group, to argue that Milgram's and Asch's findings do apply to real-life behaviour.

Generalisation of findings about one culture to other, different cultures

Since most research in psychology has been conducted in modern, western culture (North America, Australia and Europe, including the UK), it is questionable whether findings from this research should be generalised to other cultures, such as Chinese or Indian cultures. A major distinction is made in cross-cultural psychology (Smith and Harris Bond, 1999) between cultures that value individual achievement (typically western cultures) and cultures that value collective achievement (typically eastern cultures). It may not be wise to generalise from western individualist cultures to collectivist cultures.

This issue does not arise in the sciences of chemistry and physics since inert matter is the same all over the world and on different planets. However, since people are the subject matter of psychology, and people are much more varied and much less predictable, there will always be debate about generalisation of research findings in psychology.

16.6.4 Overt behaviour and private experience

Traditionally, a distinction is made between that which is observable as being amenable to the scientific approach, and that which is not observable as subjective and therefore not open to scientific inquiry. This distinction represents, on the one hand, the view of radical behaviourists who state that only that which can be objectively observed – overt behaviour – should be the object of scientific study. On the other hand, humanistic psychologists place great value on private or subjective experience and are less concerned with adopting the methods of science to study people. Generally, it is too simplistic to regard overt or observable behaviour as the domain of scientific psychology, and private experience as too subjective to be of scientific value.

Cognitive psychology attempts to investigate consciousness and thought processes such as memory and attention scientifically. These cognitive processes certainly constitute part of what we might call our private and conscious experiences of ourselves and the world around us. However, this does not seem to fully capture what we intuitively mean by the term **private experience**.

Figure 16.19 *Can a person's private experience be studied scientifically?*

In part, the areas of study of cognitive psychology neglect some essential elements of private experience. For example, William James (1890), a founding father of psychology, talked about a 'stream of consciousness'. By this he meant the second-by-second awareness we have of the world from our various senses. My stream of consciousness as I look out of the window across a Cornish harbour whilst I write this book is unique and private to me. Not only that, it is not repeatable, although I can try to recapture the sensations and feelings if I look out of the window again. Private experience as our stream of consciousness in this sense would not seem to be amenable to scientific psychology. I can try to report on my stream of consciousness by verbalising as much as I can, but this would only capture a small part of my second-to-second awareness.

Introspectionists, such as Wundt and Titchener, tried to bring scientific procedures to the study of private experience. In the end they failed because of the subjective nature of the data produced (verbal reports), and because there was no objective way of resolving disagreements between two or more people over subjective reports of the same external event (for example, how you think and feel in response to hearing a clock tick).

Ayer (1959), an influential philosopher, makes three distinctions about the sense in which mental events may be considered to be private: first, introspective reports provide the only possible evidence for mental states; second, each person has privileged and sole access to their private experiences; third, introspective reports on private experiences are subjective.

What this seems to indicate is that private experiences as reported through introspection are too subjective to allow scientific study. In contrast, overt behaviour, or behavioural (largely verbal) responses reflecting cognitive processes (as used by cognitive psychologists) are objective, and hence amenable to the scientific approach.

16.6.5 Peer review and research

One of the most important ways in which the findings of research in psychology are communicated to other psychologists, and anyone else who is interested, is through publication in research journals. The British Psychological Society (BPS) publishes 11 research journals that represent key specialist areas in psychology. These include the *British Journal of Psychology*, *British Journal of Social Psychology*, *British Journal of Clinical Psychology* and *British Journal of Developmental Psychology*. Other countries and psychology societies also publish research journals. For example, in the USA, the American Psychological Association (APA) publishes the prestigious *Journal of Personality and Social Psychology*. These journals contain a number of different reports on psychological research by different psychologists. The way in which research reports or articles appear in these journals is through a process called **peer review**.

The process of peer review of an article that a psychologist (or group of psychologists) wishes to publish in a journal is as follows:

- The psychology researcher(s) submit their article or report on their research to the editor of the journal in which they would like their research to be published.
- The editor of the journal sends the article for review to two or three psychologists who have published their own research in a similar area to that of the article submitted for publication.
- Each psychologist reviewing the article writes an independent report on it, with recommendations for improvement, stating whether or not it should be accepted for publication.
- The psychologists reviewing the article consider the adequacy of literature review, justification for the research hypotheses to be tested, adequacy of methods and statistical analysis, and whether or not the conclusions are justified by the findings. The theoretical and applied importance of the research is also evaluated.
- If the article is recommended for publication by the reviewers then it is accepted, usually with a requirement that certain amendments are made, as suggested by the reviewers. If the article is not recommended for publication in the journal it is rejected by the editor.

The time lag between acceptance of an article for publication and it appearing in the journal varies from journal to journal, but is typically one to two years. The peer review process is regarded as the most objective way for research findings to be published in journals and for the research to be communicated to anyone who is interested to read the article. This is also one of the key ways in which research evidence about a particular topic accumulates and greatly helps to generalise findings from a number of different research reports from samples to the population as a whole.

The peer review process outlined above is also used for evaluating and awarding research grants by bodies such as the Medical Research Council (MRC) and the Welcome Trust. Costed research projects are submitted by research psychologists in universities. Independent peer evaluation takes place to decide whether or not to award funding for the proposed research project.

16.6.6 Strengths and limitations of the scientific approach

Strengths

- The scientific approach is objective, with research providing accurate measurement.
- Scientific methods are replicable, so that results should be repeatable if the same procedures are used.
- The results of scientific inquiry are reliable and often generalisable to large groups or populations of people.
- The scientific approach produces theories about human thought and behaviour which allow for testable hypotheses to be derived. Theories stand or fall on the extent to which data and evidence support or refute hypotheses. The application of a scientific approach has meant that psychology has developed better and stronger theories, and advanced as a science.
- Scientific psychology has enjoyed a range of applications in areas such as health psychology, atypical psychology and criminological psychology, which

are all strongly based on a scientific approach. For example, therapies to help people with psychological disorders or cope with stress may be based on objective findings. This also allows their effectiveness to be properly assessed.

Limitations

- The scientific approach tends to view people more as machines, adopting a deterministic view of human thought and behaviour, looking for cause and effect in every aspect of human life. In consequence, the scientific approach fosters a view of people as predictable, controllable and reducible to laws and regularities of behaviour.
- The scientific approach adopts a reductionist view, assuming that complex behaviour and thought can be reduced to basic, simple, component parts. This scientific 'model' of human beings seems to take away some essential aspect of what we consider people to be about. Humanistic psychologists would say that the person should be considered as a whole.
- Many of the empirical methods of inquiry, especially the laboratory experiment in psychology, create artificial situations. This results in a lack of ecological validity and problems with attempting to generalise findings beyond the testing situation.
- The scientific approach as seen in human experimental psychology may bring with it experimenter bias and demand characteristics that do not present such problems in sciences such as physics.
- Another limitation is to do with ethical constraints that professional bodies, such as the BPS and the APA, place upon psychological research. It is entirely right that psychological research should conform to strict ethical guidelines, but it does mean that research which might be of scientific interest, simply (and rightly) cannot be undertaken using people as participants. In sciences such as physics and chemistry, ethical constraints still operate (for example, testing of nuclear bombs in the atmosphere), but the constraints are fewer. It may seem odd to cite ethical guidelines as a limitation of the scientific approach in psychology. However, it is important to be aware of both the vital importance of ethical guidelines for conducting scientific research, and the limitations ethical guidelines place on research conducted on people.

Further Reading

Introductory texts

Bell, A. (2002) *Debates in Psychology,* Chapters 2, 3, 4 and 6, Hove: Taylor & Francis.

Gross, R. (1999) *Themes, Issues and Debates in Psychology,* Chapters 3, 5, 12 and 13, London: Hodder & Stoughton.

Specialist sources

Chalmers, A.F. (1976) *What Is This Thing Called Science?,* Milton Keynes: The Open University Press.

Graham, G. (1993) *Philosophy of Mind: An Introduction,* Oxford: Blackwell Publishers.

Hospers, J. (1997) *An Introduction to Philosophical Analysis,* 4th edn., Chapters 5 and 6, London: Routledge.

Schultz, D.P. and Schultz, S.E. (2000) *A History of Modern Psychology,* 7th edn., Fort Worth, TX: Harcourt College Publishers.

Valentine, E.R. (1992) *Conceptual Issues in Psychology,* 2nd edn., Chapters 1 and 7, London: Routledge.

Methods in psychology

Chapter 17

17.1 Inferential statistics

Inferential statistical tests are used by psychologists (and other researchers) to determine the likelihood that an observed effect is due to chance. By 'observed effect' we mean a difference between two sets of scores, an association between variables or a correlation.

17.1.1 Probability and levels of significance

Consider the offer of a free holiday (all expenses paid) to Hawaii. Unfortunately there is a slight catch to the offer because the return journey might involve a fatal plane crash in which no passengers survive. With the initial offer there is only a 50% chance of safe return, but even at these odds a desperate person might go for it. What if the probability of a safe return is increased? Rather surprisingly, a 90% guarantee of a safe return is often good enough to tempt many students. At the other end of the risk-taking scale are the super-cautious students who will not accept anything less than a 100% guaranteed safe return!

We can and do estimate probabilities in real life – for example, we calculate the likelihood of rain when we decide what to wear in the morning. Although we don't normally quantify our everyday estimates of probability, they can be expressed as percentages. Such estimates can also be expressed as more than (>) x% or less than (<) x%. Consider the following and estimate the percentage likelihood in each case:

- the probability there is chewing gum stuck under the desk you are sitting at
- the probability you will get a text message during the next lesson
- the probability that you will have twins
- the probability you will get a B grade for your next homework
- the probability of finding £10,000 under your seat in the cinema
- the probability that you will take off your shoes before you get into bed tonight.

In psychological research it is important to think about probability because there is always a possibility that any research finding may have occurred by chance. This will become clear if we consider the data in Figure 17.1 and what it indicates about panic episodes in male and female phobia sufferers.

Twenty patients suffering from phobias were asked to record their experiences of panic episodes over the period of one week. Ten patients were female and the other ten were male.

If we look at the means and the raw scores in Figure 17.1 we can see that female phobia patients experience more panic episodes on average than male phobia patients. But, on closer inspection, we can see that there are some males who have more panic episodes than some of the females. We need to determine whether there is a real difference between males and females here or whether the difference in the means is due to chance. To do this, psychologists employ inferential statistical tests which determine the extent to which an observed effect is due to chance (see 17.2.3 for the tests).

Levels of significance

All statistical tests employ a significance level. This is the level at which the researcher decides whether to reject the H0 (the null hypothesis) and accept the H1

Number of panic episodes	
Females	Males
6	5
3	4
7	3
2	4
10	5
3	4
6	1
8	6
7	5
3	6
Mean 5.5	Mean 4.3
SD 2.64	SD 1.49

Figure 17.1 *Table to show the number of panic episodes experienced by female and male phobia sufferers in a week.*

(the experimental or research hypothesis), or vice versa.

Levels of significance can be expressed as decimals or percentages. The usual level of significance used in psychology is .05 or 5%.

Percentages	Decimal equivalent
5%	.05
10%	.10
1%	.01
2.5%	.025
0.1%	.001

Probability

Probability is the key to hypothesis testing.

If the probability of the observed effect being due to chance (p) is equal to or less than .05 (≤.05) then we reject the H0 and accept the H1.

If the probability of the observed effect being due to chance (p) is greater than .05 (>.05) then we accept the H0 and reject the H1.

At the 5% level of significance there is a 5% probability that the observed effect is due to chance, and a 95% probability it is due to the manipulation of the IV.

Depending on the circumstances, researchers may need to be more than 95% certain that their results are not due to chance. This would typically happen where the outcome of research could have far-reaching consequences. For example, in drug research it is important to know that an improved recovery rate is really due to a new drug and is very unlikely to have occurred simply by chance. In these circumstances researchers might decide to use a more stringent level of significance (e.g. 1% or 0.01). At the 1% level of significance there is a 1% probability that the observed effect is due to chance and a 99% probability the effect is due to the research manipulation.

Referring to some levels as more **stringent** than others when discussing different levels of significance avoids the problem of talking about 'high' and 'low' levels, which can lead to real confusion. If a researcher is really stringent it means he or she wants to eliminate as much chance as possible from the interpretation of the findings.

The usual way of expressing probability levels is shown below:

Statistical Notation	In English this means
$p < .05$	the probability of the effect being due to chance is less than 5%
$p > .05$	the probability of the effect being due to chance is more than 5%
$p = .05$	the probability of the effect being due to chance is exactly 5%
$p \leq .01$	the probability of the effect being due to chance is equal to or less than 1%
$p > .01$	the probability of the effect being due to chance is more than 1%
$p = .01$	the probability of the effect being due to chance is exactly 1%

Psychologists normally use the .05 level of significance in their research, but for every investigation they conduct they have to consider the implications of accepting the findings as due to the IV when, really, the effect is due to chance factors.

The following situations illustrate the issues involved in statistical interpretation.

Scenario 1

An occupational psychologist has devised a new incentive scheme for supermarket employees. The scheme requires considerable extra funding and is therefore quite expensive. After a year, performance data from a sample of stores using the new scheme are compared with data from a matched sample of stores where the old scheme is still in operation. Using the 0.05 level of significance, the psychologist concludes that the new scheme has significantly improved the performance compared to the old scheme. In this context the word 'significantly' has a special meaning – that is, that the difference in the performance scores is unlikely to have occurred by chance.

In interpreting the findings, the supermarket owners will need to consider that the researcher used the 0.05 level of significance. This means that they can be 95% certain that the improved performance is due to the new incentive scheme, in which case they may decide to adopt the scheme at all their stores. However, they should also be aware that there is a 5% chance that the difference in performance is not due to the new incentive scheme at all. Maybe they would like to be rather more certain of the scheme's effectiveness before they decide to adopt it in all their stores.

Scenario 2

Patients suing Dunsmore Hospital Trust for compensation argue that the Trust is to blame for infections that they suffered following their treatment at the hospital. The Hospital Trust's lawyers argue that the number of patients affected is not sufficient to say that the hospital is to blame and insist that these infections could have occurred by chance. Both sides refer to the data in Figure 17.2 to support their argument.

From the figures in the table it seems as if the risk of infection is much greater at Dunsmore than at the control hospitals. However, the hospital requires very strong evidence that the infections are definitely due to hospital treatment and not just due to chance, because the consequences of accepting responsibility in this case would be enormous. Hospital lawyers will insist that any research into the cause of infection involves the use of a very stringent level of significance (for example, 0.01 or even 0.001). On the other hand, Dunsmore patients who are seeking compensation would be happy to use a much less stringent level of significance. They would be quite content for researchers to use the 0.05 level in this case.

17.1.2 Hypothesis testing

Null and alternative hypotheses

Ideas for research usually arise from existing theory or from reading about studies that other researchers have carried out. Some investigations are focused on validating a psychological theory, either to support the theory or to refute it. Other investigations are carried out for applied purposes, enabling psychologists to make some practical contribution to an applied area of psychology like health, occupational or forensic psychology.

Starting from a general aim, a researcher then has to formulate a precise hypothesis. A hypothesis is a testable statement that should clarify exactly what is being tested and make a prediction about the relationship between two variables.

People who own at least one cat will have significantly lower stress scores on a stress questionnaire than people who do not own a cat.

A hypothesis like the one above is known as a **research** or **alternative hypothesis**. If the method used to investigate the hypothesis is experimental, then it would also be called an **experimental hypothesis**. For every research/alternative hypothesis (H1), there is a corresponding **null hypothesis** (H0). The null hypothesis predicts that the expected effect will not occur or that any differences or relationships that have been found

Post-hospitalisation infection	Dunsmore Patients	Control Patients
Yes	150	50
No	350	450

Figure 17.2 *Numbers of patients from Dunsmore Trust and a control hospital reporting infections following a stay in hospital.*

have occurred by chance. In this case, the null hypothesis would state that:

There will be no significant difference in the stress scores on a stress questionnaire between people who own at least one cat and people who do not own a cat.

Figure 17.3 *A hypothesis is a testable statement which predicts a relationship between two variables. Hypothesis: People who own at least one cat will have significantly lower stress scores on a stress questionnaire than people who do not own a cat.*

Note that the null hypothesis is not the opposite of the research hypothesis, but simply states that there will be no difference. Strictly speaking, it is the null hypothesis that is being tested in the research. According to the outcome of the study, the researcher will accept the H0 and reject the H1 (the results show that there is no effect), or reject the H0 and accept the H1 (the results show that there is an effect).

To write a clear, testable hypothesis, the researcher needs to identify the key variables in the research investigation. In the example above, one variable is whether or not the person owns at least one cat, and the other variable is the stress score on the stress questionnaire. This precise definition of exactly how variables will be measured or realised in a study is known as **operationalisation**.

A key feature of the scientific approach (see Chapter 16) is the notion that scientific statements are ones that can be falsified. According to this view, it is possible to disprove a statement or hypothesis, to show it is false, but impossible to prove that it is true. The statement 'All swans are white' is often used to help explain this point. To try to prove that this statement is true is impossible. We could search for years and years, finding millions of white swans, apparently supporting the statement, but it would take just one black swan to be hiding in the bushes for the statement to be untrue. So even though all the swans we have ever seen have been white, there is always the possibility that we might in the future come across a swan that is not white. This means that we can never prove that the statement is true. On the other hand, we would only have to find one swan that was not white to disprove the statement. This basic reasoning explains why we test the null hypothesis in research. As a consequence, where results tally with the alternative hypothesis (H1) it does not mean that we have proved that our H1 is true, but only that we have failed to disprove it.

One-tailed and two-tailed tests

A one-tailed hypothesis is a directional hypothesis that predicts an effect in a particular direction. Note that one-tailed hypotheses always contain a key word such as 'more', 'less', 'higher', or 'lower', which indicates the predicted direction of the effect. Examples of one-tailed hypotheses are given below:

People with a northern accent will be judged to be significantly ***more*** *intelligent than people with a southern accent.*

Left-handers will take significantly ***less*** *time in minutes to solve a spatial problem than right-handers.*

Participants who take a bath in the evening show significantly ***higher*** *relaxation scores than participants who take a shower.*

In correlation studies, which investigate a relationship between two variables rather than a difference between two conditions, the words 'positive' and negative' indicate that the hypothesis is one-tailed because they denote the direction of the expected correlation:

There will be a significant ***positive*** *correlation between time spent in a confined space (in minutes) and anxiety rating score.*

There will be a significant ***negative*** *correlation between number of years' driving experience and scores on a driving theory test.*

A two-tailed or non-directional hypothesis predicts an effect but does not state the direction of the effect. Examples of two-tailed hypotheses are given below:

There will be a significant difference in the time taken by left-handers and right-handers to solve a spatial problem.

There will be a significant correlation between distance travelled to work (in miles) and job satisfaction score.

There will be a significant difference in the number of bottles of sauce packed by workers on a bonus scheme and workers not on a bonus scheme.

When a statistical test is used with a non-directional hypothesis, a two-tailed test is used. When a statistical test is used with a directional hypothesis, a one-tailed test is used. If the 5% level of significance is being used with a non-directional hypothesis, there is double the probability that the differences could occur by chance because the difference could occur in either direction. This is taken into account on the tables used with statistical tests; these tables have separate sections for one-tailed and two-tailed tests. It is important to know before you carry out your analysis whether you are using a one-tailed or a two-tailed hypothesis.

The decision about whether to use a one-tailed or a two-tailed hypothesis depends on previous research. If all or most previous research and theory would lead us to expect that an effect will occur in a particular direction, then a one-tailed hypothesis is appropriate. If the results of previous research are inconsistent, sometimes showing an effect in one direction and sometimes showing an effect in the other direction, or if there is conflicting theory, then a two-tailed hypothesis is preferable.

It is more difficult to achieve significant results with a two-tailed test than it is with a one-tailed test, so you might be tempted to think that a one-tailed test is better. However, if a one-tailed test is used and the results actually go in the opposite direction to that predicted, the research has to be abandoned and a new hypothesis proposed.

17.1.3 Type I and Type II errors

In any statistical interpretation there is always some chance of error. This is because we can never be 100% certain that any observed effect is due to the experimental manipulation. Similarly, we can never be 100% certain that any observed effect is not due to the experimental manipulation.

Type I and Type II errors are statistical errors which occur when there is an incorrect interpretation of results. The concepts of Type I and Type II errors are often difficult to understand because we never know whether we have made this kind of error or not. Nevertheless, it is important to be aware they exist and that they are very important in the interpretation of research findings.

Type I and Type II errors

Type I Error

A Type I error is where the H0 is rejected and the H1 accepted when, in fact, the effect is due to chance. For this reason, a Type I error is sometimes referred to as an **error of optimists**!

The chance of a Type I error occurring is always exactly equivalent to the significance level being used. For example, at the .05 level we are 95% certain the effect is not due to chance; therefore there is at least a 5% probability it is due to chance; thus a 5% probability of a Type I error.

Type II Error

A Type II error is where the H0 is accepted and the H1 rejected when, in fact, there is a real effect but it has not been detected. For this reason, it sometimes referred to as an **error of pessimists**!

A Type II error can happen when a very stringent significance level (e.g. 0.001) is used in research. In such a case, any effect would have to be extremely strong and highly consistent for it to be significant. Using a level like this means the researcher wishes to eliminate as much chance as possible in interpretation of the findings, but it also means that sometimes there may well be an effect which the statistical test will not detect.

Another possible reason for a Type II error is the use of a small sample. If there is a very small sample – for example, only ten participants – each person's score makes such a difference to the overall outcome that a highly consistent effect is quite unlikely. Because statistical tests rely on the strength and consistency of an effect, any inconsistency would mean that a significant result is less likely. However, an insignificant result does not necessarily indicate there has not been an effect. Type II errors are quite likely when using very small samples and should always be considered when interpreting findings.

Using inferential testing and setting a level of significance is all about finding a balance between the possibility of Type I and Type II errors. Using 5% or 0.05 as the conventional level strikes this balance.

	Null hypothesis accepted	Null hypothesis rejected
Null hypothesis is true	Correct	**Type I error** (an optimistic error – the results are really due to chance, but the researcher concludes that there is an effect)
Null hypothesis is false	**Type II error** (a pessimistic error – there is an effect but it has not been detected, so the researcher concludes that there is no effect)	Correct

Figure 17.4 *The meaning of Type I and Type II statistical errors.*

17.1.4 Correlation

Positive, negative and zero correlation

Not all psychological research involves the investigation of differences. Sometimes psychologists look for relationships between two variables – for example, the relationship between height and occupational success score. In a positive correlation, as one variable increases, the other variable also increases. In the example above, this would mean that the taller people are, the more successful they are. In a negative correlation, as one variable increases, the other variable decreases. In the example above, this would mean that the taller people are, the less successful they are. In a zero correlation there is no relationship between the two variables. (See *AQA(B) Psychology for AS* by Pennington and McLoughlin, 2008, for more on correlations.)

Correlations are usually illustrated on a scattergram. The pattern of the points on a scattergram gives us a good indication of the strength and direction of the correlation, but the exact strength of the relationship between the two variables can be assessed more precisely using a statistical test. This will tell us the likelihood of the correlation having occurred by chance. Using the 0.05 level of significance, the correlation would be said to be significant if there is 5% or less probability that the correlation occurred by chance.

Using statistical tests for correlation gives a number known as a **correlation coefficient**. This will always

Figure 17.5 *1st researcher: In a Type I error the researcher concludes that there is an effect when really the effect is due to chance. This is sometimes referred to as 'an error of optimists'. 2nd researcher: In a Type II error the researcher concludes that there is no effect when really there is. This is sometimes referred to as 'an error of pessimists'.*

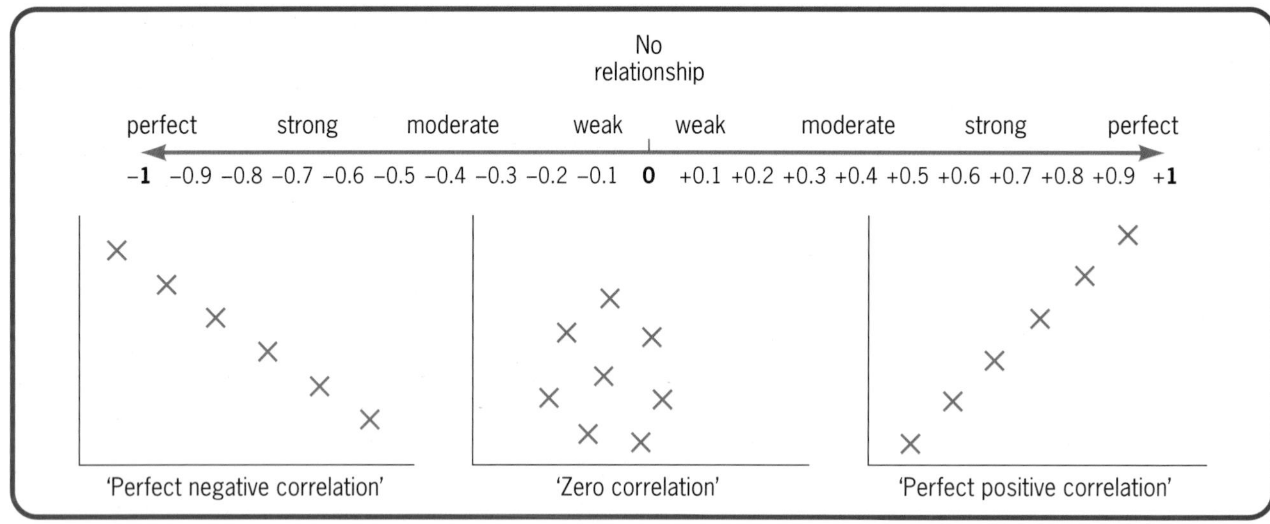

Figure 17.6 *Correlation coefficients will always have a value between −1 and +1.*

have a value somewhere between −1 and +1 (see Figure 17.6), with −1 representing a perfect negative correlation and +1 representing a perfect positive correlation.

Note that the 'positive' and 'negative' signs in front of the correlation coefficients tell us the direction of the relationship and the numerical value tells us about the strength of the relationship. Generally speaking, a correlation coefficient of less than + or – 0.3 would be considered to be fairly weak, but whether or not the correlation is significant depends upon the sample size. With very large samples, even quite low correlation coefficients may be significant.

Evaluation

- Correlations are useful for showing relationships but do not involve manipulation of any variable, so cannot be used to determine cause and effect. Quite often a third variable may be involved in a correlation. For example, if we find that there is a relationship between temperature and ratings of aggression, we might be tempted to say that increases in temperature cause aggression. However, perhaps the aggression is due to a linked factor such as increased consumption of alcohol when the weather is hotter. Remember – CORRELATION DOES NOT IMPLY CAUSATION.

17.1.5 Limitations of sampling techniques

Research involves establishing theories of human behaviour that can then be used to understand and predict how people will behave in different situations. However, although we might want to understand and predict the behaviour of people in general, for practical reasons we can only study a limited number of people. The group of people we study in an investigation is known as the **sample.** The individuals in a sample are known as **participants** because they participate in the research. This limited group is chosen from a larger group of people whose behaviour we are interested in studying. This larger group is known as the **target population.**

Ideally, the characteristics of the sample should reflect the characteristics of the population from which the sample is drawn. This then allows the researcher to **generalise** the findings of the research from the sample to the wider population. Once the target population has been identified, a technique for obtaining a sample must be used.

Limitations of sampling techniques and generalisation of results

All sampling techniques have their strengths and weaknesses, some of which have implications for generalisation of the results to the target population.

Opportunity

Here there is no attempt to ensure that the sample reflects the characteristics of the target population. Participants are selected by the researcher according to their immediate availability, so the sample is often biased; all the participants may be similar to the researcher in terms of age or background. They may even be friends or associates of the researcher and might therefore try to be especially co-operative, helping the researcher in the investigation. For these reasons, although it is frequently used, opportunity sampling is probably the least suitable method of recruiting participants. Where it is used, great caution should be exercised when attempting to generalise findings.

Random

With a small target population, the easiest way to find a random sample is to draw names from a hat. With a larger target population, everyone in the population can be allotted a number, say between 1 and 500. A computer can then be used to generate 40 numbers at random. The people with these 40 numbers would then make up the sample. With a random sample the researcher has no control over who is chosen, so there is no possibility of researcher or selector bias. However, despite the elimination of researcher bias, a randomly selected sample may still not be representative of the target population. Simply by chance it could happen that there are far more males in the sample than females, or a disproportionate number of people from a particular ethnic background.

There are additional problems with a random sample: perhaps not all members of the target population are easily available and some may not be willing to take part. This might mean that the researcher has to compromise and take members of the target population who were not part of the original selection.

Stratified

Although it is quite a time-consuming method of sampling, stratified sampling should lead to a sample that fairly represents the target population, with each subgroup being represented. In practice, however, a stratified sample can still be biased. For example, if researchers require particular demographic characteristics (age, occupation, etc.), participants may be recruited from busy areas such as shopping centres, commercial districts and colleges, where they know there will be lots of people. This would mean that people who do not normally frequent those areas would be under-represented.

Systematic

Here the researcher cannot choose who should be in the sample, so there is no researcher bias. However, the same problem exists as with stratified sampling, in that researchers will tend to recruit participants from specific locations where there will be large numbers of people. This would lead to an under-representation of people who do not normally go to those areas.

Evaluation – sampling issues

- Care should always be taken to make sure the sample fairly reflects the target population.
- **Sampling bias** occurs if a specific section of the target population is over-represented in the sample – for example, if there is a predominance of a specific age group. One way to reduce the chance of sampling bias is to use a large sample. Generally speaking, the larger the sample size, the less risk of bias.
- Reports of psychological research should include detailed description of the sampling procedure and the sample, so that the reader can assess the extent to which generalisation is possible.
- Truly random samples are very rarely possible.

Evaluation – continued

- In longitudinal research that takes place over an extended period, some participants may withdraw from the research (participant attrition). This might result in a sample bias since those that remain may be different in some way from those participants who have withdrawn.
- Care should be taken when using volunteer samples. Participants who proactively offer themselves up for psychological research may not be representative of the target population. For example, parents who respond to an advert for developmental research that is posted on a nursery school noticeboard may have certain characteristics that are not typical of all parents at the nursery.

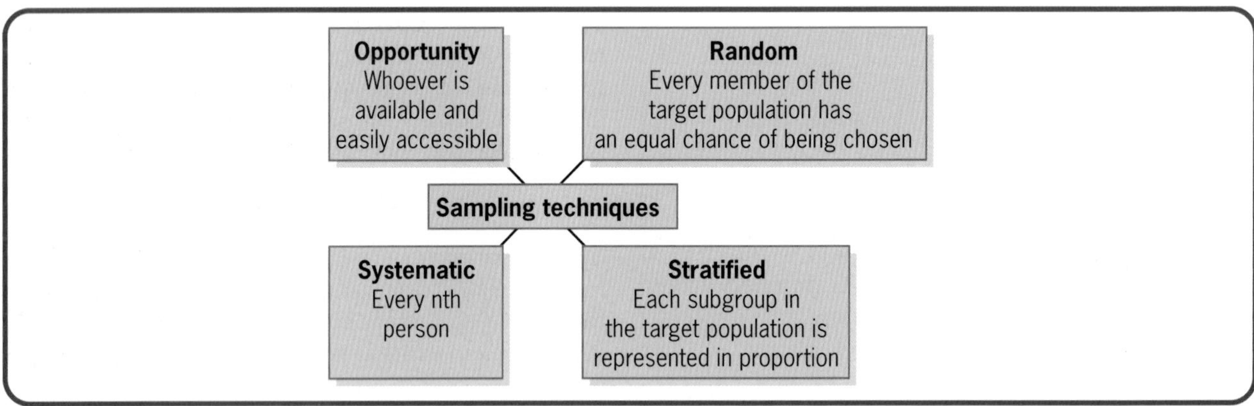

Figure 17.7 *The sampling techniques used by psychologists.*

Generalisation – other issues

The conditions under which research is conducted can also affect generalisability. For example, results obtained from research in a controlled environment such as a psychology laboratory are very difficult to generalise to any other settings. Some research findings are highly time specific. For example, Asch's conformity research in 1951 is often described as a 'child of its times' meaning that the findings were largely a product of social expectations and attitudes that prevailed in the 1950s. This means that care should be taken when generalising results over time. Researchers should also be wary of generalisation across cultures, particularly when studying social behaviours.

17.2 Statistical tests

Statistical tests are used by psychologists to determine the likelihood that any observed effect is due to chance. The outcome of the statistical test is used to decide whether or not the null hypothesis (H0) should be accepted or rejected. There are many different statistical tests for different situations, and nowadays researchers use statistical computer packages which carry out analysis of raw data from a psychological investigation. Using these packages, raw data are inputted into a spreadsheet; the computer carries out the calculations and then interprets the results. Whilst these packages are very useful, especially where there are large amounts of data, it is really important to understand the principles of statistical testing, so here we shall look at some of the tests in detail to see how they operate.

17.2.1 Factors affecting test choice

Which statistical test is used to analyse data depends on the following factors:

- The purpose of the investigation – for example, is it a study of differences, or association, or correlation? This should be clear from the aim of the investigation.

- The type of design (whether it is a related design – repeated measures or matched pairs, or an unrelated design – independent groups). In a repeated measures design, the same participants perform in each condition. In a matched pairs design, there are different participants in each condition, but for each person in Condition A there is a 'twin' person in Condition B. In an independent design, there are different people in each condition.
- The level of measurement (or type of data).

Levels of measurement (or types of data)

There are three levels of measurement:

- nominal
- ordinal
- interval (or ratio).

Nominal (or categorical) data

The numbers refer to people or events in categories. With this sort of data the participants do not get a score as such; they themselves are the scores.

Level of measurement	Example
Nominal or categorical The numbers refer to people or events in categories	The numbers of people who own cats and dogs
Ordinal Data on a numerical scale, but where the size of the unit is not defined	Fear of snakes on a rating scale of 1–10
Interval Data on a numerical scale where the units are of equal, defined size	Heart rate

Figure 17.8 *The three levels of measurement or types of data.*

An example of nominal data: The numbers of males and females who own cats or dogs

Type of animal	Males	Females
Cat	5	28
Dog	45	22

Such data can be displayed in the form of percentages and is often illustrated in bar charts or pie charts.

Ordinal data

The numbers are scores on a numerical scale and can be put into order from lowest to highest, but the units of measurement are not of defined or equal size. Ordinal measures are usually based on opinion and therefore tend to be **subjective** rather than objective.

An example of ordinal data: Ratings scales

'On a scale of 1–10, how much do you fear snakes?'

1	2	3	4	5	6	7	8	9	10
Not at all									Very much in-deed

Here we assume that someone with a score of 10 is more scared than someone with a score of 9, but we don't know the exact difference between them because there is no defined measure of 'fear of snakes'.

Completion of a rating scale involves making a subjective judgement about where we think we are on the scale. This means that ordinal scale data are not very precise.

Interval data

Interval data place scores on a numerical scale with units of **equal, defined size.** For psychology there is no need to differentiate between interval and ratio data. Good examples of interval data that are often used in psychological investigations are time-based measures, such as reaction time, heartrate and time taken to complete cognitive tasks.

The above are clearly examples of interval data. However, other examples, such as 'The number of words recalled from a list' are much less clear. This is a fairly commonly used dependent variable in psycho-

	MODE	MEDIAN	MEAN
INTERVAL	NO	NO	YES
ORDINAL	NO	YES	NO
NOMINAL	YES	NO	NO

Figure 17.9 *Table to show which measure of central tendency is appropriate for use with the different levels of measurement.*

logical studies and is very often treated as interval data. However, saying these are interval data means that we are assuming that each word on the list is equal to each of the other words on the list in terms of memorability. In fact, there are many reasons why particular words might be more memorable than others. For example, the word 'hippopotamus' is probably more memorable than 'pencil' because it is it is very long, quite distinctive and relates to a somewhat unusual creature. Whilst it is not necessarily wrong to treat 'the number of words recalled from a list' as interval data, it is worth considering whether or not it might be better to treat it as ordinal data by rank-ordering the scores.

The different levels of measurement or types of data should be treated in different ways. Figure 17.9 shows which measure of central tendency (average) is most appropriate for use with the different levels of data.

The different levels of measurement vary in terms of sophistication. Interval level data are the most sophisticated, as the unit of measurement is very precise. Ordinal level data are less sophisticated, because at this level the unit of measurement is simply a rank order and is therefore not precise. Nominal level data are the least sophisticated, because at this level individual participants do not even get a score, but are simply placed into categories. These different levels of sophistication can be illustrated by looking at the example below. Notice how it is possible to collect interval data and convert it to ordinal or even nominal level data. It would not be possible however to collect nominal level data and then make it more sophisticated. If the only information that is collected in the first place is about which category people fall into, then there is little further that can be done with that information.

Converting levels of measurement

Step 1

Interval level data are collected from a group of students who have part-time jobs at the weekend. Each student is asked how much money (£) they earned last weekend.

8	10	15	19	25	28	30	30	36	39	41	45	50	55	60

This is interval scale data because it is a fixed measure with units of defined size.

Step 2

This information can now be converted into an **ordinal scale** by putting the scores (money earned) into order and assigning a position to every score, giving first place to the lowest score.

£ earned and respective placing or order

Money earned (starting with the least)

8	10	15	19	25	28	30	30	36	39	41	45	50	55	60

Position (give 1st place to the least money earned)

1	2	3	4	5	6	7.5	7.5	9	10	11	12	13	14	15

Notice how converting the money earned into an ordinal scale like this can reduce the amount of information. If all we know about a person is their position in the order, then we have lost the more detailed information about exactly how each student earned.

Step 3

Now the data can be reduced to the least sophisticated level of measurement by putting the data into categories making it **nominal data**.

Table to show the number of students earning below £20, between £20 and £40 and above £40:

	Below £20	Between £20 and £40	Above £40
No. of students	4	6	5

Data collected	Level of measurement
Age	Interval
Anger rating on a scale of 1–7	Ordinal
A level grades	Ordinal
Number of males and females who prefer badminton or rugby	Nominal
The amount of saliva produced in response to a drop of lemon juice	Interval
The number of Fiats and BMWs involved in road accidents in May	Nominal

Figure 17.10 *Examples of the different levels of measurement.*

17.2.2 Parametric and non-parametric tests

Parametric data conform to certain boundaries (or fall within certain parameters). Statistical tests for use with parametric data are described as **powerful**, meaning that they are better able to detect a significant effect. This is because they are calculated using the actual scores rather than ranked scores. However, this sensitivity can also be a problem if the data are inconsistent or erratic. For this reason, data must be assessed to see whether they meet the three criteria for parametric testing. If they do, then a parametric test should be used for analysis. If they do not, then an equivalent non-parametric test should be used instead. Non-parametric tests are calculated using ranks, which means they are less sensitive but better able to cope with any inconsistency in the data.

In addition to being powerful, parametric tests are also described as **robust**, meaning they are able to cope with data which do not fully meet the three criteria. The only essential criterion is that the data must be interval level. Even if the other two criteria are not fully met, it can still be appropriate to use a parametric test.

The three criteria for parametric testing

- Data must be interval level.
- The distribution of scores in each condition should be normal or the data should be drawn from a population which would be expected to show a normal distribution for whatever variable is being measured.

Figure 17.11 *Parametric tests are powerful and robust.*

- The variances should be homogeneous – the spread of scores in each condition should be similar.

Checking for a normal distribution

There are three ways of determining whether data show a normal distribution:

1 Look at the data by eye – do most scores appear to cluster around the mean, with just a few at high and low extremes? Then it is probably normally distributed.

2 Calculate the mean, median and mode for the set of scores and see whether they are all very similar. In a perfect normal distribution, the three measures of central tendency are the same.

3 Plot the data on a frequency distribution bar graph and see whether it shows a normal bell-shaped distribution curve.

Taking the set of following set of scores above we can decide whether or not they show a normal distribution.

Time (in seconds) taken by 10 rats to complete a maze
14
15
17
18
18
18
19
19
20
23

Scanning the data by eye, it looks as if the distribution is fairly normal. There are a few extreme scores and a cluster of scores around 18 in the middle. The measures of central tendency are almost the same, with a mean of 18.1, a median of 18 and a mode of 18. The fact that they are all so similar indicates a normal distribution. In this example you would not expect a frequency bar graph to show a perfect normal distribution because there are so few scores; with small samples, each individual score has a big effect on the shape of the graph. However, a frequency bar graph here shows a peak in the distribution at 18, with fewer scores at the extremes (see Figure 17.12).

Checking for homogeneous variances

The requirement to have homogeneous (similar) variances simply means that two sets of scores should have a similar amount of spread around the mean. One way to check this is to see if the standard deviations (SD) for the two sets of scores are similar. Most people would agree that if there is an SD of 6.1 in one condition and an SD of 6.2 in the other condition, then the standard deviations are indeed similar. However, it is sometimes difficult to say whether or not the SDs are similar. For example, if one condition has an SD of 6.1 and the other has an SD of 5.4, are these sufficiently similar or not? Note also that the standard deviation is the square root of the variance, so whilst two SDs might look quite similar, when these are squared to give the corresponding variances they might be a lot less similar.

One way to determine whether the variances are sufficiently close for us to say that they are homogeneous is to use the F test, which tests for significant differences between the variances. The F test is a way of avoiding the guesswork in deciding whether or not two sets of scores have homogeneous variances. The F test is calculated very easily by taking the larger SD squared and dividing it by the smaller SD squared to give the F value. This is then compared to F test tables to see whether the difference between the two variances is significant or not, in other words, whether the difference is likely to have happened by chance or not.

Lack of homogeneous variances sometimes arises because there are differences between the samples in each condition. This possibility of an important difference between two groups of participants would mean that the data could be unpredictable or erratic and are therefore unsuitable for parametric testing.

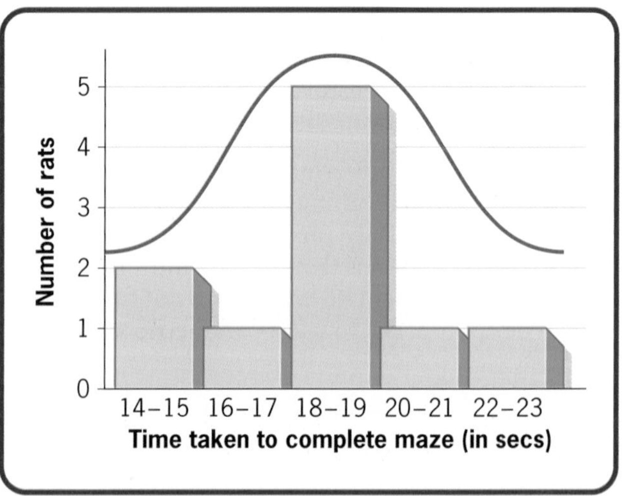

Figure 17.12 *Frequency bar graph to show the distribution of scores in the rat maze study.*

17.2.3 Choosing and using statistical tests

Figure 17.13 shows the statistical tests that A2 students are expected to know about. You would never be asked to calculate any of these tests in an examination, but you are expected to know the conditions of use for each test and should be able to interpret the results using extracts from statistical tables. This means that you need to know which test is appropriate in different circumstances and should have had some experience in calculating statistical tests and interpreting the results.

Figure 17.13 gives you the information you need to decide which test is appropriate in different situations.

In this section you will find worked examples of three of the tests the Chi-square test, the Related t test and the Spearman's rho correlation test. The corresponding statistical tables for these tests can be found in the Appendix at the back of the book. If you wish to try any of the other tests that are mentioned here you should refer to the Further Reading section at the end of this chapter for suitable textbooks.

Level of measurement	Differences		Correlation or association
	Related design	Unrelated design	
Nominal	Sign test (S)	Chi-square test X^2	Chi-square test X^2
Ordinal	Wilcoxon test (W)	Mann-Whitney (U) test	Spearman's test (rho)
Interval	Related t test (t) (parametric)	Unrelated t test (t) (parametric)	Pearson's test (r) (parametric)

Figure 17.13 *Table to show statistical tests and the circumstances in which they are appropriate.*

17.2.4 Tests for use with nominal data

The Sign test

This is a fairly crude test for a significant difference between two sets of scores. It is usually used as a preliminary to a more sensitive test for differences. The Sign test tells us whether there is a significant effect in a particular direction – for example, if a significant number of people feel better after therapy than before.

- Data should be nominal or categorical level
- Data should be related (repeated measures or matched design)

To use the Sign test table you need to know N = the number of pairs of scores.

To be significant, the calculated value of S must be **equal to or less than** the critical table value.

The Chi-square test X^2

The Chi-square test is a test for significant association between two variables or for a difference between two conditions.

- Data should be nominal or categorical level
- Data should be unrelated (the design must be independent)
- Categories should be exclusive (each person can be in only one of the categories)
- The expected scores in each cell (category on the table) should be at least five.

To use the Chi-square table you need to know that the degrees of freedom df = (number of rows – 1) x (number of columns – 1)

To be significant, the calculated value of X^2 must be **equal to or more than** the critical table value.

The Chi-square test X^2 worked example

In a study of moral understanding, a researcher sets out to compare the numbers of males and females giving different types of answers to moral dilemmas. The responses are categorised as either care-based or justice-based. The data are shown in the table below. There are two ways of wording the H1 in a study using a Chi-square analysis:

> 'There will be a significant difference in the numbers of males and females giving care-based and justice-based responses.'

or

> 'There will be a significant association between gender and type of response.'

The numbers of males and females who give care-based and justice-based responses

	Males	Females
Care-based response	10	19
Justice-based response	15	7

The frequencies in the table below are known as observed (actual) frequencies. The first step in calculating the Chi-square test is to work out the expected frequencies, that is, the frequencies that might have been expected to occur if the type of response had nothing at all to do with being male or female. The Chi-square test is calculated on the basis of the difference between the observed frequencies in the table and the frequencies that might have been expected to occur by chance.

Step 1

For each cell (box on the table), calculate the expected score (E) by multiplying the row total for that cell by the column total for that cell and dividing by the total number of people in the study (N).

a) $29 \times 25 \div 51 = 14.22$ b) $29 \times 26 \div 51 = 14.78$
c) $22 \times 25 \div 51 = 10.78$ d) $22 \times 26 \div 51 = 11.22$

Step 2

For each cell, find the numerical difference between the actual or observed frequency and the expected frequency (O – E). Ignore any sign.

a) $10 - 14.22 = 4.22$ b) $19 - 14.78 = 4.22$
c) $15 - 10.78 = 4.22$ d) $7 - 11.22 = 4.22$

Step 3

For each cell, square the answer to Step 2 and divide it by the expected frequency for that cell.

a) $4.22^2 \div 14.22 = 1.25$ b) $4.22^2 \div 14.78 = 1.21$
c) $4.22^2 \div 10.78 = 1.66$ d) $4.22^2 \div 11.22 = 1.59$

Step 4

Add the answers to Step 4 to give Chi-square X^2

$1.25 + 1.21 + 1.66 + 1.59 = 5.71$

<u>The calculated value of Chi-square is 5.71</u>

The degree of freedom in this case is $(2 - 1) \times (2 - 1) = 1$

The result should then be compared to the values on the Chi-square table (see Appendix page 385). For the result to be significant, the calculated value of Chi-square must be equal to or greater than the table value. Using the 0.05 level of significance, with a two-tailed test and 1 degree of freedom, the critical value of Chi-square is 3.84.

Since the calculated value of Chi-square (5.71) is greater than the critical table value, there is a significant difference in the numbers of males and females giving care-based and justice-based responses $p \leq .05$

	Males	Females	Row totals
Care-based response	10 (cell a)	19 (cell b)	29
Justice-based response	15 (cell c)	7 (cell d)	22
	25	26	51 Total number of participants (N)

(the probability of the difference in frequencies having occurred by chance is equal to or less than 5%). The H0 is rejected and the H1 accepted.

Note that if the hypothesis is phrased in terms of an association, you would say that there is a significant association between gender and type of response $p \leq .05$.

17.2.5 Tests for differences between two sets of scores

The Wilcoxon (W) test is:

- A test for significant difference between two sets of scores
- Data must be related (repeated or matched design)
- Used with ordinal level data

The Wilcoxon test is a non-parametric test which is calculated using ranks. It is less sensitive than its parametric equivalent, the Related t test.

To use the Wilcoxon table you will need to know that N = the number of pairs of scores.

For the calculated value of W to be significant, it must be **equal to or less than** the critical table value.

The Mann-Whitney (U) test is:

- A test for significant difference between two sets of scores
- Data must be unrelated (independent design)
- Used with ordinal level data

The Mann-Whitney test is a non-parametric test which is calculated using ranks. It is less sensitive than its parametric equivalent, the Unrelated t test.

To use the Mann-Whitney table, you will need to know that n1 and n2 = the number of scores in each condition.

For the calculated value of U to be significant, it must be **equal to or less than** the critical table value.

Related t test is:

- A test for significant difference between two sets of scores
- Data must be related (repeated or matched design)
- Data must be interval level
- As the related t test is a parametric test, data should be checked to see that they meet the criteria for parametric testing: normal distribution or drawn from a normally distributed population; homogeneous variances.

The Related t test is a parametric test which is calculated using actual scores. It is more sensitive than its non-parametric equivalent, the Wilcoxon test.

To use the t test table, you will need to know that df = the number of pairs of scores – 1.

For the calculated value of t to be significant, it must be **equal to or greater than** the critical table value.

The Unrelated t test is:

- A test for significant difference between two sets of scores
- Data must be unrelated (independent design)
- Data must be interval level
- This is a parametric test – data should be checked to see that they meet the criteria for parametric testing: normal distribution or drawn from a normally distributed population; homogeneous variances

The Unrelated t test is a parametric test which is calculated using actual scores. It is more sensitive than its non-parametric equivalent, the Mann-Whitney test.

To use the t test table, you will need to know that df = the number of scores in Condition A – 1 plus the number of scores in Condition B – 1.

For the calculated value of t to be significant, it must be **equal to or greater than** the critical table value.

Related t test worked example

A researcher wants to test the hypothesis that '*completion of a routine office task takes longer when working in a noisy environment than when working in a quiet environment*'. The data from a repeated design experiment are given in table A (opposite).

To calculate the Related t test, you need to draw up another table with two extra columns to the right-hand side (see table B opposite).

Step 1
Calculate the difference between each pair of scores and place in the differences column (d).

Step 2
Square each difference and place in the d^2 column.

Step 3
Add up the values in the d column to give the sum of d ($\sum d$) and the values in the d^2 column to give the sum of d squared ($\sum d^2$).

Step 4
Use the answers to Step 3 to calculate the formula.

$$t = \frac{\bar{d} \text{ (mean of differences)}}{\sqrt{\dfrac{\sum d^2 - \dfrac{(\sum d)^2}{n}}{n(n-1)}}}$$

Note: n = number of pairs of scores

Ignore the minus sign, it is the numerical value that matters here.

<u>The calculated value of t = 2.671</u>

The degree of freedom in this case is N – 1 = 7

The result should then be compared to the values on the t test table (see Appendix page 387). For the result to be significant, the calculated value of t must be equal to or greater than the table value. Using the 0.05 level of significance, with a one-tailed test and df = 7, the critical value of t is 1.895.

Since the calculated value of t (2.671) is greater than the critical table value, there is a significant difference between the time taken to complete a routine office task in a noisy environment and a quiet environment $p \leq .05$ (the probability of the difference having occurred by chance is equal to or less than 5%). The H0 is rejected and the H1 accepted.

A

Participant	Time in quiet condition (seconds)	Time in noisy condition (seconds)
1	15	18
2	30	30
3	26	29
4	32	40
5	18	22
6	22	20
7	25	30
8	27	29

B

Participant	Time in quiet condition (seconds) A	Time in noisy condition (seconds) B	Diff (d) A – B	d^2
1	15	18	–3	9
2	30	30	0	0
3	26	29	–3	9
4	32	40	–8	64
5	18	22	–4	16
6	22	20	2	4
7	25	30	–5	25
8	27	29	–2	4

17.2.6 Tests for correlation

Spearman's rho test

- A non-parametric test of correlation
- Data should be in related pairs
- For use with ordinal level data

To use the Spearman's table, you need to know that N = the number of pairs of scores.

For the calculated value of rho to be significant, it must be **equal to or greater than** the critical table value.

Pearson's r test

- A parametric test of correlation
- Data should be in related pairs
- Data must be interval
- As the Pearson's test is a parametric test, data should be checked to see that they meet the criteria for parametric testing: normal distribution or drawn from a normally distributed population; homogeneous variances.

To use the Pearson's table, you need to know that degrees of freedom df = number of pairs of scores – 2.

For the calculated value of r to be significant, it must be **equal to or greater than** the critical table value.

Spearman's rho test worked example

A researcher is investigating the hypothesis that '*there is a significant relationship between introversion scores and social anxiety ratings*'. Data from ten participants are presented in the first table below.

To calculate the Spearman's test, you need to draw up another table, with two extra columns to the right-hand side (see second table below).

Participant	1	2	3	4	5	6	7	8	9	10
Introversion score (out of 20)	15	19	10	9	4	16	12	13	9	8
Social anxiety rating (out of 10)	7	9	4	6	2	7	9	6	4	2

Participant	Introversion score and rank (rank A)		Social anxiety score and rank (rank B)		Diff (d) rank A – rank B	d^2
	Score	Rank	Score	Rank		
1	15	8	7	7.5	0.5	0.25
2	19	10	10	9	0	0
3	10	4.5	4	3.5	1	1
4	10	4.5	5	5	−0.5	0.25
5	4	1	2	1.5	−0.5	0.25
6	16	9	7	7.5	1.5	2.25
7	12	6	9	9	−3	9
8	13	7	6	6	1	1
9	9	3	4	3.5	−0.5	0.25
10	8	2	2	1.5	0.5	0.25

Step 1
For each condition, separately assign each score a rank, giving the lowest rank to the lowest score. If there are two scores (or more) the same, they must share the same rank as one cannot go in front of the other.

Step 2
For each pair of ranks, find the numerical difference between them. Some of these will be plus differences and some will be minus differences.

Step 3
Square the differences you calculated in Step 2. Remember that a minus number multiplied by another minus number equals a plus.

Step 4
Add all the squared values from Step 3 to give $\sum d^2$ (sum of d squared).

Step 5
Use the answer to Step 4 to calculate the following formula for rho.

$$\text{rho} = 1 - \left(\frac{6 \times \sum d^2}{n(n-1)(n+1)} \right)$$

Note that N = number of pairs of scores.

In our worked example on page 373, $\sum d^2 = 14.5$

<u>The calculated value of rho = 0.91</u>

The result should then be compared to the values on the Spearman's rho table (see Appendix page 388). For the result to be significant, the calculated value of rho must be equal to or greater than the table value. Using the 0.05 level of significance, with a two-tailed test and N = 10, the critical value of rho is .648.

Since the calculated value of rho (.91) is greater than the critical table value, there is a significant positive correlation between introversion scores and social anxiety ratings $p \leq .05$ (the probability of the correlation having occurred by chance is equal to or less than 5%). The H0 is rejected and the H1 accepted. Note that the calculated value of rho is a positive value, indicating a positive correlation.

Remember that tests for correlation should always produce a result between −1 and +1. If the value is a minus value, this indicates a negative correlation, and if the value is a plus value, this indicates a positive correlation. When using the Spearman's table, you ignore any sign and just look at the numerical value. It is the numerical value that indicates the strength of the correlation and the sign that indicates the direction (see page 362).

17.3 Issues in research

Four issues are considered in this section. First, the advantages and disadvantages of different methods of research are reviewed. This is followed by a summary of strengths and weaknesses of quantitative and qualitative methods of data collection. Third, the concepts of reliability and validity are examined. Finally, ethical issues in psychological research are discussed.

17.3.1 Strengths and limitations of different methods of research

The experimental method

An experiment involves the researcher manipulating one variable (the independent variable – IV) to examine the effect on another variable (the dependent variable – DV). Experiments are normally carried out in a carefully controlled environment, such as a laboratory, although sometimes researchers conduct field experiments in natural settings such as shopping centres or playgrounds. Field experiments are much more realistic (have higher ecological validity), but it is much more difficult to control extraneous variables in a natural setting. Despite the problems of control in field experiments, most experiments do involve the strict control of variables.

Strengths

A high level of control means that the experiment can be used to determine a **cause-and-effect relationship** between the independent variable (IV) and the dependent variable (DV). Experiments involve use of a strictly standardised procedure which means that other researchers can replicate the study. Precise operationalisation of variables means that the results can be clearly measured and verified, meaning they are objective.

Limitations

Many types of behaviour are not amenable to controlled research. For example, crowd aggression and the effects of different child-rearing styles are impossible to manipulate under experimental conditions. Laboratory experiments usually have **low ecological validity** because the experimental task and conditions are very different to the circumstances in which the behaviour occurs in everyday life. When people take part in an experiment, they are usually aware of the aim, and might therefore try to please the researcher rather than act normally. Participants often respond to what are known as 'demand characteristics' or clues about what is expected in experiments.

Interviews

Structured interviews

Here fixed questions are asked in a fixed order. All participants have exactly the same experience, which means the procedure is standardised. In practice, most interviews have some fixed questions, even if it is just basic information about age and gender.

Strengths

Large numbers of people can be interviewed quite quickly and the data can easily be collated and analysed. The interview is focused and does not stray off the topic, and the interview process can be replicated.

Limitations

Interesting answers or issues raised by the participants cannot be pursued and no follow-up questions can be asked. The process is quite formal and may be intimidating for participants.

Unstructured interviews

In this type of interview the researcher starts out with a general aim, but there are no fixed questions.

Strengths

Interesting issues that arise can be explored in more detail by use of follow-up questions. The process is less formal and therefore more comfortable for participants; this means it is probably more sensitive for investigation of delicate issues such as divorce, abortion and so on.

Limitations

Since every participant has different questions, it is difficult to make comparisons and see patterns; as such, the data may be difficult to analyse. Replication would be difficult and there is the possibility that the interview may stray off the point.

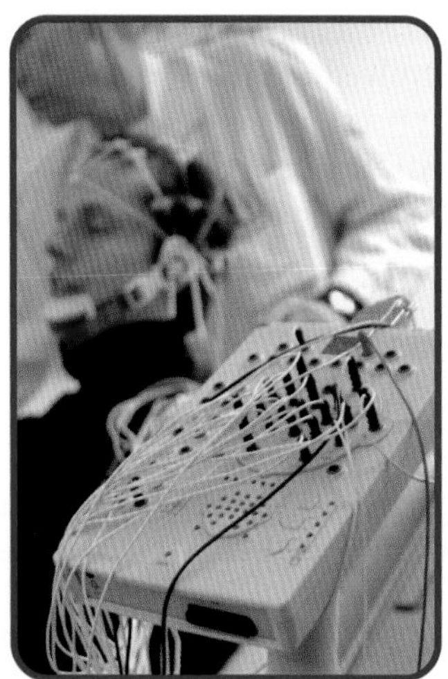

Figure 17.14 *Most experiments involve a high degree of control, enabling the researcher to infer a cause-and-effect relationship between the variables.*

Observations

Observations usually take place in a natural setting, although they can also take place in a controlled environment such as a special playroom. In a **participant** observation, the researcher takes part in the action, and in a **non-participant** observation, the observer is apart from the action.

Strengths

Natural observations have high ecological validity because behaviour is being studied in the environment where it normally occurs. This means the observational method is especially useful for social behaviours. Participant observations enable us to understand behaviour in context. Rather than just record the frequency of a behaviour we can see what has caused that behaviour to occur. Non-participant observations allow the observer to maintain greater objectivity.

Limitations

Extraneous variables might affect behaviour in natural observations. There are particular ethical problems with observational research. Participants in psychological research would normally be asked to give their informed consent, but if they know beforehand that they are going to be observed, this would lead them to behave in an artificial way. If participants are unaware that they are involved in research, they cannot exercise their right to withdraw. Subjectivity can be a problem

in participant observations, as the researcher may become too involved with the participants.

Questionnaires

Questionnaires can include **closed** and **open** questions. Closed questions feature a fixed set of response options, whereas open questions allow for any answer.

Strengths

Questionnaires can be used to gather information from large numbers of people relatively quickly. They are useful for studying behaviours and attitudes that cannot be investigated in any other way than by asking people. For example, it would be very difficult to find out about teenagers' attitudes towards condom use in any other way. Closed question responses are easy to analyse, whereas open question responses can provide rich detail and unique insight.

Limitations

Participants may give answers which are not entirely truthful because they want to appear to be socially desirable. Open question responses are difficult to analyse and may need to be laboriously categorised after the data have been collected. Response set may occur. This is where people stop reading the questions properly and just tick the same answer all the way down the page. This is most likely to occur with a long fixed-option questionnaire.

Case studies

Case studies are typically conducted by clinical, educational, occupational and cognitive psychologists and often take place over an extended period of time. They involve in-depth study of a single individual or small group. For example, an occupational psychologist might carry out a case study of an employee who is suffering from stress at work. Less usually, case studies are used to study people who are of interest because of their unusual circumstances – for example, a child who has been brought up in very deprived circumstances. Case study data can be gathered from a wide variety of sources, including formal records, interviews with the individual and with other people who know them, psychological tests and observations.

Strengths

The data are detailed and meaningful; as the case study is a real account of a person's real life, it has high validity. Patterns of change and development can be investigated over time. A single case study which goes against a theory is enough to cause that theory to be altered to take account of the new evidence.

Limitations

Each case study is unique and therefore the findings cannot be generalised to a wider population. Since some of the data are retrospective, involving the recall of past events, there is likely to be a problem with reliability. It is impossible to replicate a case study as they occur over a period of time. It is difficult to maintain objectivity, so a case study may be affected by **researcher bias** where the researcher's beliefs and expectations affect their interpretation of the data. This method also has particular ethical problems, as such cases usually involve people who are vulnerable. The usual ethical considerations of consent, right to withdraw, protection from harm and confidentiality should be taken careful account of and dealt with in the best interests of the person being studied.

Correlation studies

Correlation is a statistical technique for analysing data where two sets of numerical scores can be obtained for each participant. Correlations enable us to measure a relationship between the two sets of data or variables.

Strengths

Correlations can assess the strength of a relationship between two variables, and once we know there is a relationship, other types of study can be carried out to further investigate this relationship.

Limitations

There is no control of variables in a correlation, so correlation does not show cause and effect. Only an experiment can establish cause-and-effect relationships.

Figure 17.15 *Natural observations have high ecological validity because behaviour is being studied in a normal, everyday environment.*

Evaluation

Researchers need to consider the relative advantages and disadvantages of the various research methods when deciding how to conduct a psychological investigation. The method chosen will largely depend upon what is being studied. Interpretation of any research findings should also take account of the method that has been used to collect data, as many methods have inherent problems. For example, where any **self-report method** has been used, the data may be biased either consciously or unconsciously; people may try to appear socially desirable or respond in a way they think that they are expected to. Retrospective data, where people have to recall information from the past, may also be inaccurate because people's memories are so unreliable.

17.3.2 Strengths and limitations of qualitative and quantitative data

Quantitative data collection methods involve the collection of numerical data. Quantitative methods are usually associated with the traditional scientific approach to doing research, where hypotheses are proposed on the basis of some existing theory or research. Numerical data are then collected and subjected to statistical analysis for the purpose of testing hypotheses. The process of counting or measuring variables requires objectivity and precise operationalisation of variables. Through exact measurement and the control of any extraneous variables, researchers are able to infer a cause-and-effect relationship. Quantitative methods are objective and replicable.

Qualitative data collection methods are explorative and interpretative, involving the analysis of the meaning attached to events and the significance of experiences. As such, qualitative methods involve studying behaviour and experience within its context, since behaviour taken out of context cannot be understood in any meaningful way. In qualitative research, theories tend to come out of data collection rather than be used to guide data collection. Qualitative methods of data collection have been referred to as 'hypothesis-generating' research, as opposed to the more conventional 'hypothesis-testing' approach (Robson, 1993). A qualitative research report will include raw data – for example, transcripts of recorded interviews – along with the researcher's summaries, inferences about the meaning of the data and perhaps even the researcher's reactions and feelings. Qualitative methods are interpretative and specific.

Examples of quantitative measures

- Time taken to react to a noise stimulus.
- Number of verbal interactions between two children in a play observation.
- Number of lapses of attention reported by drivers on a motorway.

> **Examples of qualitative measures**
>
> - Descriptive account of playground interactions between two children.
> - Transcript of an interview with a person suffering from phobias.
> - Thematic analysis of diary entries for 'my first day at school'.

Whilst the traditional quantitative approach to investigation has long been dominant in psychology, many researchers now see the value in taking a more interpretative approach. Indeed there are some areas of psychology – for example, personality and counselling – where qualitative methods are seen as essential tools of investigation. Thus, the choice of a quantitative or a qualitative data collection method depends largely on what is being investigated. Increasingly, researchers who see the value in both approaches are tending to combine quantitative and qualitative methods in a single investigation. As an example, researchers looking at the effects of divorce on children might combine a quantitative measure – literacy and numeracy scores – with a qualitative measure – content of children's diaries.

In a discussion of the relative merits of quantitative and qualitative research methods, Reason and Rowan (1981) argue that quantitative methods produce results which are 'statistically significant but humanly insignificant'. In their view, taking behaviour and experience out of its context in order to be able to measure it accurately and objectively means that we lose sight of the meaning of what is being studied. They suggest that qualitative data collection methods are preferred, as 'it is much better to be deeply interesting than accurately boring'. Further support for qualitative research comes from those who argue that it is impossible for a researcher who is a human being to take a truly objective view of the behaviour and experience of other people (Banister *et al.*, 1994).

Qualitative methods are becoming increasingly accepted as part of mainstream psychology and are used particularly to investigate sensitive issues and topics where there is little existing research. The information collected can then be used to suggest hypotheses which can be tested using quantitative methods. Conversely, qualitative research might follow quantitative research, especially in cases where it has become clear that existing theory is inadequate.

17.3.3 Reliability and validity

Reliability

Reliability refers to consistency or the extent to which research findings can be repeated. Four ways of checking for reliability are described below.

i) Test-retest reliability

One method of checking the reliability of a psychological measure is **test-retest reliability**. This involves testing the same group of participants on more than

Strengths		Limitations
Easy to analyse Enables hypothesis testing Scientific Shows cause and effect Objective Enables replication	**Quantitative data collection methods**	Lacks validity Behaviour is taken out of context Less meaningful Reductionist
Strengths		**Limitations**
Valid Meaningful Holistic Rich and detailed	**Qualitative data collection methods**	Subjective Cannot be replicated Specific, therefore not amenable to generalisation

Figure 17.16 *Summary of strengths and limitations of quantitative and qualitative data collection methods.*

one occasion and checking to see whether there is a significant positive correlation between the two sets of scores. In test-retest reliability, the correlation coefficient is normally expected to be 0.7 or above.

ii) Inter-observer reliability

Reliability can also be established in observational research by using more than one observer to rate or code the different types of behaviour. It is important that an observer makes consistent observations and avoids observer bias. This can be checked by having two observers making recordings at the same time but independently. At the end of the observation period, their individual recordings can then be compared to see whether or not they are similar. If there is a strong positive correlation between the scores of the two observers then there is good **inter-rater** or **inter-observer reliability**.

iii) Split-half reliability

Reliability can also be established when using questionnaires to make sure that the questionnaire has internal reliability or consistency. This can be done in two ways. The first method is known as **split-half reliability**. Here a person's score on one randomly selected half of the questionnaire items is compared with his or her score on the other half of the items. If the questionnaire has good internal reliability, there should be a significant positive correlation between scores on the first half of the items and scores on the second half of the items.

iv) Item analysis

The second method for establishing internal reliability of a questionnaire is known as **item analysis**. Here a person's score on each individual questionnaire item is correlated with his or her overall score on the rest of the questionnaire. This enables the researcher to determine whether or not the questionnaire item is consistent with the rest of the questionnaire. Items that yield a score that is significantly positively correlated with the overall questionnaire score are considered to be consistent and reliable. Any items that are not positively correlated with the overall score on the questionnaire are deemed to be unreliable and are therefore rejected. Item analysis is a key process in the development of commercially available questionnaires.

Figure 17.17 shows an individual item analysis on an attitude questionnaire investigating attitudes to animal experiments. Four participants are asked to indicate their agreement or disagreement with the statement on a 5-point scale. Notice how for each participant, the responses to items a, b and c are consistent. Their responses to the fourth item, however, are completely out of line with their responses to the other items. This indicates that item d is testing a completely different attitude to what is being tested on the rest of the attitude questionnaire. Item d should therefore be dropped and another more suitable item put in its place.

Validity

Validity as a general concept refers to the extent to which a psychological measure measures what it is supposed to measure. For example, if we are using a test of co-ordination, does it really measure co-ordination or some other variable like agility? This type of validity is known as **internal validity** because it is concerned with issues to do with the measure itself.

Various ways of checking for internal validity are given below:

i) Face validity

This simply means whether or not, 'on the face of it', a test appears to measure what it is supposed to measure. For example, is catching a ball with one hand a good measure of spatial co-ordination? 'On the face of it', it appears to be.

ii) Content validity

This is a slightly more sophisticated version of face validity. It involves asking research colleagues (ideally ones with greater expertise) whether they think that the test measures what it is supposed to measure. Sports psychologists would be good people to ask about a measure of spatial co-ordination.

iii) Concurrent validity

One way of checking whether a test measures what it is supposed to measure is to test a group of people with the new test and test the same group of people with an established measure of the same ability. For example, we could test people on their ability to catch a ball with one hand and test them on an established measure of spatial co-ordination used by doctors or sports psychologists. If performance on each of the two measures shows a significant positive correlation, then we can assume that the new measure measures what it is supposed to measure.

iv) Criterion validity

This is where a measure is tested using a criterion group – that is, a group whose results on the test should be predictable because of special characteristics members of the group possess. In the case of our test of spatial co-ordination, a useful criterion group would be professional dancers, who we would expect to have well-developed co-ordination skills. If our test is really a valid measure of spatial co-ordination, the dancers should perform very well on the test. If they do not, we must assume that the test does not have validity because it does not appear to measure what it is supposed to measure.

v) Predictive validity

This is where performance on a test can be used to predict performance on another measure at some later date. This is most commonly seen in aptitude tests, which are used to show whether someone has the necessary skills and abilities to perform well in a certain job role. Employers often use aptitude tests as part of their selection processes. To determine predictive validity, scores on the test are correlated with performance on another measure at a later date. If there is a significant positive correlation, the test is said to have predictive validity – in other words, it can predict later performance. In the case of our example, we would expect someone who scores highly in the test of spatial co-ordination to perform well in a job that requires good spatial co-ordination, such as a forklift truck operator.

Another type of validity is **external validity**. This type of validity is concerned with the context in which behaviour is being studied and the sample that is being used in the research. You will already be familiar with the concept of **ecological validity**, which means the extent to which the behaviour is being measured in circumstances in which that behaviour would normally occur in real life. You will also be aware that data gathered using a particular sample cannot readily be generalised further than the target population from which the sample was drawn. Thus, external validity refers to the extent to which we can generalise our findings to other settings or other populations.

Figure 17.18 *How can we be sure that catching a ball with one hand is a valid measure of spatial co-ordination?*

17.3.4 Ethical considerations

The ethical guidelines covering the activities of psychologists in the UK is the Code of Ethics and Conduct (2006) produced by the British Psychological Society. This code governs the activities of all practising and research psychologists, and psychology students. It is organised under four key headings – Respect, Competence, Responsibility, Integrity – and serves the following purposes:

Item	P1	P2	P3	P4
a) Animal experiments are cruel	5	2	3	1
b) Animals are just as important as humans	5	2	3	1
c) Animal research should be banned	5	2	3	1
d) Rabbits are cuddly and fluffy	1	4	5	5

Figure 17.17 *An item analysis on an attitude questionnaire investigating attitudes to animal experiments. Notice how for each person, the response to item d is inconsistent with their other three responses.*

- It protects participants, patients and clients.
- It helps maintain and promote professional standards.
- It provides a framework within which psychologists work.
- It guides decisions about appropriate and acceptable conduct.

Much of the Code's content is applicable to those working as professional psychologists in a professional context, such as clinical, occupational or educational psychology. However, there are also guidelines for those working as researchers. These guidelines apply to everyone carrying out psychological research, including investigations carried out by students at all levels.

i) Ethical considerations related to the design and conduct of research

- **Respect**

Psychologists should respect people as individuals, taking account of factors such as gender, race, culture and religion. Unfair or prejudiced practices should be avoided.

- **Confidentiality**

Information about participants in research studies should be kept confidential, including data collected in research. This is especially important with case studies, where in-depth, personal information about a person has been gathered.

- **Consent**

Psychologists should seek informed consent from those taking part in research. Informed consent means that the people consenting know what they are consenting to. This means that prospective participants should be told about the purpose of the research before they are asked to agree to take part. Particular care should be taken with children and vulnerable adults. If they are incapable of understanding what is involved, consent should be sought from someone who is able to make decisions for them, such as a family member. It is normal practice to gain parental consent, or consent from those acting in place of parents (*in loco parentis*), if carrying out research with participants below 16 years.

- **Privacy**

This applies particularly to observational research, where psychologists should respect people's privacy, restricting their observations to locations where people might normally expect to be observed.

- **Deception**

Deception of participants should be avoided unless it is absolutely necessary for the research. Participants are deceived if they are misled about some aspect of the research. This may be deliberate, where participants are intentionally misled about some aspect of the research, or deception by omission, where the deception involves failing to tell participants about some key aspect of the investigation. If deception cannot be avoided, participants should be informed about the true nature of the research at the earliest opportunity.

- **Right to withdraw**

It is important for researchers to make it clear to participants that they have the right to withdraw themselves from research at any time. Ideally this should be explained at different points in the process: in the brief, during administration of the standardised instructions and at the time of the debriefing. In longitudinal research, which takes place over an extended period, making it very clear to participants that they have the right to withdraw is especially important. In addition, participants have the right to withdraw their data and have records of their participation destroyed if they wish. In research with young children, any attempt to evade the research situation should be taken as the child exercising his or her right to withdraw.

- **Competence**

Psychologists should give advice only if they are qualified to do so.

- **Protection from harm**

Psychologists should protect their participants from harm. There should be no risk to their psychological well-being, physical health, personal values or dignity. The general rule here is that research participants should feel no worse about themselves after having taken part in research than they did at the outset.

- **Debrief**

Psychologists should debrief research participants after the investigation, informing them in clear and understandable terms of the aims and nature of the research. A debrief is not, however, an excuse for everything that has gone before. In other words, it is not sufficient to excuse deception and harm on the grounds that a debriefing will make everything right again.

- **Integrity**

Psychologists should be honest and accurate, maintain professional boundaries and avoid exploitation.

In carrying out any investigation, psychologists should always consider whether the costs to participants outweigh the benefits to be gained from the research.

ii) Implications of research

Clearly, ethical considerations are extremely important in the design and conduct of individual pieces of research. However, there are also broader ethical issues for psychologists to consider.

> ***'Psychologists value their responsibilities to clients, to the general public, and to the profession and science of Psychology, including the avoidance of harm and the prevention of misuse or abuse of their contributions to society.'***
>
> **Ethical Principle: Responsibility**
>
> ***The Code of Ethics and Conduct* (2006), The British Psychological Society**

Psychological research is conducted with the purpose of finding out about some aspect of human behaviour or experience. The reasons for doing this will vary, depending on who is conducting the research and the context of the investigation. It might be that the research is being conducted to validate or refute an existing theory, or perhaps the intention is to further explore an issue raised in a previous investigation. Other studies will be conducted with the aim of solving a clinical or social problem, perhaps investigating the effectiveness of a therapy or providing a new educational assessment tool that can be used with primary school children.

Whatever the purpose of any individual piece of research, psychologists should be mindful of the broader consequences and implications of their investigations. To illustrate this, let us consider the implications of some well-known examples of psychological research.

Skinner's operant conditioning research (1953)

Skinner's finding that behaviour can be shaped and controlled by its consequences has had far-reaching effects in many areas of life. The use of reinforcement in token economy systems has been widely adopted in many institutional settings, including schools, prisons and psychiatric hospitals. Whilst there can undoubtedly be benefits in that the institution operates more smoothly and the life of supervising staff is made much easier, there are also major ethical problems with controlling behaviour in this way. Using a token economy in an institutional setting inevitably results in the staff having the power to deprive inmates of 'privileges' which would ordinarily be freely available to most people. In this case, then, we see how an individual piece of psychological research has been used to develop a system of social control that may appear to conflict with ideals about human rights and individual freedoms.

Milgram's research into obedience (1963)

Milgram showed that ordinary people will do harm to others if they are told to do so by an authority figure. Whilst the ethical issues related to the experiment are extremely controversial in themselves, there is also controversy about the implications of Milgram's work. In the light of Milgram's findings it had been argued that individuals should not always be held responsible for their own actions. In two well-documented cases (Adolf Eichmann and William Calley), Milgram's evidence has been used, unsuccessfully, to defend individuals accused of war crimes; in each case, the defendants argued that they were not responsible for their actions because they were simply obeying orders. Here we see how an individual piece of psychological research can have implications for decisions about personal responsibility and blame.

Loftus' research into false memory (2001)

Loftus has argued that many instances of recovered memory of alleged child abuse are, in fact, false memories. Her research has shown that people can reconstruct events they have been told about to such an extent that they believe the events actually occurred. Loftus's research was initially laboratory-based, investigating the effect of leading questions on memory. Due to the broader implications of her findings, she is now often called upon as an expert witness in legal cases involving allegations of childhood sexual abuse. Most usually, her work is used to defend individuals who have been accused of child abuse. Loftus' involvement in such legal arguments is testing her '*responsibility to the general public, and to the profession and science of Psychology, including the avoidance of harm and the prevention of misuse or abuse of their contributions to society.*'

Psychological testing

Psychological tests inevitably involve the rank ordering

of individuals, which has the potential for discrimination. At a very low point in the history of psychology, intelligence tests were used to discriminate against people seeking refuge in the USA at the time of the Second World War. Potential immigrants fleeing from Nazi occupation in Europe were required to complete written IQ tests in an unfamiliar language and were promptly deported if they did not attain the required score (Gould, 1981). Despite its controversial history, psychological testing is still very much in evidence today. Educational and occupational psychologists spend much of their working lives testing psychological variables such as intelligence, aptitude and personality. The inevitable consequence of such testing is that the tests are used to compare individuals – a happy experience for those at the positive end of the scale, but less fortunate for those at the other end of the distribution. Psychologists administering psychological tests must take great care in the disclosure and explanation of the results to individuals and other interested parties such as parents and teachers.

iii) Ethics and culture

Special ethical considerations arise when investigating other cultures and cultural differences. Berry (1969) has argued that cross-cultural research often involves an 'imposed etic' with psychologists from a predominantly western (mostly US) background attempting to explain the behaviour of other cultures in terms of theories and a body of research that has been developed in the west. In doing so, researchers are assuming that measures used in one culture will have the same meaning and validity in another, quite different culture. One example is the Strange Situation method of measuring attachment types (Ainsworth *et al.*, 1978). Some cross-cultural research indicates that the types of behaviours Ainsworth chose to record and the classification system used may not be appropriate for measuring attachment in all cultures. van Ijzendoorn and Kroonenberg (1988) analysed Strange Situation data from 32 different studies in eight countries and concluded that differing child-rearing norms between and even within cultures will lead to varying percentages of types of attachment found in any individual study.

This example shows how psychological tests and measures appropriate for one culture may not always be useful for research with another culture. It is important that researchers avoid ethnocentrism and guard against assuming the superiority of their own cultural norms and values. To reduce the likelihood that norms and expectations are imposed on other cultures, it is recommended that cross-cultural research projects involve at least one researcher from the culture being investigated. This would enable an insight into the meaning of the research situation as it is understood by members of the culture being investigated.

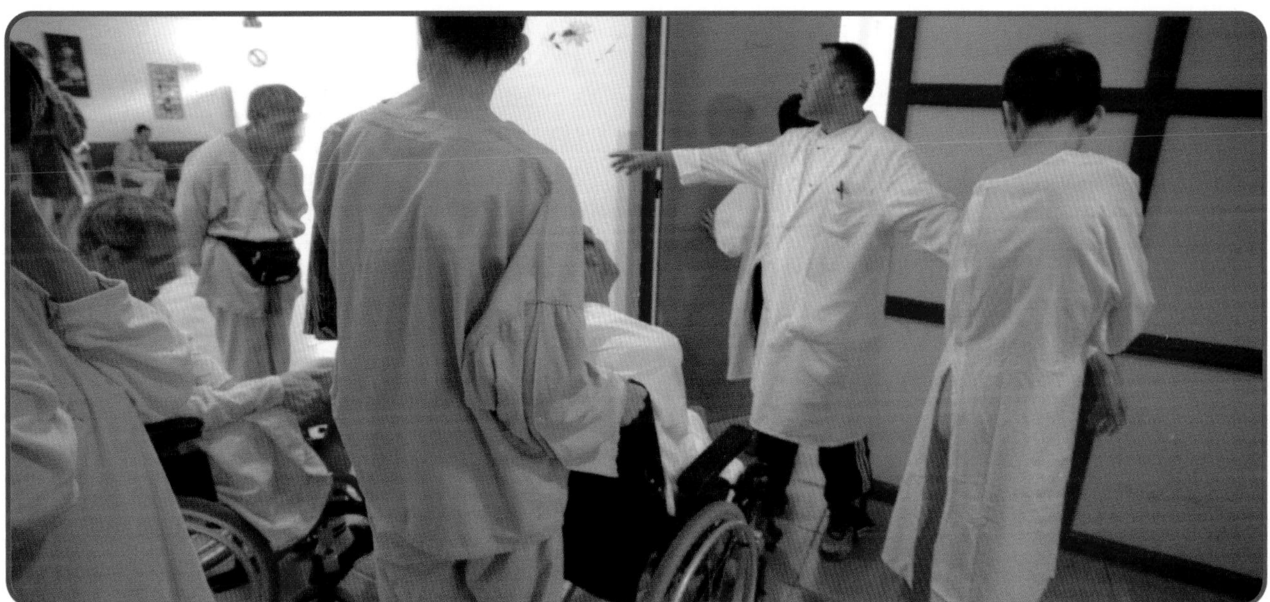

Figure 17.19 *The use of reinforcement in token economy systems has been widely adopted in many institutional settings, including schools, prisons and psychiatric hospitals.*

How Psychology Works

Choosing inferential tests

Consider the following studies and in each case decide which inferential statistical test should be used to analyse the data. Write a short paragraph explaining the reasons for your choice in each case.

An experiment to see if there is a significant difference in the time taken to complete a word puzzle with or without an audience

In one condition, participants complete the puzzle alone and have to press a stopwatch recording time in milliseconds when they have finished. In the other condition, a completely different set of participants perform the same task but with an audience of three onlookers. The two sets of data have similar standard deviations.

A study to see whether high-sugar snacks have a significant effect on alertness at work

A group of 50 office workers are asked to indicate whether they feel 'more sluggish', 'less sluggish' or 'no different' after consuming high-sugar snacks at break-time.

A study to investigate the relationship between height and business success

A sample of 50 business executives complete a rating scale which gives an overall rating of success in relation to variables such as personal satisfaction, earnings and confidence. At the top of the questionnaire, each participant's height in centimetres is recorded.

An observation of differences in male and female trolley-pushing in two different retail outlets: a food store and a DIY store

One hundred male-female couples are observed at a supermarket selling predominantly food, and another 100 couples are observed at a DIY store. In each store, the couples are observed as they are progressing along an aisle. At the midpoint along the aisle, the researcher records whether the male or the female partner is pushing the trolley.

A study to see whether there is a significant difference in attitude in patients with depression after taking medication

Thirty patients suffering from depression are asked to complete a self-report scale before they start taking medication. On the scale, each patient individually indicates the strength of their 'positive life outlook' on a scale of 1–10. After 4 weeks on medication, the same patients are asked to complete the same rating scale again. The two sets of ratings are compared to see whether or not there is any improvement in attitude.

Further Reading

Introductory texts

Coolican, H. (2004) *Research Methods and Statistics in Psychology,* London: Hodder & Stoughton.
Howitt, D. and Cramer, D. (2007) *Introduction to Statistics in Psychology,* 4th edn., Harlow: Prentice Hall.

Appendix

df	.05	.01
1	3.84	6.64
2	5.99	9.21
3	7.82	11.34
4	9.49	13.28
5	11.07	15.09
6	12.59	16.81
7	14.07	18.48
8	15.51	20.09
9	16.92	21.67
10	18.31	23.21

Figure A1: *Critical values of chi squared*

The calculated value of chi squared is significant if it is equal to or larger than the table (critical) value

Source: Lindley, D. V., & Miller, J. C. P. (1973) *Cambridge elementary statistical tables*, Cambridge University Press, Cambridge.

df	One-tailed .05	One-tailed .01	Two-tailed .05	Two-tailed .01
1	6.314	31.821	12.706	63.657
2	2.920	6.965	4.303	9.925
3	2.353	4.541	3.182	5.841
4	2.132	30747	2.776	4.604
5	2.015	3.365	2.571	4.032
6	1.943	3.143	2.447	3.707
7	1.895	2.998	2.365	3.499
8	1.860	2.896	2.306	3.355
9	1.833	2.821	2.262	3.250
10	1.812	2.764	2.228	3.169
11	1.796	2.718	2.201	3.106
12	1.782	2.681	2.179	3.055
13	1.771	2.650	2.160	3.012
14	1.761	2.624	2.145	2.977
15	1.753	2.602	2.131	2.947
16	1.746	2.583	2.120	2.921
17	1.740	2.567	2.110	2.898
18	1.734	2.552	2.101	2.878
19	1.729	2.539	2.093	2.861
20	1.725	2.528	2.086	2.845
21	1.721	2.518	2.080	2.831
22	1.717	2.508	2.074	2.819
23	1.714	2.500	2.069	2.807
24	1.711	2.492	2.064	2.797

Figure A2: *Critical values in the t-test*

	One-tailed		Two-tailed	
df	.05	.01	.05	.01
25	1.708	2.485	2.060	2.787
26	1.706	2.479	2.056	2.779
27	1.703	2.473	2.052	2.771
28	1.701	2.467	2.048	2.763
29	1.699	2.462	2.045	2.756
30	1.697	2.457	2.042	2.750

Figure A2: *continued*

Calculated value for t is significant if it is equal to or larger than the table (critical) value

Source: Lindley, D. V., and Miller, J. C. P. (1973) *Cambridge elementary statistical tables*, Cambridge University Press, Cambridge.

	One-tailed		Two-tailed	
N	**.05**	**.01**	**.05**	**.01**
5	.900	1.000	1.000	–
6	.829	.943	.886	1.000
7	.714	.893	.786	.929
8	.643	.833	.738	.881
9	.600	.783	.683	.833
10	.564	.746	.648	.794
12	.506	.712	.591	.777
14	.456	.645	.544	.715
16	.425	.601	.506	.665
18	.399	.564	.475	.625
20	.377	.534	.450	.591
22	.359	.508	.428	.562
24	.343	.485	.409	.537
26	.329	.465	.392	.515
28	.317	.448	.377	.496
30	.306	.432	.364	.478

Figure A3: *Critical values of Spearman's rho*

The calculated value of rho is significant if it is equal to or larger than the table (critical) value

Source: Olds, E. G. (1994) The 5% significance levels for sums of squares of rank differences and a correction, *Annals of Mathematical Statistics*, 20, The Institute of Mathematical Statistics

The A2 examinations are two hours long. For Unit 3 you have to answer three questions: one on child development and two on applied options. For Unit 4 you have to answer three questions: one from a choice of two on approaches, and two compulsory questions, one on debates and one on methods. Each question carries 20 marks, so you should aim to spend 40 minutes on each question in the examination.

All questions are structured in subsections. The first subsections are usually short-answer questions and the final subsection is a 12-mark question which requires extended writing.

1) Short-answer questions

These are typically worth between 2 and 6 marks.

Examples of short-answer questions:

- Outline **two** subtypes of schizophrenia.
- Explain what Gilligan meant by *ethic of care.*
- Describe what is meant by *privation.*
- Briefly discuss **one** limitation of anger management as a treatment for offending.

2) Long-answer questions

These are normally worth 12 marks. A typical 12-mark question asks for description and evaluation or discussion of a theory, an explanation, a treatment or some research. Occasionally you might see a 'Compare…' question. In the 12-mark questions, a third of the marks are for description and knowledge, and two-thirds are for evaluation/analysis/application/comparison. You should spend plenty of time on this subsection of the question.

3) Scenario questions

Some questions are designed so that students apply their knowledge of psychology to a novel situation. For example, a question might include a scenario about two people who manage stress at work in different ways. In this case, students have to apply their knowledge of coping with stress to the scenario.

4) Research methods assessment

Unit 4 has one full question on methods. This is heavily structured, with lots of subsections, mostly requiring short answers on a research scenario that has been described. There is no 12-mark subsection in the methods question. This question will test your knowledge of designing and implementing research, and of how to analyse and interpret data, and draw conclusions.

In addition, short questions on research methods will appear in other questions on both Unit 3 and Unit 4. As an example of how this would work, questions in Unit 3 might ask about conducting an observation on attachment or about how to carry out a conservation experiment.

Note that research methods questions in the Unit 3 examination will not test the research methods content of Unit 4.

Accommodation Changing an existing schema to deal with a new situation or developing a new schema.

Adaptation The child's construction of a set of schemas which accurately match his/her environment.

Addiction Where substance abuse leads to both physical and psychological addiction. See also *Physical dependence*.

Adult attachment interview An interview procedure developed to assess the type of attachment relationship a parent had as a child.

Affectionless psychopathy An inability to have feelings for another person.

Anal personality In Freudian theory, results from fixation at the anal stage and consists of the traits of orderliness, miserliness and obstinacy.

Anal stage A psychosexual stage of development in Freudian theory. It occurs during the second year of life when the child gains control of anal muscles and is being toilet-trained. Fixation at this stage may lead to the *anal personality*.

Anger management A treatment that involves learning to recognise and control anger.

Animism The belief that inanimate objects have feelings and intentions.

Antipsychotic drugs Drugs used to treat psychotic disorders such as schizophrenia.

Assimilation Adding to an existing schema or applying an existing schema to a new situation.

Atavistic form Lombroso's idea that criminals are a separate species with primitive characteristics.

Attachment An affectional tie or bond between two people, usually characterised by attachment behaviours such as proximity seeking and separation distress.

Attachment figure The preferred object of attachment – for example, a parent would most usually be an attachment figure for a young child.

Attachment Q-sort A method for measuring attachment using a set of behavioural descriptors on cards.

Autonomic nervous system Made up of the sympathetic and parasympathetic nervous systems. The sympathetic nervous system prepares the body for flight or fight. The parasympathetic nervous system supports normal and routine body functions.

Aversion therapy A form of behaviour therapy which involves pairing an unpleasant stimulus with an undesired behaviour.

Behaviour modification A psychological treatment based on operant conditioning principles of reinforcement.

Behaviour shaping Reinforcement for performance of a complex activity; reinforcement is given for successive approximations to the desired behaviour until a long sequence of behaviours is performed for a single reward.

Behaviourist approach An approach to psychology that states that behaviour is learned through association between response and consequence.

Biofeedback A technique for managing stress by gaining feedback about bodily responses, such as heart rate and blood pressure. The person tries to change their bodily responses.

Biological determinism The view that all behaviour and thought are determined by genes, the brain and nervous system.

Bipolar depression Mood disorder in which a person changes between two extreme mood states: depression and mania.

Bottom-up theory An approach to explaining cognitive processes that suggests they are influenced mainly by incoming stimuli rather than by previously stored information.

Centration The child's tendency to deal with only one aspect of a situation at a time.

Cerebral cortex Most highly developed part of the brain in human beings. To do with memory, awareness, creative thinking and problem solving.

Class inclusion An understanding that some classes of objects include other subclasses of objects. For example, the class of 'flowers' includes the class of 'roses'.

Classical conditioning A form of learning in which a stimulus (the CS) acquires the ability to cause a behavioural response originally evoked by another stimulus (the UCS).

Cognitive approach An approach to psychology that emphasises the role of thinking and understanding in behaviour.

Cognitive interview An approach to interviewing witnesses aimed at enhancing accuracy and the amount of detail recalled.

Cognitive maps Mental representations of features of a physical area.

Cognitive neuropsychology Area of psychology where the workings of the brain are linked to cognitive processes. Often people with brain damage are used to understand which cognitive processes are affected and impaired.

Cognitive processes Mental processes, which we may or may not be aware of, that are involved with thought, perception, memory and attention.

Cognitive restructuring Form of cognitive therapy used to treat stress by getting the person to replace negative and self-esteem-lowering thoughts with positive thoughts.

Communication theory Theory of attachment suggesting infants and young children attach to those with whom they are best able to communicate.

Comparative psychology Field of psychology involving the study of non-human species and extrapolation or generalisation of the findings to human behaviour.

Composite system System for construction of a facial likeness which involves combining separate facial features.

Concordance Mathematical estimation of the likelihood that a behaviour trait or characteristic is inherited. Concordance is expressed as a percentage and is based on correlation.

Confabulation Adjusting memories to fit with expectations, beliefs and stereotypes.

Conscience Part of the *superego* which tends to inhibit wrong actions and leads to guilt following wrongdoing.

Conscious In Freudian theory, that which you are aware of at any time.

Conservation Ability to understand that redistributing material does not affect its mass, number or volume.

Constructivism View of cognitive development which suggests that the child constructs a mental model of the world.

Critical period Period of time after birth during which a specific behaviour or ability is acquired or develops.

Cultural specificity Where an observation applies only to a particular culture and not to other cultures.

De-centring Ability to take into account more than one factor. Achieved in the stage of concrete operations according to Piaget.

Defence mechanisms In Freudian psychoanalysis, these operate at an unconscious level. Defence mechanisms, such as repression, help deal with inner conflicts between the id, ego and superego.

Demand characteristics Where the participants in an experiment try to guess the aim of the experiment and may behave to please (or displease) the researcher.

Depressants Act to slow down the activity of the central nervous system to make a person feel calm and relaxed. Depressants include opiates and tranquillisers such as valium.

Deprivation Losing something one has once had: in relation to attachment, the loss of an attachment figure, either short term or long term.

Determinism The view that human behaviour and thought are determined by forces beyond the person's control. See also *Soft* and *Hard determinism.*

Diathesis-stress model Diathesis refers to a genetic vulnerability that a person has for developing an illness – for example, schizophrenia. Stress is the environmental 'trigger' for the illness to occur.

Differential association theory A theory of offending which states that offending is learned through exposure to criminal norms and values.

Discovery learning Learning things by discovering them for yourself as a result of active exploration. Piaget assumed that children learn through active self-discovery during play rather than by instruction.

Disequilibrium State of cognitive imbalance that occurs when incoming information conflicts with our pre-existing understanding of the world. Leads to accommodation.

Distributive justice Moral reasoning about how material goods should be fairly divided.

Dizygotic twins Twins from two separately fertilised eggs who have the same genetic similarity as ordinary siblings (50%). Sometimes known as fraternal or non-identical twins.

Double-blind study Where the researcher administering the test or procedure is unaware of the aim of

the study. In double-blind research the results are less likely to be affected by demand characteristics and researcher expectations.

Electroconvulsive therapy Controversial treatment for severe depression which involves passing electricity through the brain to induce a seizure.

Emotion-focused strategy Strategy for coping with stress in which the individual attempts to deal with stress by controlling his/her emotional response. See also *Problem-focused strategy.*

Empirical approach Obtaining knowledge, information and data through observation and through our senses.

Endocrine system Number of glands located in different parts of the body that secrete hormones. The endocrine system is controlled by the hypothalamus.

Environment (or nurture in the nature–nurture debate). The view that all learning, behaviour and personality comes from environmental experiences.

Equilibrium A state of cognitive balance.

Evolutionary psychology The study of the evolutionary origin of human behaviour patterns – for example, sexual behaviour, jealousy and human emotions.

Existential philosophy Asks fundamental questions about what it is to be human and what is the meaning of life. Influenced the development of humanistic psychology.

Experimenter bias This occurs when the wishes, attitudes and beliefs of the experimenter influence the research procedure and/or outcome.

Expiatory punishment The view that a person has to pay for wrongdoing, possibly by harsh and arbitrary punishment.

Extinction When a behaviour ceases to be emitted or repeated.

Eyewitness testimony Verbal or written account of an event given by a person who witnessed the event.

Face recognition unit (FRU) A feature of the Bruce and Young model of face recognition containing structural information about a person's face.

False memory Memory for an event which did not take place, but which is believed to be true.

Family therapy Approach to the treatment of mental disorders in which the whole family is involved and communication patterns are identified and changed.

Fear-arousing appeals Use of fear – for example, shocking images – to prevent people behaving in certain ways – for instance, to get people to stop smoking.

Feature-analysis theory Theory of face recognition emphasising the importance of individual facial features.

Flashbulb memory Where memory for a shocking event incorporates recall of what else occurred at the time the event took place.

Folk psychology The beliefs, values, attitudes and morals held by a culture or subculture.

Forensic psychology Area of psychology involved in all aspects of criminal behaviour.

Formal operations One of Piaget's stages of cognitive development, in which the child is capable of abstract thought and thinking hypothetically.

Free will Central principle of humanistic psychology; a person is seen as having free choice. Related to the idea of personal responsibility.

Frustration–aggression hypothesis The theory that frustration results in aggression (Dollard and Miller).

Fully functioning person Proposed by Carl Rogers, a person who achieves goals, ambitions and life aspirations. A person who is able to self-actualise.

Gender concept The ability to label one's own and others' gender correctly.

General symbolic function The ability to understand that one thing can stand for another. Linked to the development of language.

Genetic engineering Changing physical, behavioural and psychological characteristics through genetic manipulation.

Genital stage Starts at puberty and in Freudian theory represents appropriate direction of the sexual instinct to heterosexual pleasure and intercourse.

Geographical approach An approach to offender profiling that uses information about crime locations to infer the likely home or base of an offender.

Gestalt psychology School of psychology holding the view that humans are best studied as organised, structured wholes and not analysed into numerous component parts. See also *Holism*.

Guided participation Type of scaffolding that occurs during the transmission of cultural practices.

Hallucinations Imaginary experiences, which may be visual, auditory or somatic.

Hard determinism Extreme determinism viewpoint that all behaviour and thought are caused by forces outside the person's control.

Hardiness Personality characteristic that protects and helps a person deal with stress. Acts as a buffer against stress.

Hereditary Traits, predispositions and characteristics inherited from parents and ancestors. Represents the nature side of the nature–nurture debate.

Heritability coefficient A number between 0 and 1.0 representing the extent to which a human characteristic is genetic in origin. A value of 1.0 means entirely genetic; a value of 0 means genetics play no role at all.

Holism The view that the whole person has to be studied rather than component parts or smaller aspects. The view of humanistic and gestalt psychologists.

Holistic form theory Theory of face recognition emphasising the importance of the face as a whole, including the general layout or configuration.

Homogeneous variances Where two sets of scores show a similar level of variability.

Horizontal décalage When a child shows cognitive abilities characteristic of more than one developmental stage.

Humanism See *Humanistic psychology*.

Humanistic psychology Known as the 'third force' in psychology, adopts the principles of free will and holism to focus on human subjective perceptions and experience. Developed by Carl Rogers and Abraham Maslow.

Hypothalamic-pituitary-andrenocortical system HPAC. HPAC is a system in the brain activated by messages from the central nervous system in response to stress.

Id The most primitive, unconscious part of the mind in Freudian theory of personality. It operates according to the pleasure principle. The sex (life) and aggressive (death) instincts originate in the id.

Ideal self The kind of person we would like to be.

Identification Adopting a range of attitudes, values and behaviours from a role model, especially a parent.

Idiographic approach An approach in psychology which recognises the uniqueness of the individual in terms of experiences, feelings, motivations, etc. Often employs qualitative methods.

Imprinting Instinctive following behaviour shown in species that are mobile from birth, whereby newborn animals follow the first large, moving object they see.

Inductive method Where single observations are made, regularities noticed and generalisations or theory inferred from the observations. Represents a common-sense view of science.

Inferential tests Statistical tests to test for a significant effect, i.e. an effect that is unlikely to have happened by chance.

Information-processing approach (to cognitive development) Focuses on quantitative changes in cognitive abilities and increased cognitive efficiency with age.

Insight Thinking or problem solving involving incubation of relevant information followed by the sudden realisation of a solution.

Interactional synchrony Where the movements and utterances of an infant and adult are synchronised in time.

Internal working model Theory of attachment whereby a child's earliest attachment relationship acts as a model for all future relationships.

Internalisation Process by which children take on an understanding of the world as a result of contact with parents, peers and others.

Interpersonal psychotherapy Used to treat people suffering from depression by changing how the person interacts with friends, intimate partner, family and work colleagues.

Interval data Where the units of measurement are of equal or defined size.

Introspection Reflecting on one's mental processes, perception, attention, etc. Used by Wilhelm Wundt over 100 years ago.

Latent stage In Freudian theory, occurs from 5–6 years until the onset of puberty. No psychosexual development is said to take place during this stage.

Leading question A question that suggests a likely answer.

Learning Relatively permanent change in the behaviour, thoughts and feelings of an organism resulting from prior experience.

Level of measurement The type of data: nominal, ordinal or interval level.

Level of significance The level of probability at which a researcher will decide to reject the H0 and accept the H1, or vice versa. The usual level of significance for psychological research is 0.05 or 5%.

Libido Freud's term meaning sexual motivation.

Light therapy Treatment for seasonal affective disorder involving exposure to bright light for 1–2 hours a day.

Limbic system Structure located deep in the brain responsible for emotion, motivation and learning.

Locus of control Personality dimension concerned with the extent to which a person thinks and feels that they are able to control what happens to them.

Longitudinal study A study which takes place over a period of time, where the researcher studies the same individual or group of participants on more than one occasion.

Maternal deprivation The loss of a mother figure or primary attachment figure. The consequences of such loss were popularised as a theory of maternal deprivation in the 1950s by John Bowlby.

Mediational processes Cognitive processes or mental events that take place between stimulus and response.

Meta analysis Research involving the collation of results from a number of separate studies to enable an overall view of findings on a particular research topic.

Meta-cognitive awareness Awareness of one's cognitive processes and abilities.

Model In social learning theory, a person being observed who can be a strong influence on another person's behaviour.

Monotropy Key feature of Bowlby's theory of attachment, according to which a child can attach to only one attachment figure.

Monozygotic twins Twins from a single egg that divides after fertilisation. Also referred to as identical twins because they have 100% of genes in common.

Moral comparison technique Children compare two contrasting stories of wrongdoing. Used by Piaget to study moral reasoning.

Moral dilemma A situation in which a person has to choose between two alternative actions, both of which involve some degree of wrongdoing.

Moral realism A stage in Piaget's theory of moral development, where children's judgments are based on the authority of parents and others, and focus on the seriousness of the consequences.

Moral relativism A stage in Piaget's theory of moral development, where children's judgements are based on their internalised moral beliefs and take account of intentions.

Morality of care Tendency to focus on the effects of actions on the feelings and needs of others, on relationships and on the prevention of harm.

Morality of justice Tendency to focus on whether or not society's rules have been broken and appropriate punishment.

Motherese Simplified and exaggerated form of language used by adults and older children when addressing young children and babies.

Nativist A philosophical view that states that human characteristics are innate or a result of nature.

Nature The influence of genetic factors, including maturation, on development.

Nature–nurture debate A disagreement about what determines psychological development. Nativists believe that *nature* is the main influence, whereas *empiricists* believe that *nurture* is the main influence.

Need for cognition is a personality variable. People high in need for cognition enjoy thinking about a task or problem and have a need to understand the world.

Negative reinforcement When a response (or behaviour) is strengthened due to the removal of an adverse (painful or unpleasant) stimulus. See also *Positive reinforcement.*

Neurotransmitters Chemicals which operate at the synapses of neurons to change neural activity.

Nominal data (categorical data) Where the unit of measurement refers to people or events in categories.

Nomothetic approach An approach in psychology that looks for similarities between people and attempts to establish general laws about human behaviour. Often employs quantitative methods and laboratory experiments.

Non-parametric test A type of statistical test that involves rank ordering the scores before calculating the test. Non-parametric tests are less sensitive than their parametric equivalents.

Normal distribution Where most scores in a set cluster around the mean, with just a few at each extreme. A typical bell-shaped distribution.

Nurture The influence of environmental factors on development.

Object concept Awareness that objects exist independently and continue to exist even when not visible.

Object relations theory Developed by the psychoanalyst Melanie Klein, takes as central concern the relationships a person has with other people, most notably parents and significant others.

Observational learning Learning through observation and imitation of the behaviour of others. Also known as social learning.

Oedipus complex Occurs during the phallic stage. The male child desires the opposite-sex parent. The resolution of the Oedipus conflict results in appropriate gender identity.

Official statistics Crime data based on all crimes reported to and recorded by the authorities.

One-tailed hypothesis A hypothesis that predicts an effect in a single direction.

Operant conditioning Type of learning that occurs through either reinforcement or punishment of a behavioural response.

Operation A powerful internal schema enabling logical thought processes – for example, in adding, subtracting, multiplying and dividing.

Oral stage A psychosexual stage of development in Freudian theory. It occurs in the first year of life and is centred around the mouth and oral pleasure. Fixation at this stage may result in an oral personality in adulthood.

Ordinal data Where the units of measurement can be ordered from lowest to highest, but the units are not of equal or defined size.

Organismic theory Treats the individual in terms of physical and mental aspects as a unified whole. Developed by Kurt Goldstein and influenced the development of humanistic psychology.

Paradigm Suggested by Thomas Kuhn to characterise a mature science. A set of shared assumptions about the subject matter and methods of inquiry of a science. Kuhn saw psychology as in a pre-science stage.

Parametric test A type of statistical test used with data that conform to parametric criteria. Parametric tests are calculated on actual scores and are therefore more sensitive than non-parametric tests.

Peak experiences Feelings of ecstasy and deep satisfaction. Some people regard peak experiences as mystical or spiritual. To do with humanistic psychology.

Peer influence Social pressure that peer groups bring to bear on a person to conform. An important factor in substance abuse.

Person identity node (PIN) A feature of the Bruce and Young model of face recognition, containing personal information about a person – for example, where they live, their job.

Person × Situation Effect Behaviour in a given situation is a result of the combined effects of personality traits and the situation the person is in at the time.

Personal growth In humanistic psychology, the idea that the person grows and changes throughout life. Personal growth comes about through self-actualisation, peak experiences and freedom from fear or threat.

Person-centred approach (or client-centred approach) In humanistic psychology, focuses on the person's subjective experience of the world. Developed by Carl Rogers.

Phallic stage Third stage of psychosexual development in Freudian theory. Here boys and girls gain pleasure from the genital area. The most important aspect of the phallic stage is the *Oedipus complex*.

Phenomenology Philosophical method developed to examine human experience and how people live their lives. Linked to subjective experience and humanistic psychology.

Phenylketonuria (PKU) An inherited disorder affecting metabolism. The damaging effects of the disorder can be completely prevented if the individual follows a strictly regulated diet from birth.

Philosophy A method of rational inquiry using logic, reason and argument to find knowledge and truth. Derived from the Greek word *philosophia*, which means the love of wisdom.

Physical dependence Where the body has got used to a substance and continued usage is needed to maintain the body in its now 'normal' state. Stopping the substance will lead to withdrawal. See also *Addiction*.

Positive regard In Rogers' person-centred humanistic approach, this is to do with how others judge and evaluate a person. See also *Unconditional positive regard*.

Positive reinforcement When a response (or behaviour) is strengthened because it is followed by a reward or reinforcement. See also *Negative reinforcement*.

Post-event contamination Where a witness's memory for an event is adversely affected after the event – for example, by leading questions.

Preconscious Thoughts and memories that can be brought to consciousness with relative ease.

Pre-operational stage The second of Piaget's stages of cognitive development, in which the child's understanding of the world is shaped by appearances rather than logical thought.

Prevention techniques Used to prevent people from becoming substance abusers. There are primary, secondary and tertiary prevention techniques.

Private experience Unique to the individual, subjective and not easily investigated using scientific procedures.

Privation Never having had the chance to form an attachment relationship with anyone.

Probability The percentage likelihood that an observed effect is due to chance.

Problem-focused strategy Strategy for coping with stress which involves addressing the source of the stress. See also *Emotion-focused strategy*.

Prochaska model Model of behaviour change concerned with helping to stop people abusing substances.

Projection A psychoanalytic defence mechanism whereby an individual projects or attributes unwanted or painful thoughts and feelings onto another person.

Pro-social behaviour Where participants are given a hypothetical situation in which there is an opportunity for doing good.

Protest, despair, detachment A sequence of behaviours seen in separation situations.

Psychic determinism Sigmund Freud's view that all thought and behaviour are determined by unconscious forces associated with the sex and death instincts.

Psychoanalytic theory A theory developed by Sigmund Freud emphasising the importance of unconscious motives.

Psychodynamic approach An approach to psychology emphasising the importance of unconscious motives.

Psychological dependence The emotional and cognitive compulsion to take a drug. See also *Physical dependence*.

Psychosexual development The development of the self, which Freud believed was strongly influenced by sexual motivation.

Psychosexual stages Freudian stages of development, including the oral stage, the anal stage and the phallic stage. The stages are linked to the sexual instinct.

Psychosocial development According to Erikson, this takes place over eight stages, from birth to old age.

Punishment Reduces the likelihood of a behaviour occurring in the future or stops it happening at all.

Purposive behaviour Behaviour performed by an organism (human or other animal) that is directed at achieving a goal or objective.

Radical behaviourism Extreme form of behaviourism solely concerned with observable behaviour as an object of scientific psychology.

Rational-emotive therapy Treatment for depression where negative, irrational thoughts are replaced with positive, rational thought (Albert Ellis). A form of cognitive therapy.

Reaction formation A psychoanalytic defence mechanism in which a person behaves in the opposite way to how he/she actually thinks or feels.

Recidivism Reoffending, usually expressed as a percentage rate of reoffending.

Reciprocal determinism A concept proposed by Albert Bandura in an attempt to bring together idiographic and nomothetic approaches.

Reciprocal punishment Punishment that reflects the nature and severity of the wrongdoing.

Recovered memory Emergence of a memory for an event of which the person had no previous recollection.

Reductionism The view that to understand human beings, psychologists have to analyse and reduce the whole to the simplest component parts. Consciousness, for example, may be reduced to the action of neurons in the brain.

Reinforcement A stimulus that increases the likelihood of behaviour occurring in the future. Positive reinforcement occurs when a behaviour is strengthened because it is followed by a reward. Negative reinforcement strengthens a behaviour because it is followed by removal of an aversive stimulus.

Reliability Consistency of a psychological measure.

Repression A psychoanalytic defence mechanism which keeps disturbing, threatening and unpleasant memories at an unconscious level and so stops such thoughts becoming conscious.

Restorative justice An approach to justice which involves the offender making amends to the victim.

Reversibility A mental operation in which a previous operation is undone.

Scaffolding Support and prompting, usually provided by an adult, which is gradually withdrawn as the child becomes more competent.

Schedules of reinforcement Include fixed and variable ratios, and fixed and variable interval schedules of reinforcement.

Schema A cognitive structure consisting of a set of linked mental representations of the world, which we use both to understand and to respond to situations.

Schizophrenia A psychotic disorder characterised by distorted perceptions of the world and loss of touch with reality. The person may hear voices and suffer hallucinations.

Seasonal affective disorder (SAD) Type of depression that typically occurs during the winter months when days are short.

Secondary drive theory A theory of attachment, according to which infants attach to those who feed them.

Self-actualisation Concerned with psychological growth and realising the true and full potential of an individual. Central to Maslow's humanistic theory of human needs.

Self-concept In humanistic psychology, this has two components: self-image and the ideal self. The ideal self is how we would like to be and may differ from how we are.

Self-disclosure The giving of personal or intimate information about oneself to others.

Self-efficacy The belief that one is able to achieve certain goals or succeed at something.

Self-esteem The evaluative dimension of the self.

Self-fulfilling prophecy A statement that becomes true simply because it has been made.

Self-image Factual or descriptive information about the self, including information about looks and social roles.

Self-management Approaches/techniques that help a person manage, for example, stress or a substance abuse problem.

Self-report measures Where information is collected by asking people about their own behaviour.

Self-worth In Rogers' person-centred theory, to do with how we value and regard ourselves. Conceptualised on a continuum from high to low.

Sensorimotor stage First of Piaget's stages of cognitive development, in which the child's understanding of the world is restricted to sensations and movements, and the here and now.

Separation anxiety A consequence of separation from an attachment figure, which continues long term and results in fear of future separations.

Skinner Box A piece of equipment developed by the radical behaviourist B.F. Skinner. A hungry animal, typically a rat, is placed in a box which contains a lever and a food tray. The rat has to learn to press the lever to get the reward of food.

Social inoculation Technique to make people resistant to persuasion and enable attitude and behaviour change. Used to help people resist the social pressure to abuse substances.

Social learning See *Observational learning*.

Social skills training A treatment involving the learning of appropriate social behaviours through demonstration and practice.

Social support Help from family, colleagues and friends to cope with and manage stress.

Sociometric study A technique to assess popularity: relationships between members of a group are assessed through interviews and then represented diagrammatically to show the popularity status of each individual.

Soft determinism A deterministic view of human behaviour, but one which also allows people to exercise a degree of free will.

Solvent abuse Use of everyday products (glues, nail varnish, etc.) to get 'high'. Solvent abuse is very dangerous because of the physically harmful effects of the chemicals.

Somatotype A body type or constitution. The theory of somatotypes was proposed by Sheldon.

Splitting A primitive defence mechanism in object relations theory in which the young infant splits objects (people) and part objects (for example, the breast) into good and bad objects.

Spontaneous recovery Where a previously learned behaviour that has been extinguished recurs in the absence of any new reinforcement.

Stage theory The view that development occurs in a universal and invariant sequence of stages.

Stimulants Substances that stimulate the central nervous system to produce feelings of euphoria and energy (e.g. amphetamines and cocaine).

Stimulus discrimination When an organism that has learned a response to a specific stimulus does *not* respond to new stimuli that are similar to the original.

Stimulus generalisation When an organism that has learned a response to a specific stimulus responds in the same way to other stimuli similar to the original stimulus.

Strange Situation A controlled observation procedure developed by Mary Ainsworth to assess type of attachment.

Stress inoculation training (SIT) A cognitive approach to stress management which integrates both cognitive and emotional responses associated with stress.

Stress management How well a person is able to cope with stress.

Sublimation A psychoanalytic defence mechanism in which unconscious sexual and aggressive thoughts are transformed and channelled into socially acceptable behaviour.

Superego In Freud's structure of the personality, made up of the ideal self and conscience. In Freudian theory, the superego develops as a result of the *Oedipus complex.*

Systematic desensitisation A behavioural therapy used to treat people with phobias or fears.

Token economy A reinforcement-based treatment which involves giving tokens for good behaviour. The tokens may later be exchanged for more tangible reinforcers, such as food.

Tolerance Where there is state of decreasing responsiveness to a frequently taken drug.

Top-down approach An approach to explaining cognitive processes that suggests they are influenced mainly by previously stored information rather than by incoming stimuli.

Transactional model of stress Stress is seen as involving a transaction between the person and their external environment.

Two-tailed hypothesis A hypothesis that predicts an effect but does not specify the direction of the effect.

Type A personality Person who is highly competitive, shows time urgency and demonstrates hostility and anger to other people.

Type B personality Person who is easygoing. Opposite to the Type A personality.

Type C personality Person who is passive, does not complain and is compliant.

Type I error A statistical error whereby the H0 is rejected when, in fact, the results are due to chance.

Type II error A statistical error whereby the H0 is accepted when, in fact, there is an effect.

Typology approach An approach to offender profiling that involves categorising offenders as either organised or disorganised.

Unconditional positive regard Accepting a person for what they are – the person is shown love and respect without being judged.

Unconscious According to Freud, the mind is largely unconscious and has the greatest influence on thoughts, feelings and behaviour. Unconscious thoughts are outside of awareness and cannot be directly brought to consciousness.

Unipolar depression Where a person experiences an extremely low mood state that lasts for weeks or longer.

Validity Where a psychological measure measures what it is supposed to measure.

Vicarious reinforcement Occurs in observational learning when the observer sees another person being reinforced for behaving in a certain way.

Victim surveys Surveys in which people are asked about their experiences as a victim of crime.

Weapon focus The tendency to focus on a weapon if one is present and therefore be unable to recall any other details of the event.

Withdrawal The unpleasant physical and psychological symptoms that occur when a person abruptly ceases taking a drug.

XYY A chromosomal abnormality in males, once linked to offending.

Zone of proximal development The gap between what a child can achieve unaided and what she/he can achieve with the help and support of other people.

ABRAHAM, K. (1916) The first pregenital stage of the libido. *Selected Papers on Psychoanalysis*, New York: Basic Books (work republished), 248–79.

ABRAMSON, L.Y., ALLOY, L.B., HANKIN, B.L., HAEFFEL, G.J., MacCOON, D.G. and GIBB, B.E. (2002) Cognitive vulnerability – stress models of depression in a self-regulatory and psychobiological context. In I.H. Gotlib and C.L. Hammen (eds.), *Handbook of Depression*, New York: Guilford Press, 268–94.

ABRAVANEL, E. and DEYONG, N. (1991) Does object modelling elicit imitative-like gestures from young infants? *Journal of Experimental Child Psychology*, 52, 22–40.

ADAMS, D.B. (1986) Vetromedial tegmental lesions abolish offense without disturbing predation or defense. *Physiology and Behaviour*, 38, 165–8.

ADAMS, H.E., WRIGHT, L.W. and LOHR, B.A. (1996) Is homophobia associated with homosexual arousal? *Journal of Abnormal Psychology*, 105, 440–5.

AINSWORTH, M.D.S., BLEHAR, M., WATERS, E. and WALL, E. (1978) *Patterns of Attachment*, Hillsdale, NJ: Erlbaum.

ALISON, L., BENNELL, C., MOKROS, A. and ORMEROD, D. (2002) The personality paradox in offender profiling. *Psychology, Public Policy and Law*, 8 (1), 115–35.

ALISON, L., SMITH, M.D. and MORGAN, K. (2003) Interpreting the accuracy of offender profiles. *Psychology, Crime and Law*, 9 (2), 185–95.

ALLISON, D.B., HESHKA, S., NEALE, M.C. and LYKKEN, D.T. (1994) A genetic analysis of relative weight among 4.020 twin pairs, with an emphasis on sex effects. *Health Psychology*, 13, 362–5.

ALLPORT, G.W. (1937) *Personality: A Psychological Interpretation*, New York: Holt.

ANDERSON, P. (1993) Management of alcohol problems: the role of the general practitioner. *Alcohol and Alcoholism*, 28, 263–72.

ANDREWS, D.A. and BONTA, J. (2006) *The Psychology of Criminal Conduct*, 4th edn., New York: Anderson Publishing, LexisNexis.

ANDREWS, D.A., ZINGER, I., HOGE, R.D., BONTA, J., GENDREAU, P. and CULLEN, F.T. (1990) Does correctional treatment work? A clinically relevant and informed meta-analysis. *Criminology*, 28, 369–404.

ANDREWS, G. and HALFORD, G.S. (1998) Children's ability to make transitive inferences: the importance of premise integration and structural complexity. *Cognitive Development*, 13, 479–513.

ASCH, S. (1951) Effects of group pressure on the modification and distortion of judgements. In H. Gretzikow (ed.), *Groups, Leadership and Men*, Pittsburgh, KS: Carnegie Press.

ASCH, S. (1955) Opinions and social pressure. *Scientific American*, 193, 5, 31–5.

ASHTON, H. (2002) Benzodiazepine abuse. In W. Caan and J. de Belleroche (eds.), *Drink, Drugs and Dependence: From Science to Clinical Practice*, London: Routledge.

ATKINSON, R.C. and SHIFFRIN, R.M. (1971) The control of short-term memory. *Scientific American*, 225 (2), 82–90.

AYER, A.J. (1959) Privacy. *Proceedings of the British Academy*, 45, 43–65.

BAGWELL, C.L., NEWCOMB, A.F. and BUKOWSKI, W.M. (1998) Preadolescent friendship and peer rejection as predictors of adult adjustment. *Child Development*, 69, 140–53.

BAHRICK, H.P. (1984) Memory for people. In J.E. Harris and P.E. Morris (eds.), *Everyday Memory, Actions and Absentmindedness*, London: Academic Press.

BAILEY, J.M., PILLARD, R.C., NEALE, M.C. and AGYEI, Y. (1993) Heritable factors influence sexual orientation in women. *Archives of General Psychiatry*, 50, 217–23.

BAILLARGEON, R. (1986) Representing the existence and the location of hidden objects: object permanence in 6- and 8-month-old infants. *Cognition*, 23, 21–41.

BAILLARGEON, R. and DEVOS, J. (1991) Object permanence in young infants: further evidence. *Child Development*, 62, 1227–46.

BAKER-WARD, L., GORDON, B.N., ORNSTEIN, P.A., LARUS, D. and CLUBB, P.A. (1993) Young children's long-term retention of a pediatric examination. *Child Development*, 64, 1519–33.

BANDURA, A. (1965) Influence of models' reinforcement contingencies on the acquisitions of imitative responses. *Journal of Personality and Social Psychology*, 1, 589–95.

BANDURA, A. (1971) *Social Learning Theory*, 2nd edn., Morristown, NJ: General Learning Press.

BANDURA, A. (1977) *Social Learning Theory*, Englewood Cliffs, NJ: Prentice Hall.

BANDURA, A. (1986) *Social Foundations of Thought and Action*, Englewood Cliffs, NJ: Prentice Hall.

BANDURA, A. (1989) Human agency in social cognitive theory. *American Psychologist*, 44, 1175–84.

BANDURA, A. (1991) Social cognitive theory of moral thought and action. In W.M. Kurtiveness and J.L. Guentz (eds.), *Handbook of Moral Behaviour and Development. Volume 1: Theory*, Hillsdale, NJ: Erlbaum.

BANDURA, A. (1995) Reflections on human agency. Keynote address presented at the IV European Congress of Psychology, Athens, Greece, July.

BANDURA, A. (1997) *Self-efficacy: The Exercise of Control*, New York: W.H. Freeman.

BANDURA, A., REESE, L. and ADAMS, N. (1982) Microanalysis of action and fear arousal as a function of differential levels of perceived self-efficacy. *Journal of Personality and Social Psychology*, 43, 5–21.

BANDURA, A., ROSS, D. and ROSS, S.A. (1961) Transmission of aggression through imitation of aggressive models. *Journal of Abnormal and Social Psychology*, 63, 575–82.

BANDURA, A., ROSS, D. and ROSS, S.A. (1963) Imitation of film-mediated aggressive models. *Journal of Abnormal and Social Psychology*, 66, 3–11.

BANISTER, P., BURMAN, E., PARKER, I., TAYLOR, M. and TINDALL, C. (1994) *Qualitative Methods in Psychology*, Buckingham: Open University Press.

BARNES, P. (1995) *Personal, Social and Emotional Development of Children*, Milton Keynes: Open University Press.

BARON, R.A. and RICHARDSON, D.R. (1994) *Human Aggression*, 2nd edn., New York: Plenum Press.

BARTLETT, F.C. (1932) *Remembering: A Study in Experimental and Social Psychology*, Cambridge: Cambridge University Press.

BARTOL, C. (1996) Police psychology: then, now and beyond. *Criminal Justice and Behaviour*, 23, 70–89.

BATESON, G., JACKSON, D.D., HALEY, J. *et al.* (1956) Toward a theory of schizophrenia. *Behavioural Science*, 1, 251–64.

BAUM, W.M. (1994) John B. Watson and behaviour analysis. In J.T. Todd and E.K. Morris (eds.), *Modern Perspectives on John B. Watson and Classical Behaviourism*, Westport, CT: Greenwood Press.

BAUMEISTER, R.F. and COVINGTON, M.V. (1985) Self-esteem, persuasion and retrospective distortion of initial attitudes. *Electronic Social Psychology*, 1, 1–22.

BECK, A. (1991) Cognitive therapy: a 30-year retrospective. *American Psychologist,* 46, 368–75.

BECK, A.T. (1976) *Cognitive Therapy and the Emotional Disorders*, New York: International Universities Press.

BECK, A.T. (1987) Cognitive models of depression. *Journal of Cognitive Psychotherapy: An International Quarterly*, 1, 5–37.

BECK, A.T. (1993) Cognitive therapy: past, present, and future. *Journal of Consulting and Clinical Psychology*, 61, 194–8.

BECK, A.T. (2002) Cognitive models of depression. In R.L. Leahy and E.T. Dowd (eds.) *Clinical Advances in Cognitive Psychotherapy: Theory and Application*. New York: Springer.

BECK, A.T. and RECTOR, N.A. (2005) Cognitive approaches to schizophrenia: theory and therapy. *Annual Review of Clinical Psychology*, 1, 577–606.

BECK, A.T. and WEISHAUR, M.E. (1995) Cognitive therapy. In R.J. Corsini and D. Wedding (eds.), *Current Psychotherapies*, 5th edn, Itasca, IL: Peacock.

BECKETT, C., MAUGHAN, B., RUTTER, M., CASTLE, J., COLVERT, E., GROOTHUES, C., KREPPNER, J., STEVENS, S., O'CONNOR, T.G. and SONUGA-BARKE, E.J.S. (2006) Do the effects of early severe deprivation on cognition persist into early adolescence? Findings from the English and Romanian Adoptees Study. *Child Development*, 77 (3), 696–711.

BEE, H. (1989) *The Developing Child*, 5th edn., New York: HarperCollins.

BEE, H. (1997) *The Developing Child*, 8th edn., New York: Addison-Wesley.

BELL, A. (2002) *Debates in Psychology*, Hove, Sussex: Taylor & Francis.

BELSKY, J. (1984) Determinants of parenting: a process model. *Child Development*, 55, 83–96.

BELSKY, J. (1988) The 'effects' of infant day-care reconsidered. *Early Child Research Quarterly*, 3, 235–72.

BENENSON, J.F. (1990) Gender differences in social networks. *Journal of Early Adolescence*, 10, 472–95.

BENENSON, J.F. and CHRISTAKOS, A. (2003) The greater fragility of 'females versus males' closest same-sex friendships. *Child Development*, 74 (4), 1123–9.

BERK, L.E. (2003) *Child Development*, 6th edn., Boston: Allyn & Bacon.

BERKMAN, L.F. and SYME, S.L. (1979) Social networks, host resistance, and mortality: a nine-year follow-up study of Alameda County residents. *American Journal of Epidemiology*, 109, 186–204.

BERRY, J.W. (1969) On cross-cultural comparability. *International Journal of Psychology*, 4, 119–28.

BIGELOW, B.J. and LA GAIPA, J.J. (1975) Children's written descriptions of friendship: a multi-dimensional analysis. *Developmental Psychology*, 11, 857–8.

BILLINGS, A.G. and MOOS, R.H. (1981) The role of coping responses and social resources in attenuating the stress of life events. *Journal of Behavioural Medicine*, 4, 139–58.

BLACKBURN, R. (1993) *The Psychology of Criminal Conduct*, Chichester: Wiley.

BLASI, A. (1980) Bridging moral cognition and moral action: a critical review of the literature. *Psychological Bulletin*, 88, 1–45.

BLATT, S.J. (1999) Personality factors in brief treatment of depression: further analysis of the NIMH-sponsored Treatment for Depression Collaborative Research Program. In D.S. Janowsky (ed.), *Psychotherapy Indications and Outcomes*, Washington, DC: American Psychiatric Press.

BLAZER, D.G., KESSLER, R.C., McGONAGLE, K.A. and SWARTZ, M.S. (1994) The prevalence and distribution of major depression in a national community sample: The National Comorbidity Study. *American Journal of Psychiatry*, 151, 979–86.

BODEN, J.M. and BAUMEISTER, R.F. (1997) Repressive coping: distraction using pleasant thoughts and memories. *Journal of Personality and Social Psychology*, 73, 45–62.

BOEHNKE, K., SILBEREISEN, R.K., EISENBERG, N., REYKOWSKI, J. and PALMONARI, A. (1989) Developmental pattern of prosocial motivation: a cross-national study. *Journal of Cross-Cultural Psychology*, 20, 219–43.

BORJESON, M. (1976) The aetiology of obesity in children. *Acta Paediatrica Scandinavica*, 65, 279–87.

BORKE, H. (1975) Piaget's mountains revisited: changes in the egocentric landscape. *Developmental Psychology*, 11, 240–3.

BORUM, M.L. (2000) A comparison of smoking cessation efforts in African Americans by resident physicians in a traditional and primary care internal medicine residency. *Journal of the American Medical Association*, 92, 131–5.

BOTVIN, G., GRIFFIN, K., DIAZ, T. and IFILL-WILLIAMS, M. (2001) Preventing binge drinking during early adolescence: one- and two-year follow-up of a school-based preventive intervention. *Psychology of Addictive Behaviour*, 15, 360–5.

BOURNE, P.G. (1974) *Addiction*, New York: Academic Press.

BOWER, T.G.R. (1979) *Human Development*, San Francisco: W.H. Freeman.

BOWER, T.G.R. (1971) The object in the world of the infant. *Scientific American*, 225 (4), 30–8.

BOWER, T.G.R. and WISHART, J.G. (1972) The effects of motor skill on object permanence. *Cognition* 1, (2), 28–35.

BOWER, T.G.R., BROUGHTON, J.M. and MOORE, M.K. (1970) The coordination of visual and tactual input in infants. *Perception and Psychophysics*, 8, 51–3.

BOWLBY, J. (1946) *Forty-four Juvenile Thieves*, London: Balliere, Tindall and Cox.

BOWLBY, J. (1951) *Maternal Care and Mental Health*, Geneva: World Health Organization.

BOWLBY, J. (1953) *Child Care and the Growth of Love*, Harmondsworth: Penguin.

BOWLBY, J. (1969) *Attachment*, London: Hogarth Press.

BRACE, N., PIKE, G. and KEMP, R. (2000) Investigating E-FIT using famous faces. In A. Czerederecka, T. Jaskiewicz-Obydzinska and J. Wojcikiewicz (eds.), *Forensic Psychology and Law*, Krakow: Institute of Forensic Research Publishers.

BRANDON, S., BOAKES, J., GLASER, D. and GREEN, R. (1998) Recovered memories of childhood sexual abuse. *The British Journal of Psychiatry*, 172, 296–307.

BRANNON, L. and FEIST, J. (1992) *Health Psychology: An Introduction to Behaviour and Health*, Belmont, CA: Wadsworth.

BREAKWELL, G.M., HAMMOND, S. and FIFE-SHAW, C. (2000) *Research Methods in Psychology*, 2nd edn., London: Sage Publications.

BREIER, A. (1995) Serotonin, schizophrenia and antipsychotic drug action. *Schizophrenia Research*, 14, 187–202.

BREMNER, J.G. (1994) *Infancy*, 2nd edn., Oxford: Blackwell.

BRITISH PSYCHOLOGICAL SOCIETY (2006) *Code of Ethics and Conduct*, Leicester: BPS Publications.

BRODY, G.H. and SHAFFER, D.R. (1982) Contributions of parents and peers to children's moral socialization. *Developmental Review*, 2, 31–75.

BROWN, D., SCHEFLIN, A.W. and HAMMOND, D.C. (1998) *Memory, Trauma and Treatment, and the Law*, New York: Norton.

BROWN, G.W., BONE, M., DALISON, B. and WING, J.K. (1966) *Schizophrenia and Social Care*, London: Oxford University Press.

BROWN, R. and KULIK, J. (1977) Flashbulb memories. *Cognition*, 5, 73–99.

BRUCE, V. and VALENTINE, T. (1986) Semantic priming of familiar faces. *Quarterly Journal of Experimental Psychology*, 38A, 125–50.

BRUCE, V. and YOUNG, A. (1986) Understanding face recognition. *British Journal of Psychology*, 77, 305–27.

BRUNER, J.S. (1966) *Towards a Theory of Instruction*, Cambridge, MA: Harvard University Press.

BUDNEY, A.J. and HIGGINS, S.T. (1988) *Therapy Manuals for Drug Addiction (Manual 2). A Community Reinforcement Plus Vouchers Approach: Treating Cocaine Addiction*, Maryland: NIDA.

BUHRICH, N., BAILEY, J.M. and MARTIN, N.G. (1991) Sexual orientation, sexual identity, and sex-dimorphic behaviors in male twins. *Behavior Genetics*, 21, 75–96.

BUHRMESTER, D. (1996) Need fulfilment, interpersonal competence, and the developmental context of early adolescent friendship. In W.M. Bukowski, A.F. Newcomb and W.W. Hartup (eds.), *The Company They Keep: Friendship in Childhood and Adolescence*, Cambridge: Cambridge University Press.

BURMAN, E. (1994) *Deconstructing Developmental Psychology*, London: Routledge.

BURTON, A.M., BRUCE, V. and JOHNSTON, R.A. (1990) Understanding face recognition with an interactive activation model. *British Journal of Psychology*, 81, 361–80.

BUSS, D.M. (1994) *The Evolution of Desire*, New York: Basic Books.

BUTZLAFF, R.L. and HOOLEY, J.M. (1998) Expressed emotion and psychiatric relapse: a meta-analysis. *Archives of General Psychiatry*, 55, 547–52.

CAAN, W. (2002) The nature of heroin and cocaine dependence. In W. Caan and J. de Belleroche (eds.), *Drink, Drugs and Dependence: From Science to Clinical Practice*, London: Routledge.

CACIOPPO, J.T. and PETTY, R.E. (1982) The need for cognition. *Journal of Personality and Social Psychology*, 42, 116–31.

CANDEL, I., MEMON, A. and AL-HARAZI, F. (2007) Peer discussion affects children's memory reports. *Applied Cognitive Psychology*, 21, 1191–9.

CANTER, D. (1994) *Criminal Shadows*, London: Harper.

CANTER, D. and GREGORY, A. (1994) Identifying the residential location of rapists. *Journal of the Forensic Science Society*, 34, 169–75.

CANTER, D. and YOUNGS, D. (2008) *Principles of Geographical Offender Profiling*, Aldershot: Ashgate.

CANTER, D., ALISON, L.J., ALISON, E. and WENTINK, N. (2004) The organized/disorganized typology of serial murder. Myth or model? *Psychology, Public Policy and Law*, 10 (3), 293–320.

CAPRA, F. (1975) *The Tao of Physics*, Berkeley, CA: Shambhale.

CAREY, G. and GOLDMAN, D. (1997) The genetics of antisocial behaviour. In D.M. Stuff, J. Breiling and J.D. Maser (eds.), *Handbook of Antisocial Behaviour*, New York: Wiley.

CARLSON, C.R. and HOYLE, R.H. (1993) Efficacy of abbreviated muscle relaxation training: a quantitative review of behavioural medicine research. *Journal of Consulting and Clinical Psychology*, 61, 1059–67.

CARROLL, K.M. and ROUNSAVILLE, B.J. (1995) Psychosocial treatments. In J.M. Oldham and M.B. Riba (eds.), *American Psychiatric Press Review of Psychiatry, Vol. 14*, Washington, DC: American Psychiatric Press.

CASSIDY, D., HARPER, G. and BROWN, S. (2005) Understanding electronic monitoring of juveniles on bail or remand to Local Authority accommodation. Home Office Online Report 21/05, London Home Office.

CASSIDY, J. (1986) The ability to negotiate the environment: an aspect of infant competence as related to quality of attachment. *Child Development*, 57, 331–7.

CECI, S. and BRUCK, M. (1993) Suggestibility of the child witness: a historical review and synthesis. *Psychological Bulletin*, 113, 403–39.

CHADWICK, O., ANDERSON, H.R., BLAND, J.M. and RAMSEY, J. (1991) *Solvent Abuse: A Population-Based Neuropsychological Study*, New York: Springer-Verlag.

CHIEN, W.T., NORMAN, I. and THOMPSON, D.R. (2004) A randomized controlled trial of a mutual support group for family caregivers of patients with schizophrenia. *International Journal of Nursing Studies*, 41 (6), 637–49.

CHOMSKY, N. (1959) Review of verbal behaviour by B.F. Skinner. *Language*, 35, 26–58.

CHOMSKY, N. (1965) *Aspects of a Theory of Syntax*, Cambridge, MA: MIT Press.

CHRISTIANSEN, K.O. (1977) A preliminary study of criminality among twins. In S.A. Mednick and K.O. Christiansen (eds.), *Biosocial Basis of Criminal Behaviour*, New York: Gardner Press.

CLARKE, A.M. and CLARKE, A.D.B. (1976) *Early Experience: Myth and Evidence*, London: Open Books.

COBB, S. and ROSE, R. (1973) Hypertension, peptic ulcer and diabetes in air traffic controllers. *Journal of the American Medical Association*, 224, 489–92.

COHEN, G. (1989) *Memory in the Real World*, Hove: Lawrence Erlbaum Associates.

COHEN, H.L. and FILIPCZAK, J. (1971) *A New Learning Environment*, San Francisco: Jossey-Bass.

COHEN, S. and HERBERT, T.B. (1996) Health psychology: psychological factors and physical disease from the perspective of human psychoneuroimmunology. *Annual Review of Psychology*, 47, 113–32.

COHEN, S. and WILLS, T.A. (1985) Stress, social support, and the buffering hypothesis. *Psychological Bulletin*, 93, 310–57.

COHEN, S., KAMARCK. T. and MERMELSTEIN, R. (1983) A global measure of perceived stress. *Journal of Health and Social Behaviour*, 24, 385–96.

COHEN, S., SHERROD, D.R. and CLARK, M.S. (1986) Social Skills and the stress-protective role of social support. *Journal of Personality and Social Psychology*, 50, 963–73.

COHEN, S., TYRRELL, D.A.J. and SMITH, A.P. (1991) Psychological stress and susceptibility to the common cold. *New England Journal of Medicine*, 325, 606–12.

COIE, J.D. and DODGE, K.A. (1983) Continuities and changes in children's social status: a five-year longitudinal study. *Merrill-Palmer Quarterly*, 29, 261–82.

COLBY, A., KOHLBERG, L., GIBBS, J. and LIEBERMAN, M. (1983) A longitudinal study of moral development. *Monographs of the Society for Research in Child Development*, 48 (1–2, Serial No. 200).

COLBY, A., KOHLBERG, L. and KAUFFMAN, K. (1987a) *The Measurement of Moral Judgment (Vol. I)*, Cambridge: Cambridge University Press.

COLBY, A., KOHLBERG, L., SPEICHER, B., HEWER, A., CANDEE, D., GIBBS, J. and POWER, C. (1987b) *The Measurement of Moral Judgment (Vol. II)*, Cambridge: Cambridge University Press.

COLE, J.O., KLERMAN, G.L. and GOLDBERG, S.C. (1964) Phenothiazine treatment in acute schizophrenia, *Archives of General Psychiatry*, 10, 246–61.

COMER, R.J. (2008) *Fundamentals of Abnormal Psychology*, 5th edn., New York: Worth.

CONDON, W.S. and SANDER, L.W. (1974) Neonate movement is synchronized with adult speech: interactional participation and language acquisition. *Science*, 183, 99–101.

COOK, R.C. (1993) The experimental analysis of cognition in animals. *Psychological Science*, 4, 174–78.

COON, D. (2002) *Psychology: A Journey*, Belmont, CA: Wadsworth, Thomson Learning.

CORWIN, D. and OLAFSON, E. (1997) Videotaped discovery of a reportedly unrecallable memory of child sexual abuse: comparison with a childhood interview taped 11 years before. *Child Maltreatment*, 2, 91–112.

COWEN, E.L., PEDERSON, A., BABIGIAN, H., IZZO, L.D. and TROST, M.A. (1973) Long-term follow-up of early detected vulnerable children. *Journal of Consulting and Clinical Psychology*, 41, 438–46.

CRAWFORD, M. and MARACEK, J. (1989) Psychology reconstructs the female: 1968–1988. *Psychology of Women Quarterly*, 13, 147–65.

CRICK, N.R. and LADD, G.W. (1993) Children's perceptions of their peer experiences: attributions, loneliness, social anxiety, and social avoidance. *Developmental Psychology*, 29, 244–54.

CRONBACH, L.J. (1957) The two disciplines of scientific psychology. *American Psychologist*, 12, 671–84.

CSIKSZENTMIHALYI, M. (1990) *Flow: The Psychology of Optimal Experience*, New York: Harper Perennial.

CUIJPERS, P., JONKERS, R., de WEERDT, I. and de JONG, A. (2002) The effects of drug abuse prevention at school: the 'Healthy School and Drugs' project. *Addiction*, 97, 67–73.

CULLEN, C. and MINCHIN, M. (2000) Prison population in 1999: a statistical review. Home Office Research Development and Statistics Directorate, No. 118, London: Home Office.

CULLEN, J.E. and SEDDON, J.W. (1981) The application of a behavioural regime to disturbed young offenders. *Personality and Individual Differences*, 2, 285–92.

CURTISS, S. (1977) *Genie: A Psycholinguistic Study of a Modern-Day 'Wild Child'*, London: Academic Press.

DAKOF, G.A. and TAYLOR, S.E. (1990) Victims' perceptions of social support: what is helpful from whom? *Journal of Personality and Social Psychology*, 58, 80–9.

DAMON, W. (1977) *The Social World of the Child*, San Francisco: Jossey-Bass.

DAMON, W. (1988) *The Handbook of Child Psychology. Volume 2 (Cognition, Perception and Language)*, 5th edn., New York: Wiley.

DANAHER, B.G. (1977) Rapid smoking and self-control in the modification of smoking behaviour. *Journal of Consulting and Clinical Psychology*, 45: 1068–75.

DANIELS, M. (1988) The myth of self-actualisation. *Journal of Humanistic Psychology*, 28, 7–28.

DASEN, P. (1975) Concrete operational development in three cultures, *Journal of Cross-Cultural Psychology*, 6, 156–72.

DAVIES, G.L. and RAYMOND, K.M. (2000) Do current sentencing practices work? *Criminal Law Journal*, 24, 236–47.

DAVIES, G., ELLIS, H. and SHEPHERD, J. (1978) Face recognition accuracy as a function of mode of representation. *Journal of Applied Psychology*, 63, 180–7.

DAVIES, G.M., VAN DER WILLICK, P. and MORRIESON, L.J. (2000) Facial composite productions: a comparison of mechanical and computer-driven systems. *Journal of Applied Psychology*, 85, 119–24.

DAWSON, M.R. (1998) *Understanding Cognitive Science*, Oxford: Blackwell Publishers.

DE CARVALHO, R.J. (1991) *The Founders of Humanistic Psychology*, New York: Praeger.

DE WOLFF, M.S. and VAN IJZENDOORN, M.H. (1997) Sensitivity and attachment: a meta-analysis on parental antecedents of infant attachment. *Child Development*, 68, 571–91.

DEARY, I. (2000) Simple information processing and intelligence. In R.J. Sternberg (ed.), *Handbook of Intelligence*, New York: Cambridge University Press.

DEVLIN, P. (1976) *Report to the Secretary of State for the Home Department Committee on Evidence of Identification in Criminal Cases*, London: HMSO.

DIGMAN, J.M. (1990) Personality structure: emergence of the five factor model. In M.R. Rozenweig and L.W. Porter (eds.), *Annual Review of Psychology*, 41, 417–40.

DOANE, J.A., FALLOON, I.R.H., GOLDSTEIN, M.J. and MINTZ, J. (1985) Parental affective style and the treatment of schizophrenia. *Archives of General Psychiatry*, 42, 34–42.

DODGE, K.A. (1983) Behavioural antecedents of peer social status. *Child Development*, 54, 1386–9.

DODGE, K.A., SCHLUNDT, D.C., SHOCKEN, I. and DELUGACH, J.D. (1983) Social competence and children's sociometric status: the role of peer group entry strategies. *Merrill-Palmer Quarterly*, 29, 309–36.

DOHERTY, M. (2001) *Criminology*, 3rd edn., London: Old Bailey Press.

DOLLARD, J. and MILLER, N.E. (1950) *Personality and Psychotherapy*, New York: McGraw-Hill.

DONALDSON, M. (1978) *Children's Minds*, London: Fontana Press.

DOUGALL, A.L. and BAUM, A. (2001) Stress, health and illness. In A. Baum, T.A. Revenson and J.E. Singer (eds.), *Handbook of Health Psychology*, Mahwah, NJ: Erlbaum, 321–37.

DOUGLAS, J.E. and BURGESS, A.E. (1986) Criminal profiling: a viable investigative tool against violent crime. *FBI Law Enforcement Bulletin*, December, 1–5.

DOUGLAS, J.E., BURGESS, A.W., BURGESS, A.G. and RESSLER, R.K. (1992) *Crime Classification Manual: A Standard System for Investigating and Classifying Violent Crime*, New York: Simon and Schuster.

DOUVAN, E. and ADELSON, J. (1966) *The Adolescent Experience*, New York: Wiley.

DRUGSCOPE (2001) *Drug Abuse Briefing – A Guide to the Non-Medical Use of Drugs in Britain*, London: Drugscope.

DRUMMOND, S. (2002) Prevention. In W. Caan and J. de Belleroche (eds.), *Drink, Drugs and Dependence: From Science to Clinical Practice*, London: Routledge.

DUCK, S.W. (1991) *Friends for Life*, Hemel Hempstead: Harvester-Wheatsheaf.

DUNN, J. (1993) *Young Children's Close Relationships Beyond Attachment*, London: Sage.

DWORETSKY, J.P. (1981) *Introduction to Child Development*, St Paul, MN: West Publishing Co.

EATON, W.W., THARA, R., FEDERMAN, E. and TIEN, A. (1998) Remission and relapse in schizophrenia: the Madras longitudinal study. *Journal of Nervous and Mental Disease*, 186, 357–63.

EISENBERG, N. (1983) Children's differentiations among potential recipients of aid. *Child Development*, 54, 594–602.

EISENBERG, N., SHELL, R., PASTERNACK, J., LENNON, R., BELLER, R. and MATHY, R.M. (1987) Prosocial development in middle childhood: a longitudinal study. *Developmental Psychology*, 23, 712–18.

ELBERS, E and STREEFLAND, L. (2000) 'Shall we be researchers again?' Identity and social interaction in a community of inquiry. In H. Cowie and G. van der Aalsvoort (eds.), *Social Interaction in Learning and Instruction*, Amsterdam: Pergamon.

ELLIS, A. (1962) *Reason and Emotion in Psychotherapy*, Secaucus, NY: Citadel Press.

ELLIS, A. (1984) Rational-emotive therapy. In R.J. Corsini (ed.), *Current Psychotherapies*, 2nd edn., Itasca, IL: Peacock Publishers.

ELLIS, A. (1989) *Inside Rational-emotive Therapy: A Critical Appraisal of the Theory and Therapy*, New York: Academic Press.

ELLIS, A. (1995) Rational-emotive therapy. In R.J. Corsini and D. Wedding (eds.), *Current Psychotherapies*, Itasca, IL: Peacock.

ELLIS, A.W. (1973) *Reading, Writing and Dyslexia: A Cognitive Analysis*, 2nd edn., London: Erlbaum.

ELLIS, H.D. (1975) Recognising Faces. *British Journal of Psychology*, 66, 409–26.

ELLIS, H.D. and SHEPHERD, J.W. (1992) Face memory – theory and practice. In M. Gruneberg and P. Morris (eds.), *Aspects of Memory*, Vol. 1, 2nd edn., London: Routledge.

ELLIS, H.D., DAVIES, G.M. and SHEPHERD, J.W. (1978) A critical examination of the Photofit system for recalling faces. *Ergonomics*, 21, 297–307.

ELLIS, H.D., SHEPHERD, J. and DAVIES, G.M. (1975) An investigation of the use of photo-fit technique for recalling faces. *British Journal of Psychology*, 66, 25–8.

ELLIS, H.D., SHEPHERD, J.W. and DAVIES, G.M. (1979) Identification of familiar and unfamiliar faces from internal and external features: some implications for theories of face recognition. *Perception*, 8, 431–9.

EMMELKAMP, P.M. (1994) Behaviour therapy with adults. In A.E. Bergin and S.L. Garfiel (eds.), *Handbook of Psychotherapy and Behaviour Change*, 4th edn., New York: Wiley.

ERICSSON, K.A. and SIMON, H.A. (1980) Verbal reports as data. *Psychological Review*, 87, 215–51.

ERIKSON, E. (1963) *Childhood and Society*, 2nd edn., New York: Norton.

ERIKSON, E. (1968) *Identity, Youth and Crisis*, New York: Norton.

ERIKSON, E. (1969) *Ghandi's Truth*, New York: Norton.

ERWIN, P. (1998) *Friendships in Childhood and Adolescence*, London: Routledge.

ESTGATE, A, and GROOME, D. (2005) *An Introduction to Applied Cognitive Psychology*, Hove: Psychology Press.

EYSENCK, H.J. (1952) The effects of psychotherapy: an evaluation. *Journal of Consulting Psychology*, 16, 319–24.

EYSENCK, H.J. (1964) *Crime and Personality*. London: Routledge and Kegan Paul.

EYSENCK, H.J. (1990) *The Decline and Fall of the Freudian Empire*, Washington, DC: Scott-Townsend.

FABREGA, H., ULRICH, R., PILKONIS, P. and MEZZICH, J. (1991) On the homogeneity of personality disorder clusters. *Comprehensive Psychiatry*, 32 (5), 373–86.

FARRINGTON, D. and DOWDS, E. (1985) Disentangling criminal behaviour and police reaction. In D. Farrington and J. Gunn (eds.), *Reactions to Crime: The Public, the Police, Courts and Prisons*, Chichester: Wiley.

FARRINGTON, D.P., BIRON, L. and LEBLANC, M. (1982) Personality and delinquency in London and Montreal. In J. Gunn and D.P. Farrington (eds.), *Abnormal Offenders, Delinquency and the Criminal Justice System*, Chichester: Wiley.

FARRINGTON, D.P., COID, J.W., HARNETT, L., JOLLIFFE, D., SOTERIOU, N., TURNER, R. and WEST, D.J. (2006) Criminal careers up to age 50 and life success up to age 48: new findings from the Cambridge Study in Delinquent Development. Home Office Research Study No 299, London: Home Office.

FARTHING, G.W. (1992) *The Psychology of Consciousness*, Englewood Cliffs, NJ: Prentice Hall.

FEMINA, D.D., YEAGAR, C.A. and LEWIS, D.O. (1990) Child abuse: adolescent records vs adult recall. *Child Abuse and Neglect*, 14, 227–31.

FEYERABEND, P.K. (1975) *Against Method: Outline of an Anarchistic Theory of Knowledge*, London: New Left Books.

FIELD-SMITH, M.E., BLAND, J.M., TAYLOR, J.C., RAMSEY, J.D. and ANDERSON, H.R. (2002) Trends in Death Associated with Abuse of Volatile Substances, No. 15 (1971–2003), London: St George's Hospital Medical School (available online at www.vsareport.org).

FINE, R. (1990) *The History of Psychoanalysis*, New York: Continuum.

FINK, M. (2001) Convulsive therapy: a review of the first 55 years. *Journal of Affective Disorders*, 63, 1–15.

FISHER, R.P. and GEISELMAN, R.E. (1992) *Memory-enhancing Techniques for Investigative Interviewing: The Cognitive Interview*, Springfield, IL: Charles C. Thomas.

FISHER, S. and GREENBERG, R.P. (1977) *The Scientific Credibility of Freud's Theories and Therapies*, New York: Basic Books.

FISHER. S. and GREENBERG, R.P. (1996) *Freud Scientifically Reappraised: Testing The Theories And Therapies*, New York: Wiley.

FIVUSH, R. and SHUKAT, J.R. (1995) Content, consistency and coherence of early autobiographical recall. In M.S. Zaragoza, J.R. Granham, G.C.N. Hall, R. Hirschman and Y.S. Ben-Yorath (eds.), *Memory and Testimony in the Child Witness*, London: Sage Publications.

FLAVELL, J.H., BEACH, D.R. and CHINSKY, J.M. (1966) Spontaneous verbal rehearsal in a memory task as a function of age. *Child Development*, 37, 283–99.

FLAY, B. (1985) Psychosocial approaches to smoking prevention: a review of findings. *Health Psychology*, 4 (5), 449–88.

FLAY, B.R., RYAN, K.B., BEST, J.A., BROWN, K.S., KERSELL, M.W., d'AVERNAS, J.R. et al. (1985) Are social-psychological smoking prevention programs effective? The Waterlook study. *Journal of Behavioural Medicine*, 8, 37–59.

FLORY, K., LYNAM, D., MILICH, R., LEUKEFELD, C. and CLAYTON, R. (2002) The relations among personality, symptoms of alcohol and marijuana abuse and symptoms of comorbid psychopathology: results from a community sample. *Experimental and Clinical Psychopharmacology*, 10 (4), 425–34.

FRALEY, R.C. and SPIEKER, S.J. (2003) Are infant attachment patterns continuously or categorically distributed? A taxometric analysis of Strange Situation behaviour. *Developmental Psychology*, 39, 387–404.

FRANKENHAUSER, M. (1975) Sympathetic adrenomedullary activity behaviour and the psychosocial environment. In P.H. Venables and M.J. Christie (eds.), *Research in Psychophysiology*, New York: Wiley.

FRANKLAND, A. and COHEN, L. (1999) Working with recovered memories. *The Psychologist*, 12 (2) 82–3.

FREUD, A. and DANN, S. (1951) An experiment in group upbringing. *Psychoanalytic Study of the Child*, 6, 127–68.

FREUD. S. (1900) *The Interpretation of Dreams*, London: Hogarth Press.

FREUD, S. (1905/1977) Fragment of an analysis of a case of hysteria (Dora). *The Pelican Freud Library, Volume 8*, Harmondsworth: Penguin.

FREUD, S. (1909/1977a) Analysis of a phobia in a five year old boy (Little Hans). *The Pelican Freud Library, Volume 8*, Harmondsworth: Penguin.

FREUD, S. (1909/1977b) Notes upon a case of obsessional neurosis (The Rat Man). *The Pelican Freud Library, Volume 9*, Harmondsworth: Penguin.

FREUD, S. (1917) Mourning and melancholia. In *Collected Papers* (Vol. 4), London: Hogarth Press and the Institute of Psychoanalysis (work published 1950), 152–72.

FREUD, S. (1922) *Beyond the Pleasure Principle*, London: Hogarth Press.

FREUD, S. (1933/1964) *New Introductory Lectures on Psychoanalysis*, Stamford edn, Vol. 22, London: Hogarth Press.

FREUD, S. (1933/1973) *New Introductory Lectures on Psychoanalysis*, Pelican Freud Library, Vol. 2, Harmondsworth: Penguin.

FREUD, S. (1961) Some psychical consequences of the anatomical distinction between the sexes. In J. Strachey (ed. and trans.), *Standard Edition of the Complete Psychological Works of Sigmund Freud* (Vol. 19), London: Hogarth Press.

FRIEDMAN, M. and ROSENMAN, R.H. (1959) Association of specific overt pattern with blood and cardiovascular findings. *Journal of the American Medical Association*, 169, 1286–96.

FRIEDMAN, M. and ROSENMAN, R.H. (1974) *Type A Behaviour and Your Heart*, New York: Knopf.

FRITH, C.D. (1992) *The Cognitive Neuropsychology of Schizophrenia*, New York: Lawrence Erlbaum.

FROMM, E. (1941) *Escape from Freedom*, New York: Holt, Rinehart and Winston.

GARCIA, J. (1989) Food for Tolman: cognition and cathexis in concert. In T. Archer and L.G. Nilsson (eds.), *Aversion Avoidance and Anxiety: Perspectives on Adversely Motivated Behaviour*, Hillsdale, NJ: Erlbaum.

GARCIA, J. and KOELLING, R. (1966) Relation of cue to consequence in avoidance learning. *Psychonomic Science*, 4, 123–4.

GARNIER, H.E. and STEIN, J.A. (2002) An 18-year model of family and peer effects on adolescent drug use and delinquency. *Journal of Youth and Adolescence*, 31 (1), 45–56.

GATCHEL, R.J., BAUM, A. and KRANTZ, D.S. (1989) *An Introduction to Health Psychology*, 2nd edn., New York: Random House.

GEISELMAN, R.E. (1999) Commentary on recent research with the cognitive interview. *Psychology, Crime and Law*, 5, 197–202.

GEISELMAN, R.E., FISHER, R.P., MACKINNON, D.F. and HOLLAND, H.L. (1985) Eye witness memory enhancement in police interview: cognitive retrieval mnemonics versus hypnosis. *Journal of Applied Psychology*, 70, 401–12.

GEISELMAN, R.E., FISHER, R.P., MACKINNON, D.F. and HOLLAND, H.L. (1986) Enhancement of eye witness memory with the cognitive interview. *American Journal of Psychology*, 99, 385–401.

GELMAN, R. (1969) Conservation acquisition: a problem of learning to attend to the relevant attributes. *Journal of Experimental Child Psychology*, 7, 167–87.

GERSON, R.P. and DAMON, W. (1978) Moral understanding and children's conduct. *New Directions for Child Development*, 2, 41–60.

GIBBS, J.C., BASINGER, K.S. and FULLER, D. (1992) *Moral Maturity: Measuring the Development of Sociomoral Reflection*, Hillsdale, NJ: Erlbaum.

GIBBS, J.C., BASINGER, K.S. and GRIME, R.L. (2002) Moral judgement maturity: from clinical to standard measures. In S.J. Lopez and C.R. Snyder (eds.), *Handbook of Positive Psychological Assessment*, Washington, DC: American Psychological Association.

GIBSON, E.J. and WALK, R.D. (1960) The 'visual cliff'. *Scientific American*, 202, 64–71.

GIBSON, J.J. (1966) *The Senses Considered as Perceptual Systems*, Boston: Houghton Mifflin.

GILLIGAN, C. (1977) In a different voice: women's conceptions of self and morality. *Harvard Educational Review*, 47, 481–517.

GILLIGAN, C. (1982) *In a Different Voice: Psychological Theory and Women's Development*, Cambridge, MA: Harvard University Press.

GLASS, D.C. and SINGER, J.E. (1972) *Urban Stress: Experiments on Noise and Social Stressors*, New York: Academic Press.

GLUECK, S. and GLUECK, E.T. (1956) *Physique and Delinquency*, New York: Dodd Meade.

GOATER, N., KING, M., COLE, E., LEAVEY, G. *et al.* (1999) Ethnicity and outcomes of psychosis. *British Journal of Psychiatry*, 175, 34–42.

GOLDFARB, W. (1943) The effects of early institutional care on adolescent personality. *Journal of Experimental Education*, 12, 106–29.

GOLDSTEIN, A. (1994) *Addiction: From Biology to Drug Policy*, New York: W.H. Freeman.

GOLDSTEIN, A.P. (1986) Psychological skill training and the aggressive adolescent. In S.J. Apter and A.P. Goldstein (eds.), *Youth Violence: Programmes and Prospects*, New York: Plenum Press.

GOLDSTEIN, J.M. and LEWINE, R.J. (2000) Overview of sex differences in schizophrenia: where have we been and where do we go to from here? In D.J. Castle, J. McGrath and J. Kulkarni (eds.), *Women and Schizophrenia*, Cambridge: Cambridge University Press.

GOLDSTEIN, J.M., SEIDMAN, L.J., O'Brien, L.M., HORTON, N.J., KENNEDY, D.N., MAKRIS, N., CAVINESS, V.S., FARAONE. S.V. and TSUANG, M.T. (2002) Impact of normal sexual dimorphisms on sex differences in structural brain abnormalities in schizophrenia assessed by magnetic resonance imaging. *Archives of General Psychiatry*, 59, 154–64.

GOLDSTEIN, K. (1939) *The Organism*, New York: American Book Company.

GOODNOW, J.J. (1969) Problems in research on culture and thought. In D. Elkind and J. Flavell (eds.), *Studies in Cognitive Development: Essays in Honour of Jean Piaget*, Oxford: Oxford University Press.

GOODWILL, A.M. and ALISON, L.J. (2006) The development of a filter model for prioritizing suspects in burglary offences. *Psychology, Crime and Law*, 12 (4), 395–416.

GORING, C. (1913) *The English Convict: A Statistical Study*, Montclair, NJ: Patterson Smith.

GOTTESMAN, I.I. (1991). *Schizophrenia Genesis: The Origins of Madness*, New York: W.H. Freeman.

GOTTESMAN, I.I. and ERLENMEYER-KIMLING, L. (2001) Family and twin strategies as a head start in defining prodromes and endophenotypes for hypothetical early interventions in schizophrenia. *Schizophrenic Research*, 51, 93–102.

GOTTESMAN, I.I. and SHIELDS, J. (1982) *Schizophrenia: The Epigenetic Puzzle*, New York: Cambridge University Press.

GOULD, S.J. (1981) *The Mismeasure of Man*, London: Penguin.

GRAY, D., SAGGERS, S., SPUTORE, B. and BOURBON, D. (2000) What works? A review of evaluated alcohol misuse interventions among Aboriginal Australians. *Addiction*, 95 (1), 11–22.

GREENFIELD, P.M. and LAVE, J. (1982) Cognitive aspects of informal education. In D.A. Wagner and H.W. Stevenson (eds.), *Cultural Perspectives on Child Development*, San Francisco: W.H. Freeman.

GREENWALD, A.G., SPANGENBERG, E.R., PRATKANIS, A.R. and ESKENAZI, J. (1991) Double-blind tests of subliminal self-help audio tapes. *Psychological Science*, 2, 119–22.

GROVE, W.M., ECKERT, E.D., HESTON, L., BOUCHARD, T.J., SEGAL, N. and LYKKEN, D.T. (1990) Heritability of substance abuse and antisocial behaviour: a study of monozygotic twins reared apart. *Biological Psychiatry*, 27, 1293–304.

GRUNEBERG, M. (1992) In J. McCrone, My family and other strangers. *The Independent on Sunday*, 1 March.

GRUZELIER, J., LEVY, J., WILLIAMS, J. and HENDERSON, D. (2001) Self-hypnosis and exam stress: comparing immune and relaxation-related imagery for influences on immunity, health, and mood. *Contemporary Hypnosis*, 18, 73–86.

GUDJONSSON, G.H. (1997) The members of the BFMS, the accusers and their siblings. *The Psychologist*, 10, 111–14.

HAIG, N.D. (1984) The effect of feature displacement on face recognition. *Perception*, 13, 505–12.

HARE, R.D. (1970) *Psychopathy: Theory and Research*, New York: Wiley.

HARE, R.D. and CONNOLLY, J.F. (1987) Perceptual asymmetrics and information processing in psychopaths. In S.A. Mednick, T.E. Moffitt and S.A. Stack (eds.), *The Causes of Crime: New Biological Approaches*, Cambridge: Cambridge University Press.

HARLOW, H.F. (1959) Love in infant monkeys. *Scientific American*, 200, 68–74.

HARTLEY, E.M., MONNELLY, E.P. and ELDERKIN, R. (1982) *Physique and Delinquent Behaviour: A Thirty-year Follow-up of William H. Sheldon's Varieties of Delinquent Youth*, New York: Academic Press.

HARTSHORNE, H. and MAY, M.S. (1928–1930) *Studies in the Nature of Character. Vol. 1: Studies in Deceit. Vol. 2: Studies in Self-Control. Vol. 3: Studies in the Organization of Character*, New York: Macmillan.

HARTUP, W.W., and STEVENS, N. (1999) Friendships and adaptation across the life span. *Current Directions in Psychological Science*, 8, 76–9.

HAZAN, C. and SHAVER, P.R. (1987) Romantic love conceptualised as an attachment process. *Journal of Personality and Social Psychology*, 52 (3), 511–24.

HEDEGAARD, M. (1996) The zone of proximal development as basis for instruction. In H. Daniels (ed.), *An Introduction to Vygotsky*, London: Routledge.

HEIDEGGER, M. (1927) *Being and Time*, New York: State University of New York Press.

HEIDER, F. (1958) *The Psychology of Interpersonal Relations*, New York: John Wiley & Sons.

HEINRICHS, R.W. and ZAKZANIS, K.K. (1988) Neurocognitive deficit in schizophrenia: a quantitive review of the evidence. *Neuropsychology*, 12 (3), 426–45.

HELWIG, C.C., ZELAZO, P.D. and WILSON, M. (2001) Children's judgements of psychological harm in normal and noncanonical situations. *Child Development*, 72, 66–81.

HELZER, J.E. and CANINO, G.J. (eds.) (1992) *Alcoholism in North America, Europe and Asia*, London: Oxford University Press.

HENDERSON, N.D. (1982) Human behaviour genetics. *Annual Review of Psychology*, 33, 403–40.

HENDRICK, V., ALTSHULER, L. and SURI, R. (1998) Hormonal changes in the postpartum and implications for postpartum depression. *Psychosomatics*, 39, 93–101.

HESS, W.R. (1957) *The Functional Organisation of the Diencephalem*, New York: Grune and Stratton.

HESSE, E. and MAIN, M. (2000) Disorganised infant, child and adult attachment: collapse in behavioural and attentional strategies. *Journal of the American Psychoanalytic Association*, 48, 1097–127.

HIGGINS, S.T., BUDNEY, A.J., BICKEL, W.K., HUGHES, J., FOERG, F. and BADGER, G. (1993) Achieving cocaine abstinence with a behavioural approach. *American Journal of Psychiatry*, 150, 753–69.

HINDE, R.A., TITMUS, G., EASTON, D. and TAMPLIN, A. (1985) Incidence of 'friendship' and behaviour with strong associates versus non-associates in pre-schoolers. *Child Development*, 56, 234–45.

HIRSTEIN, R. and RAMACHANDRAN, V.S. (1997) Capgras syndrome: a novel probe for understanding the representation of the identity and familiarity of persons. *Proceedings: Biological Sciences*, 264 (1380), 437–44, The Royal Society.

HODGES, J. and TIZARD, B. (1989) IQ and behavioural adjustment of ex-institutional adolescents. *Journal of Child Psychology and Psychiatry*, 30, 53–76.

HOFFMAN, L.W. (1974) Fear of success in males and females. *Journal of Consulting and Clinical Psychology*, 24, 353–8.

HOFFMAN, M.L. (1975) Altruistic behaviour and the parent–child relationship. *Journal of Personality and Social Psychology*, 31, 937–43.

HOFSTEDE, G. (1980) *Culture's Consequences: International Differences in Work-related Values*, Beverly Hills, CA: Sage.

HOGARTY, G.E., ANDERSON, C.M., REISS, D.J., KORNBLITH, S.J., GREENWALD, D.P., JAVNA, C.D. and MADONIA, M.J. (1986) Family psychoeducation, social skills training, and maintenance chemotherapy in the aftercare treatment of schizophrenia: I. One-year effects of a controlled study on relapse and expressed emotion. *Archives of General Psychiatry*, 43, 633–42.

HOLLAND, J.C. and LEWIS, S. (1996) Emotions and cancer: what do we really know? In D. Goleman and J. Gurin (eds.), *Mind/body Medicine: How to Use your Mind for Better Health*, Yonkers, NY: Consumer Reports Books, 85–109.

HOLLIN, C.R. (1992) *Criminal Behaviour*, Basingstoke: Falmer Press.

HOLLON, S.D., STEWART, M.O. and STRUNK, D. (2006) Enduring effects for cognitive behaviour therapy in the treatment of depression and anxiety. *Annual Review of Psychology*, 57, 285–315.

HOLMES, R.M. and DE BURGER, J. (1988) *Serial Murder*, Newbury Park, CA: Sage.

HOLMES, T.H. and RAHE, R.H. (1967) The social readjustment rating scale. *Journal of Psychosomatic Research*, 11, 213–18.

HOLSTEIN, C.B. (1976) Irreversible, stepwise sequence in the development of moral judgement: a longitudinal study of males and females. *Child Development*, 47, 51–61.

HOWITT, D. (1991) *Concerning Psychology: Psychology Applied to Social Issues*, Milton Keynes: Open University Press.

HYLAND. M.E. (1989) There is no motive to avoid success: the compromise explanation for success-avoiding behaviour. *Journal of Personality*, 57, 665–93.

IMAMOGLU, E.O. (1975) Children's awareness and usage of intention cues. *Child Development*, 46, 39–45.

INHELDER, B. and PIAGET, J. (1958) *The Growth of Logical Thinking from Childhood to Adolescence*, New York: Basic Books.

IRELAND, J. (2000) Do anger management courses work? *Forensic Update*, 63, 12–16, Leicester: The British Psychological Society.

ISABELLA, R.A., BELSKY, J. and VON EYE, A. (1989) Origins of infant–mother attachment: an examination of interactional synchrony during the infant's first year. *Developmental Psychology*, 25, 12–21.

IVERSEN, L.L. (1979) The chemistry of the brain. *Scientific American*, 241, 134–49.

JACKSON, J.L. and BERKERIAN D.A. (eds.) (1997) *Offender Profiling: Theory, Research and Practice*, Chichester: Wiley.

JACOBS, D.R., MULDOON, M.F. and RASTAM, L. (1995) Invited commentary: low blood cholesterol, nonillness mortality, and other nonatherosclerotic disease mortality: a search for causes and confounders. *American Journal of Epidemiology*, 141, 518–22.

JACOBS, P.A., BRUNTON, M., MELVILLE, H.M., BRITTAIN, R.P. and MCCLERMONT, W.F. (1965) Aggressive behaviour, mental subnormality and the XYY male. *Nature,* 208, 1351–2.

JACOBSEN, S.W. (1979) Matching behaviour in the young infant. *Child Development*, 50, 425–30.

JADACK, R.A, HYDE, J.S., MOORE, C.F. and KELLER, M.L. (1995) Moral reasoning about sexually transmitted diseases. *Child Development*, 66, 167–77.

JAMES, W. (1890) *The Principles of Psychology*, New York: Henry Holt and Company.

JANIS, I. and FESHBACH, S. (1953) Effects of fear-arousing communications. *Journal of Abnormal and Social Psychology*, 48, 78–92.

JANIS, I.L. and HOVLAND, C.I. (1959) An overview of persuasibility research. In C.I. Hovland and I.L. Janis (eds.), *Personality and Persuasibility*, New Haven, CT: Yale University Press.

JAREMKO, M.E. (2006) The use of stress inoculation training in reduction of public speaking anxiety. *Journal of Clinical Psychology*. 36, 735–8.

JENKINS, J.M., SMITH, M.A. and GRAHAM, P.J. (1989) Coping with parental quarrels. *Journal of the American Academy of Child and Adolescent Psychiatry*, 28, 182–9.

JENKINS, P. (1988) Serial murder in England, 1940–1985. *Journal of Criminal Justice*, 16, 1–15.

JOHNSON, J.G., COHEN, P., PINE, D.S., KLEIN, D.F., KASEN, S. and BROOK, J.S. (2000) Association between cigarette smoking and anxiety disorders during adolescence and early adulthood. *Journal of American Medical Association*, 284, 2348–51.

JOHNSON, S.L. and MILLER, I. (1997) Negative life events and time to recover from episodes of bipolar disorder. *Journal of Abnormal Psychology*, 106, 449–57.

JOHNSTON, D.W. (2002) Acute and chronic psychological processes in cardiovascular disease. In K.W. Schaie, H. Leventhal and S.L. Willis (eds.), *Effective Health Behaviour in Older Adults*, New York: Springer, 55–64.

KAIJ, L. (1960) *Alcoholism in Twins: Studies on the Etiology and Sequels of Alcohol Abuse*, Stockholm: Almquist & Wiksel.

KANDEL, D.B. (1978) Homophily, selection and socialization in adolescent friendships. *American Journal of Sociology*, 84, 427–36.

KANNER, A.D., COYNE, I.C., SCHAEFER, C. and LAZARUS, R.S. (1981) Comparison of two modes of stress measurement: daily hassles and uplifts versus major life events. *Journal of Behavioural Medicine*, 4, 1–39.

KAPARDIS, A. (1997) *Psychology and Law: A Critical Introduction*, Cambridge: Cambridge University Press.

KEEN, J. (2000) A practitioner's perspective. Anger management work with male young offenders. *Forensic Update*, 60. Leicester, The British Psychological Society.

KEENEY, T.J., CANNIZZO, S.R. and FLAVELL, J.H. (1967) Spontaneous and induced verbal rehearsal in a recall task. *Child Development*, 38, 953–66.

KEMP, R., MCMANUS, C. and PIGGOTT, T. (1990) Sensitivity to the displacement of facial features in negative and inverted images. *Perception*, 19, 531–43.

KEMP, R., PIKE, G.E. and BRACE, N.A. (2001) Video based identification procedures: combining best practice and practical requirements when designing identification systems. *Psychology, Public Policy and Law*, 7 (4), 802–7.

KEMP, S. and STRANGMAN, K.T. (1994) Consciousness – a folk theoretical view. *New Zealand Journal of Psychology*.

KENDLER, K., NEALE M., KESSLER, R., HEATH, A. and EAVES, L. (1992). Generalised anxiety disorder in women: a population-based twin study. *Archives of General Psychiatry*, 49, 267–72.

KENDLER, K.S., MYERS, J., PRESCOTT, C.A. and NEALE, M.C. (2001) The genetic epidemiology of irrational fears and phobias in men. *Archives of General Psychiatry*, 58, 257–65.

KENDLER, K.S., NEALE, M.C., HEATH, A.C., KESSLER, R.C. and EAVES, L.J. (1994) A twin-family study of alcoholism in women. *American Journal of Psychiatry*, 151 (5), 707–15.

KILSTROM, J. (1998) Exhumed memory. In S.J. Lynn and K.M. McConkey (eds.), *Truth and Memory*, New York: Guilford Press.

KILSTROM, J.F. (1984) Conscious, subconscious and unconscious: a cognitive view. In K.S. Bower and D. Meichenbaum (eds.), *The Unconscious Reconsidered*, New York: Wiley.

KILSTROM, J.F., BARNHARDT, M. and TATARYN, D.J. (1992) The psychological unconscious: found, lost and regained. *American Psychologist*, 47, 788–91.

KIMVAKI, M., LEINO-ARJAS, P., LUUKKONEM, R. *et al.* (2002) Work stress and risk of cardiovascular mortality: prospective cohort study of industrial employees. *British Medical Journal*, 325, 857–60.

KIND, S.S. (2008) Navigational ideas and the Yorkshire Ripper investigation. In D. Canter and D. Youngs (eds.), *Principles of Geographical Offender Profiling*, Aldershot: Ashgate.

KLAUS, H.M. and KENNELL, J.H. (1976) *Maternal Infant Bonding*, St Louis, MO: Mosby.

KLEIN, D.N., DURBIN, C.E., SHANKMAN, S.A. and SANTIAGO, N.J. (2002) Depression and personality. In I.H. Gotlib and C.L. Hammen (eds.), *Handbook of Depression*, New York: Guilford Press.

KLEIN, J. (1987) *Our Need for Others and its Roots in Infancy*, London: Routledge.

KLEIN, M. (1932) *The Psychoanalysis of Children*, London: Hogarth Press.

KLEIN, M. (1964) *Contributions to Psychoanalysis, 1921–1945*, New York: McGraw-Hill.

KLEIN, M. (1975) *Envy and Gratitude, and Other Works*, New York: Delta Books.

KLERMAN, G.L. and WEISSMAN, M.M. (1992) Interpersonal psychotherapy. In E.S. Paykel (ed.), *Handbook of Affective Disorders*, New York: Guilford Press.

KLINE, P. (1984) *Psychology and Freudian Theory: An Introduction*, London: Methuen.

KOBASA, S.C. (1979) Stressful life events, personality, and health: an inquiry into hardiness. *Journal of Personality and Social Psychology*, 37, 1–11.

KOBASA, S.C., MADDI, S.R. and KAHN, S. (1982) Hardiness and health: a prospective study. *Journal of Personality and Social Psychology*, 42 (1), 168–277.

KOHLBERG, L. (1963) The development of children's orientation towards a moral order: 1. Sequence in the development of moral thought. *Human Development*, 6, 11–33.

KOHLBERG, L. (1969) Stage and sequence: the cognitive-developmental approach to socialization. In D.A. Goslin (ed.), *Handbook of Socialization Theory and Research*, Chicago: Rand McNally.

KOHLBERG, L. (1975) The cognitive-developmental approach to moral education. *Phi Delta Kappa*, June, 670–7.

KOHLBERG, L. (1984) *Essays on Moral Development: The Psychology of Moral Development*, Vol. 2, New York: Harper and Row.

KOHLBERG, L. and KRAMER, R. (1969) Continuities and discontinuities in childhood and adult moral development. *Human Development*, 12, 93–120.

KÖHLER, W. (1929) *Gestalt Psychology*, New York: Liveright.

KOLUCHOVA, J. (1991) Severely deprived twins after 22 years of observation. *Studia Psychologica*, 33, 23–28.

KOP, W.J. and KRANTZ, D.S. (1997) Type A behaviour, hostility and coronary artery disease. In A. Baum, S. Newman, J. Weinman, R. West and C. McManus (eds.), *Cambridge Handbook of Psychology, Health and Medicine*. Cambridge: Cambridge University Press, 183–6.

KRANTZ, D.S., DUREL, L.A., DAVIA, J.E., SHAFFER, R.T., ARABIAN, J.M., DEMBROSKI, T.M. and MACDOUGALL, J.N. (1982) Propranolol medication among coronary patients: relationship to Type A behaviour and cardiovascular response. *Journal of Human Stress*, 8, 4–12.

KREPPNER, J.M., O'CONNOR, T.G., DUNN, J., ANDERSEN-WOOD, L. and the English and Romanian Adoptees (ERA) Study Team (1999) Pretend and social role play of children exposed to early severe deprivation. *British Journal of Developmental Psychology*, 17, 319–32.

KRING, A.M. and NEALE, J.M. (1996) Do schizophrenic patients show a disjunctive relationship among expressive, experiential and psychophysiological components of emotion? *Journal of Abnormal Psychology*, 105, 249–57.

KROSNICK, J.A., BETZ, A.I., JUSSIM, L.J. and LYNN, A.R. (1992) Subliminal conditioning of attitudes. *Personality and Social Psychology Bulletin*, 18, 152–63.

KRUGER, A.C. (1993) Peer collaboration: conflict, cooperation, or both? *Social Development*, 2, 165–82.

KUHN, T.S. (1970) *The Structure of Scientific Revolutions*, 2nd edn., Chicago: University of Chicago Press.

KUPERSCHMIDT, J.B. and COIE, J.D. (1990) Preadolescent peer status, aggression and school adjustment as predictors of externalising problems in adolescence. *Child Development*, 61, 1350–62.

KURLAND, H.D., YEAGER, C.T. and ARTHUR, R.J. (1963) Psychophysiologic aspects of severe behaviour disorders. *Archives of General Psychiatry*, 8, 599–604.

LACHMANN, R., LACHMANN, J.L. AND BUTTERFIELD, E.C. (1979) *Cognitive Psychology and Information Processing*, Hillsdale, NJ: Lawrence Erlbaum Associates.

LADD, G.W. and GOLTER, B.S. (1988) Parents' management of pre-schoolers' peer relations: is it related to children's social competence? *Developmental Psychology*, 24, 109–17.

LAMB, M.E. (1977) Father–infant and mother–infant interaction in the first year of life. *Child Development*, 48, 167–81.

LAMB, M.E. (1987) *The Father's Role: Cross-cultural Perspectives*, Hillsdale, NJ: Erlbaum.

LAMB, M.E. (1997) The development of father–infant relationships. In M.E. Lamb (ed.), *The Role of the Father in Child Development*, 3rd edn., New York: Wiley.

LANGE, J. (1929) *Crime as Destiny*, London: Unwin.

LAUPA, M. and TURIEL, E. (1986) Children's conceptions of adult and peer authority. *Child Development*, 57, 405–12.

LAZARUS, R.S. (1991) Cognition and motivation in emotion. *American Psychologist*, 46, 352–67.

LAZARUS, R.S. (1993) From psychological stress to the emotions: a history of changing outlooks. *Annual Review of Psychology*, 44, 1–21.

LAZARUS, R.S. (1999) *Stress and Emotion: A New Synthesis*, New York: Springer.

LEHRER, P.M., CARR, R., SARGUNARAJ, D. and WOOLFOLK, R.L. (1994) Stress management techniques: are they all equivalent, or do they have specific effects? *Biofeedback and Self-Regulation*, 19, 353–401.

LEVER, J. (1976) Sex differences in games children play. *Social Problems*, 23, 478–87.

LEVINE, R.A., DIXON, S., LEVINE, S., RICHMAN, A., LEIDERMAN, P.H., KEEFER, C.H. and BRAZELTON, T.B. (1994) *Childcare and Culture: Lessons from Africa*, New York: Cambridge University Press.

LEVINGER, G. and CLARK, J. (1961) Emotional factors in the forgetting of word association. *Journal of Abnormal and Social Psychology*, 62, 99–105.

LEVITT, M.J., GUACCI-FRANCO, N. and LEVITT, J.L. (1993) Convoys of social support in childhood and early adolescence: structure and function. *Developmental Psychology*, 29, 811–18.

LEWINSOHN, P.M. (1974) A behavioural approach to depression. In R. Friedman and M. Katz (eds.), *The Psychology of Depression: Contemporary Theory and Research*, Washington, DC: Winston Wiley.

LIEBERMAN, J., CHAKOS, M., WU, H., ALVIR, J., HOFFMAN, E., ROBINSON, D. and BILDER, R. (2001) Longitudinal study of brain morphology in first episode schizophrenia. *Biological Psychiatry*, 49, 487–99.

LIEBERMAN, J.A. (1995) Signs and symptoms: what they can tell us about the clinical course and pathophysiologic process of schizophrenia. *Archives of General Psychiatry*, 52, 361–3.

LINAZA, J. (1984) Piaget's marbles: the study of children's games and their knowledge of rules. *Oxford Review of Education*, 10, 271–4.

LINDSAY, R.C. and WELLS, G.L. (1985) Improving eyewitness identifications from lineups; simultaneous versus sequential lineup presentation. *Journal of Applied Psychology*, 70, 556–64.

LINDSAY, R.C., HAGEN, L., READ, J.D., WADE, K.A. and GARRY, M. (2004) True photographs and false memories. *Psychological Science*, 15, 149–54.

LIONE, L.A., CARTER, R.J., HUNT, M.J., BATES, G.P., MORTON, A.J. and DUNNETT, S.B. (1999) Selective discrimination learning impairments in mice expressing the human Huntingdon's disease mutation. *Journal of Neuroscience*, 19, 10428–37.

LOFTUS, E.F. (1975) Leading questions and the eyewitness report. *Cognitive Psychology*, 7, 560–72.

LOFTUS E.F. (1979) *Eyewitness Testimony*, Cambridge, MA: Harvard University Press.

LOFTUS, E.F. (2001) Imagining the past. *The Psychologist*, 4, (11), 584–7.

LOFTUS, E.F and BURNS, T. (1982) Mental shock can produce retrograde amnesia. *Memory and Cognition*, 10, 318–23.

LOFTUS, E. and KETCHAM, K. (1994) *The Myth of Repressed Memory*, New York: St Martin's Press.

LOFTUS, E.F. and PALMER, J.C. (1974) Reconstruction of automobile destruction: an example of interaction between language and memory. *Journal of Verbal Learning and Verbal Behaviour*, 13, 585–9.

LOFTUS, E.F., LOFTUS, G.R. and MESSO, J. (1987) Some facts about 'Weapon Focus'. *Law and Human Behaviour,* 11, 55–62.

LOMBROSO, C. (1876) L'uomo delinquente. In D. Putwain and A. Sammons (2002) *Psychology and Crime*, Hove: Routledge.

LONG, S.J. and SHERER, M. (1985) Social skills training with juvenile offenders. *Child and Family Behaviour Therapy*, 6 (4), 1–12.

LORENZ, K.Z. (1935) The companion in the bird's world. *Auk*, 54, 245–73.

LOZA, W. and LOZA-FANOUS, A. (1999) The fallacy of reducing rape and violent recidivism by treating anger. *International Journal of Offender Therapy and Comparative Criminology*, 43 (4), 492–502.

LUCINI, D., COVACCI, G., MILANI, R., MELA, G.S., MALLIANI, A. and PAGANI, M. (1997) A controlled study of the effects of mental relaxation on autonomic excitatory responses in healthy subjects. *Psychosomatic Medicine*, 59, 541–52.

LUNDRIGAN, S and CANTER, D. (2001) A multivariate analysis of serial murderers' disposal site location choice. *Journal of Environmental Psychology*, 21 (4), 423–32.

MACKINNON, D., JAMISON, K.R. and DePAULO, J.R. (1997) Genetics of manic depressive illness. *Annual Review of Neuroscience*, 20, 355–73.

MAIN, M. and SOLOMON, J. (1990) Procedures for identifying infants as disorganised/disoriented during the Ainsworth Strange Situation. In M.T. Greenberg, D. Cicchetti and E.M. Cummings, *Attachment in the Preschool Years*, Chicago: University of Chicago Press.

MAIN, M., KAPLAN, N. and CASSIDY, J. (1985) Security in infancy, childhood, and adulthood: a move to a level of representation. In I. Bretherton and E. Waters, (eds.), *Growing Points of Attachment Theory and Research. Monographs of the Society for Research in Child Development*, 50 (1–2, Serial No. 209).

MALPASS R.S. and DEVINE, P.G. (1981a) Guided memory in eyewitness identification. *Journal of Applied Psychology*, 66, 343–50.

MALPASS, R.S. and DEVINE, P.G. (1981b) Eyewitness identification: lineup instructions and the absence of the offender. *Journal of Applied Psychology*, 66, 482–9.

MANNING, M.M. and WRIGHT, T.L. (1983) Self-efficacy expectancies and the persistence of pain control in childbirth. *Journal of Personality and Social Psychology*, 45, 421–31.

MARIN, B.V., HOLMES, D.L., GUTH, M. and KOVAC, P. (1979) The potential of children as eyewitnesses. *Law and Human Behaviour*, 3, 295–305.

MARR, D. (1982) *Vision: A Computational Investigation into the Human Representation and Processing of Visual Information*, San Francisco: Freeman.

MARTORANO, S.C. (1977) A developmental analysis of performance on Piaget's formal operational tasks. *Developmental Psychology*, 13, 666–72.

MASLOW, A.H. (1962) *Toward a Psychology of Being*, New York: Van Nostrand.

MASLOW, A.H. (1970) *Motivation and Personality*, 2nd edn., New York: Harper and Row.

MAUTNER, T. (ed.) (2000) *The Penguin Dictionary of Philosophy*, Harmondsworth: Penguin Books.

MAZZONI, G. and MEMON, A. (2003) Imagination can cause false autobiographical memories. *Psychological Science*, 14, 186–8.

McADAMS, D.P. (2000) *The Person: An Integrated Introduction to Personality Psychology*, Forth Worth, TX: Harcourt.

McALISTER, A., PERRY, C., KILLEN, J., SLINKARD, L.A. and MACCOBY, N. (1980) Pilot study of smoking, alcohol and drug abuse prevention. *American Journal of Public Health*, 70, 719–21.

McCORMICK, J. and McPHERSON, G. (2003) The role of self-efficacy in music performance: an explanatory structural equation analysis. *Psychology of Music*, 31 (1) 37–51.

McGARRIGLE, J. and DONALDSON, M. (1974) Conservation accidents, *Cognition*, 3, 341–50.

McGILLICUDDY-DE LISI, A.V., DE LISI, R. and VAN GULIK, K. (2008) The effects of grade level, context, and family type on male and female adolescents' distributive justice reasoning. *Journal of Adolescence*, 31 (1), 107–24.

McGILLICUDDY-DE LISI, A.V., WATKINS, C. and VINCHUR, A.J. (1994) The effect of relationship on children's distributive justice reasoning. *Child Development*, 65, 1694–700.

McGILLY, K. and SIEGLER, R.S. (1990) The influence of encoding and strategic knowledge on children's choices among serial recall strategies. *Developmental Psychology*, 26, 931–41.

McGLASHAN, T.H. and FENTON, W.S. (1991) Classical subtypes for schizophrenia: literature review for DSM-IV. *Schizophrenia Bulletin*, 17, 609–23.

McGUFFIN, P., KATZ, R., WATKINS, S., and RUTHERFORD, J. (1996) A hospital-based twin register of heritability of DSM-IV unipolar depression. *Archives of General Psychiatry,* 52 (2), 129–36.

McGUIRE, W.J. (1964) Inducing resistance to persuasion: some contemporary approaches. In L. Berkowitz (ed.), *Advances in Experimental Social Psychology*, Vol. 1, New York: Academic Press.

McGURK, B.J. and McDOUGALL, C. (1981) A new approach to Eysenck's theory of criminality. *Personality and Individual Differences*, 2, 338–40.

MEDNICK, S.A., GABRIELLI, W.F. and HUTCHINGS, B. (1984) Genetic influences in criminal convictions: evidence from an adoption cohort. *Science*, 234, 891–4.

MEICHENBAUM, D. (1996) Stress inoculation training for coping with stressors. *The Clinical Psychologist*, 49, 407.

MELO, J.A., SHENDURE, J., POCIASK, K. and SILVER, L.M. (1996) Identification of sex-specific quantitative trait loci controlling alcohol preference in C57BL/6 mice. *Nature Genetics*, 13 (June), 147–53.

MELZOFF, A.N. and MOORE, M.K. (1977) Imitation of facial and manual gestures by human neonates. *Science*, 198, 75–8.

MEMON, A. and WRIGHT, D.B. (1999) Eyewitness testimony and the Oklahoma bombing. *The Psychologist,* 12, 292–5.

MERCKELBACH, A., SMEETS, T., GERAERTS, E. *et al.* (2006) I haven't thought about this for years! Dating recent recalls of vivid memories. *Applied Cognitive Psychology*, 20, 33–42.

MERCKELBACH, H., ARNTZ, A. and DE JONG, P. (1991) Conditioned experiences in spider phobics. *Behaviour Research and Therapy*, 29, 333–5.

MILGRAM, S. (1963) Behavioural study of obedience. *Journal of Abnormal and Social Psychology*, 67, 371–8.

MILLER, W.R. and SELIGMAN, M.E. (1975) Depression and learned helplessness in man. *Journal of Abnormal Psychology*, 84 (3), 228–38.

MILLER, W.R., LECKMAN, A.L., DELANEY, H.D. and TINCHOM, M. (1992) Long-term follow-up of behavioural self-control training. *Journal of Studies on Alcohol*, 51, 108–15.

MILNE, R. and BULL, R. (2002) Back to basics: a componential analysis of the original cognitive interview mnemonics with three age groups. *Applied Cognitive Psychology*, 16, 743–53.

MILNER, P. (1991). Brain-stimulation reward: a review. *Canadian Journal of Psychology*, 45, 1–36.

MODROW, J. (1992) *How to Become a Schizophrenic: The Case Against Biological Psychiatry*, Everett, WA: Apollyon Press.

MOFFITT, T.E. (1993) Adolescent-limited and life-course-persistent anti-social behaviour: a developmental taxonomy. *Psychological Review*, 100, 674–701.

MOFFITT, T.E. (2003) Life-course-persistent and adolescence-limited antisocial behaviour: a 10-year research review and a research agenda. In B.A. Lahey, T.E. Moffitt and A. Caspi (eds.), *Causes of Conduct Disorder and Juvenile Delinquency*, New York: Guilford Press.

MOHER, M., HEY, K. and LANCASTER, T. (2005) Workplace interventions for smoking cessation. *Cochrane Database of Systematic Reviews*, 2005 (Issue 2).

MOOS, R.H. and MOOS, B.S. (2004) Long-term influence of duration and frequency of participation in Alcoholics Anonymous of individuals with alcohol use disorders. *Journal of Consulting and Clinical Psychology*, 72, 81–90.

MORGENSTERN, J., LANGENBUCHER, J., LABOUVIE, E. and MILLER, K.J. (1997) The co-morbidity of alcoholism and personality disorders in a clinical population: prevalence and relation to alcohol typology variables. *Journal of Abnormal Psychology*, 106 (1), 74–84.

MORRIS, J.S., FRITH, C.D., PERRETT, D.I., ROWLAND, D., YOUNG, A.W., CALDER, A.J. and DOLAN, R.J. (1996) A differential neural response in the human amygdala to fearful and happy facial expressions. *Nature*, 383, 812–15.

MORRISON L. AND BENNET. P. (2005) *An Introduction to Health Psychology*: Englewood Cliffs, NJ: Prentice Hall Publishers.

MORROW, G.R., ASBURY, R., HAMMON, S. and DOBKIN, P. (1992) Comparing the effectiveness of behavioural treatment for chemotherapy-induced nausea and vomiting when administered by oncologists, oncology nurses, and clinical psychologists. *Health Psychology*, 11, 250–6.

MUNJACK, D.J. (1984) The onset of driving phobias. *Journal of Behaviour Therapy and Experimental Psychiatry*, 15, 305–8.

MURRAY, L. and TREVARTHEN, C. (1985) Emotional regulations of interactions between two-month-olds and their mothers. In T.M. Field and N.A. Fox (eds.), *Social Perception in Infants*, Norwood, NJ: Ablex.

MYERS, B.J. (1984) Mother–infant bonding: the status of this critical-period hypothesis. *Developmental Review*, 4, 240–74.

NAIDOO, J. and WILLS, J. (1998) *Practising Health Promotion: Dilemmas and Challenges*, London: Bailiere Tindall.

NATIONAL AUDIT OFFICE (2006) The Electronic Monitoring of Adult Offenders, Report by the Comptroller (HC 800 Session 2005–2006), London.

NATIONAL STATISTICS (2005) Available at www.statistics.gov.uk (10.09.05).

NEISSER, U. and HARSCH, N. (1992) Phantom flashbulbs: false recollections of hearing the news about Challenger. In E. Winograd and U. Neisser (eds.), *Affect and Accuracy in Recall: Studies of 'Flashbulb' Memories*, New York: Cambridge University Press.

NELSON, S.A. (1980) Factors influencing young children's use of motives and outcomes as moral criteria,. *Child Development*, 51, 823–9.

NEWMAN, L.S., DUFF, K.J. and BAUMEISTER, R.F. (1997) A new look at defensive projection: thought suppression, accessibility and biased person perception, *Journal of Personality and Social Psychology*, 72, 980–1001.

NG, D.M. and JEFFEREY, R.W. (2003) Relationships between perceived stress and health behaviours in a sample of working adults. *Health Psychology*, 22, 638–42.

NISBETT, R.E. and WILSON, T.D. (1977) Telling more than we can know: verbal reports on mental processes. *Psychological Review*, 84, 231–95.

NOLEN-HOEKSEMA, S. (2002) Gender differences in depression. In I.H. Gotlib and C.L. Hammen (eds.), *Handbook of Depression*, New York: Guilford Press.

NOMURA, H., INOUE, S., KAMIMURA, N. *et al*. (2005) A cross-cultural study on expressed emotion in carers of people with dementia and schizophrenia: Japan and England. *Social Psychiatry and Psychiatric Epidemiology*, 40 (7), 564–70.

NOVACO, R.W. (1975) *Anger Control: The Development and Evaluation of an Experimental Treatment*, Lexington, MA: Lexington Books.

NUCCI, L.P. (1996) Morality and the personal sphere of action. In E. Reed, E. Turiel and T. Brown (eds.), *Values and Knowledge*, Hillsdale, NJ: Erlbaum.

OCKENE, J.K., EMMONS, K.M., MERMELSTEIN, R.J., PERKINS, K.A., BONOLLO, D.S., VOORHEES, C.C. *et al*. (2000) Relapse and maintenance issues for smoking cessation. *Health Psychology*, 19, 17–31.

ODEN, S. and ASHER, S.R. (1977) Coaching children in social skills for friendship making, *Child Development*, 48, 495–506.

OLDS, J. and MILNER, P. (1954) Positive reinforcement produced by electrical stimulation of septal area and other regions of rat brain. *Journal of Comparative and Physiological Psychology*, 47, 419–27.

O'MALLEY, S.S., JAFFE, A.J., RODE, S. and ROUNSAVILLE, B.J. (1996) Experience of a 'slip' among alcoholics treated with naltrexone or placebo. *American Journal of Psychiatry*, 153, 281–3.

ORNE, M.T. (1962) On the social psychology of the psychological experiment: with particular reference to demand characteristics and their implications. *American Psychologist*, 17, 776–83.

OST, L. (1991) Acquisition of blood and injection phobia and anxiety response patterns in clinical patients. *Behaviour Research and Therapy*, 29, 323–32.

PAPOUSEK, H., PAPOUSEK, M. and SYMMES, D. (1991) The meaning of melodies in mothers' in tone and stress languages. *Infant Behaviour and Development*, 14, 415–40.

PARKE, R.D. and SAWIN, D.B. (1980) The family in early infancy: social interactional and attitudinal analyses. In F.A. Pedersen (ed.), *The Father–Infant Relationship: Observational Studies in a Family Context*, New York: Praeger.

PARKIN, A.J. (1993) *Memory: Phenomena, Experiment and Theory*, Oxford: Blackwell.

PATTERSON, S.M., MATTHEWS, K.A., ALLEN, M.T. and OWENS, J.F. (1995) Stress-induced hemoconcentration of blood cells and lipids in healthy women during acute psychological stress. *Health Psychology*, 14, 319–24.

PAUL, G.L. and LENTZ, R.J. (1977) *Psychosocial Treatment of Chronic Mental Patients: Miller Versus Social Learning Progress*, Cambridge, MA: Harvard University Press.

PEACOCK, E.J. and WONG, P.T.P. (1990) The stress appraisal measure (SAM): a multidimensional approach to cognitive appraisal. *Stress Medicine*, 6, 227–36.

PEDERSON, D.R., GLEASON, K.E., MORAN, G. and BENTO, S. (1998) Maternal attachment representations, maternal sensitivity, and the infant–mother attachment relationship. *Developmental Psychology*, 34, 925–33.

PENNINGTON, D.C. (2003) *Essential Personality*, London: Hodder & Stoughton.

PENNINGTON, D.C., MCLOUGHLIN, J., SMITHSON, R., ROBINSON, and BOSWELL, K. (2003) *Advanced Psychology, Child Development, Perspectives and Methods*, London: Hodder & Stoughton.

PENNINGTON, D.C. and McLOUGHLIN, J. (2008) *AQA (B) Psychology for AS*, London: Hodder Education.

PETERS, T.J. and PREEDY, V.R. (2002) Alcohol and genetic predisposition. In W. Caan and J. de Belleroche (eds.), *Drink, Drugs and Dependence: From Science to Clinical Practice*, London: Routledge.

PETERSON, C. and SELIGMAN, M.E. (1984) Causal explanations as a risk factor for depression: theory and evidence. *Psychological Review*, 91, 347–74.

PHILLIPS, A.G., COURY, A., FLORINO, D., LePIANE, F.G., BROWN, E. and FIBIGER, H.C. (1992) Self-stimulation of the ventral tegmental area enhances dopamine release in the nucleus accumbens: a microdialysis study. In P.W. Kalivas and H.H. Samson (eds.), *The Neurobiology of Drug and Alcohol Addiction. Annals of the New York Academy of Sciences*, Vol. 654, New York: New York Academy of Sciences, 199–206.

PIAGET, J. (1932) (trans. M. Gabain) *The Moral Judgment of the Child*, New York: Free Press, 1965.

PIAGET, J. (1963) *The Origins of Intelligence in Children*, New York: Norton.

PIAGET, J. and INHELDER, B. (1956) *The Child's Conception of Space*, London: Routledge and Kegan Paul.

PINEL, J.P.J. (2003) *Biopsychology*, 5th edn., Boston: Allyn & Bacon.

PINIZZOTTO, A.J. (1984) Forensic psychology: criminal personality profiling. *Journal of Police Science and Administration*, 12, 32–40.

PINIZZOTTO, A.J. and FINKEL, N.J. (1990) Criminal personality profiling: an outcome and process study. *Law and Human Behaviour*, 14, 215–34.

PLOMIN, R. (1990) *Nature and Nurture: An Introduction to Behavioural Genetics*, Pacific Grove, CA: Brooks/Cole.

PLOMIN, R. (1996) Nature and nurture. In M.R. Merrens and G.C. Brannigan (eds.), *The Developmental Psychologists: Research Adventures across the Life-span*, New York: McGraw-Hill.

PLOMIN, R., De FRIES, J.C., McCLEARN, G.E. and RUTTER, M. (1997) *Behavioural Genetics*, 3rd edn., New York: Freeman.

POOLE, D.A. and LINDSAY, D.S. (2001) Children's eyewitness reports after exposure to misinformation from parents. *Journal of Experimental Psychology: Applied*, 7, 27–50.

POPPER, K.R. (1963) *Conjectures and Reputations: The Growth of Science Knowledge*, London: Routledge and Kegan Paul.

PORTER, S., YUILLE, J.C. and LEHMAN, D.R. (1999) The nature of real, implanted, and fabricated memories for emotional childhood events. *Law and Human Behaviour*, 23, 517–37.

POSNER, M. (1978) *Chronometric Explorations of Mind*, Hillsdale, NJ: Lawrence Erlbaum Associates.

POWELL, R.A. and BOER, D.P. (1995) Did Freud misinterpret reported memories of sexual abuse as fantasies? *Psychological Reports*, 77, 563–70.

PRICE, J. (1968) The genetics of depressed behaviour. In A. Coppen and S. Walk (eds.), *Recent Development in the Affective Disorders*, Special Publication No. 2, *British Journal of Psychiatry*.

PROCHASKA, J.O., DiCLEMENTE, C.C. and NORCROSS, J.C. (1992) In search of how people change: applications to addictive behaviours. *American Psychologist*, 47, 1102–14.

PUTNAM, K.M., HARVEY, P.D., PARRELLA, M., WHITE, L., KINCAID, M., POWCHIK, P. and DAVIDSON, M. (1996) Symptom stability in geriatiric chronic schizophrenic inpatients: a one-year follow-up study. *Biological Psychiatry*, 39, 92–9.

PUTWAIN, D. and SAMMONS, A. (2002) *Psychology and Crime*. Hove: Routledge.

RAINE, A., LENCZ, T., BIHRLE, S., LACASSE, L. and COLLETTI, P. (2000) Reduced prefrontal gray matter volume and reduced autonomic activity in antisocial personality disorder. *Archives of General Psychiatry*, 57, 119–29.

RANKIN, H., HODGSON, R. and STOCKWELL, T. (1983) Cue exposure and response prevention with alcoholics: a controlled trial. *Behaviour Research and Therapy*, 21, 435–46.

REASON, P. and ROWAN, J. (eds.) (1981) *Human Enquiry: A Sourcebook in New Paradigm Research*, Chichester: Wiley.

REED, M.D. and ROWNTREE, P.W. (1997) Peer pressure and adolescent substance use. *Journal of Quantitative Criminology*, 13 (2), 143–80.

RHINEHART, L. (1999) *The Dice Man*, London: HarperCollins.

RIHMER, Z. and PESTALITY, P. (1999). Bipolar II disorder and suicidal behaviour, *The Psychiatric Clinics of North America*, 22 (3), 667–74.

ROBERTSON, J. and ROBERTSON, J. (1968) Young children in brief separation: a fresh look. *Psychoanalytic Study of the Child*, 26, 264–315.

ROBINSON, L.A. and KLESGES, R.C. (1997) Ethnic and gender differences in risk factors for smoking onset. *Health Psychology*, 16, 499–505.

ROBSON, C. (1993) *Real World Research*, Oxford: Blackwell.

ROGERS, C.R. (1951) *Client-centred Therapy: Its Current Practice, Implications and Theory*, Boston: Houghton Mifflin.

ROGERS, C.R. (1959) A theory of therapy, personality and interpersonal relationships, as developed in the client-centred framework. In S. Koch (ed.), *Psychology: A Study of Science*, Vol. 3, New York: McGraw-Hill.

ROGERS, C.R. (1961) *On Becoming a Person*, Boston: Houghton Mifflin.

ROGERS, C.R. (1977) *Carl Rogers on Personal Power*, New York: Delacorte.

ROGERS, C.R. (1980) *A Way of Being*, Boston: Houghton Mifflin.

ROGOFF, B., BAKER-SENNETT, J., LACASA, P. and GOLDSMITH, D. (1995) Development through participation in socio-cultural activity. In J. Goodnow, P. Miller and F. Kessel (eds.) *Cultural Practices as Contexts for Development*, San Francisco: Jossey-Bass.

ROKEACH, M. (1960) *The Open and Closed Mind*, New York: Basic Books.

ROSE, S.A. and BLANK, M. (1974) The potency of context in children's cognition: an illustration through conservation. *Child Development*, 45, 499–502.

ROSENHAN, D.L. (1973) On being sane in insane places. *Science*, 179 (4070), 250–8.

ROSENTHAL, R. (1966) *Experimenter Effects in Behavioural Research*, New York: Appleton-Century-Crofts.

ROSENTHAL, R. and FODE, K.L. (1963) The effects of experimenter bias on the performance of the albino rat. *Behavioural Science*, 8, 183–9.

ROSENTHAL, R. and JACOBSON, L. (1968) *Pygmalion in the Classroom: Teacher Expectations and Pupils' Intellectual Development*, New York: Holt.

ROSSMO, D.K. (1997) Geographic profiling. In J.L. Jackson and D.A. Bekerian (eds.), *Offender Profiling: Theory, Research and Practice*, Chichester, Wiley.

ROTTER, J.B. (1966) Generalised expectancies for internal versus external control of reinforcement. *Psychological Monographs*, 80 (1) (Whole No. 609).

ROTTER, J.B. (1982) *The Development and Applications of Social Learning Theory: Selected Papers*, New York: Praege.

ROWE, M. (1997) Hardiness, stress, temperament, coping and burnout in health professionals. *American Journal of Health Behaviour*, 21, 163–71.

RUBIN, Z. (1980) *Children's Friendships*, Cambridge, MA: Harvard University Press.

RUNCO, M.A., EBERSOLE, P. and MRAZ, W. (1991) Creativity and self-actualisation. *Journal of Social Behaviour and Personality*, 6, 161–7.

RUSHTON, J.P. (1988) Race differences in behaviour: a review and evolutionary analysis. *Personality and Individual Differences*, 9, 1009–24.

RUSHTON, J.P. and JENSEN A.R. (2005) Thirty years of research on race differences in cognitive ability. *Psychology, Public Policy, and Law*, 11, 235–94.

RUTTER, M. (1981) *Maternal Deprivation Reassessed*, 2nd edn., Harmondsworth: Penguin.

RUTTER, M. and the English and Romanian Adoptees Study Team (1998) Developmental catch-up and deficit after severe global early deprivation. *Journal of Child Psychology and Psychiatry*, 39, 465–76.

RUTTER, M., KREPPNER, J., CROFT, C., MURIN, M., COLVERT, E., BECKETT, C., CASTLE, J. and SONUGA-BARKE, E. (2007) Early adolescent outcomes of institutionally deprived and non-deprived adoptees. III. Quasi-autism. *Journal of Child Psychology and Psychiatry*, 48 (12), 1200–7.

RUTTER, M., TIZARD, J. and WHITMORE, K. (1970) *Education, Health and Behaviour*, London: Longman.

SALUJA, G., IACHAN, R., SCHEIDT, P.C., OVERPECK, M.D., SUN, W. and GIEDD, J.N. (2004) Prevalence of and risk factors for depressive symptoms among young adolescents. *Archives of Pediatrics and Adolescent Medicine*, 158, 760–5.

SARAFINO, E.P. (2001) *Behaviour Modification: Principles of Behaviour Change*, 2nd edn., Mountain View, CA: Mayfield.

SARAFINO, E. (2006) *Health Psychology: Biosocial Interactions*, 5th edn., New York: John Wiley and Sons.

SARASON, I.G. (1978) A cognitive social learning approach to juvenile delinquency. In R.D. Hare and D. Schalling (eds.), *Psychopathic Behaviour: Approaches to Research*, Chichester: Wiley.

SCHACHTER, S. (1977) Nicotine regulation in heavy and light smokers. *Journal of Experimental Psychology: General*, 106, 5–12.

SCHACHTER, S. and SINGER, J.E. (1962) Cognitive, social and physiological determinants of emotional state. *Psychological Review*, 69, 379–99.

SCHAFFER, D.R. (1988) *Developmental Psychology: Childhood and Adolescence*, 2nd edn., New York: Brooks/Cole Publishing Company.

SCHAFFER, H.R. and EMERSON, P.E. (1964) The development of social attachments in infancy. *Monographs of the Society for Research in Child Development*, 29, (94).

SCHAFFER, R.D. (1996) *Social Development*, Oxford: Blackwell.

SCHARFF, L., MARCUS, D.A. and MASEK, B.J. (2002) A controlled study of minimal contact thermal biofeedback treatment in children with migraine. *Journal of Pediatric Psychology*, 27 (2), 109–19.

SCHEFF, T.J. (1966) *Being Mentally Ill: A Sociological Theory*, Chicago: Aldine.

SCHIFFMAN, J., LaBRIE, J., CARTER, J., CANNON, T., SCHULSINGER, F. and PARNAS, J. (2002) Perception of parent–child relationships in high-risk families and adult schizophrenia outcome of offspring. *Journal of Psychiatric Research*, 36, 41–7.

SCHNALL, P.L., PIEPER, C., SCHWARTZ, J.E., KARASEK, R.A., SCHLUSSEL, Y., DEVEREUX, R.B. *et al*. (1990) The relationship between 'job strain', workplace diastolic blood pressure, and left ventricular mass index: results of a case-control study. *Journal of the American Medical Association*, 263, 1929–35.

SCHRAFF, L. (2002) A controlled study of minimal-contact thermal biofeedback treatment in children with migraine. *Journal of Pediatric Psychology*, 27(2), 109–19.

SCHULTZ, D.P. and SCHULTZ, G.E. (2000) *A Modern History of Psychology*, 7th edn., Fort Worth, TX: Harcourt College Publishers.

SCHUSTER, C.R. and KILBEY, M.M. (1992) Prevention of drug abuse. In J.M. Last and R.B. Wallace (eds.), *Maxcy-Rosenau-Last Public Health Prevention and Preventative Medicine*, New York: Wiley.

SELIGMAN, M.E. (1974) Depression and learned helplessness. In R.J. Freidman and M.M. Katz (eds.), *The Psychology of Depression: Contemporary Theory and Research*, Washington, DC: Winston Wiley.

SELIGMAN, M.E.P., ABRAMSON, L.Y., SEMMEL, A.R. and VAN BAEYER, C. (1979) Depressive attributional style. *Journal of Abnormal Psychology*, 88, 242–7.

SELMAN, R.L. (1980) *The Growth of Interpersonal Understanding*, New York: Academic Press.

SELYE, H. (1976) *The Stress of Life*, New York: McGraw-Hill.

SERAFICA, F.C. (1982) *Social-cognitive Development in Context*, London: Methuen.

SEXTON, T.L. and WHISTON, S.C. (1994) The status of the counselling relationship: an empirical review, theoretical implications and research directions. *The Counselling Psychologist*, 22, 6–78.

SHAROT, T., MARTORELLA, E.F., DELGADO, M.R. and PHELPS, E.A. (2007) How personal experience modulates the neural circuitry of memories of September 11. *Proceedings of National Academy of Sciences USA*, 104 (1), 389–94.

SHASTRY, B.S. (2005) Bipolar disorder: an update. *Neurochemical Interactions*, 46, 273–9.

SHEDLER, J. and BLOCK, J. (1990) Adolescent drug use and psychological health: a longitudinal inquiry. *American Psychologist*, 45 (5), 612–30.

SHEFFIELD, M., CAREY, J., PATENAUDE, W. and LAMBERT, M.J. (1995) An exploration of the relationship between interpersonal problems and psychological health. *Psychological Reports*, 76, 947–56.

SHELDON, W.H. (1949) *Varieties of Delinquent Youth*, New York: Harper.

SHEPHERD, J.W., DAVIES, G.M. and ELLIS, H.D. (1981) Studies of cue saliency. In G. Davies, H. Ellis and J. Shepherd (eds.), *Perceiving and Remembering Faces*, London: Academic Press.

SHERMAN, L.W. and STRANG, H. (2007) *Restorative Justice: The Evidence*, London: The Smith Institute.

SHETTLEWORTH, S.J. (1998) *Cognition, Evolution and Behaviour*, New York: Oxford University Press.

SHIELDS, M.M. and DUVEEN, G. (1982) The young child's image of the personal and social world: some aspects of the child's representation of persons. Paper presented at the International Sociological Association Conference, Mexico City, August 1982. In S. Meadows (1986) *Understanding Child Development*, London: Hutchinson.

SHIN, L.M., KOSSLYN, S.M., McNALLY, R.J., ALPERT, N.M., THOMPSON, W.L., RAUCH, S.L. *et al.* (1997). Visual imagery and perception in post-traumatic stress disorder: a positron emission tomographic investigation. *Archives of General Psychiatry*, 54, 233–41.

SHONTZ, F.C. (1975) *The Psychological Aspects of Physical Illness and Disability*, New York: Macmillan.

SHOSTRUM. E.L. (1963) *Personal Orientation Inventory*, San Diego: EdITS/Educational and Industrial Testing Service.

SHOSTRUM, E.L. (1977) *Manual for the Personal Orientation Dimensions*, San Diego: EdITS/Educational and Industrial Testing Service.

SIEGEL, S., HINSON, R.E., KRANK, M.D. and MCCULLY, J. (1982) Heroin 'overdose' death: contribution of drug-associated environmental cues. *Science*, 216, 436–7.

SIEGLER, R.S. (1976) Three aspects of cognitive development. *Cognitive Psychology*, 8, 481–520.

SIEGLER, R.S. (1996) *Emerging Minds: The Process of Change in Children's Thinking*, New York: Oxford University Press.

SKINNER, B.F. (1953) *Science and Human Behaviour*, New York: Macmillan.

SKINNER, B.F. (1957) *Verbal Behaviour*, New York: Appleton.

SKINNER, B.F. (1974) *About Behaviourism*, New York: Vintage Books.

SKINNER, E.A., EDGE, K., ALTMAN, J. and SHERWOOD, H. (2003) Searching for the structure of coping: a review and critique of category systems for classifying ways of coping. *Psychological Bulletin*, 129, 216–69.

SKUSE, D. (1984) Extreme deprivation in early childhood. II. Theoretical issues and a comparative review. *Journal of Child Psychology and Psychiatry*, 25, 543–72.

SMITH, C.A. and FARRINGTON, D.P. (2004) Continuities in anti-social behaviour and parenting across three generations. *Journal of Child Psychology and Psychiatry*, 45, 230–47.

SMITH, P.B. and HARRIS BOND, M.H. (1999) *Social Psychology Across Cultures*, 2nd edn., Hemel Hempstead: Harvester-Wheatsheaf.

SMITH, P.K., COWIE, H. and BLADES, M. (2003) *Understanding Children's Development*, 4th edn., Oxford: Blackwell.

SMOLENSKY, P. (1995) On the proper treatment of connectionism. In C. McDonald and G. McDonald (eds.), *Connectionism: Debates on Psychological Explanation*, Cambridge, MA: Blackwell.

SNAREY, J.R. (1995) In a communitarian voice: the sociological expansion of Kohlbergian theory, research and practice. In W.M. Kurtines and J.L. Gewirtz (eds.), *Moral Development: An Introduction*, Boston: Allyn & Bacon.

SNOW, C.E. and FERGUSON, C.A. (eds.) (1977) *Talking to Children*, Cambridge: Cambridge University Press.

SOSA, R., KENNELL, J., KLAUS, M., ROBERTSON, S. and URRUTIA, J. (1980) The effect of supportive companion on perinatal problems, length of labor and mother–infant interactions. *New England Journal of Medicine*, 303, 597–600.

SOUTHWICK, S.M., VYTHILINGHAM, M. and CHARNEY, D.S. (2005) The psychobiology of depression and resilience to stress: Implications for prevention and treatment. *Annual Review of Clinical Psychology*, 1, 255–92.

SPENCE, S.H. and MARZILLER, J.S. (1981) Social skills training with adolescent male offenders. II. Short-term, long-term and generalisation effects. *Behaviour Research and Therapy*, 19, 349–68.

STEBLAY, N., DYSART, J., FULERO, S. and LINDSAY, R.C.L. (2001) Eyewitness accuracy rates in sequential and simultaneous lineup presentations: a meta-analytic comparison. *Law and Human Behaviour,* 25, 459–73.

STEBLAY, N.M. (1997) Social influence in eyewitness recall: a meta-analytic review of lineup instruction effects. *Law and Human Behaviour*, 21, 283–97.

STEIN, C.J. and TEST, M.A. (1980) Alternative to mental hospital treatment program and clinical evaluation. *Archives of General Psychiatry*, 37, 392–7.

STEIN, J.A., NEWCOMB, M.D. and BENTLER, P.M. (1987) An 8-year study of multiple influences on drug use and drug use consequences. *Journal of Personality and Social P*sychology, 53 (6), 1094–105.

STEIN, J.F., KIMIECSK, J.C., DANIELS, J. and JACKSON, S.A. (1995) Psychological antecedents of flow in recreational sport. *Personality and Social Psychology Bulletin*, 21, 125–35.

STERNBERG, R.J. (2001) *Psychology: In Search of the Human Mind*, Fort Worth, TX: Harcourt College Publishers.

STERNBERG, R.J. and GRIGORENKO, E.L. (eds.), (1997) *Intelligence, Heredity and Environment*, New York: Cambridge University Press.

STERNBERG, S. (1966) High-speed scanning in human memory, *Science*, 153, 652–4.

STEVEN, A. (2001) *Jung: A Very Short Introduction*, Oxford: Oxford University Press.

STRAUB, R. (2007) *Health Pyschology*, 2nd edn., New York: Worth Publications.

STIRLING, J.D., HELLEWELL, J. and QURIASHI, N. (1998) Self-monitoring and the schizophrenic symptoms of alien control. *Psychological Medicine*, 28, 675–83.

STONEY, C.M., MATTHEWS, K.A., McDONALD, R.H. and JOHNSON, C.A. (1990) Sex differences in acute stress response: Lipid, lipoprotein, cardiovascular and neuroendocrine adjustments. *Psychophysiology*, 12, 52–61.

STORR, A. (2002) *Freud: a very short introduction*, Oxford: Oxford University Press.

STRANKS, J. (2005) *Stress at Work*, Oxford: Butterworth-Heinemann Publishers.

STROEBE, W. (2000) *Social Psychology and Health*, 2nd edn., Buckingham: Open University Press.

STUNKARD, A.J. (1991) Review of Schwartz, H.J. (ed.), Bulimia: psychoanalytic treatment and therapy. *Psychiatric Annals*, 19, 279.

SUOMI, S.J. and HARLOW, H.F. (1972) Social rehabilitation of isolate-reared monkeys. *Developmental Psychology* 6, 487–96.

SUTHERLAND, E.H. (1939) *Principles of Criminology*, Philadelphia: Lippincott.

SUTHERLAND, E.H. (1951) A critique of Sheldon's varieties of delinquent youth. *American Sociological Review*, 16, 10–13.

SWANN, W., STEIN-SEROUSSI, A., and GIESLER, R.B. (1992) Why people self-verify. *Journal of Personality and Social Psychology*, 62, 392–401.

SWANN, W., WENZLAFF, R., KRULL, D.S. and PELHAM, B. (1992) Allure of negative feedback: self-verification strivings among depressed persons. *Journal of Abnormal Psychology*, 101, 293–306.

SZASZ, T. (1962) *The Myth of Mental Illness*, New York: Harper and Row.

TAKAHASHI, K. (1990) Are the key assumptions of the 'Strange Situation' procedure universal? A view from Japanese research. *Human Development*, 33, 23–30.

TANAKA, J.W. and FARAH, M.J. (1993) Parts and wholes in face recognition. *Quarterly Journal of Experimental Psychology* A, 2, 225–45.

TERMAN, M. (1988). On the question of mechanism in phototherapy for seasonal affective disorder: considerations of clinical efficacy and epidemiology. *Journal of Biological Rhythms*, 3, 155–72.

THE GENERAL HOUSEHOLD SURVEY (Smoking and Drinking Among Adults) (2004) London Office for National Statistics.

THOMAS, L. and COOPER, P. (1980) Incidence and psychological correlates of intense spiritual experience. *Journal of Transpersonal Psychology*, 12, 75–85.

TIENARA, P. (1991) Interaction between genetic vulnerability and family environment: the Finnish adoptive study of family schizophrenia. *Acta Psychiatrica Scandinavica*, 84, 460–5.

TIETJEN, A. and WALKER, L. (1985) Moral reasoning and leadership among men in a Papua, New Guinea village. *Developmental Psychology*, 21, 982–92.

TIETJEN, A.M. (1986) Prosocial moral reasoning among children and adults in a Papua New Guinea society. *Developmental Psychology*, 22, 861–8.

TITCHENER, E.B. (1910) *A Textbook of Psychology*, New York: Macmillan.

TOLMAN, E.C. (1932) *Purposive Behaviour in Animals and Men*, New York: Appleton.

TOLMAN, E.C. (1948) Cognitive maps in rats and men. *Psychological Review*, 55, 189–208.

TOLMAN, E.C. and HONZIK, C.H. (1930) Insight in rats. *University of California Publications in Psychology*, 4, 215–32.

TOMKINS, S.S. (1968) Psychological models for smoking behaviour, *Review of Existential Psychology and Psychiatry*, 8 (1), 28–33.

TONIGAN, J.S., MILLER, W.R. and SCHERMER, C. (2002) Atheists, agnostics and Alcoholics Anonymous. *Journal of Studies on Alcohol*, 63, 534–41.

TORREY, E.F. (1997) *Out of the Shadows: Confronting America's Mental Illness Crisis*, New York: Wiley.

TORREY, E.F. (2001) *Surviving Schizophrenia: A Manual for Families, Consumers and Providers*, 4th edn., New York: Basic Books.

TRONICK, E.Z., MORELLI, G.A. and WINN, S. (1987) Multiple caretaking of Efe (Pygmy) infants. *American Anthropologist*, 89, 96–106.

TURIEL, E. (1978) Social regulations and domains of social concepts. In W. Damon (ed.), *New Directions for Child Development: Vol. 1 Social Cognition*, San Francisco: Jossey-Bass.

TURIEL, E. (1983) *The Development of Social Knowledge: Morality and Convention*, Cambridge: Cambridge University Press.

VAN IJZENDOORN, M.H. and DE WOLFF, M.S. (1997) In search of the absent father: meta-analyses of infant–father attachment: a rejoinder to our discussants. *Child Development*, 68, 604–9.

VAN IJZENDOORN, M.H. and KROONENBERG, P.M. (1988) Cross-cultural patterns of attachment: a meta-analysis of the strange situation. *Child Development*, 59, 147–56.

VAN IJZENDOORN, M.H., JUFFER, E. and DUYVESTEYN, M.G.C. (1995) Breaking the intergenerational cycle of insecure attachment: a review of the effects of attachment-based interventions on maternal sensitivity and infant security. *Journal of Child Psychology and Psychiatry*, 36, 225–48.

VAN WIERINGEN, J.C. (1978) Secular growth changes. In F. Falkner and J.M. Tanner (eds.), *Human Growth, Vol. 2*, New York: Plenum.

VAUGHN, B.E. and LANGLOIS, J.H. (1983) Physical attractiveness as a correlate of peer status and social competence in pre-school children. *Developmental Psychology*, 19, 561–7.

VEDHARA, K., COX, N.K.M., WILCOCK, G.K., PERKS, P., HUNT, M., ANDERSON, S. *et al.* (1999) Chronic stress in elderly carers of dementia patients and antibody response to influenza vaccination. *Lancet*, 353, 627–31.

VERGNES, N. (1975) Déclechment de reactions d'agression interspécific après lesion amygdalienne chez le rat. *Physiology and Behaviour*, 14, 271–6.

VYGOTSKY, L.S. (1978) *Mind in Society*, Cambridge, MA: Harvard University Press.

WALDROP, M.F. and HALVERSON, C.F. (1975) Intensive and extensive peer behaviour: longitudinal and cross-sectional analyses. *Child Development*, 46, 19–26.

WALKER, L.J. (1984) Sex differences in the development of moral reasoning: a critical review. *Child Development*, 55, 677–91.

WALKER, L.J. (1989) A longitudinal study of moral reasoning. *Child Development*, 60, 157–66.

WALKER, L.J., DEVRIES, B. and TREVETHAN, S.D. (1987) Moral stages and moral orientations in real-life and hypothetical dilemmas. *Child Development*, 58, 842–58.

WALLACE, J., SCHNEIDER, T. and McGUFFIN, P. (2002) Genetics of depression. In I.H. Gotlib and C.L. Hammen (eds.), *Handbook of Depression*, New York: Guilford Press.

WALLACE, P., CUTLER, S. and HAINES, A. (1988) Randomised control trial of general practitioner intervention in patients with excessive alcohol consumption. *British Medical Journal*, 287, 663ff.

WALSTER, E. (1966) The assignment of responsibility for an accident. *Journal of Personality and Social Psychology*, 5, 508–16.

WASSERMAN, E.A. (1993) Comparative cognition: beginning the second century of the study of animal cognition. *Psychological Bulletin*, 113, 211–28.

WATERS, E., MERRICK, S., TREBOUX, D., CROWELL, J. and ALBERSHEIM, L. (2000) Attachment security in infancy and early adulthood: a twenty-year longitudinal study. *Child Development*, 71, 684–9.

WATERS, E., VAUGHN, B.E., POSADA, G. and KONDO-IKEMURA, K. (1995) Caregiving, cultural and cognitive perspectives on secure-base behavior and working models: new growing points of attachment theory and research. *Monographs of the Society for Research in Child Development*, 60 (2, 3, No. 244.)

WATSON, J.B. (1919) *Psychology from the Standpoint of a Behaviourist*, Philadelphia: Lippincott.

WATSON, J.B. (1930) *Behaviourism*, New York: Norton.

WATSON, J.B. and RAYNOR, R. (1920) Conditioned emotional reactions. *Journal of Experimental Psychology*, 3, 1–4.

WEBSTER-STRATTON, C. and REID, M.J. (2003): The incredible years parents, teachers and children training series: a multifaceted treatment approach for young children with conduct problems. In A.E. Kazdin and J.R. Weisz (eds.), *Evidence-based Psychotherapies for Children and Adolescents*, New York: Guilford Press.

WEINBERGER, J.L. and SILVERMAN, L.H. (1990) Testability and empirical verification of psychoanalytic dynamic propositions through subliminal psychodynamic activation. *Psychoanalytic Psychology*, 7, 299–339.

WEINS, A.N. and MENUSTIK, C.E. (1983) Treatment outcome and patient characteristics in an aversion therapy programme for alcoholics. *American Psychologist*, 38, 1089–96.

WEITEN, W. (2002) *Psychology: Themes and Variations*, 5th edn., London: Wadsworth.

WELLS, G.L. and BRADFIELD, A.L. (1998) 'Good, you identified the suspect': feedback to eyewitnesses distorts their reports of the witnessing experience. *Journal of Applied Psychology*, 83 (3), 360–76.

WELLS, G.L., SMALL, M., PENROD, S., MALPASS, R., FUNLERO, S.D. and BRIMACOMBE, C. (1998) Eyewitness identification procedures: recommendations for line-ups and photospreads. *Law and Human Behaviour*, 22, 603–47.

WEST, D.J. and FARRINGTON, D.P. (1973) *Who Becomes Delinquent?* London: Heinemann.

WEYANDT, L.L. (2006) *The Physiological Basis of Cognitive and Behavioural Disorders*, Mahwah, NJ: Lawrence Erlbaum Associates.

WIEDENFIELD, S.A., O'LEARY, A., BANDURA, A., BROWN, S., LEVINE, S., and RASKA, K. (1990) Impact of perceived self-efficacy in coping with stressors on components of the immune system. Journal *of Personality and Social Psychology*, 39, 1082–94.

WIENS, A.N. and MENUSTIK, C.E. (1983) Treatment outcome and patient characteristics in an aversion therapy programme for alcoholism. *American Psychologist*, 38, 1089–96.

WILEMAN, S.M., EAGLES, J.M., ANDREW, J.E., HOWIE, F.L., CAMERON, I.M., McCORMACK, K. and NAJI, S.A. (2001) Light therapy for seasonal affective disorder in primary care: randomised control trial. *British Journal of Psychiatry*, 178, 311–16.

WILHELM, K. MITCHELL, P.B., NIVEN, H., FINCH, A., WEDGEWOOD, L., SCIMONE, A., BLAIR, I.P., PARKER, G., and SCHOFIELD, P.R. (2006) Life events, first depression onset and the serotonin transporter gene. *British Journal of Psychiatry*, 188, 210–15.

WILLIAMS, C.D. (1959) The elimination of tantrum behaviour by extinction procedures. *Journal of Abnormal and Social Psychology*, 59, 269.

WILLIAMS, L.M. (1994) Recall of childhood trauma: a prospective study of women's memories of child sexual abuse. *Journal of Consulting and Clinical Psychology*, 62, 1167–76.

WILLIS, J., THOMAS, P., GARRY, P.J. and GOODWIN, J.S. (1987) A prospective study of response to stressful life events in initially healthy elders. *Journal of Gerontology*, 42, 627–30.

WINDELBAND, W. (1894) *History and Natural Science*, Strasbourg: Heitz.

WINGER, G., HOFMANN, F.G. and WOODS, J.H. (1992) *Handbook on Drug and Alcohol Abuse*. New York: Oxford University Press.

WITKIN, H.A., MEDNICK, S.A., SCHULSINGER, F., BAKKESTROM, E. *et al.* (1976) XYY and XXY men: criminality and aggression. *Science*, 193, 547–55.

WOLPE, J. (1958) *Psychotherapy by Reciprocal Inhibition*, Stanford, CA: Stanford University Press.

WOOD, D.J. and MIDDLETON, D.J. (1975) A study of assisted problem-solving. *British Journal of Psychology*, 66, 181–91.

WOOD, D.J., BRUNER, J.S. and ROSS, G. (1976) The role of tutoring in problem solving. *Journal of Child Psychology and Psychiatry*, 17, 89–100.

WOODHEAD, M.M., BADDELEY, A.D. and SIMMONDS, D.C.V. (1979) On training people to recognise faces. *Ergonomics*, 22, 333–43.

WORLD HEALTH ORGANIZATION (WHO) (2000).*The World Health Report 2000: Health systems: Improving Performance*, Geneva United Nations.

WORLD HEALTH ORGANISATION (2004) Distribution of suicide rates (per 10000). Available www.who.int

WRIGHT, D.B., LOFTUS, E.F. and HALL, M. (2001) Now you see it, now you don't: inhibiting recall in the recognition of scenes. *Applied Cognitive Psychology*, 15, 471–82.

WRIGHT, D.B., OST, J. and FRENCH, C.C. (2006) Recovered and false memories. *The Psychologist*, 19 (6), 352–5.

WRIGHT, D.B., SELF, G. and JUSTICE, C. (2000) Memory conformity: exploring misinformation effects when presented by another person. *British Journal of Psychology*, 91, 189–202.

WU, J., KRAMER, G.L., KRAM, M., STECIUK, M., CRAWFORD, I.L. and PETTY, F. (1999). Serotonin and learned helplessness: a regional study of 5-HT-sub (IA), receptors and the serotonin transport site in rat brain. *Journal of Psychiatric Research*, 33 (1), 17–22.

YIN, R.K. (1969) Looking at upside-down faces. *Journal of Experimental Psychology*, 81, 141–5.

YOUNG, A. and BLOCK, N. (1996) *Unsolved Mysteries of the Mind: Tutorial Essays in Cognition*. Oxford: Taylor & Francis.

YOUNG, A. and HAY, D. (1986) Configural information in face perception. In V. Bruce (1988) *Recognising Faces*, London: Lawrence Erlbaum Associates.

YOUNG, A., HAY, D. and ELLIS, A.W. (1985) The faces that launched a thousand slips: everyday difficulties and errors in recognising people. *British Journal of Psychology*, 76, 495–523.

YUILLE, J.C. and CUTSHALL, J.L. (1986) A case study of eye-witness memory of a crime. *Journal of Applied Psychology*, 71, 291–301..

ZIMBARDO, P., HANEY, C. and BANKS, C. (1973) Interpersonal dynamics in a simulated prison. *International Journal of Criminology and Penology*, 1, 69–97.

ZIMBARDO, P.G. (1969) The human choice: individuation, reason and order versus deindividuation, impulse and chaos. In W.J. Arnold and D. Levine (eds.), *Nebraska Symposium on Motivation*, Lincoln: University of Nebraska Press

ZUCKER, R.A., ELLIS, D.A., FITZGERALD, H.E. and BINGHAM, C.R. (1996) Other evidence for at least two alcoholisms. II. Life course variation in antisociality and heterogeneity of alcoholic outcome. *Development and Psychopathology*, 8 (4), 831–48.

Index

Index

Index